CANCÚN, COZUMEL, YUCATÁN PENINSULA

Where to Stay and Eat
for All Budgets

Must-See Sights
and Local Secrets

Ratings You Can Trust

Fodor's Travel Publications   New York, Toronto, London, Sydney, Auckland
www.fodors.com

FODOR'S CANCÚN, COZUMEL, YUCATÁN PENINSULA 2005

Editor: Sarah Gold; Laura M. Kidder, senior editor

Editorial Production: Tom Holton

Editorial Contributors: Patricia Alisau, Shelagh McNally, Maribeth Mellin, Jane Onstott

Maps: David Lindroth *cartographer;* Bob Blake and Rebecca Baer, *map editors*

Design: Fabrizio La Rocca, *creative director;* Guido Caroti, *art director;* Moon Sun Kim, *cover designer;* Melanie Marin, *senior picture editor*

Production/Manufacturing: Angela L. McLean

Cover Photo: (Coastline at Tulum, Yucatan Peninsula): Robin Hill/Index Stock Imagery

ISBN 1–4000–1417–4

ISSN 1051–6336

SPECIAL SALES

This book is available for special discounts for bulk purchases for sales promotions or premiums. Special editions, including personalized covers, excerpts of existing books, and corporate imprints, can be created in large quantities for special needs. For more information, write to Special Markets/Premium Sales, 1745 Broadway, MD 6-2, New York, New York 10019, or e-mail specialmarkets@randomhouse.com.

AN IMPORTANT TIP & AN INVITATION

Although all prices, opening times, and other details in this book are based on information supplied to us at press time, changes occur all the time in the travel world, and Fodor's cannot accept responsibility for facts that become outdated or for inadvertent errors or omissions. So **always confirm information when it matters,** especially if you're making a detour to visit a specific place. Your experiences—positive and negative—matter to us. If we have missed or misstated something, **please write to us.** We follow up on all suggestions. Contact the Cancún editor at editors@fodors.com or c/o Fodor's at 1745 Broadway, New York, New York 10019.

DESTINATION CANCÚN, COZUMEL, YUCATÁN PENINSULA

C limb a Maya pyramid and get lost in one of the most brilliant civilizations of ancient Mesoamerica. Dive beneath the waves and discover the underwater treasures of one of the largest barrier reefs in the hemisphere. Stroll through the graceful old city of Mérida, where the burnished stones speak of a glorious past and where traditions are carefully guarded. Join outdoor adventurers who explore authentic indigenous communities and the untouched wilderness they live in. Bury your toes in the dazzling white sands and turquoise blue waters of the Mexican Caribbean, known the world over for its mesmerizing beauty. Visit remote islands and peninsulas with few human inhabitants and abundant wildlife. Discover a world where just a few decades ago, only archaeologists dared to tread. Witness a part of Mexico where hospitality is an art and the people are warm and inviting. Every corner of the Yucatán Peninsula richly rewards those who take the time to get to know it better. Have a fabulous trip!

Tim Jarrell, Publisher

CONTENTS

ABOUT THIS BOOK

There's no doubt that the best source for travel advice is a like-minded friend who's just been where you're headed. But with or without that friend, you'll have a better trip with a Fodor's guide in hand. Once you've learned to find your way around its pages, you'll be in great shape to find your way around your destination.

SELECTION

Our goal is to cover the best properties, sights, and activities in their category, as well as the most interesting communities to visit. We make a point of including local food-lovers' hot spots as well as neighborhood options, and we avoid all that's touristy unless it's really worth your time. You can go on the assumption that everything you read about in this book is recommended wholeheartedly by our writers and editors. Flip to On the Road with Fodor's to learn more about who they are. It goes without saying that no property mentioned in the book has paid to be included.

RATINGS

Orange stars ★ denote sights and properties that our editors and writers consider the very best in the area covered by the entire book. These, the best of the best, are listed in the Fodor's Choice section in the front of the book. Black stars ★ highlight the sights and properties we deem Highly Recommended, the don't-miss sights within any region. Fodor's Choice and Highly Recommended options in each region are usually listed on the title page of the chapter covering that region. Use the index to find complete descriptions. In cities, sights pinpointed with numbered map bullets ❶ in the margins tend to be more important than those without bullets.

SPECIAL SPOTS

Pleasures & Pastimes focuses on types of experiences that reveal the spirit of the destination. Watch for Off the Beaten Path sights. Some are out of the way, some are quirky, and all are worth your while. If the munchies hit while you're exploring, look for Need a Break? suggestions.

TIME IT RIGHT

Wondering when to go? Check On the Calendar below and chapters' Timing sections for weather and crowd overviews and best days and times to visit.

SEE IT ALL

Use Fodor's exclusive Great Itineraries as a model for your trip. (For a good overview of the entire destination, follow those that begin the book, or mix regional itineraries from several chapters.) In cities, Good Tours guide you to important sights in each neighborhood; ▶ indicates the starting points of walks and itineraries in the text and on the map.

BUDGET WELL	Hotel and restaurant price categories from ¢ to $$$$ are defined in the opening pages of each chapter—expect to find a balanced selection for every budget. For attractions, we always give standard adult admission fees; reductions are usually available for children, students, and senior citizens. Look in Discounts & Deals in Smart Travel Tips for information on destination-wide ticket schemes. Want to pay with plastic? AE, D, DC, MC, V following restaurant and hotel listings indicate whether American Express, Discover, Diners Club, MasterCard, or Visa are accepted.
BASIC INFO	Smart Travel Tips lists travel essentials for the entire area covered by the book; city- and region-specific basics end each chapter. To find the best way to get around, see the transportation section; see individual modes of travel ("Bus Travel," "Car Travel") for details. We assume you'll check Web sites or call for particulars.
ON THE MAPS	Maps throughout the book show you what's where and help you find your way around. Black and orange numbered bullets ❶ ❶ in the text correlate to bullets on maps.
BACKGROUND	In general, we give background information within the chapters in the course of explaining sights as well as in CloseUp boxes and in Understanding Cancún, Cozumel, Yucatán Peninsula at the end of the book. The Cancún at a Glance and the chronology provide insight—present and past.
FIND IT FAST	Within the book, chapters are arranged in a roughly northeast to southwest direction starting with Cancún. Chapters are divided into small regions, within which towns are covered in logical geographical order; attractive routes and interesting places between towns are flagged as En Route. Heads at the top of each page help you find what you need within a chapter.
DON'T FORGET	Restaurants are open for lunch and dinner daily unless we state otherwise; we mention dress only when there's a specific requirement and reservations only when they're essential or not accepted—it's always best to book ahead. Hotels have private baths, phone, TVs, and air-conditioning and operate on the European Plan (a.k.a. EP, meaning without meals) unless otherwise stated. We always list facilities but not whether you'll be charged extra to use them, so when pricing accommodations, find out what's included.

SYMBOLS

Many Listings

★ Fodor's Choice
★ Highly recommended
✉ Physical address
✛ Directions
📪 Mailing address
☎ Telephone
📠 Fax
🌐 On the Web
✉ E-mail
📮 Admission fee
🕗 Open/closed times
⚑ Start of walk/itinerary
Ⓜ Metro stations
▭ Credit cards

Outdoors

⛳ Golf
⛺ Camping

Hotels & Restaurants

🏨 Hotel
🛏 Number of rooms
♿ Facilities
🍽 Meal plans
✕ Restaurant
✍ Reservations
👔 Dress code
↘ Smoking
🍷 BYOB
✕🏨 Hotel with restaurant that warrants a visit

Other

☺ Family-friendly
🛈 Contact information
⇨ See also
✉ Branch address
☞ Take note

ON THE ROAD WITH FODOR'S

A trip takes you out of yourself. Concerns of life at home completely disappear, driven away by more immediate thoughts—about, say, what marvels will beguile the next day, or where you'll have dinner. That's where Fodor's comes in. We make sure that you know all your options, so that you don't miss something that's around the next bend just because you didn't know it was there. Because the best memories of your trip might well have nothing to do with what you came to Cancún to see, we guide you to sights large and small all over the region. You might set out to relax and catch the sun on a lovely white-sand beach, but back at home you find yourself unable to forget the dramatic Maya pyramids and snorkeling above beautiful coral reefs. With Fodor's at your side, serendipitous discoveries are never far away.

Our success in showing you every corner of Cancún, Cozumel, and the Yucatán Peninsula is a credit to our extraordinary writers. Although there's no substitute for travel advice from a good friend who knows your style, our contributors are the next best thing—the kind of people you would poll for travel advice if you knew them.

Patricia Alisau first visited the ruins of Chichén Itzá in a bush plane, which set the stage for numerous return trips to the Yucatán. Even today, her favorite pursuit is researching the Maya culture and scaling the towering pyramids at each new site that opens. A psychologist-turned-journalist, she was so drawn to the surrealism of Mexico that she moved to the capital. What began as a one-week vacation turned into a 20-year-plus sojourn, during which she worked as a foreign correspondent, war correspondent (Nicaragua), and feature writer for various wire services and publications in Mexico, the United States, and Europe. She updated the Caribbean Coast chapter for this book.

Journalist–turned–travel writer Shelagh McNally has lived on the Yucatán Peninsula since 1997, when she left her native Canada for a four-month Mexican vacation with her young daughter and decided to stay on and learn more about the Maya history and culture. She has covered Cancún, Cozumel, Campeche, Isla Mujeres, and elsewhere on the Caribbean coast for Fodor's, and is the author of *The Adventure Guide to Guatemala.* She has also written for the *Miami Herald, Montréal Gazette, Mundo Maya Magazine,* and other publications and Web sites in Mexico, Canada, the United Kingdom, and the United States. She updated the Cancún and Isla Mujeres chapters of this book.

Recipient of the prestigious Pluma de Plata award for writing on Mexico, Maribeth Mellin lives in San Diego near the Tijuana border in a home filled with folk art and photos from Latin America—including a snapshot of the 140-pound marlin she caught in the Sea of Cortes. She has authored travel books on Mexico, Costa Rica, Argentina, and Peru and is currently creating a fictional account of her adventures. Maribeth updated this year's Cozumel chapter.

Since earning a B.A. in Spanish language and literature, Jane Onstott has lived and traveled extensively in Latin America. She worked as director of communications and information for the Darwin Research Station in the Galapagos Islands, and studied painting in Oaxaca between 1995 and 1998. Since 1986 Jane has contributed to Fodor's guides to Mexico and South America; this year, she updated the Campeche and Mérida chapters.

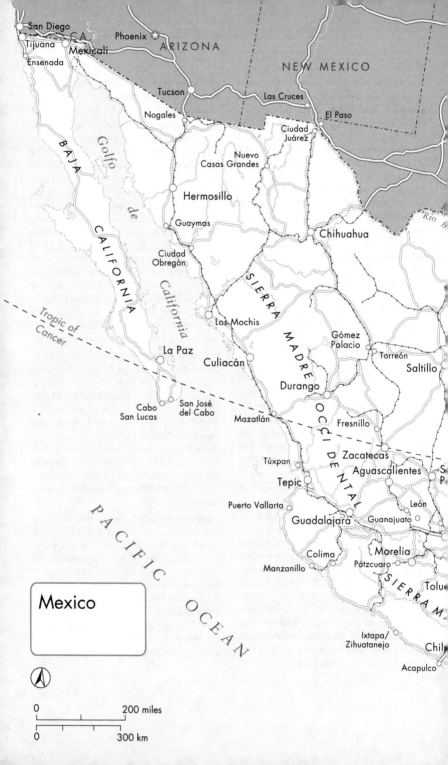

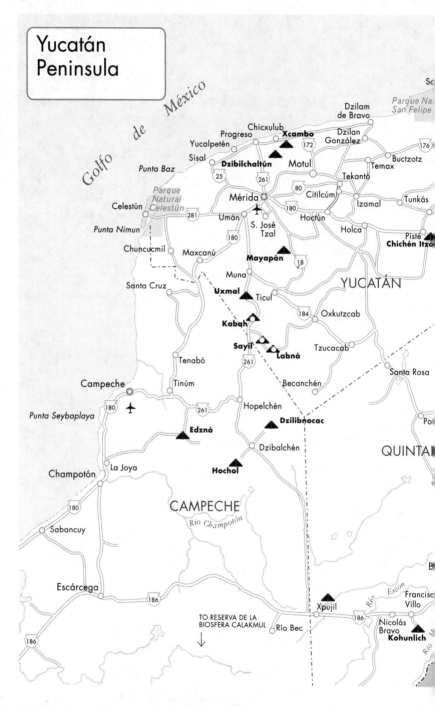

Yucatán
Peninsula

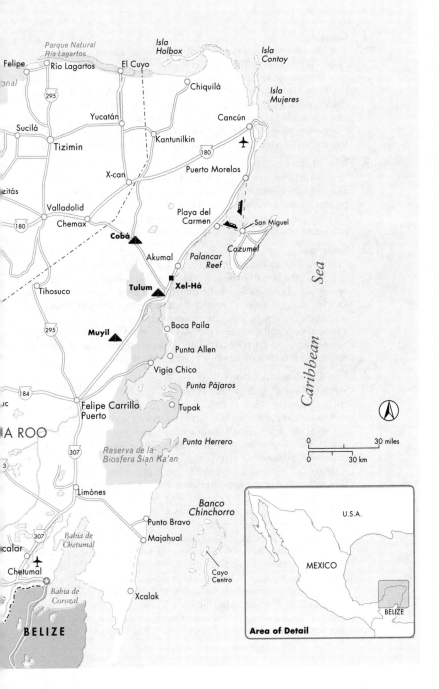

1 Cancún

The rhinestone of Mexico's Caribbean coast, Cancún, in the upper eastern portion of the Yucatán Peninsula, is currently Mexico's most popular destination. A slender, 22½-km-long (14-mi-long) barrier island called the Zona Hotelera is lined with resorts, which welcome more than 2 million visitors a year—all of whom come to enjoy water sports and gorgeous beaches by day, and folkloric performances, club-hopping, and tequila-sampling by night. Nearby, El Centro—downtown Cancún—offers authentic Mexican-Maya flavor in its markets and restaurants.

2 Isla Mujeres

Only 8 km (5 mi) across the bay from Cancún, Isla Mujeres is light-years away in temperament; it's more laid-back, less crowded, and less expensive than the flashy resorts. The main activities here are sunning on the white-sand beaches, snorkeling and diving, eating fresh seafood, and just lazing under *palapas* (thatched roofs).

3 Cozumel

Cozumel is older and mellower than Cancún, hipper than Isla Mujeres, and draws the best from both worlds. Without a doubt, the major draw on this island is scuba diving. Cozumel's reefs are the finest in the Americas, and many of them are protected national parks. Parque Chankanaab is Cozumel's showpiece, where you can see such underwater marvels as a sunken ship, and a statue of the Maya rain god Chacmool. Reef, ruins, and retailers can fill your days here, but the hopping dance clubs and bars provide plenty of action for night owls, too.

4 The Caribbean Coast

South of Cancún, golf carts and tennis courts practically disappear, and miles of pristine beach stretch as far as the eye can see. The dazzling white sands and glittering blue-green waters beckon to sun worshippers as well as snorkelers, divers, bird-watchers, and beachcombers. The Riviera Maya, a slice of coast about 113 km (70 mi) long a few miles south of Cancún, is becoming increasingly popular with visitors as well as developers. Accommodations come in every style, from jungle lodges and campgrounds to extravagant resorts. Playa del Carmen is the fastest-growing beach town on the coast, with plentiful dining options and a lively nightlife. But the natural beauty of the coast is this area's biggest draw. The Reserva Biosfera de la Sian Ka'an, a vast UNESCO site, revisits what the Yucatán was like during the days when the Maya flourished. The seaside ruins of Tulum and the towering jungle pyramids at Cobá give further glimpses into this wondrous ancient civilization. Farther south along what is known as the Costa Maya—161 km (100 mi) of pure jungle, untrammeled beaches, and teeming wildlife—development is slow. Although Majahual has a new cruise-ship port, the rest of the village is a sleepy fishing community untouched by time. The same goes for remote and lovely Xcalak, which has access to excellent diving and deep-sea fishing.

5 Mérida & Yucatán State

The Maya ruins here are some of the most spectacular in the world; both stunning Chichén Itzá and elegant Uxmal are visited by hordes of travelers each year. After spending a little time here, it becomes clear that the Maya never really left Yucatán. The old deities worshipped thousands of years ago still receive their due here (although today religious pageants meld pre-Hispanic and Christian beliefs). The capital city of Mérida, where Maya tradition commingles with colonial culture, is the perfect base for exploring the area. The music, dance, and museums here are the best in the Yucatán, and farther west along the coast, the flamingo-watching is memorable.

6 Campeche

Yucatecan life is at its mellowest in Campeche, which lies on the Yucatán's west coast and faces the Gulf of Mexico. The Maya influence here is still very strong; the ancient ruins are architecturally diverse and richly detailed, and in Becal, artisans still weave traditional hats known as *jipis*. The Reserva de la Biosfera Calakmul in southern Campeche is a primeval rain forest, where jaguar, ocelot, and puma still roam free. Spanish colonial heritage is most palpable in Campeche City, notably at the Puerta de Tierra, where locals fought off pirate attacks in the days of the buccaneers.

Highlights of Yucatán
9 to 10 Days

The Yucatán Peninsula is so diverse that in a single trip you can island-hop, explore Maya ruins and jungle wilderness, dive and snorkel in one of the world's best reef systems, beachcomb, and visit historically rich towns and museums. It's easiest to start your visit in Cancún and use it as a base for exploring the surrounding areas.

ISLA MUJERES 1 day. Lazing on the white-sand beaches and snorkeling at El Garrafón underwater park are popular pastimes here. In the 17th century, the island's reefs were used as hiding places by pirates lying in wait for passing Spanish galleons; before that, the Maya worshipped their deities on the windy bluffs overlooking the sea. Although it's steeped in history, the island's inns and restaurants prove that it has evolved into a modern-day Mexican retreat.

TULUM, XEL-HÁ 1 day. Tulum, one of the great trading cities of the ancient Maya, erected its high walls to protect precious cargo. Nearby Xel-Há, with its natural coves and inlets, was a Maya port of call, and is now a swimmer's paradise. Together they make a perfect day's outing.

RESERVA BIOSFERA DE LA SIAN KA'AN 1 day. This 1.3-million-acre UNESCO site is one of the last undeveloped coasts in North America. Conservation is at the forefront here. Take a tour and see villagers' efforts to save the spiny lobster, explore watery channels once used as part of a trade route to the sea, and watch the thousands of wild birds that have made this spot their haven.

COZUMEL 2 days. Cozumel is a scuba diving mecca, one of the top five dive spots on the globe. (In fact, Jacques Cousteau made it his headquarters for many underwater explorations.) If you're a diver, this is the place to see fabulous underwater topography—the reefs are filled with caves, canyons, tunnels, and archways—and teeming with marine life. If you'd rather stay above water, though, the island also has beaches, shops, sportfishing, and nightlife.

MÉRIDA 2 days. The Yucatán state capital reflects the confluence of traditional Maya and European colonial influences. The city's architecture is a big draw, and includes many beautifully refurbished colonial buildings. At heart, though, this remains a Maya city. If you arrive on Sunday, the best place to spend the day is the festive main plaza, where free performances of folk music and dance are given throughout the day. You can also visit open-air markets, cafés, and—for a preview of your trip to the ruins at Chichén Itzá—the Museo de Antropología y Historia.

CHICHÉN ITZÁ 1 day. One of the most famous Maya sites in the world, Chichén Itzá covers several square miles and is punctuated by stunning temples and pyramids. Thousands gather the spring and autumn equinoxes for special ceremonies honoring Kukulcán, the mystical plumed serpent god. You can wander through ancient ball courts, scale the spectacular

Castillo pyramid, and explore many other "pure Maya"-style structures adorned with latticework and stone serpents. The light-and-sound show is exceptional—especially during a full moon.

CAMPECHE CITY 1 day. The downtown area of this seaside city is full of ramparts and forts that Spanish colonists built to protect the city from pirates. Most impressive of all is the Puerta de Tierra (be sure to catch the light-and-sound show explaining the town's history). You'll also have time to travel to the Maya site of Edzná, outside town.

Maya Sites
10 to 12 Days

With a history spanning 3,000 years, the Maya are one of the world's great ancient civilizations. In this tour you can travel through time and revisit the glory of Maya dynasties—their art and culture, their sacred cities, and their architectural and engineering achievements.

MÉRIDA 2 days. Mérida was a thriving Maya city before the arrival of the Spanish conquistadores in the 16th century. It remains an important commercial hub of the Yucatán Peninsula, full of stately colonial-era architecture and museums and performances that commemorate the city's Maya culture. Surrounded by archaeological sites, nature preserves, and other charming cities, it's the perfect base from which to explore the region. You can make day trips to Chichén Itzá and Uxmal from here.

CHICHÉN ITZÁ 1 day. First settled in AD 432, Chichén Itzá was later abandoned and then rediscovered by the Itzás in 868. Under their rule and subsequent alliances, it rose to become the most important city in Yucatán from the 10th through the 12th century. The area is dominated by the spectacular Castillo ("Castle"), a pyramid and temple dedicated to Kukulcán—but there are dozens of other dazzling structures here to explore.

UXMAL & THE RUTA PUCC 1 day. Uxmal rose to prominence from the 7th to the 9th century, during the Late Classic period. The city's elegantly long, quadrangle-shape buildings embody the Pu'uc style of architecture, and details such as elaborate stone mosaic latticework and curling cornices are still intact. The highest structure is the mysterious, elliptical-shape Pirámide del Adivino, which towers 125 feet into the sky. The most famous is the Cuadrángulo de las Monjas, which served as the living quarters of a high lord of the Maya.

CAMPECHE CITY 1 day. In the colonial era, Campeche City became a prominent shipping port for goods bound for Spain. To thwart pirates, it then became a walled city—the only one in New Spain. You can tour the colonial downtown, climb the ramparts of the Baluarte de Soledad, and visit a museum filled with gorgeous jade artifacts. You can also visit the Maya ruins at Edzná, and book a tour to explore other ruins in the southern part of the state.

XPUHIL, BECÁN, HORMIGUERO & CHICANNÁ 1 day. The dramatic Chenes and Río Bec styles of Maya architecture prevail at these sites. Doorways are fashioned into fascinating monster mouths; pyramid towers, fortified walls, sculpted faces, and reliefs of the rain god Chaac stand out boldly in the isolated jungle setting. Plan to stay overnight so you have time to visit Calakmul.

RESERVA DE LA BIOSFERA CALAKMUL

1 day. Skirting the Guatemala border, Calakmul was a center of formidable Maya military power until the 7th century AD. It is one of the largest cities of the Maya empire, and, together with its surrounding biosphere reserve, stretches over a million acres. Thousands of structures in Calakmul have yet to be excavated, but its awesome size and the dramatic beauty of the surrounding landscape is apparent everywhere. Return to Campeche City after your visit.

CANCÚN 1 day. A vibrant seaside resort city, Cancún has nonstop activity from dusk to dawn. Enjoy spun-sugar sandy beaches; myriad water sports; sophisticated restaurants and bars; first-class hotels; and shopping (some in duty-free shops). Use Cancún as your hub for trips to Tulum and Cobá.

TULUM, XEL-HÁ 1 day. Tulum draws millions of tourists every year, making it the most visited archaeological site in Mexico. This former walled city is perched on a cliff overlooking the turquoise waters of the Caribbean; the view from the various stone temples and buildings is outstanding. Nearby Xel-Há, with its natural coves and inlets, is a remarkable self-contained aquatic park with dolphins, transparent lagoons, and small Maya ruins.

COBÁ, PAC CHEN 1 day. Cobá is the largest Maya site in the northern part of the Caribbean coast, at one time encompassing 70 square km (27 square mi). Once a close ally of Tikal in Guatemala, its enormous temples are the highest in the region, reaching more than 100 feet. Built around five lakes, most of the site is covered in dense jungle (only 5% of the estimated 6,500 structures have been uncovered). Well-marked footpaths lead to the excavated temples with their plazas, stucco motifs, ball courts, and sacbés—Maya roads made of limestone, which carried trade goods to neighboring cities. You'll also have time to visit the settlement of Pac Chen, where modern-day Maya choose to live in a traditionally primitive jungle village.

KOHUNLICH, LAGUNA DE BACALAR 1 day. You'll want to lodge overnight in the area, either in nearby Chetumal or at any of a number of jungle lodges here. Kohunlich is remarkable for its series of giant stucco masks embedded in its pyramids. The site is small, rarely crowded, and can be covered in half a day. Take a boat tour later in the day at the Laguna de Bacalar—the second-largest lake in Mexico, whose combination of salt and fresh water creates amazing aquamarine hues.

DZIBANCHÉ, KINICHNÁ 1 day. Dzibanché and Kinichná are two smaller sites a few miles apart. You can explore the beautiful Templo del Búho, as well as temples dedicated to Itzamná, the Maya god of the sun, in the pristine stillness of the surrounding jungle. Before leaving the region, visit the Museo de la Cultura Maya in Chetumal, the best exhibit on the life and times of this ancient culture anywhere in the country.

WHEN TO GO

°C		°F
100		212
40		105
37		98.6
30		90
25		80
20		70
15		60
10		50
5		40
0		32
-5		20
-10		10
-15		0
-20		

High season along the Mexican Caribbean runs from mid-December through the week after Easter. The most popular vacation times are Semana Santa (Holy Week, the week leading up to Easter) and the week from Christmas to New Year's. Most hotels are booked well in advance for these holiday periods, when prices are at their highest and armies of travelers swarm popular attractions. Resorts popular with college students (i.e., any place with a beach) tend to fill up in the summer months and during spring-break season (generally March through April).

Off-season price changes are considerable at the beach resorts but are less pronounced in Mérida, Campeche, and other inland regions. To avoid crowds, and high prices, the best times to go are September through mid-December, and February.

Climate

From November through March, winter temperatures hover around 27°C (80°F). Occasional winter storms can bring blustery skies and high winds, but it is generally sunny. During the early-spring months (April and May) there is a period of intense heat that tapers off in June. The hottest months, with temperatures reaching up to 43°C (110°F), start in mid-July and last until the end of September when the rainy season starts. The rainy season lasts until mid-November. Officially the tropical storm and hurricane season starts in June but usually doesn't hit the area until mid-September. Inland regions tend to be 10–15° warmer than the coast, which is perfect in winter but can be quite uncomfortable in the spring and summer months.

📶 Forecasts **Weather Channel Connection** ☎ 900/932–8437, 95¢ per minute from a Touch-Tone phone.

CANCÚN

Jan.	84F	29C	May	91F	33C	Sept.	87F	31C
	66	19		73	23		75	24
Feb.	85F	29C	June	92F	33C	Oct.	87F	31C
	68	20		75	24		73	23
Mar.	88F	31C	July	91F	33C	Nov.	86F	30C
	69	21		73	23		71	22
Apr.	88F	31C	Aug.	91F	33C	Dec.	84F	29C
	71	22		75	24		66	19

WINTER	
Dec.	The Feria de Cancún (Cancún Fair) serves as a nostalgia trip for provincials who now live along the Caribbean shore but still remember the small-town fiestas back home. Fiesta de la Concepción Inmaculada (Festival of the Immaculate Conception) is observed for six days in the villages across Quintana Roo, with processions, folkloric dances, fireworks, and bullfights. Fiesta de Nuestra Señora de Guadalupe (Festival of Our Lady of Guadalupe) is celebrated throughout Mexico. Pilgrims who journeyed to her shrine in Mexico City return home via bicycles or on foot in time for a midnight Mass followed by dance performances and fiestas. The Procesión Acuática highlights festivities at the fishing village of Celestún, west of Mérida. Navidad (Christmas) is celebrated in the Yucatán villages with processions culminating in the breaking of candy-filled piñatas. The most important day of the holiday season is December 24, Nochebuena (Holy Night), when families gather to eat a traditional midnight dinner.
Jan.	El Día de los Reyes (Three Kings' Day/Feast of the Epiphany), January 6, is the day Mexican children receive gifts brought by the three kings (the Mexican version of Santa Claus). El Día de los Reyes coincides with Mérida's Founding Day, the anniversary of the 1542 founding of the city. There, traditional gift-giving is combined with parades, fireworks, and outdoor parties. El Día de San Antonio de Abad (St. Anthony the Abbot Day), on January 17, is a religious holiday when animals are taken to churches to be blessed.
Feb.	La Candeleria, on February 2, is the date of the final Christmas fiesta, hosted by whoever got the small plastic doll called *El Niño* (literally "the child," for Baby Jesus) in his or her piece of *Rosca de Reyes* (Kings' Ring) cake on January 6.
Feb.–Mar.	Carnival festivities take place the week before Lent, with parades, floats, outdoor dancing, music, and fireworks; they're especially spirited in Mérida, Cozumel, Isla Mujeres, Campeche, and Chetumal.
SPRING	
Mar.–Apr.	Aniversario de Benito Juárez (Benito Juárez's Birthday) is the celebration of the birthday of one of Mexico's greatest heroes; parades are held on this national holiday. On the equinoxes (March 21 and September 21), shadows on the steps of the temple at Chichén Itzá create a snake that appears to be slithering down to earth. Easter is the most important holiday in Mexico. Fiestas, parades, visits to the family, and numerous religious processions and services mark the event.
Apr.–May	Holy Cross Fiestas in Celestún and Hopelchén—both in Yucatán state—include cockfights, dances, and fireworks. The Sol a Sol International Regatta, launched from St. Petersburg, Florida, arrives in

	Isla Mujeres, sparking regional dances and a general air of festivity. Billfish tournaments take place in Cozumel, Puerto Aventuras, Puerto Morelos, and Cancún.
May	Cinco de Mayo is the Mexican national holiday that honors the Mexican defeat of the French army at Puebla de los Angeles in 1862. El Día de Madres (Mother's Day) is an important holiday because of the special role mothers have in Mexico. During the last weekend in May, the Cancún Jazz Festival, an annual event since 1991, has featured such top musicians as Wynton Marsalis and Gato Barbieri.
SUMMER	
Aug.	Founder's Day celebrates the founding of Isla Mujeres with six days of races, folk dances, music, and regional cuisine.
FALL	
Sept.–Oct.	Fiesta de San Román attracts 50,000 people to Campeche to view the procession carrying the Black Christ of San Román—the city's most sacred patron saint—through the streets. *Vaquerías* (traditional cattle-branding feasts) attract aficionados to rural towns for bullfights, fireworks, and music. Día de Independencia (Independence Day), the commemoration of a historic speech, known as the *grito* (shout), by Independence leader Padre Miguel Hidalgo, is celebrated throughout Mexico with fireworks and parties. Fiesta de Cristo de las Ampollas (Christ of the Blisters) begins on September 27 and consists of two weeks or more of religious events and processions in Mérida; dances, bullfights, and fireworks take place in Ticul and other small villages.
Oct.	The 18th sees the Fiesta del Cristo de Sitilpech in Izamal, an hour from Mérida, and heralds a week of daily processions in which the image of Christ is carried from Sitilpech village to Izamal; dances and fireworks accompany the walks.
Nov.	On the Día del Muerto (Day of the Dead, or All Saints' Day), Mexicans all over the country visit cemeteries to construct marigold-strewn altars on the graves of loved ones and ancestors and to symbolically share a meal with them by leaving offerings and having graveside picnics. Bakers herald the annual return of the departed from the spirit world with pastry skulls and candy. In Mérida, a special chicken dish is prepared, roasted in a pit in the ground.
Nov.–Dec.	Fiesta de Isla Mujeres honors the island's patron saint, the Virgin of the Immaculate Conception, as members of various guilds stage processions, dances, and bullfights. Fiesta de la Virgen de Concepción (Feast of the Virgin Conception) is held each year in Champotón, Campeche.

PLEASURES & PASTIMES

Archaeology Amateur archaeologists will find heaven in the Yucatán, where remains of the ancient Maya civilization are everywhere. Whether you prefer your archaeological sites well excavated or overgrown, in remote locations or a stone's throw from major towns, you'll find them here. The region's most notable Maya ruins are at Cobá, Tulum, Chichén Itzá, and Uxmal, but smaller and less-frequented sites can be equally fascinating.

Ek Balam, 30 km (18 mi) north of Valladolid in Yucatán state, is one of the less-known but more rewarding Maya sites in the Yucatán. Only a few structures have been excavated here, but the magnitude of the site is impressive. Among the restored structures is a dazzling pyramid tower with huge stucco monster masks, which was the mausoleum for a Maya king.

The opening of the first of several planned eco-friendly jungle lodges in the Xpuhil area of Campeche has paved the way for visits to the ruins at Becán, Xpuhil, Hormiguero, and Calakmul (all of which are undergoing restoration). A luxurious ecological resort, Chicanná Ecovillage, has opened near the site of Kohunlich along the Caribbean coast, enabling adventurous visitors to experience direct links with the ancient past.

Beaches One of the biggest draws in Cancún and Yucatán state are the wonderful beaches. There are expanses of powdery white sand, rocky coves and promontories, curvaceous bays, and murky lagoons. Resorts Playa Chacmool and Playa Tortugas are on the bay side of Cancún, which is calmer if less beautiful than the windward side. Playa Norte, at the north end of Isla Mujeres, has great sunsets. Beaches on Cozumel's east coast—once used by buccaneers—are rocky, and the swimming is treacherous, but they're very private; the relatively sheltered leeward side has the widest and best beaches.

The Caribbean coast is also rimmed with exquisite beaches and coves—some hidden and pristine, others wildly popular with tourists. The sands at Puerto Morelos, Akumal, and especially Playa del Carmen, are usually filled with sunbathers. Xcalak is more remote, and has a breathtakingly beautiful location at the tip of a peninsula.

Travelers to Campeche and Progreso will find the waters of the Gulf of Mexico deep green, shallow, and tranquil. Such beaches as Payucán, Sabancuy, and Isla del Carmen are less visited by North Americans and facilities are minimal; Telchac Puerto is more developed.

Bird-Watching The Yucatán Peninsula is one of the finest areas for bird-watching in Mexico. Habitats range from planned bird sanctuaries to unmarked lagoons, estuaries, and mangrove swamps. Frigates, tanagers, warblers, and macaws inhabit Isla Contoy (off Isla Mujeres) and the Laguna Colombia on Cozumel; an even greater variety of species is to be found in the Reserva Biosfera de la Sian Ka'an on the Boca Paila peninsula south of Tulum. Along the north and west coasts of Yucatán state—at Ría Lagartos, Laguna Rosada, and Celestún—flamingos, herons, ibis, cormorants, pelicans, and peregrine falcons thrive.

Distinctive Cuisine

The mystique of Yucatecan cooking has a lot to do with the generous doses of local spices and herbs, although generally the food tends to be milder than visitors expect. Early culinary influences from France, Cuba, and New Orleans are still evident today, and have resulted in such distinctive specialties as *pollo pibil* (chicken marinated in a sour orange and annatto seed sauce and baked in banana leaves); *poc chuc* (Yucatecan pork marinated in a sour-orange sauce with pickled onions); *tikinchic* (fried fish prepared with sour orange); *panuchos* (fried tortillas filled with black beans and topped with diced turkey, chicken, or pork as well as pickled onions and avocado); *papadzules* (tortillas rolled up with hard-boiled eggs and drenched in a sauce of pumpkin seed and fried tomato); and *codzitos* (rolled tortillas in pumpkin-seed sauce). *Achiote* (annatto), cilantro (coriander), and the fiery *chile habañero* are zesty condiments. Along the Gulf coast, there's nothing finer than a dish of fresh blue crab or baby shrimp.

Yucatecans are renowned for—among other things—their love of idiosyncratic beverages. *Xtabentún,* a liqueur made of fermented honey and anise, dates back to the ancient Maya; like straight tequila, it's best drunk in small sips between bites of fresh lime. Local brews, such as the dark bock León Negra and the light Montejo, are excellent but hard to find in peninsular restaurants. On the healthier side, *chaya* is the bright-green local plant resembling spinach, often made into juice or cooked. Yucatecan *horchata*, a favorite all over Mexico, is made from milled rice and water flavored with vanilla.

Fishing

Sportfishing is popular in Cozumel and throughout the Caribbean coast. The plentiful waters of the Caribbean and the Gulf of Mexico support hundreds of species of tropical fish, making the Yucatán coastline and the outlying islands a paradise for deep-sea fishing, fly-fishing, and bonefishing. Particularly from the months of April to July, the waters off Cancún, Cozumel, and Isla Mujeres teem with sailfish, marlin, red snapper, tuna, barracuda, and wahoo, among others. Billfishing is so rich around Cozumel that it merits an annual tournament.

Farther south, along the Boca Paila peninsula, bonefishing and light-tackle saltwater fishing for banana fish, shad, permit, and sea bass are the hands-down favorites, while oysters, shrimp, and conch are plentiful in the Gulf of Mexico near Campeche and Isla del Carmen. At Progreso, on the north coast, sportfishing for grouper, dogfish, and pompano is very popular.

In the Water

All manner of water sports—jet skiing, catamaran sailing, scuba diving, snorkeling, sailboarding, waterskiing, sailing, and parasailing—are embraced in Cancún, Cozumel, Playa del Carmen, and other places along the Caribbean coast. All of these destinations (and many others) have well-equipped water-sports centers. Underwater enthusiasts come to Cozumel, Akumal, Xcalak, Xel-Há, and other parts of Mexico's Caribbean coast for the clear turquoise waters, the abundant tropical marine life, and the exquisite coral formations along the Palancar Reef system. Currents allow for drift diving, and both reefs and offshore wrecks lend themselves to dives, many of which are safe enough for neophytes. The peninsula's cenotes, or natural sinkholes, and underwater caverns also provide more unusual freshwater dive experiences.

FODOR'S CHOICE

The sights, restaurants, hotels, and other travel experiences on these pages are our editors' top picks—our Fodor's Choices. They're the best of their type in the area covered by the book—not to be missed and always worth your time. In the destination chapters that follow, you will find all the details.

LODGING

$$$$	**Ceiba del Mar Hotel & Spa**, Puerto Morelos. A butler brings Continental breakfast to your room through a discreetly hidden closet chamber.
$$$$	**Ikal del Mar**, Punta Bete. The name of this hotel means "poetry of the sea," and it's entirely appropriate. Luxurious excellence.
$$$$	**JW Marriott Cancún Resort & Spa**, Cancún. To get as impeccably manicured as the property here, just visit the spa.
$$$$	**Maroma**, Punta Maroma. Peacocks wander the grounds at this lavish hotel, and an exotic "floatarium" awaits you at the spa.
$$$$	**Presidente InterContinental Paraíso de la Bonita Resort and Thalasso**, Puerto Morelos. Sweeping ocean and jungle views, and thalassotherapy treatments in serene saltwater pools.
$$$–$$$$	**Na Balam**, El Pueblo, Isla Mujeres. Thatched palapa roofs, Mexican folk art, and a meditation room for yoga classes.
$$$	**Casa del Agua**, Puerto Aventuras. One suite has a trickling stream above the king-size bed; another has a double shower in a secluded garden.
$$$	**Presidente InterContinental Cozumel**, Cozumel. If you splurge on an oceanfront suite, you'll have a terrace only steps from the pristine white sand.
$$–$$$	**Hacienda Chichén**, Chichén Itzá, Yucatán. A converted 16th-century hacienda with its own entrance to the ruins, this hotel once served as the headquarters for the Carnegie expedition to Chichén Itzá.

BUDGET LODGING

$$	**Costa de Cocos**, Xcalak. Wind-generated electricity, and rates that include two delicious daily meals.
¢–$$	**Cabañas Copal**, Tulum. At night, sleep beneath netted palapas, and wander grounds lit by thousands of candles.

RESTAURANTS

$$$–$$$$	**Laguna Grill**, Cancún. Inventive Asian fusion entrées; a top-notch wine list; decadent desserts.
$–$$$	**Casa del Agua**, Playa del Carmen. German, Italian, and Swiss cuisine—and who could resist a dessert named "Mama Spath's Hot Love"?

$–$$$ | **Casa O's,** El Pueblo, Isla Mujeres. All the waiters at this casual surf-n-turf restaurant have names ending with the letter "o."

$–$$$ | **Gustino Italian Beachside Grill,** Cancún. A sleek, dramatic dining room—often filled with violin music—sets the stage for superb Italian fare.

$–$$$ | **La Pigua,** Campeche City. Don't miss the *camarones al coco* (coconut-encrusted shrimp) at this plant-filled lunch spot.

BUDGET RESTAURANTS

$–$$ | **El Pórtico del Peregrino,** Mérida. Smokers get the street view at this 30-year Mérida institution—but everyone gets incredible local seafood.

ARCHAEOLOGY

Chichén Itzá, Yucatán. Known worldwide as one of the most magnificent ancient cities built by the Maya.

Cobá, Riviera Maya. The Maya stone temples and pyramids here are surrounded by thick, wild jungle.

Edzná, southeast of Campeche City. This Maya ruin site is dominated by the 102-foot Pirámide de los Cinco Pisos or five-story pyramid.

Ex-Convento y Iglesia de San Antonio de Padua, Mérida. This enormous 16th-century monastery is perched on—and built from—the remains of a Maya pyramid devoted to Itzamná, god of the heavens.

Fuerte de San Miguel, Campeche City. When this towering fort was completed in 1801, pirates immediately stopped attacking the city.

Tulum, Riviera Maya. This ruined Maya city is built high on a cliff overlooking the Caribbean.

Uxmal, Yucatán. Some of the finest examples of Pu'uc architecture can be seen at this ancient Maya site: The temples and 125-foot pyramid are adorned with ornate stone mosaics and friezes, cornices, rows of columns, and vaulted arches.

EXCURSIONS

Pak Chen, southeast of Cobá. A jungle settlement of modern-day Maya who live in traditional—and primitive—style.

Reserva de la Biosfera Calakmul, southwest of Xpujil. Some 350 species of butterflies and 75 different reptiles make their home in this natural preserve; luckily, the venomous snakes only come out at night.

SMART TRAVEL TIPS

Finding out about your destination before you leave home means you won't squander time organizing everyday minutiae once you've arrived. You'll be more streetwise when you hit the ground as well, better prepared to explore the aspects of Cancún, Cozumel, and the Yucatán Peninsula that drew you here in the first place. The organizations in this section can provide information to supplement this guide; contact them for up-to-the-minute details, and consult the A to Z sections in each chapter for facts on the various topics as they relate to the different regions. Happy landings!

ADDRESSES

The Mexican method of naming streets can be exasperatingly arbitrary, so **be patient when searching for addresses.** Streets in the centers of many colonial cities are laid out in a grid surrounding the *zócalo* (main square) and often have different names on opposite sides of the square. Other streets simply acquire a new name after a certain number of blocks or when they cross a certain street. Numbered streets are usually designated *norte* (north), *sur* (south), *oriente* (east), or *poniente* (west) on either side of a central avenue.

Blocks are often labeled numerically, according to distance from a chosen starting point, as in "la Calle de Pachuca," "2a Calle de Pachuca," and so on. Many Mexican addresses have "s/n" for *sin número* (no number) after the street name. This is common in small towns where there aren't many buildings on a block.

Addresses all over Mexico are written with the street name first, followed by the street number (or "s/n"). A five-digit *código postal* (postal code) precedes, rather than follows, the name of the city: *Hacienda Paraíso, Calle Allende 211, 68000 Oaxaca.* Apdo. (*apartado*) means box; Apdo. Postal, or A. P., means post-office box number.

In many cities, most addresses include their *colonia* (neighborhood), which is abbreviated as Col. Other abbreviations used in addresses include: Sm (*Super Manzan*, meaning block or square); Av. (*avenida,* or avenue); Calz. (*calzada,* or road); Fracc. (*fraccionamiento,* or housing estate); and Int. (interior).

Mexican states have postal abbreviations of two or more letters. To send mail to the regions of Mexico covered in this book, you can use the following: Campeche: Camp.; Quintana Roo: Q. Roo; Yucatán: Yuc.

AIR TRAVEL

Almost all flights to Cancún have stopovers at hub airports (Houston, Dallas, Miami, Chicago, Los Angeles, or Atlanta), where you must change planes and transfer luggage. Some flights go to Mexico City, where you must pass through customs before transferring to a domestic flight to Cancún. This applies to air travel from the United States, Canada, the United Kingdom, Australia, and New Zealand. Be sure to have all your documents in order for entry into the States, otherwise you may be turned back.

BOOKING

When you book, look for nonstop flights and remember that "direct" flights stop at least once. Try to avoid connecting flights, which require a change of plane. Two airlines may operate a connecting flight jointly, so ask whether your airline operates every segment of the trip; you may find that the carrier you prefer flies you only part of the way. To find more booking tips and to check prices and make online flight reservations, log on to www.fodors.com.

CARRIERS

You can reach the Yucatán either by U.S., Mexican, or regional carriers. The most convenient flight from the United States is a nonstop one on a domestic or Mexican airline. Booking a carrier with stopovers adds several hours to your travel time. Flying within the Yucatán, although not cost efficient, saves you precious time if you are on a tight schedule. A flight from Cancún to Mérida, for example, can cost as much as one from Mexico City to Cancún. Select your hub city for exploring before making your reservation from abroad.

All the major airlines listed here fly to Cancún. Aeroméxico, American, Continental, and Mexicana also fly to Cozumel. Aeroméxico, Delta, and Mexicana fly to Mérida.

Within the Yucatán, Aerocaribe serves Cancún, Cozumel, Mérida, Chichén Itzá, Palenque, Chetumal, and Playa del Carmen. Flight service from the new Kuau airport near Pisté connects to Palenque, Cancún, and Cozumel. Aeroméxico flies to Campeche and Ciudad del Carmen from Mexico City. Aviacsa serves Cancún, Chetumal, and Mérida.

🔢 Major Airlines **Aeroméxico** ☎ 800/237-6639. **American** ☎ 800/433-7300. **Continental** ☎ 800/231-0856. **Delta** ☎ 800/221-1212. **Mexicana** ☎ 800/531-7921. **Northwest** ☎ 800/447-4747. **US Airways** ☎ 800/428-4322.

🔢 Within the Yucatán **Aerocaribe** ☎ 998/884-2000, 55/5536-9046 in Mexico City. **Aerocozumel** ☎ 998/884-2000. **Aeroméxico** ☎ 800/021-2622, 55/5625-2622 in Mexico City. **Aviacsa** ☎ 01800/021-4010. **Mexicana** ☎ 01800/509-8960, 55/5448-1050 in Mexico City.

CHECK-IN & BOARDING

Always **find out your carrier's check-in policy.** Plan to arrive at the airport about 2 hours before your scheduled departure time for domestic flights and 2½ to 3 hours before international flights. You may need to arrive earlier if you're flying from one of the busier airports or during peak air-traffic times.

There are three departure terminals at Cancún airport. If you are flying to Mexico City to catch a connecting flight you will be leaving from the Domestic Departures Terminal. This is at the east end of the main terminal (also known as the International Departures Terminal). Regular flights leave from the main terminal. Charter flights leave from a separate terminal, ½ km (¼ mi) west of the main terminal. In peak season lines can be long and slow-moving; plan accordingly. Be sure to ask your airline about your check-in location and departure terminal. To avoid delays at airport-security checkpoints, try not to wear any metal. Jewelry, belt and other buckles, steel-toe shoes, barrettes, and underwire bras are among the items that can set off detectors.

Assuming that not everyone with a ticket will show up, airlines routinely overbook planes. When everyone does, airlines ask for volunteers to give up their seats. In return, these volunteers usually get a several-hundred-dollar flight voucher, which can be used toward the purchase of another ticket, and are rebooked at no further charge on the next flight out. If there are not enough volunteers, the airline must choose who will be denied boarding. The first to get bumped are passengers who checked in late and those flying on discounted tickets, so get to the gate and check in as early as possible, especially during peak periods.

Always **bring a government-issued photo ID** to the airport; even when it's not required, a passport is best.

CUTTING COSTS

The least-expensive airfares to Cancún are priced for round-trip travel and must usually be purchased in advance. Some airlines also have a 30-day restriction for discount tickets. After 30 days the price goes up. Airlines generally allow you to change your return date for a fee; most low-fare tickets, however, are nonrefundable. It's smart to call a number of airlines and check the Internet; when you are quoted a good price, book it on the spot—the same fare may not be available the next day, or even the next hour. Always check different routings and look into using alternate airports. Also, price off-peak flights, which may be significantly less expensive than others. Travel agents, especially low-fare specialists, are helpful.

Consolidators are another good source. They buy tickets for scheduled flights at reduced rates from the airlines, then sell them at prices that beat the best fare available directly from the airlines. Sometimes you can even get your money back if you need to return the ticket. Carefully read the fine print detailing penalties for changes and cancellations, purchase the ticket with a credit card, and confirm your consolidator reservation with the airline.

When you fly as a courier, you trade your checked-luggage space for a ticket deeply subsidized by a courier service. There are restrictions on when you can book and

how long you can stay. Some courier companies list with membership organizations, such as the Air Courier Association and the International Association of Air Travel Couriers; these require you to become a member before you can book a flight. Most courier traffic to Mexico goes to Mexico City, where you can catch a cheap domestic flight into Cancún.

7 Consolidators **AirlineConsolidator.com** ☎ 888/468-5385 ⊕ www.airlineconsolidator.com; for international tickets. **Best Fares** ☎ 800/576-8255 or 800/576-1600 ⊕ www.bestfares.com; $59.90 annual membership. **Cheap Tickets** ☎ 800/377-1000 or 888/922-8849 ⊕ www.cheaptickets.com. **Expedia** ☎ 800/397-3342 or 404/728-8787 ⊕ www.expedia.com. **Hotwire** ☎ 866/468-9473 or 920/330-9418 ⊕ www.hotwire.com. **Now Voyager Travel** ✉ 45 W. 21st St., 5th fl., New York, NY 10010 ☎ 212/459-1616 ⊕ www.nowvoyagertravel.com. **Onetravel.com** ⊕ www.onetravel.com. **Orbitz** ☎ 888/656-4546 ⊕ www.orbitz.com. **Priceline.com** ⊕ www.priceline.com. **Travelocity** ☎ 888/709-5983 in the U.S., 877/282-2925 in Canada, 0870/111-7060 in the U.K. ⊕ www.travelocity.com.

7 Courier Resources **Air Courier Association/Cheaptrips.com** ☎ 800/282-1202 ⊕ www.aircourier.org or www.cheaptrips.com; $29 annual membership. **International Association of Air Travel Couriers** ☎ 308/632-3273 ⊕ www.courier.org; $45 annual membership.

ENJOYING THE FLIGHT

State your seat preference when purchasing your ticket, and then repeat it when you confirm and when you check in. For more legroom, you can request one of the few emergency-aisle seats at check-in, if you are capable of lifting at least 50 pounds—a Federal Aviation Administration requirement of passengers in these seats. Seats behind a bulkhead also offer more legroom, but they don't have under-seat storage. Don't sit in the row in front of the emergency aisle or in front of a bulkhead, where seats may not recline.

Ask the airline whether a snack or meal is served on the flight. If you have dietary concerns, request special meals when booking. These can be vegetarian, low-cholesterol, or kosher, for example. It's a good idea to pack some healthful snacks and a small (plastic) bottle of water in your carry-on bag. On long flights, try to maintain a normal routine, to help fight jet lag. At night, get some sleep. By day, eat light meals, drink water (not alcohol), and **move around the cabin** to stretch your legs. For additional jet-lag tips consult *Fodor's FYI: Travel Fit & Healthy* (available at bookstores everywhere).

Smoking policies vary from carrier to carrier. All airlines flying into Mexico currently prohibit smoking on their flights.

Most of the larger U.S. airlines no longer offer meals on flights to the Yucatán Peninsula. The flights are considered short-haul flights because there is a stopover at a hub airport (where you can purchase your own overpriced meals). The snacks provided on such flights are measly at best, so you may want to **bring food on board** with you. Aeroméxico and Mexicana both provide full meals. All flights aboard Mexican airlines are no-smoking.

FLYING TIMES

Cancún is 3½ hours from New York and Chicago, 4½ hours from Los Angeles, 3 hours from Dallas, 11¾ hours from London, and 18 hours from Sydney. Add another 1–4 hours if you change planes at one of the hub airports and have a long layover. Flights to Cozumel and Mérida are comparable in length.

HOW TO COMPLAIN

If your baggage goes astray or your flight goes awry, complain right away. Most carriers require that you **file a claim immediately.** The Aviation Consumer Protection Division of the Department of Transportation publishes *Fly-Rights,* which discusses airlines and consumer issues and is available online. You can also find articles and information on mytravelrights.com, the Web site of the nonprofit Consumer Travel Rights Center.

🛪 Airline Complaints **Aviation Consumer Protection Division** ✉ U.S. Department of Transportation, C-75, Room 4107, 400 7th St. SW, Washington, DC 20590 ☎ 202/366-2220 ⊕ airconsumer.ost.dot.gov. **Federal Aviation Administration Consumer Hotline** ✉ for inquiries: FAA, 800 Independence Ave. SW, Washington, DC 20591 ☎ 800/322-7873 ⊕ www.faa.gov.

RECONFIRMING

Check the status of your flight before you leave for the airport. You can do this on your carrier's Web site, by linking to a flight-status checker (many Web booking services offer these), or by calling your carrier or travel agent. Always confirm international flights at least 72 hours ahead of the scheduled departure time. Charter flights, especially those leaving from Cancún, are notorious for last-minute changes. Be sure to ask for an updated telephone number from your charter company before you leave so you can call to check for any changes in flight departures. Most recommend you call within 48 hours. This check-in also applies for the regular airlines, although their departure times are more regular. Their changes are usually due to weather conditions rather than seat sales.

AIRPORTS

Cancún Aeropuerto Internacional (CUN) and Cozumel Aeropuerto Internacional (CZM) are the area's major gateways. The inland Hector José Vavarrette Muñoz Airport (MID), in Mérida, is a good size and closest to the major Maya ruins. Campeche, Chetumal, and Playa del Carmen have smaller airports served primarily by domestic carriers. The ruins at Palenque and Chichén Itzá also have airstrips that handle small planes.

Fly into the airport closest to where you'll be doing most of your travel. Airfares to Cancún, Mérida, and Cozumel don't differ much, and the airports serving these three are no more than 20 minutes from downtown. Car rentals are a bit less expensive in Mérida than in Cancún and Cozumel, but not enough to warrant a four-hour drive to Cancún if it's your hub.

🛪 Airport Information **Cancún Aeropuerto Internacional** ☎ 998/886-0341. **Cozumel Aeropuerto Internacional** ☎ 987/872-0485. **Hector José Vavarrette Muñoz Airport** ☎ 999/946-1340.

DUTY-FREE SHOPPING

Cancún and Cozumel are duty-free shopping zones with more variety and better prices than the duty-free shops at the airports.

BOAT & FERRY TRAVEL

The Yucatán is served by a number of ferries and boats. Most popular are the efficient speedboats that run between Playa del Carmen and Cozumel or from Puerto Juárez, Punta Sam, and Isla Mujeres. Smaller and less efficient boat carriers are also available in many places.

FARES & SCHEDULES

Most carriers follow schedules, with the exception of boats going to the smaller, less-visited islands. However, departure times can vary with the weather and the number of passengers.

For specific fares and schedules, *see* Boat & Ferry Travel *in* the A to Z section in each chapter.

BUS TRAVEL

The Mexican bus network is extensive and also the best means of getting around, since passenger trains have just about become obsolete. Service is frequent and tickets can be purchased on the spot (except during holidays and on long weekends, when advance purchase is crucial). Bring something to eat on long trips in case you don't like the restaurant where the bus stops; **bring toilet tissue;** and **wear a sweater,** as the air-conditioning is often set on high. Most buses play videos or television continually until midnight, so if you are bothered by noise **bring earplugs.** Smoking is prohibited on a growing number of Mexican buses, though the rule is occasionally ignored.

CLASSES

Buses range from comfortable, fast, air-conditioned coaches with bathrooms, televisions, and complimentary beverages (*especial,* deluxe, and first-class) to dilapidated "vintage" buses (second-class), which stop at every village along the way and pick up anyone who flags them from the highway. On the more rural routes passengers will include chickens, pigs, or baby goats. A second-class bus ride can be interesting if you're not in a hurry and want to see the sights and experience the local culture. The fare is usually at least 20% cheaper. For comfort's sake alone, travelers planning a long-distance haul

are advised to buy first-class or especial tickets. Several truly first-class bus companies offer service connecting Mexico's major cities. ADO (Autobuses del Oriente) is the Yucatán's principal first-class bus company.

FARES & SCHEDULES

Bus travel in the Yucatán, as throughout Mexico, is inexpensive by U.S. standards, with rates averaging $2–$5 per hour depending on the level of luxury (or lack of it). Schedules are posted at bus stations; the bus leaves more or less around the listed time. Often, if all the seats have been sold, the bus will leave early. Check with the driver.

RESERVATIONS

Most bus tickets, including first-class or especial and second-class, can be reserved in advance in person at ticket offices. ADO allows you to reserve tickets 48 hours in advance over the Internet. ADO and ADO GL (deluxe service) travel to Cancún, Chiapas, Oaxaca, Tampico, Veracruz, Villahermosa, and Yucatán from Mexico City.
🚍 Bus Information **ADO** ☎ 55/5133-2424. **ADO GL** ☎ 01800/702-8000 toll-free in Mexico, 55/5785-9659 ⊕ www.adogl.com.mx.

BUSINESS HOURS

In well-traveled places such as Cancún, Isla Mujeres, Playa del Carmen, Mérida, and Cozumel, businesses generally are open during posted hours. In more off-the-beaten-path areas, neighbors can tell you when the owner will return.

BANKS & OFFICES

Banks are open weekdays 9–5. Some banks open on Saturday morning. Most banks will exchange money only until noon. Most businesses are open weekdays 9–2 and 4–7.

GAS STATIONS

Most gas stations are open 24 hours. However, in the remote areas, some gas stations close from midnight until 6 AM.

MUSEUMS & SIGHTS

Most museums throughout Mexico are closed on Monday and open 8–5 the rest of the week. But it's best to call ahead or ask at your hotel. Hours of sights and attractions in this book are denoted by a clock icon, ☾.

PHARMACIES

The larger pharmacies in Cancún and Cozumel are usually open daily 8 AM–10 PM, and each of the big cities has at least one 24-hour pharmacy. Smaller pharmacies are often closed on Sunday.

SHOPS

Stores in the tourist areas such as Cancún and Cozumel are usually open 10–9 Monday through Saturday and on Sunday afternoon. Shops in more traditional areas, such as Campeche and Mérida and the Yucatán, close weekdays between 1 PM and 4 PM, opening again in the evening. They are generally closed Sunday.

CAMERAS & PHOTOGRAPHY

Mexico, with its majestic landscapes and ruins (don't miss taking photos of the ruins at Tulum and Chichén Itzá) and varied cityscapes, is a photographer's dream. Mexicans seem amenable to having picture-taking visitors in their midst, but you should always **ask permission before taking pictures in churches or of individuals.** They may ask you for a *propina*, or tip, in which case a few pesos is customary. (Note that most indigenous peoples don't ever want to be photographed; taking pictures is also forbidden in some churches.) If you're bashful about approaching strangers, photograph people with whom you interact: your waiter, your desk clerk, the vendor selling you crafts. Even better, have a traveling companion or a passerby photograph you *with* them. Also, **don't snap pictures of military or high-security installations** anywhere in the country. It's forbidden.

To avoid the blurriness caused by shaky hands, get a mini-tripod—they're available in sizes as small as 6 inches. (Although cameras are permitted at archaeological sites, many of them strictly prohibit the use of tripods.) Buy a small beanbag to support your camera on uneven surfaces. If you plan to take photos on some of the country's many beaches, bring a skylight (81B or 81C) or polarizing filter to minimize haze and light problems. If you're visiting forested areas, bring high-speed film to compensate for low light under the tree canopy and invest in a telephoto lens to photograph wildlife; standard zoom lenses in the 35–88 range won't capture enough detail.

Casual photographers should **consider using inexpensive disposable cameras** to reduce the risks inherent in traveling with sophisticated equipment. One-use cameras with panoramic or underwater functions are also nice supplements to a standard camera and its gear.

The *Kodak Guide to Shooting Great Travel Pictures* (available at bookstores everywhere) is loaded with tips.
📷 Photo Help **Kodak Information Center** ☎ 800/242-2424 ⊕ www.kodak.com.

EQUIPMENT PRECAUTIONS

Don't pack film or equipment in checked luggage, where it is much more susceptible to damage. X-ray machines used to view checked luggage are extremely powerful and therefore are likely to ruin your film. Try to ask for hand inspection of film, and keep videotapes and computer disks away from metal detectors. Carry an extra supply of batteries, and be prepared to turn on your camera, camcorder, or laptop to prove to airport security personnel that the device is real.

Humidity and heat are problems for cameras in this region. Always **keep your camera, film, tape, and computer disks out of the sun.** Try to **keep sand out of your camera.** You may want to invest in a special filter to protect your lens from sand. After a trip to the beach be sure to clean your lens, since salt air can leave a film on the lens and grains of sand may scratch it. Keep a special cleansing solution and cloth for this purpose. Also, as petty crime can be a problem, **keep a close eye on your gear.**

FILM & DEVELOPING

Film is widely available in Cancún, Cozumel, Playa del Carmen, Campeche City, and Mérida, and all have one-hour photo development places. (Check to see that all the negatives were developed into pictures; sometimes a few are missed.) Prices are a bit more expensive than those in the United States. Fuji and Kodak are the most popular brands with prices for a roll of 36-exposure color print film starting at about $5. The more sophisticated brands of film, such as Advantix, will be available at American outlet stores such as Wal-Mart and Costco. These stores also offer bulk packages of film.

VIDEOS

The local standard for videotape in Mexico is the same as in the United States. All videos are NTSC (National Television Standards Committee). Prices are a bit more expensive than those in the United States, starting at around $5.50 for a 90-minute tape. American outlet stores like Wal-Mart and Costco will have more variety and lower prices. Be careful buying DVDs while in Mexico. Most have been programmed for use only in Latin America and will not play on your machine back home.

CAR RENTAL

An economy car with no air-conditioning, manual transmission, and unlimited mileage begins at $50 a day or about $300 a week in Cancún; in Mérida, rates are about $35 a day or $210 a week; and in Campeche, $30 a day or $200 a week. Count on about $10 a day more with air-conditioning and automatic transmission. This does not include tax, which is 10% in Cancún and on the Caribbean coast and 15% elsewhere. The most common and least-expensive brand of car here is the Volkswagen Beetle. If you reserve online before your departure you can save up to 50% and often get upgraded.

🚗 **Alamo** 🕾 800/522-9696 ⊕ www.alamo.com. **Avis** 🕾 800/331-1084 in the U.S., 800/879-2847 in Canada, 0870/606-0100 in the U.K., 02/9353-9000 in Australia, 09/526-2847 in New Zealand ⊕ www.avis.com. **Budget** 🕾 800/527-0700 in the U.S., 0870/156-5656 in the U.K. ⊕ www.budget.com. **Dollar** 🕾 800/800-6000 in the U.S., 0124/622-0111 in the U.K., where it's affiliated with Sixt, 02/9223-1444 in Australia ⊕ www.dollar.com. **Hertz** 🕾 800/654-3001 in the U.S., 800/263-0600 in Canada, 0870/844-8844 in the U.K., 02/9669-2444 in Australia, 09/256-8690 in New Zealand ⊕ www.hertz.com. **National Car Rental** 🕾 800/227-7368 in the U.S., 0870/600-6666 in the U.K. ⊕ www.nationalcar.com.

CUTTING COSTS

For a good deal, book through a travel agent who will shop around. Also, price local car-rental companies—whose prices may be lower still, although their service and maintenance may not be as good as those of major rental agencies—and research rates on the Internet. Remember to ask about required deposits, cancellation penalties, and drop-off charges if you're planning to pick up the car in one city and leave it in another. If you're traveling during a holiday period, also make sure that a confirmed reservation guarantees you a car.

Do look into wholesalers, companies that do not own fleets but rent in bulk from those that do and often offer better rates than traditional car-rental operations. Prices are best during off-peak periods. Rentals booked through wholesalers often must be paid for before you leave home.

🚗 **Local Agencies Buster Renta Car** 🕾 998/849-7221. **Econorent** 🕾 998/887-6487. **Executive** 🕾 998/886-0065 or 998/884-2699 in Cancún, 999/946-1387 in Mérida ⊕ www.executive.com.mx. **Localiza** 🕾 998/886-0248 or 998/886-0244 in Cancún ⊕ www.localizarentacar.com.
🚗 **Wholesaler Auto Europe** 🕾 800/223-5555 or 207/842-2000 ⊕ www.autoeurope.com.

INSURANCE

When driving a rented car you are generally responsible for any damage to or loss of the vehicle. You also may be liable for any property damage or personal injury that you may cause while driving. Before you rent, see what coverage you already have under the terms of your personal auto-insurance policy and credit cards.

Regardless of any coverage afforded to you by your credit-card company, you must **obtain Mexican auto-liability insurance.** This is usually sold by car-rental agencies and included in the cost of the car. Be sure that you have been provided with proof of such insurance; if you drive without it, you are not only liable for damages, but you're also breaking the law. If you are in a car accident and you don't have insurance, you may be placed in jail until you are proven innocent. If anyone is injured you will remain in jail until you make retribution to all injured parties and their families—which will likely cost you thousands of dollars. Mexican laws favor nationals.

REQUIREMENTS & RESTRICTIONS
In Mexico the minimum driving age is 18, but most rental-car agencies require you to be between 21 and 25. Your own driver's license is acceptable, but an international driver's license is a good idea. It's available from the U.S. and Canadian automobile associations, and, in the United Kingdom, from the Automobile Association or Royal Automobile Club.

SURCHARGES
Before you pick up a car in one city and leave it in another, ask about drop-off charges or one-way service fees, which can be substantial. Note, too, that some rental agencies charge extra if you return the car before the time specified in your contract. To avoid a hefty refueling fee, fill the tank just before you turn in the car, but be aware that gas stations near the rental outlet may overcharge. It's almost never a deal to buy the tank of gas that's in the car when you rent it; the understanding is that you'll return it empty, but some fuel usually remains.

CAR TRAVEL
Though convenient, cars are not a necessity in this part of Mexico. Cancún offers excellent bus and taxi service; Isla Mujeres is too small to make a car practical. Cars are not needed in Playa del Carmen because the downtown area is quite small and the main street is blocked off to vehicles. You will need a car in Cozumel only if you wish to explore the eastern side of the island. Cars are actually a burden in Mérida and Campeche City because of the narrow cobbled streets and the lack of parking spaces. Driving is the easiest way to explore other areas of the region, especially those off the beaten track. But even then a car is not absolutely necessary, as there is good bus service.

Before setting out on any car trip, **check your vehicle's fuel, oil, fluids, tires, and lights.** Gas stations and mechanics can be hard to find, especially in more remote areas. Consult a map and have your route

in mind as you drive. Be aware that there is no formal driver's education in Mexico. This makes for many bad drivers on the roads who think nothing of tailgating, speeding, and weaving in and out of traffic. **Drive defensively** and keep your cool. When stopped for traffic or at a red light, always **leave sufficient room between your car and the one ahead** so you can maneuver to safety if necessary.

EMERGENCY SERVICES
The Mexican Tourism Ministry operates a fleet of some 350 pickup trucks, known as Angeles Verdes, or the Green Angels, to render assistance to motorists on the major highways. You can call the Green Angels directly or call the Ministry of Tourism's hotline and they will dispatch them. The bilingual drivers provide mechanical help, first aid, radio-telephone communication, basic supplies and small parts, towing, and tourist information. Services are free, and spare parts, fuel, and lubricants are provided at cost. Tips are always appreciated.

The Green Angels patrol fixed sections of the major highways twice daily 8 AM to dusk, later on holiday weekends. If your car breaks down, **pull as far as possible off the road,** lift the hood, hail a passing vehicle, and ask the driver to **notify the patrol.** Most bus and truck drivers will be quite helpful. Do not accept rides from strangers. If you witness an accident, do not stop to help but instead find the nearest official.

🛈 **Angeles Verdes** ☎ 800/903–9200 Ministry of Tourism hotline, 55/5250–8221.

GASOLINE
Pemex, Mexico's government-owned petroleum monopoly, franchises all gas stations, so prices throughout the Yucatán are the same. Prices tend to be about 30% higher than those in the United States. Gas is always sold in liters and you must pay in cash since none of the Pemex stations accept foreign credit cards. Premium unleaded gas is called *super*; regular unleaded gas is *magna sin.* At some of the older gas stations you may find leaded fuel called *nova.* Avoid using this gas; it's very hard on your engine. Fuel quality is generally

lower than in the United States and Europe. Vehicles with fuel-injected engines are likely to have problems after driving extended distances. A fuel-injection cleaner-supplement is sold in most of the larger cities and is highly recommended.

There are no self-service stations in Mexico. When you have your tank filled, **ask for a specific amount in pesos** to avoid being overcharged. Check to make sure that the attendant has set the meter back to zero and that the price is shown. Watch the attendant check the oil as well—to make sure you actually need it—and watch while he pours it into your car. **Never pay before the gas is pumped,** even if the attendant asks you to. Always **tip your attendant** a few pesos. Finally, keep your gas tank full, because gas stations are not plentiful in this area. If you run out of gas in a small village and there's no gas station for miles, ask if there's a store that sells gas from containers.

PARKING

Always **park your car in a parking lot,** or at least in a populated area. Tip the parking attendant or security guard a few dollars and ask him to look after your car. **Never park your car overnight on the street.** Never leave anything of value in an unattended car. There is usually a parking attendant available who will watch your car for a few pesos. Sometimes there are attendants who will wash your car and keep an eye on it for about $2.

ROAD CONDITIONS

The road system in the Yucatán Peninsula is extensive and generally in good repair. Carretera 307 parallels most of the Caribbean coast from Punta Sam, north of Cancún, to Tulum; here it turns inward for a stretch before returning to the coast at Chetumal and the Belize border. Carretera 180 runs west from Cancún to Valladolid, Chichén Itzá, and Mérida, then turns southwest to Campeche, Isla del Carmen, and on to Villahermosa. From Mérida, the winding, more scenic Carretera 261 also leads to some of the more off-the-beaten-track archaeological sites on the way south to Campeche and Francisco Escárcega, where it joins Carretera 186 going east to

Chetumal. These highways are two-lane roads. Carretera 295 (from the north coast to Valladolid and Felipe Carrillo Puerto) is also a good two-lane road.

The *autopista,* or *carretera de cuota,* a four-lane toll highway between Cancún and Mérida, was completed in 1993. It runs roughly parallel to Carretera 180 and cuts driving time between Cancún and Mérida—otherwise about 4½ hours—by about 1 hour. Tolls between Mérida and Cancún can run as high as $24, and the stretches between highway exits are long. Be careful when driving on this road, as it retains the heat from the sun and can make your tires blow if they have low pressure or worn threads.

Many secondary roads are in bad condition—unpaved, unmarked, and full of potholes. If you must take one of these roads, the best course is to **allow plenty of daylight hours and never travel at night.** Slow down when approaching towns and villages—which you are forced to do by the *topes* (speed bumps)—because small children and animals are everywhere. Children selling oranges, nuts, or other food will almost certainly approach your car. Some people feel that it's best not to buy from them, reasoning that if the children can make money this way, they will not go to school. Others choose to buy from them on the theory that they would probably go to school if they could afford it and need the meager profits to survive. Judge for yourself.

ROAD MAPS

Maps published by Pemex are available in bookstores and papelerías, but gas stations don't sell them. The best guide is Guía Roji.

RULES OF THE ROAD

There are two absolutely essential points to remember about driving in Mexico. First and foremost is to **carry Mexican auto insurance.** If you injure anyone in an accident, you could well be jailed—whether it was your fault or not—unless you have insurance. Second, **if you enter Mexico with a car, you must leave with it.** In recent years, the high rate of U.S. vehicles being sold illegally in Mexico has caused the Mexican government to enact stringent regulations for bringing a car into the country. You must be in your foreign vehicle at all times when it is driven. You cannot lend it to another person. Do not, under any circumstances, let a national drive your car. It is illegal for Mexicans to drive foreign cars and if they are caught by the police your car will be impounded by customs and you will be given a very stiff fine to pay. Newer models of vans, SUVs, and pickup trucks can be impossible to get back once impounded.

You must cross the border with the following documents: title or registration for your vehicle; a birth certificate or passport; a credit card (AE, DC, MC, or V); a valid driver's license with a photo. The title holder, driver, and credit-card owner must be one and the same—that is, if your spouse's name is on the title of the car and yours isn't, you cannot be the one to bring the car into the country. For financed, leased, rental, or company cars, you must **bring a notarized letter of permission** from the bank, lien holder, rental agency, or company. When you submit your paperwork at the border and pay the $22 charge on your credit card, you'll receive a car permit and a sticker to put on your vehicle, all valid for up to six months. You may go back and forth across the border during this six-month period, as long as you check with immigration and bring all your permit paperwork with you. If you are planning to stay and keep your car in Mexico for longer than six months, however, you will have to get a new permit before the original one expires.

One way to minimize hassle when you cross the border with a car is to **have your paperwork done in advance** at a branch of Sanborn's Mexican Insurance; look in the Yellow Pages for an office in almost every town on the U.S.–Mexico border. You'll still have to go through some of the procedures at the border, but all your paperwork will be in order, and Sanborn's express window will ensure that you get through relatively quickly. There's a $10 charge for this service. The fact that you

drove in with a car is stamped on your tourist card, which you must give to immigration authorities at departure. If an emergency arises and you must fly home, there are complicated customs procedures to face.

When you sign up for Mexican car insurance, you should receive a booklet on Mexican rules of the road. It really is a good idea to read it to avoid breaking laws that differ from those of your country. If an oncoming vehicle flicks its lights at you in daytime, slow down: it could mean trouble ahead. When approaching a narrow bridge, the first vehicle to flash its lights has right of way. One-way streets are common. One-way traffic is indicated by an arrow; two-way, by a double-pointed arrow. Other road signs follow the widespread system of international symbols.

Mileage and speed limits are given in kilometers: 100 kph and 80 kph (62 mph and 50 mph, respectively) are the most common maximums. A few of the toll roads allow 110 kph (68 mph). In cities and small towns, observe the posted speed limits, which can be as low as 20 kph (12 mph). Seat belts are required by law throughout Mexico.

SAFETY ON THE ROAD

Never drive at night in remote and rural areas. While there are few *banditos* on the roads here, there are large potholes, free-roaming animals, cars with no working lights, road-hogging trucks, and difficulty in getting assistance. If you must travel at night, use the toll roads whenever possible; although costly, they're much safer.

Some of the biggest hassles on the road might be from police who pull you over for supposedly breaking the law, or for being a good prospect for a scam. Remember to **be polite**—displays of anger will only make matters worse—and be aware that a police officer might be pulling you over for something you didn't do. Although efforts are being made to fight corruption, it's still a fact of life in Mexico, and the $5 it costs to get your license back is definitely supplementary income for the officer who pulled you over with no intention of taking you down to police headquarters.

If you're stopped for speeding, the officer is supposed to take your license and hold it until you pay the fine at the local police station. But the officer will always prefer a *mordida* (small bribe) to wasting his time at the station. If you decide to dispute a charge that seems preposterous, do so with a smile, and tell the officer that you would like to talk to the police captain when you get to the station. The officer usually will let you go rather than go to the station. However, if you're in a hurry, you may choose to negotiate a payment.

When crossing the streets by foot, **look both ways for oncoming traffic,** even with the light. Although pedestrians have the right of way by law, drivers disregard it. And more often than not, if a driver hits a pedestrian, he'll drive away as fast as he can without stopping, to avoid jail. Many Mexican drivers don't carry auto insurance, so you'll have to shoulder your own medical expenses.

CHILDREN IN CANCÚN
Traveling with children opens doors in Mexico that often remain closed to single travelers. If they enjoy travel in general, your children will do well throughout the Yucatán.

Note that Mexico has one of the strictest policies about children entering the country. All children, including infants, must have proof of citizenship (a birth certificate) for travel to Mexico. All children up to age 18 traveling with a single parent must also have a notarized letter from the other parent stating that the child has his or her permission to leave their home country. If the other parent is deceased or the child has only one legal parent, a notarized statement saying so must be obtained as proof. In addition, parents must now fill out a tourist card for each child over the age of 10 traveling with them.

If you are renting a car, don't forget to **arrange for a car seat** when you reserve. For general advice about traveling with children, consult *Fodor's FYI: Travel with Your Baby* (available in bookstores everywhere).

BABY-SITTING
Most hotels offer baby-sitting services, especially if there is a kids' club at the hotel. The sitters will be professionally trained nannies who speak English. Rates range from $10 to $20 (U.S.) per hour.

🚩 Agency **Cancún Baby Sitting Services,** c/o Veronica C. Flores ✉ Torres Cancún 15, Sm 28 ☎ 998/880-9098 🌐 www.cancun-baby-sitting-services.com.

FLYING
If your children are two or older, ask about children's airfares. As a general rule, infants under two not occupying a seat fly at greatly reduced fares or even for free. But if you want to guarantee a seat for an infant, you have to pay full fare. Consider flying during off-peak days and times; most airlines will grant an infant a seat without a ticket if there are available seats. When booking, confirm carry-on allowances if you're traveling with infants. In general, for babies charged 10% to 50% of the adult fare you are allowed one carry-on bag and a collapsible stroller; if the flight is full, the stroller may have to be checked or you may be limited to less.

Experts agree that it's a good idea to use safety seats aloft for children weighing less than 40 pounds. Airlines set their own policies: if you use a safety seat, U.S. carriers usually require that the child be ticketed, even if he or she is young enough to ride free, because the seats must be strapped into regular seats. And even if you pay the full adult fare for the seat, it may be worth it, especially on longer trips. Do **check your airline's policy about using safety seats during takeoff and landing.** Safety seats are not allowed everywhere in the plane, so get your seat assignments as early as possible.

When reserving, request children's meals or a freestanding bassinet (not available at all airlines) if you need them. But note that bulkhead seats, where you must sit to use the bassinet, may lack an overhead bin or storage space on the floor.

FOOD
The more populated areas, such as Cancún, Mérida, Campeche City, Cozumel,

and Playa del Carmen, have U.S. fast-food outlets, and most restaurants that serve tourists have a special children's menu with the usual chicken fingers, hot dogs, and spaghetti. Yucatecan cuisine also has plenty of dishes suited for children's taste buds. It's common for parents to share a plate with their children, so no one will look twice if you order one meal with two plates.

LODGING

Most hotels in the Yucatán Peninsula allow children under 12 to stay in their parents' room at no extra charge, but others charge for them as extra adults; be sure to **find out the cutoff age for children's discounts.** Most of the chain hotels offer services that make it easier to travel with children. These include connecting family rooms, wading pools and playgrounds, and kids' clubs with special activities and outings. Check with your hotel before booking to see if the price includes the services you're interested in.

🚹 Best Choices **Fiesta Americana Mérida** ✉ Av. Colón 451, at Paseo Montejo, 97000 Mérida ☎ 800/343-7821 or 999/942-1111 ⊕ www.fiestaamerican. com. **Gran Caribe Real Club** ✉ Blvd. Kukulcán, Km 5.5, 77500 Cancún ☎ 998/881-7300 ⊕ www.real. com.mx. **Occidental Caribbean Village** ✉ Blvd. Kukulcán, Km 13.5, Zona Hotelera, 77500 Cancún, Quintana Roo ☎ 800/645-1179 or 998/848-8000 ⊕ www.tropicalsands.com/resorts/allegro.

PRECAUTIONS

Since children are particularly prone to diarrhea, be especially careful with their food and beverages. Peel all fruits, cook vegetables, and stay away from ice unless it comes from a reliable source. Ice cream from vendors should also be avoided. Infants and young children may be bothered by the heat and sun; make sure they drink plenty of fluids, wear sunscreen, and stay out of the sun at midday (⇨ Health).

SIGHTS & ATTRACTIONS

The larger tourist areas have plenty of activities for children, including museums, zoos, aquariums, and theme parks. Places that are especially appealing to children are indicated by a rubber-duckie icon (🐤) in the margin.

SUPPLIES & EQUIPMENT

Fresh milk is hard to find—most of the milk here is reconstituted and sold in cartons. Most other necessities, including *pañales desechables* (disposable diapers) and *fórmula infantil* (infant formula), can be found in almost every small town.

COMPUTERS ON THE ROAD

If you are traveling with your laptop, watch it carefully. The biggest danger, aside from theft, is the constantly fluctuating electricity, which will eventually damage your hard drive. Invest in a Mexican surge protector (available at most electronics stores for about $45) that can handle the frequent brownouts and fluctuations in voltage. The surge protectors you use at home probably won't give you much protection. It's best to leave repairs until you are back home.

CONSUMER PROTECTION

Whether you're shopping for gifts or purchasing travel services, **pay with a major credit card** whenever possible, so you can cancel payment or get reimbursed if there's a problem (and you can provide documentation). If you're doing business with a particular company for the first time, contact your local Better Business Bureau and the attorney general's offices in your state and (for U.S. businesses) the company's home state as well. Have any complaints been filed? Finally, if you're buying a package or tour, always **consider travel insurance** that includes default coverage (⇨ Insurance).

The Mexican consumer protection agency, the Procuraduría Federal de Consumidor (PROFECO), also helps foreigners. However, the complaint process with PROFECO is cumbersome and can take up to several months to resolve.

🚹 BBBs **Council of Better Business Bureaus** ✉ 4200 Wilson Blvd., Suite 800, Arlington, VA 22203 ☎ 703/276-0100 ⊕ www.bbb.org. **Procuraduría Federal de Consumidor (PROFECO)** ☎ 998/884-2634 in Cancún, 55/5547-1084 in Mexico City.

CRUISE TRAVEL

Cozumel and Playa del Carmen have become increasingly popular ports for

Caribbean cruises. The last few years have seen many changes in the cruise business. Several companies have merged and several more are suffering financial difficulties. Due to heavy traffic, Cozumel and Playa del Carmen have limited the amount of traffic coming into their ports. Currently only Cunard, Carnival, and Norwegian Cruise lines sail direct to Cozumel. Carnival and Cunard leave from Galveston, New Orleans, and Miami while Norwegian departs from Houston. Princess, Royal Caribbean International, and Celebrity Cruises dock at Cozumel for only a few hours as a port of call on their Caribbean cruises.

To learn how to plan, choose, and book a cruise-ship voyage, consult *Fodor's FYI: Plan & Enjoy Your Cruise* (available in bookstores everywhere).

🛈 Cruise Lines **Carnival Cruise Lines** ☎ 800/304–2319 ⊕ www.cruise-carnival.net. **Cunard** ☎ 800/728-6273 ⊕ www.cunard.com. **Norwegian** ☎ 800/327-7030 ⊕ www.ncl.com. **Princess** ☎ 800/774–6237 ⊕ www.princess.com. **Royal Caribbean International** ☎ 800/398–9819 ⊕ www.royalcaribbean.com.

DISCOUNT CRUISES

Usually, the best deals on cruise bookings can be found by consulting a cruise-only travel agency.

🛈 Agency **National Association of Cruise Only Travel Agencies** (NACOA) ⊠ 3191 Coral Way, Suite 622, Miami, FL 33145 ☎ 305/446-7732.

CUSTOMS & DUTIES

When shopping abroad, keep receipts for all purchases. Upon reentering the country, **be ready to show customs officials what you've bought.** Pack purchases together in an easily accessible place. If you think a duty is incorrect, appeal the assessment. If you object to the way your clearance was handled, note the inspector's badge number. In either case, first ask to see a supervisor. If the problem isn't resolved, write to the appropriate authorities, beginning with the port director at your point of entry.

IN AUSTRALIA

Australian residents who are 18 or older may bring home A$400 worth of souvenirs and gifts (including jewelry), 250

cigarettes or 250 grams of cigars or other tobacco products, and 1,125 ml of alcohol (including wine, beer, and spirits). Residents under 18 may bring back A$200 worth of goods. Members of the same family traveling together may pool their allowances. Prohibited items include meat products. Seeds, plants, and fruits need to be declared upon arrival.

🛈 **Australian Customs Service** ☏ Regional Director, Box 8, Sydney, NSW 2001 ☎ 02/9213-2000 or 1300/363263, 02/9364-7222 or 1800/020-504 quarantine-inquiry line ⊕ www.customs.gov.au.

IN CANADA

Canadian residents who have been out of Canada for at least seven days may bring in C$750 worth of goods duty-free. If you've been away fewer than seven days but more than 48 hours, the duty-free allowance drops to C$200. If your trip lasts 24 to 48 hours, the allowance is C$50. You may not pool allowances with family members. Goods claimed under the C$750 exemption may follow you by mail; those claimed under the lesser exemptions must accompany you. Alcohol and tobacco products may be included in the seven-day and 48-hour exemptions but not in the 24-hour exemption. If you meet the age requirements of the province or territory through which you reenter Canada, you may bring in, duty-free, 1.5 liters of wine *or* 1.14 liters (40 imperial ounces) of liquor *or* 24 12-ounce cans or bottles of beer or ale. Also, if you meet the local age requirement for tobacco products, you may bring in, duty-free, 200 cigarettes and 50 cigars. Check ahead of time with the Canada Customs and Revenue Agency or the Department of Agriculture for policies regarding meat products, seeds, plants, and fruits.

You may send an unlimited number of gifts (only one gift per recipient, however) worth up to C$60 each duty-free to Canada. Label the package UNSOLICITED GIFT—VALUE UNDER $60. Alcohol and tobacco are excluded.

🛈 **Canada Customs and Revenue Agency** ⊠ 2265 St. Laurent Blvd., Ottawa, Ontario K1G 4K3 ☎ 800/461-9999, 204/983-3500, or 506/636-5064 ⊕ www.ccra.gc.ca.

IN MEXICO

Upon entering Mexico, you'll be given a baggage declaration form and asked to itemize what you're bringing into the country. You are allowed to bring in 3 liters of spirits or wine for personal use; 400 cigarettes, 25 cigars, or 200 grams of tobacco; a reasonable amount of perfume for personal use; one movie camera and one regular camera and 12 rolls of film for each; and gift items not to exceed a total of $300. If driving across the U.S. border, gift items must not exceed $50. You aren't allowed to bring firearms, meat, vegetables, plants, fruit, or flowers into the country. You can bring in one of each of the following items without paying taxes: a cell phone, a beeper, a radio or tape recorder, a musical instrument, a laptop computer, a portable copier or printer, and a typewriter. Compact discs are limited to 20 and DVDs to five.

Mexico also allows you to bring one cat, one dog, or up to four canaries into the country if you have two things: 1) a pet health certificate signed by a registered veterinarian in the United States and issued not more than 72 hours before the animal enters Mexico; and 2) a pet vaccination certificate showing that the animal has been treated for rabies, hepatitis, pip, and leptospirosis. Aduana Mexico (Mexican Customs) has a striking and informative Web site, though everything is in Spanish.

🛈 **Aduana Mexico** ⊕ www.aduanas.sat.gob.mx. **Mexican Consulate** ⊠ 2401 W. 6th St., Los Angeles, CA 90057 ☎ 231/351-6800 ⊕ www.consulmex-la.com ⊠ 27 E. 39th St., New York, NY 10016 ☎ 212/217-6400 ⊕ www.consulmexny.com.

IN NEW ZEALAND

All homeward-bound residents may bring back NZ$700 worth of souvenirs and gifts; passengers may not pool their allowances, and children can claim only the concession on goods intended for their own use. For those 17 or older, the duty-free allowance also includes 4.5 liters of wine or beer; one 1,125-ml bottle of spirits; and either 200 cigarettes, 250 grams of tobacco, 50 cigars, *or* a combination of the three up to 250 grams. Meat products, seeds, plants, and fruits must be declared upon arrival to the Agricultural Services Department.

🛈 **New Zealand Customs** ⊠ Head office: The Customhouse, 17–21 Whitmore St., Box 2218, Wellington ☎ 0800/428-786 or 09/300-5399 ⊕ www.customs.govt.nz.

IN THE U.K.

From countries outside the European Union, including Mexico, you may bring home, duty-free, 200 cigarettes or 50 cigars; 1 liter of spirits or 2 liters of fortified or sparkling wine or liqueurs; 2 liters of still table wine; 60 ml of perfume; 250 ml of toilet water; plus £145 worth of other goods, including gifts and souvenirs. Prohibited items include meat products, seeds, plants, and fruits.

🛈 **HM Customs and Excise** ⊠ Portcullis House, 21 Cowbridge Rd. E, Cardiff CF11 9SS ☎ 0845/010-9000 or 0208/929-0152, 0208/929-6731 or 0208/910-3602 complaints ⊕ www.hmce.gov.uk.

IN THE U.S.

U.S. residents who have been out of the country for at least 48 hours may bring home, for personal use, $800 worth of foreign goods duty-free, as long as they haven't used the $800 allowance or any part of it in the past 30 days. This exemption may include 1 liter of alcohol (for travelers 21 and older), 200 cigarettes, and 100 non-Cuban cigars. Family members from the same household who are traveling together may pool their $800 personal exemptions. For fewer than 48 hours, the duty-free allowance drops to $200, which may include 50 cigarettes, 10 non-Cuban cigars, and 150 ml of alcohol (or 150 ml of perfume containing alcohol). The $200 allowance cannot be combined with other individuals' exemptions, and if you exceed it, the full value of all the goods will be taxed. Antiques, which the U.S. Bureau of Customs and Border Protection defines as objects more than 100 years old, enter duty-free, as do original works of art done entirely by hand, including paintings, drawings, and sculptures. This doesn't apply to folk art or handicrafts, which are in general dutiable.

You may also send packages home duty-free, with a limit of one parcel per addressee per day (except alcohol or tobacco products or perfume worth more than $5). You can mail up to $200 worth of goods for personal use; label the package PERSONAL USE and attach a list of its contents and their retail value. If the package contains your used personal belongings, mark it AMERICAN GOODS RETURNED to avoid paying duties. You may send up to $100 worth of goods as a gift; mark the package UNSOLICITED GIFT. Mailed items do not affect your duty-free allowance on your return.

To avoid paying duty on foreign-made high-ticket items you already own and will take on your trip, register them with customs before you leave the country. Consider filing a Certificate of Registration for laptops, cameras, watches, and other digital devices identified with serial numbers or other permanent markings; you can keep the certificate for other trips. Otherwise, bring a sales receipt or insurance form to show that you owned the item before you left the United States.

🔒 **U.S. Bureau of Customs and Border Protection** ✉ for inquiries and equipment registration: 1300 Pennsylvania Ave. NW, Washington, DC 20229 ⊕ www.customs.gov ☎ 877/287-8667 or 202/354-1000 ✉ for complaints: Customer Satisfaction Unit, 1300 Pennsylvania Ave. NW, Room 5.5D, Washington, DC 20229.

DISABILITIES & ACCESSIBILITY

For people with disabilities, traveling in the Yucatán can be both challenging and rewarding. Travelers with mobility impairments used to venturing out on their own should not be surprised if locals try to prevent them from doing things. This is mainly out of concern; most Mexican families take complete care of relatives who use wheelchairs, so the general public is not accustomed to such independence. Additionally, very few places in the Yucatán have handrails, let alone special facilities and means of access. Although some of the newer hotels are accessible to wheelchairs, not even Cancún offers wheelchair-accessible transportation. Knowing how to ask for assistance is extremely important. If you are not fluent in Spanish, be sure to take along a pocket dictionary. Travelers with vision impairments who have no

knowledge of Spanish probably need a translator; people with hearing impairments who are comfortable using body language usually get along very well.

LODGING

Le Meridien, and the Occidental Caribbean Village in Cancún, the Presidente InterContinental Cozumel, and the Fiesta Americana Mérida are the only truly wheelchair-accessible hotels in the region. Individual arrangements must be made with other hotels.

🔒 **Best Choices Fiesta Americana Mérida** ✉ Av. Colón 451, at Paseo Montejo, 97000 Mérida, Yucatán ☎ 800/343-7821 or 999/942-1111 ⊕ www.fiestaamericana.com. **Le Meridien** ✉ Retorno Del Rey, Lote 37, 77500 Cancún, Quintana Roo ☎ 800/543-4300 or 998/881-2200 ⊕ www.meridienCancún.com.mx. **Occidental Caribbean Village** ✉ Blvd. Kukulcán, Km 13.5, Zona Hotelera, 77500 Cancún, Quintana Roo ☎ 01800/645-1179 or 998/848-8000 ⊕ www.tropicalsands.com/resorts/allegro. **Presidente InterContinental Cozumel** ✉ Carretera Chankanaab, Km 6.5, 77600 Cozumel, Quintana Roo ☎ 800/327-0200 or 987/872-0322 ⊕ www.interconti.com.

RESERVATIONS

When discussing accessibility with an operator or reservations agent, ask hard questions. Are there any stairs, inside *or* out? Are there grab bars next to the toilet *and* in the shower/tub? How wide is the doorway to the room? To the bathroom? For the most extensive facilities meeting the latest legal specifications, opt for newer accommodations. If you reserve through a toll-free number, consider also calling the hotel's local number to confirm the information from the central reservations office. Get confirmation in writing when you can.

SIGHTS & ATTRACTIONS

Few beaches, ruins, and sites around the Yucatán are accessible for people who use wheelchairs. The most accessible museums are found in Mérida (although there are stairs and no ramp) and in Cancún. Xcaret is wheelchair accessible; special transport is available but must be arranged in advance.

🔒 **XCaret Guest Services** ✉ Blvd. Kukulcán, Km 2.5, Zona Hotelera, Cancún ☎ 998/899-1900 🖷 998/898-1901 ✐ info@grupoxcaret.com.

TRANSPORTATION

There isn't any special transportation for travelers who use wheelchairs. Public buses are simply out of the question, there are no special buses, and some taxi drivers are not comfortable helping travelers with disabilities. Have your hotel arrange for a cab.

⚠ Complaints Aviation Consumer Protection Division (⇨ Air Travel) for airline-related problems. **Departmental Office of Civil Rights** ✉ for general inquiries, U.S. Department of Transportation, S-30, 400 7th St. SW, Room 10215, Washington, DC 20590 ☎ 202/366-4648 ⊕ www.dot.gov/ost/docr/index. htm. **Disability Rights Section** ✉ NYAV, U.S. Department of Justice, Civil Rights Division, 950 Pennsylvania Ave. NW, Washington, DC 20530 ☎ 800/514-0301, 800/514-0383 TTY, 202/514-0383 TTY, 202/514-0301 ADA information line ⊕ www.ada.gov. **U.S. Department of Transportation Hotline** ☎ 800/778-4838 or 800/455-9880 TTY for disability-related air-travel problems.

TRAVEL AGENCIES

In the United States, the Americans with Disabilities Act requires that travel firms serve the needs of all travelers. Some agencies specialize in working with people with disabilities.

⚠ Travelers with Mobility Problems Access Adventures/B. Roberts Travel ✉ 206 Chestnut Ridge Rd., Scottsville, NY 14624 ☎ 585/889-9096 ⊕ www.brobertstravel.com, run by a former physical-rehabilitation counselor. **CareVacations** ✉ No. 5, 5110-50 Ave., Leduc, Alberta, Canada T9E 6V4 ☎ 877/478-7827 or 780/986-6404 ⊕ www. carevacations.com, for group tours and cruise vacations. **Flying Wheels Travel** ✉ 143 W. Bridge St., Box 382, Owatonna, MN 55060 ☎ 507/451-5005 ⊕ www.flyingwheelstravel.com.

⚠ Travelers with Developmental Disabilities New Directions ✉ 5276 Hollister Ave., Suite 207, Santa Barbara, CA 93111 ☎ 888/967-2841 or 805/967-2841 ⊕ www.newdirectionstravel.com.

DISCOUNTS & DEALS

The best discounts you will find in Cancún are those offered on the various coupons handed out—often by welcoming committees at airports. These coupons offer discounts on restaurants, gifts, and entrance fees to local attractions.

Be a smart shopper and compare all your options before making decisions. A plane ticket bought with a promotional coupon from travel clubs, coupon books, and direct-mail offers or purchased on the Internet may not be cheaper than the least-expensive fare from a discount ticket agency. And always keep in mind that what you get is just as important as what you save.

DISCOUNT RESERVATIONS

To save money, look into discount reservations services with Web sites and toll-free numbers, which use their buying power to get a better price on hotels, airline tickets (⇨ Air Travel), even car rentals. When booking a room, always **call the hotel's local toll-free number** (if one is available) rather than the central reservations number—you'll often get a better price. Always ask about special packages or corporate rates.

When shopping for the best deal on hotels and car rentals, look for guaranteed exchange rates, which protect you against a falling dollar. With your rate locked in, you won't pay more, even if the price goes up in the local currency.

⚠ Airline Tickets Air 4 Less ☎ 800/AIR4LESS; low-fare specialist.

⚠ Hotel Rooms Accommodations Express ☎ 800/444-7666 or 800/277-1064 ⊕ www. accommodationsexpress.com. **Hotels.com** ☎ 800/246-8357 ⊕ www.hotels.com. **Quikbook** ☎ 800/789-9887 ⊕ www.quikbook.com. **Steigenberger Reservation Service** ☎ 800/223-5652 ⊕ www.srs-worldhotels.com. **Turbotrip.com** ☎ 800/473-7829 ⊕ www.turbotrip.com.

PACKAGE DEALS

Don't confuse packages and guided tours. When you buy a package, you travel on your own, just as though you had planned the trip yourself. Fly/drive packages, which combine airfare and car rental, are often a good deal. In cities, ask the local visitor's bureau about hotel packages that include tickets to major museum exhibits or other special events.

EATING & DRINKING

The restaurants we list are the cream of the crop in each price category. Properties indicated by a ✕🏠 are lodging establishments whose restaurant warrants a special trip.

MEALS & SPECIALTIES

Desayuno can be either a breakfast sweet roll and coffee or milk or a full breakfast of an egg dish such as *huevos a la mexicana* (scrambled eggs with chopped tomato, onion, and chiles), *huevos rancheros* (fried eggs on a tortilla covered with salsa), or *huevos con jamón* (scrambled eggs with ham), plus juice and tortillas. Lunch is called *comida* or *almuerzo* and is the biggest meal of the day. Traditional businesses close down between 2 PM and 4 PM for this meal. It usually includes soup, a main dish, and dessert. Regional specialties include *pan de cazón* (baby shark shredded and layered with tortillas, black beans and tomato sauce), in Campeche; *pollo pibíl* (chicken marinated in sour orange and baked in banana leaves), in Mérida; and *tikinchic* (fish in a sour-orange sauce), on the coast. Restaurants in tourist areas also serve American-style food such as hamburgers, pizza, and pasta. The lighter evening meal is called *cena*.

MEALTIMES

Most restaurants are open daily for lunch and dinner during high season (December–April), but hours tend to be more erratic during the rest of the year. It's always a good idea to **phone ahead.**

Unless otherwise noted, the restaurants listed in this guide are open daily for lunch and dinner.

PAYING

Most small restaurants do not accept credit cards. Larger chain restaurants and those catering to tourists take credit cards, but their prices reflect the fee placed on all credit-card transactions.

RESERVATIONS & DRESS

Reservations are always a good idea; we mention them only when they're essential or not accepted. Book as far ahead as you can, and reconfirm as soon as you arrive. (Large parties should always call ahead to check the reservations policy.) We mention dress only when men are required to wear a jacket or a jacket and tie.

WINE, BEER & SPIRITS

Almost all restaurants in the region serve beer and some also offer wine. Larger restaurants have beer, wine, and spirits. Mexico does not make any wine, but many restaurants offer a good range of Chilean, Spanish, Italian, and French wines at reasonable prices. You pay more for imported liquor such as vodka, brandy, and whiskey; tequila and rum are less expensive. Small lunch places called *loncherias* don't sell liquor, but you can bring your own as long as you are discreet. Almost all corner stores sell beer and tequila; grocery stores carry all brands of beer, wine, and spirits. Liquor stores are rare and usually carry specialty items. You must be 18 to buy liquor, but this rule is often overlooked.

ECOTOURISM

Ecoturismo is fast becoming a buzzword in the Mexican tourism industry, even though not all operators and establishments employ practices that are good for the environment. For example, in the Riviera Maya, an area south of Cancún, hotel developments greatly threaten the ecosystem, including the region's coral reefs. Nevertheless, President Vicente Fox has pledged to support more ecotourism projects, and recent national conferences have focused on this theme.

DOLPHIN ENCOUNTERS

One of the most heavily advertised activities in Cancún is swimming with dolphins. The water parks offering such "dolphin encounters" often bill the experience as "educational" and "enchanting," and every year, thousands of tourists who understandably love dolphins pay top dollar to participate in the activity. Many environmental and anti-cruelty organizations, however, including the Humane Society of the United States, Greenpeace, WDCS (Whale and Dolphin Conservation Society), and CSI (Cetacean Society International), have spoken out against such dolphin encounters. One contention these organizations make is that several water parks have broken international laws regulating the procurement of dolphins from restricted areas; another is that the confined conditions at such parks have put dolphins' health at risk. Some of the animals are kept in overcrowded pens and suffer from stress-related diseases; others have died from illnesses that may have come from human contact; some have even behaved aggressively toward the tourists swimming with them.

These organizations believe that keeping any dolphins in captivity is wrong, and have been pressuring the water parks to adhere to international regulations and treat their dolphins with better care. Until conditions improve, however, you may wish to visit dolphins at a facility like Xcaret, which has a track record of handling its animals humanely—or applying the current $100-plus fee for this activity toward a snorkeling or whale-watching trip, where you can see marine life in its natural state.

Cetacean Society International ⊕ http://csi-whalesalive.org. **Greenpeace** ⊕ www.greenpeace.org. **Humane Society of the United States** ⊕ www.hsus.org. **Whale and Dolphin Conservation Society** ⊕ www.wdcs.org.

ELECTRICITY

Electrical converters are not necessary, because Mexico operates on the 60-cycle, 120-volt system; however, many outlets have not been updated to accommodate three-prong and polarized plugs (those with one larger prong), so **bring an adapter.** When in Mexico **purchase a surge protector** for valuable electronic equipment such as computers and stereos.

EMBASSIES

Australia **Australian Embassy** ⊠ Calle Rubén Darío 55, Col. Polanco, Mexico City 11580 ☎ 55/5531-5225 ⊕ www.mexico.embassy.gov.au/quienes/mx/index.html.

Canada **Canadian Embassy** ⊠ Calle Schiller 529, Col. Polanco, Mexico City 11580 ☎ 55/5724-7900 ⊕ www.canada.org.mx.

Mexico **Mexican Embassies** **Australia** ⊠ 14 Perth Ave., Yarralumla ACT 2600 ☎ 02/6273-3963 or 02/6273-3905 🖷 02/6273-1190 ⊕ www.embamexau.com. **Canada** ⊠ 45 O'Connor St., Suite 1500, Ottawa K1P 3M6 ☎ 513/233-8988 🖷 613/235-9123 ⊕ www.embamexcan.com. **New Zealand** ⊠ 111 Customhouse Quay, Level 8, Wellington ☎ 644/472-0555 🖷 644/496-3559 ⊕ www.mexico.org.nz. **United Kingdom** ⊠ 42 Hertford St., London W1J 7JR ☎ 44/20-7499-8586 ⊕ www.

embamex.co.uk. **United States** ⊠ 1911 Pennsylvania Ave, Washington, D.C. 20006 ☎ 202/736-1000 🖷 202/234-4498.

New Zealand **New Zealand Embassy** ⊠ Jaime Balmes No. 8, 4th fl., Colonia Los Morales, Col. Polanco, 11510 Mexico City ☎ 55/5283-9460.

United Kingdom **British Embassy** ⊠ Av. Río Lerma 71, Col. Cuauhtémoc, 06500 Mexico City ☎ 55/5207-2089 ⊕ www.embajadabritanica.com.mx.

United States **U.S. Embassy** ⊠ Paseo de la Reforma 305, Col. Cuauhtémoc, 06500 Mexico City ☎ 55/5080-2000 ⊕ www.usembassy-mexico.gov/emenu.html.

EMERGENCIES

It's helpful, albeit daunting, to know ahead of time that you're not protected by the laws of your native land once you're on Mexican soil. However, if you get into a scrape with the law, you can call the Citizens' Emergency Center in the United States. In Mexico, you can also call the 24-hour English-speaking hotline of the Mexico Ministry of Tourism (Sectur). The hotline can provide immediate assistance as well as general, nonemergency guidance. **In an emergency, call** ☎ 06 from any phone.

Air Ambulance Network ☎ 800/327-1966 or 95800/010-0027 ⊕ www.airambulancenetwork.com. **Angeles Verdes** (emergency roadside assistance in Mexico City) ☎ 55/5250-8221 or 55/5520-8555. **Citizens' Emergency Center** ☎ 202/647-5226 weekdays 8:15 AM-10 PM EST and Sat. 9 AM-3 PM, 202/647-4512 after hrs and Sun. **Global Life Flight** ☎ 01800/305-9400 toll-free in Mexico, 888/554-9729 in the U.S., 877/817-6843 in Canada ⊕ www.globallifeflight.com. **Mexico Ministry of Tourism** ☎ 01800/903-9200 toll-free in Mexico.

ETIQUETTE & BEHAVIOR

In the United States, being direct, efficient, and succinct are highly valued traits. In Mexico, where communication tends to be more diplomatic and subtle, this style is often perceived as rude and aggressive. People will be far less helpful if you lose your temper or complain loudly, as such behavior is considered impolite. Remember that things move at a much slower rate here. There is no stigma attached to being late. Try to accept this pace gracefully.

Learning basic phrases such as *por favor* (please) and *gracias* (thank you) in Spanish will make a big difference.

BUSINESS ETIQUETTE

Business etiquette is much more formal and traditional in Mexico than in the United States. Personal relationships always come first, so developing rapport and trust is essential. A handshake is an appropriate greeting, along with a friendly inquiry about family members. With established clients, do not be surprised if you are welcomed with a kiss on the check or full hug with a pat on the back. Mexicans love business cards—be sure to present yours in any business situation. Without a business card you may have trouble being taken seriously. In public always be respectful of colleagues and keep confrontations private. Meetings may or may not start on time, so be patient with delays. When invited to dinner at the home of a customer or business associate, it's not necessary to bring a gift.

GAY & LESBIAN TRAVEL

Gender roles in Mexico are rigidly defined, especially in rural areas. Openly gay couples are a rare sight, and two people of the same gender may have trouble getting a *cama matrimonial* (double bed) at hotels. All travelers, regardless of sexual orientation, should be extra cautious when frequenting gay-friendly venues, as police sometimes violently crash these clubs, and there's little recourse or sympathy available to victims. The companies below can help answer your questions about safety and travel to the Yucatán.

🏳 Gay- & Lesbian-Friendly Travel Agencies **Different Roads Travel** ✉ 8383 Wilshire Blvd., Suite 520, Beverly Hills, CA 90211 ☎ 800/429-8747 Ext. 14 or 323/651-5557 Ext. 14 ✍ lgernert@tzell.com. **Kennedy Travel** ✉ 130 W. 42nd St., Suite 401, New York, NY 10036 ☎ 800/237-7433 or 212/840-8659 ⊕ www.kennedytravel.com. **Now, Voyager** ✉ 4406 18th St., San Francisco, CA 94114 ☎ 800/255-6951 or 415/626-1169 ⊕ www.nowvoyager.com. **Skylink Travel and Tour** ✉ 1455 N. Dutton Ave., Suite A, Santa Rosa, CA 95401 ☎ 800/225-5759 or 707/546-9888; serving lesbian travelers.

GUIDEBOOKS

Plan well and you won't be sorry. Guidebooks are excellent tools—and you can take them with you. You may want to check out color-photo-illustrated *Fodor's Exploring Mexico*, which is thorough on culture and history. It's available at online retailers and bookstores everywhere.

HEALTH

Medical clinics in all the main tourist areas have English-speaking personnel. Many of the doctors in Cancún have studied in Miami and speak English fluently. You will pay much higher prices than average for the services of English-speaking doctors or for clinics catering to tourists. Campeche and the more rural areas have few doctors who speak English.

DIVERS' ALERT

Do not fly within 24 hours of scuba diving.

FOOD & DRINK

In Mexico the major health risk, known as *turista,* or traveler's diarrhea, is caused by eating contaminated fruit or vegetables or drinking contaminated water. So **watch what you eat.** Stay away from ice, uncooked food, and unpasteurized milk and milk products, and **drink only bottled water** or water that has been boiled for at least 10 minutes (insist on this by saying *"quiero el agua hervida por diez minutos"*), even when you're brushing your teeth. Mild cases may respond to Imodium (known generically as loperamide or Lomotil) or Pepto-Bismol (not as strong), both of which you can buy over the counter; keep in mind, though, that these drugs can complicate more serious illnesses. Drink plenty of purified water or tea; chamomile tea (*te de manzanilla*) is a good folk remedy and it's readily available in restaurants throughout Mexico. In severe cases, rehydrate yourself with Gatorade or a salt-sugar solution (½ teaspoon salt and 4 tablespoons sugar per quart of water). If your fever and diarrhea last longer than three days, see a doctor—you may have picked up a parasite that requires prescription medication.

When ordering cold drinks at untouristed establishments, **skip the ice:** *sin hielo.* (You can usually identify ice made commercially from purified water by its uniform shape and the hole in the center.) Hotels with water-purification systems will post signs to that effect in the rooms. *Tacos al pastor*—thin pork slices grilled on a spit and garnished with the usual cilantro, onions, and chile peppers—are delicious but dangerous. It's also a good idea to pass up *ceviche*, raw fish cured in lemon juice—a favorite appetizer, especially at seaside resorts. The Mexican Department of Health warns that marinating in lemon juice does not constitute the "cooking" that would make the shellfish safe to eat. Also, be wary of hamburgers sold from street stands, because you can never be certain what meat they are made with (horse meat is common).

MEDICAL PLANS

No one plans to get sick while traveling, but it happens, so consider signing up with a medical-assistance company. Members get doctor referrals, emergency evacuation or repatriation, hotlines for medical consultation, cash for emergencies, and other assistance.

Medical Assistance Companies International SOS Assistance ⊕ www.internationalsos.com ⊠ **United States** ⊠ 8 Neshaminy Interplex, Suite 207, Trevose, PA 19053 ☎ 800/523–8930 or 215/244–1500, 215/245–4707 for emergencies ⊠ **United Kingdom** ⊠ Landmark House, Hammersmith Bridge Rd., 6th fl., London W6 9DP ☎ 020/8762–8000, 020/8762–8008 for emergencies ⊠ **Singapore** ⊠ 331 N. Bridge Rd., 17–00, Odeon Towers, Singapore 188720 ☎ 6338–7800, 6338–7800 for emergencies.

OVER-THE-COUNTER REMEDIES

Farmacias (pharmacies) are the most convenient place for such common medicines as *aspirina* (aspirin) or *jarabe para la tos* (cough syrup). You'll be able to find many U.S. brands (e.g., Tylenol, Pepto-Bismol, etc.), especially at American chain outlets such as Wal-Mart. There are pharmacies in all small towns and on practically every corner in larger cities.

PESTS & OTHER HAZARDS

It's best to be cautious and go indoors at dusk (called the "mosquito hour" by lo-

cals). An excellent brand of *repellente de insectos* (insect repellent) called Autan is readily available; do not use it on children under age two. If you want to bring a mosquito repellent from home, make sure it has at least 10% DEET or it won't be effective. If you're hiking in the jungle, wear repellent and long pants and sleeves; if you're camping in the jungle use a mosquito net and invest in a package of mosquito coils (sold in most stores). Another local flying pest is the *tabaño*, a type of deerfly, which resembles a common household fly with yellow stripes. Some people swell up after being bitten, but taking an antihistamine can help. Some people may also react to ant bites. Watch out for the small red ants, in particular, as their bites can be quite irritating. Scorpions also live in the region; their sting is similar to a bee sting. They are not poisonous but can cause strong reactions in small children. Those who are allergic to bee stings should go to the hospital. Again, antihistamines help. Clean all cuts carefully, as the rate of infection is much higher here. The Yucatán has many poisonous snakes and the coral snake, easily identified by its black and red markings, should be avoided at all costs; its bite is fatal. If you are planning any jungle hikes, be sure to wear hard-sole shoes and stay on the path. For more remote areas hire a guide and make sure there is an anti-venom kit accompanying you on the trip.

Other hazards to travelers in Mexico are sunburn and heat exhaustion. The sun is strong here; it takes fewer than 20 minutes to get a serious sunburn. Avoid the sun between 11 AM and 3 PM all year-round. Wear a hat and use sunscreen. You should **drink more fluid than you do at home**—Mexico is probably hotter than what you're used to and you will perspire more. Rest in the afternoons and stay out of the sun to avoid heat exhaustion. The first signs of dehydration and heat exhaustion are dizziness, extreme irritability, and fatigue.

SHOTS & MEDICATIONS

According to the U.S. government's National Centers for Disease Control and

Prevention (CDC) there is a limited risk of malaria and dengue fever in certain rural areas of the Yucatán Peninsula, especially the states of Campeche and Quintana Roo. Travelers in mostly urban or easily accessible areas need not worry. However, if you plan to visit remote regions or stay for more than six weeks, **check with the CDC's International Travelers' Health Hotline.** In areas where mosquito-borne diseases like malaria and dengue are prevalent, use mosquito nets, wear clothing that covers the body, apply repellent containing DEET, and use spray for flying insects in living and sleeping areas. You might **consider taking antimalarial pills,** but the side effects are quite strong and the current strain of Mexican malaria can be cured with the right medication. There is no vaccine to combat dengue, although the strain found in Quintana Roo is not life-threatening.

⚡ Health Warnings National Centers for Disease Control and Prevention (CDC) ⊠ National Center for Infectious Diseases, Division of Quarantine, Travelers' Health, 1600 Clifton Rd. NE, Atlanta, GA 30333 ☎ 877/394–8747 international travelers' health hotline, 404/498–1600 Division of Quarantine, 800/311–3435 other inquiries ⊕ www.cdc.gov/travel.

HOLIDAYS

The lively celebration of holidays in Mexico interrupts most daily business, including banks, government offices, and many shops and services, so plan your trip accordingly: New Year's Day; February 5, Constitution Day; May 5, Anniversary of the Battle of Puebla; September 1, the State of the Union Address; September 16, Independence Day; October 12, Day of the Race; November 1, Day of the Dead; November 20, Revolution Day; December 12, Feast of Our Lady of Guadalupe; and Christmas Day.

Banks and government offices close during Holy Week (the Sunday before Easter until Easter Sunday), especially the Thursday and Friday before Easter Sunday. Some private offices close from Christmas to New Year's Day; government offices usually have reduced hours and staff.

INSURANCE

The most useful travel-insurance plan is a comprehensive policy that includes coverage for trip cancellation and interruption, default, trip delay, and medical expenses (with a waiver for preexisting conditions).

Without insurance you'll lose all or most of your money if you cancel your trip, regardless of the reason. Default insurance covers you if your tour operator, airline, or cruise line goes out of business. Trip-delay covers expenses that arise because of bad weather or mechanical delays. Study the fine print when comparing policies.

If you're traveling internationally, a key component of travel insurance is coverage for medical bills incurred if you get sick on the road. Such expenses aren't generally covered by Medicare or private policies. U.K. residents can buy a travel-insurance policy valid for most vacations taken during the year in which it's purchased (but check preexisting-condition coverage). British and Australian citizens need extra medical coverage when traveling overseas.

Always **buy travel policies directly from the insurance company;** if you buy them from a cruise line, airline, or tour operator that goes out of business you probably won't be covered for the agency or operator's default, a major risk. Before making any purchase, review your existing health and home-owner's policies to find what they cover away from home.

⚡ Travel Insurers In the United States: Access America ⊠ 6600 W. Broad St., Richmond, VA 23230 ☎ 800/284–8300 ⊕ www.accessamerica. com. **Travel Guard International** ⊠ 1145 Clark St., Stevens Point, WI 54481 ☎ 800/826–1300 or 715/345–0505 ⊕ www.travelguard.com.

⚡ In Australia: Insurance Council of Australia ⊠ Insurance Enquiries and Complaints, Level 3, 56 Pitt St., Sydney, NSW 2000 ☎ 1300/363683 or 02/9251–4456 ⊕ www.iecltd.com.au.

In Canada: **RBC Insurance** ⊠ 6880 Financial Dr., Mississauga, Ontario L5N 7Y5 ☎ 800/565–3129 ⊕ www.rbcinsurance.com.

In New Zealand: **Insurance Council of New Zealand** ⊠ 111–115 Customhouse Quay, Level 7, Box 474, Wellington ☎ 04/472–5230 ⊕ www.icnz.org.nz.

In the United Kingdom: **Association of British Insurers** ✉ 51 Gresham St., London EC2V 7HQ ☎ 020/7600-3333 ⊕ www.abi.org.uk.

LANGUAGE

Spanish is the official language, although Indian languages are spoken by approximately 8% of the population and some of those people speak no Spanish at all. Basic English is widely understood by most people employed in tourism, less so in the less-developed areas. At the very least, shopkeepers will know the numbers for bargaining purposes. As in most other foreign countries, knowing the mother tongue has a way of opening doors, so **learn some Spanish words and phrases.** Mexicans welcome even the most halting attempts to use the language.

Castilian Spanish—which is different from Latin American Spanish not only in pronunciation and grammar but also in vocabulary—is most widely taught outside Mexico. In terms of grammar, Mexican Spanish ignores the *vosotros* form of the second person plural, using the more formal *ustedes* in its place. As for pronunciation, the lisped Castilian "c" or "z" is dismissed in Mexico as a sign of affectation. The most obvious differences are in vocabulary: Mexican Spanish has thousands of indigenous words and uses *¿mande?* instead of *¿cómo?* (excuse me?). Also, be aware that words or phrases that are harmless or everyday in one country can offend in another. Unless you are lucky enough to be briefed on these nuances by a native coach, the only way to learn is by trial and error. Most Mexicans are very forgiving of errors and will appreciate your efforts.

LANGUAGE-STUDY PROGRAMS

There is a recommended Spanish-language study center in Playa del Carmen, the Playalingua del Caribe. Students can stay at the center while they learn or lodge with a local family.

🎵 Program **Playalingua del Caribe** ✉ Calle 20 Norte between Avs. 5A and 10A, Playa del Carmen 77710 ☎ 984/873-3876 ⊕ www.playalingua.com.

LANGUAGES FOR TRAVELERS

A phrase book and language-tape set can help you get started. *Fodor's Spanish for Travelers* (available at bookstores everywhere) is excellent.

LODGING

The price and quality of accommodations in Mexico vary from superluxurious, international-class hotels and all-inclusive resorts to modest budget properties, seedy places with shared bathrooms, *casas de huéspedes* (guesthouses), youth hostels, and *cabañas* (beach huts). You may find appealing bargains while you're on the road, but if your comfort threshold is high, look for an English-speaking staff, guaranteed dollar rates, and toll-free reservation numbers.

The lodgings we list are the cream of the crop in each price category. Properties are assigned price categories based on the range from their least-expensive standard double room at high season (excluding holidays) to the most expensive. We always list the facilities that are available—but we don't specify whether they cost extra; when pricing accommodations, **always ask what's included and what costs extra.** Lodgings are denoted in the text with a house icon, 🏠; establishments with restaurants that warrant a special trip have ✕🏠.

Assume that hotels operate on the **European Plan** (EP, with no meals) unless we specify that they use either the **Continental Plan** (CP, with a Continental breakfast), the **Modified American Plan** (MAP, with breakfast and dinner), the **Full American Plan** (FAP, with all meals included), or **all-inclusive** (AI, including all meals and most activities).

APARTMENT & VILLA RENTALS

If you want a home base that's roomy enough for a family and comes with cooking facilities, **consider a furnished rental.** These can save you money, especially if you're traveling with a group. Home-exchange directories sometimes list rentals as well as exchanges.

Local rental agencies can be found in Isla Mujeres, Cozumel, and Playa del Carmen. They specialize in renting out apartments, condos, villas, and private homes.

🚩 International Agents **At Home Abroad** ✉ 405 E. 56th St., Suite 6H, New York, NY 10022 ☎ 212/421–9165 ⊕ www.athomeabroadinc.com. **Hideaways International** ✉ 767 Islington St., Portsmouth, NH 03801 ☎ 800/843–4433 or 603/430–4433 ⊕ www.hideaways.com; annual membership $145. **Vacation Home Rentals Worldwide** ✉ 235 Kensington Ave., Norwood, NJ 07648 ☎ 800/633–3284 or 201/767–9393 ⊕ www.vhrww. com. **Villanet** ✉ 1251 N.W. 116th St., Seattle, WA 98177 ☎ 800/964–1891 or 206/417–3444 ⊕ www.rentavilla.com. **Villas and Apartments Abroad** ✉ 370 Lexington Ave., Suite 1401, New York, NY 10017 ☎ 800/433–3020 or 212/897–5045 ⊕ www.ideal-villas.com.

Villas International ✉ 4340 Redwood Hwy., Suite D309, San Rafael, CA 94903 ☎ 800/221–2260 or 415/499–9490 ⊕ www.villasintl.com.

🚩 Local Agents **Akumal Villas** ✉ Carretera 307, Km 104, 77600 Akumal, Quintana Roo ☎ 984/875–9012 ⊕ www.akumal-villas.com. **Caribbean Realty** ✉ Centro Commercial Marina, Puerto Aventuras 77750 ☎ 984/873–5098 ⊕ www.caribbean-realty.com. **Cozumel Vacation Villas** ✉ 3300 Airport Rd., Boulder, CO 80301 ☎ 800/224–5551 or 303/442–7644 🖷 303/442–0380 ⊕ www.cozumel-villas.com.

Lost Oasis Property Rentals ✉ 77400 Isla Mujeres, Quintana Roo ☎ 998/877–0951 ⊕ www.lostoasis.net/. **Playa Beach Rentals** ✉ Retorno Copan Lote 71, 77110 Playa del Carmen, Quintana Roo 🖷🖷 984/873–2952 ⊕ www.playabeachrentals.com.

Turquoise Waters ✉ AKA Liza Piorkowski, 77500 Puerto Morelos, Quintana Roo ☎ 877/215–0052 or 998/874–4794 ⊕ www.turquoisewater.com.

BED-AND-BREAKFASTS

B&Bs are relatively new to Mexico and consequently there are only a handful found throughout the Yucatán peninsula. The establishments listed in this guide are closer to small hotels that offer breakfast.

CAMPING

There are no official campgrounds in the Yucatán. Since all beachfront is federal property, you can legally camp on the beach. However, there are no services and this can be a dangerous practice, especially for women traveling alone. Those wishing to sleep out on the beach in safety and comfort should contact Kai Luum II. Las Ruinas Camp Grounds in Playa del Carmen have palapas, tents, and RV spaces.

🚩 **Kai Luum II** ✉ La Posada del Capitán Lafitte, off Carretera 307 at Km 62, 77400, Quintana Roo reservations: **Turquoise Reef Group** ☎ Box 2664, Evergreen, CO 81439 ☎ 800/538–6802 ⊕ www.mexicoholiday.com. **Las Ruinas Camp Grounds** ✉ Calle 2 and Av. 5 Norte, 77400 Playa del Carmen, Quintana Roo ☎ 984/873–0405.

HOME EXCHANGES

If you would like to exchange your home for someone else's, **join a home-exchange organization,** which will send you its updated listings of available exchanges for a year and will include your own listing in at least one of them. It's up to you to make specific arrangements.

🚩 Exchange Clubs **HomeLink International** ☎ Box 47747, Tampa, FL 33647 ☎ 800/638–3841 or 813/975–9825 ⊕ www.homelink.org; $110 yearly for a listing, online access, and catalog; $70 without catalog. **Intervac U.S.** ✉ 30 Corte San Fernando, Tiburon, CA 94920 ☎ 800/756–4663 ⊕ www.intervacus.com; $105 yearly for a listing, online access, and a catalog; $50 without catalog.

HOSTELS

No matter what your age, you can save on lodging costs by staying at hostels. In some 4,500 locations in more than 70 countries around the world, Hostelling International (HI), the umbrella group for a number of national youth-hostel associations, offers single-sex, dorm-style beds and, at many hostels, rooms for couples and family accommodations. Membership in any HI national hostel association, open to travelers of all ages, allows you to stay in HI-affiliated hostels at member rates; one-year membership is about $28 for adults (C$35 for a two-year minimum membership in Canada, £13.50 in the United Kingdom, A$52 in Australia, and NZ$40 in New Zealand); hostels charge about $10–$30 per night. Members have priority if the hostel is full; they're also eligible for discounts around the world, even on rail and bus travel in some countries.

F Organizations **Hostelling International–Canada** ✉ 205 Catherine St., Suite 400, Ottawa, Ontario K2P 1C3 ☎ 800/663-5777 or 613/237-7884 ⊕ www.hihostels.ca.

Hostelling International–USA ✉ 8401 Colesville Rd., Suite 600, Silver Spring, MD 20910 ☎ 301/495-1240 ⊕ www.hiayh.org. **YHA Australia** ✉ 422 Kent St., Sydney, NSW 2001 ☎ 02/9261-1111 ⊕ www.yha.com.au.

YHA England and Wales ✉ Trevelyan House, Dimple Rd., Matlock, Derbyshire DE4 3YH U.K. ☎ 0870/870-8808, 0870/770-8868, or 0162/959-2700 ⊕ www.yha.org.uk. **YHA New Zealand** ✉ Level 1, Moorhouse City 166 Moorhouse Avenue, Box 436, Christchurch ☎ 0800/278-299 or 03/379-9970 ⊕ www.yha.org.nz.

HOTELS

Hotel rates are subject to the 10%–15% value-added tax, in addition to a 2% hotel tax. Service charges and meals generally aren't included in the hotel rates.

The Mexican government categorizes hotels, based on qualitative evaluations, into *gran turismo* (superdeluxe, or five-star-plus, properties, of which there are only about 30 nationwide); five-star down to one-star; and economy class. Keep in mind that many hotels that might otherwise be rated higher have opted for a lower category to avoid higher interest rates on loans and financing.

High- versus low-season rates can vary significantly. In the off-season, Cancún hotels can cost one-third to one-half what they cost during peak season. Keep in mind, however, that this is also the time that many hotels undergo necessary repairs or renovations.

Hotels in this guide have private bathrooms with showers, unless stated otherwise; bathtubs aren't common in inexpensive hotels and properties in smaller towns.

RESERVING A ROOM

Reservations are easy to make in this region over the Internet. If you call hotels in the larger urban areas, there will be someone who speaks English. In more remote regions you will have to make your reservations in Spanish.

F Local Contacts **Cancún Hotel/Motel Association** ✉ Plaza San Angel, Av. Acanceh, Sm 15, 77500 ☎ 998/884-9347. **Cozumel Island Hotel Association** ✉ Calle 2 Norte 15A 77600 ☎ 987/872-3132. **Hotels Tulum** ⊕ www.hoteltulum.com.

F Toll-Free Numbers **Best Western** ☎ 800/528-1234 ⊕ www.bestwestern.com. **Choice** ☎ 800/424-6423 ⊕ www.choicehotels.com. **Days Inn** ☎ 800/325-2525 ⊕ www.daysinn.com. **Doubletree Hotels** ☎ 800/222-8733 ⊕ www.doubletree.com. **Four Seasons** ☎ 800/332-3442 ⊕ www.fourseasons.com. **Hilton** ☎ 800/445-8667 ⊕ www.hilton.com. **Holiday Inn** ☎ 800/465-4329 ⊕ www.sixcontinentshotels.com. **Hyatt Hotels & Resorts** ☎ 800/233-1234 ⊕ www.hyatt.com. **Inter-Continental** ☎ 800/327-0200 ⊕ www.intercontinental.com. **Le Meridien** ☎ 800/543-4300 ⊕ www.lemeridien-hotels.com. **Marriott** ☎ 800/228-9290 ⊕ www.marriott.com. **Nikko Hotels International** ☎ 800/645-5687 ⊕ www.nikkohotels.com. **Omni** ☎ 800/843-6664 ⊕ www.omnihotels.com. **Radisson** ☎ 800/333-3333 ⊕ www.radisson.com. **Ritz-Carlton** ☎ 800/241-3333 ⊕ www.ritzcarlton.com. **Sheraton** ☎ 800/325-3535 ⊕ www.starwood.com/sheraton. **Westin Hotels & Resorts** ☎ 800/228-3000 ⊕ www.starwood.com/westin. **Wyndham Hotels & Resorts** ☎ 800/822-4200 ⊕ www.wyndham.com.

MAIL & SHIPPING

Mail can be sent from your hotel or the local post office. Be forewarned, however, that mail service to, within, and from Mexico is notoriously slow and can take anywhere from 10 days to 12 weeks. **Never send anything of value to or from Mexico via the mail,** including cash, checks, or credit-card numbers.

POSTAL RATES

It costs 8.50 pesos (about 90¢) to send a postcard or letter weighing under 20 grams to the United States or Canada; it's 10.50 ($1) to Europe and 11.50 ($1.20) to Australia.

RECEIVING MAIL

To receive mail in Mexico, you can have it sent to your hotel or use *poste restante* at the post office. In the latter case, the address must include the words "a/c Lista de Correos" (general delivery), followed by the city, state, postal code, and country. To use this service, you must first register with the post office at which you wish to receive your mail. Mail is held for 10 days, and a list of recipients is posted daily. Postal codes for the main Yucatán destinations are as follows: Cancún, 77500; Isla Mujeres, 77400; Cozumel, 77600; Campeche, 24000; Mérida, 97000. Keep in mind that the mail service in Mexico is very slow and can take up to 12 weeks to deliver mail.

Holders of American Express cards or traveler's checks can have mail sent to them in care of the local American Express office. For a list of offices worldwide, write for the *Traveler's Companion* from American Express.

🚩 **American Express** ✉️ Box 678, Canal Street Station, New York, NY 10013 ⊕ www.americanexpress.com.

SHIPPING PARCELS

Hotel concierges can recommend international carriers, such as DHL, Estafeta, or Federal Express, which give your package a tracking number and ensure its arrival back home.

Despite the promises, *overnight* courier service is rare in Mexico. It's not the fault of the courier service, which may indeed have the package there overnight. Delays occur at customs. Depending on the time of year, all courier packages are opened and inspected. This can slow everything down. You can expect one- to three-day service in Cancún and two- to four-day service elsewhere. **Never send cash through the courier services.**

🚩 Major Services **AeroMexpress** ☎ 998/886–0123. **DHL** ☎ 998/887-1906 ⊕ www.dhl.com. **Estafeta** ☎ 998/884-1167. **Federal Express** ☎ 998/887-4003 ⊕ www.federalexpress.com.

MONEY MATTERS

Prices in this book are quoted most often in U.S. dollars. We would prefer to list costs in pesos, but because the value of the currency fluctuates considerably, what costs 90 pesos today might cost 120 pesos in six months.

If you travel only by air or package tour, stay at international hotel-chain properties, and eat at tourist restaurants, you might not find Mexico such a bargain. If you want a closer look at the country and aren't wedded to standard creature comforts, you can spend as little as $25 a day on room, board, and local transportation. Speaking Spanish is also helpful in bargaining situations and when asking for dining recommendations.

Cancún is one of the most expensive destinations in Mexico. Cozumel is on par with Cancún, and Isla Mujeres in turn is slightly less expensive than Cozumel. You're likely to get the best value for your money in Mérida and the other Yucatán cities less frequented by visitors, like Campeche. For obvious reasons, if you stay at international chain hotels and eat at restaurants designed with tourists in mind (especially hotel restaurants), you may not find the Yucatán such a bargain.

Peak-season sample costs: cup of coffee, 10 pesos–20 pesos; bottle of beer, 20 pesos–50 pesos; plate of tacos with trimmings, 25 pesos–60 pesos; grilled fish platter at a tourist restaurant, 35 pesos–80 pesos; 2-km (1-mi) taxi ride, 20 pesos.

Prices throughout this guide are given for adults. Substantially reduced fees are almost always available for children, students, and senior citizens. For information on taxes, *see* Taxes.

ATMS

ATMs (*cajeros automáticos*) are becoming more commonplace. Cirrus and Plus are the most frequently found networks. Before you leave home, **ask what the transaction fee will be** for withdrawing money in Mexico. (It's usually $3 a pop.)

Many Mexican ATMs cannot accept PINs (personal identification numbers) with more than four digits; if yours is longer, **ask your bank about changing your PIN (*número de clave*) before you leave home,** and keep in mind that processing such a change often takes a few weeks. If your PIN is fine yet your transaction still can't be completed—a regular occurrence—chances are that the computer lines are busy or that the machine has run out of money or is being serviced.

For cash advances, plan to use Visa or MasterCard, as many Mexican ATMs don't accept American Express. Some may not accept foreign credit cards for cash advances or may impose a cap of $300 per transaction. The ATMs at Banamex, one of the oldest nationwide banks, tend to be the most reliable. Bancomer is another bank with many ATM locations, but they usually provide only cash advances. The newer Serfín banks have reliable ATMs that accept credit cards as well as Plus and Cirrus cards. *See also* Safety, on avoiding ATM robberies.

CREDIT CARDS

Credit cards are accepted in most tourist areas. Smaller, less expensive restaurants and shops, however, tend to take only cash. In general, credit cards aren't accepted in small towns and villages, except in hotels. Diners Club is usually accepted only in major chains; the most widely accepted cards are MasterCard and Visa. When shopping, you can usually get better prices if you **pay with cash.**

At the same time, when traveling internationally you'll **receive wholesale exchange rates** when you make purchases with credit cards. These exchange rates are usually better than those that banks give you for changing money. In Mexico the decision to pay cash or use a credit card might depend on whether the establishment in which you are making a purchase finds bargaining for prices acceptable. To avoid fraud, it's wise to **make sure that "pesos" is clearly marked on all credit-card receipts.**

Before you leave for Mexico, be sure to **find out your credit-card companies' toll-free card-replacement numbers** that work at home as well as in Mexico; they could be impossible to find once you get to Mexico, and the calls you place to cancel your cards can be long ones. **Carry these numbers separately from your wallet** so you'll have them if you need to call to report lost or stolen cards.

Throughout this guide, the following abbreviations are used: **AE,** American Express; **DC,** Diners Club; **D,** Discover; **MC,** MasterCard; and **V,** Visa.

F Reporting Lost Cards **American Express** ☎ 800/528-2122 ⊕ www.americanexpress.com. **Diners Club** ☎ 702/797-5532 ⊕ www.dinersclub. com. **Discover** ☎ 800/347-2683. **MasterCard** ☎ 800/307-7309 ⊕ www.mastercard.com. **Visa** ☎ 800/847-2911 ⊕ www.visa.com.

CURRENCY

At this writing, the peso was still "floating" after the devaluation enacted by the Zedillo administration in late 1994. Although exchange rates have been as favorable as 10.6 pesos to US$1, 7.2 pesos to C$1, 16.6 pesos to £1, 6.4 pesos to A$1, and 5.8 pesos to NZ$1, the market and prices continue to adjust. Check with your bank or the financial pages of your local newspaper for current exchange rates. For quick estimates of how much something costs in U.S. dollar terms, divide prices given in pesos by 10. For example, 50 pesos would be about $5.

Mexican currency comes in denominations of 10-, 20-, 50-, 100-, 200-, 500-, and 1,000-peso bills. Coins come in denominations of 1, 5, 10, and 20 pesos and 5, 10, 20, and 50 centavos. Many of the coins and bills are very similar, so check carefully.

U.S. dollar bills (but not coins) are widely accepted in border towns and in many parts of the Yucatán, particularly in Cancún and Cozumel, where you'll often find prices in shops quoted in dollars. However, you'll get your change in pesos. Many tourist shops and market vendors as well as virtually all hotel service personnel also accept dollars.

CURRENCY EXCHANGE

For the most favorable rates, **change money through banks.** Although ATM transaction fees may be higher abroad than at home, ATM rates are excellent because they're based on wholesale rates offered only by major banks. You won't do as well at exchange booths in airports or rail and bus stations, in hotels, in restaurants, or in stores. To avoid lines at airport exchange booths, get a bit of local currency before you leave home.

Most banks only change money on weekdays until noon (though they stay open until 5), while *casas de cambio* (private exchange offices) generally stay open until 6 or 9 and often operate on weekends. Bring your photo ID or passport when you exchange money. Bank rates are regulated by the federal government and are therefore invariable, while casas de cambio have slightly more variable rates. Exchange houses in the airports and in areas with heavy tourist traffic tend to have the worst rates, often considerably lower than the banks. Some hotels also exchange money, but for providing you with this convenience they help themselves to a bigger commission than banks.

When changing money, count your bills before leaving the bank, and don't accept any partially torn, ink-marked, or taped-together bills; they will not be accepted anywhere. Also, many shop and restaurant owners are unable to make change for large bills. Enough of these encounters may compel you to request *billetes chicos* (small bills) when you exchange money.

Exchange Services International Currency Express ⌧ 427 N. Camden Dr., Suite F, Beverly Hills, CA 90210 ☎ 888/278-6628 orders ⊕ www. foreignmoney.com. **Thomas Cook International Money Services** ☎ 800/287-7362 orders and retail locations ⊕ www.us.thomascook.com.

TRAVELER'S CHECKS

Do you need traveler's checks? It depends on where you're headed. If you're going to rural areas and small towns, go with cash; traveler's checks are best used in cities. Lost or stolen checks can usually be replaced within 24 hours. To ensure a speedy refund, buy your own traveler's checks—don't let someone else pay for them: irregularities like this can cause delays. The person who bought the checks should make the call to request a refund. Unless you are planning on only traveling in very remote areas, American denominations are fine. In smaller establishments you will not receive American dollars when you cash your check but will be given the equivalent in pesos. You must always show a photo ID when cashing traveler's checks.

PACKING

Pack light, because you may want to save space for purchases: the Yucatán is filled with bargains on clothing, leather goods, jewelry, pottery, and other crafts.

Bring lightweight clothes, sundresses, bathing suits, sun hats or visors, and cover-ups for the Caribbean beach towns, but also pack a jacket or sweater to wear in the chilly, air-conditioned restaurants, or to tide you over during a rainstorm or an unusual cool spell. For trips to rural areas or Mérida, where dress is typically more conservative and shorts are considered inappropriate, women may want to pack one longer skirt. If you plan to visit any ruins, **bring comfortable walking shoes** with rubber soles. Lightweight rain gear is a good idea during the rainy season. Cancún is the dressiest spot on the peninsula, but even fancy restaurants don't require men to wear jackets.

Pack sunscreen, sunglasses, and umbrellas for the Yucatán. Other handy items—especially if you are traveling on your own or camping—include toilet paper, facial tissues, a plastic water bottle, and a flashlight (for occasional power outages or use at campsites). Snorkelers should consider bringing their own equipment unless traveling light is a priority; shoes with rubber soles for rocky underwater surfaces are also advised.

In your carry-on luggage, pack an extra pair of eyeglasses or contact lenses and enough of any medication you take to last a few days longer than the entire trip. You may also ask your doctor to write a spare prescription using the drug's generic name, as brand names may vary from country to country. In luggage to be checked, **never pack prescription drugs, valuables, or undeveloped film.** And don't forget to carry with you the addresses of offices that handle refunds of lost traveler's checks. Check *Fodor's How to Pack* (available at online retailers and bookstores everywhere) for more tips.

To avoid customs and security delays, carry medications in their original packaging. Don't pack any sharp objects in your carry-on luggage, including knives of any size or material, scissors, and corkscrews, or anything else that might arouse suspicion.

To avoid having your checked luggage chosen for hand inspection, don't cram bags full. The U.S. Transportation Security Administration suggests packing shoes on top and placing personal items you don't want touched in clear plastic bags.

CHECKING LUGGAGE

You're allowed to carry aboard one bag and one personal article, such as a purse or a laptop computer. Make sure what you carry on fits under your seat or in the overhead bin. Get to the gate early, so you can board as soon as possible, before the overhead bins fill up.

Baggage allowances vary by carrier, destination, and ticket class. On international flights, you're usually allowed to check two bags weighing up to 70 pounds (32 kilograms) each, although a few airlines allow checked bags of up to 88 pounds (40 kilograms) in first class. Some international carriers don't allow more than 66 pounds (30 kilograms) per bag in business class and 44 pounds (20 kilograms) in economy. On domestic flights, the limit is usually 50 to 70 pounds (23 to 32 kilograms) per bag. In general, carry-on bags shouldn't exceed 40 pounds (18 kilograms). Most airlines won't accept bags that weigh more than 100 pounds (45 kilograms) on domestic or international flights. Check baggage restrictions with your carrier before you pack.

Airline liability for baggage is limited to $2,500 per person on flights within the United States. On international flights it amounts to $9.07 per pound or $20 per kilogram for checked baggage (roughly $640 per 70-pound bag), with a maximum of $634.90 per piece, and $400 per passenger for unchecked baggage. You can buy additional coverage at check-in for about $10 per $1,000 of coverage, but it often excludes a rather extensive list of items, shown on your airline ticket.

Before departure, itemize your bags' contents and their worth, and label the bags with your name, address, and phone number. (If you use your home address, cover it so potential thieves can't see it readily.) Include a label inside each bag and **pack a copy of your itinerary.** At check-in, make sure each bag is correctly tagged with the destination airport's three-letter code. Because some checked bags will be opened for hand inspection, the U.S. Transportation Security Administration recommends that you leave luggage unlocked or use the plastic locks offered at check-in. TSA screeners place an inspection notice inside searched bags, which are resealed with a special lock.

If your bag has been searched and contents are missing or damaged, file a claim with the TSA Consumer Response Center as soon as possible. If your bags arrive damaged or fail to arrive at all, file a written report with the airline before leaving the airport.

🔁 **Complaints** U.S. Transportation Security Administration Consumer Response Center ☎ 866/289-9673 ⊕ www.tsa.gov.

PASSPORTS & VISAS

When traveling internationally, carry your passport even if you don't need one (it's always the best form of ID) and **make two photocopies of the data page** (one for someone at home and another for you, carried separately from your passport). If you lose your passport, promptly call the nearest embassy or consulate and the local police.

U.S. passport applications for children under age 14 require consent from both parents or legal guardians; both parents must appear together to sign the application. If only one parent appears, he or she must submit a written statement from the other parent authorizing passport issuance for the child. A parent with sole authority must present evidence of it when applying; acceptable documentation includes the child's certified birth certificate listing only the applying parent, a court order specifically permitting this parent's travel with the child, or a death certificate for the nonapplying parent. Application forms and instructions are available on the Web site of the U.S. State Department's Bureau of Consular Affairs (⊕ www.travel.state.gov).

ENTERING MEXICO

For stays of up to 180 days, Americans must prove citizenship through either a valid passport, certified copy of a birth certificate, or voter-registration card (the last two must be accompanied by a government-issue photo ID). Minors traveling with one parent need notarized permission from the absent parent. For stays of more than 180 days, all U.S. citizens, even infants, need a valid passport to enter Mexico. Minors also need parental permission.

Canadians need only proof of citizenship to enter Mexico for stays of up to six months. U.K. citizens need only a valid passport to enter Mexico for stays of up to three months.

Mexico has instituted a $20 visitor fee (not to be confused with the VAT taxes or with the airport departure tax) that applies to all visitors—except those entering by sea at Mexican ports who stay less than 72 hours, and those entering by land who do not stray past the 26-km–30-km (16-mi–18-mi) checkpoint into the country's interior. For visitors arriving by air, the fee, which covers visits of more than 72 hours and up to 30 days, is usually tacked on to the airline ticket price. You must pay the fee each time you extend your 30-day tourist visa. The fee is usually automatically added into the cost of your plane ticket, but check with your travel agent or airline carrier.

You get the standard tourist visas on the plane without even asking for them. They're also available through travel agents and Mexican consulates and at the border if you're entering by land. The visas can be granted for up to 180 days, but this is at the discretion of the Mexican immigration officials. Although many officials will balk if you request more than 90 days, be sure to ask for extra time if you think you'll need it; going to a Mexican immigration office to renew a visa can easily take a whole day.

PASSPORT OFFICES

The best time to apply for a passport or to renew is in fall and winter. Before any trip, check your passport's expiration date, and, if necessary, renew it as soon as possible.

🛂 **Australian Citizens** Passports Australia ☎ 131-232 ⊕ www.passports.gov.au.

🛂 **Canadian Citizens** Passport Office ✉ to mail in applications: 200 Promenade du Portage, Hull, Québec J8X 4B7 ☎ 800/567-6868 or 819/994-3500 ⊕ www.ppt.gc.ca.

🛂 **New Zealand Citizens** New Zealand Passports Office ☎ 0800/225-050 or 04/474-8100 ⊕ www.passports.govt.nz.

🛂 **U.K. Citizens** U.K. Passport Service ☎ 0870/521-0410 ⊕ www.passport.gov.uk.

🛂 **U.S. Citizens** National Passport Information Center ☎ 888/362-8668 or 888/498-3648 TTY [calls are $5.50 each], 900/225-5674 or 900/225-7778 TTY [calls are 55¢ per min for automated service, $1.50 per min for operator service] ⊕ www.travel.state.gov.

RESTROOMS

Expect to find clean flushing toilets, toilet tissue, soap, and running water at public restrooms in the major tourist destinations and at tourist attractions. Although many markets, bus and train stations, and the like have public facilities, you may have to pay a couple of pesos for the privilege of using a dirty toilet that lacks a seat, toilet paper (keep tissues with you at all times), and possibly even running water. You're better off popping into a restaurant, buying a little something, and using its restroom, which will probably be simple but clean and adequately equipped.

SAFETY

The Yucatán remains one of the safest areas in Mexico. But even in resort areas like Cancún and Cozumel, you should use common sense. Wear a money belt, make use of hotel safes when available, and carry your own baggage whenever possible unless you are checking into a hotel. Leave expensive jewelry at home, since it often entices thieves and will mark you as a "*rico turista*" who can afford to be overcharged.

When traveling with all your money, be sure to keep an eye on your belongings at all times and distribute your cash and any valuables between a deep front pocket, an inside jacket or vest pocket, and a hidden money pouch. Do not reach for your money pouch once in public. If you carry a purse, choose one with a zipper and a thick strap that you can drape across your body; adjust the length so that the purse sits in front of you at or above hip level.

Avoid driving on desolate streets, and don't travel at night, pick up hitchhikers, or hitchhike yourself. Use luxury buses (rather than second- or third-class vehicles), which take the safer toll roads. It's best to take only registered hotel taxis or have a hotel concierge call a *sitio* (stationed cab). If you plan on hiking in remote areas, leave an itinerary with your hotel and hire a local guide to help you. Several of the more deserted beaches in the Playa del Carmen area are not safe and should be avoided by single women.

Use ATMs during the day and in big, enclosed commercial areas. Avoid the glass-enclosed street variety of banks where you may be more vulnerable to thieves who force you to withdraw money for them. This can't be stressed strongly enough.

Bear in mind that reporting a crime to the police is often a frustrating experience unless you speak excellent Spanish and have a great deal of patience. If you're victimized, contact your local consular agent or the consular section of your country's embassy in Mexico City.

WOMEN IN THE YUCATÁN PENINSULA

A woman traveling alone will be the subject of much curiosity, since traditional Mexican women do not venture out unless accompanied by family members or friends. Violent crimes against women are rare here, but you should still be cautious. Part of the machismo culture is being flirtatious and showing off in front of *compadres,* and lone women are likely to be subjected to catcalls, although this is less true in the Yucatán than in other parts of Mexico.

Although annoying, it is essentially harmless. The best way to get rid of unwanted attention is to simply ignore the advances. Avoid direct eye contact with men on the streets—it invites further acquaintance. It's best not to enter into a discussion with harassers, even if you speak Spanish. When the suitor is persistent say "no" to whatever is said, walk briskly, and leave immediately for a safe place, such as a nearby store. Dressing conservatively may help; clothing that seems innocuous to you, such as brief tops or Bermuda shorts, may be inappropriate in more conservative rural areas. Never go topless on the beach unless it is a recognized nude beach with lots of other people and **never** alone on a beach—no matter how deserted it appears to be. Mexicans, in general, do not nude sunbathe, and men may misinterpret your doing so as an invitation.

SENIOR-CITIZEN TRAVEL

There are no established senior-citizen discounts in Cancún, so ask for any hotel or travel discounts before leaving home.

To qualify for age-related discounts, mention your senior-citizen status up front when booking hotel reservations (not when checking out) and before you're seated in restaurants (not when paying the bill). Be sure to have identification on hand. When renting a car, ask about promotional car-rental discounts, which can be cheaper than senior-citizen rates.

🔢 Educational Programs **Elderhostel** ⊠ 11 Ave. de Lafayette, Boston, MA 02111-1746 ☎ 877/426–8056, 877/426–2167 TTY, 978/323–4141 international callers ⊕ www.elderhostel.org. **Interhostel** ⊠ University of New Hampshire, 6 Garrison Ave., Durham, NH 03824 ☎ 800/733–9753 or 603/862–1147 ⊕ www.learn.unh.edu.

SHOPPING

You often get better prices by paying with cash (pesos or dollars) or traveler's checks because Mexican merchants frequently tack the 3%–6% credit-card company commission on to your bill. If you can do without plastic, you may even get the 12% sales tax lopped off.

If you are just window-shopping, use the phrase "*Sólo estoy mirando, gracias*" (so-lo ess-*toy* mee-*ran*-do, *gras*-yas; I'm just looking, thank you). This will ease the high-pressure sales pitch that you invariably get in most stores.

Most prices are fixed in shops, but bargaining is expected at markets. Start by offering half the price, and let the haggling begin. Keep in mind, though, that many small-town residents earn their livelihoods from the tourist trade; rarely are the prices in such places outrageous. Shopping around is a good idea, particularly in crafts markets where things can be very competitive. Just be sure to examine merchandise closely: some "authentic" items—particularly jewelry—might be poor imitations. And don't plan to use your ceramic plates, bowls, and cups for anything other than decoration—most items have high levels of lead in them.

KEY DESTINATIONS

Cozumel is famous for its jewelry, and there are many good deals to be found on diamonds and other precious gemstones. For authentic arts and crafts, you must journey inland to Mérida and Campeche. To buy hammocks, shoes, and pottery directly from artisans go to the tiny village of Ticul, one hour south of Mérida. Perhaps the richest source of crafts and the least-visited area is La Ruta de los Artesanos in Campeche along Carretera180. Here you will find villages filled with beautiful crafts: Calkiní, famed for its lovely pottery; Nunkiní, known for its beautiful woven mats and rugs; Pomuch, with its famous bakery; and Becal, where the renowned Panama hats are woven by locals.

SMART SOUVENIRS

T-shirts and other commonplace souvenirs abound in the area. But there are also some unique gifts to be found. This area is well known for its vanilla. There is also a special variety of bees on the peninsula that produces Yucatecan honey—a rich, aromatic honey that is much sought after. Supermarkets and outdoor markets carry a variety of brands, which are priced considerably less than in the United States.

The Yucatecan hammock is considered the finest in the world and comes in a variety of sizes, color, and materials. You can find the best hammocks from street vendors or at the municipal markets. Prices start from $16 and go up to $60. Don't pass up any opportunity to purchase a Panama hat—most start around $35. A hand-embroidered *huipile* (the traditional dress of Maya women) or a *guayabera* shirt both make lovely souvenirs. Prices depend on the material and amount of embroidery done. The simplest dresses and shirts start at $20 and can go as high as $150. You can also pick up handwoven shawls for under $20.

Mexico is also famous for its amber. Most of the "amber" sold by street merchants is plastic, but there are several fine amber shops to be found in Playa del Carmen. Prices depend on the size of the amber.

WATCH OUT

If you pay with a credit card, watch that your card goes through the machine only once. If there's an error and a new slip needs to be done make sure the original is destroyed before your eyes. Another favorite scam is to ask you to wait while the clerk runs next door to use their phone or verify your number. Often they are making extra copies. Don't let your card leave the store without you.

Items made from tortoiseshell (or any sea turtle products) and black coral aren't allowed into the United States. Neither are birds or wildlife curios such as stuffed iguanas or parrots. Cowboys boots, hats, and sandals made from the leather of endangered species such as crocodiles will also be taken from you at customs. Both the U.S. and Mexican governments also have strict laws and guidelines about the import/export of antiquities. The same applies to paintings by such Mexican masters as Diego Rivera and Frida Kahlo, which, like antiquities, are defined as part of the national patrimony.

Although Cuban cigars are readily available, American visitors will have to enjoy them while in Mexico. However, Mexico has been producing some fine alternatives to Cuban cigars. If you're bringing any Mexican cigars back to the States, make sure they have the correct Mexican seals on both the individual cigars and on the box. Otherwise they may be confiscated.

SIGHTSEEING GUIDES

In the states of Quintana Roo and the Yucatán most of the tour guides found outside the more popular ruins are not official guides. Some are professionals, but others make it up as they go along (which can be highly entertaining). Official guides will be wearing a name tag and identification issued by INAH, Instituto Nacional de Antropología e Historia (National Institute of Anthropology and History). These guides are excellent and can teach you about the architecture and history of the ruins. At the smaller ruins, guides are usually part of the research or maintenance teams and can give you an excellent tour.

All guides in Campeche have been trained by the state and are very knowledgeable. They must be booked through the Campeche tourist office. Costs vary. At the smaller sites usually a $5 to $10 tip will suffice. At the larger ruins the fees can run as high as $30. Those charging more are scam artists. The larger ruins have the more aggressive guides. Turn them down with a very firm *No, gracias,* and if they persist, lose them at the entrance gate.

STUDENTS IN THE YUCATÁN PENINSULA

Unless you are enrolled in a local school (and therefore considered a resident), there aren't many established discounts for students. Cancún offers deals for *spring breakers* on hotels, meals, and drinks but this is only for a few weeks in spring. 🎫 IDs Services **STA Travel** ✉ 10 Downing St., New York, NY 10014 ☎ 800/777−0112 24-hr service center, 212/627−3111 ⊕ www.sta.com. **Travel Cuts** ✉ 187 College St., Toronto, Ontario M5T 1P7 Canada ☎ 800/592−2887 in the U.S., 416/979−2406 or 866/246−9762 in Canada ⊕ www.travelcuts.com.

TAXES

AIRPORT TAXES

An air-departure tax of $18—not to be confused with the fee for your tourist visa—or the peso equivalent must be paid at the airport for international flights from Mexico. For domestic flights the departure tax is around $10. It's important that you save a little cash for this transaction, as traveler's checks and credit cards are not accepted. Many travel agencies and airlines automatically add this cost to the ticket price, but check with them before your departure.

HOTELS

Hotels in the state of Quintana Roo charge a 12% tax, which is a combined 10% Value Added Tax with the 2% hotel tax; in Yucatán and Campeche, expect a 17% tax since the VAT is 15% in these states.

VALUE-ADDED TAX (VAT)

Mexico has a value-added tax (VAT), or IVA (*impuesto de valor agregado*), of 15% (10% along the Cancún–Chetumal corridor). Many establishments already include the IVA in the quoted price. Occasionally (and illegally) it may be waived for cash purchases.

TELEPHONES

Most phones in Mexico now have Touch-Tone (digital) circuitry, especially in the larger cities and tourist areas. If you think you'll need to access an automated phone system or voice mail in the United States or elsewhere and you don't know what phone service will be available, it's a good idea to take along a Touch-Tone simulator (you can buy one for about $17 at most electronics stores).

AREA & COUNTRY CODES

The country code for Mexico is 52. When calling a Mexico number from abroad, dial the country code and then all of the numbers listed for the entry.

DIRECTORY & OPERATOR ASSISTANCE

Directory assistance is 040 nationwide. For international assistance, dial 00 first for an international operator and most likely you'll get one who speaks English; tell the operator in what city, state, and country you require directory assistance, and he or she will connect you.

INTERNATIONAL CALLS

To make an international call, dial 00 before the country code, area code, and number. The country code for the United States and Canada is 1, the United Kingdom 44, Australia 61, New Zealand 64, and South Africa 27.

LOCAL & LONG-DISTANCE CALLS

The cheapest and most dependable method for making local or long-distance calls is to buy a prepaid phone card and dial direct (*See* Phone Cards). Another option is to find a *caseta de larga distancia*, a telephone service usually operated out of a store such as a papelería, pharmacy, restaurant, or other small business; look for the phone symbol on the door. Casetas may cost more to use than pay phones, but you have a better chance of immediate success. To make a direct long-distance call, tell the person on duty the number you'd like to call, and she or he will give you a rate and dial for you. Rates seem to vary widely, so shop around. Sometimes you can make collect calls from casetas, and sometimes you cannot, depending on the individual operator and possibly your degree of visible desperation. Casetas will generally charge 50¢–$1.50 to place a collect call (some charge by the minute); it's usually better to call *por cobrar* (collect) from a pay phone.

LONG-DISTANCE SERVICES

AT&T, MCI, and Sprint access codes make calling long-distance relatively convenient, but you may find the local access number blocked in many hotel rooms. First ask the hotel operator to connect you. If the hotel operator balks, ask for an international operator, or dial the international operator yourself. One way to improve your odds of getting connected to your long-distance carrier is to travel with more than one company's calling card (a hotel may block Sprint, for example, but not MCI). If all else fails, call from a pay phone.

🚹 Access Codes **AT&T Direct** ☎ 01800/288-2872 or 01800/462-4240 both toll-free in Mexico. **MCI WorldPhone** ☎ 95800/674-7000. **Sprint** ☎ 01800/234-0000 or 01800/877-8000 both toll-free in Mexico.

PHONE CARDS

In most parts of the country, pay phones accept prepaid cards, called Ladatel cards, sold in 30-, 50- or 100-peso denominations at newsstands or pharmacies. Many pay phones accept only these cards; coin-only pay phones are usually broken. Still other phones have two unmarked slots, one for a Ladatel (a Spanish acronym for "long-distance direct dialing") card and the other for a credit card. These are only for Mexican bank cards, but some accept Visa or MasterCard. Mexican pay phones do not accept U.S. phone cards.

To use a Ladatel card, simply insert it in the appropriate slot, dial 001 (for calls to the States) or 01 (for calls in Mexico) and the area code and number you're trying to reach. Local calls may also be placed with the card. Credit is deleted from the card as you use it, and your balance is displayed on a small screen on the phone.

TOLL-FREE NUMBERS

Toll-free numbers in Mexico start with an 800 prefix. To reach them, you need to dial 01 before the number. In this guide, Mexico-only toll-free numbers appear as follows: 01800/123-4567. Some toll-free numbers use 95 instead of 01 to connect. The 800 numbers listed simply 800/123-4567 work north of the border only.

TIME

Mexico has two time zones. The west coast and middle states are on Pacific Standard Time. The rest of the country is on Central Standard Time, which is one hour behind Pacific Time.

TIPPING

When tipping in Mexico, remember that the minimum wage is the equivalent of $3 a day and that most workers in the tourism industry live barely above the poverty line. There are also Mexicans who think in dollars and know, for example, that in the United States porters are tipped about $2 a bag. Many of them expect the peso equivalent from foreigners and may complain if they feel they deserve more—you and your conscience must decide.

What follows are some guidelines. Naturally, larger tips are always welcome: porters and bellhops, 10 pesos per bag at airports and moderate and inexpensive hotels and 20 pesos per person at expensive hotels; maids, 10 pesos per night (all hotels); waiters, 10%–15% of the bill, depending on service (make sure a service charge hasn't already been added, a practice that's particularly common in resorts); bartenders, 10%–15% of the bill, depending on service (and, perhaps, on how many drinks you've had); taxi drivers, 5–10 pesos is nice, but only if the driver helps you with your bags as tipping cabbies isn't necessary; tour guides and drivers, at least 50 pesos per half day; gas-station attendants, 3–5 pesos unless they check the oil, tires, and so on, in which case tip more; parking attendants, 5–10 pesos, even if it's for valet parking at a theater or restaurant that charges for the service.

TOURS & PACKAGES

Because everything is prearranged on a prepackaged tour or independent vacation, you spend less time planning—and often get it all at a good price.

BOOKING WITH AN AGENT

Travel agents are excellent resources. But it's a good idea to collect brochures from several agencies, as some agents' suggestions may be influenced by relationships with tour and package firms that reward them for volume sales. If you have a special interest, find an agent with expertise in that area; the American Society of Travel Agents (ASTA, ⇨ Travel Agencies) has a database of specialists worldwide. You can log on to the group's Web site to find an ASTA travel agent in your neighborhood.

Make sure your travel agent knows the accommodations and other services of the place being recommended. Ask about the hotel's location, room size, beds, and whether it has a pool, room service, or programs for children, if you care about these. Has your agent been there in person or sent others whom you can contact?

Do some homework on your own, too: local tourism boards can provide information about lesser-known and small-niche operators, some of which may sell only direct.

BUYER BEWARE

Each year consumers are stranded or lose their money when tour operators—even large ones with excellent reputations—go out of business. So check out the operator. Ask several travel agents about its reputation, and try to **book with a company that has a consumer-protection program.** (Look for information in the company's brochure.) In the United States, members of the National Tour Association and the United States Tour Operators Association are required to set aside funds to cover payments and travel arrangements in the event that the company defaults. It's also a good idea to choose a company that participates in the American Society of Travel Agents' Tour Operator Program; ASTA will act as mediator in any disputes between you and your tour operator.

Remember that the more your package or tour includes, the better you can predict the ultimate cost of your vacation. Make sure you know exactly what is covered, and beware of hidden costs. Are taxes, tips, and transfers included? Entertainment and excursions? These can add up.

◪ Tour-Operator Recommendations **American Society of Travel Agents** (⇨ Travel Agencies). **National Tour Association** (NTA) ⊠ 546 E. Main St., Lexington, KY 40508 ☎ 800/682-8886 or 859/226-4444 ⊕ www.ntaonline.com. **United States Tour Operators Association** (USTOA) ⊠ 275 Madison Ave., Suite 2014, New York, NY 10016 ☎ 212/599-6599 ⊕ www.ustoa.com.

THEME TRIPS

◪ Adventure **TrekAmerica** ⌂ Box 189, Rockaway, NJ 07866 ☎ 800/221-0596 or 973/983-1144 ⊕ www.trekamerica.com.

◪ Art & Archaeology **Far Horizons Archaeological & Cultural Trips** ⌂ Box 91900, Albuquerque, NM 87199-1900 ☎ 800/552-4575 or 505/343-9400 ⊕ www.farhorizon.com. **Maya Sites** ☎ 877/620-8715 or 719/256-5186 ⊕ www.mayasites.com. **The Mayan Traveler** ⊠ 5 Grogan's Park, Suite 102, The Woodlands, TX 77380 ☎ 800/451-8017 or 281/367-3386 🖷 281/298-2335 ⊕ www.themayantraveler.com.

◪ Bicycling **Aventuras Tropicales de Sian** ⊠ 37 S. Clearwater Rd., Grand Marais, MN 55604 ☎ 800/649-4166 or 218/388-9455 ⊕ www.boreal.org/yucatan. **Backroads** ⊠ 801 Cedar St., Berkeley, CA 94710-1800 ☎ 800/462-2848 or 510/527-1555 ⊕ www.backroads.com.

◪ Ecotourism **Ecoturismo Yucatán** ⊠ Calle 3 No. 235, between Calles 32A and 34, Col. Pensiones,

97219 Mérida ☎ 999/925-2772 or 999/925-2187
⊕ www.mexonline.com/ecoyuc.htm. **Emerald
Planet** ✉ 2602 Timberwood Dr. No. 16, Fort Collins,
CO 80528 ☎ 888/883-0736 or 970/204-4484
⊕ www.emeraldplanet.com.

🎣 Fishing **Costa de Cocos** ✉ 2 km [1 mi] outside
of Xcalak, Quintana Roo ⊕ www.costadecocos.com.
Fishing International ✉ 1825 4th St., Santa Rosa,
CA 95404 ☎ 800/950-4242 or 707/542-4242
📠 707/526-3474 ⊕ www.fishinginternational.com.
🎣 Spas **Spa-Finders** ✉ 91 5th Ave., Suite 301,
New York, NY 10003-3039 ☎ 800/255-7727 or 212/
924-6800.

TRAVEL AGENCIES

A good travel agent puts your needs first.
Look for an agency that has been in business at least five years, emphasizes customer service, and has someone on staff
who specializes in your destination. In
addition, **make sure the agency belongs
to a professional trade organization.**
The American Society of Travel Agents
(ASTA)—the largest and most influential
in the field with more than 20,000 members in some 140 countries—maintains
and enforces a strict code of ethics and
will step in to help mediate any agent-
client disputes involving ASTA members
if necessary. ASTA (whose motto is
"Without a travel agent, you're on your
own") also maintains a Web site that includes a directory of agents. (If a travel
agency is also acting as your tour operator, *see* Buyer Beware *in* Tours and
Packages.)

🎣 Local Agent Referrals **American Society of
Travel Agents (ASTA)** ✉ 1101 King St., Suite 200,
Alexandria, VA 22314 ☎ 800/965-2782 24-hr hotline, 703/739-2782 ⊕ www.astanet.com. **Association of British Travel Agents** ✉ 68-71 Newman
St., London W1T 3AH ☎ 020/7637-2444 ⊕ www.
abta.com. **Association of Canadian Travel Agencies** ✉ 130 Albert St., Suite 1705, Ottawa, Ontario
K1P 5G4 ☎ 613/237-3657 ⊕ www.acta.ca. **Australian Federation of Travel Agents** ✉ 309 Pitt
St., Level 3, Sydney, NSW 2000 ☎ 02/9264-3299
⊕ www.afta.com.au. **Travel Agents' Association
of New Zealand** ✉ Tourism and Travel House,
Level 5, 79 Boulcott St., Box 1888, Wellington 6001
☎ 04/499-0104 ⊕ www.taanz.org.nz.

VISITOR INFORMATION

Learn more about foreign destinations by
checking government-issued travel advisories and country information. For a
broader picture, consider information
from more than one country.

🎣 Mexico Tourism Board **Canada** ✉ 1 Pl. Ville
Marie, Suite 1931, Montréal, Québec H3B 2C3
☎ 514/871-1052 ✉ 2 Bloor St. W, Suite 1502,
Toronto, Ontario M4W 3E2 ☎ 416/925-0704 ✉ 999
W. Hastings St., Suite 1110, Vancouver, British
Columbia V6C 2W2 ☎ 604/669-2845.

United Kingdom ✉ Wakefield House, 41 Trinity Sq.,
London EC3N 4DJ ☎ 020/7488-9392.

United States ☎ 800/446-3942 ⊕ www.visitmexico.
com ✉ 21 E. 63rd St., 3rd fl., New York, NY 10021
☎ 212/821-0304 ✉ 300 N. Michigan Ave., 4th fl.,
Chicago, IL 60601 ☎ 312/606-9252 ✉ 2401 W. 6th
St., 5th fl., Los Angeles, CA 90057 ☎ 213/351-2069
✉ 4507 San Jacinto, Suite 308, Houston, TX 77004
☎ 713/772-2581 ✉ 5975 Sunset Dr., Suite 305,
South Miami, FL 33143 ☎ 786/621-2909.

🎣 Government Advisories **Australian Department
of Foreign Affairs and Trade** ☎ 02/6261-1299 Consular Travel Advice Faxback Service ⊕ www.dfat.
gov.au.

Consular Affairs Bureau of Canada ☎ 800/267-
6788 or 613/944-6788 ⊕ www.voyage.gc.ca. **New
Zealand Ministry of Foreign Affairs and Trade**
☎ 04/439-8000 ⊕ www.mft.govt.nz.

U.K. Foreign and Commonwealth Office ✉ Travel
Advice Unit, Consular Division, Old Admiralty Bldg.,
London SW1A 2PA ☎ 020/7008-0232 or 020/
7008-0233 ⊕ www.fco.gov.uk/travel. **U.S. Department of State** ✉ Overseas Citizens Services Office,
Room 4811, 2201 C St. NW, Washington, DC 20520
☎ 888/407-4747, 202/647-5225 interactive hotline
⊕ www.travel.state.gov; enclose a cover letter with
your request and a business-size SASE.

WEB SITES

Do check out the World Wide Web when
planning your trip. You'll find everything
from weather forecasts to virtual tours of
famous cities. Be sure to visit Fodors.com
(⊕ www.fodors.com), a complete travel-
planning site. You can research prices and
book plane tickets, hotel rooms, rental
cars, vacation packages, and more. In ad-

dition, you can post your pressing questions in the Travel Talk section. Other planning tools include a currency converter and weather reports, and there are loads of links to travel resources.

There are two official Web sites for Mexico: ⊕ www.mexico-travel.com and ⊕ www.visitmexico.com have information on tourist attractions and activities, and an overview of Mexican history and culture. If you would like to get a feel for the country's political climate, check out the president's site at ⊕ www.presidencia.gob.mx; he also has a site for children at ⊕ www.elbalero.gob.mx. For more information specifically on the Yucatán Peninsula, try ⊕ www.yucatantoday.com, ⊕ www.mayan-riviera.com, or ⊕ www.cancun.com. All are fairly comprehensive sites with information on nightlife, hotel listings, archaeological sites, area history, and other useful information for travelers.

CANCÚN

MOST BOUNDLESS BEACHES
Boulevard Kukulcán's 20 km of sand
and surf ⇨*p.9*

BEST PLACE TO BARGAIN
El Centro's Mercado Veintiocho ⇨*p.37*

DISCO INFERNO
Wild Nights at Coco Bongo ⇨*p.30*

GENTLEMEN, START YOUR ENGINES
The racetrack at Go Karts Cancún ⇨*p.33*

TORO! TORO!
Wednesday afternoons at the bullring ⇨*p.33*

Updated by
Shelagh
McNally

FLYING INTO CANCÚN, YOU SEE NOTHING BUT GREEN TREETOPS for miles. It's clear from the air that this resort was literally carved out of the jungle. When development began in the early 1970s, the beaches were deserted except for birds and iguanas. Now luxury hotels, malls, and restaurants line the oceanfront. More vacationers come here than to any other part of Mexico, and many come again and again.

Not much was written about Cancún before its birth as a resort. The Maya people settled the area during the Late Preclassic era, around AD 200, and remained until the 14th or 15th century, but little is known about them. Other explorers seem to have overlooked it—it doesn't appear on early navigators' maps. It was never heavily populated, perhaps because its terrain of mangroves and marshes (and resulting swarms of mosquitoes) discouraged settlement. Some minor Maya ruins were discovered in the mid-19th century, but archaeologists didn't get around to studying them until the 1950s.

In 1967, the Mexican government, under the leadership of Luis Echeverría, commissioned a study to pinpoint the ideal place for an international Caribbean resort. The computer chose Cancún, and the Cinderella transformation began. At the time, the area's only residents were the three caretakers of a coconut plantation. In 1972 work began on the first hotel, and the island and city grew from there.

Today's Cancún has two different sides. On the mainland is the actual Ciudad Cancún (Cancún City). Its commercial center, known as El Centro, offers an authentic glimpse into the sights and sounds of Mexico. The other half, the Zona Hotelera (Hotel Zone), is the tourist heart. It's actually a 22½-km (14-mi) barrier island off the Yucatán Peninsula. A separate northern strip called Punta Sam, north of Puerto Juárez (where some ferries to Isla Mujeres depart), is sometimes referred to as the Zona Hotelera Norte (Northern Hotel Zone).

During the day you can shop, eat, and lounge in the year-round tropical warmth: the sun shines an average of 240 days a year, and temperatures linger at about 27°C (80°F). The reefs off Cancún and nearby Cozumel, Puerto Morelos, and Isla Mujeres are great places to dive, and Cancún also makes a relaxing base for visiting the ruins of Chichén Itzá, Tulum, and Cobá. At night you can sample Yucatecan food and watch folkloric dance performances, knock back tequila slammers, or listen to great jazz.

Cancún's success hasn't come without a price. Its lagoons and mangrove swamps have been polluted; a number of species, such as conch and lobster, are dwindling; and parts of the coral reef are dead. And although the beaches still appear pristine for the most part, an increased effort will have to be made to preserve the beauty that is the resort's prime appeal.

EXPLORING CANCÚN

The Zona Hotelera is a small island shaped roughly like the numeral 7. The top extends east from the mainland into the Caribbean; the Punta Cancún–Punta Nizuc strip has a slight north–northeast arc. Hotel de-

Archaeological Sites

The Yucatán is more than a perfect place for a beach vacation. The many Maya ruins scattered throughout the peninsula also make it an area of special historical interest. Many of these ruins are within easy driving distance of Cancún, and are well worth a visit.

The closest Maya site is the ancient coastal city of Tulum, which is about a two-hour drive south of Cancún. This is one of the last of the Maya cities, and was a bustling center of Maya trade spotted from the sea by Spanish conquistadores when they landed in the 1500s. The ruins, perched high on a cliff overlooking the Caribbean, include several striking examples of Maya architecture; the Templo de los Frescos, with its vaulted temple roof and its walls showing faint traces of Maya paintings, is especially dazzling. Historians say the name of the city roughly translates as "City of the Dawn."

Set a bit farther inland from Tulum are the ruins of Cobá (Maya for "water stirred by the winds"). This ancient city is situated on five lakes, and was once one of the most powerful cities in the region with a strong alliance to Tikal in Guatemala. There are over 6,500 structures at Cobá, many of them huge temples and pyramids that have been partly engulfed by the surrounding jungle. So far, however, only 5 percent of the ruins have been explored. One of these, a pyramid called Nohoch Mul, is one of the tallest in the area—approximately 12 stories high—and the view from the top stretches far across the jungly landscape. Another group of structures, Las Pinturas Group, is buried deep in the trees and has friezes on the inner and outer walls dating back to 600 BC.

Most spectacular of all the area's Maya sites, however, are the ruins at Chichén Itzá, about a four-hour drive southwest of Cancún. Settled by a particularly mysterious Maya group, the Itzás, in around AD 868, Chichén was the most important city in the Yucatán between the 10th and the 12th centuries. The site, which is approximately 6 square km (2½ square mi), contains several hundred structures, and although only about 40 of them have been fully explored, they are some of the most breathtaking examples of Maya architecture existing today. Among them are what is thought to be the largest ball court in Mesoamerica; several temples; a round observatory; and the extraordinary 98-foot pyramid known as El Castillo ("the castle"), which dwarfs all the other buildings in the complex. This pyramid has four staircases, one on each side, and is topped by a temple dedicated to the serpent god Kukulcán. At the spring and autumn equinoxes, sunlight strikes one of the many serpent statues so that its shadow seems to undulate down the northern staircase of the pyramid; thousands of visitors flock to the site each year to witness the sight.

Beaches

The Mexican government might have designed the resort, but nature provided its most striking features—its cool, white, limestone sand and clear turquoise sea. Except for the tip of Punta Cancún, Cancún Island is one long beach. These long stretches of silky sand and crystal waters can tempt you to immediately dive in—although this probably isn't a wise thing to do on the eastern coast, as these beaches have dangerous riptides and currents. The windward beaches that fringe the Bahía de Mujeres are the safest places to indulge, as they have the calmest water. One thing you may notice that's special about Cancún beaches is how cool the sand remains, no matter how hot the sun is. This is because the sand is actually made from finely ground coral reef crustaceans, which make the sand porous, fluffy, and unable to absorb heat. All beaches are federal property and are open to everyone.

Dining

One of the best things about Cancún is its diversity of restaurants. Many restaurants present a hybrid cuisine that combines fresh fish from local waters, elements of Yucatecan and Mexican cuisines, and a fusion of French, Italian, and North and South American influences. Steak houses are popular venues here, but so are sushi bars. There are many choices for elegant dining in upscale restaurants with European-style service, and plenty of romantic spots, too (many restaurants overlook either the ocean or Laguna Nichupté, and are perfect for a sunset cocktail or starlit dinner). For those looking for a livelier good time, there are places where the perpetual New Year's Eve atmosphere includes singing, dancing waiters who often drag diners into the fun. Fiesta dinners are a weekly staple at many hotels, so you can sample Mexican favorites without venturing out. If you enjoy watching culinary artistry at work, there are dinner spots where waiters prepare meals table-side or mix flaming cocktails with great flourish. Downtown Cancún offers equally romantic restaurants at lower prices but also the opportunity to try out new flavors (watch those chiles!) with the locals.

Hotels

With more than 25,000 hotel rooms and over 110 hotels, Cancún has accommodations to suit every personality, as well as every pocketbook. One thing many hotels do have in common, however, is architecture; especially in the Zona Hotelera, it tends to be an appealing if somewhat kitschy cross between Mediterranean style and a developer's interpretation of Maya style. Typical Mediterranean structures—low, solid, rectangular, with flat, red-tile roofs; Moorish arches; and white stucco walls covered with exuberantly pink bougainvillea—are embellished with palapas, columns, latticework, and beveled cornices. Inside are contemporary-style furniture and pastel hues. All-inclusive resorts are popular here, and each one offers something different; some are intimate, honeymoon-type couples destinations; others are great for families with children. Many of the familiar upscale chains have hotels here offering complete luxury and comfort; but for those who wish to experience a more genuinely local lifestyle, downtown Cancún has some modest hotels that are still lovely and charming.

Nightlife

Cancún is a party town. From early evening until dawn the whole Zona pulses with music. Salsa, reggae, hip-hop, mariachi, jazz, disco, rock and roll—it's all here. Mexicans love music and dancing is an integral part of the culture, so let yourself relax and join in the fun. Local discos give you the chance to dance the night away and even practice your salsa technique. If you don't want to dance then you can certainly enjoy the terrific bands and musicians playing throughout the Zona Hotelera and downtown. Cancún attracts some of Mexico's most talented musicians, who come to perform in the lobby bars and restaurants. Many of these lobby bars also have two-for-one drink deals at happy hour, and bar-hopping in the big resorts is a great way to check out the different kinds of music. To see how the locals party, head to the Latin clubs.

For couples there are cruises where you can dine and dance under the stars. Generally the clubs and discos don't close until 2 or 3 AM, so there's plenty of time to get into the groove.

Water Sports
Cancún is one of the water-sports capitals of the world, and, with the Caribbean on one side of the island and the still waters of Laguna Nichupté on the other, it's no wonder. The most popular activities are snorkeling and diving along the coral reef just off the coast, where schools of colorful tropical fish and other marine creatures live. If you want to view the mysterious underwater world but don't want to get your feet wet, a glass-bottom boat or "submarine" is the ticket. You can also fish, sail, jet ski, parasail, or windsurf. If you prefer your water chlorinated, lots of hotels also have gorgeous pools—many featuring waterfalls, Jacuzzis, and swim-up bars serving cool drinks. Several hotels offer organized games of water polo and volleyball as well as introductory scuba courses in their pools.

---

velopment began at the north end (close to the mainland), headed east toward Punta Cancún, and then moved south to Punta Nizuc. At the south end of the Zona Hotelera, the road curves west toward the highway and airport. Downtown Cancún—El Centro—is 4 km (2½ mi) west of the Zona Hotelera on the mainland.

A system of lagoons separates the Zona Hotelera from the mainland. Nichupté, the largest (about 29 square km, or 18 square mi), contains both fresh and salt water. Bojórquez is nestled inside the northeastern elbow. Laguna Río Inglés is south of Nichupté. Bahía de Mujeres lies north of the Zone; the bay, which is 9 km (5½ mi) wide, separates Cancún from Isla Mujeres.

Boulevard Kukulcán is the main drag in the Zona Hotelera, and because the island is so narrow—less than 1 km (½ mi) wide—you can see both the Caribbean and the lagoons from either side of it. Regularly placed kilometer markers alongside Boulevard Kukulcán indicate where you are. The first marker (Km 1) is near downtown on the mainland; Km 20 lies at the south end of the Zone at Punta Nizuc. The area in between consists entirely of hotels, restaurants, shopping complexes, marinas, and time-share condominiums. It's not the sort of place you can get to know by walking, although there is a bicycle-walking path that starts downtown at the beginning of the Zona Hotelera and continues through to Punta Nizuc. The beginning of the path parallels a grassy strip of Boulevard Kukulcán decorated with reproductions of ancient Mexican art, including the Aztec calendar stone, a giant Olmec head, the Atlantids of Tula, and a Maya Chacmool (reclining rain god).

South of Punta Cancún, Boulevard Kukulcán becomes a busy road, difficult to cross on foot. It's also punctuated by steeply inclined driveways that turn into the hotels, most of which are set at least 100 yards from the road. The lagoon side of the boulevard consists of scrubby stretches of land alternating with marinas, shopping centers, and restaurants. Because there are so few sights, there are no orientation tours of Cancún: just do the local bus circuit to get a feel for the island's layout.

When you first visit El Centro, the downtown layout might not be self-evident. It is not based on a grid but rather on a circular pattern. The whole city is divided into districts called Super Manzanas (abbreviated Sm in this book), each with its own central square or park. The main streets curve around the manzanas, and the smaller neighborhood streets curl around the parks in horseshoe shapes. Avenida Tulum is the main street—actually a four-lane road with two northbound and two southbound lanes. The inner north and south lanes, separated by a meridian of grass, are the express lanes. Along the express lanes, smaller roads lead to the outer lanes, where local shops and services are. This setup makes for some amazing traffic snarls, and it can be quite dangerous crossing at the side roads. Instead, cross at the speed bumps placed along the express lanes that act as pedestrian walkways.

Avenidas Bonampak and Yaxchilán are the other two major north–south streets that parallel Tulum. The three major east–west streets are Avenidas Cobá, Uxmal, and Chichén. They are marked along Tulum by huge traffic circles, each set with a piece of sculpture.

Numbers in the text correspond to numbers in the margin and on the Cancún map.

A Good Tour

Cancún's scenery consists mostly of beautiful beaches and crystal-clear waters, but there are also a few intriguing historical sites tucked away among the modern hotels. In addition to the attractions listed below, two modest vestiges of the ancient Maya civilization are worth a visit, but only for dedicated archaeology buffs. Neither is identified by name. On the 12th hole of Pok-Ta-Pok golf course (Boulevard Kukulcán, Km 6.5)—the name means "ball game" in Maya—stands a ruin consisting of two platforms and the remains of other ancient buildings. And the ruin of a tiny Maya shrine is cleverly incorporated into the architecture of the Hotel Camino Real, on the beach at Punta Cancún.

You don't need a car in Cancún, but if you've rented one to make extended trips, start in the Zona Hotelera at **Ruinas del Rey ❶** ▸. Drive north to **Yamil Lu'um ❷**, and then stop in at the **Cancún Convention Center ❸**, with its anthropology and history museum, before heading farther north to the **Museo de Arte Popular ❹**, in El Embarcadero marina, and finally turning west to reach **El Centro ❺**.

What to See

❸ **Cancún Convention Center.** This strikingly modern venue for cultural events is the jumping-off point for a 1-km (½-mi) string of shopping malls that extends west to the Presidente InterContinental Cancún. The **Instituto Nacional de Antropología e Historia** (National Institute of Anthropology and History; ☎ 998/883–0305), a small, ground-floor museum, traces Maya culture with a fascinating collection of 1,000- to 1,500-year-old artifacts from throughout Quintana Roo. Admission to the museum is about $3; it's open Tuesday–Sunday 9–7. Guided tours are available in English, French, German, and Spanish. ✉ *Blvd. Kukulcán, Km 9, Zona Hotelera* ☎ 998/883–0305.

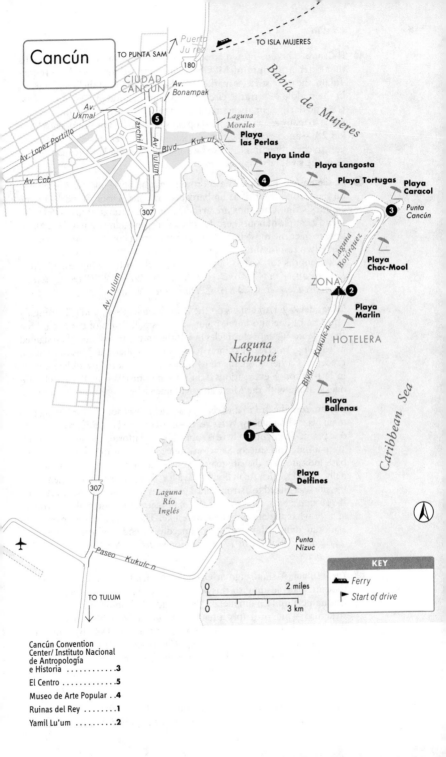

Cancún

TO PUNTA SAM

Puerto Juárez

TO ISLA MUJERES

180

CIUDAD CANCÚN

Av. Bonampak

Bahía de Mujeres

Av. Uxmal

Yaxchilán

Blvd. Kukulcán

Laguna Morales

Playa las Perlas

Av. López Portillo

Av. Tulum

Av. Cob

5

Playa Linda

4

Playa Langosta

Playa Tortugas

Playa Caracol

3

Punta Cancún

307

ZONA

Laguna Bojórquez

Playa Chac-Mool

2

Playa Marlin

HOTELERA

Laguna Nichupté

Blvd. Kukulcán

Playa Ballenas

1

Caribbean Sea

Playa Delfines

Laguna Río Inglés

307

Punta Nizuc

Paseo Kukulcán

TO TULUM

KEY	
🚢	*Ferry*
🚩	*Start of drive*

0 — 2 miles

0 — 3 km

❺ El Centro. The downtown area is a combination of markets and malls that offer a glimpse of Mexico's emerging urban lifestyle. Avenida Tulum, the main street, is marked by a huge sculpture of shells and starfish in the middle of a traffic circle. The sculpture, one of Cancún's icons, is particularly dramatic at night when the lights are turned on. It's also home to many restaurants and shops as well as Mercado Veintiocho (Market 28)—an enormous crafts market just off Avenidas Yaxchilán and Sunyaxchén. Bargains can also be found along Avenida Yaxchilán as well as in the smaller shopping centers.

★ ❹ Museo de Arte Popular. The enormous, entrancing Folk Art Museum is on the second floor of El Embarcadero marina. Original works by the country's finest artisans are arranged in fascinating tableaux; plan to spend a couple of hours here. It's open daily, and admission is $10. Allow time to visit the museum's shop. Other marina complex attractions include two restaurants, a rotating scenic tower, the Teatro Cancún, and ticket booths for Xcaret, a snorkeling park on Isla Mujeres. ✉ *Blvd. Kukulcán, Km 4, Zona Hotelera* ☎ *998/849–4848* ⊕ *www. elembarcadero.com* 🎫 *$10* ⊗ *Daily 9* AM–9 PM.

🔺 ▶ ❶ Ruinas del Rey. Large signs on the Zona Hotelera's lagoon side, roughly opposite El Pueblito hotel, point out the small Ruins of the King. First entered into Western chronicles in a 16th-century travelogue, then sighted in 1842 by American explorer John Lloyd Stephens and his draftsman, Frederick Catherwood, the ruins were finally explored by archaeologists in 1910, though excavations didn't begin until 1954. In 1975 archaeologists, along with the Mexican government, began restoration work.

Dating from the 3rd to 2nd century BC, del Rey is notable for having two main plazas bounded by two streets—most other Maya cities contain only one plaza. The pyramid here is topped by a platform, and inside its vault are paintings on stucco. Skeletons interred both at the apex and at the base indicate that the site may have been a royal burial ground. Originally named Kin Ich Ahau Bonil, Maya for "king of the solar countenance," the site was linked to astronomical practices in the ancient Maya culture. If you don't have time to visit the major sites, this one will give you an idea of what the ancient cities were like. The ruins are now part of an elaborate dinner show, which you needn't attend to visit the structures. ✉ *Blvd. Kukulcán, Km 17, Zona Hotelera* ☎ *998/883–2080* 🎫 *$4.50* ⊗ *Daily 8–5.*

🔺 ❷ Yamil Lu'um. A small sign at Occidental Caribbean Village directs you to a dirt path leading to this site, which is on Cancún's highest point (the name Yamil Lu'um means "hilly land"). Although it comprises two structures—one probably a temple, the other probably a lighthouse—this is the smallest of Cancún's ruins. Discovered in 1842 by John Lloyd Stephens, the ruins date from the late 13th or early 14th century. ✉ *Blvd. Kukulcán, Km 12, Zona Hotelera* ☎ *No phone* 🎫 *Free.*

BEACHES

Cancún Island is one long continuous beach. By law the entire coast of Mexico is federal property and open to the public. In reality, security guards discourage locals from using the beaches outside hotels. Some all-inclusives distribute neon wristbands to guests; those without a wristband aren't actually prohibited from being on the beach—just from entering or exiting via the hotel. Everyone is welcome to walk along the beach, as long as you get on or off from one of the public points. Although these points are often miles apart, one way around the situation is to find a hotel open to the public, go into the lobby bar for a drink or snack, and afterward go for a swim along the beach. All of the beaches can also be reached by public transportation; just let the driver know where you are headed.

Most hotel beaches have lifeguards, but, as with all ocean swimming, use common sense—even the calmest-looking waters can have currents and riptides. Overall, the beaches on the windward stretch of the island—those facing the Bahía de Mujeres—are best for swimming; farther out, the undertow can be tricky. *Don't* swim when the red or black danger flags fly; yellow flags indicate that you should proceed with caution, and green or blue flags mean the waters are calm.

Playa las Perlas is the first beach on the drive heading east from El Centro along Boulevard Kukulcán. It's a relatively small beach with waters protected by the Bahía de Mujeres and is popular with locals. There aren't many public facilities here, and most of the water-sports activities are available only to those staying at the nearby resorts such as Club las Perlas or the Blue Bay Getaway. At Km 4 on Boulevard Kukulcán, **Playa Linda** is where the ocean meets the fresh water of the Nichupté lagoon to create the Nichupté Channel. There's lots of boat activity along the channel, and the ferry to Isla Mujeres leaves from the adjoining Embarcadero marina, so the area isn't safe for swimming—although it's a great place to people-watch. Small, placid **Playa Langosta,** which starts at Boulevard Kukulcán's Km 4, has calm waters that make it an excellent place for a swim, although it has no public facilities. **Playa Tortugas,** the last "real" beach along the east–west stretch of the Zona Hotelera, has lots of hotels with lots of sand in between. There are restaurants, changing areas, and restrooms at either end of the beach (it stretches between about Km 6 and Km 8 on Boulevard Kukulcán). The swimming is excellent, and many people come here to sail, snorkel, kayak, paraglide, and use Wave Runners.

Playa Caracol, the outermost beach in the Zona Hotelera, is a beach only in name. The whole area has been eaten up by development—in particular the monstrous Xcaret ferry dock. This beach is also hindered by the rocks that jut out from the water marking the beginning of Punta Cancún, where Boulevard Kukulcán turns south. Heading down from Punta Cancún onto the long, southerly stretch of the island, **Playa Chacmool** is the first beach on the Caribbean's open waters. It's close to several shopping centers and the party zone, so there are plenty of restaurants nearby. The shallow clear water makes it tempting to walk far out into the ocean, but be careful—there's a strong current and undertow. **Playa Marlin,** at Km 13 along Boulevard Kukulcán, is in the heart of the Zona Hotelera and accessible via area resorts (access is easiest at Occidental Carribean Village). It's a seductive beach with turquoise waters and silky sands, but like most beaches facing the Caribbean, the waves are strong, and the currents are dangerous. There aren't any public facilities.

Playa Ballenas starts off with some rather large rocks at about Km 14 on Boulevard Kukulcán, but it widens shortly afterward and extends down for another breathtaking—and sandy—3 km (5 mi). The wind here is strong, making the surf rough, and several hotels have put up ropes and buoys to help swimmers make their way safely in and out of the water. Access is via one of the hotels, such as Le Meridien or JW Marriott. **Playa Delfines** is the final beach, at Km 20 where Boulevard Kukulcán curves into a hill. There's an incredible lookout over the ocean; on a clear day you can see at least four shades of blue in the water, though swimming is treacherous unless one of the green flags is posted. Since few people actually make it down from the parking lot, Playa Delfines is often deserted, making it perfect for solitary sunbathing.

WHERE TO EAT

Cancún attracts chefs—as well as visitors—from around the globe, so the area has choices to suit just about every palate (from Provençal cuisine to traditional Mexican and American diner fare). Fusion menus, however, are especially popular. When traditional Mexican flavors are combined with Swiss, Italian, and Asian cuisine, delicious dishes are often the result. Some of the best can be found at Le Basilic, where French chef Henri Charvet works his magic; Laguna Grill, the domain of Swiss master chef Alex Rudin; Gustino Italian Beachside Grill, headed by Richard Sylvester of Austria; and Labná, where Carlos Hannon brings Yucatecan cuisine to new heights.

Both the Zona Hotelera and El Centro have plenty of great places to eat. There are some pitfalls: restaurants that line Avenida Tulum are often noisy and crowded, gas fumes make it hard to enjoy alfresco meals, and Zona Hotelera chefs often cater to what they assume is a visitor preference for bland food. The key to eating well is to find the local haunts, most of which are in El Centro. The restaurants in the Parque de las Palapas, just off Avenida Tulum, serve expertly prepared Mexican food. Farther into the city center, you can find fresh seafood and traditional fare at dozens of small, reasonably priced restaurants in the Mercado Veintiocho (Market 28).

Unless otherwise stated, restaurants serve lunch and dinner daily. Large breakfast and brunch buffets are among the most popular meals in the Zona Hotelera. With prices ranging from $3 to $15 per person, they are a good value—if you eat on the late side, you won't need to eat again until dinner. They are especially pleasant at palapa restaurants on the beach.

Prices

	WHAT IT COSTS In Dollars			
	$$$$	**$$$**	**$$**	**$**	**¢**
AT DINNER	over $25	$15–$25	$10–$15	$5–$10	under $5

Per person, for a main course at dinner, excluding tax and tip.

What to Wear

Dress is casual in Cancún, but many restaurants do not allow bare feet, short shorts, bathing suits, or no shirt. At upscale restaurants, pants, skirts, or dresses are favored over shorts at dinnertime.

Zona Hotelera

American Casual

¢–$$ ✕ **Johnny Rockets.** This transplanted 1950s-style American diner serves great hamburgers and genuine malted milk shakes. Hot dogs, sandwiches, and salads are also on the menu, along with good old-fashioned American apple pie. The jukeboxes add just the right touch. The one drawback is the slow service. ⊠ *La Isla Shopping Village, Blvd. Kukulcán, Km 12.5, Zona Hotelera* ☎ *998/883–5576* ▭ *MC, V.*

Cajun

$$–$$$$ ✕ **Blue Bayou.** Mexico's first Cajun restaurant is still very popular. Five levels of intimate dining areas are done in wood, rattan, and bamboo—all set against a backdrop of waterfalls and greenery. Specialties include Cancún jambalaya, blackened grouper, herb crawfish Louisiana, plantation duckling, and chicken Grand Bayou. There's live jazz nightly and dancing on weekends. ⊠ *Hyatt Cancún Caribe, Blvd. Kukulcán, Km 10.5, Zona Hotelera* ☎ *998/848–7800* ⌣ *Reservations essential* ▭ *AE, DC, MC, V* ☺ *No lunch.*

Contemporary

$$$$ ✕ **Club Grill.** The dining room is romantic and quietly elegant—with rich wood, fresh flowers, crisp linens, and courtyard views—and the classic dishes have a distinctly Mexican flavor. The cream of lobster soup infused with coconut is a good starter, and the filet mignon and roast duck with Yucatán honey are excellent entrées. The tasting menu offers a small selection of all the courses paired with wines and followed by wickedly delicious desserts. ⊠ *Ritz-Carlton Cancún, Blvd. Kukulcán, Km 14 (Retorno del Rey 36), Zona Hotelera* ☎ *998/881–0808* ▭ *AE, MC, V* ☺ *No lunch.*

★ **$$$–$$$$**   ✕ **Le Basilic.** The sophisticated dishes served in this elegant, oak and marble dining room are the creations of French chef Henri Charvet. The spinach tart with a hint of curry is the perfect start to a meal; the quail stew with fresh figs and roast loin of lamb seasoned with bacon are supremely satisfying. Reservations are recommended. ⊠ *Blvd. Kukulcán, Km 9.5, Lote 6, Zona Hotelera* ☎ *998/881–3200 Ext. 4220* ▭ *AE, MC, V.*

$$$–$$$$
Fodor'sChoice
★   ✕ **Laguna Grill.** Intricate tile work adorns this restaurant's floors and walls, and a natural stream divides the open-air dining room, which overlooks the lagoon. The menu here is as imaginative as the setting; culinary wizard Alex Rudin whips up such innovative appetizers as shrimp and vegetable tempura with carrot sherbet and sea scallops with truffle emulsion. Ingenious entrées include Thai spiced salmon, lamb shank with curry mash, honey-mustard pork loin, and rib-eye steak with lobster satay. The wine menu is excellent as well, and be sure to finish off your meal with a decadent dessert. ⊠ *Blvd. Kukulcán, Km 15.6, Zona Hotelera* ☎ *998/885–0267* ▭ *AE, MC, V.*

French

$$$–$$$$ ✕ **Aioli.** Dining is relaxed and stylish at this restaurant, with its green-and-taupe plaids, white linens, contemporary table settings, and creative Provençal dishes. Try the duck breast in a potato *galette* (buckwheat pancake) and lavender sauce or Moroccan-style rack of lamb. Fresh fish is grilled to perfection, and the wine list is extensive. The breakfast buffet is superb. ☒ *Le Meridien, Blvd. Kukulcán, Km 14 (Retorno del Rey, Lote 37), Zona Hotelera* ☎ *998/881–2260* ▤ *AE, DC, MC, V.*

Italian

$$$–$$$$ ✕ **La Madonna.** This dramatic-looking restaurant is a fine place to enjoy a selection of martinis and cigars. The menu is Italian "with a Swiss twist." Enjoy saffron risotto or salmon fettuccine alongside large statues reminiscent of Greek caryatids and a massive reproduction of the Mona Lisa. The service can be chilly at times. ☒ *La Isla Shopping Village, Blvd. Kukulcán, Km 12.5, Zona Hotelera* ☎ *998/883–4837* ⟁ *Reservations essential* ▤ *AE, D, MC, V.*

$$–$$$$ ✕ **Casa Rolandi.** The secret to this restaurant's success is its creative handling of Swiss and northern Italian cuisine. Be sure to try the carpaccio *di salmone alla Rolandi* (thin slices of fresh salmon with extra-virgin oil), the homemade lasagna, or the homemade ravioli *ripieni di carne di capriolo* (stuffed with venison). Appetizers are also tempting: there's puff bread from a wood-burning oven, and a huge salad and antipasto bar. The beautiful dining room and attentive service further add to the dining experience. ☒ *Plaza Caracol, Blvd. Kukulcán, Km 8.5, Zona Hotelera* ☎ *998/883–2557* ▤ *AE, D, MC, V.*

$–$$$ ✕ **La Dolce Vita.** This grand dame of Cancún restaurants delivers on the promise of its name (which means "the sweet life" in Italian). It has a classic style: candlelit tables adorned with fine linen and china, soft music, and discreet waiters. The menu offers superior Italian fare, including gnocchi in a four-cheese sauce, lobster fettuccine, and Bolognese-style lasagna; the wine list is also excellent. The service is top-notch whether you dine indoors or on the terrace overlooking the lagoon. ☒ *Blvd. Kukulcán, Km 14.5, Zona Hotelera* ☎ *998/885–0161* ▤ *AE, D, MC, V.*

$–$$$ ✕ **Gustino Italian Beachside Grill.** Everything works in harmony to create a memorable dining experience at this restaurant. You walk down a dramatic staircase to a brick-and-wood entrance; then continue past the wine cellar and open-air kitchen to the dining room where leather furniture and sleek table settings are set off by artistic lighting. Chef Richard Sylvester's menu is full of tantalizing choices; standout appetizers include *ostriche gustino* (black-shelled oysters with lemon) and swordfish carpaccio, while the pappardelle pasta with sun-dried tomatoes, seafood risotto, and roasted lamb wrapped in prosciutto are all excellent entrées. The waitstaff is impeccable; the violin music adds a romantic touch. Reservations are recommended. ☒ *JW Marriott Resort, Blvd. Kukulcán, Km 14.5, Zona Hotelera* ☎ *998/848–9600 Ext. 6649* ▤ *AE, MC, V* ⊘ *No lunch.*

FodorsChoice ★

Japanese

$$$–$$$$ ✕ **Mitachi.** The moonlight on the water, the sounds of the surf, the superbly attentive staff, and the artwork by Japanese ceramist Mineo

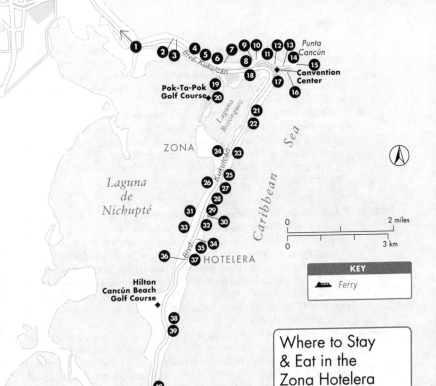

Where to Stay
& Eat in the
Zona Hotelera

Mizumo all help to make this restaurant feel like a sanctuary. Traditional Japanese dishes are served with care, especially the tempura, grilled fish, and beef tenderloin. The sushi and sashimi are also top-notch. ⊠ *Hilton Cancún, Blvd. Kukulcán, Km 17 (Retorno Lacandones), Zona Hotelera* ☎ *998/881–8000 Ext. 72* ▤ *AE, D, MC, V.*

$–$$$ ✕ **Mikado.** Sit around the *teppanyaki* tables and watch the utensils fly as showmen chefs prepare steaks, seafood, vegetables, and rice. The menu includes Thai specialties as well as Japanese classics. The sushi, tempura, grilled salmon, and beef teriyaki are feasts fit for a shogun. ⊠ *Marriott Casa Magna, Blvd. Kukulcán, Km 14.5, Zona Hotelera* ☎ *998/881–2000* ▤ *DC, MC, V* ⊗ *No lunch.*

Mexican

$$–$$$$ ✕ **La Destileria.** Be prepared to have your perceptions of tequila changed forever. In what looks like an old-time Mexican hacienda, you can sample from a list of 100 varieties—in shots or in superb margaritas—while visiting the tequila museum and store. The traditional Mexican menu focuses on wonderfully fresh fish and seafood; highlights include the sea scallops with avocado and habanero chiles, and grilled tuna done Maya style. The chicken in pistachio mole is also excellent. ⊠ *Blvd. Kukulcán, Km 12.65 (across from Plaza Kukulcán), Zona Hotelera* ☎ *998/885–1087* ▤ *AE, MC, V.*

$$–$$$$ ✕ **La Joya.** The dramatic interior of this restaurant has three levels of stained-glass windows, a fountain, artwork, and beautiful furniture from central Mexico. The food is traditional but creative; one especially popular dish is the Angus beef marinated in honey. The pan-seared pork loin and red snapper fillet are also wonderful. ⊠ *Blvd. Kukulcán, Km 9.5, Zona Hotelera* ☎ *998/881–3222* ▤ *DC, MC, V.*

$$–$$$ ✕ **Maria Bonita.** Colorful tile work, ceramics, paintings, and a glass-enclosed patio with a water view make this the perfect spot to enjoy such Mexican dishes as chicken almond mole (with chocolate, almonds, and chiles). The menu explains the different chiles used in many of the regional dishes. The bar is spacious and stocked with fine tequila; be sure to try the tamarind margaritas. ⊠ *Hotel Camino Real, Punta Cancún, Blvd. Kukulcán, Km 9, Zona Hotelera* ☎ *998/848–7000* ▤ *AE, D, MC, V* ⊗ *No lunch.*

$–$$$ ✕ **La Casa de las Margaritas.** With folk art and traditional textiles adorning every inch of space, this restaurant lets you know you're in for a truly Mexican dining experience. There's live music nightly, so this is not the place for a quiet meal. The kitchen creates contemporary Mexican entrées such as marinated chicken strips with tequila flambé, and desserts such as *tres leche* (three milk) cake or key lime pie. It's a great place to stop for dinner and margaritas while visiting La Isla Shopping Village. ⊠ *La Isla Shopping Village, Blvd. Kukulcán, Km 12.5, Zona Hotelera* ☎ *998/883–3222* ▤ *MC, V.*

$–$$$ ✕ **Hacienda el Mortero.** With its cheerful and welcoming staff, strolling mariachi band, and traditional menu, this casual restaurant is the quintessential Mexican dining spot. The tortilla soup is delicious, as is the beef fillet "chemita" with its four chile peppers. Fish lovers should definitely try the pescado Veracruzana, fresh grouper prepared Veracruz-style with olives, garlic, and fresh tomatoes. ⊠ *Blvd. Kukulcán, Km 9, Zona Hotelera* ☎ *998/848–9800* ▭ *AE, MC, V.*

$–$$$ ✕ **Iguana Wana.** Art from around Mexico fills this upbeat contemporary café. There are extensive, inexpensive all-you-can-eat breakfast buffets along with special vegetarian and children's menus. The fajita and grilled dishes are especially good, and there's a tempting selection of beers and tequilas. During the day, televised sports provide the entertainment; in the evening, there's live music. ⊠ *Plaza Caracol, Blvd. Kukulcán, Km 8.5, Zona Hotelera* ☎ *998/883–0829* ▭ *AE, D, MC, V.*

Seafood

$–$$$$ ✕ **Lorito Joe's.** This restaurant has a lovely terrace overlooking the Laguna Nichupté and surrounding mangroves. A crab-and-lobster all-you-can-eat buffet is displayed on two giant oyster shells. Don't overlook the regular menu, however, or you might miss such choices as coconut shrimp, crab cakes, broiled soft-shell crab, and Alaska king crab served with lemon butter and mustard sauce. ⊠ *Blvd. Kukulcán, Km 14.5, Zona Hotelera* ☎ *998/885–1536* ▭ *AE, MC, V.*

$$$ ✕ **La Brisa Mesquite Grill.** A winding pathway under a palapa brings you to this idyllic restaurant alongside Bahía de Mujeres. The view, the sea breezes, and the large selection of fresh wood-grilled seafood make eating here a feast for the senses. Chilean sea bass, Atlantic turbot, Pacific mahimahi, and swordfish are just a few of the choices. ⊠ *Blvd. Kukulcán, Km 9, Punta Cancún (next to Camino Real Hotel), Zona Hotelera* ☎ *998/888–7000* ▭ *AE, MC, V.*

Steak

$$$–$$$$ ✕ **Palm Restaurant.** This classic steak house, with its mahogany bar, private dining room, and caricature artwork, evokes 1920s New York. The house specialties are the porterhouse steaks and birdbath-size martinis, although the veal parmigiana and fresh Nova Scotia lobster are also very good. ⊠ *Blvd. Kukulcán, Km 7.5 (next to Presidente InterContinental Cancún hotel), Zona Hotelera* ☎ *998/848–8747* ▭ *AE, MC, V.*

$$–$$$$ ✕ **Cambalache.** This boisterous Argentine steak house is renowned for its tender, juicy steaks. Other highlights include short ribs and the dorado or grouper stuffed with cheese and mushrooms. Vegetarians may wish to go elsewhere—there are very few menu choices that don't include meat. ⊠ *Forum-by-the-Sea, Blvd. Kukulcán, Km 9.5, Zona Hotelera* ☎ *998/883–0897* ▭ *AE, MC, V.*

$$–$$$$ ✕ **Porterhouse Grill.** With its beige walls, wooden floors, and elegantly set tables, this eatery resembles a New York steak house. Choose your steak from the display case, and watch as it's prepared in the open-grill kitchen. If the porterhouse or filet mignon is too much, try the rack of lamb or duck breast. The only greens served are in the crisp Caesar salad. The wine list is superb, as are the martinis. ⊠ *Blvd. Kukulcán, Km 12, Zona Hotelera* ☎ *998/848–9300* ▭ *MC, V.*

$–$$$ ✕ **Rio Churrascaria Steak House.** You could easily pass over this haven for meat lovers because of its simple look. The Brazilian-style menu is based around more than 20 different kinds of grilled meats, which are slowly cooked on skewers over charcoal and then sliced right onto your plate. Choices include Angus and USDA-certified beef, pork, and chicken as well as an excellent oyster cocktail and king crab salad. Vegetarians won't be happy here. ⊠ *Blvd. Kukulcán, Km 3.5, Zona Hotelera* ☎ *998/849–9040* ▭ *AE, MC, V.*

El Centro

Cafées

$–$$ ✕ **Roots.** This is a favorite hangout for both locals and tourists, who come to enjoy Cancún's fusion jazz and flamenco music scene. It also doubles as a classy café serving fresh salads, soups, sandwiches, and pastas with an international flair. Enjoy the Athens salad, Chinese chicken, Mexican fish, or German sausage. ⊠ *Av. Tulipanes 26, Sm 22* ☎ *998/884–2437* ▭ *D, MC, V* ☉ *Closed Sun. No lunch.*

¢–$ ✕ **La Pasteleteria-Crepería.** This small café offers fresh salads and terrific soups and crepes. The cream of mushroom soup followed by the turkey breast crepe makes a perfect lunch. There's also a bakery that makes decadent desserts. ⊠ *Av. Cobá 7, Sm 25* ☎ *998/884–3420* ▭ *AE, V.*

¢–$ ✕ **Ty-Coz.** Tucked behind the Comercial Mexicana and across from the bus station on Avenida Tulum, this restaurant serves excellent Continental breakfasts with croissants and freshly brewed coffee. Lunches are a combination of sandwiches and salads served on freshly baked baguettes. Pictures of the Brittany region of France adorn the walls of the bright dining room. ⊠ *Av. Tulum, Sm 2* ☎ *No phone* ▭ *No credit cards.*

Caribbean

$–$$$ ✕ **La Habichuela.** Elegant yet cozy, the much-loved Green Bean restaurant is full of Maya sculptures and local trees and flowers. Don't miss the famous *crema de habichuela* (a rich, cream-based seafood soup) or the *cocobichuela* (lobster and shrimp in a light curry sauce served inside a coconut). Finish off your meal with Xtabentun, a Maya liqueur made with honey and anise. ⊠ *Av. Margaritas 25, Sm 22* ☎ *998/884–3158* ▭ *AE, MC, V.*

Chinese

¢–$$ ✕ **Hong Kong.** If you're missing your favorite take-out Chinese food, then head over to Hong Kong. You can order from the take-out counter or sit in the cozy restaurant filled with plants. It serves the usual egg rolls, fried rice, sweet-and-sour chicken, and garlic spareribs. The food may not be particularly inspired, but it's fresh and reasonably priced. ⊠ *Av. Cobá 97, Sm 21* ☎ *998/884–1871* ▭ *D, MC, V.*

Eclectic

$–$$ ✕ **Mesón del Vecindario.** This sweet little restaurant, tucked away from the street, resembles a Swiss A-frame house. The menu has all kinds of cheese and beef fondues along with terrific salads, fresh pasta, and baked goods. Breakfasts are hearty and economical. This remains a popular restaurant with locals. ⊠ *Av. Uxmal 23, Sm 3* ☎ *998/884–8900* ▭ *AE, MC, V* ☉ *Closed Sun.*

Italian

$$–$$$$ ✕ **Locanda Paolo.** Flowers and artwork lend warmth to this sophisticated restaurant, and the staff is attentive without being fussy. The cuisine is innovative southern Italian. Don't even think of passing up the black

THE HOT STUFF:
TEQUILA AND CHILE PEPPERS

TEQUILA IS THE NATIONAL DRINK OF MEXICO, and chances are you will be offered a glass sooner or later. There are hundreds of tequilas available, ranging from the super-smooth to the pretty harsh varieties. To be considered authentic, tequila must come from the state of Jalisco and have a seal of certification. There are basically three types, all of which are made from the blue agave plant. Blanco (white) or plata (silver) tequila is fresh from the still and retains most of the flavor of the agave plant. Sometimes a caramel coloring is added to this tequila and then it is known as joven (young). Reposado (rested) is tequila that has been aged in a white oak cask anywhere between two months and a year. It has a mellow flavor and pale color. Añejo (aged) tequila has been aged in an oak cask for between one and four years. The aging process allows it to take on an amber color and a smooth taste. Muy añejo (very aged) refers to tequila aged between three to five years. Some companies also refer to this type as reserva; it is considered the highest quality caliber of tequila.

Liquor made from any other kind of agave plant is known as mezcal. It, too, comes in varying degrees of smoothness.

The traditional method many people use for drinking tequila—licking salt off the backs of their hands, then drinking, then sucking on lime wedges—is not the Mexican way. Most Mexicans prefer to sip añejo tequila in a brandy snifter so the aroma can be savored. Blanco and reposado are usually served with sangrita, which is a mix of tomato and orange juice with salt and lime. All tequilas should be enjoyed at room temperature and are always sipped, even when put into the small shot glasses known as cabalitos. It's considered crass to chug your tequila unless you are drinking a harsh joven—in which case the idea is to get it down as quickly as possible. Most of the places offering all-you-can-drink menus will be serving joven—which can leave you with a wicked hangover. Reposado is the favored tequila in margaritas because it is somewhat smooth, but many places do use joven combined with a premixed lime juice and lots of salt and crushed ice to mask the harshness. Again, drinking these can make you feel a little rough the morning after. An authentic margarita will have minimal ice, freshly squeezed lime juice, and just a hint of salt around the rim that should be tasted with each sip to enhance the flavor of the drink.

Before tasting anything with chiles be sure to ask ¿Es muy picante? (Is it very hot?) The answer is often yes, so start off with small quantities. The mildest chiles are the pimiento green or red peppers. Next up in the heat scale are poblano chiles, which are mildly spicy. These are usually stuffed with cheese and served as poblanos rellenos. The serrano chile is used in many restaurant's salsas, and can be very hot. But slender, green jalapeño chiles, often used in sauces, are even hotter. Another steaming-hot chile is the chipotle, which has a smoky flavor—but which still packs less of a punch than the habanero chile, used in many Yucatecan dishes. The deadliest of all is the rubio (white) chile—most gringos simply can't handle it.

Since a chile's heat comes not from the actual pepper itself, but from the oil of the seeds inside, when your mouth is on fire it's best to eat a piece of bread or tortilla to soak up the oil. Salt also helps. Vast quantities of beer or tequila will only spread the flame—although after a while, you may not care or notice.

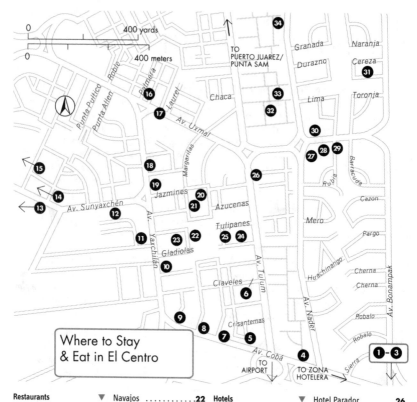

Where to Stay & Eat in El Centro

pasta in calamari sauce or the penne with basil and tomato sauce. Also delicious are the steamed lobster in garlic sauce and the lemon dorado (mahimahi). ✉ *Av. Bonampak 145, between Avs. Uxmal and Cobá, Sm 3* ☎ *998/887–2627* ☰ *AE, D, DC, MC, V.*

$–$$ ✕ **Lucky Luciano.** Although it's off the beaten track, this spot is well worth the trip. The homemade pastas and ravioli are superb. Or you can be adventurous and try the fillet steak cooked with a pistachio-and-cheese sauce. Salads are large and fresh. Take a cab here since it's hard to reach on foot. ✉ *Calle Tlaquepaque (at the corner of Calle Andres Q. Roo), Sm 45* ☎ *998/880–5858* ☰ *AE, V.*

$–$$ ✕ **Stefano's.** This cozy little bistro has reliably good Italian food at reasonable prices. Delicious and hearty pizzas are cooked in a wood oven, and pastas are prepared fresh each day. Enjoy the chicken medallions topped with crabmeat, or the spinach-and-cheese cannelloni. Dine inside amid European art or outside in the small patio garden. The lunch specials are quite a bargain. ✉ *Av. Bonampak 177, Sm 4* ☎ *998/887–9964* ☰ *AE, V.*

Japanese

¢–$$ ✕ **Yamamoto.** The fresh sushi here rivals any found in the area. The restaurant also offers traditional Japanese dishes such as beef teriyaki and tempura for those who prefer their food cooked. ✉ *Av. Uxmal 31, Sm 3* ☎ *998/887–3366* ☰ *D, MC, V.*

Mexican

$$–$$$$ ✕ **La Parrilla.** With its palapa-style roof, flamboyant live mariachi music, and energetic waiters, this place is a Cancún classic. The menu isn't fancy, but it offers good, basic Mexican food. Two reliably tasty choices are the mixed grill (chicken, steak, shrimp) and the grilled Tampiqueña-style steak; for accompaniment, you can choose from a wide selection of tequilas. ✉ *Av. Yaxchilán 51, Sm 22* ☎ *998/884–5398* ☰ *AE, D, MC, V.*

★ $–$$$ ✕ **Labná.** Yucatecan cuisine reaches new and exotic heights here, with fabulous dishes prepared by chef Carlos Hannon. The *papadzules*—tortillas stuffed with eggs and covered with pumpkin sauce—are a delicious starter; for an entrée, try the savory *loganza de Valladolid* (spicy sausage from the village of Valladolid) or *poc chuc*, tender pork loin in a sour orange sauce. *Guayaba* (guava) mousse and Xtabentun-infused Maya coffee make for a happy ending. ✉ *Av. Margaritas 29, Sm 22* ☎ *998/892–3056* ☰ *AE, D, MC, V.*

$–$$$ ✕ **Perico's.** Bar stools are topped with saddles, caricature busts of political figures line the walls, and waiters dressed as *zapatas* (revolutionaries) serve flaming desserts at this zany and popular restaurant. The Mexican menu is passable, but the real draw are the mariachi and marimba bands that play every night from 7—everyone jumps up to join the conga line. Your reward for galloping through the restaurant and nearby streets is a free shot of tequila. ✉ *Av. Yaxchilán 61, Sm 25* ☎ *998/884–3152* ☰ *AE, MC, V.*

$–$$ ✕ **La Guadalupana.** Enjoy steak, fajitas, tacos, and other Mexican traditional dishes at this lively cantina. It's decorated with art and photos of famous bull fighters—very appropriate since it's alongside a bullring—and is usually filled with music and an animated crowd. ✉ *Av. Bonampak (Plaza de Toros), Sm 4* ☎ *998/887–0660* ☰ *MC, V.*

¢–$$ ✕ **El Tacolote.** This popular *taqueria* (taco stand) sells delicious fajitas, grilled kebabs, and all kinds of tacos. The salsa, which comes free with every meal, is fresh and *muy picante* (very hot). This is a great lunch stop. ✉ *Av. Cobá 19, Sm 22* ☎ 998/887–3045 ▭ *MC, V.*

¢–$ ✕ **Bisquets Obregon.** With its cheery lunch counter and two levels of tables, this cafeteria-style spot is *the* place to have breakfast downtown. Begin your day early (food is served starting at 7 AM) with hearty Mexican classics such as huevos rancheros (eggs sunny-side up on tortillas, covered with tomato salsa). The *cafe con leche* (coffee with hot milk) is also delicious—and just watching the waiters pour it is impressive. ✉ *Av. Náder 9, Sm 2* ☎ 998/887–6876 ▭ *MC, V.*

Pizza

¢–$$ ✕ **Rolandi's.** The wood-burning ovens are in clear view at this bright red-and-yellow sidewalk eatery. There are 15 varieties of pizza to choose from—if you can't make up your mind, try the delicious one made with Roquefort cheese. Homemade pasta dishes are also very good. Anything on the menu can be delivered to your hotel. ✉ *Av. Cobá 12, Sm 3* ☎ *998/884–4047* ▭ *MC, V.*

Seafood

$–$$$ ✕ **El Cejas.** The seafood is fresh at this fun open-air eatery and the clientele is lively—often joining in song with the musicians who stroll among the tables. If you've had a wild night, try the *vuelva la vida*, or "return to life" (conch, oysters, shrimp, octopus, calamari, and fish with a hot tomato sauce). The ceviche and hot, spicy shrimp soup are both good as well, though the quality can be inconsistent. ✉ *Mercado Veintiocho, Av. Sunyaxchén, Sm 26* ☎ 998/887–1080 ▭ *No credit cards.*

Vegetarian

$ ✕ **Navajos.** This outdoor restaurant serves simple, light food. Breakfast includes yogurt, sweet breads, and fruit plates; the lunch and dinner menus feature soups, sandwiches, and salads. There are also daily specials at great prices. As the name suggests, the decor has a Native American motif. ✉ *Av. Alcatraces 18 (behind the Parque de las Palapas), Sm 25* ☎ *998/887–7269* ▭ *AE, MC, V.*

¢–$ ✕ **100% Natural.** Looking for something light and healthy? Head to one of these cheery open-air restaurants, done up with plenty of plants and modern Maya sculptures. The menus emphasize soups, fruit and veggie salads, fresh fruit drinks, and other nonmeat items, though egg dishes, sandwiches, grilled chicken and fish, and Mexican and Italian specialties are also available. ✉ *Zona Hotelera: Kukulcán Shopping Plaza, Blvd. Kukulcán, Km 13.5* ☎ *998/885–2903* ✉ *Forum-by-the-Sea, Blvd. Kukulcán, Km 9.5* ☎ *998/883–1180* ✉ *El Centro: Av. Sunyaxchén 62, Sm 25* ☎ *998/884–3617* ▭ *D, MC, V.*

WHERE TO STAY

You might find it bewildering to choose among the many hotels in Cancún, not least because brochures and Web sites make them sound—and look—alike. For luxury and amenities, the Zona Hotelera is the place to stay. Boulevard Kukulcán, the district's main thoroughfare, is artfully landscaped with palm trees, sculpted bushes, waterfalls, and tiered pools. The hotels pride themselves on delivering endless opportunities for fun; most have water sports, golf, tennis, kids' clubs, fitness centers, spas, shopping, entertainment, dining, and tours and excursions (along with warm attentive Mexican service). None of this comes cheaply, however; hotels in the Zona Hotelera are expensive.

If proximity to El Centro is a priority, stay in the north end. Many of the malls are within walking distance, and taxis to downtown and to the ferries at Puerto Juárez cost less than from hotels farther south. If you prefer something more secluded, the south end is less developed.

In the modest Centro, local color outweighs facilities. The hotels here are basic and much less expensive than those in the Zona. Many have free shuttle service to the beach, and Ki Huic—Cancún's crafts market—and authentic Mexican restaurants are close by.

Prices

Many hotels have all-inclusive packages, as well as theme-night parties complete with food, beverages, activities, and games. Mexican, Italian, and Caribbean themes seem to be the most popular. Take note, however, that the larger the all-inclusive resort, the blander the food. (It's difficult to provide inventive fare when serving hundreds of people.) For more memorable dining, you may need to leave the grounds. Another thing to keep in mind is that many of the larger and more popular all-inclusives will no longer guarantee an ocean-view room when you book your reservation. If this is crucial to your stay, then check that all rooms have ocean views at your chosen hotel, or book only at places that will guarantee a view.

For most of the hotels, it's best to make reservations at least one month in advance and up to three months in advance for the Christmas season. Many of the larger chain hotels also offer special Internet deals, with rates dropping considerably when you make online reservations.

WHAT IT COSTS In Dollars				
	$$$$	**$$$**	**$$**	**$**	**¢**
FOR 2 PEOPLE	over $250	$150–$250	$75–$150	$50–$75	under $50

All prices are for a standard double room in high season, based on the European Plan (EP) and excluding service and 12% tax (10% Value Added Tax plus 2% hospitality tax).

Isla Blanca/Punta Sam

The area north of Cancún is slowly being developed into an alternative hotel zone, known informally as Zona Hotelera Norte. This is an idea area for a tranquil beach vacation since the shops, restaurants, and nightlife of Cancún are about 45 minutes away by cab.

★ $$ ▦ **Chalet Maya.** These gorgeous waterfront bungalows are on the virgin beaches of Isla Blanca—9 km (5½ mi) north of Punta Sam. The property is designed to feel like a sanctuary, so there are no televisions or phones. Bungalows are individually decorated with hand-carved sculptures. A charming on-site restaurant offers moderately priced, delicious meals. The hotel offers bird-watching trips to nearby Isla Contoy and snorkeling or fishing trips out to the reef. ⊠ *Isla Blanca, Km 9, Punta Sam 77400* ☎ *998/850–4610* 🖷 *998/850–4819* ⊕ *www.chaletmaya. com* 🖙 *20 rooms* ⸖ *Restaurant, pool, boating; no a/c, no room phones, no room TVs* ▭ *MC, V* ⦿ *CP.*

Zona Hotelera

★ **$$$$** 🏨 **Fiesta Americana Grand Coral Beach.** This distinctive salmon-colored hotel is a perennial favorite. Despite its vastness, it has a cozy lobby with stained-glass skylights, sculptures, plants, and mahogany furniture. Rooms are large and marble-floored, and decorated in tones of soothing slate-blue and beige. Small sitting rooms open onto balconies that overlook the Bahía de Mujeres and gardens. The beach here is small, but there's a 660-foot pool surrounded by a lush exotic flower garden. Exceptional dining is only steps away at the hotel's restaurant, Le Basilic. ⊠ *Blvd. Kukulcán, Km 9.5, Zona Hotelera, 77500* ☎ *998/ 881–3200 or 800/343–7821* 🖷 *998/881–1401* ⊕ *www.fiestaamericana. com* 🖙 *602 rooms, 60 suites* ⸖ *5 restaurants, cable TV with video games, pool, health club, hair salon, spa, beach, 5 bars, baby-sitting, children's programs (ages 4–12), Internet, business services, car rental, free parking* ▭ *AE, D, DC, MC, V.*

$$$$ 🏨 **Gran Meliá Cancún.** A sheer black marble wall and a waterfall flank this boldly modern version of a Maya temple. The ultrachic atrium is filled with plants and sunlight (there's a pyramid skylight overhead). Ivory and pastel hues softly brighten rooms, all of which have plush carpets and private balconies or terraces. This is one of the area's largest hotels, and houses a convention center and six meeting halls—so don't come expecting an intimate setting. ⊠ *Blvd. Kukulcán, Km 16, Zona Hotelera, 77500* ☎ *998/881–1100* 🖷 *998/881–1140* ⊕ *www.solmelia.es* 🖙 *700 rooms, 64 suites* ⸖ *5 restaurants, cable TV with video games, 9-hole golf course, tennis court, 2 pools, health club, spa, beach, paddle tennis, volleyball, 3 bars, shops, baby-sitting, convention center, car rental, travel services* ▭ *AE, DC, MC, V.*

$$$$ 🏨 **Hilton Cancún Beach & Golf Resort.** All rooms here have balconies or terraces with views—either of the ocean or of the resort's championship 18-hole, par-72 golf course. Lavish, interconnected pools wind through palm-dotted lawns, ending at the magnificent beach. For total luxury consider staying at the Beach Club, with its 80 oceanfront villas. In the evening enjoy incredible Japanese fare at the romantic seaside restaurant, Mitachi. ⊠ *Blvd. Kukulcán, Km 17 (Retorno Lacandones), Zona Hotelera, 77500* ☎ *998/881–8000 or 800/445–8667* 🖷 *998/881–8080* ⊕ *www.hilton. com* 🖙 *426 rooms, 4 suites* ⸖ *2 restaurants, cable TV with video games, 18-hole golf course, 2 tennis courts, 7 pools, fitness classes, gym, hair salon, hot tubs, sauna, beach, 3 bars, lobby lounge, shops, children's programs (ages 4–12), car rental* ▭ *AE, DC, MC, V* ⦿ *CP.*

$$$$ 🏨 **JW Marriott Cancún Resort & Spa.** Outside this lavish hotel, manicured
Fodor'sChoice lawns lead to lovely fountains and pools. Inside is a plush lobby, with
★ large vaulted windows that let sunlight stream in. The ocean-view rooms

are elegant in light gold, jade, and taupe tones, and the marble bathrooms have spalike showers. If you want even more pampering, visit the spa for massages and facials. In the evening you can dine at the delicious Gustino Italian Beachside Grill. ⊠ *Blvd. Kukulcán, Km 14.5, Zona Hotelera, 77500* ☎ *998/848–9600 or 800/228–9290* 🖷 *998/848–9601* ⊕ *www.marriott.com* ⇨ *423 rooms, 36 suites* ⌂ *3 restaurants, cable TV with video games, tennis court, gym, hair salon, hot tubs, spa, beach, dock, bar, shops, children's programs (ages 4–12), Internet, meeting rooms, travel services* ⊟ *AE, DC, MC, V.*

★ **$$$$** ⊞ **Le Meridien.** High on a hill, this refined yet relaxed hotel is an artful blend of art deco and Maya styles; there's lots of wood, glass, and mirrors. Rooms have spectacular ocean views. The many thoughtful extras—such as water of a different temperature in each of the swimming pools—make a stay here special. The Spa del Mar is the area's best, with the latest European treatments and an outdoor hot tub and waterfall. The Aioli restaurant serves fabulous French food. ⊠ *Blvd. Kukulcán, Km 14 (Retorno del Rey, Lote 37), Zona Hotelera, 77500* ☎ *998/881–2200 or 800/543–4300* 🖷 *998/881–2201* ⊕ *www.meridiencancun.com.mx* ⇨ *187 rooms, 26 suites* ⌂ *3 restaurants, cable TV with video games, 2 tennis courts, 3 pools, gym, health club, hot tub, spa, beach, 2 bars, shops, children's programs (ages 4–12)* ⊟ *AE, MC, V.*

$$$$ ⊞ **Ritz-Carlton Cancún.** The sumptuous carpets, rich European antiques, and elegant oil paintings may cause you to forget that you're in Mexico. Rooms are done in shades of teal, beige, and rose and have wall-to-wall carpeting, large balconies overlooking the Caribbean, and marble bathrooms with separate tubs and showers. In the evening, the Club Grill serves a wonderful dinner. ⊠ *Blvd. Kukulcán, Km 14 (Retorno del Rey 36), Zona Hotelera, 77500* ☎ *998/881–0808 or 800/241–3333* 🖷 *998/881–0815* ⊕ *www.ritzcarlton.com* ⇨ *365 rooms, 40 suites* ⌂ *3 restaurants, 3 tennis courts, pro shop, 2 pools, health club, hot tub, spa, beach, 2 bars, shops* ⊟ *AE, D, DC, MC, V.*

$$$$ ⊞ **Sun Palace.** This adults-only, all-inclusive resort is set up like a camp, with daily activities posted in the lobby and coordinators to direct you toward game rooms, tennis courts, exercise and water-sports equipment, and the pool. Rooms have ocean views but no balconies or room service. Staying here gets you free access to the hotel's sister resorts, including Beach Palace, Cancún Palace, and Moon Palace. Book your reservations over the Internet or through a travel agent to get a better price. ⊠ *Blvd. Kukulcán, Km 20, Zona Hotelera, 77500* ☎ *998/885–1555 or 877/505–5515* 🖷 *998/885–2425* ⊕ *www.palaceresorts.com* ⇨ *227 rooms, 19 suites* ⌂ *3 restaurants, cable TV, 3 tennis courts, pool, gym, hot tub, beach, billiards, Ping-Pong, recreation room* ⊟ *AE, D, MC, V* ⊠ *AI.*

$$$ ⊞ **Fiesta Americana Cancún.** This consistently popular hotel has everything going for it: perfect location, gracious service, and good restaurants. It's been designed to resemble a Mexican village, with a brown-and-yellow color scheme. The public areas are decorated with marble from Mexico, which is offset by Guadalajara stained glass. Rooms have rattan furniture, marble floors, colorful rugs, and decorative art. All face the calm northern waters of Bahía de Mujeres, which are excellent for swimming. ⊠ *Blvd. Kukulcán, Km 8.5, Zona Hotel-*

era, 77500 ☎ *998/881–1400 or 800/343–7821* 🖷 *998/881–1401*
⊕ *www.fiestaamericana.com* ⇗ *236 rooms, 16 suites* 🍴 *3 restaurants,*
cable TV with video games, pool, health club, hair salon, spa, beach, 3
bars, baby-sitting, children's programs (ages 4–12), business services,
car rental, free parking ▭ *AE, D, DC, MC, V.*

$$–$$$$ 🏨 **Omni Cancún Hotels & Villas.** This pleasant, pink 10-story hotel is sur-
rounded by smaller villas. The cozy lobby has marble floors, wood fur-
niture, and a sea-green-and-pink color scheme that continues into the
rooms. More expensive rooms have balconies; all have either ocean or
lagoon views. The flexible rules allow you to choose between an all-in-
clusive option or European-plan rates if you prefer to eat outside the
grounds. The villas have fully equipped kitchens. Highlights of this
hotel include its tri-level pool, fitness center, and spa. ⊠ *Blvd. Kukul-*
cán, Km 16.5, Zona Hotelera, 77500 ☎ *998/881–0600* 🖷 *998/885–*
0059 ⊕ *www.omnihotels.com* ⇗ *331 rooms, 15 villas* 🍴 *3 restau-*
rants, 3 snack bars, cable TV, 2 tennis courts, pool, gym, spa, beach,
dock, 2 bars, shops ▭ *AE, DC, MC, V* 🍴 *AI, EP.*

$$$ 🏨 **Fiesta Americana Condesa.** The Condesa is easily recognized by the
118-foot-tall palapa that covers its lobby. Despite the rustic roof, the
rest of the hotel's architecture is extravagant, with marble pillars,
stained-glass awnings, and swimming pools joined by arched bridges.
The three seven-story towers overlook an inner courtyard with hanging vines and fountains. Standard rooms share balconies with ocean views
and are done up in off-white stucco with blue and pink accents. Suites
have hot tubs on their terraces. ⊠ *Blvd. Kukulcán, Km 16.5, Zona Hotel-*
era, 77500 ☎ *998/881–4200* 🖷 *998/885–1800* ⊕ *www.fiestaamericana.*
com ⇗ *476 rooms, 25 suites* 🍴 *4 restaurants, some kitchenettes, cable*
TV with video games, 3 tennis courts, 3 pools, gym, spa, beach, 3 bars,
children's programs (ages 3–12), travel services ▭ *AE, MC, V.*

$$$ 🏨 **Gran Caribe Real Resort.** This beach resort has all-inclusive packages
geared to families; the children's program is among the best in Cancún.
The bright lobby restaurants have stained-glass windows, hanging
plants, and elegant furniture. Sunny comfortable suites all have ocean
views. Staying here also gives you access to Costa Real Hotel & Suites
in Cancún and Porto Real Resort in Playa del Carmen. Be warned: this
is not the place for peace and quiet. ⊠ *Blvd. Kukulcán, Km 5.5, Zona*
Hotelera, 77500 ☎ *998/881–7300* 🖷 *998/881–7399* ⊕ *www.*
grancaribereal.com ⇗ *466 rooms, 34 suites* 🍴 *2 restaurants, cable TV*
with video games, 2 tennis courts, 2 pools, gym, spa, beach, dock, 2 bars,
theater, video game room, shops, children's programs (ages 2–12) ▭ *AE,*
MC, V 🍴 *AI.*

$$$ 🏨 **Hyatt Cancún Caribe Villas & Resort.** This intimate crescent-shape re-
sort has a white marble lobby and comfy contemporary rooms uphol-
stered in pale colors. Beach-level rooms have gardens, and the beachfront
villas have private kitchens and dining-living areas. Be sure to have at
least one meal in the Blue Bayou restaurant. ⊠ *Blvd. Kukulcán, Km 10.5,*
Zona Hotelera, 77500 ☎ *998/848–7800 or 800/633–7313* 🖷 *998/*
883–1514 ⊕ *www.hyatt.com* ⇗ *226 rooms, 28 villas* 🍴 *3 restaurants,*
some kitchens, cable TV with video games, 3 tennis courts, 3 pools, hair
salon, hot tubs, beach, dock, 2 bars, shop ▭ *AE, DC, MC, V.*

$$$ ☷ **Hyatt Regency Cancún.** This hotel's 14-story cylindrical tower on Punta Cancún is easy to spot. Inside, the building is striking: a central atrium filled with tropical greenery provides a 360-degree view of the surrounding sea and lagoon; there's also an enormous two-level pool with a waterfall. Cilantro, the hotel's waterfront restaurant, serves a good breakfast buffet. Soothing blue, green, and beige tones prevail in the rooms. The property is close to the convention center and several shopping malls. ⊠ *Blvd. Kukulcán, Km 8.5, Zona Hotelera, 77500* ☎ *998/883–0966 or 800/233–1234* 🖷 *998/883–1349* ⊕ *www.hyatt.com* ⌖ *300 rooms* ⌕ *2 restaurants, cable TV with video games, pool, health club, beach, 3 bars, recreation room* ▤ *AE, MC, V.*

$$$ ☷ **Krystal Cancún.** This hotel on Punta Cancún is in the heart of the Zona Hotelera, within walking distance of three major shopping malls and dozens of restaurants. The split-level lobby has marble pillars and leads to two towers where the guest rooms are. All rooms have ocean views and are modestly furnished in earth tones with contemporary furniture. Although the beach is small, there are three spacious pools with poolside service. The hotel houses four restaurants, as well as the popular Bull Dog Rock 'n Roll Club. ⊠ *Blvd. Kukulcán, Km 9, Lote 9, Zona Hotelera, 77500* ☎ *998/883–1133 or 800/232–9860* 🖷 *998/883–1790* ⊕ *www.krystal.com.mx* ⌖ *322 rooms* ⌕ *4 restaurants, cable TV with video games, 2 tennis courts, pool, gym, hot tub, sauna, beach, 4 bars, dance club, shops* ▤ *AE, DC, MC, V.*

$$$ ☷ **Marriott Casa Magna.** The sister property to the JW Marriott, this hotel has sweeping grounds that lead up to an eclectically designed six-story hotel. The lobby has large windows, crystal chandeliers, hanging vines, and contemporary furniture. Rooms have a rose, mauve, and earth-tone color scheme with tile floors and soft rugs. All have ocean views, and most have balconies. Three restaurants overlook the pool area and the ocean; check out Mikado, the Japanese steak house, whose chefs perform dazzling table-side displays. Sports fans can visit the Champion Sports Bar next door. ⊠ *Blvd. Kukulcán, Km 14.5, Zona Hotelera, 77500* ☎ *998/881–2000 or 888/236–2427* 🖷 *998/881–2085* ⊕ *www.marriott. com* ⌖ *414 rooms, 36 suites* ⌕ *3 restaurants, cable TV with video games, 2 tennis courts, health club, hair salon, hot tubs, sauna, beach, dock, bar, shops* ▤ *AE, DC, MC, V.*

$$$ ☷ **Occidental Caribbean Village.** This 300-room all-inclusive hotel offers a beachfront family resort with terrific amenities. All rooms in the hotel's three-tower compound have balconies with ocean views, double beds, and small sitting areas done up in sunset colors. The superb beach offers snorkeling and deep-sea fishing, and there are two large pools. If you stay here you are also allowed to visit the other Allegro resorts in Cancún, Playa del Carmen, and Cozumel, as part of a "Stay at One, Play at Four" promotion. The hotel has three rooms specially equipped for people with disabilities. ⊠ *Blvd. Kukulcán, Km 13.5, Zona Hotelera, 77500* ☎ *998/848–8000 or 01800/645–1179* 🖷 *998/ 885–8003* ⊕ *www.tropicalsands.com/resorts/allegro* ⌖ *300 rooms* ⌕ *4 restaurants, 3 snack bars, cable TV, 2 tennis courts, pool, gym, beach, 3 bars, shops, children's program (ages 4–12), dive shop, snorkeling, windsurfing* ▤ *AE, DC, MC, V* ⎜◎⎟ *AI.*

$$$ ⊡ **Presidente InterContinental Cancún.** It's hard to miss the striking yellow entrance of this hotel. Inside, lavish marble and Talavera pottery fill the public areas, and larger-than-average rooms have royal-blue or beige color schemes with wicker furniture and area rugs on stone floors. Most don't have balconies, but those on the first floor have patios and outdoor hot tubs. Suites have contemporary furnishings, in-room VCRs and DVD players, and spacious verandas. The pool has a waterfall in the shape of a Maya pyramid, and the beach is peaceful. ⊠ *Blvd. Kukulcán, Km 7.5, Zona Hotelera, 77500* ☎ *998/848–8700 or 888/567–8725* 🖶 *998/883–2602* ⊕ *www.interconti.com* 🛏 *299 rooms, 6 suites* ♢ *2 restaurants, cable TV with video games, some in-room VCRs, tennis court, 2 pools, gym, hair salon, hot tubs, beach, bar, shops* ⊟ *AE, MC, V.*

$$$ ⊡ **Villas Tacul.** These villas—originally built for visiting dignitaries—are surrounded by well-trimmed lawns and landscaped gardens that lead to the beach. Each villa has a kitchen, two to five bedrooms, tile floors, colonial-style furniture, wagon-wheel chandeliers, and tinwork mirrors. Less expensive rooms without kitchens are also available, but they aren't nearly as pleasant (and are farther from the beach). ⊠ *Blvd. Kukulcán, Km 5.5, Zona Hotelera, 77500* ☎ *998/883–0000 or 800/842–0193* 🖶 *998/849–7070* ⊕ *www.villastacul.com.mx* 🛏 *23 villas, 79 rooms* ♢ *Restaurant, kitchens, cable TV, 2 tennis courts, pool, beach, basketball, bar* ⊟ *AE, D, MC, V.*

$$$ ⊡ **Westin Regina Resort Cancún.** On the southern end of the Zona Hotelera, this low-rise hotel is more secluded than most. The lobby has dramatic sculptures displayed against vivid pink or blue backdrops. Both the stylish lobby bar and the restaurant have stunning ocean views. Rooms are even more elegant, with cozy beds dressed in soft white linens, oak tables and chairs, and pale marble floors extending to ocean-view balconies. This is one of the few hotels with direct access to both the beach and Laguna Nichupté. For added privacy consider staying at the Royal Beach Club, a separate area on the grounds that has 48 rooms. ⊠ *Blvd. Kukulcán, Km 20, Zona Hotelera, 77500* ☎ *998/848–7400 or 888/625–5144* 🖶 *998/885–0296* ⊕ *www.starwood.com/westin* 🛏 *278 rooms, 15 suites* ♢ *4 restaurants, cable TV with video games, 2 tennis courts, 5 pools, gym, health club, 6 hot tubs, beach, 3 bars, children's programs (ages 4–12)* ⊟ *AE, MC, V.*

$$–$$$ ⊡ **Continental Villas Plaza.** This property is older and a bit less luxurious than some of Cancún's other choices, but it remains a popular and comfortable all-inclusive resort. The architecture is a blend often seen in Cancún: Mexican hacienda meets Miami meets Mediterranean. Rooms are a good size with bright furnishings, balconies (not all are ocean view), and large bathrooms. There are also smaller and more intimate villas with kitchenettes. The beach here is particularly pleasant, and the sports center offers everything from jet skiing to parasailing. ⊠ *Blvd. Kukulcán, Km 11.5, Zona Hotelera, 77500* ☎ *998/881–5500 or 866/385–0256* 🖶 *998/881–5501* ⊕ *www.hotels-cancun.com/continental-plaza* 🛏 *638 rooms, 26 villas* ♢ *4 restaurants, 3 pools, cable TV, dive shop, snorkeling, jet skiing, waterskiing, parasailing, tennis courts, hair salon, beach, racquetball, 3 bars, children's programs (ages 4–12), business services, car rental, free parking* ⊟ *AE, D, DC, MC, V* ¶◎¶ *AI.*

$$–$$$ 🏨**Golden Crown Paradise Spa.** Romantic rooms at this all-inclusive, adults-only resort have private Jacuzzis, and are warmly decorated with sunset colors, flower arrangements, and rich wood furniture. Small sitting areas open up onto balconies with ocean or lagoon views. The beach here is small, but there's a comfortable pool area with two tiers of deck chairs and palapas. The spa offers massages and facials and the restaurants are bright and airy. This hotel provides great luxury at a reasonable price. ⊠ *Blvd. Kukulcán, Km 14.5 (Retorno Del Rey, Lote 37), Zona Hotelera, 77500* ☎*998/885–0909 or 800/882–8215* ⊕*998/885–1919* ⊕*www. crownparadise.com* ⤳ *214 rooms* ♨ *4 restaurants, cable TV, miniature golf, tennis courts, pools, spa, beach, billiards, 4 bars, Internet, car rental, travel services, free parking; no kids* ⊟ *AE, D, DC, MC, V* ⦿❙ *AI.*

$$–$$$ 🏨**El Pueblito Beach Hotel.** Built on a hill, this all-inclusive resort has striking landscaping: pathways lined with tropical foliage lead to terraced pools with waterfalls and stone archways (and also to a long, separate water slide for children). Rooms, which are large for the price, have marble floors and simple rattan furnishings; a few have kitchenettes. Ask about the European plan, which excludes meals and can lower the cost of the room. ⊠ *Blvd. Kukulcán, Km 17.5, Zona Hotelera, 77500* ☎*998/885–8800* ⊕*998/885–0422* ⊕*www.pueblitohotels.com* ⤳*350 rooms* ♨ *3 restaurants, some kitchenettes, cable TV, tennis court, 5 pools, beach, bar, shops, travel services* ⊟ *AE, MC, V* ⦿❙ *AI.*

$$ 🏨**Calinda Beach Cancún.** At the spot where Laguna Nichupté meets the Caribbean Sea, this otherwise no-frills hotel has one spectacular draw: its beach. It's quiet, with calm waters perfect for swimming, and within walking distance of shops and restaurants. The hotel also has a patio garden surrounding the pool; rooms are on the small side but do have marble floors, comfortable beds, and balconies overlooking the ocean. If you can stand to forego some luxurious extras, this place is a good bargain for the Zona Hotelera. ⊠ *Blvd. Kukulcán, Km 8.5, Zona Hotelera, 77500* ☎*998/849–4510* ⊕*998/883–1857.* ⊕ *http://cancun.calinda. beach.hotels-by.com* ⤳ *470 rooms* ♨ *2 restaurants, cable TV, 2 pools, 3 bars, free parking* ⊟ *AE, D, DC, MC, V.*

$$ 🏨**Holiday Inn Express.** Within walking distance of the Pok-Ta-Pok golf course, this hotel was built to resemble a Mexican hacienda—but with a pool instead of a courtyard at its center. Rooms have either patios or small balconies that overlook the pool and deck. All rooms are bright in blues and reds; furnishings are modern. Although not luxurious, it's perfect for families in which Dad wants to golf, Mom wants to shop, and the kids want to hit the beach. A free shuttle runs to the shops and beaches, which are five minutes away; taxis are inexpensive alternatives. ⊠ *Paseo Pok-Ta-Pok, Zona Hotelera, 77500* ☎ *998/883–2200* ⊕ *998/ 883–2532* ⊕ *www.sixcontinentshotels.com/h/d/ex/hd/cnnex* ⤳ *119 rooms* ♨ *Restaurant, cable TV, pool* ⊟ *AE, MC, V* ⦿❙ *BP.*

$ 🏨**Suites Sina.** These economical suites are in front of Laguna Nichupté and close to the Pok-Ta-Pok golf course. Each unit has comfortable furniture, a kitchenette, a dining-living room with a sofa bed, a balcony or a terrace, and double beds. Outside is a central pool and garden. ⊠ *Club de Golf, Calle Quetzal 33, Zona Hotelera, 77500* ☎ *998/883–1017 or 877/666–9837* ⊕ *998/883–2459* ⤳ *33 suites* ♨ *Kitchenettes, cable TV, pool* ⊟ *AE, MC, V.*

El Centro

$$ ▣ **Antillano.** This small well-kept hotel has a cozy lobby bar and a decent-size pool. Each of its rooms has wood furniture, one or two double beds, a sink area separate from the bath, and tile floors. The quietest rooms face the interior—avoid the noisier ones overlooking Avenida Tulum. ⊠ *Av. Tulum and Calle Claveles, Sm 21, 77500* ☎ *998/884–1532* 🖷 *998/884–1878* ⊕ *www.hotelantillano.com* ⤹ *48 rooms* ♨ *Cable TV, pool, bar, shops, baby-sitting* ⊟ *AE, D, MC, V.*

$$ ▣ **Radisson Hotel Hacienda.** Rooms in this pink, hacienda-style building are on the generic side but do have pleasant Mexican accents like wall prints and flower arrangements. The rooms overlook a large pool surrounded by tropical plants. The gym has state-of-the-art equipment and the business center offers e-mail access. The daily breakfast buffet is popular with locals, and there's a shuttle to the beach. ⊠ *Av. Nader 1, Sm 2, 77500* ☎ *998/887–4455 or 888/201–1718* 🖷 *998/884–7954* ⊕ *www.radisson.com* ⤹ *248 rooms* ♨ *2 restaurants, cable TV, tennis court, pool, gym, hair salon, 2 bars, nightclub, laundry facilities, car rental, travel services, business services* ⊟ *AE, DC, MC, V.*

$ ▣ **Cancún Inn El Patio.** This charming inn has the feel of an old Mexican residence. The entrance leads off a busy street into a central patio, landscaped with trees, flowers, and a lovely tiled fountain. Off to one side is a comfortable dining-living room. Upstairs, large, airy rooms are furnished with Spanish-style furniture and Mexican photos and ceramics. Downtown attractions are within walking distance, and the helpful owners, who live on-site, can direct you to them: among the most popular are the nearby bullring and Parque de las Palapas, the open-air central square where local musicians play and festivals are held under the giant palapa. ⊠ *Av. Bonampak 51, Sm 2, 77500* ☎ *998/884–3500* 🖷 *998/884–3540* ⊕ *www.cancun-suites.com* ⤹ *18 rooms* ♨ *Cable TV, recreation room* ⊟ *MC, V.*

$ ▣ **Hotel Bonampak.** Named after one of the famous Maya ruins, this comfortable hotel is on the edge of the Zona Hotelera, just minutes away from the beach by bus or taxi. The bullring and open-air markets are within walking distance. Rooms are basic, with a rose-and-taupe color scheme. There are no patios or terraces, but the windows do look out onto the medium-size pool and garden below. Each floor has a large, bright, airy sitting area. The staff is helpful. Salad lovers can find sustenance at the Ensalada Rico restaurant, right on the premises. ⊠ *Av. Bonampak 225, Sm 4, 77500* ☎🖷 *998/884–0280* ⤹ *80 rooms* ♨ *Restaurant, cable TV, pool, laundry facilities, laundry service, free parking* ⊟ *AE, MC, V.*

★ $ ▣ **Hotel El Rey del Caribe.** Thanks to the use of solar energy, a water-recycling system, and composting toilets, this hotel has very little impact on the environment—and its luxuriant garden blocks the heat and noise of downtown. Hammocks hang poolside, and wrought-iron tables and chairs dot the grounds. Rooms are small but pleasant. El Centro's shops and restaurants are within walking distance. ⊠ *Avs. Uxmal and Nader, Sm 2, 77500* ☎ *998/884–2028* 🖷 *998/884–9857* ⊕ *www.reycaribe.com* ⤹ *25 rooms* ♨ *Kitchenettes, cable TV, pool, hot tub* ⊟ *MC, V.*

$ ▣ **Maria de Lourdes.** It may look a bit worn, but this hotel has reasonable rates and a convenient location. Basic rooms are each furnished with two queen-size beds. Rooms overlooking the street are noisy, but they're brighter and airier than those facing the hallways. A decent-size swimming pool is surrounded by tables, where guests often play cards. ⊠ *Av. Yaxchilán 80, Sm 22, 77500* ☎ *998/884–4744* 🖷 *998/884–1242* ⊕ *www.hotelmariadelourdes.com* ⬎ *57 rooms* ⚐ *Restaurant, cable TV, pool, bar, parking (fee)* ▭ *No credit cards.*

¢–$ 🖬 **Hotel Margaritas.** This lovely hotel is just steps away from several restaurants and Parque de las Palapas. Its largish rooms are decorated with elegant marble tiles, floral bedspreads, and Mexican folk art. The pool is on the small side but there is a lovely palapa restaurant with a brick oven, which serves great pizza. The buffets are also good and reasonably priced. ⊠ *Av. Yaxchilán 41, Sm 22, 77500* ☎ *998/884–9333* 🖷 *998/884–1324* ⊕ *www.margaritascancun.com* ⬎ *99 rooms, 3 suites* ⚐ *Restaurant, cable TV, pool, bar* ▭ *MC, V.*

¢–$ 🖬 **Hotel Parador.** Rooms at this centrally located hotel line two narrow hallways, which lead to a pool, garden, and palapa bar. Rooms are spare but functional; the bathrooms are large and the showers hot. You can walk to all the nightlife in minutes, and the bus to the Zona Hotelera stops right outside. ⊠ *Av. Tulum 26, Sm 5, 77500* ☎ *998/884–9696* 🖷 *998/884–9712* ⊕ *www.hotelparador.com.mx* ⬎ *66 rooms* ⚐ *Restaurant, cable TV, pool, bar* ▭ *MC, V.*

¢–$ 🖬 **Suites Cancún Centro.** You can rent suites or rooms by the day, week, or month at this quiet hotel. Even though is abuts the lively Parque de las Palapas, the hotel manages to remain tranquil with a lovely and private courtyard filled with flowers and plants. All the suites open up onto the courtyard. Tiled bathrooms are small but pleasant, and there are king-size as well as single beds. Suites have fully equipped kitchenettes along with sitting and dining areas. Some rooms only have fans, so be sure to ask when you make reservations. ⊠ *Calle Alcatraces 32, Sm 22, 77500* ☎ *998/884–2301* 🖷 *998/884–7270* ⬎ *30 suites* ⚐ *Kitchenettes, cable TV, no a/c in some rooms* ▭ *MC, V.*

¢ 🖬 **Hotel Colonial.** The colonial-style buildings of this small economy hotel are centered around a charming fountain and garden. Rooms are comfortable but simple, each with a double bed, dresser, and bathroom. What it lacks in luxury it makes up for in value and location; you are five minutes away from all the downtown concerts, clubs, restaurants, shops, and attractions. ⊠ *Av. Tulipanes 22, Sm 21, 77500* ☎ *998/884–1535* 🖷 *998/884–1535* ⬎ *46 rooms* ⚐ *Restaurant, cable TV, free parking* ▭ *D, MC, V.*

¢ 🖬 **Hotel Cotty.** This very basic hotel is just minutes from the bus station downtown. Rooms have two double beds each (a bit on the soft side), hot showers, and cable TV. Ask for a room at the back since they are quieter. There is a cafeteria on-site that serves good basic Mexican meals such as roasted chicken, tortillas, and beans. ⊠ *Av. Uxmal 44, Sm 22, 77500* ☎ *998/884–0550* 🖷 *998/884–1319* ⬎ *38 rooms* ⚐ *Cafeteria, cable TV, free parking* ▭ *No credit cards.*

¢ 🖬 **Hotel Tankah.** Just around the corner from Mercado Veintiocho (Market 28), this basic hotel has clean, simple rooms with comfortable beds, air-conditioning, good showers, and cable TV. Some even have small sitting areas. The lobby is pleasant, with Mexican-style arches and a small garden; the staff is friendly and helpful. ⊠ *Av. Tankah, Lotes 69 and*

70, Sm 24, 77500 ☎ 998/884–4446 🖷 998/884–3065 ⤴ 40 rooms ⚫ Cable TV ▭ No credit cards.

¢ 🏨 **Mexico Hostels.** The cheapest place to stay in Cancún, this clean but cramped hostel is four blocks from the main bus terminal. Some rooms are lined with bunk beds and share baths; others are more private. There are lockers to secure your belongings, and access to a full kitchen, a lounge area, laundry facilities, and the Internet on-site. Those who want to sleep outdoors can share a space with 20 others under a palapa roof. The hostel is open 24 hours. ✉ Calle Palmera 30 (off Av. Uxmal), Sm 23, 77500 ☎ 998/887–0191, 212/699–3825 Ext. 7860 🖷 425/962–8028 ⊕ www.mexicohostels.com ⤴ 64 beds ⚫ Café, lounge, laundry facilities, Internet; no a/c ▭ No credit cards ⏐⊙⏐ CP.

¢ 🏨 **Soberanis Hotel.** Rooms here are uncluttered, with modern furniture and white tile floors. There's also a hostel section, with four bunks to a room and lockers. The neighboring cybercafé has a travel agency and bulletin board with info posted by other travelers. Downtown banks, shops, and restaurants are within walking distance. ✉ Av. Cobá, Sm 22, 77500 ☎🖷 998/884–4564 ⊕ www.soberanis.com.mx ⤴ 78 rooms ⚫ Restaurant, room service, some cable TV, Internet, meeting room, free parking ▭ MC, V ⏐⊙⏐ CP.

NIGHTLIFE & THE ARTS

Nightlife

Many restaurants in Cancún double as party centers, and there are also discos with DJs and light shows, and nightclubs where live bands play. There are several familiar chain clubs, including Hard Rock, Margaritaville, and Carlos n' Charlie's, but there are many other, more unique nightspots that cater to locals as well as tourists.

Dinner Cruises

AquaWorld's **Cancún Queen** (✉ AquaWorld Marina, Blvd. Kukulcán, Km 15.2, Zona Hotelera ☎ 998/848–8300) is the only paddle wheeler in Mexico. It offers cruises of the lagoon, complete with a three-course dinner. The 62-foot galleon **Columbus** (✉ Royal Yacht Club, Blvd. Kukulcán, Km 16.6, Zona Hotelera ☎ 998/849–4621) offers lobster dinner cruises at sunset (5 PM) and star cruises at 8 PM. On the **Capitán Hook** (✉ El Embarcadero, Blvd. Kukulcán, Km 4.5, Zona Hotelera ☎ 998/849–4451 or 998/849–4452), you can watch a pirate show and enjoy a lobster dinner aboard a replica of an 18th-century Spanish galleon.

Discos

Cancún wouldn't be Cancún without its glittering discos, which generally start jumping about 10:30. **La Boom** (✉ Blvd. Kukulcán, Km 3.5, Zona Hotelera ☎ 998/883–1152) is always the last place to close; it has a video bar with a light show and weekly events such as dance contests. The **Bull Dog Night Club** (✉ Krystal Cancún hotel, Blvd. Kukulcán, Km 9, Lote 9, Zona Hotelera ☎ 998/883–1133) has an all-you-can-drink bar, the latest dance music, and an impressive laser-light show. The wild, wild **Coco Bongo** (✉ Blvd. Kukulcán, Km 9.5, across the street from Dady'O, Zona Hotelera ☎ 998/883–5061) has no chairs, but there are plenty of tables that everyone dances on. The floor show billed as "Las Vegas meets Hollywood" has some impressive performances.

Glazz (⊠ La Isla Shopping Village, Blvd. Kukulcán, Km 12.5, Zona Hotelera ☎ 998/883–1881) is an upscale restaurant and club with a large dance floor, where all kinds of music is played. The menu is ghastly and pretentious, but the dancing and cocktails are terrific. **Hijack** (⊠ Plaza la Fiesta, Blvd. Kukulcán, Km 9, Zona Hotelera ☎ 998/883–5801) plays classic disco so you can indulge your Saturday-night fever, Cancún style.

Dady'O (⊠ Blvd. Kukulcán, Km 9.5, Zona Hotelera ☎ 998/883–3333) has been around for a while but is still very "in" with the younger set. Next door to Dady'O, **Dady Rock** (⊠ Blvd. Kukulcán, Km 9.5, Zona Hotelera ☎ 998/883–3333) draws a high-energy crowd with live music, a giant TV screen, contests, and food specials. **Fat Tuesday** (⊠ Blvd. Kukulcán, Km 6.5, Zona Hotelera ☎ 998/849–7199), with its large daiquiri bar and live and taped disco music, is another place to dance the night away.

Music

☺ To mingle with locals and hear great music for free, head to the **Parque de las Palapas** (⊠ Bordered by Avs. Tulum, Yaxchilán, Uxmal, and Cobá, Sm 22) in El Centro. Every Friday night at 7:30 there's live music that ranges from jazz to salsa to Caribbean. There are often shows on Sunday, too, when families gather at the plaza.

Azucar (⊠ Hotel Camino Real, Blvd. Kukulcán, Km 9, Zona Hotelera ☎ 998/883–0100) showcases the very best Latin American bands. Go just to watch the locals dance (the beautiful people tend to turn up here really late). Proper dress is required—no jeans or sneakers. The **Blue Bayou Jazz Club** (⊠ Blvd. Kukulcán, Km 10.5, Zona Hotelera ☎ 998/883–0044), the lobby bar in the Hyatt Cancún Caribe, has nightly jazz. **Mambo Café** (⊠ Av. Tulum, Plaza las Americas, 2nd fl., Sm 4 ☎ 998/887–7894), which opens its doors after 10 PM, plays hot salsa music so you can practice your moves with the locals.

El Centro's classy **Roots Bar** (⊠ Av. Tulipanes 26, near Parque de las Palapas, Sm 22 ☎ 998/884–2437) is the place to go for jazz, fusion, flamenco, and blues.

The **Royal Bandstand** (⊠ Blvd. Kukulcán, Km 13.5, Royal Sands Hotel, Zona Hotelera ☎ 998/848–8220) is the place for ballroom dancing. Its terrific live band plays golden oldies, romantic favorites, and latest hits. There is a dinner menu offered as well if you get hungry.

Tragar Bar (⊠ Laguna Grill, Blvd. Kukulcán, Km 15.6, Zona Hotelera ☎ 998/885–0267) in the Laguna Grill has a DJ after 10 PM on weekends; if you show up early, you can sample some terrific cocktails at the plush aquarium bar.

Restaurant Party Centers

The following restaurants all serve decent food—but the real draw is the nightly parties that often have live music until dawn.

At **Carlos n' Charlie's** (⊠ Blvd. Kukulcán, Km 5.5, Zona Hotelera ☎ 998/849–4124), zany waiters perform on stage with live rock bands. **Champi-**

ons (✉ Marriott Casa Magna hotel, Blvd. Kukulcán, Km 14.5, Zona Hotelera ☎ 998/881–2000 Ext. 6341) has a giant sports screen with 40 monitors, a live DJ, pool tables, cold beer, and dancing until the wee hours. **Mango Tango** (✉ Blvd. Kukulcán, Km 12.5, Zona Hotelera ☎ 998/883–0303) has a Las Vegas–style dinner theater show with Caribbean music and dance. **Pat O'Brien's** (✉ Blvd. Kukulcán, Km 11.5, Zona Hotelera ☎ 998/883–0418) brings the New Orleans party scene to the Zone with live rock bands and its famous cocktails. **Señor Frog's** (✉ Blvd. Kukulcán, Km 12.5, Zona Hotelera ☎ 998/883–1092) is known for its crazy souvenir drinks.

The Arts

♻ The **Casa de Cultura** (✉ Prolongación Av. Yaxchilán, Sm 26 ☎ 998/884–8364) hosts local cultural events, including art exhibits, dance performances, plays, and concerts, throughout the year.

Film

Most movies that play in Cancún are Hollywood blockbusters shown in English with Spanish subtitles, although some of the more popular movies are now being dubbed into Spanish. Look for *En Inglés* displayed alongside the title on the marquee or in newspaper listings. The ticket seller will usually tell you when you are buying a ticket for a Spanish movie instead of an English one. All children's movies are dubbed in Spanish.

♻ In the Zona Hotelera, **Cinemark Cancún** (✉ La Isla Shopping Village, Blvd. Kukulcán, Km 12.5, Zona Hotelera ☎ 998/883–5604 or 998/883–5603 ⊕ www.cinemark.com.mx) has five large screens.

Downtown, at Plaza las Americas, **Cinepolis** (✉ Av. Tulum, Sm 4 and Sm 9 ☎ 998/884–4056) has the largest selection of movies, with 12 screens. **Tulum Plus** (✉ Av. Tulum 10, Sm 2 ☎ 998/884–3451) is a small movie theater with six large screens and cheaper prices than many other, newer theaters. It gives the traditional Mexican half-time intermission.

Performances

The **Gran Meliá Cancún** (✉ Blvd. Kukulcán, Km 12, Zona Hotelera ☎ 998/885–1160) presents a light-and-sound show based on the Maya culture every Tuesday and Thursday evening. Call for ticket prices and times.

♻ Every weeknight the **Teatro de Cancún** (✉ El Embarcadero, Blvd. Kukulcán, Km 4, Zona Hotelera ☎ 998/849–4848) presents two shows: *Voces y Danzas de Mexico* (*Voices and Dances of Mexico*), a colorful showcase of popular songs and dances from different cities in Mexico, as well as *Traducíon del Caribe* (*Caribbean Tradition*), which highlights the rhythms, music, and dance of Cuba, Puerto Rico, and other Caribbean destinations. Tickets for each performance are $29. Dinner packages are also available.

SPORTS & THE OUTDOORS

Boating & Sailing

There are lots of ways to get your adrenaline going on the waters of Cancún. You can arrange to go parasailing (about $35 for eight minutes), waterskiing ($70 per hour), or jet skiing ($70 per hour, or $60 for Wave Runners). Paddleboats, kayaks, catamarans, and banana boats are readily available, too.

Aqua Fun (⊠ Blvd. Kukulcán, Km 16.5, Zona Hotelera ☎ 998/885–2930) maintains a large fleet of water toys such as Wave Runners, Jet Skis, speedboats, kayaks, and Windsurfers. **AquaWorld** (⊠ Blvd. Kukulcán, Km 15.2, Zona Hotelera ☎ 998/848–8300 ⊕ www.aquaworld.com.mx.) rents boats and water toys and offers parasailing and tours aboard a submarine. **El Embarcadero** (⊠ Blvd. Kukulcán, Km 4, Zona Hotelera ☎ 998/849–4848), the marina complex at Playa Linda, is the departure point for ferries to Isla Mujeres and several tour boats.

Marina Asterix (⊠ Blvd. Kukulcán, Km 4.5, Zona Hotelera ☎ 998/883–4847) gives tours to Isla Contoy and Isla Mujeres, and snorkeling trips.

Marina Manglar (⊠ Blvd. Kukulcán, Km 20, Zona Hotelera ☎ 998/885–1808) offers a Jet Ski jungle tour.

Bullfighting

The Cancún **bullring** (⊠ Blvd. Kukulcán and Av. Bonampak, Sm 4 ☎ 998/884–8372 or 998/884–8248), a block south of the Pemex gas station, hosts year-round bullfights. A matador, *charros* (Mexican cowboys), a mariachi band, and flamenco dancers entertain during the hour preceding the bullfight (from 2:30 PM). Tickets cost about $40. Fights are held Wednesday at 3:30.

Fishing

Some 500 species—including sailfish, wahoo, bluefin, marlin, barracuda, and red snapper—live in the waters off Cancún. You can charter deep-sea fishing boats starting at about $350 for four hours, $450 for six hours, and $550 for eight hours. Rates generally include a captain and first mate, gear, bait, and beverages.

Marina Barracuda (⊠ Blvd. Kukulcán, Km 14.1, Zona Hotelera ☎ 998/885–343), which has one of Cancún's largest fishing fleets, offers deepsea and fly-fishing. **Marina Punta del Este** (⊠ Blvd. Kukulcán, Km 10.3, Zona Hotelera ☎ 998/883–1210) is right next to the convention center. **Marina del Rey** (⊠ Blvd. Kukulcán, Km 15.5, Zona Hotelera ☎ 998/885–0273) offers boat tours and has a small market and a souvenir shop. **Mundo Marino** (⊠ Blvd. Kukulcán, Km 5.5, Zona Hotelera ☎ 998/883–0554) is the marina closest to downtown and specializes in deep-sea fishing.

Go-Carts

About 20 minutes south of Cancún, speed demons can get their fix at **Go Karts Cancún.** There's a racetrack where Honda-engine go-carts reach speeds of up to 120 kph (70 mph), and also a smaller track with slower carts for children. Your choice of cart and track determines the price, which is by the hour. If you don't have a car to get here, a taxi ride should cost about $5 to $10 from downtown (and considerably more from the Zona Hotelera). Buses leave every 20 minutes from the downtown terminal and cost about $1.20. Check to make sure your bus is not a direct route and will let you off. ⊠ *Cancún–Puerto Morelos Hwy./Carretera 307, Km 7.5, Bonfil* ☎ *998/882–1275* ◷ *Daily 10–10.*

Golf

Cancún's main golf course is at **Pok-Ta-Pok** (⊠ Blvd. Kukulcán between Km 6 and Km 7, Zona Hotelera ☎ 998/883–1230). The club has fine views of both sea and lagoon; its 18 holes were designed by Robert Trent Jones Sr. The club also has a practice green, a swimming pool, tennis courts, and a restaurant. The greens fees start at $80 ($45 after 2 PM); electric cart, $30; and caddies, $20. There is an 18-hole championship golf course at the **Hilton Cancún Beach & Golf Resort** (⊠ Blvd. Kukulcán, Km 17, Zona Hotelera ☎ 998/881–8016); greens fees are $100 ($65 for hotel guests), carts are included, and club rentals run from $20 to $30. The 13-hole executive course (par 53) at the **Gran Meliá Cancún** (⊠ Blvd. Kukulcán, Km 12, Zona Hotelera ☎ 998/885–1160) forms a semicircle around the property and shares its beautiful ocean views. The greens fee is about $20.

☾ If you're looking for a less strenuous golf game, **Mini Golf Palace** (⊠ Blvd. Kukulcán, Km 14.5, Zona Hotelera ☎ 998/881–3600 Ext. 6655) has a complete 36-hole mini-golf course around pyramids, waterfalls, and a river on the grounds of the Cancún Palace.

Health Clubs

Most deluxe hotels have health clubs, although some are quite small and not open to the public. Most of the larger hotels, including the JW Marriott and Le Meridien, sell day passes to their spas and gyms.

Running

If the idea of jogging in the intense heat of Cancún sounds appealing, there is a 14-km (9-mi) track that extends along half the island, running parallel to Boulevard Kukulcán from the Punta Cancún area into Cancún City. Every December Cancún puts on an international marathon called the **Most Beautiful Marathon in the World.** The route goes through both the Zona Hotelera and downtown. For more information contact the **Cancún Conventions and Visitors Bureau** (⊠ Avs. Cobá and Náder, El Centro, Sm 4 ☎ 998/884–6531 🖷 998/887–6648).

MAADMAN Cancún is a challenging triathlon event, usually hosted in early October: a 3.8-km (2.28-mi) ocean swim, followed by a 180-km (108-mi) bike ride along the highway, and then a 42.2-km (25.3-mi) run along Boulevard Kukulcán. The winner of the race is declared the MAADMAN of Cancún; for the rest of us, there are spectator benches. For more information contact www.maadman.com.

Snorkeling & Scuba Diving

The snorkeling is best at Punta Nizuc, Punta Cancún, and Playa Tortugas, although you should be careful of the strong currents at Tortugas. You can rent gear for about $10 per day from many of the scuba-diving places as well as at many hotels.

Scuba diving is popular in Cancún, though it's not as spectacular as in Cozumel. Look for a scuba company that will give you lots of personal attention: smaller companies are often better at this than larger ones. Regardless, ask to meet the dive master, and check the equipment and certifications thoroughly. A few words of caution about one-hour courses that many resorts offer for free: such courses *do not* prepare you to dive in the ocean, no matter what the high-pressure concession operators tell you. If you've caught the scuba bug, prepare yourself properly by investing in several lessons.

Barracuda Marina (⊠ Blvd. Kukulcán, Km 14, Zona Hotelera ☎ 998/885–3444) has a two-hour Wave Runner jungle tour through the mangroves, which ends with snorkeling at the Punta Nizuc coral reef. The fee (which starts at $35) includes snorkeling equipment, life jackets, and refreshments. **Scuba Cancún** (⊠ Blvd. Kukulcán, Km 5, Zona Hotelera ☎ 998/884–7508) specializes in diving trips and offers NAUI, CMAS, and PADI instruction. It's operated by Luis Hurtado, who has more than 35 years of experience. A two-tank dive starts at $64. **Solo Buceo** (⊠ Blvd. Kukulcán, Km 9.5, Zona Hotelera ☎ 998/883–3979) charges $60 for two-tank dives and has NAUI, SSI, and PADI instruction. The outfit goes to Cozumel, Akumal, and Isla Mujeres. Extended trips are available from $130.

SHOPPING

The *centros comerciales* (malls) in Cancún are fully air-conditioned and as well kept as similar establishments in the United States or Canada. Like their northerly counterparts, they also sell just about everything: designer clothing, beachwear, sportswear, jewelry, music, video games, household items, shoes, and books. Some even have the same terrible mall food that is standard north of the border. Prices are fixed in shops. They're also generally—but not always—higher than in the markets, where bargaining for better prices is a possibility.

There are many duty-free stores that sell designer goods at reduced prices—sometimes as much as 30% or 40% below retail. Although prices for handicrafts are higher here than in other cities and the selection is limited, you can find handwoven textiles, leather goods, and handcrafted silver jewelry.

A note of caution about tortoiseshell products: the turtles from which they're made are an endangered species, and it's illegal to bring tortoiseshell into the United States and several other countries. Simply refrain from buying anything made from tortoiseshell. Also be aware that there are some restrictions regarding black coral. You must purchase it from a recognized dealer.

Shopping hours are generally weekdays 10–1 and 4–7, although more stores are increasingly staying open throughout the day rather than closing for siesta. Many shops keep Saturday-morning hours, and some are now open on Sunday until 1. Centros comerciales tend to be open weekdays 9 AM or 10 AM to 8 PM or 9 PM.

Districts, Markets & Malls

Zona Hotelera

There is only one open-air market in the Zona Hotelera. **Coral Negro** (⊠ Blvd. Kukulcán, Km 9, Zona Hotelera), next to the convention center, is a collection of about 50 stalls selling crafts items. It's open daily until late evening. Everything here is overpriced, but bargaining does work.

ON MEXICO TIME

Mexicans are far more relaxed about time than their counterparts north of the border are. Although mañana translates as "tomorrow," it is often used to explain why something is not getting done or not ready. In this context, mañana means, "Relax—it'll get taken care of eventually." If you make an appointment in Mexico, it's understood that it's for half an hour later. For example, if you make a date for 9, don't be surprised if everyone else shows up at 9:30. The trick to enjoying life on Mexican time is: don't rush. And be sure to take advantage of the siesta hour between 1 PM and 4 PM. How else are you going to stay up late dancing?

Plaza Flamingo (✉ Blvd. Kukulcán, Km 11.5, across from the Hotel Flamingo, Zona Hotelera ☎ 998/883–2855) is a small plaza beautifully decorated with marble. Inside are a few designer emporiums, duty-free shops, an exchange booth, sportswear shops, restaurants, and boutiques selling Mexican handicrafts.

Forum-by-the-Sea (✉ Blvd. Kukulcán, Km 9.5, Zona Hotelera ☎ 998/883–4428) is a sparkling, three-level entertainment and shopping plaza in the Zona. There is a large selection of brand-name stores and restaurants here, all in a circuslike atmosphere.

The glittering, ultratrendy, and ultraexpensive **La Isla Shopping Village** (✉ Blvd. Kukulcán, Km 12.5, Zona Hotelera ☎ 998/883–5025) is on the Laguna Nichupté under a giant canopy. A series of canals and small bridges is designed to give the place a Venetian look. In addition to shops, the mall has a marina, an aquarium, a disco, restaurants, and movie theaters. You won't find any bargains here, but it's a fun place to window-shop.

Plaza Kukulcán (✉ Blvd. Kukulcán, Km 13, Zona Hotelera ☎ 998/885–2200) is a seemingly endless mall, with around 80 shops, six restaurants, a liquor store, and a video arcade. The plaza is also notable for the many cultural events and shows that take place in the main public area.

Leading off Plaza Caracol is the oldest and most varied commercial center in the Zona, **Plaza Mayafair** (✉ Blvd. Kukulcán, Km 8.5, Zona Hotelera ☎ 998/883–2801). Mayafair has a large open-air center filled with shops, bars, and restaurants. An adjacent indoor shopping mall is decorated to resemble a rain forest, complete with replicas of Maya stelae.

The largest and most contemporary of the malls, **Plaza Caracol** (✉ Blvd. Kukulcán, Km 8.5, Zona Hotelera ☎ 998/883–1038) is north of the convention center. It houses about 200 shops and boutiques, including two pharmacies, art galleries, a currency exchange, and folk art and jewelry shops, as well as a café and restaurants. Boutiques include Benetton, Bally, Gucci, and Ralph Lauren, with prices lower than those of their U.S. counterparts. You can rest your feet upstairs at the café, where there are often afternoon concerts, or have a meal at one of the fine restaurants.

Plaza la Fiesta (⊠ Blvd. Kukulcán, Km 9, Zona Hotelera ☎ 998/883–2116) has 20,000 square feet of showroom space, and over 100,000 different products for sale. This is probably the widest selection of Mexican goods in the hotel zone, and includes leather goods, silver and gold jewelry, handicrafts, souvenirs, and swimwear. There are some good bargains here.

El Centro

There are lots of interesting shops downtown along Avenida Tulum (between Avenidas Cobá and Uxmal). **Fama** (⊠ Av. Tulum 105, Sm 21 ☎ 998/884–6586) is a department store that sells clothing, English books and magazines, sports gear, toiletries, liquor, and *latería* (crafts made of tin). The oldest and largest of Cancún's crafts markets is **Ki Huic** (⊠ Av. Tulum 17, between Bancomer and Bital banks, Sm 3 ☎ 998/884–3347). It is open daily 9 AM–10 PM and houses about 100 vendors. **Mercado Veintiocho** (Market 28), just off Avenidas Yaxchilán and Sunyaxchén, is a popular souvenir market filled with shops selling many of the same items found in the Zona Hotelera but at half the price. **Ultrafemme** (⊠ Av. Tulum and Calle Claveles, Sm 21 ☎ 998/885–1402) is a popular downtown store that carries duty-free perfume, cosmetics, and jewelry. It also has branches in the Zona Hotelera at Plaza Caracol, Plaza Flamingo, Plaza Kukulcán, and La Isla Shopping Village.

Plaza las Americas (⊠ Av. Tulum, Sm 4 and Sm 9 ☎ 998/887–3863) is the largest shopping center in downtown Cancún. Its 50-plus stores, three restaurants, eight movie theaters, video arcade, fast-food outlets, and five large department stores will—for better, for worse—make you feel right at home.

Plaza Bonita (⊠ Av. Tulum 260, Sm 7 ☎ 998/884–6812) is a small outdoor plaza next door to Mercado Veintiocho (Market 28). It has many wonderful specialty shops carrying Mexican goods and crafts.

Plaza Cancún 2000 (⊠ Av. Tulum 42, Sm 7 ☎ 998/884–9988) is a local shopping mall popular with locals. There are some great bargains to be found here on shoes, clothes, and cosmetics.

Specialty Shops

Galleries

The **Huichol Collection** (⊠ Forum-by-the-Sea, Blvd. Kukulcán, Km 9.5, Zona Hotelera ☎ 998/883–5856) sells handcrafted beadwork and embroidery made by the Huichol Indians of the West Coast. You can also watch a visiting tribe member doing this amazing work. **Arte Popular** (⊠ Plaza Flamingo, Blvd. Kukulcán, Km 11, Zona Hotelera ☎ 998/883–2824) sells crafts and art from around Mexico. **The Attic** (⊠ La Isla Shopping Village, Blvd. Kukulcán, Km 12.5, Zona Hotelera ☎ 998/883–5466), found in Las Margaritas Restaurant, specializes in gold and silver jewelry from Taxco, as well as traditional Mexican art. The **Iguana Wana** restaurant (⊠ Plaza Caracol, Blvd. Kukulcán, Km 8.5, Zona Hotelera ☎ 998/883–0829) displays a small collection of art for sale.

Grocery Stores

The few grocery stores in the Zona Hotelera tend to be expensive. It's better to shop for groceries downtown. **Chedraui** (⊠ Av. Tulum, Sm 21 ⊠ Plaza las Americas, Av. Tulum, Sm 4 and Sm 9 ☎ 998/887–2111 for both locations) is a popular department store with two central locations. **Mega Comercial Mexicana** (⊠ Avs. Tulum and Uxmal, Sm 2 ☎ 998/884–4524 ⊠ Avs. Kabah and Mayapan, Sm 21 ☎ 998/880–9164) is one of the major Mexican grocery store chains, with three locations. The most convenient is at Avenidas Tulum and Uxmal, across from the bus station; its largest store is farther north on Avenida Kabah, which is open 24 hours.

If you are a member in the States, you can visit **Costco** (⊠ Avs. Kabah and Yaxchilán, Sm 21 ☎ 998/881–0250). **Sam's Club** (⊠ Av. Cobá, Lote 2, Sm 21 ☎ 998/881–0200) has plenty of bargains on groceries and souvenirs. Most locals shop at **San Francisco de Asís** (⊠ Av. Tulum 18, Sm 3 ⊠ Mercado Veintiocho, Avs. Yaxchilán and Sunyaxchén, Sm 26 ☎ 998/884–1155 for both locations) for its many bargains on food and other items. **Wal-Mart** (⊠ Av. Cobá, Lote 2, Sm 21 ☎ 998/884–1383) is a popular shopping spot.

CANCÚN A TO Z

To research prices, get advice from other travelers, and book travel arrangements, visit www.fodors.com.

ADDRESSES

In Cancún addresses, "Sm" stands for Super Manzana, literally a group of houses. All neighborhoods are classified with an Sm number (Sm 23, Sm 25, and so on). Each Sm has its own park or square, and the area streets are fashioned around the park.

AIR TRAVEL

AIRPORT The Aeropuerto Internacional Cancún is 16 km (9 mi) southwest of the heart of Cancún and 10 km (6 mi) from the Zona Hotelera's southernmost point.

🚹 **Aeropuerto Internacional Cancún** ⊠ Carretera Cancún–Puerto Morelos/Carretera 307, Km 9.5 ☎ 998/886–0028.

AIRPORT The public-transport options are taxis or *colectivos* (vans); buses aren't
TRANSFERS allowed into the airport due to an agreement with the taxi union. A counter at the airport exit sells colectivo and taxi tickets; prices range from $15 to $75, depending on the destination and driver. Don't hesitate to barter with the cab drivers. The colectivos have fixed prices and usually wait until they are full before leaving. They start at the far end of the Zona Hotelera, dropping off passengers along the way. It's slow but cheaper than a cab. Getting back to the airport for your departure is less ex-

pensive; taxi fares range from about $15 to $22. Hotels post current rates. Be sure to agree on a price before getting into a cab.

CARRIERS   Aeroméxico flies nonstop to Cancún from Los Angeles. American has nonstop service from Chicago, New York, Dallas, and Miami. Continental offers daily direct service from Houston. Mexicana's nonstop flights are from Los Angeles and Miami. From Cancún, Mexicana subsidiaries Aerocaribe and Aerocozumel fly to Cozumel, the ruins at Chichén Itzá, Mérida, and other Mexican cities. Aerocosta flies to mainland cities, ruins, and haciendas.

🛪 **Aerocaribe/Aerocozumel** ☎ 998/884-2000 El Centro, 998/886-0083 airport. **Aerocosta** ☎ 998/884-0383. **Aeroméxico** ☎ 998/884-3571 El Centro, 998/886-0161 airport. **American** ☎ 998/883-4460 airport, 800/904-6000. **Continental** ☎ 998/886-0006. **Mexicana** ☎ 998/881-9093 El Centro, 998/886-0068 airport. **United Airlines** ☎ 800/003-0777.

BOAT & FERRY TRAVEL

From either the Embarcadero dock or the Xcaret dock (both are owned by the same company) in the Zona Hotelera, you can take a shuttle boat to the main dock at Isla Mujeres. Ferries carry vehicles and passengers between Cancún's Punta Sam and Isla's dock, and other ferries carry passengers from Puerto Juárez.

BUS TRAVEL

Frequent, reliable public buses run between the Zona Hotelera and El Centro from 6 AM to midnight; the cost is 75¢. There are designated stops—look for blue signs with white buses in the middle—but you can also flag down drivers along Boulevard Kukulcán. Take Ruta 8 (Route 8) to reach Puerto Juárez and Punta Sam for the ferries to Isla Mujeres. Take Ruta 1 (Route 1) to and from the Zona Hotelera. Ruta 1 buses will drop you off anywhere along Avenida Tulum, and you can catch a connecting bus into El Centro. Try to have the correct change and be careful of drivers trying to shortchange you. Also, hold on to the tiny piece of paper the driver gives you. It's your receipt, and bus company officers sometimes board buses and ask for all receipts.

Autocar and Publicar, in conjunction with the Cancún tourist board, has published an excellent pocket guide called "TheMAP" that shows all the bus routes to points of interest in Cancún and surrounding area. The map is free and is easiest to find at the airport. Some of the mid-range hotels carry copies and if you are lucky you may find one on a bus.

First- and second-class buses arrive at the downtown bus terminal from all over Mexico. ADO and Playa Express are the main companies servicing the coast. Buses leave every 20 minutes for Puerto Morelos and Playa del Carmen. Check the schedule for departure times for Tulum, Chetumal, Cobá, Valladolid, Chichén Itzá, and Mérida.

🚌 **ADO** ☎ 998/887-1149. **Bus terminal** ✉ Avs. Tulum and Uxmal, Sm 23 ☎ 998/887-1149. **Playa Express** ☎ 998/884-0994.

CAR RENTAL

Most rental cars are standard-shift subcompacts and jeeps; air-conditioned cars with automatic transmissions should be reserved in advance (though bear in mind that some smaller car-rental places have only standards). Rates average around $55 per day but can be as high as $75 daily if you haven't reserved a car; you can save a great deal on a rental by booking before you leave home, particularly over the Internet. It's also a good idea to shop around. In addition to the rental agencies, the Car Rental Association can help you arrange a rental.

⚑ Major Agencies **Avis** ☎ 998/886-0222. **Budget** ☎ 998/886-0226 airport. **Hertz** ☎ 998/884-1326 airport. **National** ☎ 998/886-0152 airport. **Thrifty** ☎ 998/886-0333 airport.

⚑ Local Agencies & Contacts **Buster Renta Car** ✉ Plaza Nautilus Kukulcán, Km 3.5, Zona Hotelera ☎ 998/849-7221. **Car Rental Association** ✉ La Costa 28, Sm 2 ☎ 998/887-3109. **Econorent** ✉ Av. Bonampak at Av. Cobá, Sm 4 ☎ 998/887-6487. **Executive** ✉ Av. Yaxchilán 160, Sm 20 ☎ 998/884-2699. **Localiza Rent a Car** ✉ Airport, International Terminal ☎ 998/886-0248. **Zipp Rental Cars** ✉ Avalon Grand, Blvd. Kukulcán, Km 11.5, Zona Hotelera ☎ 998/849-4193.

CAR TRAVEL

Driving in Cancún isn't for the faint of heart. Traffic moves at a breakneck speed; adding to the danger are the many one-way streets, *glorietas* (traffic circles), sporadically working traffic lights, ill-placed *topes* (speed bumps), numerous pedestrians, and large potholes. Be sure to observe speed limits as traffic police are vigilant and eager to give out tickets. As well as being risky, car travel is expensive, since it often necessitates tips for valet parking, gasoline, and costly rental rates.

Although driving in Cancún isn't recommended, exploring the surrounding areas on the peninsula by car is. The roads are excellent within a 100-km (62-mi) radius. Carretera 180 runs from Matamoros at the Texas border through Campeche, Mérida, Valladolid, and into Cancún. The trip from Texas can take up to three days. Carretera 307 runs south from Cancún through Puerto Morelos, Tulum, and Chetumal, then into Belize. Carretera 307 has several Pemex gas stations between Cancún and Playa del Carmen. For the most part, though, the only gas stations are near major cities and towns, so keep your tank full. When approaching any community, watch out for the speed bumps—hitting them at top speed can ruin your transmission and tires.

CONSULATES

⚑ Canadian Consulate ✉ Plaza Caracol 11, 3rd fl., Zona Hotelera ☎ 998/883-3360, 800/706-2900 emergencies. **U.K. Consulate** ✉ Royal Sands Hotel, Blvd. Kukulcán, Km 13.5, Zona Hotelera ☎ 998/881-0100. **U.S. Consulate** ✉ Plaza Caracol, 3rd fl., Zona Hotelera ☎ 998/883-0272.

EMERGENCIES

⚑ Emergency Services **Fire Department** ☎ 998/884-9480. **General Emergencies** ☎ 06. **Highway Police** ☎ 998/884-0710. **Immigration Office** ☎ 998/884-1749. **Municipal Police** ☎ 998/884-1913. **Red Cross** ✉ Avs. Xcaret and Labná, Sm 21 ☎ 998/884-1616. **Traffic Police** ☎ 998/884-0710.

⚑ Hospitals **Ameri Med** ✉ Plaza las Americas, Sm 4 ☎ 998/881-3400. **Hospital Amat** ✉ Av. Náder 13, Sm 3 ☎ 998/887-4422. **Hospital Americano** ✉ Retorno Viento 15, Sm 4 ☎ 998/884-6133. **Total Assist** ✉ Claveles 5, Sm 22 ☎ 998/884-1092.

☎ Pharmacies **Farmacia Cancún** ⊠ Av. Tulum 17, Sm 22 ☎ 998/884-1283. **Farmacia Extra** ⊠ Plaza Caracol, Blvd. Kukulcán, Km 8.5, Zona Hotelera ☎ 998/883-2827. **Paris** ⊠ Av. Yaxchilán 32, Sm 3 ☎ 998/884-3005. **Roxanna's** ⊠ Plaza Flamingo, Blvd. Kukulcán, Km 11.5, Zona Hotelera ☎ 998/885-1351.

ENGLISH-LANGUAGE MEDIA

You can pick up many helpful publications at the airport, malls, tourist kiosks, and many hotels. Indeed, you can't avoid having them shoved into your hands. Most are stuffed with discount coupons offering some savings. The best of the bunch is *Cancún Tips,* a free pocket-size guide to hotels, restaurants, shopping, and recreation. Although it's loaded with advertising and coupons, the booklet, published twice a year in English and Spanish, has some useful information. The accompanying *Cancún Tips Magazine* has informative articles about local attractions. The *Mapa Pocket Guide* is handy for its Zona Hotelera map and some local contact information. Since the folks who own the parks of Xcaret, Xel-Há, El Embarcadero, and Garrafón publish this guide, they often leave out information on any competitors while heavily promoting their own interests. *Map@migo* has an excellent map of the Zona Hotelera as well as El Centro. It's a handy brochure filled with numbers and coupons to restaurants. Along the same lines in a smaller, booklet format, *Passport Cancún* also has helpful numbers and information along with more coupons.

MAIL, INTERNET & SHIPPING

The *correos* (post office) is open weekdays 8–5 and Saturday 9–1; there's also a Western Union office in the building and a courier service. Postal service to and from Mexico is extremely slow. Avoid sending or receiving parcels—and never send checks or money through the mail. Invariably they are stolen. Your best bet for packages, money, and important letters is to use a courier service such as DHL or Federal Express.

You can receive mail at the post office if it's marked "Lista de Correos, Cancún, 77500, Quintana Roo, Mexico." If you have an American Express card, you can have mail sent to you at the American Express Cancún office for a small fee. The office is open weekdays 9–6 and Saturday 9–1. To send an e-mail or hop online, try Web@Internet, which is downtown.

Most hotels offer Internet service but at exorbitant rates. Some go as high as $25 per hour. Most of the Internet cafés in the Zona Hotelera charge by the minute and have computers that take at least 10 minutes to boot up. Compu Copy, in the Zona Hotelera, is open daily 9–9. Downtown, the Internet Café is open Monday–Saturday 11–10, and Infonet is open daily 10 AM–11 PM. Rates at all three start at $2 per hour. Head to El Centro if you need to send more than one e-mail.

☎ Cybercafés **Compu Copy** ⊠ Plaza Kukulcán, Blvd. Kukulcán, Km 13, Zona Hotelera ☎ 998/885-0055. **Infonet** ⊠ Plaza las Americas, Av. Tulum, Sm 4 and Sm 9 ☎ 998/887-9130. **Internet Café** ⊠ Av. Tulum behind Comercial Mexicana, across from the bus station, Sm 2 ☎ 998/887-3167. **Web@Internet** ⊠ Av. Tulum 51, El Centro, Sm 26 ☎ 998/887-2833.

⊞ Mail Services American Express ✉ Av. Tulum 208, at Calle Agua, Sm 4 ☎ 998/ 884-4554 or 998/884-1999. **Correos** ✉ Avs. Sunyaxchén and Xel-Há, Sm 26 ☎ 998/ 884-1418. **DHL** ✉ Av. Tulum 200, El Centro, Sm 26 ☎ 998/887-1813. **Federal Express** ✉ Av. Tulum 9, El Centro, Sm 22 ☎ 998/887-3279. **Western Union** ✉ Avs. Sunyax- chén and Xel-Há, Sm 26 ☎ 998/884-1529.

MONEY MATTERS

Banks are generally open weekdays 9 to 5; money-exchange desks have hours from 9 to 1:30. Automatic teller machines (ATMs) usually dis- pense Mexican money; some newer ones also dispense dollars. ATMs at the smaller banks are often out of order, and if your personal iden- tification number has more than four digits, your card may not work. Also, don't delay in taking your card out of the machine. ATMs are quick to eat them up, and it takes a visit to the bank and a number of forms to get them back. If your transactions require a teller, arrive at the bank early to avoid long lines. Banamex and Bital both have El Centro and Zona Hotelera offices and can exchange or wire money.

⊞ Banks Banamex Downtown ✉ Av. Tulum 19, next to City Hall, Sm 1 ☎ 998/884- 6403 ✉ Plaza Terramar, Blvd. Kukulcán, Km 37, Zona Hotelera ☎ 998/883-3100. **Bital** ✉ Av. Tulum 15, Sm 4 ☎ 998/881-4103 ✉ Plaza Caracol, Blvd. Kukulcán, Km 8.5, Zona Hotelera ☎ 998/883-4652.

MOPED TRAVEL

Riding a moped in Cancún is extremely dangerous, and you may risk serious injury by using one in either the Zona or downtown. If you have never ridden a moped or a motorcycle before, *this is not the place to learn.* Mopeds rent for about $25 a day; you are required to leave a credit- card voucher for security. You should receive a crash helmet, which by law you must wear. Read the fine print on your contract; companies will hold you liable for all repairs or replacement in case of an accident and will not offer any insurance to protect you.

TAXIS

Taxi rides within the Zona Hotelera cost $5–$9; between the Zona Hotel- era and El Centro, they run $8 and up; and to the ferries at Punta Sam or Puerto Juárez, fares are $15–$20 or more. Prices depend on distance, your negotiating skills, and whether you pick up the taxi in front of a hotel or save a few dollars by going onto the avenue to hail one your- self (look for green city cabs). Most hotels list rates at the door; con- firm the price with your driver *before* you set out. If you lose something in a taxi or have questions or a complaint, call the Sindicato de Taxis- tas. Don't be disappointed if your lost item stays lost. Most locals as- sume that something lost means it doesn't have to be returned. Some drivers ask for such outrageously high fares it's not worth trying to bar- gain with them. Just let them go and flag down another cab.

⊞ Sindicato de Taxistas ☎ 998/888-6985.

TELEPHONES

Most hotels charge the equivalent of between 50¢ and $1 for each local call you make from your room. In addition, there is usually a hefty ser- vice charge on long-distance calls, and it can add up quickly. The cheapest way to make a phone call—local or long distance—is from a TELMEX public phone. These public phones are found on almost every other street corner and outside of every hotel. To use the phones you must purchase a Ladatel phone card, sold in blocks of about $3, $5, $10, and $20. A more expensive alternative to the phone card is the *caseta de larga distancia*—the long-distance telephone office. There are casetas in Plaza Kukulcán, Plaza Mayafair, and Plaza Caracol and one at the downtown bus terminal. These places have specially designed booths where you take your call after the number has been dialed by a clerk. A service fee of $3.50–$5 is added on top of the steep long-distance charge. The booths do, however, offer more privacy and comfort than many public-phone booths.

TOURS

BOAT TOURS   Day cruises to Isla Mujeres generally include snorkeling, shopping, and lunch. Caribbean Carnaval runs a nightly cruise with music and dinner for $60. Capitán Hook runs a nighttime cruise around the bay with lobster or steak dinner and pirate show; it costs $60 or $70, depending on your dinner choice.

🚩 **Capitán Hook** ✉ Playa Langosta, Blvd. Kukulcán, Km 3, Zona Hotelera ☎ 998/849-4452. **Caribbean Carnaval** ✉ Fat Tuesday, Blvd. Kukulcán, Km 6.5, Zona Hotelera ☎ 998/884-3760.

ECOTOURS   The 500,000-acre Reserva Ecológica El Edén, 48 km (30 mi) northwest of Cancún, is in the area known as Yalahau. The reserve was established by one of Mexico's leading naturalists, Arturo Gómez-Pompa, and his nephew, Marco Lazcano-Barrero, and is dedicated to research and conservation. It offers excursions for people interested in exploring wetlands, mangrove swamps, sand dunes, savannas, and tropical forests. Activities include bird-watching, animal-tracking, stargazing, and archaeology. Rates are based on activities and the number of nights you stay at the station. For more information on tours contact **Reserva Ecológica El Edén** (✆ Box 770, 77500 Cancún, Quintana Roo ☎🗃 998/880-5032 ⊕ http://maya.ucr.edu/pril/el_eden/home.html).

Eco Colors runs adventure tours to the wildlife reserves at Isla Holbox and Sian Ka'an, El Eden and to remote ruins on the peninsula. It also offers bird-watching, kayaking, camping, and biking excursions around the peninsula.

🚩 **Eco Colors** ✉ Calle Camarón 32, Sm 27 ☎🗃 998/884-9580 ⊕ www.ecotravelmexico.com.

PLANE TOURS   Promocaribe (a subsidiary of the Promotora Caribena corporation) flies one-day tours between Cancún and Guatemala City, continuing on to Flores and the ruins at Tikal. A round-trip fare of $267 includes all ground transfers, departure taxes, entrance fees at the ruins, a tour guide, and lunch.

🚩 **Fees & Schedules Promotora Caribena** ✉ Plaza Centro, Av. Nader 8, Sm 5 ☎ 998/884-4741 🗃 998/884-4714 ⊕ www.promocaribe.com.

SUBMARINE   *Sub See Explorer* is a "floating submarine" that takes you for a one-TOURS   hour reef cruise. Experience the beauty of Cancún's reef and watch the exotic fish while staying dry. The $35 price includes lunch and refreshments. Tours leave on the hour daily 9–3 PM. Call AquaWorld for information.

🛈 Fees & Schedules *AquaWorld* ☎ 998/848-8300.

TRAVEL AGENCIES

🛈 Local Agent Referrals **Travel Agency Association** ✉ Plaza México, Av. Tulum 200, Suite 301, Sm 5 ☎ 998/887-1670 🖷 998/884-3738.

🛈 Local Agents **Intermar Caribe** ✉ Avs. Tulum and Cobá, Sm 4 ☎ 998/884-4266. **Mayaland Tours** ✉ Av. Robalo 30, Sm 3 ☎ 998/987-2450. **Olympus Tours** ✉ Av. Bonampak 107, Sm 3 ☎ 998/881-9030.

VISITOR INFORMATION

🛈 **Cancún Visitors and Convention Bureau Visitor** ✉ Avs. Nader and Cobá, Sm 5 ☎ 998/884-6531 ⊕ www.ovccancun.org. **Quintana Roo State Tourism Office** ✉ Calle Pecari 23, Sm 20 ☎ 998/881-9000.

ISLA MUJERES

2

BEST STROLL ON THE SUNNY SIDE
The boardwalk at El Malecón ⇨*p.51*

GET YOUR HEART RACING
Swimming with sharks at Playa Tiburon ⇨*p.51*

SEASIDE SERENITY
Na Balam's meditation room ⇨*p.56*

GLIDERS ABOVE AND BELOW
Birds and manta rays at Isla Contoy ⇨*p.64*

O, WHAT A MEAL!
The fresh seafood at Casa O's ⇨*p.54*

Updated by
Shelagh
McNally

IT'S SLEEPY, UNASSUMING, AND MAGICAL, resisting change in a region where change has come quickly. Isla Mujeres (*ees*-lah moo-*hair*-ayce) is only 8 km (5 mi) across the bay from Cancún, yet it's an ocean away in attitude. Swimming or snorkeling, exploring the remnants of the island's past, drinking cold beer with the locals, eating fresh seafood, and lazing under a thatched roof are the liveliest activities here.

This fish-shape island is only about 8 km (5 mi) long by 1 km (½ mi) wide. It has flat sandy beaches on its northern end and steep rocky bluffs to the south. Its name means "Island of Women," although no one knows who dubbed it that. Many believe it was the ancient Maya, who were said to use the island as a religious center for worshipping Ixchel (ee-*shell*), the Maya goddess of rainbows, the moon, and the sea, and the guardian of fertility and childbirth. Another popular legend has it that the Spanish conquistador Hernández de Córdoba named the island when he landed here in 1517 and found hundreds of female-shape clay idols dedicated to Ixchel and her daughters. Others say the name dates from the 17th century, when pirates stashed their women on Isla before heading out to rob the high seas.

After its popularity waned with buccaneers and smugglers, Isla settled into life as a quiet fishing village. In the 1950s it became a favorite vacation spot for Mexicans. Americans discovered it soon afterward, and in the 1960s Isla became well known among hippies and backpackers. As Cancún grew so did Isla. During the late 1970s, the number of day-trippers coming over from the mainland increased, turning the island into a small-scale tourist haven.

Although Isla continues to undergo development, it still primarily attracts visitors who prefer such seaside pleasures as scuba diving, snorkeling, and relaxing on the beach to spending time in fast-paced Cancún. And its inhabitants, *isleños* (islanders; pronounced ees-*lay*-nyos), cherish Isla's history and culture. Most wish to continue the legacy of Ramon Bravo, the late shark expert, ecologist, and filmmaker who fought to keep Isla a peaceful, authentically Mexican getaway.

EXPLORING ISLA MUJERES

To get your bearings, think of Isla Mujeres as an elongated fish, the head being the southeastern tip, the northwest prong the tail. The minute you step off the boat, you get a sense of how small Isla is. Directly in front of the ferry piers is the only town, known simply as El Pueblo. It extends the full width of the northern "tail" and is sandwiched between sand and sea to the south, west, and northeast, with no high-rises to block the views. Past El Pueblo's T-shirt and souvenir shops and bounded by Avenidas Morelos, Bravo, Guerrero, and Hidalgo is the *zócalo* (main square), the ideal place to take in daily life. In the evenings, locals congregate in front of the church while their children run around the playground or play basketball. On holidays and weekends the square is set up for dances, concerts, and fiestas. The main road is Avenida Rueda Medina, which runs the island's length; southeast of a village known as

Beaches

The minute you set foot on Playa Norte's silky sand and gaze out over that stretch of blue water and sky, you'll feel the tension melting. Here you can wade out into placid waters or relax at congenial *palapa* (thatch-roofed) bars with drinks and snacks. Plenty of people simply rent a beach chair, stake out a spot, and stay there until sundown. Sunsets here are spectacular.

The western beaches of Playa Lancheros and Playa Tiburon are great places to dine on the grilled catch of the day. Both beaches face the bay. The water here is deeper and the sand not as soft, but you can still relax underneath one of the many palm trees. Restaurants here are classic beach stands where no one cares whether you're wearing a shirt or shoes. On Sunday, both beaches fill with locals enjoying their day off.

Bird-Watching

About 45 minutes north of Isla Mujeres, Isla Contoy (Isle of Birds) is a national wildlife park and bird sanctuary. The tiny island is an unspoiled spot with sand dunes, mangroves, and coconut trees. It's a favorite of bird-watchers, who come to see the 70-plus local species. Climb the observation tower and see the frigate hovering in the wind or watch a patient heron stalking its prey in the mangroves. This is a chance to step back in time and experience this coast when the birds outnumbered humans and the coconut trees outnumbered hotels.

Island Dining

Perhaps it's the fresh air and sunlight that whets the appetite, making the simple Isla meals so delicious. Food on Isla Mujeres is what you would expect on a small island: plenty of fresh fish, shrimp, and grilled lobster. You'll also find pleasant variations on pasta, pizza, steak, and sandwiches. Bright mornings, sweet fruits, fresh coffee, and baked goods make breakfast on Isla a treat as well. Like island life, meals don't need to be complicated.

Fishing

Deep-sea fishing is not a sport for the fainthearted. Big-game fish are the acrobats of the sea and will twist, turn, pull, and jump—fighting to their last breath to escape the hook. The warm currents around Isla attract a variety of big-game fish in spring and early summer and fishermen flock to Isla in search of the grand slam—catching three different species in one outing (most coveted are sailfish, and white and blue marlin). During the rest of the year, you can fish for barracuda and tuna, as well as shad, sailfish, grouper, red snapper, and wahoo.

El Colonia, it turns into Carretera El Garrafón. Smaller street names and other address details don't really matter much here.

Numbers in the text correspond to numbers in the margin and on the Isla Mujeres map.

A Good Tour

The best way to explore the entire island is to take a taxi or rent a moped or golf cart. You can walk to Isla's historic **Cementerio** ❶ ▶ by going northwest from the ferry piers on Avenida López Mateos. Then head southeast (by car or other vehicle) along Avenida Rueda Medina past the piers to reach the Mexican naval base, where you can see flag ceremonies at sunrise and sunset. Just don't take any pictures—it's illegal to photograph military sites in Mexico. Continue southeast; 2½ km (1½ mi) out of town is **Laguna Makax** ❷, on the right.

At the lagoon's southeast end, a dirt road on the left leads to the remains of the **Hacienda Mundaca** ❸. About a block west, where Avenida Rueda Medina splits, is a statue of Ramon Bravo, the first diver to explore the Cave of the Sleeping Sharks. Bravo, who passed away in 1998, was Isla's first environmentalist; he started campaigning to protect the island's natural treasures as early as 1950. He remains a hero to many islanders. If you turn right (northwest) and follow the road for about ½ km (¼ mi), you'll reach Playa Tiburon. If you turn left (southwest), you'll see Playa Lancheros almost immediately. Both are good swimming beaches.

Continue southeast past Playa Lancheros to **El Garrafón National Park** ❹. Slightly more than ½ km (¼ mi) farther along the same road, on the windward side of the tip of Isla Mujeres, is the site of a small Maya ruin, once a temple dedicated to Ixchel, the Santuario Maya a la Diosa Ixchel. Although little remains here, the ocean and bay views are still worth the stop—although you must pay to see them. Follow the paved eastern perimeter road northwest back into town. Known as either the Corredor Panorámico (Panoramic Highway) or Carretera Perimetral al Garrafón (Garrafón Perimeter Highway), this is a scenic drive with a few pull-off areas along the way. This side of the island is quite windy, with strong currents and a rocky shore, so swimming is not recommended. The road curves back into Avenida Rueda Medina near the naval base.

What to See

❶ **El Cementerio.** Isla's unnamed cemetery, with its century-old gravestones, is on Avenida López Mateos, the road that runs parallel to Playa Norte. Many of the tombstones are covered with carved angels and flowers; the most elaborate and beautiful mark the graves of children. Hidden among them is the tomb of the notorious Fermín Mundaca. This 19th-century slave trader—who's often billed more glamorously as a pirate—carved his own skull-and-crossbones gravestone with the ominous epitaph: AS YOU ARE, I ONCE WAS; AS I AM, SO SHALL YOU BE. Mundaca's grave is empty, however; his remains lie in Mérida, where he died. The monument is tough to find—ask a local to point out the unidentified marker.

☺ ❹ **El Garrafón National Park.** Much of the coral reef at this national marine park has died—a result of too many snorkelers—and so the fish have to be bribed with food. There's no longer much for snorkelers here, but the park does have kayaks and ocean playground equipment, as well as a three-floor facility with restaurants, bathrooms, and gift shops. Be prepared to spend big money here. The basic entry fee doesn't include snorkel gear, lockers, or food; the deluxe package is overpriced. Bring a book if you intend to spend a whole day here. (The Garrafón Beach Club next door is a much cheaper alternative; the snorkeling is at least equal to that available in the park.)

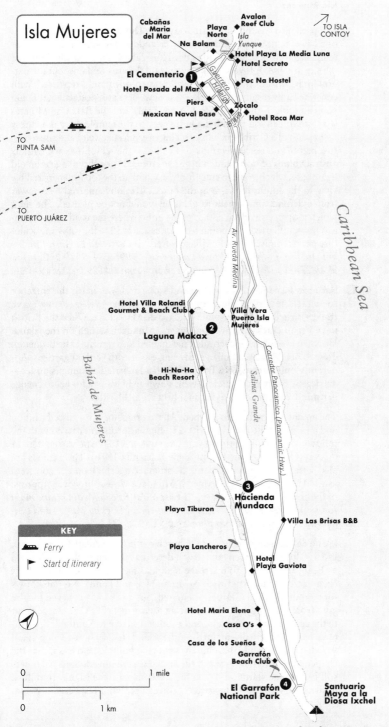

Isla Mujeres

TO ISLA CONTOY

Cabañas Maria del Mar

Avalon Reef Club

Playa Norte

Isla Yunque

Na Balam

Hotel Playa La Media Luna

Hotel Secreto

Greteria Hidalgo

El Cementerio ❶

Poc Na Hostel

Hotel Posada del Mar

Piers

Zócalo

Mexican Naval Base

Hotel Roca Mar

TO PUNTA SAM

TO PUERTO JUÁREZ

Caribbean Sea

Bahía de Mujeres

Av. Rueda Medina

Hotel Villa Rolandi Gourmet & Beach Club

Villa Vera Puerto Isla Mujeres

Laguna Makax ❷

Hi-Na-Ha Beach Resort

Corredor Panorámico (Panoramic Hwy.)

Salina Grande

Hacienda Mundaca ❸

Playa Tiburon

Villa Las Brisas B&B

Playa Lancheros

Hotel Playa Gaviota

Hotel Maria Elena

Casa O's

Casa de los Sueños

Garrafón Beach Club

El Garrafón National Park ❹

Santuario Maya a la Diosa Ixchel

Punta Sur

KEY
🛥 *Ferry*
▶ *Start of itinerary*

0 — 1 mile

0 — 1 km

The park also has the **Santuario Maya a la Diosa Ixchel,** the sad vestiges of a Maya temple once dedicated to the goddess Ixchel. Unsuccessful attempts to restore it were made after Hurricane Gilbert greatly damaged the site in 1988. A lovely walkway around the area remains, but the natural arch beneath the ruin has been blasted open and "repaired" with concrete badly disguised as rocks. The views here are spectacular, though: you can look to the open ocean on one side and the Bahía de Mujeres (Bay of Women) on the other. On the way to the temple there is a cutesy re-creation of a Caribbean village selling overpriced jewelry and souvenirs. Just before you reach the ruins you will pass the sculpture park with its abstract blobs of iron painted in garish colors. Inside the village is an old lighthouse, which you can enter for free. Climb to the top for an incredible view to the south; the vista in the other direction is marred by a tower from a defunct amusement ride. Ixchel would not be pleased. The ruin, which is open daily 9 to 5:30, is at the point where the road turns northeast into the Corredor Panorámico. Admission is $3 to the ruins and sculpture park. Admission to the village is free. ✛ *Carretera El Garrafón, 2½ km (1½ mi) southeast of Playa Lancheros* ☎ *998/884–9420 in Cancún, 998/877–1100 to the park* ⊕ *www.garrafon.com* ☕ *$29* ⊙ *Daily 9–5:30.*

 Hacienda Mundaca. A dirt drive and stone archway mark the entrance to what's left of a mansion constructed by 19th-century slave trader–turned–pirate Fermín Mundaca de Marechaja. When the British navy began cracking down on slavers, Mundaca settled on the island. He fell in love with a local beauty nicknamed La Trigueña (The Brunette). To woo her, Mundaca built a sprawling estate with verdant gardens. Apparently unimpressed, La Trigueña instead married a young islander— and legend has it that Mundaca went slowly mad waiting for her to change her mind. He ended up dying in a brothel in Mérida.

The actual hacienda has vanished. All that remains are a rusted cannon and a ruined stone archway with a triangular pediment carved with the following inscription: HUERTA DE LA HACIENDA DE VISTA ALEGRE MDCC-CLXXVI (Orchard of the Happy View Hacienda 1876). The gardens are also suffering from neglect, and the animals in a small on-site zoo seem as tired as the rest of the property. Mundaca would, however, approve of the cover charge; it's piracy. ⊠ *East of Av. Rueda Medina (take main road southeast from town to S-curve at end of Laguna Makax and turn left onto dirt road)* ☎ *No phone* ☕ *$2.50* ⊙ *Daily 9 AM–dusk.*

Iglesia de Concepion Inmaculada (Church of the Immaculate Conception). In 1890 local fishermen landed at a deserted colonial settlement known as Ecab, where they found three identical statues of the Virgin Mary, each carved from wood with porcelain face and hands. No one knows for certain where the statues originated, but it is widely believed they're gifts from the conquistadores during a visit in 1770. One statue went to the city of Izamal, Yucatán, and another was sent to Kantunikin, Quintana Roo. The third remained on the island. It was housed in a small wooden chapel while this church was being built; legend has it that the chapel burst into flames when the statue was removed. Some islanders still believe the statue walks on the water around the island from dusk until dawn, looking for her sisters. You can pay your respects daily from

10 AM until 11:30 AM and then from 7 PM until 9 PM. ☒ *Avs. Morelos and Bravo, south side of zócalo.*

❷ **Laguna Makax.** Pirates are said to have anchored their ships in this lagoon while waiting to ambush hapless vessels crossing the Spanish Main (the geographical area in which Spanish treasure ships trafficked). These days the lagoon houses a local shipyard and provides a safe harbor for boats during hurricane season. It's off Avenida Rueda Medina about 2½ km (1½ mi) south of town, across the street from a Mexican naval base and some *salinas* (salt marshes).

☪ **El Malecón.** To enjoy the drama of Isla's eastern shore while soaking up some rays, stroll along this mile-long boardwalk. It's the beginning of a long-term improvement project and will eventually encircle the island. Currently, it runs from Half Moon Bay to El Colonia, with several benches and look-out points. You can visit El Monumento de Tortugas (Turtle Monument) along the way.

BEACHES

Playa Norte is easy to find: simply head north on any of the north–south streets in town until you hit this superb beach. The turquoise sea is as calm as a lake here, and you can wade out for 40 yards in waist-deep water. According to isleños, Hurricane Gilbert's only good deed was to widen this and other leeward-side beaches by blowing sand over from Cancún. Enjoy a drink and a snack at one of the area's palapa bars; Buho's is especially popular with locals and tourists who gather to chat, eat fresh seafood, drink cold beer, and watch the sunset. Tarzan Water Sports rents out snorkeling gear, Jet Skis, floats, and sailboards. Seafriends offers snorkeling classes and kayaks. Several outfits also rent out lounge chairs and umbrellas for about $10 per day.

There are two beaches between Laguna Makax and El Garrafón National Park. **Playa Lancheros** is a popular spot with an open-air restaurant where locals gather to eat freshly grilled fish. The beach has grittier sand than Playa Norte, but more palm trees. The calm water makes it the perfect spot for children to swim—although it's best if they stay close to shore, since the ocean floor drops off steeply. The souvenir stands here are fairly low key and run by local families. There is a small pen with domesticated and quite harmless *tiburones gatos*—nurse sharks. (These sharks are tamer than the *tintoreras,* or blue sharks, which live in the open seas, have seven rows of teeth, and weigh up to 1,100 lbs.) You can swim with them or get your picture taken for $1. **Playa Tiburon,** like Playa Lancheros, is on the west coast facing Bahía de Mujeres, and so its waters are also exceptionally calm. It's a more developed beach with a large, popular seafood restaurant (through which you actually enter the beach). There are several souvenir stands selling the usual T-shirts as well as handmade seashell jewelry. On certain days there are women who will braid your hair or give you a temporary henna tattoo. This beach also has two sea pens with the sleepy and relatively tame nurse sharks. You can have a low-key and very safe swim with these sharks—and get your picture taken doing so—for $2.

WHERE TO EAT

Dining on Isla is a casual affair. Restaurants tend to serve simple meals: seafood, pizza, salads, and Mexican dishes, mostly prepared by local cooks. Fresh ingredients and hospitable waiters make up for the island's lack of elaborate menus and master chefs.

Locals often eat their main meal during siesta hours, between 1 and 4, and then have a light dinner in the evening. Unless otherwise stated, restaurants are open daily for lunch and dinner. Some restaurants open late and close early Sunday; others are closed Monday. Most restaurants welcome children and will cater to their tastes.

Prices

	WHAT IT COSTS In Dollars				
	$$$$	$$$	$$	$	¢
AT DINNER	over $25	$15–$25	$10–$15	$5–$10	under $5

Per person, for a main course at dinner, excluding tax and tip.

What to Wear

Generally, restaurants on the island are informal, though shirts and shoes are required in most indoor dining rooms. Some, but not all, outdoor terraces and palapas request that swimsuits and feet be covered.

El Pueblo

$–$$$ ✕ **Mamacita.** Although it's run by an English chef, the menu at this casual restaurant is full of popular Mexican dishes such as burritos, fajitas, and tacos; there are also excellent vegetarian choices and daily specials. Everything is served fresh, so expect to wait while it's being prepared. ⊠ *Av. Matamoros 19A, at Av. Hidalgo* ☎ *No phone* ▭ *D, MC, V.*

$–$$$ ✕ **Rolandi's Pizzeria.** It serves consistently good pizzas, calzones, and pastas. The grilled fresh fish and shrimp are also recommended, and so is the garlic bread—a puffed pita oozing butter and garlic. It's a friendly, casual spot in the heart of downtown, the perfect stop for a drink and some people-watching. ⊠ *Av. Hidalgo 110, between Avs. Francisco Madero and Abasolo* ☎ *998/877–0430* ▭ *AE, D, MC, V.*

$–$$$ ✕ **Velazquez.** This family-owned restaurant on the beach is open until dusk and serves the island's freshest seafood. You haven't eaten Yucatecan until you've tried the regional specialty *tikinchic* (fish marinated in a sour-orange sauce and chile paste then cooked in a banana leaf over an open flame). Feasting on fish while you sit outside and watch the boats go by is the true Isla experience. ⊠ *Av. Rueda Medina, 2 blocks northwest of ferry docks* ☎ *No phone* ▭ *No credit cards.*

$–$$$ ✕ **Zazil Ha.** This consistently good restaurant serves both vegetarian and traditional Mexican dishes. You can dine downstairs under the trees or upstairs under a palapa roof. Enjoy fresh couscous with vegetables, stuffed red peppers with polenta, or grapefruit and avocado salad. The breakfast menu includes Mexican egg dishes, beans, tortillas, and other choices. ⊠ *Na Balam hotel, Calle Zazil-Ha 118* ☎ *998/877–0279* ⊟ *AE, MC, V.*

$–$$ ✕ **Bamboo.** This fusion restaurant serves excellent Thai food as well as Mexican classics. Enjoy the spring rolls, chicken skewers in a spicy peanut sauce, or a thick grilled steak. The beer is *super* cold. Locals like to hang out here in the evenings. ⊠ *Av. Hidalgo 12A, between Avs. Mateos and Guerrero* ☎ *No phone* ⊟ *No credit cards.*

$–$$ ✕ **Fayne's.** This funky restaurant serves delicious island fare such as garlic shrimp, stuffed calamari, and grilled fish. There's also a well-stocked bar with an aquarium and an art gallery upstairs. ⊠ *Av. Hidalgo 12A, between Avs. Mateos and Guerrero* ☎ *No phone* ⊟ *No credit cards.*

$–$$ ✕ **Jax Bar & Grill/Jax Upstairs Lounge.** Downstairs this palapa-roof restaurant is a lively sports bar with cold beer, bar food, and satellite TV. Upstairs in the lounge, things are even more laid back. Enjoy fresh sushi and seafood while listening to smooth jazz and blues. ⊠ *Av. Adolfo Mateos 42* ☎ *998/887—1218* ⊟ *MC, V.*

$ ✕ **Amigos Pizza.** The place for the pizza connoisseur, Amigos serves classic combinations with some interesting twists (for example, some pizzas are topped with shrimp). Pick your favorite from 14 varieties, or opt for one of several pasta dishes. There's also a simple but satisfying breakfast menu. ⊠ *Av. Hidalgo between Avs. Matamoros and Abasolo* ☎ *No phone* ⊟ *No credit cards.*

¢–$ ✕ **Angelo.** Stop here for fresh pasta prepared by an Italian expat. Try the Gorgonzola pasta with four different cheeses, the ravioli stuffed with cheese, or the tomato penne. It will be hard to choose just one dish; they're all delicious. ⊠ *Av. Hidalgo 12A, between Avs. Mateos and Guerrero* ☎ *No phone* ⊟ *No credit cards.*

¢–$ ✕ **Café Cito.** Blue-and-white shells decorate tabletops, photos and watercolors line the walls, and wind chimes dangle from the rafters. Breakfast choices include fresh waffles, fruit-filled crepes, and egg dishes, as well as great cappuccino and espresso. The chef whips up different lunch specials daily. Afterward, you can go next door for a tarot reading with Sabrina. ⊠ *Avs. Juárez and Matamoros* ☎ *998/877–0438* ⊟ *No credit cards.*

¢–$ ✕ **Café El Nopalito.** The eggs are done to perfection, the coffee is aromatic, the bread is homemade, and the juices are fresh. You can also indulge in French toast, yogurt, and granola. There's no need to rush; you can sit for a while and chat with owner Anneliese Warren, or drop into the crafts store next door. ⊠ *Av. Guerrero 17* ☎ *998/877–0555* ⊟ *No credit cards* ⊗ *No dinner.*

¢–$ ✕ **La Cazuela M&J.** At this eatery next to the Hotel Roca Mar, the Caribbean is the backdrop for terrific food. Breakfast choices include fresh juice, fruit, crepes, and omelets. Or try La Cazuela, the specialty created by chef-owner Marco Fraga; it's somewhere between an omelet and a soufflé. Grilled chicken with homemade barbecue sauce and thick juicy hamburgers are on the lunch menu. ⊠ *Calle Nicolas Bravo, Zona Maritima* ☎☎ *998/ 877–0101* ⊟ *No credit cards* ⊗ *Closed Mon. No dinner.*

¢–$ ✕ **Don Chepo.** Mexican grill cuisine (tacos, fajitas, and steak) is offered in this lively restaurant. The *arracera* is a fine cut of meat that's grilled and served with rice, salad, baked potato, warm tortillas, and beans.

The service is good, and the beer is cold. ⊠ *Avs. Hidalgo and Francisco Madero* ☎ *No phone* ▭ *MC, V.*

¢–$ ✕ **Fredy's Restaurant & Bar.** This friendly, family-run restaurant specializes in simple fish, seafood, and traditional Mexican dishes. Everything is fresh, the bar is well stocked, and occasionally there's live music. ⊠ *Av. Hidalgo just below Av. Mateos* ☎ *998/810–1691* ▭ *No credit cards.*

¢–$ ✕ **Loncheria Poc-chuc El Original.** Specialties at this family-owned spot include such traditional Yucatecan dishes as *panuchos* (a type of open-face tortilla with beans and chicken) as well as fish tacos and other Mexican fare. Sandwiches are also available, and you can order two beers for the price of one all day. ⊠ *Avs. Juárez and Abasolo* ☎ *No phone* ▭ *No credit cards.*

¢–$ ✕ **Taquería.** For delicious Yucatecan specialties—*sabutes* (fried corn tortillas smothered in chicken and salsa), *tortas* (sandwiches), panuchos, or tamales—check out this hole-in-the-wall eatery. The two sisters who do the cooking don't speak English but can communicate using sign language. ⊠ *Av. Juárez, 1 block south of cemetery* ☎ *No phone* ▭ *No credit cards.*

¢ ✕ **Los Aluxes Cafe.** Enjoy an early-morning or late-night cappuccino or espresso with a freshly baked dessert. Linger at a café table or get your java to go. The prices here are *cheap.* ⊠ *Av. Matamoros 87* ☎ *No phone* ▭ *No credit cards.*

¢ ✕ **Aqui Estoy.** The substantial pizzas here have thick crusts and are smothered in cheese and fresh vegetables or pepperoni. For dessert, try a slice of apple pie. It's a great place for a quick and filling snack for a few dollars. ⊠ *Av. Matamoros 85* ☎ *No phone* ▭ *No credit cards.*

Elsewhere on the Island

★ $$–$$$$ ✕ **Casa Rolandi.** Of the many delicious items on the northern Italian menu, the carpaccio *di tonno alla Giorgio* (thin slices of tuna with extra-virgin olive oil and lime juice) is particularly good, as are the lasagna and shrimp-filled black ravioli. The restaurant extends out to an open-air deck over the beach; the sunset views are spectacular. ⊠ *Hotel Villa Rolandi Gourmet & Beach Club, Fracc. Laguna Mar Makax, Sm 7* ☎ *998/877–0100* ▭ *AE, D, MC, V.*

$–$$$ ✕ **Casa O's.** The entrance to this casual yet stylish restaurant crosses a
Fodor'sChoice   small stream and down to a three-tiered circular dining room overlooking
★   the bay. Enjoy the sunset while dining on excellent fresh snapper or grouper or on fresh lobster chosen from the on-site pond. The Black Angus steaks will satisfy your beef cravings; the roasted lamb is equally delicious. Be sure to try the incredible key lime pie. The restaurant is named for its waiters—all their names end in the letter "o." ⊠ *Carretera El Garrafón s/n* ☎ *998/888–0170* ▭ *MC, V.*

WHERE TO STAY

Hotels focus on providing a relaxed, tranquil beach vacation. Many have simple rooms, usually with ceiling fans, and some have air-conditioning, but few have TVs or phones. Generally, modest budget hotels can be found in town, while the more expensive resorts are around Punta

Where to Stay
& Eat in El Pueblo

TO
ISLA YUNQUE

Carlos Lazo

Av. Vicente Guerrero

Av. Hidalgo

Av. Matamoros

Av. Abasolo

Av. Madero

Av. Benito Juárez

Av. Mateos

Av. Morelos

Av. Bravo

Av. Rueda Medina

Caribbean Sea

Malecón

Iglesia de la
Concepcion
Inmaculada

Ferry
Terminal

0   300 yards
0   300 meters

Norte or the peninsula near the lagoon. Local travel agents can provide information about luxury condos and residential homes for rent—an excellent option if you're planning a long stay.

Prices

	WHAT IT COSTS In Dollars				
	$$$$	$$$	$$	$	¢
FOR 2 PEOPLE	over $250	$150–$250	$75–$150	$50–$75	under $50

All prices are for a standard double room in high season, based on the European Plan (EP) and excluding service and 12% tax (10% Value Added Tax plus 2% hospitality tax).

El Pueblo

$$$$ 🏨 **Avalon Reef Club.** This gorgeous all-inclusive is on a tiny island at the northern tip of Isla Mujeres. Regular rooms in the hotel tower are small without balconies, but the seaside suites have balconies with extraordinary ocean views. Be warned: this is a time-share resort and preference for reservations is given to those who bought into its "Paradise Found" program. Sales pitches are relentless, but if you can be stalwart in your refusal, you may be able to enjoy this lovely hotel. ⊠ *Calle Zacil-Ha s/n, Isla Yunque, 77400* ☎ *998/999–2050 or 888/497–4325* 🖷 *998/ 999–2052* ⊕ *www.avalonresorts.net* ⇔ *83 rooms, 6 suites, 55 villas* ♨ *Restaurant, some in-room hot tubs, some kitchenettes, cable TV, pool, gym, beach, car rental* ⊟ *AE, D, MC, V* |⊙| *AI.*

$$$–$$$$ 🏨 **Na Balam.** Each room in the main building has a thatched palapa roof, **Fodor'sChoice** Mexican folk art, a large bathroom, an eating area, and a spacious bal-★ cony or patio facing the ocean. The beach here is private, with its own bar serving snacks and drinks. Across the street are eight more spacious rooms surrounding a pool, a garden, and a meditation room where yoga classes are held. ⊠ *Calle Zacil-Ha 118, 77400* ☎ *998/877–0279* 🖷 *998/ 877–0446* ⊕ *www.nabalam.com* ⇔ *31 rooms* ♨ *Restaurant, pool, beach, bar; no room phones, no room TVs* ⊟ *AE, MC, V.*

★ $$$ 🏨 **Hotel Secreto.** It's airy, modern, and intimate. It's also not such a secret anymore, so reserve far in advance. All rooms have floor-to-ceiling windows, veiled king-size four-poster beds, and balconies overlooking Half Moon Bay. Mexican artwork really pops out from predominantly white backdrops. The cozy dining room is alongside a small ocean-side pool. ⊠ *Sección Rocas, Lote 11, Half Moon Bay, 77400* ☎ *998/877– 1039* 🖷 *998/877–1048* ⊕ *www.hotelsecreto.com* ⇔ *9 rooms* ♨ *Restaurant, pool, bar; no a/c, no room phones, no room TVs* ⊟ *AE, MC, V* |⊙| *CP.*

$$ 🏨 **Cabañas María del Mar.** One of Playa Norte's first hotels has rooms on the beach in a three-story tower, rooms in thatch-roofed cabañas by the pool, and rooms facing the street and restaurant in a three-story "castle." Each accommodation has merits; when making reservations ask for specifics on features and amenities. Locals favor the restaurant-bar, Buho's, for drinks and moderately priced meals. The hotel also rents mopeds and golf carts. ⊠ *Av. Arq. Carlos Lazo 1, 77400* ☎ *998/877– 0179* 🖷 *998/877–0213* ⊕ *www.cabanasdelmar.com* ⇔ *24 tower rooms,*

31 cabaña rooms, 18 castle rooms ⚐ Restaurant, refrigerators, 2 pools, beach, video game room ☰ MC, V ⦿ CP.

$$ ⊞ **Hotel Playa la Media Luna.** This breezy three-story bed-and-breakfast is on Half Moon Beach, just south of Playa Norte. All 18 guest rooms are done in soft pastel colors with king-size beds and balconies or terraces that look out onto the ocean and pool. Thatch roofs and wooden walkways give the place a castaway feel. Breakfast is served in a sunny dining room. The hotel also offers small, clean, but spartan rooms with no view for $25 per night. ⊠ *Sección Rocas, Punta Norte, 77400* ☎ *998/877–0759* 🖷 *998/877–1124* ⊕ *www.playamedialuna.com* ⤴ *18 rooms ⚐ Dining room, pool, beach; no room phones ☰ AE, MC, V ⦿ CP.*

$–$$ ⊞ **Casa Isleño II Apartments.** These fully equipped apartments are just minutes from the main pier and downtown, yet private and quiet. Each has a full kitchen, small sitting area, king-size bed, and hammock—perfect for setting up a home base. ⊠ *Av. Guerrero Norte 3A, 77400* 🖷🖷 *998/877–70265* ⊕ *www.isla-mujeres.net/casaisleno/home.htm* ⤴ *3 apartments ⚐ Kitchenettes, microwaves; no room phones, no room TVs ☰ No credit cards.*

$–$$ ⊞ **Hotel Roca Mar.** You can smell, hear, and see the ocean from the simply furnished guest rooms of this quintessential beach hotel. The courtyard—filled with plants, birds, and benches—overlooks the ocean, too. ⊠ *Calle Nicolas Bravo, Zona Maritima, 77400* 🖷🖷 *998/877–0101* ⊕ *http://mjmnet.net/hotelrocamar/home.htm* ⤴ *31 rooms ⚐ Restaurant, fans, pool, beach, snorkeling; no a/c in some rooms, no room phones, no room TVs ☰ AE, MC, V.*

$ ⊞ **Hotel Frances Arlene.** This small hotel is a perennial favorite with visitors. The Magaña family takes great care to maintain the property—signs everywhere remind you of the rules. Rooms surround a pleasant courtyard and are outfitted with double beds, bamboo furniture, and refrigerators. Some have kitchenettes. The beach and downtown are a short stroll away. ⊠ *Av. Guerrero 7, 77400* 🖷🖷 *998/877–0310* ⤴ *11 rooms ⚐ Fans, some kitchenettes, refrigerators ☰ MC, V.*

$ ⊞ **Hotel Posada del Mar.** Rooms in this venerable hotel are fresh and clean. Stone archways by the pool frame the water and gardens. The restaurant faces Playa Norte; shops and restaurants are a short walk away. ⊠ *Av. Rueda Medina 15A, 77400* ☎ *998/877–0770* 🖷 *998/877–0266* ⊕ *www.posadadelmar.com* ⤴ *42 rooms ⚐ Restaurant, pool ☰ AE, D, MC, V.*

¢–$ ⊞ **Hotel Belmar.** Rooms are cozy with comfortable beds, excellent showers, and views of downtown. Front rooms have terraces that open up onto the main street where you can watch all the action. Ask for a back room for more tranquillity. Room service is direct from the Pizza Rolandi restaurant just downstairs. ⊠ *Av. Hidalgo Norte 110, between Avs. Madero and Abasolo, 77400* ☎ *998/877–0430* 🖷 *998/977–0429* ⊕ *www.rolandi.com* ⤴ *12 rooms ⚐ Room service, fans, laundry service, cable TV ☰ MC, V.*

¢ ⊞ **Hotel Carmelina.** With its bright purple doors and window frames, this three-story budget hotel is hard to miss. Its renovated rooms have bathrooms and comfortable double beds. Third-floor rooms have excellent views. ⊠ *Avs. Juárez and Francisco Madero, 77400* ☎ *998/877–0006* ⤴ *25 rooms ⚐ Fans; no room phones ☰ No credit cards.*

¢ ⊞ **Hotel Xul-Ha.** It's a heart-of-town hotel that's just steps away from all the nightlife. Rooms are basic but clean and comfortable, with two double beds, private bathrooms, and ceiling fans. There is a small garden on-site. ⊠ *Av. Hidalgo 23, 77400* ☎ *998/877–0075* ⤴ *12 rooms* ⚲ *Fans; no a/c, no room phones, no room TVs* ⊟ *No credit cards.*

¢ ⊞ **Poc-Na.** The island's co-ed youth hostel is one of El Pueblo's best deals. Poc-Na has hammocks and mattresses in a dormitory. Proximity to Playa Norte and shops, restaurants, and bars is a bonus for young travelers. ⊠ *Av. Matamoros 15, 77400* ☎ *998/877–0090 or 998/877–0059* ⊕ *www.hostels.com/en/mx.ot.html* ⤴ *14 beds* ⚲ *Dining room, Internet; no a/c, no room phones, no room TVs* ⊟ *No credit cards.*

¢ ⊞ **Posada Isla Mujeres.** Rooms at this small hotel, which is near many restaurants and bars, are basic but clean and comfortable. ⊠ *Av. Juárez 14, between Avs. Abasolo and Francisco Madero, 77400* ☎ *No phone* ⤴ *15 rooms* ⚲ *Fans; no a/c, no room phones, no room TVs* ⊟ *No credit cards.*

¢ ⊞ **Roca Teliz.** This hotel is tucked away behind a small souvenir store. Its six rooms open onto a central courtyard; all have two double beds and local Mexican crafts ⊠ *Av. Hidalgo 93, 77400* ☎☎ *998/877–0101* ⤴ *6 rooms* ⚲ *Fans; no a/c, no room phones* ⊟ *No credit cards.*

Elsewhere on the Island

$$$$ ⊞ **La Casa de los Sueños.** What started out as a B&B is now a high-end spa and meditation center. A large interior courtyard leads to a sunken, open-air lounge area done in sunset colors; this, in turn, extends to a terrace with a cliff-side swimming pool overlooking the ocean. Each room has unique crafts and artwork from all over Mexico. Spa treatments include massages, body wraps, and facials. The restaurant serves dishes that fuse Asian and Mexican flavors. ⊠ *Carretera El Garrafón, 77400* ☎ *998/ 877–0651 or 800/551–2558* ☐ *998/877–0708* ⊕ *No web* ⤴ *9 rooms* ⚲ *Dining room, fans, pool, beach, dock, snorkeling, boating, bicycles; no a/c, no room phones, no room TVs, no kids, no smoking* ⊟ *AE, MC, V.*

$$$$ ⊞ **Hotel Villa Rolandi Gourmet & Beach Club.** A private yacht delivers you from Cancún's Embarcadero Marina to this property. Each of its elegant, brightly colored suites has an ocean view, a king-size bed, and a sitting area that leads to a balcony with a heated whirlpool bath. Showers have *six* adjustable heads and can be converted into saunas. Both the Casa Rolandi restaurant and the garden pool overlook the Bahía de Mujeres; a path leads down to an intimate beach. ⊠ *Fracc. Laguna Mar Makax, 77400* ☎ *998/877–0700 or 998/877–0500* ☐ *998/877–0100* ⊕ *www.rolandi.com* ⤴ *20 suites* ⚲ *Restaurant, in-room hot tubs, cable TV, pool, gym, spa, beach, dock, boating; no kids under 13, no smoking* ⊟ *AE, MC, V* ⦿ *MAP.*

$$$$ ⊞ **Villa Vera Puerto Isla Mujeres.** Yachties love this hideaway. Rooms are awash in rose and blue and have cozy seating areas. The large pool, which has a fountain and swim-up bar, is surrounded by a garden and lawn. Paths lead to the dock and the lagoon, where a shuttle boat ferries you to a beach club that faces Cancún. Families are warmly welcomed. ⊠ *Puerto de Abrigo, Laguna Makax, 77400* ☎ *998/287–3340 or 800/ 508–7923* ⊕ *www.puertoislamujeres.com* ⤴ *17 suites, 4 villas* ⚲ *Restau-*

rant, in-room hot tubs, some kitchenettes, cable TV, in-room VCRs, 3 pools, beach, marina ☰ *AE, MC, V* ⑩ *CP.*

$$–$$$ ⊞ **Hi-Na-Ha Beach Resort.** This intimate hotel, facing the Bahía de Mujeres with the Laguna Makax at the back, is arranged like a luxurious home. Suites have queen-size beds; villas have two bedrooms, fully equipped kitchens, dining rooms, and gorgeous furniture. All have ocean-view balconies. Cable television is available upon request for an additional charge. With its lovely garden, pool, restaurant, and dock, this is a perfect family retreat. ✉ *Fracc. Laguna Mar Makax, Sm 7, Mz 75, 77400* ☎ *998/877–0615* ⊕ *www.villashinaha.com* ⌕ *10 suites, 2 villas* ♨ *Restaurant, fans, kitchenettes, massage, beach, boating, bar; no room phones, no room TVs* ☰ *MC, V.*

$$ ⊞ **Villa Las Brisas B&B.** The ocean views are dramatic from this romantic eastern-coast hideaway. Rooms have king-size beds, hammocks, conch-head showers, ceiling fans, and refrigerators. A restaurant and a small pool are on-site. It's a bit of a jaunt to downtown, but the hotel can arrange for a taxi or a golf-cart rental for you. ✉ *Carretera Perimetral al Garrafón, 77400* ☎ *998/888–0342* ⊕ *www.villalasbrisas.com* ⌕ *6 rooms* ♨ *Fans, refrigerators; no a/c, no room phones, no room TVs* ☰ *MC, V* ⑩ *CP.*

$ ⊞ **Playa Gaviota.** The real plus at this hilltop hotel is the beach, with its barbecue area, palapas, and gorgeous sunset views. Each blue-and-white suite has a kitchenette, two queen-size beds, a small dining area, and a large terrace facing the ocean. There are also smaller and older (but still comfortable) cabins on the beach. The owners, a quiet Mexican family, live on-site. ✉ *Carretera El Garrafón, Km 4.5, 77400* ☎ *998/877–0216* ⊕ *www.lostoasis.net/gaviota.htm* ⌕ *10 suites, 3 cabins* ♨ *Fans, kitchenettes, beach, cable TV; no room phones* ☰ *No credit cards* ⑩ *CP.*

¢–$ ⊞ **Hotel & Beach Club Garrafón de Castilla.** The snorkeling at the beach club of this small family-owned hotel is better than what you're likely to experience at El Garrafón National Park next door. In addition, the beach here is bigger, with easy water access. Rooms have double beds and balconies overlooking the water; some have refrigerators. Decorations are minimal, but the overall effect is bright, cheery, and comfortable. ✉ *Carretera Punta Sur, Km 6, 77400* ☎ *998/877–0107* 🖷 *998/877–0508* ⊕ *www.isla-mujeres.net/castilla/home.htm* ⌕ *14 rooms* ♨ *Snack bar, minibars, some refrigerators, beach, dive shop, snorkeling; no room phones, no room TVs* ☰ *MC, V.*

¢ ⊞ **Hotel Maria Elena.** Rooms are bright and cheery in this south-end hotel. All have king-size beds and balconies overlooking the bay. There's also a small garden and a deck. ✉ *Carretera El Garrafón, Km 5.5, 77400* ☎ *998/888–0471* ⌕ *28 rooms* ♨ *Fans; no room phones* ☰ *No credit cards.*

NIGHTLIFE & THE ARTS

Nightlife

Isla has developed a healthy nightlife with a variety of clubs from which to choose. **La Adelita** (✉ Av. Hidalgo Norte 12A ☎ No phone) is a popular gathering spot for enjoying local music while trying out a variety of tequila and cigars. **Buho's** (⊠ Cabañas María del Mar, Av. Arq. Carlos Lazo 1 ☎ 998/877–1479) remains the favorite restaurant on Playa Norte for a relaxing sunset drink. There is a small bar and a large television at **Chiles Loco** (⊠ Av. Hidalgo 81, Local A4 ☎ No phone). **Jax Bar & Grill** (⊠ Av. Adolfo Mateos 42, near the lighthouse ☎ 998/887–1218) has live music, cold beer, good bar food, and satellite TV with ESPN.

Dance the night away with the locals at **Nitrox** (⊠ Av. Matamoros 87, ☎ No phone). Wednesday night is salsa night and the weekend is a blend of disco, techno, and house. Equally relaxing is **Las Palapas Beach Bar** (⊠ Playa Norte at Av. Hidalgo ☎ No phone) where the beer is cold and the scenery stunning. **La Peña** (⊠ Calle Nicolas Bravo, Zona Maritima ☎ 998/845–7384) is just across from the main square and has a lovely terrace bar that faces the eastern shore. They serve a variety of sinful cocktails and great music. **El Sombrero de Gomar** (⊠ Av. Hidalgo 5 ☎ 998/877–0627) has a bar well stocked with beer and tequila; its central location makes it a perfect spot for people-watching.

The Arts

The island celebrates many religious holidays and festivals in El Pueblo's zócalo, usually with live entertainment. Carnival, held annually in February, is spectacular fun. Other popular events include the springtime regattas and fishing tournaments. Founding Day, August 17, marks the island's official founding by the Mexican government. Isla's cemetery is among the best places to mark the Día de los Muertos (Day of the Dead) on November 1. Families decorate the graves of loved ones with marigolds and their favorite objects from life, then hold all-night vigils to commemorate their lost loved ones.

Casa de la Cultura (⊠ Av. Guerrero ☎ 998/877–0639) has art, drama, yoga, and folkloric-dance classes year-round. It's open Monday–Saturday 9–1 and 4–8.

SPORTS & THE OUTDOORS

Boating

Puerto Isla Mujeres (⊠ Puerto de Abrigo, Laguna Makax ☎ 998/877–0330 ⊕ www.puerto-isla.co) is a full-service marina for vessels up to 170 feet. Services include mooring, a fuel station, a 150-ton lift, customs assistance, hookups, 24-hour security, laundry and cleaning services, and boatyard services. If you prefer to sleep on land, the Villa Vera Puerto Isla Mujeres resort is steps away from the docks. The shallow waters of Playa Norte make it a pleasant place to kayak. You can rent kayaks—as well as sailboats and paddleboats starting at $20 for the day—from **Tarzan Water Sports** located in the middle of Playa Norte.

Fishing

Captain Anthony Mendillo Jr. (⊠ Av. Arq. Carlos Lazo 1 ☎ 998/877–0213) provides specialized fishing trips aboard his 29-foot vessel, the *Keen M*. **Sea Hawk Divers** (⊠ Av. Arq. Carlos Lazo ☎ 998/877–0296) runs fishing trips—for barracuda, snapper, and smaller fish—that start at $200 for a half day. The **Sociedad Cooperativa Turistica** (☎ 998/

IN SEARCH OF THE DEAD

EL DÍA DE LOS MUERTOS (the Day of the Dead) is often billed as "Mexican Halloween," but it's much more than that. The festival, which takes place October 31 through November 2, is a hybrid of pre-Hispanic and Christian beliefs that honors the cyclical nature of life and death. Local celebrations are as varied as they are dynamic, often laced with warm tributes and dark humor.

To honor departed loved ones at this time of year, families and friends create ofrendas, altars adorned with photos, flowers, candles, liquor, and other items whose colors, smells, and potent nostalgia are meant to lure their spirits back for a family reunion. The favorite foods of the deceased are also included, prepared extra spicy so that the souls can absorb the essence of these offerings. Although the ofrendas and the colorful calaveritas (skeletons made from sugar that are a treat for Mexican children) are common

everywhere, the holiday is observed in so many ways that a definition of it depends entirely on what part of Mexico you visit.

In a sandy Isla Mujeres cemetery, Marta, a middle-age woman wearing a tidy pantsuit and stylish sunglasses, rests on a fanciful tomb in the late-afternoon sun. "She is my sister," Marta says, motioning toward the teal-and-blue tomb. "I painted this today." She exudes no melancholy; rather she's smiling, happy to be spending the day with her sibling.

Nearby, Juan puts the final touches—vases made from shells he's collected—on his father's colorful tomb. A glass box holds a red candle and a statue of the Virgin Mary, her outstretched arms pressing against the glass as if trying to escape the flame. "This is all for him," Juan says, motioning to his masterpiece, "because he is a good man."

— David Downing

877–0239) provides four hours of fishing close to shore for $100; eight hours farther out is $240.

Snorkeling & Scuba Diving

DIVE SITES Most area dive spots are also described in detail in *Dive Mexico* magazine, which is available in many local shops. The coral reefs at El Garrafón National Park have suffered tremendously because of human negligence, boats dropping their anchors (now an outlawed practice), and the effects of Hurricane Gilbert in 1988. Some good snorkeling can be had near Playa Norte on the north end.

Isla is a good place for learning to dive, since the snorkeling is close to shore. Offshore, there's excellent diving and snorkeling at Xlaches (pronounced *ees*-lah-chayss) reef, due north on the way to Isla Contoy. One of Contoy's most alluring dives is the Cave of the Sleeping Sharks, east of the northern tip. The cave was discovered by an island fisherman known as Vulvula and extensively explored by Ramon Bravo, a local diver, cinematographer, and Mexico's foremost expert on sharks. The cave is a fascinating 150-foot dive for experienced divers only.

CloseUp
SHHH . . . DON'T WAKE THE SHARKS

THE UNDERWATER CAVERNS off Isla Mujeres attract a dangerous species of shark—though nobody knows exactly why. Stranger still, once the sharks swim into the caves they enter a state of relaxed nonaggression seen nowhere else. Naturalists have two explanations, both involving the composition of the water inside the caves—it contains more oxygen, more carbon dioxide, and less salt. According to the first theory, the decreased salinity causes the parasites that plague sharks to loosen their grip, allowing the remora fish (the sharks' personal vacuum cleaner) to eat the parasites more easily. Perhaps the sharks relax in order to facilitate the cleaning, or maybe their deep state of relaxation is a side effect of having been scrubbed clean.

Another theory is that the caves' combination of fresh- and saltwater may produce euphoria, similar to the effect scuba divers experience on extremely deep dives. Whatever the sharks experience while "sleeping" in the caves, they pay a heavy price for it: a swimming shark breathes automatically and without effort (water is forced through the gills as the shark swims), but a stationary shark must laboriously pump water to continue breathing. If you dive in the Cave of the Sleeping Sharks, be cautious: many are reef sharks, the species responsible for the largest number of attacks on humans. Dive with a reliable guide and be on your best diving behavior.

At 30 feet to 40 feet deep and 3,300 feet off the southwestern coast, the coral reef known as Los Manchones is a good dive site. During the summer of 1994, an ecology group hoping to divert divers and snorkelers from El Garrafón commissioned the creation of a 1-ton, 9¾-foot bronze cross, which was sunk here. Named the Cruz de la Bahía (Cross of the Bay), it's a tribute to everyone who has died at sea. Another option is the Barco L-55 and C-58 dive, which takes in sunken World War II boats just 20 minutes off the coast of Isla.

DIVE SHOPS The PADI-affiliated **Coral Scuba Dive Center** (⊠ Av. Matamoros 13A ☎ 998/877–0763) sells two-tank dives ($60), shipwreck dives, and snorkel trips. **Mundaca Divers** (⊠ Av. Francisco Madero 10 ☎ 998/877–0607) has a good reputation with professional divers and employs a PADI instructor. A two-tank dive costs $60.

Sea Hawk Divers (⊠ Av. Arq. Carlos Lazo ☎ 998/877–0296) runs dive ($55 for two tanks) and snorkel trips, has a PADI instructor, and will also set up accommodations for divers in pleasant rooms starting at $45 per day during low season, $65 during high. **Seafriends** (⊠ Playa Norte ☎ No phone) is a small cooperative dive operation that runs dives ($55 for two tanks); the PADI introduction course is available for $65.

SHOPPING

Aside from seashell art and jewelry, Isla produces few local crafts. The streets are filled with souvenir shops selling T-shirts, garish ceramics, and seashells glued onto a variety of objects. But amidst all the junk, you may find good Mexican folk art, hammocks, textiles, and silver jewelry. Most stores are small family operations that don't take credit cards, but everyone gladly accepts American dollars. Stores that do take credit cards sometimes tack on a fee to offset the commission they must pay. Hours are generally Monday–Saturday 10–1 and 4–7, although many stores stay open during siesta hours (1–4).

Books

Cosmic Cosas (⊠ Av. Matamoros 82 ☎ 998/877–0806) is the island's only English-language bookstore. The friendly shop offers two-for-one book trades (no Harlequin romances) and e-mail and computer services. It also rents out board games—a great option for keeping children occupied on rainy days. It's also the official headquarters for the Isla Animal Organization, so don't be surprised to see dogs and cats on the premises. The store is open Tuesday–Sunday 10 AM to 9 PM.

Crafts

Artesanías Arcoiris (⊠ Avs. Hidalgo and Juárez ☎☎ No phone) has Mexican blankets and other handicrafts. Staffers here also braid hair. Look for Mexican ceramics and onyx jewelry at **Artesanías Lupita** (⊠ Av. Hidalgo 13 ☎☎ No phone). Many local artists display their works at the public **Artesanías Market** (⊠ Avs. Matamoros and Arq. Carlos Lazo ☎ No phone) where you can find plenty of bargains.

Artesanías El Nopal (⊠ Avs. Guerrero and Matamoros ☎ 998/877–0555) has fine Mexican handicrafts hand-picked by the owner. If you want flattering swimsuits, sportswear, and sandals head over to **Vicky's Store** (⊠ Av. Francisco Madero between Avs. Hidalgo and Juárez ☎☎ 998/845–5054).

Grocery Stores

For fresh produce, the **Mercado Municipal** (municipal market; ⊠ Av. Guerrero Norte near the post office ☎ No phone) is your best bet. It's open daily until noon. **Super Express** (⊠ Av. Morelos 3, in the plaza ☎ 998/877–0127), Isla's main grocery store, is well stocked with all the basics.

Jewelry

Jewelry on Isla ranges from tasteful creations to junk. Bargains are available, but beware of street vendors—most of their wares, especially the amber, are fake. **Gold and Silver Jewelry** (⊠ Av. Hidalgo 58 ☎☎ No phone) specializes in precious stones such as sapphires, tanzanite, and amber in a variety of settings. **Joyeria Maritz** (⊠ Av. Hidalgo between Avs. Morelos and Francisco Madero ☎☎ No phone) sells jewelry from Taxco (Mexico's silver capital) and crafts from Oaxaca at reasonable prices. **Van Cleef & Arpels** (⊠ Avs. Juárez and Morelos ☎ 998/877–0331) stocks rings, bracelets, necklaces, and earrings with precious stones set in 18K gold. Many of the designs are innovative; prices are often lower than in the United States. Across the street is the Silver Shop, a sister store offering designer pieces at bargain prices.

SIDE TRIP TO ISLA CONTOY

Some 30 km (19 mi) north of Isla Mujeres, Isla Contoy (Isle of Birds) is a national wildlife park and bird sanctuary. Just 6 km (4 mi) long and less than 1 km (about ½ mi) wide, the island is a protected area—the number of visitors is carefully regulated in order to safeguard the flora and fauna. Isla Contoy has become a favorite among bird-watchers, snorkelers, and nature lovers who come to enjoy its unspoiled beauty.

More than 70 bird species—including gulls, pelicans, petrels, cormorants, cranes, ducks, flamingos, herons, doves, quail, spoonbills, and hawks—fly this way in late fall, some to nest and breed. Although the number of species is diminishing—partly as a result of human traffic, partly from the effects of Hurricane Gilbert—Isla Contoy remains a treat for bird-watchers.

The island is rich in sea life as well. Snorkelers will see brilliant coral and fish. Manta rays, which average about 5 feet across, are visible in the shallow waters. Surrounding the island are large numbers of shrimp, mackerel, barracuda, flying fish, and trumpet fish. In December, lobsters pass through in great (though diminishing) numbers, on their southerly migration route.

Sand dunes inland from the east coast rise as high as 70 feet above sea level. Black rocks and coral reefs fringe the island's east coast, which drops off abruptly 15 feet into the sea. The west coast is fringed with sand, shrubs, and coconut palms. At the north and the south ends, you find nothing but trees and small pools of water.

The island is officially open to visitors daily from 9 to 5:30; overnight stays aren't allowed. Other than the birds and the dozen or so park rangers who live here, the island's only residents are iguanas, lizards, turtles, hermit crabs, and boa constrictors.

Everyone landing on Isla Contoy must purchase a $5 authorization ticket; the price is usually included in the cost of a guided tour. Check with your tour operator to make sure that you'll actually land on the island; many larger companies simply cruise past. The best tours leave directly from Isla Mujeres; these operators know the area and therefore are more committed to protecting Isla Contoy. Tours that leave from Cancún can charge up to three times as much for the same service.

Once on shore, visit the outdoor museum, which has a small display of animals along with photographs of the island. Climb the nearby tower for a bird's-eye view. Remember to obey all rules in order to protect the island: it's a privilege to be allowed here. Government officials may someday stop all landings on Isla Contoy in order to protect its fragile environment.

ISLA MUJERES A TO Z

To research prices, get advice from other travelers, and book travel arrangements, visit www.fodors.com.

AIR TRAVEL

AIRPORT   The island has a small landing strip for private planes and military aircraft, so the Aeropuerto Internacional Cancún (Cancún International Airport) is really the only option. Three companies can pick you up at the Cancún airport in an air-conditioned van and deliver you to the ferry docks at Puerto Juárez: AGI Tours, Executive Services, and Best Day. Fares start at $18 one-way ($36 round-trip); reservations are recommended.

🔝 **Aeropuerto Internacional Cancún** ⊠ Carretera Cancún–Puerto Morelos/Carretera Hwy. 307, Km 9.5 ☎ 998/886-0028.

AIRPORT   If you aren't in a rush, consider booking a *colectivo* at the airport. These
TRANSFERS   12-passenger white vans are the cheapest transportation option. You won't leave until the van is full, but that doesn't take long. The downside: vans drop off passengers in the city's Hotel Zone first before heading over to Puerto Juárez. The entire trip takes about 45 minutes. You can also opt to get off in the Hotel Zone and take the fast Isla ferry that leaves from the Xcaret docks at Playa Caracol. Look for the colectivos just outside the international terminal. The cost of the trip is $9 per person.

🔝 **AGI Tours** ☎ 998/877-6967. **Best Day** ☎ 998/881-7037. **Executive Services** ☎ 998/877-0959.

BIKE, MOPED & GOLF CART TRAVEL

You can rent bicycles on Isla, but keep in mind that it's hot here and the roads have plenty of speed bumps. Don't ride at night; many roads don't have streetlights, so drivers have a hard time seeing you. Most moped rental places carry bicycles starting at about $5.50 an hour.

Mopeds are the most popular mode of transportation. Most rental places charge $22–$27 a day, or $5.50–$11 per hour, depending on the moped's make and age. Most tourist prefer golf carts—a fun way to get around the island, especially when traveling with children. Ciro's Motorent and P'pe's Rentadora have rates as low as $40 for 24 hours. Although motorists are generally accommodating, be prepared to move to the side of the road to let vehicles pass. Whether walking or driving, exercise caution when traveling through the streets—the locals like to drive their mopeds at breakneck speeds.

🔝 **Ciro's Motorent** ⊠ Av. Guerrero Norte 11, at Av. Matamoros ☎ 998/877-0578. **Cardenas Rent-a-car** ⊠ Av. Guerrero 105 ☎ 998/877-0079. **El Sol** ⊠ Av. Francisco Madero 5 ☎ 998/877-0068. **P'pe's Rentadora** ⊠ Av. Hidalgo 19 ☎ 998/877-0019.

BOAT & FERRY TRAVEL

The Isla ferries are actually speedboats that run between the main dock on the island and Puerto Juárez on the mainland. *Miss Valentina* and *Caribbean Lady* are small air-conditioned cruisers able to make the crossing in just under 20 minutes, depending on weather. A one-way ticket costs $3.50 and the boats leave daily, every 30 minutes from 6:30 AM to 8:30 PM with a late ferry at 11:30 PM for those returning from partying in Cancún. Don't buy your ticket from anyone on the dock; all official tickets are sold on board by young girls easily identified by their uniforms and money belts. They accept American dollars but your change will be given in Mexican pesos.

Always check the times posted at the dock. Schedules are subject to change, depending on the season and weather. Boats also wait until there are enough passengers to make the crossing worthwhile, but this delay never lasts long. Both docks have porters who will carry your luggage and load it on the boat for a tip. (They're easy to spot; they're the ones wearing T-shirts with the slogan "Will carry bags for tips.") One dollar per person for between 1–3 bags is the usual gratuity. To avoid long lines with Cancún day-trippers, catch the early-morning ferry or the ferry after 5 PM. The docks get busy from 11 AM until 3 PM.

Fast, expensive shuttles to Isla's main dock leave from El Embarcadero marina complex in Cancún's Zona Hotelera and from the Xcaret office complex. The cost is between $10 and $15 round-trip, and the voyage takes about 30 minutes.

Municipal ferries carry vehicles (although you don't really need a car on the island) and passengers between Isla's dock and Punta Sam, north of Cancún. The ride takes about 45 minutes, and the fare is $1.50 per person and about $15–$20 per vehicle, depending on the size of your car. The ferry runs four times a day and docks just a few steps from the main dock.

🚢 **Isla Ferry office** ☎ 998/877-0065. **Isla Shuttle service** ☎ 998/883-3448.

BUS TRAVEL

Municipal buses run at 20- to 30-minute intervals daily between 6 AM and 10 PM, generally following the ferry schedule. The route goes from the Hotel Posada del Mar on Avenida Rueda Medina out to Colonia Salinas (an area of salt marshes near the naval base) on the windward side. The service does not continue farther south to any of the beaches or hotels past El Colonia village. Service is slow because the buses make frequent stops to let passengers on and off. Fares are about 25¢.

🚌 **Municipal buses** ☎ 998/877-0307 on Isla, 998/884-5542 in Cancún.

CAR TRAVEL

There aren't any car-rental agencies on the island, and there's little reason to bring a car here. Taxis are inexpensive, and the island is small, making bikes, mopeds, and golf carts good ways to get around.

EMERGENCIES

🚑 **Centro de Salud** (Health Center) ✉ Av. Guerrero 5, on the plaza ☎ 998/877-0001. **Police** ☎ 998/877-0082. **Port Captain** ☎ 998/877-0095. **Red Cross Clinic** ✉ Colonia La Gloria, south side of island ☎ 998/877-0280. **Tourist/Immigration Department** ✉ Av. Rueda Medina ☎ 998/877-0307.

🚑 **Late-Night Pharmacies Farmacia Isla Mujeres** ✉ Av. Juárez 8 ☎ 998/877-0178. **Farmacia Lily** ✉ Av. Francisco Madero 17 ☎ 998/877-0116.

ENGLISH-LANGUAGE MEDIA

Islander is a small monthly publication (free) with maps, phone numbers, a history of the island, and other useful information. You can pick up a copy at the tourist office or at your hotel.

MAIL, INTERNET & SHIPPING

The *correos* (post office) is open weekdays 8–7 and Saturday 9–1. You can have mail sent to "Lista de Correos, Isla Mujeres, Quintana Roo, Mexico"; the post office will hold it for 10 days, but note that it can take up to 12 weeks to arrive. There aren't any courier services on the island; for Federal Express or DHL, you have to go to Cancún.

Internet service is available in downtown stores, hotels, and offices. The average price is 15 pesos per hour. Cafe Internet and Cosmic Cosas have the fastest computers.

🖪 Cybercafés **Cafe Internet** ⊠ Av. Hidalgo 15 ☎ 998/877-0461. **Cosmic Cosas** ⊠ Av. Matamoros 82 ☎ 998/877-0349.

🖪 Services **Correos** ⊠ Avs. Guerrero and López Mateos, ½ block from market ☎ 998/877-0085.

MONEY MATTERS

Bital, the island's only bank, is open weekdays 8:30–6 and Saturday 9–2. Its ATM often runs out of cash or has a long line, especially on Sunday, so plan accordingly. Bital exchanges currency Monday–Saturday 10–noon. You can also exchange money at Cunex Money Exchange, which is open weekdays 8:30–7 and Saturday 9–2.

🖪 Bank **Bital** ⊠ Av. Rueda Medina 3 ☎ 998/877-0005.

🖪 Exchange Service **Cunex Money Exchange** ⊠ Av. Francisco Madero 12A, at Av. Hidalgo ☎ 998/877-0474.

TAXIS

Taxis line up by the ferry dock around the clock. Fares run $2 to $3 from the ferry to hotels along Playa Norte. A taxi to the south end of the island should be about $5.50. You can also hire a taxi for an island tour for about $16.50 an hour. Some taxis have begun overcharging in an effort to recoup revenue lost to golf-cart rentals. Always establish the price before getting into the cab. If it seems too high, decline the ride; you'll always be able to find another. If you think you've been overcharged or mistreated, contact the taxi office.

🖪 **Sitio de Taxis** (Taxi Syndicates) ⊠ Av. Rueda Medina ☎ 998/877-0066.

TELEPHONES

Isla's area code is 998. You need only dial the seven digits for local calls, and Cancún and the mainland are no longer considered long distance. (Note that some printed materials may still carry the old area code, 9877. If you're having trouble connecting, check to make sure you're dialing the new code.) To contact cell phones you must dial 0–44 followed by the area code and number.

Isla has plenty of phones. Those that encourage you to "pick up and dial 0" charge ridiculously high prices—sometimes as much as $8 per minute. It's better to use the TELMEX phones that accept Ladatel phone cards. Many local stores sell cards with blocks of time worth $3, $5, $10, and $20; with these cards, you can dial directly to anywhere in the world. All TELMEX phones have display screens in Spanish. To switch to English instructions, press the button with the ABC icon.

To reach the United States or Canada, dial 00, then the area code and number. To place a collect call, dial 090 for an international operator from any phone booth (no card is required) and ask for *para cobrar* (literally, "to charge"). All international operators speak English. Once connected, the rate is about $2 per minute to the States and $4 per minute to Canada.

TOURS

Cooperativa Lanchera runs four-hour trips to the lighthouse, the turtles at Playa Lancheros, the coral reefs at Los Manchones, and El Garrafón for about $28 per person, including lunch. Cooperativa Isla Mujeres rents boats for a maximum of four hours and six people ($120). An island tour with lunch (minimum six people) costs $20 per person. Sundreamers has full- and half-day tours around the island on its 52-foot catamaran. Prices start at $30 per person and include food and drinks.

Sociedad Cooperativa Isla Mujeres and La Isleña launch boats to Isla Contoy daily at 8:30 AM and return at 4 PM. Groups are a minimum of 6 and a maximum of 12 people. Captain Jaime Avila Canto, a local Isla Contoy expert, provides an excellent tour for large groups aboard his boat the *Anett.*

The trip to Isla Contoy takes about 45 minutes, depending on the weather and the boat; the cost is $38–$50. Sociedad Cooperativa Isla Mujeres tour operators provide a fruit breakfast on the boat and stop at Xlaches reef on the way to Isla Contoy for snorkeling (gear is included). As you sail, your crew trolls for the lunch it cooks on the beach—you may be in for anything from barracuda to snapper (beer and soda are also included). While the catch is being barbecued, you have time to explore the island, snorkel, check out the small museum and biological station, or just laze under a palapa.

🛈 Operators Captain Jaime Avila Canto ✉ Av. Lic Jesús Martínez Ross 38 ☎ 998/ 877-0478. **Cooperativa Isla Mujeres** ✉ Av. Rueda Medina ☎ 998/877-0274. **Cooperativa Lanchera** ✉ Waterfront near dock ☎ No phone. **La Isleña** ✉ Avs. Morelos and Juárez, ½ block from pier ☎ 998/877-0578. **Sociedad Cooperativa Isla Mujeres** ✉ Pier ☎ 998/877-0500. **Sonadoras del Sol** (Sundreamers) ✉ Av. Juárez 9 ☎ 998/ 877-0736 ⊕ www.sundreamers.com.

TRAVEL AGENCIES

Mundaca Travel sells bus tickets and arranges airport transfers and tours. If has become primarily a real-estate outfit so if you're interested in buying on Isla, they are the people to see.

🛈 Local Agency Mundaca Travel ✉ Av. Hidalgo ☎ 998/877-0025, 998/877-0026, or 888/501-4952 🖷 998/877-0076.

If you want to rent a home or apartment on Isla, there are several rental agencies handling properties. The Web site **www.lostoasis.net** is run by an American transplant. It lists fully equipped apartments and houses for rent and also handles reservations for hotel rooms. You may also want to check out the rentals at **www.islabeckons.com.** Most rental homes have fully equipped kitchens, bathrooms, and bedrooms. You can opt for a house downtown or a more secluded one on the eastern coast.

VISITOR INFORMATION

The Isla Mujeres tourist office is open weekdays 8–8 and weekends 8–noon and has general information about the island.

🛈 **Isla Mujeres Tourist Office** ✉ Av. Rueda Medina 130 🖶 998/877–0307 ⊕ www. isla-mujeres.net.

COZUMEL

3

A WATERY WONDERLAND
32 km of diving and snorkeling reefs ⇨*p.97*

GET JAZZED
Evenings at the Havana Club ⇨*p.93*

GET CRAFTY
Los Cinco Soles crafts market ⇨*p.100*

LOOK, MA, NO HANDS!
Kids' banana boat rides at Mr. Sancho's
Beach Club ⇨*p.81*

LINGER OVER LUNCH
at the Playa Bonita beach café ⇨*p.84*

Updated by
Maribeth
Mellin

COZUMEL STRIKES A BALANCE between the sophistication of Cancún and the relaxed lifestyle of Isla Mujeres. The island has white-sand beaches, excellent snorkeling and scuba diving, luxury resorts and modest hotels, fine restaurants and family eateries, great shops, and a few Maya ruins. It's particularly popular among underwater enthusiasts, who come to explore some of the world's best coral reefs.

Signs of development are everywhere; fast-food outlets, satellite television, and widespread use of English indicate that the island caters to North American tastes. Still, Cozumel has taken steps to preserve its culture and protect its environment and wildlife. Despite the influence of docking cruise ships—shops and restaurants along the main road practically drag customers in—the island's earthy charm and tranquillity remain intact.

A 490-square-km (189-square-mi) island 19 km (12 mi) east of the Yucatán peninsula, Cozumel is mostly flat, with an interior covered by parched scrub, low jungle, and marshy lagoons. White beaches with calm waters line the island's leeward (western) side, which is fringed by a spectacular reef system; the windward (eastern) side, facing the Caribbean Sea, has rocky strands and powerful surf. A handful of Maya ruins provide the only sightseeing beyond the island's glorious natural attractions. San Miguel is the only town.

Cozumel's name comes from the Maya "Ah-Cuzamil-Peten" ("land of the swallows"). For the Maya, who lived here intermittently between about AD 600 and AD 1200, the island was a center for trade and navigation, but it was also a sacred place. Pilgrims from all over Mesoamerica came to honor Ixchel, the goddess of fertility, childbirth, the moon, and rainbows. Viewed as the mother of all other gods, Ixchel was often depicted with swallows at her feet. Maya women, who were expected to visit Ixchel's site at least once during their lives, made the dangerous journey from the mainland by canoe. Cozumel's main exports were salt and honey; at the time, both were considered more valuable than gold.

In 1518 Spanish explorer Juan de Grijalva arrived on Cozumel, looking for slaves. His tales of treasure inspired Hernán Cortés, Mexico's most famous Spanish explorer, to visit the island the following year. There he met Geronimo de Aguilar and Gonzales Guerrero, Spanish men who had been shipwrecked on Cozumel years earlier. Initially enslaved by the Maya, the two were later accepted into their community. When Cortés and his company landed, Aguilar reportedly jumped into the ocean and swam to the ship, while Guerrero refused to leave his Maya wife and children. Aguilar joined forces with Cortés, helping set up a military base on the island and using his knowledge of the Maya to defeat them. Guerrero died defending his adopted people; the Maya still consider him a hero. By 1570, most Maya islanders had been massacred by Spaniards or killed by disease. By 1600 the island was abandoned.

In the 17th and 18th centuries, pirates found Cozumel to be the perfect hideout. Two notorious buccaneers, Jean Laffite and Henry Morgan, favored the island's safe harbors and hid their treasures in the Maya's catacombs and tunnels. They laid siege to numerous cargo ships, many of which now lie in the briny depths near the island. By 1843, Cozumel had again been abandoned. Five years later, 20 families fleeing Mexico's brutal War of the Castes resettled the island; their descendants still live on Cozumel.

By the early 20th century, the island began capitalizing on its abundant supply of *zapote* (sapodilla) trees, which produce chicle, prized by the chewing-gum industry (think Chiclets). Shipping routes began to include Cozumel, whose deep harbors made it a perfect stop for large vessels. Jungle forays in search of chicle led to the discovery of ruins; soon archaeologists began visiting the island as well. Meanwhile, Cozumel's importance as a seaport diminished as air travel grew, and demand for chicle dropped off with the invention of synthetic chewing gum.

For decades Cozumel was another backwater where locals fished, hunted alligators and iguanas, and worked on coconut plantations to produce *copra*, the dried kernels from which coconut oil is extracted. Cozumeleños subsisted largely on seafood, still a staple of local economy. During World War II, the U.S. Army built an airstrip and maintained a submarine base here, accidentally destroying some Maya ruins. Then, in the 1960s, the underwater explorer Jacques Cousteau helped make Cozumel a vacation spot by featuring its incredible reefs on his television show. Today Cozumel is among the world's most popular diving locations.

EXPLORING COZUMEL

Cozumel is 53 km (33 mi) long and 15 km (9 mi) wide. Its paved roads, except for the one to Punta Molas, are excellent. The dirt roads are another story; they're too deeply rutted for most rental cars, and in the rainy season, flash flooding makes them even tougher to navigate.

Outside its developed areas, Cozumel consists of sandy or rocky beaches, quiet coves, palm groves, lagoons, swamps, scrubby jungle, and a few low hills (the highest elevation is 45 feet). Brilliantly feathered tropical birds, lizards, armadillos, coati (raccoonlike mammals), deer, and small foxes populate the undergrowth and mangroves. Several minor Maya ruins dot the island's eastern coast, including El Caracol, which was an ancient lighthouse.

The town of San Miguel earned its name a century ago, when workers unearthed a statue of St. Michael on the saint's feast day, September 29. Legend has it that Juan de Grijalva, the first Spanish explorer to reach the island, gave the statue to locals in 1518. Today it's displayed in the town church.

Cozumel's main road is Avenida Rafael E. Melgar, which runs along the island's western shore. South of San Miguel, the road is known as Carretera Chankanaab or Carretera Sur; it runs past hotels, shops, and the international cruise-ship terminals. South of town, the road splits into two parallel lanes, with the right lane reserved for slower motor-scooter and bicycle traffic. After Parque Chankanaab, the road passes several excellent beaches and a cluster of resorts. At Cozumel's southernmost point, the road turns northeast; beyond that point, it's known simply

3

Beaches

Swimmers glide through schools of tiny silver fish in the shallow, crystal-clear water alongside the beaches on the northwest side of Cozumel. On land, hammocks swing beneath palms and sunbathers sip frosty piña coladas or tall glasses of *limonada* (lemonade). Close to town, the sand is replaced by limestone shelves jutting over the water, which doesn't discourage tourists from claiming lounge chairs where they sit under shade umbrellas for hours while reading the latest thrillers or simply napping. Most hotels that don't have big beaches provide ladders down to excellent snorkeling spots, where parrot fish crunch on coral.

Local kids play on the sand and jump into the water from the ferry pier downtown, but this isn't the cleanest place to explore the sea. Better to continue on south where hotels are interspersed with beach clubs that have restaurants, bars, rental water-sports equipment, and all sorts of activities. Few beaches in this area are secluded or private. Most of the coast has been gobbled up by hotels, beach clubs, and restaurants. Surprisingly, the fish aren't discouraged from gathering around all this activity. Instead, they've grown fat and friendly and are very accustomed to munching on stale bread and other human offerings. Music fills the air throughout the day at most beach clubs while customers race about on Wave Runners, paddle along the shore in kayaks, and dance on the sand.

Cozumel's windward side is the place for those seeking solitude and natural beauty. The rough surf of the Caribbean pounds against the limestone shore, creating pocket-size beaches perfect for solitary sunbathing. The water can be rough here; pay attention to the tides, currents, and sudden drop-offs in the ocean floor. Use caution and stick to wading and swimming in the shallow water.

Island Dining

The aromas of sizzling shrimp, grilled chicken and steak, spicy sauces, and crisp pizza fill the air of San Miguel in the evening. Waiters deliver platters of enchiladas, tacos, and fajitas to sidewalk tables along pedestrian walkways, where strollers eye others' dinners while deciding where to stop for a meal. At rooftop restaurants, groups gather over Cajun and Italian feasts; along the shoreline, lobster and the catch of the day are the delicacies of choice. There's no shortage of dining choices on Cozumel, where entrepreneurs from Louisiana, Texas, Switzerland, and Italy have decided to make a go of their dreams. Foods familiar to American taste buds abound. In fact, in can be hard to find authentic regional cuisine. Yucatecan dishes such as cochinita pibíl (pork with achiote spice), *queso relleno* (Gouda cheese stuffed with ground meat), and *sopa de lima* (lime soup) rarely appear on tourist-oriented menus, but are served at small family-owned eateries in San Miguel. Look for groups of local families gathered at wobbly tables in tiny cafés to find authentic Mexican cooking. Even the finest chefs tend to emphasize natural flavors and simple preparations rather than fancy sauces and experimental cuisine. Trends aren't important here. There are places where you can wear your finest sundress or silky Hawaiian shirt and dine by candlelight, for sure. But clean shorts and shirts with buttons are considered dress-up clothing suitable for most establishments. At the finer restaurants, guitarists or trios play soft ballads while customers savor lobster salad, filet mignon, and chocolate mousse. But the most popular dining spots are combination restaurant-bars in the Carlos 'n Charlie's style, where diners fuel up on barbecued ribs and burgers before burning those calories away on the dance floor.

Lodging

Windows open to the sound of the sea, ceiling fans stirring the breeze, a hammock swinging on a waterfront balcony—such are the simple pleasures of Cozumel's hotels. Leave the glitz and glamour to Cancún; simplicity is the draw here. The most expensive hotels charge surprisingly low room rates, yet offer all the comforts a traveler needs. They don't have Egyptian cotton sheets and Bulgari toiletries, but they do have housekeepers who take great pleasure in shaping rolled towels into snakes and elephants and decorating beds with hibiscus flowers. It's the small touches that make Cozumel's hotels so special.

Although hotel chains now have branches on the island, there's nothing cookie-cutter about their style. The Presidente InterContinental is beloved for its freshly raked beaches, home-baked breads, and loyal, generous staff members. Fiesta Americana Cozumel Dive Resort aims to please the always-wet set with an excellent dive shop and rooms designed to accommodate wet gear. Meliá Cozumel All-Inclusive Golf & Beach Resort has plenty of facilities for families; Iberostar is designed with sandy pathways so guests rarely need to don shoes.

Many of the island's best hotels are mom-and-pop operations with fewer than 100 rooms. Many have a high percentage of return guests who request their favorite rooms and greet bellhops and waiters like old friends. Even the most modest, budget-level hotels give the feeling the management will do all it can to make guests comfortable and happy. Meanwhile, all-inclusive hotels hug the beaches along the southwest coast. Guests here have a different island experience, since they don't need to leave the property for meals, activities, or entertainment. Rent a car for a day or two if you're staying far from San Miguel, and spend some time exploring downtown and the windward side of the island. It would be a shame to miss the charms of Cozumel.

Scuba Diving & Snorkeling

First comes the giant step, a leap from a dry boat into the warm Caribbean Sea. Then the slow descent to white sand framed by rippling brain coral and waving purple sea fans. Lean back and look up toward the sea's surface. The water off Cozumel is so clear you can see puffy white clouds in the sky even when you're submerged 20 feet.

With more than 30 charted reefs whose depths average 50–80 feet and water temperatures around 24°C–27°C (75°F–80°F) during peak diving season (June–August, when hotel rates are coincidentally at their lowest), Cozumel is far and away *the* place to dive in Mexico. More than 60,000 divers come here each year to explore the underwater coral formations, caves, sponges, sea fans, and tropical fish.

Because of the diversity of coral formations and the dramatic underwater peaks and valleys, divers consider Cozumel's Palancar Reef (promoters now call it the Maya Reef) to be one of the top five in the world. Sea turtles headed to the beach to lay their eggs swim beside divers in May and June. Fifteen-pound lobsters wave their antennae from beneath coral ledges. They've been protected in Cozumel's National Marine Park for so long they've lost all fear of humans. Long green moray eels still appear rather menacing as they bare their fangs at curious onlookers, and snaggle-toothed barracuda look ominous as they swim by. But all in all, diving off Cozumel is relaxing, rewarding, and so addictive you simply can't dive here just once.

Snorkelers have nearly as much fun as divers in Cozumel's calm waters. There's good snorkeling off nearly every hotel beach, with views of brilliantly colored fingerlings, parrot fish, sergeant majors, angelfish, and squirrel fish, along with elk coral, conch, sea fans, and sand dollars. Most hotels have snorkeling classes in their swimming pools and rent snorkel gear. All you need is a pair of fins, a mask, a snorkel, and a sense of curiosity.

---

as "the coastal road." North of San Miguel, Avenida Rafael E. Melgar becomes Carretera Norte along the North Hotel Zone and ends near the Cozumel Country Club.

Alongside Avenida Rafael E. Melgar in San Miguel is the 14-km (9-mi) walkway called the *malecón*. The sidewalk by the water is relatively uncrowded; the other side, packed with shops and restaurants, gets clogged with crowds when cruise ships are in port. Avenida Juárez, Cozumel's other major road, stretches east from the pier for 16 km (10 mi), dividing town and island into north and south.

San Miguel is laid out in a grid. *Avenidas* are roads that run north or south; they're numbered in increments of five. A road that starts out as an "avenida norte" turns into an "avenida sur" when it crosses Avenida Juárez. *Calles* are streets that run east–west; those north of Avenida Juárez have even numbers (Calle 2 Norte, Calle 4 Norte) while those south have odd numbers (Calle 1 Sur, Calle 3 Sur).

Plaza Central, or *la plaza*, the heart of San Miguel, is directly across from the docks. Residents congregate here in the evenings, especially on Sunday, when free concerts begin at 8. Shops and restaurants abound in the square. Heading inland (east) takes you away from the tourist zone and toward the residential sections. The heaviest commercial district is concentrated between Calle 10 Norte and Calle 11 Sur to beyond Avenida Pedro Joaquin Coldwell.

Numbers in the text correspond to numbers in the margin and on the Cozumel map.

A Good Tour

Taxis are costly on Cozumel, so it's worth renting a car for a couple of days. Be aware that most car-rental companies will void your insurance if you leave the paved roads to drive to Punta Molas or other hard-to-reach locations.

Head south from **San Miguel** ❶ ▶ to **Parque Chankanaab** ❷. Continue past the park to reach the beaches: Playa Corona, Playa San Clemente,

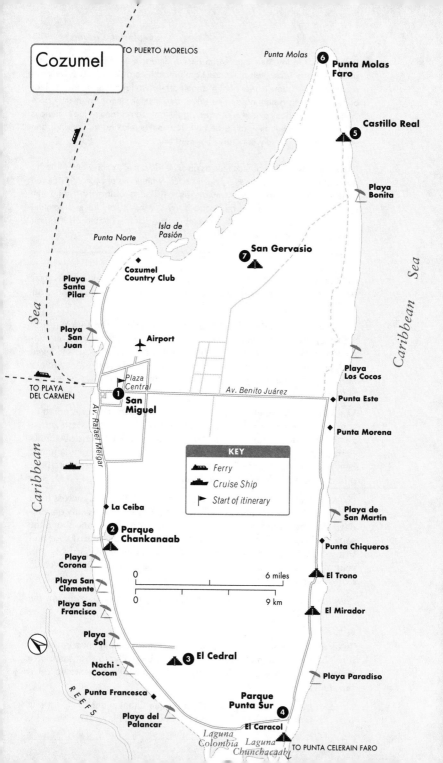

Playa San Francisco, and Playa Sol. Stay on the road to reach the village of **El Cedral ❸**. A red arch on the left marks the turnoff.

Back on the coast road, continue south until you reach the turnoff for Playa del Palancar, where the famous reef lies offshore. Continue to the island's southernmost tip to reach **Parque Punta Sur ❹**. The park encompasses Laguna Colombia and Laguna Chunchacaab as well as an ancient Maya lighthouse, El Caracol, and the modern lighthouse, Faro de Celarain. Leave your car at the gate and use the public buses or bicycles to enter the park.

At Punta Sur the road swings north. Not far from the Parque Punta Sur entrance are the minuscule ruins of **El Mirador** (The Balcony) and **El Trono** (The Throne). The road also passes several beaches: Playa Paraíso, Punta Chiqueros, Playa de San Martín, and Punta Morena. At Punta Este, the coast road intersects with Avenida Juárez, which crosses the island to the opposite coast. Follow this road back to San Miguel.

North of Punta Morena, an inaccessible dirt road runs along the rest of the windward coast to **Punta Molas**. Don't try to drive here; instead, arrange for an off-road-vehicle tour. The area includes several marvelously deserted beaches, including Ixpal Barco, Los Cocos, Hanan Reef, and Ixlapak. Beyond them is **Castillo Real ❺**, a small Maya site. Farther north are a few other minor ruins, including a lighthouse, **Punta Molas Faro ❻**, at the island's northern tip.

Take Avenida Juárez from Punta Este past the Army airfield to the turnoff for the ruins of **San Gervasio ❼**. Turn right and follow this well-maintained road for 7 km (4½ mi) to reach the ruins. To return to San Miguel, go back to Avenida Juárez and keep driving west.

What to See

🏛 ❺ **Castillo Real.** A Maya site on the coast near the island's northern end, the "royal castle" includes a lookout tower, the base of a pyramid, and a temple with two chambers capped by a false arch. The waters here harbor several shipwrecks, and it's a fine spot for snorkeling because there are few visitors to disturb the fish. Note, however, that you can't get here by car; plan to explore the area on a guided tour.

🏛 ❸ **El Cedral.** Spanish explorers discovered this site, once the hub of Maya life on Cozumel, in 1518. Later, it became the island's first official city, founded in 1847. Today it's a farming community with small houses and gardens that show little evidence of its past glory. Conquistadores tore down much of the temple and, during World War II, the U.S. Army Corps of Engineers destroyed the rest to make way for the island's first airport. All that remains of the Maya ruins is one small structure with an arch; look inside to see faint traces of paint and stucco. Nearby is a green-and-white cinder-block church, decorated inside with crosses shrouded in embroidered lace; legend has it that Mexico's first Mass was held here. Each May there's a fair here with dancing, bullfights, and a cattle show. More small ruins are hidden in the surrounding jungle, but you need a guide to find them. Check with nearby locals who offer excellent tours on horseback. ⊠ *Turn at Km 17.5 off Carretera Sur or*

Av. Rafael E. Melgar, then drive 3 km (2 mi) inland to the site ☎ No phone ☞ *Free* ⊙ *Daily dawn–dusk.*

Isla de Pasión (Passion Island). This tiny island in Abrigo Bay, east of Punta Norte, is part of a state reserve. It's difficult to reach, but it has secluded beaches and good bird-watching, and fishing is permitted. There are no facilities. Ask a local tour company to arrange a visit.

★ ☼ **Museo de la Isla de Cozumel.** Cozumel's island museum is housed on two floors of a former luxury hotel. One floor is dedicated to natural history, with exhibits on the island's origins, endangered species, topography, and coral reef ecology. Upstairs, exhibits of Maya artifacts, conquistadores' swords, cannons, and maritime instruments illustrate Cozumel's history. Another upstairs exhibit depicts the island in the 20th century. Guided tours are available. ✉ *Av. Rafael E. Melgar between Calles 4 and 6 Norte* ☎ *987/872–1475* ⊕ *www.cozumelparks.com.mx* ☞ *$3* ⊙ *Daily 9–5.*

need a break? On the terrace off the second floor of the Museo de la Isla de Cozumel, the **Restaurante del Museo** (☎ 987/872–0838) serves breakfast and lunch from 7 to 2. The Mexican fare is enhanced by a great waterfront view, and the café is as popular with locals as tourists.

★ ☼ ❷ **Parque Chankanaab.** A short drive from San Miguel, Chankanaab (which means "small sea") is a national park with a saltwater lagoon, an archaeological park, and a botanical garden. Established in 1980, it's among Mexico's oldest marine parks.

Scattered throughout the archaeological park are reproductions of a Maya village, and of Olmec, Toltec, Aztec, and Maya stone carvings. The botanical garden has more than 350 plant species. Enjoy a cool walk through pathways leading to the lagoon, home to 60-odd species of marine life, including fish, coral, turtles, and various crustaceans.

Swimming is no longer allowed in the lagoon; the area's ecosystem has become quite fragile since the collapse of the underwater tunnels that linked the lagoon to the sea. But you can swim, scuba dive, or snorkel at the beach. Sea Trek and Snuba programs allow nondivers to spend time underwater while linked up to an above-water oxygen system (there's an extra charge for this activity). There's plenty to see under the sea: a sunken ship, crusty old cannons and anchors, a statue of Maya Chacmool (the revered rain god), and a sculpture of the Virgin del Mar (Virgin of the Sea). Hordes of brilliantly colored fish swim around the coral reef. To preserve the ecosystem, park rules forbid touching the reef or feeding the fish.

Close to the beach are four dive shops, two restaurants, three gift shops, a snack stand, and dressing rooms with lockers and showers. There's also a sea-lion enclosure and an aviary. A small but worthwhile museum nearby offers exhibits on coral, shells, and the park's history as well as some sculptures. Arrive early—the park fills up fast, particularly when the cruise ships dock. ✉ *Carretera Sur, Km 9* ☎ *987/872–2940* ⊕ *www.cozumelparks.com.mx* ☞ *$10* ⊙ *Daily 7–5.*

🐢 ❹ **Parque Punta Sur.** The 247-acre national preserve, at Cozumel's southernmost tip, has numerous birds and animals, including crocodiles, flamingos, egrets, and herons. Cars aren't allowed, so use park transportation: bicycles or public buses. From observation towers you can spot crocodiles and birds in **Laguna Colombia** or **Laguna Chunchacaab.** Or visit the ancient Maya lighthouse, **El Caracol,** constructed to whistle when the wind blows in a certain direction. At the park's (and the island's) southernmost point is the **Faro de Celarain,** a lighthouse that is now a museum of navigation. Climb the 134 steps to the top; it's a steamy effort, but the views are incredible. Beaches here are wide and deserted, and there's great snorkeling offshore. Snorkeling equipment is available for rent, as are kayaks. The park also has an excellent restaurant, an information center, a small souvenir shop, and restrooms. In summer, when the turtles are nesting, the park runs a special evening program; it costs $55 per person to see a film on sea turtles and then watch them nesting. Without a rental car, expect to pay about $40 for a round-trip taxi ride from San Miguel. Food and drinks are not allowed. ⊠ *Southernmost point in Punta Sur Park and the coastal road* ☎ *987/872–2940 or 987/872–0914* ⊕ *www.cozumelparks.com.mx* 🔳 *$10* ⊗ *Daily 9–5.*

❻ **Punta Molas Faro** (Molas Point Lighthouse). The lighthouse, at Cozumel's northernmost point, is an excellent spot for sunbathing and bird-watching. The jagged shoreline and open sea offer magnificent views, making it well worth the cost of a guided tour. Don't try to get here on your own; the narrow, rutted road is impassable in a car.

⛰ ❼ **San Gervasio.** Surrounded by a forest, these remarkable ruins comprise Cozumel's largest remaining Maya and Toltec site. San Gervasio was once the island's capital and ceremonial center, dedicated to the fertility goddess Ixchel. The Classic- and Postclassic-style buildings were continuously occupied from AD 300 to AD 1500. Typical architectural features include limestone plazas and arches atop stepped platforms, as well as stelae and bas-reliefs. Be sure to see the "hands" temple with red handprints all over its altar. Plaques clearly describe each ruin in Maya, Spanish, and English. At the entrance there's a snack bar and craft shops. ⊠ *From San Miguel, take the cross-island road (follow signs to the airport) east to San Gervasio access road; turn left and follow road for 7 km (4½ mi)* 🔳 *$5.50* ⊗ *Daily 8–5.*

★ ❶ **San Miguel.** Although highly commercialized and packed with tourists, Cozumel's only town has retained some of the flavor of a Mexican village. Stroll along the malecón and take in the ocean breeze. The main square is where townspeople and visitors hang out, particularly on Sunday night, when musical groups join the assortment of food and souvenir vendors.

BEACHES

Cozumel's beaches vary from sandy treeless stretches to isolated coves to rocky shores. Most of the development on the island is on the leeward (western) side, where the coast is relatively sheltered by the main-

THE QUIETER COZUMEL

BLAZING WHITE CRUISE SHIPS parade in and out of Cozumel as if competing in a big-time regatta. Rare is the day there isn't a white behemoth looming on the horizon. Typically, thousands of day-trippers wander along the waterfront, packing franchise jewelry and souvenir shops and drinking in tourist-trap bars. Precious few explore the beaches and streets favored by locals.

Travelers staying in Cozumel's one-of-kind hotels experience a totally different island. They quickly learn to stick close to the beach and pool when more than two ships are in port (some days the island gets six). If you're lucky enough to stay overnight, consider these strategies for avoiding the crowds.

–Time your excursions. Go into San Miguel for early breakfast and errands, then stay out of town for the rest of the day. Wander back after you hear the ships blast their departure warnings (around 5 PM or 6 PM).

–Dive in. Hide from the hordes by slipping underwater. But be sure to choose a small dive operation that travels to less popular reefs.

–Drive on the wild side. Rent a car and cruise the windward coast, still free of rampant construction. You can picnic and sunbathe in privacy on beaches hidden by limestone outcroppings. Use caution when swimming; the surf can be rough.

–Frequent the "other" downtown. The majority of Cozumel's residents live and shop far from San Miguel's waterfront. Avenidas 15, 20, and 25 are packed with taco stands, stationery stores (or papelerías), farmacias, and neighborhood markets. Driving here is a nightmare. Park on a quieter side street and explore the shops and neighborhoods to glimpse a whole different side of Cozumel.

---

land. Beach clubs have sprung up on the southwest coast; a few charge admission despite the fact that Mexican beaches are public property. However, admission is usually free, as long as you buy food and drinks. Beware of tour buses in club parking lots—they indicate that hordes of cruise-ship passengers have taken over the facilities. Clubs offer typical tourist fare: souvenir shops, *palapa* (thatch-roofed) restaurants, kayaks, and cold beer. Reaching beaches on the windward (eastern) side is more difficult, but the solitude is worth the effort.

Leeward Beaches

The best sand beaches lie along the southern half of Cozumel's west coast.

Playa Santa Pilar, which runs along the northern hotel strip and ends at Punta Norte, has long stretches of pure white sand and shallow water. But there's little privacy here, as hotels line the beach. **Playa San Juan,** south of Playa Santa Pilar, has a rocky shore with no easy ocean access. It's usually crowded with guests from nearby hotels. **Playa Azul,** beside the hotel of the same name, is among the north coast's few publicly accessible beaches. It has a small restaurant and is packed with families on weekends. Next to Parque Chankanaab is **Playa Corona,** which shares the park's access to the Yucab reef. Snorkeling equipment is available for rent, and the restaurant here serves conch and shrimp ceviche. The crowds that visit Chankanaab haven't yet discovered this tranquil neighbor.

South of Parque Chankanaab and Playa San Clemente is **Playa San Francisco,** an inviting 5-km (3-mi) stretch of sandy beach that's among the longest and finest on Cozumel. Encompassing beaches known as Playa Maya and Santa Rosa, it's typically packed with cruise-ship passengers in high season. On Sunday locals flock here to eat fresh fish and hear live music. Amenities include two outdoor restaurants, a bar, dressing rooms, gift shops, volleyball nets, beach chairs, and water-sports equipment rentals. Divers use this beach as a jumping-off point for the San Francisco reef and Santa Rosa wall. However, the abundance of turtle grass in the water makes this a less-than-ideal spot for swimming.

Playa Sol (⊠ Carretera Sur, Km 15.5 ☎ 987/872–9030 ⊕ www.playasol. com.mx) is a serious tourist trap, with good reason. It has a fine beach with excellent swimming; in addition, snorkelers can view an underwater archaeological park with replicas of famous Maya structures. The park has a small zoo, kayak and sailboat rentals, nearly every water toy imaginable, a large playground, and a decent restaurant. With plenty of planned activities and loud music, this beach isn't tranquil, but it's a great place to party. Arrive early to avoid the crowds. Admission to the facilities is $6; an all-you-can-eat package is $35.

★ There's no admission charge to enter **Mr. Sancho's Beach Club** (⊠ Carretera Sur, Km 15 ☎ 987/879–0021 ⊕ www.mrsanchos.com). Its beach is similar to the one at Playa Sol; in addition, the club provides swimming, snorkeling, scuba diving, Wave Runners, and glass-bottom boat rides. Every water toy known buzzes by; kids particularly enjoy riding on banana boats that are dragged behind speedboats. Guides lead horseback and ATV rides into the jungle and along the beach, and the restaurant holds a lively, informative tequila seminar at lunchtime. Grab a swing seat at the beach bar and sip a mango margarita, settle into the 30-person hot tub, or nap through a massage. Showers and lockers are available, and souvenirs aplenty are for sale.

Nachi-Cocom (☎ 987/872–0555), south of Playa Sol, has a wide, uncluttered, and shallow beach, a freshwater pool, lounge chairs, a dive shop, a restaurant, and a beach bar. It gets around charging an admission by having a food-or-beer minimum of $10 per adult and $5 per child.

South of the resorts lies the mostly ignored (and therefore serene) Punta Francesca, on the outskirts of **Playa del Palancar.** Offshore is the famous Palancar Reef. There's also a water-sports center and a bar-café. Playa del Palancar keeps prices low to draw divers, who are often more bargain-minded than other visitors.

Windward Beaches

The east coast of Cozumel presents a splendid succession of mostly deserted rocky coves and narrow powdery beaches poised dramatically against the turquoise Caribbean. Swimming can be treacherous here if you go out too far—in some parts, a deadly undertow can sweep you out to sea in minutes. But Cozumel's beaches are perfect for solitary sunbathing.

Note that Playa Bonita refers to two different areas, depending on whom you talk to. This is what the locals call the beach at Punta Chiqueros, where there's a restaurant that goes by the name Playa Bonita. The beach near Castillo Real bears the same name. Several casual restaurants dot the coast; all close after sunset.

Playa Paraíso (also known as Playa Bosh) is the southernmost of Cozumel's windward beaches. This windswept place is good for beachcombing or sunbathing. Afterward, cool off with a cold beer and shrimp quesadillas at the Paradise Cafe or Rastas, a reggae bar.

North of El Mirador, **Punta Chiqueros** is a half-moon-shape cove sheltered by an offshore reef. Part of a longer beach that most locals call Playa Bonita, it has fine sand, clear water, and moderate waves. Come here to swim, watch the sunset, and eat fresh fish at the restaurant, also called Playa Bonita.

Not quite 5 km (3 mi) north of Punta Chiqueros, a long stretch of beach begins along the Chen Río Reef. Turtles come to lay their eggs on the section known as **Playa de San Martín** (although some locals call it Chen Río, after the reef). During full moons in May and June, the beach is blocked by soldiers or ecologists to prevent the poaching of the turtle eggs. Directly in front of the reef is a small bay with clear waters and surf that's relatively mild, thanks to a protective rock formation. This is a particularly good spot for swimming. A restaurant, also called Chen Río, serves cold drinks and decent seafood.

About 1 km (½ mi) to the north, the island road turns hilly, providing panoramic ocean views. Coconuts, a hilltop restaurant, offers additional lookout spots as well as good food.

Surfers and boogie-boarders have adopted **Punta Morena**, north of Playa de San Martín, as their official hangout. The pounding surf creates great waves, and the local restaurant serves typical surfer food (hamburgers, hot dogs, and french fries). The owners allow camping here, although it's not actually legal.

The beach at **Punta Este** has been nicknamed Mezcalitos, after a much-loved area restaurant. (The Mezcalito Café serves seafood and beer and has a very pleasant staff.) Punta Este is a typical windward beach—great for beachcombing but unsuitable for swimming.

WHERE TO EAT

Dining options on Cozumel reflect the island's nature: breezy and relaxed with few pretensions. Most restaurants emphasize fresh ingredients, simple presentation, and amiable service. Nearly every menu includes seafood; for a regional touch go for *pescado tixin-xic* (fish spiced with achiote and baked in banana leaves). Only a few tourist-area restaurants serve regional Yucatecan cuisine, though nearly all carry standard Mexican tacos, enchiladas, and huevos rancheros. The restaurants, many owned by foreigners, cater to tourist tastes by serving up piles of barbecued ribs and chicken, platters of pasta and pizza, and the inevitable steaks (best when imported or marinated and grilled). Breakfasts are among the island's best meals, with hotels presenting lavish buffets and small restaurants serving waffles and crispy hash browns. Chain restaurants—including McDonald's, Subway, TGI Friday's, and the Hard Rock Cafe, among others—have popped up on Cozumel as well. Even so, budget meals are harder and harder to find, especially near the waterfront. The best dining experiences are usually in small, family-owned restaurants that seem to have been here forever.

Prices

Many restaurants accept credit cards; café-type places generally don't. Tip: Don't follow cab drivers' dining suggestions; they're often paid to recommend restaurants.

	WHAT IT COSTS In Dollars				
	$$$$	**$$$**	**$$**	**$**	**¢**
AT DINNER	over $25	$15–$25	$10–$15	$5–$10	under $5

Per person, for a main course at dinner, excluding tax and tip.

Reservations & Dress

Casual dress and no reservations are the rule in most Cozumel restaurants. In $$$$ restaurants you wouldn't be out of place if you dressed up, and reservations are advised.

Zona Hotelera Norte

$$–$$$$ ✕ **La Cabaña del Pescador Lobster House.** Walk the gangplank to this palapa restaurant with seashells and nets hanging from the walls. Yes, it's kitschy, but worth it if you're craving lobster, even though it may be frozen. There's really no menu here—just crustaceans sold by weight (at market prices). You pay for the lobster; veggies and rice are included in the price. Another local favorite is La Cabaña's sister establishment, the less expensive Guacamayo King Crab House next door. ✉ *Carretera Costera Norte, Km 4, across from Playa Azul Golf and Beach Resort* ☎ 987/872–0795 ▭ *AE, MC, V* ☷ *No lunch.*

Zona Hotelera Sur

★ **$$$–$$$$** ✕ **Arrecife.** Some locals celebrate every special occasion with dinner at this subtly elegant restaurant, where a guitarist plays familiar ballads—listen for the Beatles and Eric Clapton in the mix. The unusual and delicious warm lobster salad served over mashed potatoes is a full meal for light eaters; any beef dish will satisfy a hearty yet discerning appetite. Save room for one of the special flambéed coffees, prepared table-side. Reservations are recommended. ✉ *Carretera Chankanaab, Km 6.5* ☎ 987/872–0322 ▭ *AE, D, DC, MC, V* ☷ *No lunch.*

$–$$ ✕ **Coconuts.** The T-shirts and bikinis hanging from the palapa roof at this windward-side hangout are a good indication of the place's spirit. Jimmy Buffet tunes accompany partying crowds downing *cervezas* (beers) and fish tacos, shrimp quesadillas, and fajitas. Assign a designated driver and hit the road home before dark (there are no streetlights).

✉ *East-coast road near the junction with the road to town* ☎ *No phone* ▤ *No credit cards* ⊗ *No dinner.*

★ ⟳ ¢–$ ✕ **Playa Bonita.** Locals gather on Sunday afternoons at this casual beach café. The water is usually calm here, and families alternate between swimming and lingering over long lunches of ceviche and fried fish. Weekdays are quieter, and this is a good place to spend the day if you want access to food, drinks, and showers, but aren't into the rowdy beach-club scene. ✉ *East-coast road* ☎ *No phone* ▤ *No credit cards* ⊗ *No dinner.*

San Miguel

$$–$$$$ ✕ **Pepe's Grill.** Practically a landmark, Pepe's has a nautical theme, complete with model boats, and ship's wheels and weather vanes covering the walls. The upstairs dining room's tall windows provide an exceptional view of sunsets. Start with Caesar salad prepared at your table, then move on to chateaubriand, T-bone steaks, or prime rib, all done to perfection. This place is popular with cruise-ship crowds, so expect long lines. ✉ *Av. Rafael E. Melgar and Calle Adolfo Rosado Salas* ☎ *987/872–0213* ⌕ *Reservations not accepted* ▤ *AE, MC, V* ⊗ *No lunch.*

$$–$$$ ✕ **La Veranda.** Romantic and intimate, this wooden Caribbean house has comfortable rattan furniture, soft lighting, and good music. Sit inside or enjoy the evening out on the terrace. Start with poblano chiles stuffed with goat cheese or Roquefort quesadillas, then move on to shrimp curry or jerk chicken. The menu changes as the chef experiments with new dishes, which are sometimes overambitious. ✉ *Calle 4 Norte 140, between Avs. 5 and 10 Norte* ☎ *987/872–4132* ▤ *MC, V.*

$–$$$ ✕ **Casa Mission.** Like a country hacienda in mainland Mexico, this large estate is part private home and part restaurant. It's also a botanical garden with mango and papaya trees and a small zoo with caged birds and a pet lion (kept out of view). The setting, with tables lining the veranda, outshines the food. Stalwart fans rave about huge platters of fajitas and grilled fish. It's out of the way, so take a cab. ✉ *Av. Juárez and Calle 55A* ☎ *987/872–3248* ▤ *AE, MC, V* ⊗ *No lunch.*

$–$$$ ✕ **La Cocay.** The name is Maya for "firefly," and like its namesake, this place is a bit magical. The chef creates a new menu every four to five weeks; dishes might include seared tuna or rack of lamb with a red-onion sauce. The sophisticated restaurant has wood tables, wrought-iron chairs, soft lighting, and an open kitchen. Desserts are fantastic, and the wine list has a good selection. ✉ *Calle 19 No. 1100, at Av. 25* ☎ *987/872–5533* ▤ *No credit cards* ⊗ *Closed Sun. and Mon. and Oct. No lunch.*

$–$$$ ✕ **French Quarter.** Owner Mike Slaughter is here nightly making sure that everyone is happily sated with bodacious portions of home-style gumbo, jambalaya, and crawfish étouffée. The beef is imported; satisfy your cravings with a ribeye and a spinach salad. Dine outside on the cool rooftop terrace or inside with the colorful murals. The bar stocks imported beer and wine at reasonable prices. ✉ *Av. 5 Sur between Calles Adolfo Rosado Salas and 3* ☎ *987/872–6321* ▤ *AE, MC, V* ⊗ *No lunch.*

★ $–$$$ ✕ **Guido's.** Chef Ivonne Arenal works wonders with fresh fish—if the wahoo with spinach is on the menu, don't miss it. But Guido's is best known for its pizzas baked in a wood-burning oven, which makes sections of the indoor dining room rather warm. Sit in the pleasantly overgrown courtyard instead, and order a pitcher of sangria to go with the puffy garlic bread. ⊠ *Av. Rafael E. Melgar 23, between Calles 6 and 8 Norte* ☎ *987/872–0946* 🖃 *AE, D* ⊙ *Closed Sun.*

$–$$ ✕ **Plaza Leza.** Let the hours slip away as you savor great Mexican food and watch the action in the square. For more privacy, go indoors to the somewhat secluded, cozy inner patio for everything from *poc chuc* (tender pork loin in a sour orange sauce), enchiladas, and lime soup to chicken sandwiches and coconut ice cream. Breakfast is available here as well. ⊠ *Calle 1 Sur, south side of Plaza Central* ☎ *987/872–1041* 🖃 *MC, V.*

$–$$ ✕ **Las Tortugas.** The motto at this simple eatery is "delicious seafood at accessible prices," and Las Tortugas lives up to it. The menu consists primarily of fish, lobster, and conch caught by local fishermen, and it changes according to what's available. Fajitas and other traditional Mexican dishes are also options. ⊠ *Av. 30 and Calle 19 Sur* ☎ *987/ 872–1242* 🖃 *MC, V* ⊙ *Closed Mon.*

$ ✕ **Ambientes Cozumel.** Blissfully powerful air-conditioning cools the art-filled dining room and an indigenous cayumito tree shades the courtyard. Pita sandwiches are the specialty—try one stuffed with flank steak and manchego cheese, or the crab rolls with bacon. The bartender makes a mean mango margarita. ⊠ *Av. 10 between Calles Adolfo Rosado Salas and 3 Sur* ☎ *987/872–3621* 🖃 *MC, V.*

$ ✕ **La Perlita.** The ceviche and whole fried fish are as fresh as can be at this neighborhood seafood market and restaurant. Lunch is the main meal and the crowd is largely made up of families and local workers on break. Take a taxi—it's far from downtown and hard to find. ⊠ *Av. 65 Norte 49, between Calles 8 and 10* ☎ *987/872–3452* 🖃 *MC, V* ⊙ *No dinner.*

¢–$$$ ✕ **Costa Brava.** This casual café on a side street serves excellent fresh seafood from the catch of the day to garlic conch and king crab. Go for the simplest preparations. You can't go wrong with grilled fish *mojo de ajo* (with butter and garlic), or anything garlicky, including the soup. The breakfast special is a great deal. ⊠ *Calle 7 Sur 57, between Avs. Rafael E. Melgar and 5 Sur* ☎ *987/872–3549* 🖃 *AE, MC, V.*

¢–$$$ ✕ **La Choza.** Purely Mexican in design and cuisine, this family-owned restaurant is a favorite for mole *rojo* (with cinnamon and chiles) and *cochinita pibíl* (marinated pork baked in banana leaves). Leave room for the chilled chocolate pie or the equally intriguing avocado pie. ⊠ *Calle Adolfo Rosado Salas 198, at Av. 10* ☎ *987/872–0958* 🖃 *AE, MC, V.*

¢–$ ✕ **Casa Denis.** This little yellow house near the plaza has long been the purview of budget travelers seeking Yucatecan *pollo pibíl* (spiced chicken baked in banana leaves) and other local favorites. *Tortas* (sandwiches) and tacos are a real bargain. Sit at one of the outdoor tables and watch the shoppers dash about as you relax. ⊠ *Calle 1 Sur 132, between Avs. 5 and 10* ☎ *987/872–0067* 🖃 *No credit cards.*

¢–$ ✕ **Cocos Cozumel.** Start the day with a bountiful breakfast at this cheery café, where the coffee is strong, the muffins enormous, and the egg dishes perfectly prepared. If you've come early enough to beat the heat, sit at a table under the front awning and watch the town come to life. The restaurant is open 7 AM–1 PM. ⊠ *Av. 5 Sur 180* ☎ *987/872–0241* ⚶ *Reservations not accepted* 🖃 *No credit cards* ⊙ *Closed Mon. and Sept. and Oct. No dinner.*

¢–$ ✕ **El Foco.** Here's a fun spot to grab a cerveza and a bite to eat. This traditional Mexican joint is essentially a *taquería* (taco stand), offering soft tacos stuffed with pork, chorizo, cheese, or chiles. The graffiti on the walls provides the entertainment. ⊠ *Av. 5 Sur 13B, between Calles Adolfo Rosado Salas and 3 Sur* 🕾 *No phone* ⊟ *No credit cards.*

¢–$ ✕ **Garden of Eatin'.** Just when you think you can't bear another taco, along comes this bright, cheery, green-and-yellow café with its healthful veggie choices. All ingredients are washed in purified water, and the veggie sandwich (eggplant, goat cheese, and pine nuts) is especially good. Create your own sandwich or choose from a menu that includes roast beef with Dijon mustard and smoked salmon with avocado. Salads include the Mediterranean with feta cheese and summer spinach with chicken, or you can create your own from a long list of ingredients. ⊠ *Calle Adolfo Rosado Salas between Avs. Rafael E. Melgar and 5 Sur* 🕾 *987/ 878–4020* ⊟ *No credit cards* ⊙ *Closed Sun.*

★ ¢–$ ✕ **Jeanie's Waffles & Raul's Tacos.** This is a wonderful place to start the day. Tables in the dining room and on the terrace face the sea; sidewalk tables have a view of traffic and travelers walking to and from town. The waffles are fresh, light, and yummy, and available in more variations than you can imagine. Jeanie's husband Raul takes over in the evening with a menu of ceviche, tacos, and other reasonably priced Mexican dishes. ⊠ *Av. Rafael E. Melgar and Calle 11* 🕾 *044–987/871–2133 cell phone* ⊟ *No credit cards.*

¢–$ ✕ **Rock 'n Java Caribbean Café.** The extensive breakfast menu includes such delights as whole-wheat French toast and cheese blintzes. For lunch or dinner consider the vegetarian tacos or linguine with clam sauce, or choose from more than a dozen salads. There are also scrumptious pies, cakes, and pastries baked here daily. Enjoy your healthful meal or sinful snack while sitting on the wrought-iron studio chairs. ⊠ *Av. Rafael E. Melgar 602-6* 🕾 *987/872–4405* ⊟ *No credit cards* ⊙ *Closed Sun.*

¢–$ ✕ **El Turix.** Off the beaten track, about 10 minutes by cab from downtown, this simple place is worth the trip for a chance to experience true Yucatecan cuisine served by the amiable owners, Rafael and Maruca. Don't miss the pollo pibíl or the poc chuc. There are also daily specials, and paella is available on request (call 24 hours ahead). ⊠ *Av. 20 Sur between Calles 17 and 19* 🕾 *987/872–5234* ⊟ *No credit cards* ⊙ *Closed Oct. No lunch.*

WHERE TO STAY

All of Cozumel's hotels are on the leeward (west) and south sides of the island, though construction has begun on some small properties on the windward (east) side. The larger resorts are north and south of San Miguel; the less expensive places are in town. Divers and snorkelers tend to congregate at the southern properties, while swimmers and families prefer the hotels to the north, where smooth white-sand beaches face calm, shallow water.

Cozumel has more than 3,600 hotel rooms, plus private homes, condos, villas, and apartments available for rent. Before booking, call around or check the Internet for bargains on air, hotel, and dive packages, especially in the off-season (April to June and September to November). Make Christmas reservations at least three months ahead.

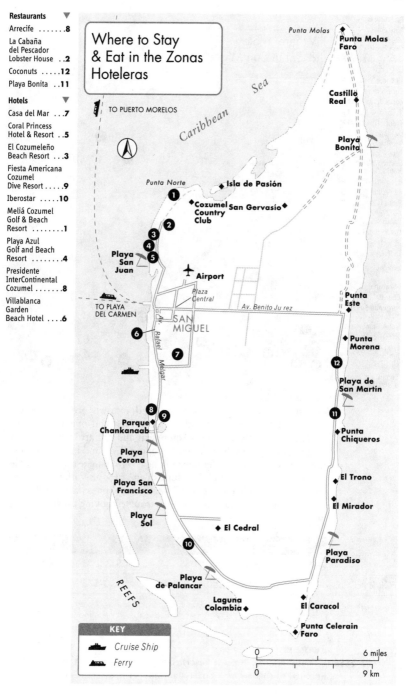

Where to Stay & Eat in the Zonas Hoteleras

TO PUERTO MORELOS

Punta Molas

Punta Molas Faro

Caribbean Sea

Castillo Real

Playa Bonita

Punta Norte

Isla de Pasión

❶

Cozumel Country Club **San Gervasio** ◆

❷

❸

❹

Playa San Juan

❺

✈ **Airport**

Plaza Central

TO PLAYA DEL CARMEN

SAN MIGUEL

Av. Rafael Melgar

Av. Benito Juárez

Punta Este

❻

❼

Punta Morena

⓬

Playa de San Martín

⓫

❽ ❾

Parque Chankanaab ◆

Punta Chiqueros

Playa Corona

El Trono

Playa San Francisco

El Mirador

Playa Sol

◆ **El Cedral**

⓾

Playa Paradiso

Playa de Palancar

REEFS

Laguna Colombia ◆

◆ **El Caracol**

Punta Celerain Faro

KEY

Cruise Ship

Ferry

0   6 miles

0   9 km

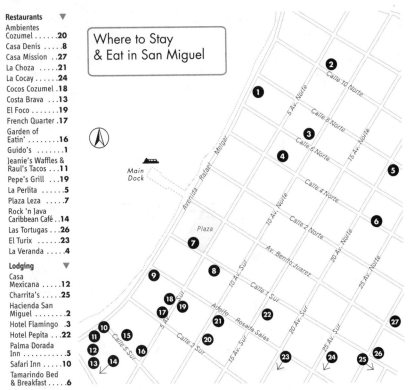

Restaurants ▼
Ambientes
Cozumel **20**
Casa Denis **8**
Casa Mission . .**27**
La Choza **21**
La Cocay **24**
Cocos Cozumel .**18**
Costa Brava . . .**13**
El Foco **19**
French Quarter .**17**
Garden of
Eatin' **16**
Guido's **1**
Jeanie's Waffles &
Raul's Tacos . . .**11**
Pepe's Grill . . .**19**
La Perlita **5**
Plaza Leza **7**
Rock 'n Java
Caribbean Café . .**14**
Las Tortugas . . .**26**
El Turix **23**
La Veranda **4**

Lodging ▼
Casa
Mexicana **12**
Charrita's **25**
Hacienda San
Miguel **2**
Hotel Flamingo .**3**
Hotel Pepita . . .**22**
Palma Dorada
Inn **5**
Safari Inn **10**
Tamarindo Bed
& Breakfast **6**

Where to Stay
& Eat in San Miguel

Some of the resort hotels (north and south of town) are affiliated with
international chains, while others are owned and operated by local
families. All rent water-sports equipment and can arrange excursions.
Nearly all properties have air-conditioning, TVs, and in-room phones;
more costly properties offer no-smoking rooms, on-site tour companies,
and transportation rentals, and furnish guest rooms with in-room hair
dryers, safes, minibars, satellite TV, and telephones. In-room Internet
access is still rare, and you may have trouble hooking up your laptop.

Prices

	WHAT IT COSTS In Dollars				
	$$$$	**$$$**	**$$**	**$**	**¢**
FOR 2 PEOPLE	over $250	$150–$250	$75–$150	$50–$75	under $50

All prices are for a standard double room in high season, based on the European
Plan (EP) and excluding service and 12% tax (10% Value Added Tax plus 2% hospitality tax).

Zona Hotelera Norte

$$–$$$$ 🏨 **Coral Princess Hotel & Resort.** Great snorkeling off the rocky shore-
line makes this a north coast standout. Princess Villas have two bed-

rooms, two bathrooms, kitchen, and terrace; Coral Villas have one bedroom, a kitchen-dining area, and a terrace. These large rooms are often taken by time-share owners, though there's no pressure to attend a sales demo. Room service will deliver a reasonably priced 5-gallon jug of purified water, a great money saver for extended stays. Except for 61 studios, all rooms overlook the ocean. ⊠ *Carretera Costera Norte, Km 2.5, 77600* ☎ *987/872–3200 or 800/253–2702* 🖷 *987/872–2800* ⊕ *www.coralprincess.com* ⇨ *100 rooms, 37 villas, 2 penthouses* ⚬ *Restaurant, snack bar, room service, in-room safes, some kitchens, refrigerators, cable TV, 2 pools, gym, dive shop, dock, snorkeling, volleyball, bar, laundry service, car rental* ▭ *AE, MC, V.*

$$$ ⬚ **Meliá Cozumel All-Inclusive Golf & Beach Resort.** A long white-sand beach with clear, shallow water fronts this full-scale resort. Spacious rooms are cool and comfortable, with ocean-view balconies. Families congregate around the kids' club and pool; grown-ups go for the quieter pool by the beach. The golf course is across the street. The fresh french fries are in big demand at the grill, and the food at the buffets is better than in the specialty restaurant. ⊠ *Carretera Costera Norte, Km 5.8, 77600* ☎ *987/872–9870 or 800/336–3542* 🖷 *987/872–1599* ⊕ *www.solmelia. com* ⇨ *147 rooms* ⚬ *2 restaurants, snack bar, in-room safes, refrigerators, cable TV, 2 tennis courts, 2 pools, gym, fitness classes, steam bath, beach, dive shop, snorkeling, windsurfing, boating, bicycles, horseback riding, 5 bars, theater, children's programs (ages 2–12), laundry service, meeting rooms, car rental* ▭ *AE, MC, V* ⦿ *AI.*

★ $$$ ⬚ **Playa Azul Golf and Beach Resort.** The bright airy rooms of this boutique hotel face the ocean or gardens and have mirrored niches, wicker furnishings, and sun-filled terraces. Master suites have hot tubs. Small palapas shade lounge chairs on the beach, and you can arrange snorkeling and diving trips at the hotel's own dock. The Palma Azul restaurant serves Continental meals, and all rooms have coffeemakers. Golf packages are available. ⊠ *Carretera Costera Norte, Km 4, 77600* ☎ *987/ 872–0043* 🖷 *987/872–0110* ⊕ *www.playa-azul.com* ⇨ *34 rooms, 16 suites* ⚬ *Restaurant, room service, in-room safes, some in-room hot tubs, minibars, pool, beach, dive shop, dock, snorkeling, billiards, 2 bars, laundry service, car rental* ▭ *AE, MC, V.*

$$–$$$ ⬚ **El Cozumeleño Beach Resort.** This all-inclusive resort is geared toward families (children under seven stay free), with lots of activities—especially on the long beach. Rooms are large and fitted with contemporary pine furniture; most have ocean views and terraces. Included in the package: all meals and drinks, snorkel and scuba lessons, miniature golf, tennis, kayaking, windsurfing, a game room, and children's camp. There is an additional charge for dive trips to the reefs. ⊠ *Carretera Costera Norte, Km 4.5, 77600* ☎ *987/872–0050 or 800/437–3923* 🖷 *987/872–0381* ⊕ *www.elcozumeleno.com* ⇨ *252 rooms* ⚬ *2 restaurants, snack bar, cable TV, miniature golf, tennis court, 3 pools, gym, 6 hot tubs, beach, dive shop, boating, windsurfing, 2 bars, recreation room, shops, children's programs (ages 2–12), laundry service, car rental* ▭ *AE, MC, V* ⦿ *AI.*

Zona Hotelera Sur

$$$ ⬚ **Iberostar.** Jungle greenery surrounds this all-inclusive resort at Cozumel's southernmost point. Rooms are small but pleasant, with wrought-iron details, one king-size or two queen-size beds, and a terrace or patio with hammocks. There isn't much privacy, though, as paths through the resort wind around the rooms. But this is the most enjoyable all-inclusive on the south coast. Guests don sandals and cover-ups to dine, but otherwise are utterly casual and relaxed. ⊠ *Carretera Chankanaab, Km 17, past El Cedral turnoff, 77600* ☎ *987/872–9900 or 888/923–2722* 🖷 *987/872–9909* ⊕ *www.iberostar.com* ⇨ *300 rooms* ⌂ *3 restaurants, in-room safes, 2 tennis courts, 2 pools, health club, hot tub, spa, beach, dive shop, dock, windsurfing, boating, bicycles, 3 bars, theater, children's programs (ages 4–12), car rental* ▤ *AE, D, MC, V* ⊚ *AI.*

$$$ 🏨 **Presidente InterContinental Cozumel.** The long driveway edged by palms
Fodor'sChoice and vines lets you know that this comfortable luxury resort protects its
★ guests' privacy and serenity. Rooms are stylish and contemporary, with white cedar furnishings and private terraces or balconies; most overlook the ocean. Splurge on an oceanfront suite; terraces lead right to quiet sands. Couples and families often opt for at least one private candlelit dinner on the beach. The pool is modest, but the snorkeling and dive shop are superb, and the restaurants are highly recommended. ⊠ *Carretera Chankanaab, Km 6.5, 77600* ☎ *987/872–9500 or 800/327–0200* 🖷 *987/ 872–2928* ⊕ *www.interconti.com* ⇨ *253 rooms, 7 suites* ⌂ *2 restaurants, snack bar, room service, in-room safes, minibars, 2 tennis courts, pool, gym, hot tub, beach, dive shop, dock, snorkeling, 3 bars, shops, children's programs (ages 4–12), laundry service, concierge, Internet, business services, meeting rooms, car rental, no-smoking rooms* ▤ *AE, DC, MC, V.*

$$ 🏨 **Fiesta Americana Cozumel Dive Resort.** A walkway over the road links this hotel to the dive shop, dock, beach, pool, and restaurant. Standard rooms are large, with light-wood furnishings; all have oceanfront balconies, some with hammocks. Casitas along jungle paths have balconies with hammocks and outdoor lockers for dive gear. ⊠ *Carretera Chankanaab, Km 7.5, 77600* ☎ *987/872–2622 or 800/343–7821* 🖷 *987/ 872–2666* ⊕ *www.fiestaamericana.com* ⇨ *172 rooms, 54 casitas* ⌂ *3 restaurants, room service, in-room safes, minibars, 2 tennis courts, 2 pools, gym, hot tub, beach, dive shop, dock, snorkeling, 3 bars, laundry service, meeting room, car rental, travel services* ▤ *AE, MC, V.*

$$ 🏨 **Villablanca Garden Beach Hotel.** The architecture is striking here—from the hotel's white facade to the guest rooms with sleeping and living areas separated by archways. All rooms have sunken bathtubs; some include refrigerators and private terraces. The hotel's beach club, which is across the street from the main building, has three dive shops. An innovative meal plan includes vouchers for dinner at several popular restaurants. ⊠ *Carretera Chankanaab, Km 3, 77600* ☎ *987/872–0730 or 888/ 599–3483* 🖷 *987/872–0865* ⊕ *www.villablanca.net* ⇨ *25 superior rooms, 15 standard rooms, 1 penthouse, 5 villas* ⌂ *Restaurant, fans, some kitchens, some refrigerators, tennis court, pool, beach, dock, bicycles, laundry service* ▤ *AE, D, MC, V* ⊚ *MAP.*

$–$$ 🏨 **Casa del Mar.** The cheerful rooms at this three-story hotel are decorated with Mexican artwork and yellow-tile headboards; each has a small balcony. The bi-level cabanas, which sleep three or four, are a good deal. The hotel accommodates divers with an in-house dive shop and gear-storage areas. The beach is across the street, and hotel guests get discounts at Nachi Cocom Beach Club on the south coast. ⊠ *Carretera*

Chankanaab, Km 4, 77600 ☎ *987/872–1900 or 800/437–9606* 🖨 *987/ 872–1855* ⊕ *www.casadelmarcozumel.com* 🛏 *98 rooms, 8 cabanas* ⚘ *Restaurant, fans, pool, hot tub, dive shop, 2 bars, laundry service, meeting room, car rental* ⊟ *AE, D, MC, V.*

San Miguel

$$–$$$ 🏨 **Casa Mexicana.** The dramatic staircase leading up to the windswept lobby and well-designed guests rooms make this place a standout. The rooms, decorated in subtle blues and yellows, are equipped with irons and ironing boards, hair dryers, and Internet access. Some face the ocean; others overlook the pool and terrace. The price includes a full buffet breakfast. Two sister properties, Hotel Bahía and Suites Colonial, offer equally comfortable but less expensive suites with kitchenettes (the Bahía has ocean views; the Colonial is near the square). You can contact all three hotels using the central reservation number. ⊠ *Av. Rafael E. Melgar Sur 457, between Calles 5 and 7, 77600* ☎ *987/872–0209 or 877/228–6747* 🖨 *987/872–1387* ⊕ *www.casamexicanacozumel.com* 🛏 *90 rooms* ⚘ *In-room data ports, in-room safes, minibars, pool, gym, laundry service, concierge, business services, car rental* ⊟ *AE, D, MC, V* ❏❘ *BP.*

$ 🏨 **Charrita's.** This bed-and-breakfast is in a residential neighborhood 11 blocks from the beach. Each of the three comfortable rooms is individually decorated and has a private bath. Upstairs there's a terrace for sunbathing or taking in sunsets. Guests rave about the huge Mexican breakfast included in the room rate. The on-site restaurant, open to the public, serves burritos, chile con carne, and other Tex-Mex food, and it stocks 50 brands of tequila. ⊠ *Calle 11 and Av. 55 Bis, 77600* ☎ *987/872–4760* ⊕ *www.cozumelbandb.com* 🛏 *3 rooms* ⚘ *Restaurant* ⊟ *No credit cards* ❏❘ *BP.*

$ 🏨 **Hacienda San Miguel.** Continental breakfast is delivered to your room at this small gem of a hotel, where two-story buildings surround a lush courtyard. Extra in-room touches include bathrobes, coffeemakers, purified water, wrought-iron balconies, and hand-carved furnishings. The management arranges car rentals at lower-than-usual rates, and guests get discounts at the affiliated Mr. Sancho's Beach Club. You can use the office phone, but you won't be able to hook up your laptop. ⊠ *Calle 10 Norte 500, at Av. 5, 77600* ☎ *987/872–1986* 🖨 *987/872–7043* ⊕ *www. haciendasanmiguel.com* 🛏 *7 studios, 3 junior suites, 1 master suite* ⚘ *In-room safes, kitchenettes, car rental; no room phones* ⊟ *MC, V.*

$ 🏨 **Hotel Flamingo.** You get a lot for your pesos at this stellar, almost-budget hotel, including a rooftop sundeck with water view and a courtyard with barbecue and group dining facilities (bring your own catch of the day). Three blocks from the ferry in the heart of downtown, the hotel has a beach club at Playa Azul. Large rooms are done in bright colors with wrought-iron furnishings. Those in front have balconies but can be noisy. Spanish lessons and dive packages are available. ⊠ *Calle 6 Norte 81, near the Cozumel Museum, 77600* ☎ *987/872–1264 or 800/ 806–1601* ⊕ *www.hotelflamingo.com* 🛏 *21 rooms* ⚘ *Fans, Internet; no a/c in some rooms* ⊟ *AE, D, MC, V.*

¢–$ 🏨 **Tamarindo Bed & Breakfast.** The owners have blended elements of Mexico and France. Many rooms have hammocks; all rooms are pleasantly furnished. Bungalows and apartments are for rent closer to the waterfront. The staff arranges diving expeditions, and there's a rinse tank as well as gear-storage facilities. Breakfast includes French-pressed coffee, and guests can use the communal outdoor kitchenette with barbecue. ⊠ *Calle 4 Norte 421, between Avs. 20 and 25, 77600* 🖃 *987/872–3614* ⊕ *www.cozumel.net/bb/tamarind/* ⥲ *5 rooms* ⚖ *Fans, massage, bicycles, laundry service; no a/c in some rooms* ▭ *MC, V* 🍽 *CP.*

¢ 🏨 **Hotel Pepita.** One of Cozumel's first hotels, this is bargain lodging: clean, basic rooms with air-conditioning, cable TV, and refrigerators and a plant-filled courtyard with places to sit. Discounts are given for longer stays. ⊠ *Av. 15 Sur 120, 77600* 🖃 *987/872–0098* 🖷 *987/872–0098* ⥲ *20 rooms* ⚖ *Fans, refrigerators, cable TV* ▭ *No credit cards.*

¢ 🏨 **Palma Dorada Inn.** This family-owned budget inn gives guests as many amenities as they care to purchase. The best suites come with air-conditioners and fully equipped kitchenettes. The least expensive have fans and three single beds. Jugs of purified water sit in the hallways, and you can use the communal microwave and request an iron or hair dryer. The waterfront is a half block away. ⊠ *Calle Adolfo Rosado Salas 44, 77600* 🖃 *987/872–0330* 🖷 *987/872–0248* 📧 *pdinn@prodigy.net.mx* ⥲ *14 rooms, 3 suites* ⚖ *Some fans; no a/c in some rooms, no TV in some rooms* ▭ *MC, V.*

¢ 🏨 **Safari Inn.** Above the Aqua Safari dive shop on the waterfront, this small hotel has comfy beds, powerful hot-water showers, air-conditioning, and the camaraderie of fellow scuba fanatics. The owner also operates Condumel, a small, comfortable condo complex that's perfect for setting up house for one night, a week, or longer. Rates are reasonable and the setting is peaceful, with excellent snorkeling. ⊠ *Av. Rafael E. Melgar and Calle 5, 77600* 🖃 *987/872–0101* 🖷 *987/872–0661* ⊕ *www.aquasafari.com* ⥲ *12 rooms* ⚖ *Dive shop, snorkeling* ▭ *MC, V.*

NIGHTLIFE & THE ARTS

Nightlife

Bars

Sports fans come to bet on their favorite teams, watch the games, and catch the ESPN news at **All Sports** (⊠ Av. 5 Norte and Calle 2 🖃 987/869–2246). **Cactus** (⊠ Av. Rafael E. Melgar 145 🖃 987/872–5799) has a disco, live music, and a bar that stays open until 5 AM.

Karaoke draws an amusing crowd to the bar at the **Hotel Cozumel & Resort** (⊠ Carretera Costera Sur, Km 1.7 🖃 987/872–2900), where happy-hour drinks and munchies are served in early evening. The singing gets going much later. **Señor Frog's** and **Carlos 'n Charlie's** (⊠ Av. Rafael E. Melgar and Punta Langosta 🖃 987/872–0191) attract lively crowds who want loud rock and a liberated, anything-goes dancing scene.

Similar in style and noise level, **Fat Tuesdays** (⊠ Av. Juárez between Av. Rafael E. Melgar and Calle 3 Sur 🖃 987/872–5130) draws crowds day and night for frozen daiquiris, ice-cold beers, and blaring rock.

A CEREMONIAL DANCE

WOMEN REGALLY DRESSED in embroidered, lace-trimmed dresses and men in their best guayabera shirts carry festooned trays on their heads during the Baile de las Cabezas de Cochino (dance of the pig's head) at the Fería del Cedral. The trays are festooned with trailing ribbons, papeles picados (paper cutouts), piles of bread, and, in some cases, the head of a barbecued pig.

The pig is a sacrificial offering to God, who supposedly saved the founders of this tiny Cozumel settlement. According to legend, the tradition began during the 19th-century War of the Castes, when Yucatán's Maya rose up against their oppressors. The enslaved Maya killed most of the mestizos in the mainland village of Sabán. Casimiro Cardenas, a wealthy young man, survived while clutching a small wooden cross. He promised he would establish an annual religious festival once he found a new home.

Today the original religious vigils and novenas blend into the more secular fair, which runs from April 27 to May 3. Festivities include horse races, bullfights, and amusement park rides, and stands selling hot dogs, corn on the cob, and cold beer. Celebrations peak during the ritualistic dance, which is usually held on the final day.

The music begins with a solemn cadence as families enter the stage, surrounding one member bearing a multi-tiered tray. The procession proceeds in a solemn circle as the participants proudly display their costumes and offerings. Gradually, the beat quickens and the dancing begins. Grabbing the ends of ribbons trailing from the trays, children, parents, and grandparents twirl in ever-faster circles until the scene becomes a whirling blend of grinning, sweaty faces and bright colors.

Discos

Cozumel's oldest disco, **Neptune Dance Club** (⊠ Av. Rafael E. Melgar and Av. 11 ☎ 987/872–1537), is the island's classiest night spot, with a dazzling light-and-laser show. **Viva Mexico** (⊠ Av. Rafael E. Melgar ☎ 987/872–0799) has a DJ who spins Latin and American dance music until the wee hours. There's also an extensive snack menu.

Live Music

Sunday evenings 8–10, locals head for the zócalo to hear mariachis and island musicians playing tropical tunes. Salsa bands perform on some nights, adding a Latin beat to the night scene at **Cafe Salsa** (⊠ Av. 10 between Av. Juárez and Calle 2 ☎ No phone). The band at the **Hard Rock Cafe** (⊠ Av. Rafael E. Melgar between Av. Juárez and Calle 2, 2nd fl. ☎ 987/872–5273) often rocks until near dawn. Air-conditioning is a major plus.

★ For sophisticated jazz, smart cocktails, and great cigars, check out the **Havana Club** (⊠ Av. Rafael E. Melgar between Calles 6 and 8, 2nd fl. ☎ 987/872–1268). Beware of ordering imported liquors such as vodka and scotch; drink prices are very high.

The food isn't the draw at **Joe's Lobster House** (⊠ Av. Rafael E. Melgar, across from the ferry pier ☎ 987/872–3275), but the reggae and salsa bring in the crowds nightly, from 10:30 until dawn.

The Arts

The arts scene on Cozumel tends to focus on the local culture; every Thursday during high season there's a folkloric dance performance at the **Fiesta Americana Cozumel Dive Resort** (☎ 987/872–2622). The whole island explodes with music, costumes, dancing, parades, and parties for Carnival, which marks the start of Lent. Visitors from around the world are encouraged to dress up and catch the fever.

Movies

Locals say the best thing to happen in years is the opening of **Cineopolis** (⊠ Av. Rafael E. Melgar ☎ 987/869–0799). The modern, multiscreen theater shows current hit films in Spanish and English and has afternoon matinees and nightly shows.

SPORTS & THE OUTDOORS

Most people come to Cozumel for the water sports—scuba diving, snorkeling, and fishing are particularly popular. Services and equipment rentals are available throughout the island, especially through major hotels and water-sports centers such as **Scuba Du** (⊠ At the Presidente InterContinental and El Cozumeleño hotels ☎ 987/872–0050).

Fishing

The waters off Cozumel swarm with more than 230 species of fish, making this one of the world's best deep-sea fishing destinations. During billfish migration season, from late April through June, blue marlin, white marlin, and sailfish are plentiful, and world-record catches aren't uncommon.

Deep-sea fishing for tuna, barracuda, wahoo, and dorado is good year-round. You can go bottom-fishing for grouper, yellowtail, and snapper on the shallow sand flats at the island's north end; you can fly-fish for bonefish, tarpon, snook, grouper, and small sharks in the same area. Regulations forbid commercial fishing, sportfishing, spear fishing, and collecting marine life in certain areas around Cozumel. It's illegal to kill certain species within marine reserves, including billfish, so be prepared to return some prize catches to the sea.

Charters

You can charter high-speed fishing boats for $400 for a half day or $550 for a full day (with a maximum of six people). Your hotel can help arrange daily charters—some offer special deals, with boats leaving from their own docks. **Albatros Deep Sea Fishing** (☎ 987/872–7904 or 888/333–4643) is a local outfit specializing in fishing trips. Full-day rates include the boat and crew, tackle and bait, and lunch with beer and soda. **Marathon Fishing & Leisure Charters** (☎ 987/872–1986) is popular with fishermen. Full-day rates include the boat and crew, tackle and bait, and lunch with beer and soda.

3 Hermanos (☎ 987/872–6284) specializes in deep-sea and fly-fishing trips.

Golf

The **Cozumel Country Club** (✉ Carretera Costera Norte, Km 5.8 ☎ 987/872–9570 ⊕ www.cozumelcountryclub.com.mx) has an 18-hole championship golf course. The gorgeous fairways amid mangroves and a lagoon are the work of the Nicklaus Design Group. The greens fee is $149, which includes a golf cart. Many hotels offer golf packages.

☺ If you're not a fan of miniature golf, **Cozumel Mini-Golf** (✉ Calle 1 Sur 20 ☎ 987/872–6570) might convert you. The jungle-theme course has banana trees, birds, two fountains, and a waterfall. Order your drinks via walkie-talkie; they'll be delivered as you try for that hole in one. Admission is $5; it's open Monday–Saturday 10 AM–11 PM and Sunday 5 PM–11 PM.

Scuba Diving

The options for divers on Cozumel include deep dives, drift dives, shore dives, wall dives, and night dives, as well as theme dives focusing on ecology, archaeology, sunken ships, and photography. More than 100 shops serve divers, so look for high safety standards and documented credentials. The best places offer small groups and individual attention. Next to your equipment, your dive master is the most important consideration for your adventure, particularly if you're new to the sport. Make sure he or she has PADI or NAUI certification (or FMAS, the Mexican equivalent). Be sure to bring your own certification card; all reputable shops require customers to show them before diving. If you forget, you may be able to call the agency that certified you and have the card number faxed to the shop. If you feel ill during or after your dive, tell the instructor, who may refer you to a medical center specializing in such problems.

There's a reputable recompression chamber at the **Buceo Médico Mexicano** (✉ Calle 5 Sur 21B ☎ 987/872–1430 24-hr hotline). The **Cozumel Recompression Chamber** (✉ San Miguel Clinic, Calle 6 between Avs. 5 and 10 ☎ 987/872–3070) is a fully equipped recompression center. These chambers, which aim for a 35-minute response time from reef to chamber, treat decompression sickness, commonly known as "the bends," which occurs when you surface too quickly and nitrogen bubbles form in the bloodstream. Recompression chambers are also used to treat nitrogen narcosis, collapsed lungs, and overexposure to the cold. Consider getting DAN (Divers Alert Network) insurance, which covers accidents.

Many hotels and dive shops offer Discover Scuba or other introductory dive classes, often called a "resort course." The classes usually last between two and four hours and cover the basics of using scuba gear and breathing underwater in a swimming pool. Most include a beach or boat dive. Once you've completed the course, you may be allowed to participate in more instructor-led drives, but you shouldn't descend more than 40 feet. Resort courses cost about $50–$60. Many dive shops also offer full open-water certification classes, which take at least four days of intensive classroom study and pool practice. Basic certification courses cost about $350, while advanced certification courses cost as much as $700. You can also do your classroom study at home, then make your training and test dives on Cozumel.

Much of the reef area off Cozumel is included in a National Marine Park. Boats aren't allowed to anchor around the reefs, and visitors can't touch the coral or take anything from the reefs. When diving, stay at least 3 feet above the reef—not just because coral can sting or cut you, but also because it's easily damaged and grows very slowly; it has taken 2,000 years to reach its present size. Some dive operators do not allow customers to wear gloves or carry dive knives as an extra measure to protect reefs and marine life.

Dive Shops & Operators

Most dive shops can provide everything you need for an underwater adventure. Equipment rental is relatively inexpensive, ranging from $6 for tanks or a lamp to about $8–$10 for a regulator and BC. Underwater-camera rentals can cost as much as $35, video-camera rentals run about $75, and professionally shot and edited videos of your own dive are about $160. You can choose from two-tank boat trips and specialty dives ranging from $45 to $60. Most companies also offer one-tank afternoon and night dives for $30–$35. The dive shops handle more than 1,000 divers per day; many run "cattle boats" packed with lots of divers and gear. It's worth the extra money to go out with a smaller group on a fast boat, especially if you're experienced.

Because dive shops tend to be competitive, it's well worth your while to shop around. Many hotels have their own on-site operations, and there are dozens of dive shops in town. **ANOAAT** (Aquatic Sports Operators Association; ☎ 987/872–5955) has listings of affiliated dive operations. Before signing on, ask experienced divers about the place, check credentials, and look over the boats and equipment.

Aqua Safari (✉ Av. Rafael E. Melgar 429, between Calles 5 and 7 Sur ☎ 987/872–0101) is among the island's oldest and most professional shops. It provides PADI certification, classes on night diving, deep diving and other interests, and individualized dives. **Blue Bubble** (✉ Av. 5 Sur and Calle 3 Sur ☎ 987/872–1865) offers several departure times in the morning—a blessing for those who hate early wake-up calls.

Del Mar Aquatics (✉ Carretera Costera Sur, Km 4 ☎ 987/872–5949) offers dive instructions and boat and shore dives. It operates at El Cid La Ceiba hotel, among the best places for shore and night dives. **Dive Cozumel** (✉ Calle Adolfo Rosado Salas 72, at Av. 5 Sur ☎ 987/872–4567) specializes in cave diving for highly experienced divers, along with regular open-water dives for the less proficient. **Eagle Ray Divers** (✉ Avs. Chichén and Pamuul ☎ 987/872–5735 ⊕ www.eagleraydivers.com) offers snorkeling trips and dive instruction.

Pepe Scuba (⊠ Carretera Costera Norte, Km 2.5 ☎ 987/872–3200) operates out of the Coral Princess Hotel and offers boat dives and several options for resort divers. **Proscuba** (⊠ Calle 3 Norte 299, between Avs. 15 and 20 ☎ 987/872–5994) is a small family-run operation offering personalized service.

Yucatech Divers (⊠ Av. 15 Sur 144 ☎ 987/872–5659) can take you cave diving on Cozumel and the mainland.

Reef Dives

Cozumel's reefs stretch for 32 km (20 mi), beginning at the international pier and continuing to Punta Celarain at the island's southernmost tip. Following is a rundown of Cozumel's main dive destinations.

Chankanaab Reef. This inviting reef lies south of Parque Chankanaab, about 350 yards offshore. Large underground caves are filled with striped grunt, snapper, sergeant majors, and butterfly fish. At 55 feet, there's another large coral formation that's often filled with crabs, lobster, barrel sponges, and angelfish. Drift a bit farther south to see the Balones de Chankanaab, balloon-shape coral at 70 feet. This is an excellent place for beginners.

Colombia Reef. Several miles off Palancar, the reef reaches 82–98 feet and is best suited for experienced divers who want to take some deep dives. Its underwater structures are as varied as those of Palancar Reef, with large canyons and ravines to explore. Clustered near the overhangs are large groupers, jacks, rays, and an occasional sea turtle.

Maracaibo Reef. Considered the most difficult of all the Cozumel reefs, Maracaibo is a thrilling dive—you don't even see the ledge of the reef until you go 60 feet below the surface. At the southern end of the island, this reef lends itself to drift dives because of its length. Although there are shallow areas, only advanced divers who can cope with the current should attempt Maracaibo. Dive shops don't stop here on their regular trips, so you must make advance reservations.

Palancar Reef. The most famous of Cozumel's reefs is about 2 km (1 mi) offshore. Palancar is actually a series of varying coral formations with about 40 dive locations. It's filled with winding canyons, deep ravines, narrow crevices and archways, tunnels, and caves. Black and red coral and huge elephant-ear and barrel sponges are among the attractions at the bottom. A favorite of divers is the section called Horseshoe, where a series of coral heads form a natural horseshoe shape at the top of the drop-off. Visibility here ranges to 150 feet, making it one of the Caribbean's most spectacular dives.

Paraíso Reef. About 330 feet offshore, running parallel to the international cruise-ship pier, this reef averages 30–50 feet. It's a perfect spot to dive before you head for deeper drop-offs such as La Ceiba and Villa Blanca. There are impressive formations of star and brain coral as well as sea fans, sponges, sea eels, and yellow rays. It's wonderful for night diving.

Paseo El Cedral. Also known as Cedar Pass, this flat reef, northeast of Palancar Reef, has gardenlike valleys full of fish, with angelfish, lobster, and thick-lipped grouper. At depths of 35–55 feet, you can also spot sea turtles, moray eels, and rays.

Plane Wreck. During a 1977 Mexican film shoot, this 40-passenger Convair airplane was sunk about 300 feet away from La Ceiba pier. Because it's so close to the shore and in shallow depths—only 9–30 feet—it's a favorite training ground for neophyte divers and a good spot for shore and night dives. Enormous coral structures and colorful sponges surround the wreck.

San Francisco Reef. Considered Cozumel's shallowest wall dive (35–50 feet), this 1-km (½-mi) reef runs parallel to Playa San Francisco and has many varieties of reef fish. It requires using a dive boat.

Santa Rosa Wall. A site for experienced divers, north of Palancar, Santa Rosa is renowned for deep dives and drift dives; at 50 feet there's an abrupt yet sensational drop-off to enormous coral overhangs. The strong current drags you along the tunnels and caves, where there are huge sponges, angelfish, groupers, and rays—maybe even a shark.

Tormentos Reef. The abundance of sea fans, sponges, sea cucumbers, arrow crabs, green eels, groupers, and other marine life—against a terrifically colorful backdrop—makes this a perfect spot for underwater photography. This variegated reef has a maximum depth of around 70 feet.

Yucab Reef. South of Tormentos Reef, this relatively shallow reef is close to shore, making it an ideal spot for beginners. About 400 feet long and 55 feet deep, it's teeming with queen angelfish and sea whip swimming around the large coral heads. The one drawback is the strong current, which can reach 2 or 3 knots.

Snorkeling

Snorkeling equipment is available at nearly all hotels and beach clubs as well as at Parque Chankanaab, Playa San Francisco, and Parque Punta Sur. Gear rents for less than $10 a day. Snorkeling tours run about $60 and take in the shallow reefs off Palancar, Chankanaab, Colombia, and Yucab.

Cozumel Sailing (✉ Carretera Norteat the marina ☎ 987/869–2312) offers sailing tours with open bar, lunch, snorkeling, and beach time for $60. Sunset cruises aboard *El Tucan* are also available; they include unlimited drinks and live entertainment and cost about $25.

Fury Catamarans (✉ Carretera Sur beside Casa del Mar hotel ☎ 987/872–5145) runs snorkeling tours from its 45-foot catamarans. Rates begin at about $58 per day and include equipment, a guide, soft drinks, beer, and margaritas and a beach party with lunch.

SHOPPING

Cozumel's main shopping area is downtown on the waterfront along Avenida Rafael E. Melgar and on some side streets around the plaza; there are more than 150 shops in this area alone. There are also small clusters of shops at Plaza del Sol (east side of the main plaza), Villa Mar (north side of the main plaza), and Plaza Confetti (south side of the main plaza). Glitzy malls at the cruise-ship piers aim to please passengers seeking jewelry, perfume, sportswear, and low-end souvenirs sold at high-end prices. As a rule, the newer, trendier stores line the waterfront, and the area around Avenida 5A houses the better crafts shops.

Downtown shops are geared toward tourists. Most accept U.S. dollars as readily as pesos, and many goods are priced in dollars. To get better prices, pay with cash or traveler's checks—some shop tack a hefty surcharge on credit-card purchases. But if you're buying something expensive and there isn't a surcharge, you get the best exchange rate with a credit card. MasterCard and Visa are the two most popular, followed by American Express. Avoid buying from street vendors—the quality of their merchandise leaves much to be desired.

There are three cruise-ship docks (one in the center of town), and there are usually several ships in port daily. Expect shops, restaurants, and streets to be crowded and hard to maneuver between 10 AM and 2 PM. Come back later, when things are calmer, for more leisurely dining and shopping. Traditionally, stores are open from 9 to 1 (except Sunday) and 5 to 9, but a number of them, especially those nearest the pier, tend to stay open all day and on weekends, particularly during high season. Most shops are closed Sunday morning.

Don't pay much attention to written or verbal offers of "20% discounts, today only" or "only for cruise-ship passengers"—they're nothing but bait to get you inside. Similarly, many larger stores advertise "duty-free" wares, but these are of greater interest to Mexicans from the mainland than to Americans, since the prices tend to be higher than retail prices in the United States.

One last caveat: Don't buy black coral—it's overpriced and an endangered species. You may be barred from bringing it to the United States and other countries.

Markets

★ ℂ There's a **crafts market** (⊠ Calle 1 Sur behind the plaza) in town, which sells a respectable assortment of Mexican wares. The market across the street from **Puerto Maya,** where some cruise ships dock, has some crafts at good prices. Bargains are best after the ships have departed. For fresh produce try the **Mercado Municipal** (⊠ Calle Adolfo Rosadao Salas between Avs. 20 and 25 Sur ☎ No phone), open Monday–Saturday 8–5.

Shopping Malls

Punta Langosta (⊠ Av. Rafael E. Melgar 551, at Calle 7), a fancy multilevel shopping mall, is across the street from the cruise-ship dock. An enclosed pedestrian walkway leads over the street from the ships to the center, which houses several jewelry and sportswear stores, TGI Friday's, and Carlos 'n Charlie's. The center is designed to lure cruise-ship passengers into shopping in air-conditioned comfort and has decreased traffic for local businesses. **Forum Shops** (✉ Av. Rafael E. Melgar and Calle 10 Norte ☎ 987/869–1687) is a flashy marble-and-glass mall with jewels glistening in glass cases and an overabundance of eager salesclerks. Diamonds International and Tanzanite International have shops in the Forum and all over Avenida Rafael E. Melgar, as does Roger's Boots, a leather store. There's a Havana Club restaurant and bar upstairs, where shoppers select expensive cigars. **Puerto Maya** (✉ Carretera Surat the southern cruise dock) is another mall for passengers. This one isn't geared to street traffic; it's close to the ships at the end of a huge parking lot.

Specialty Stores

Clothing

Several trendy sportswear stores line Avenida Rafael E. Melgar between Calles 2 and 6. **Exotica** (✉ Av. Juárez at the plaza ☎ 987/872–5880) has high-quality sportswear and shirts with nature-theme designs. **Lolha** (✉ Calle 1 Sur between Avs. 10 and 15 ☎ 987/872–7174) has a collection of Brazilian swimwear and sundresses. **Mr. Buho** (✉ Av. Rafael E. Melgar between Calles 6 and 8 ☎ 987/869–1601) specializes in white and black clothes and has well-made guayabera shirts and cotton dresses.

Poco Loco (✉ Av. Rafael E. Melgar 18, at Juárez 2A ☎ 987/872–5499) sells casual wear and beach bags.

Crafts

The showrooms at **Anji** (✉ Av. 5 between Calles Adolfo Rosado Salas and 1 Sur ☎ 987/869–2623) are filled with imported lamps, carved animals, and clothing from Bali.

★ ☾ **Bugambilias** (✉ Av. 10 Sur between Calles Adolfo Rosado Salas and 1 Sur ☎ 987/872–6282) sells handmade Mexican linens. **Los Cinco Soles** (✉ Av. Rafael E. Melgar and Calle 8 Norte ☎ 987/872–0132) is the best one-stop shop for crafts from around Mexico. Several display rooms, covering almost an entire block, are filled with clothing, furnishings, home decor items, and jewelry. Latin music CDs and English-language novels are displayed at **Fama** (✉ Av. 5 between Calle 2 and the plaza ☎ 987/872–2050), which also has sandals, swimsuits, and souvenirs.

The **Hammock House** (✉ Av. 5 and Calle 4 ☎ No phone) has long been a local curiosity thanks to its bright-blue exterior and the inventory that hangs out front. Manuel Azueta Vivas has been selling hammocks here for more than four decades.

Indigo (✉ Av. Rafael E. Melgar 221 ☎ 987/872–1076) carries a large selection of purses, belts, vests, and shirts from bright blue, purple, and green Guatemalan fabrics. They also have wooden masks.

Librería del Parque (✉ Av. 5 at the plaza ☎ 987/872–0031) is Cozumel's best bookstore; it carries the *Miami Herald, USA Today,* and English and Spanish magazines and books.

Mayan Feather (✉ Av. 5 and Calle 2 Norte ☎ No phone) has reasonably priced original paintings on feathers from area birds. At **Miguelon e Hijos Taller de Joyeria y Camafeos** (✉ Calle 5 Sur between Avs. 10 and 15 ☎ 044–987/800–1853 cell phone) artists create fascinating jewelry and art objects by carving intricate designs in shells.

El Porton (✉ Av. 5 Sur and Calle 1 Sur ☎ 987/872–5606) has a stunning collection of masks and unusual crafts. Look for antiques and high-quality silver jewelry at **Shalom** (✉ Av. 10 No. 25 ☎ 987/872–3783). **Talavera** (✉ Av. 5 Sur 349 ☎ 987/872–0171) carries tiles from the Yucatán, masks from Guerrero, brightly painted wooden animals from Oaxaca, and carved chests from Guadalajara.

Grocery Stores

The main grocery store, **Chedraui** (✉ Carretera Chankanaab, Km 1.5 and Calle 15 Sur ☎ 987/872–3655), is open daily 8 AM–10 PM and also carries clothing, kitchenware, appliances, and furniture.

Jewelry

Diamond Creations (✉ Av. Rafael E. Melgar Sur 131 ☎ 987/872–5330) lets you custom-design a piece of jewelry from a collection of loose diamonds, emeralds, rubies, sapphires, or tanzanite. The shop and its affiliates, Tanzanite International, Diamond Creations, and Silver International, have multiple locations along the waterfront and in the shopping malls—in fact, you can't avoid them.

Look for silver, gold, and coral jewelry—especially bracelets and earrings—at **Joyería Palancar** (✉ Av. Rafael E. Melgar Norte 15 ☎ 987/872–1468). **Luxury Avenue (Ultrafemme)** (✉ Av. Rafael E. Melgar 341 ☎ 987/872–1217) sells high-end goods including watches and perfume. **Pama** (✉ Av. Rafael E. Melgar Sur 9 ☎ 987/872–0090), near the pier, carries imported luxury items.

Quality gemstones and striking designs are the strong points at **Rachat & Romero** (✉ Av. Rafael E. Melgar 101 ☎ 987/872–0571).

Innovative designs and top-quality stones are available at **Van Cleef & Arpels** (✉ Av. Rafael E. Melgar Norte across from the ferry ☎ 987/872–6540).

Viva Mexico (✉ Av. Rafael E. Melgar and Calle Adolfo Rosada Salas ☎ 987/872–0791) sells souvenirs and handicrafts from all over Mexico; it's your best one-stop souvenir shopping option for standard T-shirts, blankets, and trinkets.

COZUMEL A TO Z

To research prices, get advice from other travelers, and book travel arrangements, visit www.fodors.com.

AIR TRAVEL

AIRPORT The **Aeropuerto Internacional de Cozumel** is 3 km (2 mi) north of San Miguel.

🛈 Aeropuerto Internacional de Cozumel ☎ 987/872–0928.

AIRPORT At the airport, the *colectivo,* a van that seats up to eight, takes arriving
TRANSFERS passengers to their hotels; the fare is about $7–$20. If you want to avoid
waiting for the van to fill or for other passengers to be dropped off, you
can hire an *especial*—an individual van. A trip in one of these to hotel
zones costs about $20–$25; to the city it's about $10; and to the all-in-
clusives at the far south it's about to $30. Taxis to the airport cost be-
tween $10 and $30 from the hotel zones and approximately $5 from
downtown.

CARRIERS Continental has two nonstop flights from Houston on Saturday and one
daily nonstop flight from Houston the rest of the week. US Airways flies
nonstop daily from Charlotte, North Carolina, to Cozumel and nonstop from Philadelphia on Saturday. American Airlines has seasonal nonstop flights daily from Dallas. Aerocaribe flies between Cozumel, Cancún,
and Mexico City twice daily. Charter flights to Chichén Itzá, Tulum,
Palenque, and Belize can be arranged through Aerolamsa.
🛪 **Aerocaribe** ☎ 987/872-0503. **Aerolamsa** ☎ 987/872-1781. **American** ☎ 800/
882-8880. **Continental** ☎ 987/872-0847. **US Airways** ☎ 800/622-1015.

BOAT & FERRY TRAVEL

Passenger-only ferries to Playa del Carmen leave Cozumel's main pier
approximately every hour on the hour from 5 AM to 10 PM (no ferries
at 11 AM, 1, 7, and 9 PM). They leave Playa del Carmen's dock also about
every hour on the hour, from 6 AM to 11 PM (no service at 7 AM, noon,
2 PM, and 8 PM). The trip takes 45 minutes. Call to verify the times. Bad
weather sometimes prompts cancellations.

There are car ferries from Puerto Morelos and Punta Venado. The trip
takes three to five hours. Service is more frequent from Punta Venado.
The fare starts at about $60 for small cars (more for larger vehicles) and
$6 per passenger.
🛪 **Car Ferry** ☎ 987/872-0950. **Cozumel's main pier** ☎ 987/872-1508 or 987/872-
1588. **Playa del Carmen dock** ☎ 987/873-0067.

BUS TRAVEL

Public buses do not operate in the hotel zones along the leeward coast;
local bus service runs mainly within the town of San Miguel, although
there is a route from town to the airport. Service is irregular but inexpensive.

CAR RENTAL

🛪 **Major Agencies Avis** ☎ 987/872-0219. **Hertz** ☎ 987/872-3888.
🛪 **Local Agencies Aguila Rentals** ✉ Av. Rafael E. Melgar 685 ☎ 987/872-0729. **Fiesta** ✉ Calle 11 No. 598 ☎ 987/872-0433.

CAR TRAVEL

There are several excellent paved roads, but dirt roads—such as the one
to Punta Molas—aren't well maintained; proceed with great caution, especially after rain. Most car-rental companies have a policy that voids your
insurance when you leave the paved roads and journey to off-road points.
If you rent a four-wheel-drive vehicle, make sure it works properly.

EMERGENCIES

General Emergency Numbers **Air Ambulance** ☎ 987/872-4070. **Police** ✉ Anexo del Palacio Municipal ☎ 987/872-0409.

Hospitals & Clinics **Centro Medico de Cozumel** (Cozumel Medical Center) ✉ Calle 1 Sur 101, corner of Av. 50 ☎ 987/872-3545 or 987/872-5370. **Centro de Salud** ✉ Av. 20 Sur and Calle 11 ☎ 987/872-0140. **Medical Specialties Center** ✉ Av. 20 Norte 425 ☎ 987/872-1419 or 987/872-2919. **Red Cross** ✉ Calle Adolfo Rosada Salas and Av. 20 Sur ☎ 987/872-1058.

Late-Night Pharmacies **Farmacia Canto** ☎ 987/872-5377. **Farmacia Dori** ✉ Calle Adolfo Rosado Salas between Avs. 15 and 20 Sur ☎ 987/872-0559. **Farmacia Joaquin** ✉ North side of plaza ☎ 987/872-2520.

Recompression Chambers **Buceo Médico Mexicano** ✉ Calle 5 Sur 21B ☎ 987/872-1430 24-hr hotline. **Cozumel Recompression Chamber** ✉ San Miguel Clinic, Calle 6 between Avs. 5 and 10 ☎ 987/872-3070.

ENGLISH-LANGUAGE MEDIA

Most shops and hotels around town offer the *Blue Guide to Cozumel,* a free publication with good information and maps of the island and downtown.

MAIL, INTERNET & SHIPPING

The local correos (post office), six blocks south of the plaza, is open weekdays 8–8, Saturday 9–5, and Sunday 9–1. For packages and important letters, you're better off using DHL. You can hop online at Coffee Net.

Cybercafés **Calling Station** ✉ Av. Rafael E. Melgar 27, at Calle 3 Sur ☎ 987/872-1417. **Coffee Net** ✉ Av. Rafael E. Melgar s/n ☎ 987/872-6394.

Mail Services **Correos** ✉ Calle 7 Sur and Av. Rafael E. Melgar ☎ 987/872-0106. **DHL** ✉ Av. Rafael E. Melgar and Av. 5 Sur ☎ 987/872-3110.

MONEY MATTERS

Most of the banks are in the main square and are open weekdays 9 to 4 or 5. Many change currency all day. Most have ATMs. The American Express exchange office is open weekdays 9–5. After hours, you can change money at Promotora Cambiaria del Centro, which is open Monday–Saturday 8 AM–9 PM.

Banks **Banamex** ✉ Av. 5 Norte at the plaza ☎ 987/872-3411. **Bancomer** ✉ Av. 5 Norte at the plaza ☎ 987/872-0550. **Banco Serfín** ✉ Calle 1 Sur between Avs. 5 and 10 Sur ☎ 987/872-0930. **Bancrecer** ✉ Calle 1 Sur, between Avs. 5 and 10 ☎ 987/872-4750. **Bital** ✉ Av. Rafael E. Melgar 11 ☎ 987/872-0142.

Exchange Services **American Express** ✉ Punta Langosta, Av. Rafael E. Melgar 599 ☎ 987/869-1389. **Promotora Cambiaria del Centro** ✉ Av. 5 Sur between Calles 1 Sur and Adolfo Rosado Salas ☎ No phone.

MOPED TRAVEL

Mopeds are popular here, but also extremely dangerous because of heavy traffic, potholes, and hidden stop signs; accidents happen all too frequently. Mexican law requires all riders to wear helmets (it's a $25 fine if you don't). If you do decide to rent a moped, drive slowly, check for oncoming traffic, and don't ride when it's raining or if you've had any alcoholic beverages. Mopeds rent for about $25 per day; insurance is included.

Moped Rentals **Auto Rent** ✉ Carretera Costera Sur ☎ 987/872-0844 Ext. 712. **Ernesto's Scooter Rental** ✉ Carretera Costera Sur, Km 4 ☎ 987/872-3152. **RC Scooter**

Rentals ✉ Av. 30 Norte 700, between Calles 7 and 11 Sur ☎ 987/872-5009. **Rentadora Cozumel** ✉ Calle Adolfo Rosado Salas 3B ☎ 987/872-1503 ✉ Av. 10 Sur and Calle 1 ☎ 987/872-1120. **Rentadora Marlin** ✉ Av. Adolfo López Mateos ☎ 987/872-1586.

TAXIS

Cabs wait at all the major hotels, and you can hail them on the street. The fixed rates run about $2 within town; $8–$20 between town and either hotel zone; $10–$30 from most hotels to the airport; and about $20–$40 from the northern hotels or town to Parque Chankanaab or Playa San Francisco. The cost from the cruise-ship terminal by La Ceiba to San Miguel is about $10.

Drivers quote prices in pesos or dollars—the peso rate may be cheaper. Tipping isn't necessary. Despite the established taxi fares, many of the younger and quite aggressive cab drivers have begun charging double or even triple these rates. Be firm on a price before getting into the car. Drivers carry a rather complicated rate sheet with them that lists destinations by zone. Ask to see the sheet if the price seems unreasonably high.

TELEPHONES

Phone numbers throughout Mexico have a three-digit area code (987) and seven-digit local number. Some of the older printed material on Cozumel does not reflect this change.

The least-expensive way to make an international call is to buy a TELMEX phone card (sold in blocks of 500, 1,000, and 2,000 pesos) and use the TELMEX public phones. The TELMEX phones can be hard to find, as they are being replaced with private services' blue and red phones that urge you to "pick up and dial 0" and have very high rates. However, you can make local calls from these phones using peso coins. Local calls start at the equivalent of about 10¢. An alternative to the phone card is the *caseta de larga distancia*—the long-distance telephone office. There's an office on Calle 1, on the south side of the plaza; it's open daily 8–1 and 4–9. These offices have specially designed booths where you take your call after the number has been dialed by a clerk.

More expensive than the TELMEX phones but handier is the Calling Station, at Avenida Rafael E. Melgar 27, at Calle 3 Sur. It also offers videotape and cell-phone rentals, currency exchange, and Internet access and is open daily 8 AM–11 PM during high season.

TOURS

ATV & JEEP TOURS You can travel to the northern part of the island as part of Dune Buggy Tours and Wild Tours' all-terrain-vehicle excursions. Rates start at about $90 for a single passenger, or $70 per person for two passengers with Wild Tours. Rates with Dune Buggy Tours start at $89 per person. Both tours include a light lunch, drinks, a visit to one of the northern Maya ruins, and a beach stop. Whether you take an ATV or a dune buggy, the ride through the jungle is exhilarating and the scenery incredible. Tickets are available through any local travel agent.

🎫 **Dune Buggy Tours** ☎ 987/872-5735. **Wild Tours** ☎ 987/872-56747 or 800/202-4990.

BOAT & SUBMARINE TOURS
Atlantis Submarine runs 1½-hour submarine rides that explore the Chankanaab Reef and surrounding area; tickets for the tours are $72. ✈ **Atlantis Submarines** ✉ Carretera Sur, Km 4, across from Hotel Casa del Mar ☎ 987/872-5671 ⊕ www.goatlantis.com.

HORSEBACK TOURS
Aventuras Naturales runs two-hour guided horseback tours. Prices start at $50 and visit Maya ruins and the jungle. Rancho Buenavista provides four-hour rides through the jungle starting at $65 per person. ✈ **Aventuras Naturales** ✉ Av. 35 No. 1081 ☎ 987/872-1628. **Rancho Buenavista** ✉ Av. Rafael E. Melgar and Calle 11 Sur ☎ 987/872-1537.

ORIENTATION
Tours of the island's sights, including the San Gervasio ruins, El Cedral, Parque Chankanaab, and the Museo de la Isla de Cozumel, cost about $50 a person and can be arranged through travel agencies. Fiesta Holidays, which has representatives in most major hotels, sells several tours. Another option is to take a private tour of the island via taxi, which costs about $70 for the day. ✈ **Fiesta Holidays** ✉ Calle 11 Sur 598, between Avs. 25 and 30 ☎ 987/872-0923.

TRAVEL AGENCIES

✈ **Local Agents Fiesta Holidays** ✉ Calle 11 Sur 598, between Avs. 25 and 30 ☎ 987/872-0923. **IMC** ✉ Calle 2 Norte 101-8 ☎ 987/872-1535. **Turismo Aviomar** ✉ Av. 5 Norte 8, between Calles 2 and 4 ☎ 987/872-5445.

VISITOR INFORMATION

The state tourism office, Fidecomiso, is open weekdays 9–2:30. The Cozumel Island Hotel Association provides information on affiliated hotels and tour operators. ✈ **Cozumel Island Hotel Association** ✉ Calle 2 Norte and Av. 15 ☎ 987/872-3132. **Fidecomiso** ✉ Upstairs at Plaza del Sol, at east end of main square ☎☎ 987/872-0972 ⊕ www.islacozumel.com.mx.

THE CARIBBEAN COAST

4

Updated by
Patricia Alisau

ABOVE ALL ELSE, BEACHES ARE WHAT DEFINE THE EAST COAST of the Yucatán Peninsula—soft, blinding white strands of sand embracing clear turquoise waters; shores that curve into calm lagoons, coves, and inlets; waves that crash against cliffs; mangrove swamps with minuscule islands where only the birds hold sway alongside freshwater cenotes (sinkholes). Paralleling the coast, a coral reef teems with kaleidoscopic marine life swimming lazily among the shipwrecks and relics left by pirates. Landscapes change from savanna to wetland to scrubby limestone terrain to jungle.

Mexico's Caribbean coast is in the state of Quintana Roo (pronounced keen-*tah*-nah *roh*-oh), bordered on the northwest by the state of Yucatán, on the west by Campeche, and on the south by Belize. Quintana Roo existed as only a territory of the country until politicians decided to develop the area for tourism. It officially became a state in 1974—the same year the first two hotels popped up in Cancún, where development was first focused.

Coastal destinations are varied and eccentric. Puerto Morelos has the relaxed atmosphere of a Mexican fishing village. Playa del Carmen is filled with resorts—some of them all-inclusive—that are as glitzy and hectic as those in Cancún and Cozumel, embodying the coast's *vida loca* (crazy life). The beaches here, from Punta Tanchacté to Tulum, are beloved by scuba divers, snorkelers, bird-watchers, and beachcombers. Rustic but comfortable fishing and scuba-diving lodges on the secluded Boca Paila and Xcalak peninsulas have a well-deserved reputation for excellent bonefishing and superb diving on virgin reefs. All this despite the fact that the coast is under siege from developers, and the environment is starting to suffer.

Against this backdrop is Maya culture. Although the modern Maya live in the cities and villages along the coast, their history can be seen at the ruins. At Tulum, dramatic ruins sit on a bluff overlooking the Caribbean, welcoming the sunrise each morning. Cobá, a short distance inland, has towering jungle-shrouded pyramids, testaments to its importance as a center of commerce in the ancient Maya world. Farther south, digs at Kohunlich have unearthed temples, palaces, and pyramids that have vestiges of the distinct Río Bec architectural style mixed with other styles. These structures have been restored but are still largely unvisited. At the Belizean border is the capital of Quintana Roo—Chetumal. Although it's a modern city, a sprinkling of brightly painted wooden houses left over from an earlier era combine with the sultry sea air to make it seem more Central American than Mexican.

During your trek along the coast, you're likely to encounter expats from around the world, many running lodges and restaurants where you'd least expect to find them. Chat with them for a bit and find out how they succumbed to the spell of the Caribbean coast.

Exploring the Caribbean Coast

The coast is divided into two major areas. The stretch from Punta Tanchacté to Punta Allen, at the tip of the Reserva de la Biosfera Sian Ka'an, is called the Riviera Maya. It has the most sites and places to lodge. The more southern stretch, from Punta Allen to Chetumal, has been dubbed the Costa Maya. This is where civilization thins out and you can find the most alluring landscapes. The Río Bec Route starts west of Chetumal and continues into Campeche.

About the Restaurants

Restaurants here vary from quirky beachside affairs with outdoor tables and *palapas* (thatch roofs) to more elaborate and sophisticated establishments. In addition to being relaxed, restaurants offer a few bargains. Fresh local fish—grouper, dorado, red snapper, and sea bass—is tasty and inexpensive. Shrimp, lobster, oysters, and other shellfish, on the other hand, can be expensive as they're often flown in frozen from the Gulf.

Tourism and an expatriate presence mean that an assortment of flavorful foods are available in some surprising places, such as Bacalar and Tulum. Playa del Carmen and Puerto Aventuras have more-urbane restaurants, as well as fast-food places serving pizza, burgers, and pasta.

Dress is casual at most places. Smaller cafés and fish eateries may not accept credit cards or travelers checks, especially in remote beach villages. Bigger establishments and those in hotels normally accept plastic.

About the Hotels

Many resorts are in remote areas; if you haven't rented a car and want to visit local sights or restaurants, you may find yourself at the mercy of the hotel shuttle service (if there is one) or waiting for long stretches of time for the bus or spending large sums on taxis.

The rule seems to be that the larger the hotel, the more bland the food. To avoid *turista* (traveler's diarrhea), be especially wary of creamed dishes or mayonnaise-based foods that have been sitting for hours in an all-inclusive buffet. Smaller hotels and inns are often family run and full of character; a stay in one of them may well give you the chance to mix with the locals.

Hotel rates can drop as much as 50% in the low season (September to approximately mid-December). In high season, it's virtually impossible to find low rates, especially in Playa del Carmen. During Christmas week, prices rise as much as $100 a night. The good news? More hotels now include breakfast in their rates.

Addresses listed throughout this chapter are the street addresses. Mailing addresses aren't generally used as mail service is unreliable. You are much safer making reservations via a Web site or by fax or e-mail.

WHAT IT COSTS In Dollars				
$$$$	**$$$**	**$$**	**$**	**¢**
RESTAURANTS over $25	$15–$25	$10–$15	$5–$10	under $5
HOTELS over $250	$150–$250	$75–$150	$50–$75	under $50

Restaurant prices are per person, for a main course at dinner, excluding tax and tip. Hotel prices are for a standard double room in high season, based on the European Plan (EP) and excluding service and 12% tax (which includes 10% Value added tax plus 2% hospitality tax).

4

Numbers in the text correspond to numbers in the margin and on the Mexico's Caribbean Coast map.

Three to five days gives you enough time to visit most of the Riviera Maya, from Punta Tanchacté to Tulum. With seven days you can cover the entire coast; even longer visits allow you to see every attraction and village. Playa del Carmen is a convenient base—it's closest to the ruins of Tulum and Cobá, and it has the best bus, taxi, and rental-car services outside Cancún. You need a car to venture south of Tulum, preferably a four-wheel-drive vehicle that can negotiate ruts and puddles the size of small Maya settlements.

If you have 3 days

Get a room in ▣ **Playa del Carmen** ⑥ and then visit **Akumal** ⑪ for diving or deep-sea fishing, snorkeling, or swimming. Later in the day cycle on a rented mountain bike or drive to the tiny lagoon of Yalkú, which was around during the time of the Maya traders. On Day 2, head to the cenote at **Xel-Há** ⑬, where you can snorkel, swim, sunbathe, and see some modest ruins. In the afternoon visit the underground caves at Aktun-Chen. On Day 3 head for **Tulum** ⑮ to take in the cliff-side Castillo temple. Afterward, climb down to the small adjacent beach for a dip in the ocean. In the afternoon head over to Tulum's hotel area, where you can lunch on fresh fish and enjoy a long walk along the shore.

If you have 5 days

Station yourself in ▣ **Playa del Carmen** ⑥. Begin your travels with a visit to **Xcaret** ⑦, a Disney-like ecological theme park where you can snorkel in a cenote and watch a flashy folkloric performance at night. Spend the morning of Day 2 at **Tulum** ⑮; in the afternoon cool off at **Xel-Há** ⑬ or at one of the numerous cenotes along Carretera 307. On Day 3, explore the beaches at **Paamul** ⑧ and **Xpu-há** ⑩ and continue on to **Akumal** ⑪ and Yalkú. Spend Day 4 at the Maya village of **Pac Chen** ⑰ in the morning and, after lunch, head for the ruins at **Cobá** ⑯. On Day 5, take a tour of the **Reserva de la Biosfera Sian Ka'an** ⑱.

If you have 7 days

Follow the five-day itinerary. On Day 6 drive to the enormous Laguna de Bacalar to marvel at its transparent layers of turquoise, green, and blue waters—figure about three hours to drive straight through. Visit the colonial San Felipe Fort in the village of **Bacalar** ㉔ and spend the night in ▣ **Chetumal** ㉕, visiting the Museo de la Cultura Maya. On Day 7, travel to **Kohunlich** ㉖, known for its huge stucco masks of ancient Maya rulers and the surrounding jungle's ruins. Head into the nearby farmlands to visit the majestic pyramids of **Dzibanché** and **Kinichná** ㉗. Then drive back up the coast to ▣ **Playa del Carmen** ⑥, stopping at the Cenote Azul, Mexico's largest sinkhole, and at **Muyil** ⑲, with its small Maya temple and remote lagoon.

Timing

High season or not, if you're driving, start early in the day to beat the tour buses; most come from nearby Cancún and Playa del Carmen, Mexico's most popular resorts. The new cruise-ship terminal near Xcaret is also putting more buses on the road. Be sure to get to your overnight stop before dark. September and October are hurricane months so expect plenty of rain—and mosquitoes.

THE RIVIERA MAYA

It takes patience to discover the coast's treasures. Beaches and towns aren't easily visible from the main highway—the road from Cancún to Tulum is 1 km–2 km (½ mi–1 mi) from the coast. Thus there's little to see but dense vegetation; lots of billboards; many roadside markets; and signs marking entrances to businesses, ruins, resorts, beaches, and campgrounds.

The Mexican government under the old ruling PRI (Institutional Revolutionary Party) sold vast tracts of land and beaches to corporations, and they have built huge resorts. So far there are 22,000 hotel rooms in the Riviera Maya area, which stretches from Punta Tanchacté south to Punta Allen. The frenzy of building has affected the wildlife as well as the beachside Maya communities, which have had to relocate to the jungle. The government even launched four planned towns with low-cost housing and other public services meant for the growing number of people—many local Maya—who now work in the region's tourism industry.

The highway from Playa del Carmen to Tulum is lined with what seems like a giant barbed-wire fence punctuated with security gates. Many battles are taking place along the coast as environmentalists fight to preserve what land and wildlife are left against the onslaught of progress and keep the beaches open to everyone. Thanks to the federal government's foresight, 1.3 million acres of coastline and jungle have been set aside as the Reserva de la Biosfera Sian Ka'an. Whatever may happen elsewhere along the coast, this protected area gives the wildlife, and the travelers who seek the Yucatán of old, someplace to go.

Apart from the decidedly U.S. influence—thanks to Cancún—in northern Quintana Roo, the music, food, and cultural traditions of the Caribbean coast are Yucatecan. Although the beach resorts' international restaurants and modern malls flourish within a few kilometers of small Maya settlements, the Maya culture remains intact.

Aside from Playa del Carmen, there isn't much in the way of nightlife on the coast unless you happen upon some entertainment in a fancy hotel bar. Nor is shopping sophisticated here. There's little in the way of high-quality crafts, except in Playa del Carmen and its vicinity, where the number of good folk-art shops has been increasing.

Punta Tanchacté

❶ *28 km (17 mi) south of Cancún.*

The Riviera Maya experience starts at Punta Tanchacté (pronounced tan-chak-*te*), with small hotels on long stretches of beach caressed by

4

Archaeology

This corner of the Yucatán has some fantastic sites—cities built when the Maya controlled the trade routes in the region and beyond. Tulum, the last city to be built; Cobá, an important trade center; and Kohunlich, a political center with majestic stucco masks, are all breathtaking. Dzibanché and nearby Kinichná were powerful cities that dominated the southern coast during the Classic period. Trade ties linked Chacchoben to Tikal in Guatemala, and this led to a strong strategic alliance.

Temples with hidden chambers, fading murals that once told the tale of regents and kings, stelae carved with images of deities, and the sounds of wildlife hidden in the jungles intermingle at these sites. The temples flank grand plazas that were once the setting for religious pageantry. Royal tombs and ball courts hold mysteries that archaeologists are still trying to unravel. Roads have been carved out of the jungle to create easy access, especially on the southern coast. It's best to visit ruins early in the morning, before the tour buses arrive and the temperature rises. Regardless of when you visit, bring water and bug repellent.

Beaches

With the exception of those in more developed communities such as Puerto Morelos, Playa del Carmen, Akumal, and Puerto Aventuras, most beaches are uncrowded and have long expanses of platinum sand. South of Tulum, the beaches are even more deserted.

The Yucatán Peninsula is pure limestone, formed millions of years ago. And beneath the earth's surface is a complex river system that flows through cenotes, caves, and caverns. Many of these are so close to the shore that you can snorkel in fresh water very close to the ocean.

Snug little inlets and coves often create ideal conditions for swimming or snorkeling. One such cove is Akumal; another is Paamul. Farther south, in Tulum, the coast is wild, but the beaches are pristine and soothing. In Boca Paila, fly fishermen take advantage of the flats right off the beach for some vigorous bonefishing. At the tip of the Xcalak Peninsula, coconut palms grow practically to the water's edge. Giant sea turtles come ashore at night to lay their eggs on the beaches at Akumal, Xcaret, and especially at Xcacel.

Coastal Cuisine

At one time, rustic palapas serving freshly grilled fish offered *the* dining experience along the Caribbean coast. With the onslaught of luxury lodgings, this has changed. In the ever-more-populous Playa del Carmen, for example, menus invariably have a mix of Italian, Argentine, American, and vegetarian dishes alongside Yucatecan and Mexican standbys. Resort restaurants take international to a new level with Continental and Asian fare.

Dining is still defined by seafood, which is supplied fresh to coastal restaurants from numerous fishing villages, especially Punta Allen, where the lobster is famous. The best fish is found in no-frills eateries right on the beach here, simply prepared and good. Elsewhere preparations vary greatly—your grouper, dorado, or jumbo shrimp may be grilled, breaded, buttered, or served with garlic or other spices. Most restaurants will also cook your own deep-sea catches for you.

Fishing

The Caribbean coast draws anglers from all parts. If you want to go fly-fishing, you can rent boats from locals who have beachside stalls, especially at Boca Paila. Area fishing lodges also have their own boats and crews at hand to charter. Charter captains at the marina in Chetumal—the only marina along the coast—can take you out to deep waters for marlin, bonito, dorado, and sailfish. The Boca Paila Peninsula is great for a week of serious fishing, especially for the feisty bonefish. Farther south, Majahual is good for deep-water sportfishing and the Xcalak Peninsula is famous for fly-fishing. Coastal waters also teem with permit, snook, and tarpon.

Lodging

Although there's a range of accommodations—from campsites and strictly functional palapas and bungalows to mid-range hotels, luxury resorts, and condominiums—the northern coast has become one of the most expensive areas in Mexico and Central America. Many of the luxury properties are in Puerto Morelos, Punta Bete, Playa del Carmen, Akumal, and Puerto Aventuras. And more high-end resorts, especially all-inclusives, are being built outside these towns in prime beach areas.

Tulum has several tranquil ecological hotels. South of here, though, what few hotels there are tend to be either very primitive or very expensive. More properties are being built in Majahual, especially since the cruise-ship pier went into operation. These tend to be eco-lodges, though, much like those at Tulum. Bacalar has midsize hotels, though few of these are new. The Xcalak Peninsula is filling up with decent inns geared to those who dive or are interested in other outdoor activities. It's rare to find rooms with air-conditioning or a TV, but the trade-off is often a beautiful beach right outside your door.

Chetumal, a commercial center, has a respectable number of quality lodgings. On the flip side are a few holdouts that appear to have been last renovated during the War of the Castes. The latter category—popular with backpackers—reflects the town's origins as a stop for traders en route to or from Central America.

Nature

Untouched reefs, lagoons, cenotes, and caves along the Caribbean and down the Río Hondo (Hondo River, along the border between Mexico, Belize, and Guatemala) are filled with alligators, giant turtles, sharks, and tropical fish. The Río Hondo is also an official manatee sanctuary. You can spot this threatened animal and other creatures on a downriver kayak trip.

Farther north, near the Laguna de Bacalar, is the Fauna Studies Center, a nature preserve where tapir, great curassow, white-tailed deer, and toucan have been bred successfully in captivity. It's easy to stumble across yellow, blue, and scarlet butterflies; singing cicadas and orioles; sparkling dragonflies; kitelike frigates; and night owls nesting in the trees. In the jungle and the seaside marshes you can catch glimpses of parrots, toucans, terns, herons, and ibis. You can also spot wild pigs, foxes, turkeys, iguanas, lizards, and snakes in forest clearings. Jaguars, monkeys, white-tailed deer, armadillos, tapir, wild boars, peccaries, ocelots, raccoons, and badgers inhabit more isolated reaches.

At dusk, colorless crabs scuttle sideways toward the coconut groves over pale white limestone sand, while tiny persistent mosquitoes and gnats bore through the smallest rips in window screens, tents, and mosquito nets. The seasons are marked here by the wildlife: northern songbirds return in winter, newborn jellyfish invade beaches in spring, clouds of butterflies are born in the early summer heat, and sea turtles crowd the beaches throughout summer to lay thousands of eggs. It all unfolds before your eyes.

Scuba Diving & Snorkeling

The transparent turquoise-and-emerald waters here are strewn with rose, black, and red coral reefs as well as sunken pirate ships. Schools of black, gray, and gold angelfish; luminous green-and-purple parrot fish; earth-color manta rays; and scores of other jewel-tone species seem oblivious to curious humans and their underwater cameras. The visibility in these waters reaches 100 feet, so you can actually see the marine life without getting wet.

Akumal and Puerto Morelos have good dive sites. Tankah is known for its exotic Gorgonian Gardens, at a depth of from 20 feet to 80 feet. Everything seems to be in constant motion—not only the hundreds of tiny fish but also the sea fans, candelabras, and sponges. Banco Chinchorro, Mexico's largest coral atoll, also has superb dives. The isolated reef across from the Xcalak Peninsula is a graveyard of vessels that have foundered on the corals over the centuries. The reef is filled with conches, anemones, sea rods, moray eels, coral heads, precious black coral, and about 500 varieties of fish. Sea turtles nest each year on nearby beaches.

A series of cenotes lies just off the highway between Playa del Carmen and Tulum. They're favorites with divers, snorkelers, and swimmers. Highway signs make them easy to find. Or you can dive in the biggest cenote of them all, the Cenote Azul, which is known for its caves and is near Bacalar.

---

turquoise waters. It's quieter here than in Cancún, and you can walk for miles with only the birds for company.

Where to Stay

$$$$ 🏨 **Escape Paraiso Maya Hotel.** On a secluded beach, this low-key hotel has ocean views, lush grounds, and palapa-covered walkways. Rooms are filled with Maya designs and colorful art and have either two twin beds or one double as well as a tiny bathroom. The pools are small but still pleasant, as is the outdoor hot tub. Activities such as diving, kayaking, sailing, and evening shows are offered, and the food is excellent. A shuttle transports you to nearby Puerto Morelos, Cancún, or Playa del Carmen. ✉ *Carretera 307, Km 27.5* 📠 *998/872–8088* ⊕ *www.renthotel.com* ⇌ *60 rooms* ⚹ *Restaurant, in-room safes, 2 pools, outdoor hot tub, beach, dive shop, snorkeling, windsurfing, boating, volleyball, bar, dance club, theater, laundry service* ➾ *MC, V* ⏐○⏐ *AI.*

$–$$ 🏨 **Sand Castle.** An atrium with a high, arched ceiling overlooks the beach at this Mediterranean-style property. You can rent the whole complex (which can sleep 10 people), a floor, or a studio. The first-floor villa has

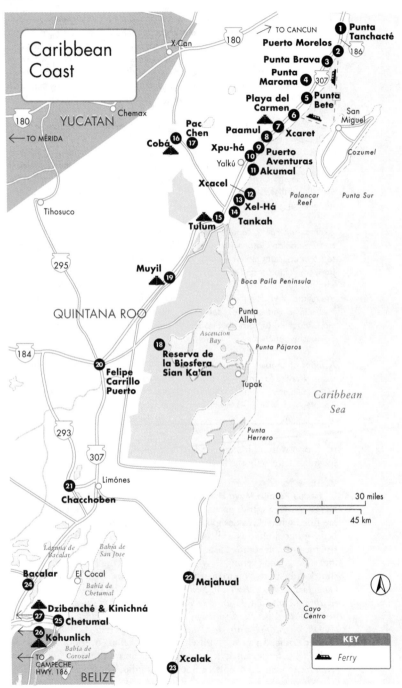

Caribbean Coast

TO CANCUN

Punta Tanchacté **1**
Puerto Morelos
Punta Brava **3**
Punta Maroma **4**
Playa del Carmen **5** Punta Bete
6
Paamul **7** Xcaret
8
Xpu-há **9** Puerto Aventuras
10
11 Akumal
Xcacel
12
13 Xel-Há
14 Tankah
Tulum **15**
Pac Chen **17**
Cobá **16**
Muyil **19**

2

X-Can

180

186

307

San Miguel

Cozumel

Palancar Reef

Punta Sur

YUCATAN

Chemax

180

TO MÉRIDA

Yalkú

Tihosuco

295

QUINTANA ROO

Boca Paila Peninsula

Punta Allen

Ascencion Bay

Punta Pájaros

18 Reserva de la Biosfera Sian Ka'an

Tupak

Caribbean Sea

184

20 Felipe Carrillo Puerto

293

307

Limónes

21 Chacchoben

0   30 miles
0   45 km

Laguna de Bacalar

Bahía de San José

Bacalar **24**

El Cocal

Bahía de Chetumal

22 Majahual

Cayo Centro

27 Dzibanché & Kinichná
25 Chetumal
26 Kohunlich

Bahía de Corozal

TO CAMPECHE, HWY. 186

BELIZE

Xcalak **23**

KEY

Ferry

a full-size kitchen, a living room, two bedrooms, 2½ large bathrooms, and a small patio facing the ocean. The upstairs studios have private baths, kitchenettes, large sundecks, and a balcony atrium. A separate casita for two is also available. ⊠ *Carretera 307, Km 27.5* ☎ *998/872–8093 or 998/872–8094* 🖨 *998/872–8093* ⊕ *www.villasandcastle.com* 🛏 *1 villa, 2 studios, 1 casita* ♨ *Pool, hot tub, massage, beach, snorkeling, shop, Internet; no room phones, no room TV* ▤ *MC, V.*

Puerto Morelos

❷ *8 km (5 mi) south of Punta Tanchacté.*

For years, Puerto Morelos was known as the small, relaxed coastal town where the car ferry left for Cozumel. This lack of regard actually helped it avoid overdevelopment, though now the construction of all-inclusive resorts nearby may spoil the fishing-village aura. And more people are discovering that Morelos, exactly halfway between Cancún and Playa del Carmen, makes a great base for exploring the region.

In ancient times this was one of the points of departure for pregnant Maya women making pilgrimages by canoe to Cozumel, the sacred isle of the fertility goddess, Ixchel. Remnants of Maya ruins exist along the coast here, but nothing has been restored. The town itself is small but colorful, with a central plaza surrounded by shops and restaurants; its trademark is a leaning lighthouse.

Puerto Morelos's greatest appeal lies out at sea: a superb coral reef only 1,800 feet offshore is an excellent place to snorkel and scuba dive. Its proximity to shore means that the waters here are calm and safe, though the beach isn't as attractive as others as it isn't regularly cleared of seaweed and turtle grass. Still, you can walk for miles here and see only a few people. In addition, the mangroves in back of town are home to 36 species of birds, making it a great place for bird-watchers.

☾ The biologists running the **Croco-Cun** (⊠ Carretera 307, Km 30 ☎ 998/884–4782) crocodile farm and zoo just north of Puerto Morelos have collected specimens of many of the reptiles and some of the mammals indigenous to the area. They offer immensely informative tours—you may even get to handle a baby crocodile or feed the deer. Be sure to wave hello to the 500-pound crocodile secure in his deep pit. The farm is open daily 8:30–5:30; admission is $6.

South of Puerto Morelos, the 150-acre **Jardín Botánico del Dr. Alfredo Barrera Marín** (Dr. Alfredo Barrera Marín Botanical Garden; ⊠ Carretera 307, Km 36 ☎ No phone), named for a local botanist, exhibits the peninsula's plants and flowers, which are labeled in English, Spanish, and Latin. There's also a tree nursery, a remarkable orchid and epiphyte garden, a reproduction of a *chiclero* (gum arabic collector), an authentic Maya house, and an archaeological site. A nature walk goes directly through the mangroves for some great bird-watching (bring that bug spray). A tree-house lookout offers a spectacular view—but the climb isn't for those afraid of heights. The garden is open daily 9–5, and admission is $5.

CloseUp
A SHORT HISTORY OF THE MAYA

THE MAYA SETTLED *in the lowlands of Guatemala, Mexico, and Belize before they moved north onto the Yucatán Peninsula. That puts the* height of the Classic period in the north at a time when the southern centers were being abandoned. The following divisions are commonly used by archaeologists who study the Maya.

Preclassic Period (2000 BC–AD 100): *At this time, farming replaced the nomadic lifestyle as the Maya adopted some of the ways of the Olmec, a more advanced culture. Monumental buildings with corbeled (false) arches and roof combs appeared, as did the first hieroglyphics and a calendar system.*

Classic Period (AD 100–AD 1000): *The Maya eventually developed their own art, language, science, and architecture. Trade routes were established helping the economy to grow. With the cult of the ruler, government became centralized; cities began to resemble small kingdoms or city-states. A distinct class system emerged, with the wealthiest living in elaborate ceremonial sites and the peasants in the rural areas. Regents had temples and pyramids constructed to chronicle their feats in war and to honor the gods. Buildings were placed on superstructures atop stepped platforms and were often decorated with bas-reliefs and ornate frescoes. The population's growing dependence on agriculture inspired the creation of the highly accurate Maya calendar, based on planting cycles. Examples of great Classic architecture are Yaxchilán, near Chiapas, and Uxmal and Sayil, both in Yucatán state.*

Postclassic Period (AD 1000–AD 1521): *Every flourishing civilization has its decline. Here, increased military activity and the growth of conquest states were the telltale signs. Powers from other Mexican cultures became part of the ruling bodies of the small sovereign states. This led to an increasingly warlike society, more elaborate temples and palaces, and a greater number of human sacrifices— especially after the Aztecs conquered the Yucatán. At the same time, the quality of Maya craftsmanship fell; for example, carved-stone building facades were replaced by carved stucco. Eventually many of the sites were abandoned. Chichén Itzá and Mayapán, both in Yucatán state, are representative of Postclassic architecture.*

Where to Stay & Eat

★ **$–$$$** ✕ **Casa del Mar.** The food at this family-run restaurant is some of the town's best. Choices include delicious empanadas, chicken fajitas, fresh salads, pastas, and incredible steaks that rival anything at the larger steak houses in Cancún (and for half the price). There's a palapa bar on a terrace that leads down to the beach. ⊠ *Calle Heriberto Frias 6* ☎ *998/ 871–0522* ▭ *D, MC, V.*

¢–$ ✕ **Twin Delphines Taquería & Restaurant.** You can watch the moon rise as you eat a delicious dinner at this open-air restaurant run by a local Mexican chef. The menu, which changes according to the season and what's available, offers specialties such as marinated shark with sautéed vegetables. When the weather is bad, this place is closed. ⊠ *Twin Delphines Aquarium, Av. Rafael Melgar s/n* ☎ *No phone* ▭ *No credit cards.*

$$$$ 🏨 **Ceiba del Mar Hotel & Spa.** For peace and quiet, this resort on a se-
Fodor'sChoice cluded beach is just the ticket. Rooms are in eight thatch-roofed build-
★ ings, and all have ocean-view terraces. Painted tiles, wrought ironwork, and bamboo details complement hardwood furnishings from Guadalajara. The whole effect is very Maya, though. A first-class spa offers massage and beauty treatments. There's also butler service, and your Continental breakfast is discreetly delivered to your room through a hidden closet chamber. ⊠ *Av. Niños Heroes s/n* ☎ *998/872–8060 or 877/545–6221* 🖷 *998/872–8061* ⊕ *www.ceibadelmar.com* ⇋ *120 rooms, 6 suites* ⚿ *2 restaurants, in-room safes, cable TV with movies, tennis court, pool, hot tub, spa, beach, dive shop, bar, shop, laundry service, concierge, meeting room, car rental, travel services* ▭ *AE, MC, V* ¹⊚¹ *CP.*

$$$$ 🏨 **Presidente InterContinental Paraiso de la Bonita Resort and Thalasso.**
Fodor'sChoice Eclectic is the byword at this luxury all-suites hotel. A pair of stone
★ dragons guards the entrance, and the spacious two-room guest quarters—all with sweeping sea and jungle views—are outfitted with furnishings from Asia, Africa, the Mediterranean, or the Caribbean. The restaurants, which are among the best in the Riviera Maya, adroitly blend Asian and Mexican flavors. The knockout spa has thalassotherapy treatments, some of which take place in specially built saltwater pools. ⊠ *Carretera 307, Km 328* ☎ *998/872–8300 or 800/327–7777* 🖷 *998/ 872–8301* ⊕ *www.paraisodelabonitaresort.com* ⇋ *90 suites* ⚿ *2 restaurants, in-room data ports, in-room safes, cable TV, golf privileges, tennis court, pool, health club, hot tub, massage, sauna, spa, steam room, beach, snorkeling, fishing, bar, laundry service, Internet, meeting room, airport shuttle, car rental, travel services, free parking; no kids under 13* ▭ *AE, DC, MC, V.*

$ 🏨 **Casa Caribe.** This small hotel is a few blocks from the town center and five minutes from the beach. Breezy rooms have king-size beds, coffeemakers, and large tile baths. Terraces have hammocks and views of the ocean or the mangroves. You can use the large kitchen, huge terrace, and the lounge area. The grounds include a walled courtyard and a fragrant tropical garden. ⊠ *Avs. Javier Rojo Gómez and Ejercito Mexicano, 3 blocks north of town* ☎ *998/871–0049, 763/441–7630 in U.S.* ⊕ *www.us-webmasters.com/casa-caribe* ⇋ *6 rooms* ⚿ *Fans, refrigerators, bar; no a/c, no room phones, no room TVs* ▭ *No credit cards.*

¢ 🏨 **Casita del Mar.** This hotel has an incredible beach, a lovely pool, and a great restaurant. Rooms are average size, with either twin beds or one king-size bed. Bathrooms are exceptionally clean and well done. Ask for one of the ocean-facing units, which have fantastic beach views and are perfect for watching the sunrise. The price of a room varies according to whether you have a sea view and whether you want a full breakfast included. ⊠ *Calle Heriberto Frias 6, 4 blocks north of town* 🏨 *998/ 871–0301* ⊕ *www.mayanriviera.com/hotels/Casita* ⇨ *17 rooms* ⊿ *Restaurant, some cable TV, pool, beach, snorkeling, fishing, laundry service; no room phones* ⊟ *AE, MC, V* ❁ *BP, EP.*

¢ 🏨 **Hotel Inglaterra.** The pluses at the Inglaterra are that it's clean, secure, and close to the beach. It also has free tea and coffee and a large, sunny upstairs deck. The staff can be cranky, though, and the hotel is sparse. Rooms are basic with one double and one single bed, a functional bathroom, ceiling fans, and absolutely no view (or air) from the windows. Four minisuites have air-conditioning, and there's a communal kitchen. ⊠ *Av. Niños Héroes 29* 🏨 *998/871–0418* ⇨ *14 rooms, 4 minisuites* ⊿ *Fans; no a/c in some rooms, no TV in some rooms* ⊟ *No credit cards.*

¢ 🏨 **Hotel Ojo de Agua.** It's a peaceful family-run hotel on the beach, and it's a great bargain, too. Half the rooms have kitchenettes; all the rooms are done in cheerful colors and have ceiling fans and views of the sea and courtyard gardens. An open-air restaurant serves good regional Mexican dishes along with American food. The beach offers superb snorkeling directly out front, including the Ojo de Agua, an underwater cenote shaped like an eye. ⊠ *Av. Javier Rojo Gómez, Sm 2, Lote 16* 🏨 *998/ 871–0027* 🏨 *998/871–0202* ⊕ *www.ojo-de-agua.com* ⇨ *36 rooms* ⊿ *Restaurant, some kitchenettes, pool, beach* ⊟ *D, MC, V.*

Sports & the Outdoors

Enrique at the PADI-affiliated **Almost Heaven Adventures** (🕾 998/871– 0230), in the main square by the currency exchange office, can set up snorkeling and diving trips. Instruction ranges from an $85 beginner course to a $275, four-day, open-water course; dives cost $45 for one tank, $65 for two tanks. **Brecko's** (⊠ Casita del Mar, Calle Heriberto Frias 6 🕾 998/871–0301) offers snorkeling and deep-sea fishing in a 25-foot boat. Snorkeling trips start at $15–$20 and fishing trips at $200. **David Sanchez** (🕾 998/860–0542), a PADI-certified dive master, is also a good bet for scuba-diving trips. A two-tank dive that lasts roughly 2½ hours costs $60. On a day trip with **H.E.A.D. South** (High Energy Adventure Day; 🕾 998/871–0483), Billy Alexander takes you out to snorkel at beaches with Spanish shipwrecks or to explore nearby cenotes. Trips start at $65. **Sub-Aqua Explorers** (🕾 998/871–0018) can set up scuba-diving excursions. Rates start at $60.

Shopping

Alma Libre Libros (⊠ Av. Tulum on main plaza 🕾 998/871–0264) is the only English-language bookstore on the coast, with more than 20,000 titles in stock. You can trade in your books for 25% of their cover prices and replenish your holiday reading. It's open October–April, Tuesday–Saturday 9–noon and 6–9.

The **Collectivo de Artesanos de Puerto Morelos** (Puerto Morelos Artists' Cooperative; ⊠ Avs. Javier Rojo Gómez and Isla Mujeres ☎ No phone) is a series of palapa-style buildings where local artisans sell their jewelry, hand-embroidered clothes, hammocks, and other items. You might find some real bargains here. It's open daily from 8 AM until dusk.

Rosario & Marco's Art Shoppe (⊠ Av. Javier Rojo Gómez 14 ☎ No phone), close to the ferry docks, is run by the eponymous couple from their living room. They paint regional scenes such as markets, colonial homes, and flora and fauna as well as portraits. Marco also creates replicas of Spanish galleons.

Punta Brava

❸ *7 km (4½ mi) south of Puerto Morelos on Carretera 307.*

Punta Brava is also known as South Beach in Puerto Morelos. It's a long, winding beach strewn with seashells. On windy days, its shallow waters are whipped up into waves large enough for bodysurfing.

Where to Stay

$$$$ 🏨 **El Dorado Royale.** This resort has been eclipsed by newer, more luxurious resorts, but the staff is friendly and the location—amid 500 acres of jungle and on a long, unspoiled beach—is great. Junior suites have Mexican furnishings, small sitting rooms, king-size beds, hot tubs, coffeemakers, and ocean-facing terraces. Casitas have domed roofs, king-size beds, DVD players, and oceanfront palapa terraces. Five restaurants serve à la carte menus filled with exceptional dishes. There's free shuttle service to Cancún and Playa del Carmen. ⊠ *Carretera 307, Km 45, Punta Brava* ☎ *998/872–8030 or 800/290–6679* 📠 *998/872–8031* ⊕ *www.eldorado-resort.com* 🛏 *304 junior suites, 73 casitas* ⚐ *5 restaurants, room service, some in-room hot tubs, 2 tennis courts, 8 pools, spa, beach, snorkeling, boating, bicycles, 6 bars, shop, laundry service, Internet, car rental, travel services; no kids* ☐ *AE, DC, MC, V* ¶⊙¶ *AI.*

Punta Maroma

❹ *2 km (1 mi) south of Punta Brava.*

On a bay where the winds don't reach the waters, this gorgeous beach remains calm even on blustery days. To the north you can see the land curve out to another beach, Playa del Secreto; to the south the curve that leads eventually to Punta Bete is visible.

Where to Stay & Eat

$$$$ ✕🏨 **Maroma.** It's an elegant, extravagant hotel, where peacocks wander jungle walkways and the scent of flowers fills the air. Rooms, which have small sitting areas, are filled with whimsical decorative items and original artwork. The king-size beds are draped in mosquito nets. A full breakfast is served on each room's private terrace. The restaurant excels at such dishes as lobster bisque and honeyed rack of lamb. A cutting-edge "flotarium" (a tank of water where you float deprived of light or sound) has been added to the spa. If you want to learn Span-

Fodor's Choice
★

ish, you can sign up for the private classes, which are held on the beach. ⊠ *Carretera 307, Km 51* ☎ *998/872–8200 or 866/454–9351* ☒ *998/872–8221* ⊕ *www.maromahotel.com* ⟿ *56 rooms, 8 villas ⚫ 2 restaurants, room service, golf privileges, pool, gym, hot tub, spa, beach, snorkeling, windsurfing, boating, fishing, horseback riding, bar, library, theater, laundry service, airport shuttle; no room phones, no kids ▤ AE, D, MC, V* ⫶⊙⫶ *BP.*

Punta Bete

❺ *13 km (8 mi) south of Punta Maroma on Carretera 307, then about 2 km (1 mi) off main road.*

The one concession to progress here has been a slight improvement in the road. Take this bumpy 2-km (1-mi) ride through the jungle to arrive at a 7-km-long (4½-mi-long) isolated beach dotted with bargain bungalow-style hotels and thatch-roofed restaurants. A few more-comfortable accommodations are available if you want to spare yourself some grit in your belongings.

Where to Stay

$$$$ 🏨 **Ikal del Mar.** The name, which means "poetry of the sea" is apt: this
FodorśChoice romantic jungle lodge on Punta Bete's beach vibrates with under-
★ stated luxury and sophistication. Guests have included European heads of state, who seem to cherish the privacy and serenity. Villas are named after poets and have thatched ceilings with intricate woodwork, sumptuous Egyptian-cotton sheets, Swiss piqué robes, and tony Molton Brown soaps and shampoos. Beside the sea near temple ruins, the spa delicately fuses Maya healing lore and ancient techniques into its treatments. The restaurant serves excellent Mediterranean-Yucatecan cuisine and has an outstanding wine cellar. ⊠ *Playa Xcalacoco, 9 km (5½ mi) north of Playa del Carmen* ☎ *984/877–3000 or 888/230–7330* ☒ *984/877–3009, 713/528–3697 in U.S.* ⊕ *www.ikaldelmar.com* ⟿ *29 rooms, 1 suite ⚫ Restaurant, in-room data ports, cable TV, pool, fitness classes, gym, spa, beach, dive shop, bar, laundry service, concierge, car rental, travel services, free parking; no kids under 16 ▤ AE, D, MC, V.*

$$$ 🏨 **Posada del Capitán Lafitte.** This warm, family-friendly resort is named after a pirate known to have frequented local waters. Guest quarters are in duplexes and three- or four-unit cabanas—opt for a newer cabana on the beach's tranquil north end. All units have balconies and hammocks, and some are practically flush with the ocean for wonderful views. One of the first resorts on the Riviera Maya, this hotel has aged gracefully; just try to disregard the tacky cement fortresslike structure that marks the highway turnoff. ⊠ *Carretera 307, Km 62* ⊡ *reservations: Turquoise Reef Group, Box 2664, Evergreen, CO 80439* ☎ *303/674–8735 or 800/538–6802* ☒☒ *984/873–0212* ☒ *303/674–8735 in U.S.* ⊕ *www.mexicoholiday.com* ⟿ *62 rooms ⚫ Restaurant, fans, minibars, pool, beach, dive shop, snorkeling, boating, fishing, horseback riding, bar, Internet, car rental; no a/c in some rooms, no TV in some rooms ▤ AE, MC, V* ⫶⊙⫶ *MAP.*

$$ ⌂ **Kai Luum II.** The lazy man's answer to camping out, this much-loved vacation spot has "tentalapas"—large canvas tents under palapa roofs with ocean-view porches, hammocks, and double beds with fluffy pillows. Bathrooms are shared, and there's no electricity. The restaurant, which serves Yucatecan specialties, is under a giant palapa lit by oil lamps. ⊠ *Carretera 307, Km 62, beyond Posada del Capitán Lafitte* ⌂ *reservations: Turquoise Reef Group, Box 2664, Evergreen, CO 80439* ☎ *303/674–8735 or 800/538–6802* ⊕ *www.mexicoholiday.com* ⤶ *29 tents* ⎔ *Restaurant, beach, snorkeling, fishing, bar; no a/c, no room phones, no room TVs, no kids under 16* ⊟ *AE, MC, V* ⋒ *MAP* ⊙ *Closed Sept. and Oct.*

¢–$ ⌂ **Cocos Cabañas.** Enjoy tranquillity and seclusion in these cozy palapa bungalows 30 yards from the beach. Although small, the bungalows are colorful and bright and have a bath, a netting-draped queen- or king-size bed, hammocks, and a terrace that leads to a garden. Breakfast, lunch, and dinner are served at the Grill Bar, whose menu includes fresh fish dishes as well as Italian fare. The place is owned and managed by a former Swiss chef, so the service and the food are excellent. ⊠ *Playa Xcalacoco, follow signs and take dirt road off Carretera 307, Km 42, for about 3 km (2 mi)* ☎ *998/874–7056* ⎙ *998/887–9964* ⤶ *5 bungalows* ⎔ *Restaurant, fans, pool, beach, snorkeling, fishing; no a/c, no room phones, no room TVs* ⊟ *No credit cards.*

¢ ⌂ **Xcalacoco Juanitos.** You're really roughing it on the beach here. The place is secluded and a bit grungy, rooms are spartan, and there are no private baths and no electricity (kerosene lamps light up the nights). That said, rooms have double beds, hammocks, and small porches, and you can't beat the price or the beach, which you'll probably have all to yourself. There are also camping facilities with showers. ⊠ *Playa Xcalacoco, follow signs and take dirt road off Carretera 307, Km 42, for about 3 km (2 mi)* ☎ *984/100–4487* ⤶ *7 cabanas* ⎔ *Restaurant, beach; no a/c, no room phones, no room TVs* ⊟ *No credit cards.*

Playa del Carmen

6 *10 km (6 mi) south of Punta Bete, 68 km (42 mi) south of Cancún.*

Once upon a time, Playa del Carmen was a fishing village with a ravishing deserted beach. The villagers fished and raised coconut palms to produce copra, and the only foreigners who ventured here were beach bums. These days, however, it's one of Latin America's fastest-growing communities, with a population of more than 135,000 and a pace almost as hectic as Cancún's. The beach is still delightful—alabaster-white sand, turquoise-blue waters—it's just not deserted.

Hotels, restaurants, and shops multiply faster than you can say "Kukulcán." Some businesses are branches of Cancún establishments whose owners have taken up permanent residence in Playa or commute daily between the two places. Other businesses are owned by American and European expats who came here years ago. It makes for a varied, international community.

Avenida 5, the first street parallel to the beach, is a colorfully tiled pedestrian walkway with shops, cafés, and street performers; small hotels and stores stretch north from this avenue. Avenida Juárez, running east–west from the highway to the beach, is the main commercial zone for the Riviera Maya corridor. Here, locals visit the food shops, pharmacies, auto-parts and hardware stores, and banks that line the curbs. People traveling the coast by car usually stop here to stock up on supplies—its banks, grocery stores, and gas stations are the last ones until Tulum.

The ferry pier, where the hourly boats arrive from and depart for Cozumel, is another busy part of town. The streets leading from the dock have shops, restaurants, cafés, a hotel, a basketball court, and food stands. Take a stroll north from the pier along the beach to find the serious sun worshippers. On the pier's south side is the edge of the sprawling Playacar complex. The development is a labyrinth of residences and all-inclusive resorts bordered by an 18-hole championship golf course. The excellent 32-acre **Xaman Ha Aviary** (⊠ Paseo Xaman-Ha, Playacar ☎ 984/873–0593), in the middle of the Playacar development, is home to more than 30 species of native birds. It's open daily 9–5, and admission is $8.

Where to Eat

★ $$–$$$ ✕ **Blue Lobster.** You can chose your dinner live from a tank and if it's grilled, you pay by the weight—the average is $10–$50 a platter. At night, the candlelit dining room draws a good crowd. People come not only for the lobster but also for the ceviche, mussels, jumbo shrimp, or imported T-bone steak. Ask for a table on the terrace overlooking the street. ⊠ *Calle 12 and Av. 5* ☎ *984/873–1360* ▭ *AE, MC, V* ☾ *No lunch.*

$–$$$ ✕ **Casa del Agua.** Gunther Spath, the patriarch of the Swiss family that
Fodor'sChoice   founded this restaurant, learned his trade as manager of Las Palapas hotel
★   north of Playa del Carmen. His praiseworthy German, Italian, and Swiss dishes include sliced chicken Zurich with spaetzle and mushroom gravy and the ever-popular steak Roquefort. Finish up with Mama Spath's Hot Love, an ice-cream-and-hot-blueberry dessert. ⊠ *Av. 5 and Calle 2* ☎ *984/803–0232* ▭ *MC, V.*

$–$$$ ✕ **Media Luna.** The Canadian couple that runs this stylish restaurant has combined Toronto-style preparations of vegetarian, fish, and chicken dishes with Mexican flavors. Choices include curried root-vegetable puree with cilantro cream and black-crusted fish with steamed rice. Dine alfresco on the second-floor balcony or people-watch from the street-level dining room. There are fixed-price lunches ($5) and dinners ($10) daily. ⊠ *Av. 5 between Calles 12 and 14* ☎ *984/873–0526* ▭ *No credit cards.*

$–$$$ ✕ **La Parrilla.** Excellent Mexican fare is the draw at this boisterous, touristy restaurant. The smell of sizzling *parrilla mixta* (a grilled, marinated mixture of lobster, shrimp, chicken, and steak) can make it difficult to resist grabbing one of the few available tables. Also tempting are the strong margaritas, the friendly service, and the live music. ⊠ *Av. 5 and Calle 8* ☎ *984/873–0687* ▭ *AE, D, MC, V* ☾ *No lunch.*

$-$$$ ✕ **Sur.** This two-story enclave of food from the Pampas region of Argentina is a trendy spot. Sky-blue tablecloths and plants complement hardwood floors in the intimate upstairs dining room. Entrées come with four sauces, dominant among them *chimichurri*, made with oil, vinegar, and finely chopped herbs. Start off with meat or spinach empanadas or Argentine sausage, followed by a sizzling half-pound *churrasco* (top sirloin steak). Finish the meal with warm caramel crepes. ⊠ *Calle Corozon between Calles 12 and 14* ☎ *984/803–2995* ⊟ *D, MC, V* ⊘ *No lunch Sun.*

★ **$-$$$** ✕ **Yaxche.** One of Playa's best restaurants has copies of hand-carved stelae from famous ruins and murals of Maya gods and kings. Maya dishes such as *halach winic* (chicken in a spicy four-pepper sauce) are superb. Finish your meal with a Maya Kiss (Kahlúa and Xtabentun, the local liqueur flavored with anise and honey). ⊠ *Calle 8 and Av. 5* ☎ *984/873–2502* ⊟ *AE, MC, V.*

$-$$ ✕ **Casa Tucan.** This sidewalk restaurant may be small—it has only 10 tables—but is nonetheless refined. Homemade Italian and Greek dishes are the specialty; try the spanakopita served with salad or the grilled salmon with brandy sauce. Everything is fresh; even the herbs are homegrown. ⊠ *Calle 4 between Avs. 10 and 15* ☎ *984/873–0283* ⊟ *D, MC, V.*

$-$$ ✕ **Palapa Hemingway.** A mural of Che Guevara sporting a knife and fork looms larger than life in this palapa seafood restaurant focused on Cuba and its revolution. The grilled shrimp, fish, and steaks are good choices, as are the fresh salads, pastas, and chicken dishes. ⊠ *Av. 5 between Calles 12 and 14* ☎ *984/873–0004* ⊟ *MC, V.*

$ ✕ **Sabor.** The salads, sandwiches, and baked goods are tasty, and the open-air location—with a bird's-eye view of busy Avenida 5—is great. Although the interior is plain, the service is fast and efficient. Seats at breakfast and lunch are hard to find; if you don't like rap music, you should avoid breakfasting here anyway. ⊠ *Av. 5 between Calles 2 and 3* ☎ *No phone* ⊟ *No credit cards.*

$-$$ ✕ **Señor Frog's.** From a table at this restaurant beside the pier you can watch the Cozumel ferries arrive while dining on oysters Rockefeller, barbecued ribs, pizza, or a sandwich. The ultracasual, sprawling place gets lively in the evening thanks, in part, to the zany antics of the waiters and the DJ, who spins dance music after 10. People come here for fun and food, and it doesn't disappoint. ⊠ *Plaza Marina shopping center* ☎ *984/873–0930* ⊟ *AE, MC, V.*

¢-$ ✕ **Hot.** If this place were a still-life painting, it would be titled *Two Sidewalk Tables and a Grill.* It opens at 6 AM and whips up great egg dishes (the chile-and-cheese omelet is particularly good), baked goods, and hot coffee. Salads and sandwiches are lunch options. ⊠ *Calle 10 between Avs. 5 and 10* ☎ *984/876–4370* ⊟ *No credit cards* ⊘ *No dinner.*

¢ ✕ **Café Sasta.** This sweet little café serves fantastic coffee drinks (cappuccino, espresso, mocha blends), teas, light sandwiches, and baked goods. The staff is very pleasant—something that's becoming rare in Playa. ⊠ *Av. 5 between Calles 8 and 10* ☎ *984/873–3030* ⊟ *No credit cards.*

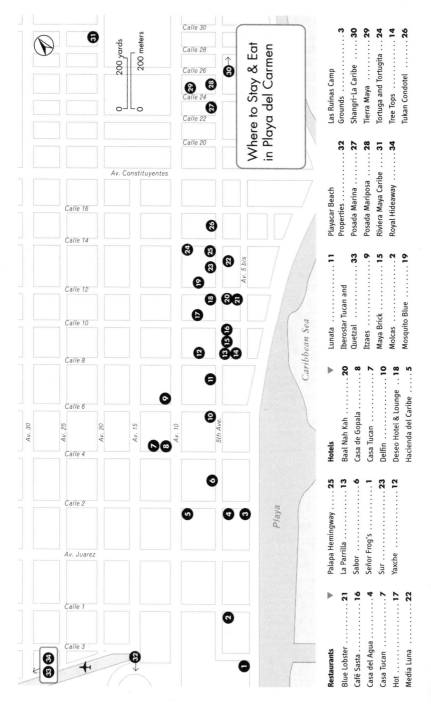

Calle 30
Calle 28
Calle 26
Calle 24
Calle 22
Calle 20

Av. Constituyentes

Calle 16
Calle 14
Calle 12
Calle 10
Calle 8
Calle 6
Calle 4
Calle 2

Av. Juarez

Calle 1
Calle 3

Av. 30
Av. 25
Av. 20
Av. 15
Av. 10
5th Ave.
Av. 5 bis

Caribbean Sea

Playa

200 yards
200 meters

Where to Stay & Eat in Playa del Carmen

Restaurants ▶

Blue Lobster **21**
Café Sasta **16**
Casa del Agua **4**
Casa Tucan **7**
Hot **17**
Media Luna **22**
Palapa Hemingway **25**
La Parrilla **13**
Sabor **6**
Señor Frog's **1**
Sur **23**
Yaxche **12**

Hotels ▶

Baal Nah Kah **20**
Casa de Gopala **8**
Casa Tucan **7**
Delfin **10**
Deseo Hotel & Lounge . . **18**
Hacienda del Caribe **5**
Lunata **11**
Iberostar Tucan and
Quetzal **33**
Itzaes **9**
Maya Brick **15**
Molcas **2**
Mosquito Blue **19**

Playacar Beach
Properties **32**
Posada Marina **27**
Posada Mariposa **28**
Riviera Maya Caribe . . . **31**
Royal Hideaway **34**

Las Ruinas Camp
Grounds **3**
Shangri-La Caribe **30**
Tierra Maya **29**
Tortuga and Tortugita . . **24**
Tree Tops **14**
Tukan Condotel **26**

Where to Stay

IN TOWN ★ $$$ **Lunata.** An elegant entrance, Spanish-tile floors, and hand-tooled furniture from Guadalajara greet you at this classy inn. Guest rooms have sitting areas, dark hardwood furnishings, high-quality crafts, orthopedic mattresses, and terraces—some with hammocks. Service is personal and gracious. Breakfast is laid out in the garden each day. ⊠ *Av. 5 between Calles 6 and 8* ☎ *984/873–0884* ⌸ *984/873–1240* ⊕ *www. lunata.com* ⫏ *10 rooms* ⌂ *Refrigerators, cable TV, laundry service, car rental* ▤ *AE, MC, V* ⦿ *CP.*

$$$ **Shangri-La Caribe.** Shangri-La used to be on the outskirts of Playa, but now it's considered part of northern downtown. It remains a tranquil beachside resort with attractive whitewashed bungalows and plenty of European guests. Rooms have comfortable beds, tile floors, baths, and balconies or patios with hammocks. The restaurants serve Mexican and international fare. ⊠ *Calle 38 between Av. 5 and Zona Playa* ⫐ *reservations: Turquoise Reef Group, Box 2664, Evergreen, CO 80439* ☎ *984/873–0611 or 800/538–6802* ⌸ *984/873–0500* ⊕ *www. shangrilacaribe.net* ⫏ *97 rooms, 10 suites* ⌂ *3 restaurants, 2 pools, beach, dive shop, snorkeling, fishing, laundry service, airport shuttle (fee), car rental; no a/c in some rooms, no room phones, no room TVs* ▤ *AE, MC, V* ⦿ *MAP.*

$$–$$$ **Deseo Hotel & Lounge.** The Deseo is somewhere between cutting-edge and corny. It starts with a Maya-pyramid stairway that cuts through a stark modern building. The steps lead to a minimalist, white-on-white, open-air lobby, with huge daybeds for sunning, a trendy bar, and the pool, which is lit with purple lights at night. Each of the austere guest rooms has a bed, a lamp, and clothesline hung with flip-flops, earplugs (the bar has its own DJ), bananas, and a beach bag. Suites are large and have clawfoot tubs. ⊠ *Av. 5 and Calle 12* ☎ *984/879–3620* ⌸ *984/879–3621* ⊕ *www.hoteldeseo.com* ⫏ *15 rooms, 3 suites* ⌂ *Room service, in-room safes, minibars, pool, bar, lounge, car rental, travel services; no phones in some rooms, no TV in some rooms, no kids* ▤ *AE, MC, V.*

$$ **Hacienda del Caribe.** This hotel evokes an old Yucatecan hacienda— albeit a colorful one—with wrought-iron balconies, stained-glass windows, and Talavera tile work. Guest rooms have such unique details as headboards with calla lily motifs and painted tile sinks. The pool is right off the lobby and surrounded by a small restaurant. The beach is a half block away. ⊠ *Calle 2 between Avs. 5 and 10* ☎ *984/873–3132* ⌸ *984/ 873–1149* ⊕ *www.haciendadelcaribe.com* ⫏ *27 rooms, 5 suites* ⌂ *Restaurant, fans, in-room safes, cable TV, pool, car rental, free parking* ▤ *D, MC, V.*

$$ **Itzaes.** Although this modern hotel in a colonial-style building has amenities geared toward business travelers, divers also like to stay here as it's two blocks from the beach. The lobby opens onto a marble, vine-draped atrium with several homey sitting areas as well as a tapas bar. Extra-spacious rooms have tile floors, two double beds, desks, and hair dryers. The staff is warm and efficient. ⊠ *Av. 10 and Calle 6* ☎ *984/ 873–2397* ⌸ *984/873–2373* ⊕ *www.itzaes.com* ⫏ *16 rooms* ⌂ *In-room data ports, minibars, cable TV, pool, hot tub, concierge, car rental* ▤ *MC, V* ⦿ *BP.*

$$ ⊡ **Molcas.** Steps from the ferry docks, this colonial-style hotel has been in business since the early 1980s and has aged gracefully. Rooms have dark-wood furniture and face the pool, the sea, or the street. The second-floor pool area is glamorous, with white tables, umbrellas, and uniformed waiters. Although it's in the heart of town, the hotel is well insulated from noise. ⊠ *Av. 5 and Calle 1 Sur* ☎ 984/873–0070 🖨 984/873–0138 ⊕ *www.molcas.com* ⟿ *25 rooms* ⌂ *Restaurant, refrigerators, pool, beach, bar* ▭ *AE, MC, V.*

$$ ⊡ **Mosquito Blue.** It's simultaneously casual, exotic, and elegant. The lobby and guest quarters have Indonesian details, mahogany furniture, and soft lighting. King-size beds and great views round out the rooms. The open-air bar is a soothing spot—it's sheltered by a thatched roof and surrounded by pastel walls in a cloistered courtyard near one of the swimming pools. The restaurant serves Mexican and Italian cuisine. ⊠ *Calle 12 between Avs. 5 and 10* ☎ 984/873–1335 ⊕ *www. mosquitoblue.com* ⟿ *46 rooms, 1 suite* ⌂ *Restaurant, cable TV, 2 pools, massage, dive shop, bar, laundry service, car rental, travel services; no kids under 16* ▭ *AE, MC, V.*

$$ ⊡ **Tierra Maya.** The Spanish owners have transformed this small inn just three blocks from the beach into a little work of art, with burned-orange and ocher color schemes, stucco Maya masks, batik wall hangings, and rustic wood-frame beds. All guest rooms have balconies overlooking the garden and pool area, which also has a thatch-roofed restaurant, a reading pavilion, and a *temazcal* (sweat lodge). The temazcal ceremony led by a shaman costs $70 and includes purification rituals, massage, and fruit juices. The apartment and the suite have kitchenettes. ⊠ *Calle 24 between Avs. 5 and 10* ☎ 984/873–3960 ⊕ *www.hoteltierra maya.com* ⟿ *21 rooms, 1 suite, 1 apartment* ⌂ *Restaurant, fans, in-room safes, some kitchenettes, cable TV, pool, massage, bar, concierge, Internet, free parking* ▭ *MC, V.*

$$ ⊡ **Tukan Condotel Villas and Beach Club.** There's an immense jungle-clad garden at the rustic entrance, which leads to a lobby and sitting area. The small, simple rooms and suites are well separated from one another and have private terraces, tiny kitchenettes, tile floors, and painted wood furniture. (Make sure you choose a newly painted room as mold settles in fast in the tropics.) The garden has a pool and a natural cenote. The included buffet breakfast is served at the Tucan Maya restaurant, to one side of the hotel. ⊠ *Av. 5 between Calles 14 and 16* ☎ 984/873–0417 🖨 984/873–0668 ⊕ *www.eltukanconotel.com* ⟿ *56 rooms, 39 suites* ⌂ *Kitchenettes, cable TV, pool, bar; no a/c in some rooms* ▭ *MC, V* ⊘ *BP.*

$–$$ ⊡ **Baal Nah Kah.** True to its Maya name, which means "home hidden among the gum trees," this small hotel is quite homey. You can use the large kitchen, the sitting room, and the barbecue pit. The five bedrooms and one studio are on different levels, affording complete privacy. Two rooms have spacious balconies with ocean views; all have tile baths, double or king-size beds, and Mexican details. There's a small café next door, and the beach is a block away. ⊠ *Calle 12 near Av. 5* ☎ 984/873–2343 🖨 984/873–0050 ⊕ *www.playabedandbreakfast.*

com ⟲ *5 rooms, 1 studio* ♦ *Fans; no a/c in some rooms, no TV in some rooms* ▭ *No credit cards.*

$ ▦ **Delfín.** One of the area's longer-lived hotels retains the laid-back charm of old Playa. It's covered with ivy and looks fresh and smart. Sea breezes cool the bright rooms and mosaics lend touches of color. Some rooms also have wonderful ocean views. Restaurants and shops are close by. The management is exceptionally helpful. ⊠ *Av. 5 and Calle 6* ▦▦ *984/873–0176* ⊕ *www.hoteldelfin.com* ⟲ *14 rooms* ♦ *Fans, in-room safes, refrigerators, travel services; no a/c in some rooms, no room phones* ▭ *MC, V.*

$ ▦ **Posada Mariposa.** Not only is this Italian-style property in the quiet north end of town impeccable and comfortable, but it's also well priced. Rooms center on a garden with a small fountain. All have ocean views, queen-size beds, wall murals, luxurious bathrooms, and shared patios. Suites have full kitchens. Sunset from the rooftop is spectacular, and the beach is five minutes away. ⊠ *Av. 5 No. 314, between Calles 24 and 26* ▦▦ *984/873–3886* ⊕ *www.posada-mariposa.com* ⟲ *18 rooms, 6 suites* ♦ *Cable TV; no room phones* ▭ *No credit cards.*

$ ▦ **Riviera Maya Caribe.** It may not have the splash and dash of other Playa hotels, but this small property is very pleasant. It's in a quiet neighborhood and just two blocks from the beach. Rooms have tile floors, cedar furnishings, and spacious baths; suites also have hot tubs. Amenities include a coffee shop and a beach club. ⊠ *Av. 10 and Calle 30* ▦ *984/873–1193, 800/822–3274 in U.S. and Canada* ▦ *984/873–2311* ⊕ *www.hotelrivieramaya.com* ⟲ *17 rooms, 5 suites* ♦ *Coffee shop, room service, fans, in-room safes, minibars, cable TV, pool, hot tubs, dive shop, bicycles, laundry service, Internet, car rental* ▭ *MC, V.*

$ ▦ **Tortuga and Tortugita.** European couples tend to favor this inn on a quiet side street. Mosaic stone pathways wind through gardens, and colonial-style hardwood furnishings gleam throughout. Rooms are small but have balconies and are well equipped; junior suites have hot tubs. The restaurant specializes in seafood. ⊠ *Calle 14 and Av. 10* ▦ *984/873–1484* ▦ *984/873–0793* ⊕ *www.hotellatortuga.com* ⟲ *36 rooms, 9 junior suites* ♦ *Restaurant, fans, in-room safes, cable TV, pool, hot tubs, billiards, car rental, travel services; no kids under 15* ▭ *AE, MC, V.*

$ ▦ **Tree Tops.** Rooms are behind a jungly garden, which has a cenote right in the middle of it. The beach is nearby, too. Despite all the surrounding nature, the hotel is right in the heart of Playa's shopping and dining area. Units are fresh, painted in soft shades with cream-color tile floors, double beds, and spacious tubs. Small terraces have hammocks. There are also simple, less-expensive palapa rooms without air-conditioning, TV, or phones. ⊠ *Calle 8 between Av. 5 and the beach* ▦ *984/873–3195* ▦ *984/873–0351* ⊕ *www.treetopshotel.com* ⟲ *15 rooms, 2 suites, 1 bungalow* ♦ *Some refrigerators, some cable TV, pool; no a/c in some rooms, no phones in some rooms, no TV in some rooms* ▭ *MC, V.*

¢–$ ▦ **Casa de Gopala.** It's a great place to experience the laid-back rhythm of the old Playa. Once you pass through the wooden doors, you enter a private jungle that's cool and tranquil. Rooms are spacious, bright, and airy, with large windows, two double beds, and Mexican accents. There's no pool, but you can use the one at the Casa Tucan hotel. ⊠ *Calle 2 between Avs. 10 and 15* ☎☎ *984/873–0054* ⊕ *www. casadegopala.com* ➵ *16 rooms* ⟁ *Fans; no a/c in some rooms, no room phones, no room TVs* ⊟ *No credit cards.*

¢–$ ⊞ **Las Ruinas Camp Grounds.** It's near the beach, and it's the only authorized campground in town. Lodging options include cabanas (with baths), palapa and tent spaces (with communal baths), and RV spaces. A Continental breakfast comes with rooms. Restaurants are right outside the door, and Avenida 5 is a half block away. ⊠ *Calle 2 and Av. 5 Norte* ☎☎ *984/873–0405* ➵ *24 rooms* ⟁ *No a/c in some rooms, no room phones, no room TVs* ⊟ *No credit cards* ⫶❶⫶ *CP, EP.*

★ ¢ ⊞ **Casa Tucan.** For the price, it's hard to beat this warm, eclectic, German-managed hotel a few blocks from the beach. The gardens are home to rabbits, ducks, birds, and turtles. Mexican fabrics are put to good use in the cheerful rooms and apartments. The property also has a yoga palapa, a TV bar, a language school, a book exchange, and a specially designed pool that's used for classes by the staff at the on-site dive center. ⊠ *Calle 4 between Avs. 10 and 15* ☎ *984/873–0283* ⊕ *www. traveleasymexico.com* ➵ *24 rooms, 4 apartments* ⟁ *Restaurant, pool, dive shop, bar, recreation room, shops; no a/c in some rooms, no room phones, no room TVs* ⊟ *MC, V.*

¢ ⊞ **Maya Brick.** The best thing about this hotel is that it's in the middle of Avenida 5 yet it's still surprisingly quiet. Rooms are small, with double beds and private baths, and open onto the garden and small pool. Being next to a dive school, it attracts divers. You get a free diving lesson in the pool. ⊠ *Av. 5 between Calles 8 and 10* ☎ *984/873–0011* ⊟ *984/873–2041* ⊕ *www.mayabric.com* ➵ *29 rooms* ⟁ *Restaurant, fans, pool; no a/c in some rooms, no room phones, no room TVs* ⊟ *MC, V.*

¢ ⊞ **Posada Marina.** Popular with Italian budget travelers, this friendly, three-story, family–style hotel in the tranquil north part of Avenida 5 has small rooms done in shades of yellow as well as a patio garden with benches. Each floor has a sitting area looking out to sea. The cozy restaurant serves Italian cuisine. ⊠ *Av. 5 Norte between Calles 22 and 24* ☎ *984/873–3240* ⊕ *www.alphauniversal.com/posadamarina* ➵ *20 rooms* ⟁ *Restaurant; no a/c, no room phones, no room TVs* ⊟ *No credit cards.*

PLAYACAR ⊞ **Iberostar Tucan and Quetzal.** This unique resort has preserved its nat-
$$$$ ural surroundings—among the resident animals are flamingos, ducks, hens, turtles, toucans, and monkeys. Landscaped pool areas and fountains surround the open-air restaurant and reception area. Spacious rooms have cheerful Caribbean color schemes and patios overlooking dense vegetation. The four restaurants serve decent Mexican and international fare. ⊠ *Fracc. Playacar, Playacar* ☎ *984/873–0200 or 888/ 923–2722* ⊟ *984/873–0424* ⊕ *www.iberostar.com* ➵ *700 rooms* ⟁ *4 restaurants, room service, fans, in-room safes, minibars, cable TV, 2 tennis courts, 4 pools, health club, spa, beach, dive shop, snorkeling, windsurfing, boating, basketball, 2 bars, lounge, library, nightclub, recreation*

room, shops, baby-sitting, children's programs (ages 4–12), laundry service, concierge, Internet, meeting rooms, free parking ⊟ *AE, D, MC, V* ⊚| *AI.*

★ **$$$$** ⊞ **Royal Hideaway.** On a breathtaking stretch of beach, this 13-acre resort has exceptional amenities and superior service. Art and artifacts from around the world fill the lobby, and streams, waterfalls, and fountains dot the grounds. Rooms are in two- and three-story colonial-style villas, each with its own concierge, who will make reservations for you at the five on-site restaurants. Gorgeous rooms have two queen-size beds, sitting areas, and ocean-view terraces. The resort is wheelchair accessible. ⊠ *Fracc. Playacar, Lote 6, Playacar* ☎ *984/873–4500 or 800/858–2258* ⊟ *984/873–4506* ⊕ *www.allegroresorts.com* ⊅ *192 rooms, 8 suites* ♨ *5 restaurants, in-room data ports, cable TV, 2 tennis courts, 2 pools, exercise equipment, hot tub, spa, beach, snorkeling, windsurfing, bicycles, 3 bars, library, recreation room, theater, shops, laundry service, concierge, meeting rooms, Internet, travel services, free parking; no kids* ⊟ *AE, MC, V* ⊚| *AI.*

$$$ ⊞ **Playacar Beach Properties.** You can rent a furnished condo or house on the beach at this upscale resort area. Units have from one to four bedrooms as well as air-conditioning and maid service; they start at $175 a night (for a one-bedroom). There's a five-night minimum stay during high season, and reservations must be made at least six months in advance. The rest of the year, the minimum stay is only three nights. A 50% deposit is required. ⊠ *Av. 10 Sur at entrance to Playacar,* ☎ *984/873–0418* ⊟ *984/873–0148* ⊕ *www.playacarbeachproperties. com* ⊟ *MC, V.*

Nightlife

Alux (⊠ Av. Juárez and Calle 55 Sur ☎ 984/803–0713) has a bar, disco, and restaurant and is built into a cavern. **Apasionado** (⊠ Av. 5 ☎ 984/803–1101) has live jazz Wednesday through Sunday nights. At the **Blue Parrot** (⊠ Calle 12 and Av. 1 ☎ 984/873–0083) there's live music every night until midnight; the bar sometimes stays open until 3 AM. **Capitán Tutix** (⊠ Calle 4 Norte near Av. 5 ☎ 984/803–1595) is a beach bar designed to resemble a ship. Good drink prices and live music keep things humming until dawn.

To party off the beach check out **Coco Bongo** (⊠ Calle 6 between Avs. 5 and 10 ☎ 984/973–3189), a dance club that plays the latest Cuban sounds. For smooth jazz, head to the **Frida Bar** (⊠ Av. 5 and Calle 12 ☎ 984/973–2222), where the music happens Wednesday through Saturday. Folks take to the dance floor at **Señor Frog's** (⊠ Plaza Marina shopping center ☎ 984/876–2116), where the DJ spins music loud and clear until the wee hours.

Sports & the Outdoors

GOLF Playa's golf course is an 18-hole, par-72 championship course designed by Robert Von Hagge. The greens fee is $150; there's also a special twilight fee of $90. Information is available from the **Casa Club de Golf** (☎ 984/873–0624 or 998/881–6088).

HORSEBACK RIDING **Rancho Dos Amigos** (☎ 984/883–1138) offers horseback expeditions on the beach and in the jungle. The two-hour trips start at $35 and include food, drinks, and bilingual guides. Two-hour rides along beaches and jungle trails are run by **Rancho Loma Bonita** (☎ 984/887–5465) start at $45.

MOUNTAIN BIKING You can rent bicycles from **Universal Rent** (⊠ Av. 10 between Calles 12 and 14 ☎ 984/879–3358). The best (and safest) bike path is through Playacar.

SCUBA DIVING The PADI-affiliated **Abyss** (⊠ Calle 12 ☎ 984/873–2164) offers training ($80 for an introductory course) in addition to dive trips ($38 for one tank, $56 for two tanks) and packages. The oldest shop in town, **Tank-Ha Dive Shop** (⊠ Av. 5 between Calles 8 and 10 ☎☎ 984/873–5037) has PADI-certified teachers and runs diving and snorkeling trips to the reefs and caverns. A one-tank dive costs $35; for a two-tank trip it's $55; and for a cenote two-tank trip it's $90. Dive packages are also available. **Yucatek Divers** (⊠ Av. 15 Norte between Calles 2 and 4 ☎ 984/873–1363), which is affiliated with PADI, specializes in cenote dives and diving packages and works with divers who have disabilities. Introductory courses start at $75 for a one-tank dive and go as high as $350 for a four-day beginner course in open water.

SKYDIVING Thrill seekers can take the plunge high above Playa in a tandem sky dive (you're hooked up to the instructor the whole time). **SkyDive** (⊠ Plaza Marina 32 ☎ 984/873–0192) even videotapes your trip so you have proof that you did it.

Shopping

Avenida 5 between Calles 4 and 10 is the best place to shop along the coast. Boutiques sell folk art and textiles from around Mexico, and clothing stores carry lots of sarongs and beachwear made from Indonesian batiks. A shopping area called Calle Corozon, between Calles 12 and 14, has a pedestrian street, art galleries, restaurants, and boutiques.

Amber Mexicano (⊠ Av. 5 between Calles 4 and 6 ☎☎ 984/873–2357) has amber jewelry crafted by a local designer who imports the amber from Chiapas. **La Calaca** (⊠ Av. 5 between Calles 6 and 8 ⊠ Av. 5 and Calle 4 ☎ 984/873–0177 for both) has an eclectic collection of wooden masks and other carvings. The playful devils and angels are of note. **Etenoha Amber Gallery** (⊠ Av. 5 between Calles 8 and 10 ☎☎ 984/879–3716), run by a Swiss-Italian couple, has rustic-looking amber jewelry from Chiapas. Some of the stones have insects inside them, a characteristic that's highly prized by collectors. **Mango, Mango** (⊠ Av. 5 between Calles 6 and 8 ☎ 984/873–1240) sells high-style evening wear, swimsuits, and sportswear for women. **Mayan Arts Gallery** (⊠ Av. 5 between Calles 6 and 8 ☎ 984/879–3389) has an extensive collection of hand-carved Maya masks and *huipiles* (the traditional, white, sacklike dresses worn by Maya women) from Mexico and Guatemala.

The **Opals Mine** (⊠ Av. 5 between Calles 4 and 6 ☎ 984/879–5041 ⊠ Av. 5 and Calle 12 ☎ 984/803–3658) has fire, white, pink, and orange opals from the Jalisco State as well as turquoise. You can buy loose stones or commission pieces of jewelry. **Santa Prisca** (⊠ Av. 5 between Calles 2 and 4 ☎ 984/873–0960) has silver jewelry, flatware, trays, and decorative items from the town of Taxco. Some pieces are set with semiprecious stones. **Selva y Mar** (⊠ Av. 5 between Calles 4 and 6 ☎ 984/873–0525) showcases beaded masks made by Mexico's Huichol Indians. **Telart** (⊠ Av. Juárez 10 ☎ 984/873–0066) carries textiles from all over Mexico. **Xbal** (⊠ Av. 5 and Calle 14 ☎ 984/803–3352) is filled with attractive men's and women's cotton shirts, skirts, blouses, and shorts.

Xcaret

🚠 ⏱ **7** *11 km (6½ mi) south of Playa del Carmen.*

Once a sacred Maya city and port, Xcaret (pronounced *ish*-car-et) is now a 250-acre ecological theme park on a gorgeous stretch of coastline. It's the coast's most heavily advertised attraction, with its own buses, magazines, and stores. Though billed as "nature's sacred paradise," it's expensive, contrived, and crowded.

Highlights include an aviary, a butterfly pavilion, botanical gardens, riding stables, an aquarium with a sea-turtle nursery, a nursery for abandoned flamingo eggs, a man-made beach, a dive center with myriad sporting activities, a replica Maya village, a small zoo, some Maya ruins, and an underground river ride where you snorkel through a series of caves.

There's also a dolphinarium, where you can attend a dolphin workshop and touch swimming dolphins (although not swim with them) for $90 a person; book early as only 36 people a day are allowed to participate. A cruise-ship port, being constructed in partnership with the Carnival Corporation, is partially up and running; when it's finished it will be able to berth four ships.

Evenings see folkloric extravaganzas that begin with a reenactment of the Maya ball game, followed by an ancient fire ball game and a performance by the famed Voladores de Papantla (Fliers of Papantla) from Veracruz. The finale consists of regional folk dances performed by a 200-member dance troupe. An optional dinner ($24 a person) is served during the show.

Plan to spend the day and plenty of money. The hefty entrance fee covers only access to the grounds and the exhibits; all other activities and equipment—from lockers to snorkel and swim gear to horseback riding—are extra. You can buy tickets from any travel agency or major hotel along the coast. ☎ 998/881–2451 in Cancún ⊕ www.xcaret.net 💰 $49 (including show) ⏱ Daily 8:30 AM–9 PM.

Paamul

8 *10 km (6 mi) south of Xcaret.*

Beachcombers and snorkelers are fond of Paamul (pronounced paul-*mool*), a crescent-shape lagoon with clear, placid waters sheltered by a coral reef. Shells, sand dollars, and even glass beads—some from the sunken pirate ship at Akumal—wash onto the sandy parts of the beach.

In June and July you can see one of Paamul's chief attractions: sea-turtle hatchlings.

Where to Stay

$ ⊡ **Cabañas Paamul.** It's a rustic, secluded hostelry on a perfect white-sand beach. Ten bungalows face the sea, each with two double beds, ceiling fans, and hammocks. A large palapa houses the restaurant. Farther along the beach are 10 no-frills cabanas, which offer still more privacy. The property includes 140 RV hookups (gas, water, and drainage, $20 a day) as well as tent sites ($6 a day) and a full-service dive shop with PADI and NAUI certification courses. ⊠ *Carretera 307, Km 85* ☎ *984/875–1051* ⤳ *10 bungalows, 10 cabanas* ⚮ *Restaurant, fans, beach, dive shop, bar, laundry service; no a/c in some rooms, no room phones, no room TVs* ⊟ *No credit cards.*

Puerto Aventuras

❾ *5 km (3 mi) south of Paamul.*

While the rest of the coast has been caught up in development fever, Puerto Aventuras has been quietly doing its own thing. It has emerged as a popular vacation spot, particularly for families. It's not, however, the place to experience Yucatecan culture as it's like any planned community in the United States. The 900-acre self-contained resort is built around a 95-ship marina. It has a beach club, an 18-hole golf course, restaurants, shops, a great dive center, tennis courts, doctors, and a school. The **Museo CEDAM** displays coins, sewing needles, nautical devices, clay dishes, and other artifacts from 18th-century sunken ships. All recoveries were by members of the Mexican Underwater Expeditions Club (CEDAM), founded in 1959 by Pablo Bush Romero. ⊠ *North end of the marina behind the centro commercial* ☎☎ *984/873–5000* ⊠ *Donation* ☉ *Daily 10–1 and 3:30–5:30.*

The Maya-owned and -operated eco-park called **Cenotes Kantún Chi** has cenotes and underground caverns that are great for snorkeling and diving. The site includes some small Maya ruins and a botanical garden. The place is not at all slick, so it's a break from the coast's more commercial attractions. ⊠ *Carretera 307, 3 km (2 mi) south of Puerto Aventuras* ☎☎ *984/873–0021* ⊠ *$3* ☉ *Daily 8:30–5.*

Where to Stay & Eat

$$–$$$$ ✕ **Café Olé International.** The laid-back hub of Puerto Aventuras is a terrace café with a varied menu. Chicken chimichurri and coconut shrimp are good lunch or dinner choices; rib-eye cuts are also popular. In high season, musicians from around the world play until the wee hours on Sunday. ⊠ *Across from Omni Puerto Aventuras hotel* ☎ *984/873–5125* ⊟ *MC, V.*

$$$$ ⊡ **Omni Puerto Aventuras.** Simultaneously low key and elegant, this resort is a great place for some serious pampering. Each room has a king-size bed, a sitting area, an ocean-view balcony or terrace, and a hot tub. The beach is steps away, and the pool seems to flow right into the sea. A golf course and a marina are within walking distance. Breakfast and a newspaper arrive at your room every morning by way of a cubbyhole

to avoid disturbing your slumber. Ask about the all-inclusive plan. ✉ *Carretera 307, Km 269.5 (on beach near marina)* ☎ *984/873–5101 or 800/THE–OMNI* 🖷 *984/873–5102* ⊕ *www.omnihotels.com* ⟿ *30 rooms* ⌂ *2 restaurants, café, room service, cable TV, pool, gym, beach, dive shop, 2 bars, shop, baby-sitting, laundry service, meeting room, free parking* 🖃 *AE, MC, V* ⏏ *CP, AI.*

$$$ 🏨 **Casa del Agua.** This small, discreet, romantic hotel, lovingly designed
Fodor'sChoice by a Mexican painter, has one of the coast's most sumptuous beaches.
★ Each of the four large suites is strikingly different from the next. The Arroyo suite has a stream of water running above a round king-size bed; the Caleta has a double shower in a secluded garden; the Cenote promotes relaxation with its meditation room and to-die-for ocean view; and the Cascada commands a stunning vista of Puerto Aventuras from its L-shape balcony. ✉ *East of marina* ☎ *984/873–5184* ⊕ *www. casadelagua.com* ⟿ *4 suites* ⌂ *Room service, fans, minibars, massage, spa, beach, laundry services, Internet, airport shuttle; no room TVs, no kids* 🖃 *No credit cards* ⏏ *BP.*

Sports & the Outdoors

Aquanuts (✉ Center Complex, by marina 🖷🖷 984/873–5280) is a full-service dive shop that specializes in cave and cenote diving and offers certification courses. Dives start at $37 and courses at $349.

Xpu-há

⑩ *3 km (2 mi) south of Puerto Aventuras.*

Xpu-há (pronounced shpoo-*ha*) used to be a tranquil little beach until developers turned it into an overpriced eco-park, which subsequently closed. Since then, two megaresorts have invaded the beach, one of which hijacked a popular cenote that happened to lie on its property and is no longer open to the public.

Where to Stay

$$$$ 🏨 **Copacabana.** This lavish all-inclusive resort was designed around the surrounding jungle, cenotes, and beach. The lobby has bamboo furniture and a central waterfall underneath a giant palapa roof. Rooms have beautiful wood furniture, king-size beds, and private terraces with jungle views. Three large pools, separated from the outdoor hot tubs by an island of palm trees, look out onto the spectacular beach. The food is exceptional and served à la carte in two of the restaurants. ✉ *Carretera 307, Km 264.5* ☎ *984/875–1800 or 866/321–6880* 🖷 *984/875–1818* ⊕ *www.hotelcopacabana.com* ⟿ *224 rooms* ⌂ *4 restaurants, room service, fans, in-room safes, cable TV, golf privileges, 3 pools, gym, hot tubs, massage, beach, snorkeling, windsurfing, boating, volleyball, 4 bars, dance club, shops, children's programs (ages 4–12), laundry service, meeting rooms, travel services* 🖃 *D, MC, V* ⏏ *AI.*

$ 🏨 **Hotel Villas del Caribe.** Leon, the laid-back manager, makes sure you're well looked after at this throwback to simpler days. Rooms are basic, with double beds, simple furniture, and hot water. There's great, inexpensive food (especially the fish) at Café del Mar on the beach morning, noon, and night. Yoga classes are an option. ✉ *Carretera 307, Xpu-*

há X-4 (look for sun sign) ☎ *984/873–2194* ⊕ *www.hotelvillasdelcaribe. com* ➹ *14 rooms* ⌂ *Restaurant, beach, massage, bar; no room phones, no room TVs* ⊟ *No credit cards.*

Akumal

⑪   *37 km (23 mi) south of Playa del Carmen.*

In Maya, Akumal (pronounced ah-koo-*maal*) means "place of the turtle," and for hundreds of years this beach has been a nesting ground for turtles (the season is June–August and the best place to see them is on Half Moon Bay). The place first attracted international attention in 1926, when explorers discovered the *Mantanceros*, a Spanish galleon that sank in 1741. In 1958, Pablo Bush Romero, a wealthy businessman who loved diving these pristine waters, created the first resort, which became the headquarters for the club he formed—the Mexican Underwater Expeditions Club (CEDAM). Akumal soon attracted wealthy underwater adventurers who flew in on private planes and searched for sunken treasures.

These days Akumal is probably the most Americanized community on the coast. It consists of three areas: Half Moon Bay, with its pretty beaches, terrific snorkeling, and large number of rentals; Akumal Proper, a large resort with a market, grocery stores, laundry facilities, a pharmacy; and Akumal Aventuras, to the south, with more condos and homes. The original Maya community has been moved to a planned town across the highway.

Devoted snorkelers may want to walk the unmarked dirt road to **Yalkú**, a couple of miles north of Akumal in Half Moon Bay. A series of small lagoons that gradually reach the ocean, Yalkú is an eco-park that's home to schools of parrot fish in superbly clear water with visibility to 160 feet. It has restrooms and an entrance fee of about $8.

Where to Stay & Eat

$–$$ ✕ **Que Onda.** A Swiss-Italian couple created this northern Italian restaurant at the end of Half Moon Bay. Dishes are served under a palapa and include great homemade pastas, shrimp flambéed in cognac with a touch of saffron, and vegetarian lasagna. Que Onda also has a neighboring six-room hotel that's creatively furnished with Mexican and Guatemalan handicrafts. ⊠ *Caleta Yalkú, Lotes 97–99; enter through Club Akumal Caribe, turn left, and go north to very end of road at Half Moon Bay* ☎ *984/875–9101* ⊟ *MC, V* ☉ *Closed Tues.*

¢–$ ✕ **Turtle Bay Café & Bakery.** This funky café has delicious (and healthful) breakfasts and lunches. The real specialties are the smoothies and fresh baked goods. It has a garden to sit and drink coffee in, and its location by the ecological center makes it the closest thing to a downtown Akumal has. ⊠ *Plaza Ukana I, Loc. 15 (beginning of Half Moon Bay road)* ☎ *No phone* ⊟ *No credit cards* ☉ *No dinner.*

$$–$$$$ ▥ **Villas Akumal.** These white-stucco, thatch-roofed condos in a beachside residential development offer all the comforts of home and are perfect for extended stays (there are special rates if you book for a week). Units vary in size and configuration but most have cool tile floors, fabrics in tropical colors and prints, wicker furniture, and well-equipped kitchens. Many also have terraces with dynamite sea views—especially beautiful on evenings when the moon is full. On summer nights you can watch nesting sea turtles. ⊠ *Carretera Cancún–Tulum, Km 104, Fracc. Akumal C, Playa Jade* ☎ *55/5202–3600 Ext. 224 in Mexico City* ☎ *55/ 5202–8200 in Mexico City* ⊕ *www.lasvilasakumal.com* ⇗ *8 3-bedroom suites, 10 2-bedroom suites, 8 studios* ⟡ *Kitchen, cable TV, pool, beach, snorkeling, boating, concierge, airport shuttle, car rental, travel services, free parking* ⊟ *AE, MC, V.*

$$$ ▨ **Club Oasis Akumal.** One of the region's all-inclusive pioneers, this hotel with Yucatecan architecture, remains intimate and understated, with abundant tropical plants and flowers as well as mahogany railings, doors, furniture, and floors. Rooms are spacious and have terraces, king-size beds, and sitting areas. Bathrooms have tile showers with Moorish arches and windows and beach views. The beach is a hub for water-sports activities, and there's an exotic open-air ocean-side massage area. ⊠ *South of Akumal, off Carretera 307 at Km 251* ☎ *984/875–7300* ☎ *984/875–7302* ⊕ *www.oasishotels.com.mx* ⇗ *182 rooms* ⟡ *2 restaurants, cable TV, tennis court, 4 pools, massage, beach, dive shop, snorkeling, bicycles, 2 bars, baby-sitting, laundry service, car rental, travel services* ⊟ *AE, MC, V* ⦿ *AI.*

$$ ▨ **Club Akumal Caribe & Villas Maya.** Pablo Bush Romero established this resort in the 1960s to house his diving buddies, and it still has pleasant accommodations and a congenial staff—not to mention some of the best rates along the Riviera Maya. Rooms have rattan furniture, large beds, tile work, and ocean views. The bungalows are surrounded by gardens and have lots of beautiful Mexican tile. The secluded one-, two-, and three-bedroom units, called Villas Flamingo, are on Half Moon Bay and have kitchenettes as well as a separate beach and pools. Dive and meal-plan packages available. ⊠ *Carretera 307, Km 104* ☎ *984/875– 9012, 800/351–1622 in U.S. and Canada, 800/343–1440 in Canada* ☎ *915/581–6709* ⊕ *www.hotelakumalcaribe.com* ⇗ *21 rooms, 40 bungalows, 4 villas, 1 condo* ⟡ *Restaurant, grocery, ice cream parlor, pizzeria, snack bar, fans, some kitchenettes, refrigerators, pool, beach, 2 dive shops, bar, baby-sitting, children's programs (ages 2–12); no room phones, no TV in some rooms* ⊟ *AE, MC, V.*

$$ ▨ **Vista Del Mar.** Each small room has an ocean view, a terrace, a king-size bed, and colorful Guatemalan-Mexican accents. Next door are more expensive condos with Spanish-colonial touches. The spacious one-, two-, and three-bedroom units have full kitchens, living and dining rooms, and oceanfront balconies. ⊠ *South end of Half Moon Bay* ☎ *984/875–9060 or 877/425–8625* ☎ *984/875–9061* ⊕ *www.akumalinfo. com* ⇗ *15 rooms, 8 condos* ⟡ *Restaurant, grocery, some kitchenettes, minibars, refrigerators, cable TV with movies, pool, beach, dive shop; no room phones* ⊟ *AE, MC, V.*

Sports & the Outdoors

The **Akumal Dive Center** (⊠ About 10 mins north of Club Akumal Caribe ☎ 984/875–9025) is the area's oldest and most experienced dive operation, offering reef or cenote diving, fishing, and snorkeling. Dives cost from $33 (one tank) to $110 (four tanks); a two-hour fishing trip for as many as four people runs $99.

en route

Aktun-Chen is Maya for "the cave with cenote inside." These amazing underground caves, estimated to be about 5 million years old, are the area's largest. You walk through the underground passages, past stalactites and stalagmites, until you reach the cenote with its various shades of deep green. You don't want to miss this one. ⊠ *Carretera 307, Km 107* ☎ *984/884–0444* ⊕ *www. aktunchen.com* ✉ *$8 (including 1-hr tour)* ⊙ *Daily 8:30–4.*

Xcacel

⓬ *7 km (4½ mi) south of Akumal.*

Xcacel (pronounced *ish*-ka-shell) is one of the few remaining nesting grounds for the endangered Atlantic green and loggerhead turtles. For years it was a federally protected zone, until it was sold—illegally—in 1998 to a Spanish conglomerate. The group immediately tried to push through an elaborate development plan that would have destroyed the nesting grounds. This prompted Greenpeace, in cooperation with biologists, scientists, and other locals, to fight an international campaign, which they won, to save the turtles. You can visit the turtle center or offer to volunteer. The Friends of Xcacel Web site (www.turtles.org/xcacel. htm) has more information.

Xel-Há

⓭ *3 km (2 mi) south of Laguna de Xcacel.*

Brought to you by the people who manage Xcaret, Xel-Há (pronounced shel-*hah*) is a natural aquarium made from coves, inlets, and lagoons cut from the limestone shoreline. The name means "where the water is born," and a natural spring here flows out to meet the saltwater, creating a perfect habitat for tropical marine life. Scattered throughout the park are small Maya ruins, including Na Balaam, known for a yellow jaguar painted on one of its walls. Low wooden bridges over the lagoons allow for leisurely walks around the park, and there are spots to rest or swim. Although there seems to be fewer fish each year, and the mixture of fresh- and saltwater can cloud visibility, there is still enough here to impress novice snorkelers.

The place gets overwhelmingly crowded, so come early. The grounds are well equipped with bathrooms, restaurants, and a shop. At the entrance you will receive specially prepared sunscreen that won't kill the fish; other sunscreens are prohibited. For an extra charge, you can "interact" (not swim) with dolphins. There's also an all-inclusive package with a meal, a towel, a locker, and snorkel equipment for $61. ☎ *984/ 875–6000* ⊕ *www.xelha.com.mx* ✉ *$25–$31* ⊙ *Daily 9–5:30.*

The squat structures of the compact, little-visited **Xel-Há Archaeological Site** are thought to have been inhabited from about 300 BC–AD 100, until about AD 1200–AD 1521. The most interesting sights are on the north end of the ruins, where remains of a Maya *sacbé* (road) and mural paintings in the **Jaguar House** sit near a tranquil, deep cenote. The site takes about 45 minutes to visit. ☎ *No phone* ✉ *$3; free Sun.* ⊙ *Daily 8–5.*

Tankah

🔟 *9½ km (6 mi) south of Xel-Há on the dirt road off Carretera 307.*

In ancient Maya times, Tankah (pronounced *taan*-ka), which is between Xel-Há and Tulum, was a more important trading city than Tulum. Many centuries later, it evolved into a beach without too much development. Since electricity was brought in in 2001, all this has changed. The growing number of very small hotels offers rooms and cabanas at reasonable prices.

Where to Stay & Eat

$$ ✕🏠 **Casa Cenote.** Mostly known as a restaurant ($)—and still the only place to eat on the beach—Casa Cenote is beside a large fresh- and salt-water cenote full of fish. You can go for a snorkeling trip and then rest in the shade while you wait for your meal. The simple menu includes burgers, chicken, fish, beer, and margaritas. Sunday sees an all-you-can-eat Texas barbecue for $12. Guest rooms have *equipal* furniture (leather furniture from Jalisco State) and small patios facing the beach. The price of a room not only includes a full breakfast, but also use of kayaking and snorkel equipment. ⊠ *Turn left at end of dirt road from Carretera 307 into Tankah (look for Casa Cenote sign)* ☎ *998/874–5170* ⊕ *www. casacenote.com* 🛏 *7 rooms* ⌂ *Restaurant, beach, dive shop, snorkeling, boating; no a/c in some rooms, no room phones, no room TVs* ▭ *MC, V* ⦿ *BP.*

★ **$$** 🏠 **Blue Sky.** Guest quarters have such one-of-a-kind pieces as Cuban oil paintings, Guatemalan bedspreads, handblown vases, inlaid-silver mirrors, and chairs hand-tooled of native *chichén* wood. A couple of suites have sofa beds. The open-air dining room is swept of mosquitoes by a special carbon-dioxide machine developed by the U.S. military. ⊠ *Bahía Tankah, past Casa Cenote* ☎ *998/801–4004 or 877/792–9237* 📠 *984/ 873–5225* ⊕ *www.blueskymexico.com* 🛏 *6 rooms, 2 suites* ⌂ *Restaurant, beach, snorkeling, boating, bicycles, library, shop, Internet; no room phones, no room TVs* ▭ *MC, V* ⦿ *CP.*

$$ 🏠 **Tankah Dive Inn.** A friendly former cowboy from east Texas runs this guesthouse on a windswept beach. There's great diving just off the shore, so the inn is geared toward (and popular with) divers. Rooms are large, bright, and comfortable though not luxurious. The view from the upstairs restaurant–living room is spectacular. The restaurant turns out great steak, fajita, and coconut shrimp meals. The owner offers open-water diving and resort courses. ⊠ *Bahía Tankah 16* ☎ *998/804– 9006* ⊕ *www.tankah.com* 🛏 *5 rooms* ⌂ *Restaurant, beach, dive shop, snorkeling, bar; no a/c, no room phones, no room TVs* ▭ *No credit cards* ⦿ *CP.*

Tulum

🔟 *2 km (1 mi) south of Tankah, 130 km (81 mi) south of Cancún.*

Fodor'sChoice
★

Tulum (pronounced tool-*lum*) is the Yucatán Peninsula's most-visited Maya ruin, attracting more than 2 million people annually. This means you have to share the site with roughly half of the tourist population of

Quintana Roo on any given day, even if you arrive early. Though most of the architecture is of unremarkable Postclassic (AD 1000–AD 1521) style, the amount of attention that Tulum receives is not entirely undeserved. Its location by the blue-green Caribbean is breathtaking.

At the entrance you can hire a guide, but keep in mind that some of their information is more entertaining than historically accurate. (Disregard that stuff about virgin sacrifices atop the altars.) Because you aren't allowed to climb or enter the fragile structures—only three really merit close inspection anyway—you can see the ruins in two hours. You might, however, want to allow extra time for a swim or a stroll on the beach.

Tulum is one of the few Maya cities known to have been inhabited when the conquistadores arrived in 1518. In the 16th century, it functioned as a safe harbor for trade goods from rival Maya factions; it was considered neutral territory where merchandise could be stored and traded in peace. The city reached its height when traders, made wealthy through the exchange of goods, for the first time outranked Maya priests in authority and power. When the Spaniards arrived, they forbade the Maya traders to sail the seas, and commerce among the Maya died.

Tulum has long held special significance for the Maya. A key city in the League of Mayapán (AD 987–AD 1194), it was never conquered by the Spaniards, although it was abandoned about 75 years after the conquest. For 300 years thereafter, it symbolized the defiance of an otherwise subjugated people; it was one of the last outposts of the Maya during their insurrection against Mexican rule in the War of the Castes, which began in 1846. Uprisings continued intermittently until 1935, when the Maya ceded Tulum to the government.

The first significant structure is the two-story **Templo de los Frescos,** to the left of the entryway. The temple's vault roof and corbel arch are examples of classic Maya architecture. Faint traces of blue-green frescoes outlined in black on the inner and outer walls refer to ancient Maya beliefs (the clearest frescoes are hidden from sight now that you can't walk into the temple). Reminiscent of the Mixtec style, the frescoes depict the three worlds of the Maya and their major deities and are decorated with stellar and serpentine patterns, rosettes, and ears of maize and other offerings to the gods. One scene portrays the rain god seated on a four-legged animal—probably a reference to the Spaniards on their horses.

The largest and most famous building, the **Castillo** (Castle), looms at the edge of a 40-foot limestone cliff just past the Temple of the Frescoes. Atop it, at the end of a broad stairway, is a temple with stucco ornamentation on the outside and traces of fine frescoes inside the two chambers. (The stairway has been roped off, so the top temple is inaccessible.) The front wall of the Castillo has faint carvings of the Descending God and columns depicting the plumed serpent god, Kukulcán, who was introduced to the Maya by the Toltecs. To the left of the Castillo is the **Templo del Dios Descendente**—so called for the carving of a winged god plummeting to earth over the doorway.

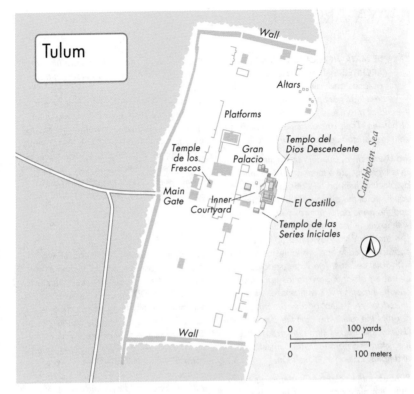

The tiny cove to the left of the Castillo and Temple of the Descending God is a good spot for a cooling swim, but there are no changing rooms. A few small altars sit atop a hill at the north side of the cove and have a good view of the Castillo and the sea. On the highway about 4 km (2½ mi) south of the ruins is the present-day village of Tulum. As Tulum's importance as a commercial center increases, markets, restaurants, shops, services, and auto-repair shops continue to spring up along the road. Growth hasn't been kind to the pueblo, however: it's rather unsightly, with a wide four-lane highway running down the middle. Despite this blight, it has a few good restaurants.

🎟 *$9; use of video camera extra* ⏱ *Daily 8–5.*

Where to Stay & Eat

★ **$$–$$$$** ✕ **Restaurante Oscar y Lalo.** A couple of miles outside Tulum, at Bahías de Punta Soliman, is this wonderful restaurant run by two friends, Oscar and Lalo. The seafood is excellent—this is supposedly the only place for miles that serves king crab—and the pizza is divine. If you're inspired to sleep on the beach, there are campsites. RVs are also welcome, though there aren't any hookups. ✉ *Carretera 307 north of Tankah (look for faded white sign)* ☎ *984/871–2209* 🚫 *No credit cards.*

CloseUp

MAYA ARCHITECTURE

THE MAYA WERE OUTSTANDING ARCHITECTS. *They erected immense palaces and towering pyramids in less-than-hospitable climates without the aid of metal tools, the wheel, or beasts of burden. Their ancient cities still resound with the magnificence of their cultures.*

Río Usumacinta. Builders of pyramids of this style typically gave them additional height by placing them on hillsides or crests—as you'll see at the otherworldly Palenque—and the principal structures were covered with exquisite bas-reliefs carved in stone. The small one-story pyramid-top temples characteristically had vestibules and rooms with vault ceilings. The wide, spacious chambers inside the pyramids had smaller attached rooms filled with bas-reliefs of important events that occurred during the reign of the ruler who built the pyramid. Río Usumacinta friezes slope inward, rather than standing perpendicular. Finest examples: Palenque, Yaxchilán.

Río Bec. Influenced by Guatemala's Peten style, the pitch of these pyramids is rather steep, and the foundations are elaborately decorated. The stairways on the outside of some pyramids were built for aesthetic rather than practical purposes, and were "false" (unclimbable). The principal structures were long, one-story affairs containing two or sometimes three tall towers. Each was capped by a large roof comb emboldened with a dramatic stucco facade. Río Bec is found only in what is now the state of Campeche. Finest examples: Calakmul, Xpujil.

Chenes. Found mainly in Campeche, this style likewise had long single-story structures. In this case they were divided into three distinct sections, each with its own doorway charmingly surrounded by a face of the rain god, Chaac, whose mouth is the entrance. Finest examples: Hochob, Chicanná.

Puuc. Uxmal is the most striking illustration of the beautifully proportioned Puuc style. Commonly found in the state of Yucatán, it looks like the "typical" Maya style. The buildings were designed in a low-slung quadrangle shape and had many rooms. Exterior walls were probably kept plain to show off the friezes above, which were lavishly embellished with stone-mosaic deities surrounded by geometric and serpentine motifs. The corners of buildings were characteristically lined with the curl-nosed Chaac. Finest examples: Uxmal, Labná, Kabah, Sayil.

Northeast Yucatán. The fusion of two Maya groups—the early Chichén Maya and later Itzá Maya—produced this Late Classic (AD 800–AD 1000) style famously exemplified by Chichén Itzá. Here new forms such as columns and grand colonnades were introduced. Palaces with row upon row of columns carved in the form of serpents looked over private patios, platforms were dedicated to the planet Venus, and pyramids were offered to Kukulcán (the plumed serpent god borrowed from the Toltecs, who called him Quetzalcóatl). Chichén Itzá is also famous for its carved-stone Chacmool (a reclining figure with an offering tray carved in its middle)—another Itzá addition. Finest examples: Chichén Itzá, Mayapán.

Quintana Roo Coast. Although somewhat influenced by the Itzá Maya, a unique style eventually evolved here. The large, squat-looking, one-story buildings have interior columns, wood-beam-supported ceilings, and numerous figures of the descending or Upside Down god that began appearing in the Postclassic era (AD 900–AD 1521).

$–$$ ✕ **Vita e Bella.** Italian tourists travel miles out of their way to eat at this utterly rustic place, with plastic tables and chairs beside the sea. The menu headlines 15 pasta dishes and pizza prepared in a wood-burning oven with such toppings as squid, lobster, and Italian sausage. Since the place is run by an Italian couple, you know the food is authentic. There's wine, beer, and margaritas to sip with your supper, too. ⊠ *Carretera Tulum Ruinas, Km 1.5* ☎ *984/877–8145* ▭ *No credit cards.*

★ **$$$** ✕▦ **Las Ranitas.** Stylish and ecologically correct Las Ranitas (The Little Frogs) creates its own power through wind-generated electricity, solar energy, and recycled water. Each chic room has gorgeous tile and fabric from Oaxaca. Terraces overlook gardens and the ocean, and jungle walkways lead to the breathtaking beach. The pièce de résistance is the French chef, who creates incredible French and Mexican cuisine ($$–$$$). ⊠ *Carretera Tulum–Boca Paila, Km 9 (last hotel before the Reserva de la Biosfera Sian Ka'an)* ☎▤ *984/877–8554* ⊕ *www.lasranitas. com* ➬ *13 rooms, 2 suites* ⚤ *Restaurant, pool, beach, snorkeling, paddle tennis; no a/c, no room phones* ▭ *No credit cards* ⦿ *CP* ⊙ *Closed mid-Sept.–mid-Nov.*

$$ ✕▦ **Zamas.** On the wild, isolated Punta de Piedra (Rock Point), with ocean views as far as the eye can see, this kick-back-and-groove hotel draws Americans. The romantically rustic cabanas—with bare-bulb lighting, mosquito nets over spartan beds, big tile bathrooms, and bright Mexican colors—are nicely distanced from one another. The restaurant ($–$$$) has an eclectic Italian-Mexican-Yucatecan menu and fresh fish. ⊠ *Carretera Tulum–Boca Paila, Km 5* ☎ *984/871–2067, 415/387– 9806 in U.S.* ⊕ *www.zamas.com* ➬ *15 cabanas* ⚤ *Restaurant, beach, bar, snorkeling, car rental; no a/c, no room phones* ▭ *No credit cards.*

$$ ▦ **Cabañas La Conchita.** The simple cabanas have exposed-wood beams, window frames, and floors as well as comfortable bathrooms with plenty of hot water. All cabanas are at the water's edge in a lovely inlet. The full tropical breakfast is the perfect complement to roughing it mildly on the beach. ⊠ *Carretera Tulum–Boca Paila, Km 4.5* ☎ *984/871–2092* ⊕ *www.differentworld.com* ➬ *8 rooms* ⚤ *Restaurant, some fans, beach, bicycles; no a/c, no room phones, no room TVs* ▭ *No credit cards* ⦿ *BP.*

¢–$$ ▦ **Cabañas Copal.** At this sensational eco-hotel on a rugged cliff, you
Fodor's Choice can sleep in dirt- or cement-floored palapas sheltered from the jungle
★ elements by mosquito nets and thatched roofs. Some baths are shared, and there's no electricity in some. Rooms are bigger and more elegant than palapas, with hardwood floors, hand-carved furniture, and a kind of primitive whirlpool bath. At night thousands of candles light the walkways and grounds. Wellness programs, exercise classes, and spa treatments include yoga, dream classes, and Maya massages; there's also a flotation chamber and a temazcal (sweat lodge). ⊠ *Carretera Tulum Ruinas, Km 5 (turn right at fork in highway; hotel is less than 1 km (½ mi) on right)* ☎ *984/806–4406 or 984/806–8247* ⊕ *www.cabanascopal.com* ➬ *45 palapas, 15 rooms* ⚤ *Restaurant, fitness classes, massage, beach, snorkeling, fishing, bar, Internet; no a/c, no room phones, no room TVs* ▭ *No credit cards.*

Cobá

Fodor'sChoice
★

🔵 **16** *49 km (30 mi) northwest of Tulum.*

Cobá (pronounced ko-*bah*), Maya for "water stirred by the wind," flourished from AD 800 to AD 1100, with a population of as many as 55,000. Now it stands in solitude, with the jungle having taken many of its buildings. Cobá is often overlooked by visitors who opt, instead, to visit better-known Tulum. But this site is much grander and less crowded, giving you a chance to really immerse yourself in ancient culture. Cobá exudes stillness, the silence broken by the occasional shriek of a spider monkey or the call of a bird. Processions of huge army ants cross the footpaths as the sun slips through openings between the tall hardwood trees, ferns, and giant palms.

Near five lakes and between coastal watchtowers and inland cities, Cobá exercised economic control over the region through a network of at least 16 *sacbéob* (white stone roads), one of which measures 100 km (62 mi) and is the longest in the Maya world. The city once covered 70 square km (27 square mi), making it a noteworthy sister state to Tikal in northern Guatemala, with which it had close cultural and commercial ties. It's noted for its massive temple-pyramids, one of which is 138 feet tall, the largest and highest in northern Yucatán. The main groupings of ruins are separated by several miles of dense vegetation, so the best way to get a sense of the immensity of the city is to scale one of the pyramids. It's easy to get lost here, so stay on the main road; *don't* be tempted by the narrow paths that lead into the jungle unless you have a qualified guide with you.

The first major cluster of structures, to your right as you enter the ruins, is the **Cobá Group**, whose pyramids are around a sunken patio. At the near end of the group, facing a large plaza, is the 79-foot-high temple, which was dedicated to the rain god, Chaac; some Maya people still place offerings and light candles here in hopes of improving their harvests. Around the rear to the left is a restored ball court, where a sacred game was once played to petition the gods for rain, fertility, and other boons.

Farther along the main path to your left is the **Chumuc Mul Group**, little of which has been excavated. The principal pyramid here is covered with the remains of vibrantly painted stucco motifs (*chumuc mul* means "stucco pyramid"). A kilometer (½ mi) past this site is the **Nohoch Mul Group** (Large Hill Group), the highlight of which is the pyramid of the same name, the tallest at Cobá. It has 120 steps—equivalent to 12 stories—and shares a plaza with Temple 10. The Descending God (also seen at Tulum) is depicted on a facade of the temple atop Nohoch Mul, from which the view is excellent.

Beyond the Nohoch Mul Group is the **Castillo**, with nine chambers that are reached by a stairway. To the south are the remains of a ball court, including the stone ring through which the ball was hurled. From the main route follow the sign to **Las Pinturas Group**, named for the still-discernible polychrome friezes on the inner and outer walls of its large, patioed pyramid. An enormous stela here depicts a man standing with his feet on two prone captives. Take the minor path for 1 km (½ mi) to the Macanxoc Group, not far from the lake of the same name. The main pyramid at Macanxoc is accessible by a stairway.

Cobá is a 35-minute drive northwest of Tulum along a pothole-filled road that leads straight through the jungle. You can comfortably make your way around Cobá in a half day, but spending the night in town is highly advised, as doing so will allow you to visit the ruins in solitude when they open at 8 AM. Even on a day trip, consider taking time out for lunch to escape the intense heat and mosquito-heavy humidity of the ruins. Buses depart to and from Cobá for Playa del Carmen and Tulum at least twice daily. Taxis to Tulum are still reasonable (about $16). ⌨ $4; *use of video camera $6; $2 fee for parking* ☉ *Daily 8–5.*

Where to Stay & Eat

¢–$ ✕ **El Bocadito.** The restaurant closest to the ruins is owned and run by a gracious Maya family, which serves simple, traditional cuisine. A three-course fixed-price lunch costs $4. Look for such classic dishes as *pollo pibíl* (chicken baked in banana leaves) and *cochinita pibíl* (pork baked in banana leaves). ⊠ *On road to ruins* ☎ 987/874–2087 ☰ *No credit cards* ☉ *No dinner.*

$ ▥ **Uolis Nah.** This small thatch-roofed complex has extra-large, quiet rooms with high ceilings, two beds, hammocks, and tile floors. You're less than 2 km (1 mi) from the Tulum highway but away from the noise, and there's lots of privacy. An extra person in a double room costs $11 more. ⊠ *On road to ruins* ☎ 984/879–5685 ⊕ *www.uolisnah.com* ☞ *7 rooms* ⚗ *Fans, kitchenettes, car rental; no a/c, no room phones, no room TVs* ☰ *No credit cards.*

Pac Chen

⛰ ⑰ *20 km (13 mi) southeast of Cobá.*

Fodor'sChoice ★

You can only visit Pac Chen (pronounced pak *chin*) on trips organized by Alltournative, an ecotour company based in Playa del Carmen. The unusual, soft-adventure experience is definitely worth your while. Pac Chen is a Maya jungle settlement of 125 people who still live in round thatch huts; there's no electricity or indoor plumbing, and the roads aren't paved. The inhabitants, who primarily make their living farming pineapple, beans, and plantains, still pray to the gods for good crops. Alltournative also pays them by the number of tourists it brings in, though no more than 80 people are allowed to visit on any given day. This money has made the village self-sustaining and has given the people an alternative to logging and hunting, which were their main means of livelihood before.

The half-day tour starts with a trek through the jungle to a cenote where you grab on to a harness and Z-line to the other side. Next is the Jaguar cenote, set deeper into the forest, where you must rappel down the cavelike sides into a cool underground lagoon. You'll eat lunch under an open-air palapa overlooking another lagoon, where canoes await. The food include such Maya dishes as grilled *achiote* (annatto seed) chicken, fresh tortillas, beans, and watermelon.

Reserva de la Biosfera Sian Ka'an

★ ⑱ *15 km (9 mi) south of Tulum to the Punta Allen turnoff and within Sian Ka'an.*

The Sian Ka'an ("where the sky is born," pronounced see-an caan) region was first settled by the Maya in the 5th century AD. In 1986 the Mexican government established the 1.3-million-acre Reserva de la Biosfera Sian Ka'an as an internationally protected area. The next year, it was named a World Heritage Site by the United Nations Educational, Scientific, and Cultural Organization (UNESCO); later, it was extended by 200,000 acres. The Riviera Maya and Costa Maya split the biosphere reserve; Punta Allen and north belong to the Riviera Maya, and everything south of Punta Allen is part of the Costa Maya.

The Sian Ka'an reserve constitutes 10% of the land in Quintana Roo and covers 100 km (62 mi) of coast. Hundreds of species of local and migratory birds, fish, other animals and plants, and fewer than 1,000 residents (primarily Maya) share this area of freshwater and coastal lagoons, mangrove swamps, cays, savannas, tropical forests, and a barrier reef. There are approximately 27 ruins (none excavated) linked by a unique canal system—one of the few of its kind in the Maya world in Mexico. This is one of the last undeveloped stretches of North American coast. To see its sites you must take a guided tour. Several kinds of tours, including bird-watching and kayaking trips, are offered on site through the reserve's visitor center; other privately run tours are also available. (*See* Tours *in* The Caribbean Coast A to Z section of this chapter.)

Many species of the once-flourishing wildlife have fallen into the endangered category, but the waters here still teem with rooster fish, bonefish, mojarra, snapper, shad, permit, sea bass, and crocodiles. Fishing the flats for wily bonefish is popular, and the peninsula's few lodges also run deep-sea fishing trips.

To explore on your own, follow the road past Boca Paila to the secluded 35-km (22-mi) coastal strip of land that's part of the reserve. You'll be limited to swimming, snorkeling, and camping on the beaches, as there are no trails into the surrounding jungle. The narrow, extremely rough dirt road down the peninsula is filled with monstrous potholes and after a rainfall is completely impassable. Don't attempt it unless you have four-wheel drive. Most fishing lodges along the way close for the rainy season in August and September, and accommodations are hard to come by. The road ends at Punta Allen, a fishing village whose main catch is spiny lobster, which was becoming scarce until ecologists taught the local fishing cooperative how to build and lay special traps to conserve the species. There are several small, expensive guesthouses. If you haven't booked ahead, start out early in the morning so you can get back to civilization before dark.

Where to Stay

$$$$ ⌂ **Boca Paila Fishing Lodge.** Home of the "grand slam" (fishing lingo for catching three different kinds of fish in one trip), this charming lodge has nine cottages, each with two double beds, couches, bathrooms, and screened-in sitting areas. Boats and guides for fly-fishing and bonefishing are provided; you can rent tackle at the lodge. Meals consist of fresh fish dishes and Maya specialties, among other things. From January through June and October through December a 50% deposit is required, and the minimum stay is one week (there's no required deposit and only a three-night minimum stay the rest of the year). ⊠ *Boca Paila Peninsula* ✆ *reservations: Frontiers, Box 959, Wexford, PA 15090* ☎ *724/935–1577 or 800/245–1950* ⊕ *www.frontierstravel.com* ⇱ *9 cottages* ⟁ *Restaurant, beach, snorkeling, fishing, bar, laundry service, airport shuttle; no a/c in some rooms, no room phones, no room TVs* ▤ *No credit cards unless arranged with Frontiers* ⊖ *AI.*

★ **$$$$** ⊡ **Casa Blanca Lodge.** This American-managed lodge is on a rocky outcrop on remote Punta Pájaros Island—reputed to be one of the best places in the world for light-tackle saltwater fishing. Modern guest rooms have tile-and-mahogany bathrooms. An open-air thatch-roofed bar welcomes anglers with drinks, fresh fish dishes, fruit, and vegetables at the start and end of the day. Only weeklong packages can be booked March through July. Rates include a charter flight from Cancún, all meals, a boat, and a guide; nonfishing packages are cheaper. A 50% prepayment fee is required. ⊠ *Punta Pájaros* ✆ *reservations: Frontiers, Box 959, Wexford, PA 15090* ☎ *724/935–1577, 800/245–1950 to Frontiers* ⊕ *www.frontierstravel. com* ⇱ *9 rooms* ⟁ *Restaurant, beach, snorkeling, fishing, bar, laundry service; no room phones, no room TVs* ▤ *MC, V* ⊖ *AI.*

Muyil

⑲ *24 km (15 mi) south of Tulum.*

This photogenic archaeological site at the northern end of the Reserva de la Biosfera Sian Ka'an is underrated. Once known as Chunyaxché, it's now called by its ancient name, Muyil (pronounced mool-*hill*). It dates from the Late Preclassic era, when it was connected by road to the sea and served as a port between Cobá and the Maya centers in Belize and Guatemala. A 15-foot-wide sacbé, built during the Postclassic period, extended from the city to the mangrove swamp and was still in use when the Spaniards arrived.

Structures were erected at 400-foot intervals along the white limestone road, almost all of them facing west, but there are only three still standing. At the beginning of the 20th century, the ancient stones were used to build a chicle (gum arabic) plantation, which was managed by one of the leaders of the War of the Castes. The most notable site at Muyil today is the remains of the 56-foot **Castillo**—one of the tallest on the Quintana Roo coast—at the center of a large acropolis. During excavations of the Castillo, jade figurines representing the moon and fertility goddess Ixchel were found. Recent excavations at Muyil have uncovered some smaller structures.

The ruins stand near the edge of a deep-blue lagoon and are surrounded by nearly impenetrable jungle—bring bug repellent. You can drive down a dirt road on the side of the ruins to swim or fish in the lagoon. The bird-watching is also exceptional here. ▤ *$4; free Sun.* ☉ *Daily 8–5.*

THE COSTA MAYA

The coastal area south of Punta Allen is more purely Maya than the stretch between Cancún and Punta Allen. Fishing collectives and close-knit communities carry on ancient traditions, and the proximity to Belize lends a Caribbean flavor, particularly in Chetumal, where you'll hear both Spanish and a Caribbean patois. The Costa Maya also encompasses the southern part of the Reserva de la Biosfera Sian Ka'an. A multimillion-dollar government initiative proposes to support ecotourism and sustainable development projects here, perhaps preventing resorts from winning out entirely over wildlife. The first of the government projects was the glitzy cruise-ship port at Majahual. Other projects include the excavation and opening of more archaeological sites.

Felipe Carrillo Puerto

20 *60 km (37 mi) south of Muyil.*

Formerly known as Chan Santa Cruz, Felipe Carrillo Puerto—the Costa Maya's first major town—is named after the man who became governor of Yucatán in 1920. He was hailed a hero after instituting a series of reforms to help the impoverished *campesinos* (farmers or peasants). Assassinated by the alleged henchman of the presidential candidate of an opposing party in 1923, he remained a popular figure long after his death.

The town was a political, military, and religious asylum during the 1846 War of the Castes; rebels fled here after being defeated at Mérida. It was also in this town that the famous cult of the Talking Cross took hold. The Talking Cross was a sacred symbol of the Maya; it was believed that a holy voice emanated from it, offering guidance and instruction. In this case the cross appeared emblazoned on the trunk of a cedar tree, and the voice urged the Indians to keep fighting. (The voice was actually an Indian priest and ventriloquist, Manual Nahuat, prompted by the Maya rebel José Maria Barrera.) Symbolic crosses were subsequently placed in neighboring villages, including Tulum, inspiring the Maya. They continued fighting until 1915, when the Mexican army finally gave up. The Cruzob Indians ruled Quintana Roo as an independent state, much to the embarrassment of the Mexican government, until 1935, when the Cruzob handed Tulum over and agreed to Mexican rule.

Felipe Carrillo remains very much a Maya city, with even a few old-timers who cling to the belief that one day the Maya will once again rule the region. It exists primarily as the hub of three highways, and the only vestige of the momentous events of the 19th century is the small uncompleted temple—on the edge of town in an inconspicuous, poorly marked park—begun by the Indians in the 1860s and now a monument to the War of the Castes. The church where the Talking Cross was originally housed also stands. Several humble hotels, some good restaurants, and a gas station may be incentives for stopping here on your southbound trek.

CASTE WARS

When Mexico achieved independence from Spain in 1821, the Maya didn't celebrate. The new government didn't return their lost land, and it didn't treat them with respect. In 1846, a Maya rebellion began in Valladolid. A year later, they had killed hundreds and the battle raged on. (The Indians were rising up against centuries of being relegated to the status of "lower caste" people. Hence the conflict was called the Guerra de las Castas or Caste Wars.

Help for the embattled Mexicans arrived with a vengeance from Mexico City, Cuba, and the United States. By 1850, the Maya had been mercilessly slaughtered, their population plummeting from 500,000 to 300,000. Survivors fled to the jungles and held out against the government until its troops withdrew in 1915. The Maya controlled Quintana Roo from Tulum, their headquarters, and finally accepted Mexican rule in 1935.

Where to Stay & Eat

¢ ✕🏨 **El Faisán y El Venado.** The price is right at this clean and comfortable hotel. The restaurant ($–$$) does a brisk business with the locals because it's centrally located and has good Yucatecan specialties such as *poc chuc* (pork marinated in sour-orange sauce), *bistec a la yucateca* (Yucatecan-style steak), and pollo pibíl. ⊠ *Av. Benito Juárez 781* 📠 *983/834–0702* 🛏 *35 rooms* ⚑ *Restaurant, fans, refrigerators, cable TV; no a/c* ⊟ *No credit cards.*

Chacchoben

㉑ *33 km (21 mi) southwest of Felipe Carrillo Puerto.*

Chacchoben ("red corn," pronounced *cha*-cho-ben), one of the more recent archaeological sites to undergo excavation, is an ancient city that was a contemporary of Kohunlich and the most important trading partner with Guatemala north of the Bacalar Lagoon area. So far three buildings and a residential section in remarkably good condition have been unearthed. The lofty **Templo Mayor,** the main temple, was dedicated to the Maya sun god Itzamná and once held a royal tomb. (When archaeologists found it, though, it had already been looted.) Most buildings were constructed in the early Classic period around AD 200 in the Peten style, although the city could have been inhabited as early as 200 BC. The inhabitants made a living growing cotton and extracting gum arabic and copal resin from the trees. ⊠ *Carretera 307, take Calle Lazaro Cardenas Exit south of Cafetal, turn right on Carretera 293, continue 9 km (5½ mi)* 📠 *No phone* 🎟 *$3* ☉ *Daily 8–5.*

Majahual

㉒ *71 km (44 mi) southeast of Felipe Carrillo Puerto on Carretera 307 to the Majahual Exit south of Limones; turn left and continue 56 km (35 mi).*

The road to Majahual (pronounced ma-ha-wal) is long. But if you follow it, you'll get a chance to see one of the coast's last authentic fishing villages. Majahual is very laid-back, with inexpensive accommodations, dirt roads, backpackers, and lots of small restaurants serving fresh fish. It's what Playa del Carmen must have been 30 years ago. Activities include lounging, fishing, snorkeling, and diving. With an upscale residential area, an airport that's built (but lying abandoned) in a northern field, and a cruise-ship dock and passengers-only shopping plaza north of the main part of town, this place seems slated to be the next Cozumel. Come and enjoy it while it remains a quaint village.

Where to Stay

$$ 🏨 **Maya Ha Resort.** This modern dive resort rises disconcertingly from the jungle and is a glimpse of things to come in Majahual. The owners, who hail from Austin, Texas, chose architecture based on such Maya sites as Chichén Itzá and Kabah. In the restaurant-pool area is a giant pyramid decorated with reproductions of stelae found at famous ruins; it offers a spectacular view. The suites have double beds and refrigerators. There's a state-of-the-art dive shop, and packages are available. A temazcal helps you to work out the kinks after a dive. ⊕ *Follow dirt road, Carretera Antigua a Xcalak, from Majahual about 10 km (6 mi) or turn off at checkpoint and follow paved coastal road, Carretera Nueva a Xcalak, 15 km (9 mi); at junction, turn left onto dirt road and drive about 2 km (less than 1 mi)* ☎ *512/443–2977 or 877/443–1600* 📠 *983/831–0065* ⊕ *www.mayaharesort.com* 🛏 *14 suites* ☖ *Restaurant, refrigerators, pool, massage, dive shop, boating, bar, laundry service, Internet, airport shuttle; no room TVs, no room phones* ⊟ *AE, MC, V.*

★ ¢ 🏨 **Cabañas de Tio Phil.** Solar energy and wind power drive things at this small complex, whose heart is the main building's big, inviting front porch. The attractive cabanas have thatched roofs, wooden floors, two beds with mosquito netting, and tile bathrooms with wall murals and plenty of hot water. The staff is friendly; one of them might even offer to cook your catch of the day. The kitchen serves breakfast; its big oven is used to cook pizza in the evenings. ⊠ *Carretera Antigua a Xcalak, Km 2* ☎ *983/835–7166* ✉ *tiophilhome@hotmail.com* 🛏 *7 cabanas* ☖ *Restaurant, snorkeling, fishing; no a/c in rooms, no room phones, no room TVs* ⊟ *No credit cards.*

Xcalak

㉓ *Carretera 307 to the Majahual exit south of Limones; turn left, go 56 km (35 mi) to the checkpoint, and turn south (left) onto highway for 60 km (37 mi).*

It's quite a journey to get to Xcalak (pronounced *ish*-ka-lack), but it's worth the effort. This national reserve is on the tip of a peninsula that divides Chetumal Bay from the Caribbean. Flowers, birds, and butter-flies are abundant here, and the terrain is marked by savannas, marshes, streams, and lagoons dotted with islands. There are also fabulously deserted beaches. Visitor amenities are few; the hotels cater mostly to rugged types who come to bird-watch on Bird Island or to dive at Banco Chinchorro, a coral atoll and national park some two hours northeast by boat.

Where to Stay

$$ **Costa de Cocos.** Wind generates the electricity at this small collection

Fodor's Choice of cabanas, 2 km (1 mi) north of Xcalak. Each unit has a double bed

★ and a bathroom; a family unit has two bathrooms. Owners Dave and Ilana Randall are knowledgeable about the peninsula and the offshore reef, and they can help you plan fishing trips, sea-kayak outings, bird-watching excursions, or diving courses with PADI instructors. Rates include two delicious meals. Reserve well in advance for stays here. ⊠ *Xcalak Peninsula, follow Carretera 307 to sign for Majahual, turn right at paved coast road to Xcalak* ☎ *983/831–0110* ⊕ *www.costadecocos.com* ➭ *14 cabanas* ☖ *Restaurant, fans, beach, dive shop, dock, snorkeling, boating, Internet; no a/c, no room phones, no room TVs* ▭ *No credit cards* ▮◎▮ *MAP.*

$–$$ **Playa Sonrisa.** This American-owned property has deluxe beachfront or garden-view cabanas and suites—all with wood furniture, tile floors, and blue color schemes. You can snorkel off the dock, and the staff can arrange fishing and scuba diving trips. Breakfast is served overlooking the beach, where clothing is optional. ⊠ *Xcalak Peninsula, 54 km (33 mi) south of Majahual, 5 km (3 mi) north of Costa de Cocos* ☎☎ *983/ 838–1872* ⊕ *www.playasonrisa.com* ➭ *2 rooms, 2 cabanas, 2 suites* ☖ *Restaurant, fans, some refrigerators, beach, dock, snorkeling; no a/c in some rooms, no room phones, no room TVs* ▭ *MC, V* ▮◎▮ *CP.*

$–$$ **Sin Duda.** Sin Duda is on a beach that's both wild and lovely. Rooms have single or double beds, trundle beds, and plenty of closet space. You and other guests have access to a fully equipped kitchen as well as to a dining area and a balcony. For more privacy, opt for Studio 6, which is in a separate building, or Apartment 7 or 8, which have their own kitchens and living rooms. All guest quarters are adorned with Mexican pottery and other collectibles. ⊠ *Xcalak Peninsula, 54 km (33 mi) south of Majahual, 15 km (9 mi) north of Costa de Cocos* ☍ *reservations: 34 N. Ferndale, Mill Valley, CA 85712* ☎ *415/380–9031 in U.S.* ☎☎ *983/831–0006* ⊕ *www.sindudavillas.com* ➭ *5 rooms, 1 studio, 2 apartments* ☖ *Some kitchens, beach, snorkeling, fishing; no a/c, no room phones, no room TVs* ▭ *No credit cards* ▮◎▮ *CP.*

Bacalar

24 *112 km (69 mi) south of Felipe Carrillo Puerto, 40 km (25 mi) north-west of Chetumal.*

Founded in AD 435, Bacalar (pronounced *baa*-ka-lar) is one of Quintana Roo's oldest settlements. **Fuerte de San Felipe** (San Felipe Fort) is an 18th-century stone fort built by the Spaniards using stones from the nearby Maya pyramids. It was constructed as a haven against pirates and marauding Indians, though during the War of the Castes it was a Maya stronghold, putting its stones in their hands once more. Today the monolithic structure, which overlooks the enormous Laguna de Bacalar, houses government offices and a museum with exhibits on local history (ask for someone to bring a key if museum doors are locked). ☎ *No phone* 🎫 *$2* ☉ *Tues.–Sun. 10–6.*

Seawater and freshwater mix in the 56-km-long (35-mi-long) **Laguna de Bacalar,** intensifying the aquamarine hues that have earned it the nickname of Lago de los Siete Colores (Lake of the Seven Colors). Drive along the lake's southern shores to enter the affluent section of the town of Bacalar, with elegant waterfront homes. Also in the vicinity are a few hotels and campgrounds.

Just beyond Bacalar is Mexico's largest sinkhole, **Cenote Azul,** 607 feet in diameter, with clear blue waters that afford unusual visibility even at 200 feet below the surface. With all its underwater caves, the cenote (open daily 8–8) attracts divers who specialize in this somewhat tricky type of dive. At **Restaurant Cenote Azul** you can linger over fresh fish and a beer while gazing out over the deep blue waters or enjoy a swim off its docks. A giant all-inclusive resort keeps threatening to open here; try to visit before the tranquillity disappears.

Where to Stay

★ **$$–$$$** 🏨 **Rancho Encantado.** On the shores of Laguna Bacalar, 30 minutes north of Chetumal, the enchanting Rancho consists of Maya-theme *casitas* (cottages) that have Oaxacan furnishings, a patio, a hammock, a refrigerator, a sitting area, and a bathroom. Breakfast and dinner are included in the room rate (no red meat is served). You can swim and snorkel off the private dock leading into the lagoon or tour the ruins in southern Yucatán, Campeche, and Belize. Pick a room close to the water or your nights will be marred by the sound of trucks zooming by. ✉ *Off Carretera 307 at Km 3 (look for turnoff sign)* ✆ *reservations: Box 1256, Taos, NM 87571* ☎ *983/831–0037 or 800/505–6292* 📠 *505/ 776–5878* ⊕ *www.encantado.com* 🛏 *12 casitas* 🍴 *Restaurant, refrigerators, hot tub, massage, boating, bar, laundry service, travel services; no a/c in some rooms, no room phones, no room TVs* 🖃 *AE, MC, V* 🍽 *MAP.*

¢ 🏨 **Laguna.** This brightly colored, eclectic hotel outside Bacalar is just like a summer lodge. Rooms are simple, clean, and comfortable; cabins are on a hill overlooking the lagoon. A garden path leads down to a dock-restaurant area where you can swim or use the canoes. The staff is hospitable. ✉ *Carretera 307, Km 40* ☎ *983/834–2206* ⊕ *www. bacalarmosaico.com* 🛏 *3 cabins, 29 rooms* 🍴 *Restaurant, fans, dock, boating; no a/c in some rooms, no room phones, no room TVs* 🖃 *MC, V.*

Chetumal

❷❺ *58 km (36 mi) south of Bacalar.*

Chetumal (pronounced *chet*-too-maal) is the final-stop town on the Costa Maya. Originally called Payo Obis, it was founded by the Mexican government in 1898 in a partially successful attempt to gain control of the lucrative trade of precious hardwoods, arms, and ammunition and as a military base against rebellious Indians. The city, which overlooks the Bay of Chetumal at the mouth of the Río Hondo, was devastated by a hurricane in 1955 and rebuilt as the capital of Quintana Roo and the state's major port. Though Chetumal remains the state capital, it attracts few visitors other than those en route to Central America or those traveling to the city on government business.

At times, Chetumal feels more Caribbean than Mexican; this isn't surprising, given its proximity to Belize. Many cultural events between the two countries are staged. Further, a population that includes Afro-Caribbean and Middle Eastern immigrants has resulted in a mix of music (reggae, salsa, calypso) and cuisines (Yucatecan, Mexican, and Lebanese). Although Chetumal's provisions are modest, the town has a number of parks on a waterfront that's as pleasant as it is long: the Bay of Chetumal surrounds the city on three sides. The downtown area has been spruced up, and mid-range hotels and visitor-friendly restaurants have popped up along Boulevard Bahía and on nearby Avenida Héroes. Tours are run to the fascinating nearby ruins of Kohunlich, Dzibanché, and Kinichná, a trio dubbed the "Valley of the Masks."

Paseo Bahía, Chetumal's main thoroughfare, runs along the water for several miles. A walkway runs parallel to this road and is a popular gathering spot at night. If you follow the road it turns into the Carretera Chetumal–Calderitas and, after 16 km (11 mi), leads to the small ruins of **Oxtankah.** Some archaeologists believe this is the city where the Chaktemal kingdom was started by Gonzalo Guerrero, father of the Mestizo race (later known as Mexicans). The city's prosperity peaked between AD 300 and AD 600. It's open daily 8–5; admission is $3.

The **Museo de la Cultura Maya,** a sophisticated, interactive museum dedicated to the complex world of the Maya, is outstanding. Displays, which have explanations in Spanish and English, trace Maya architecture, social classes, politics, and customs. The most impressive display is the three-story Sacred Ceiba Tree. The Maya use this symbol to explain the relationship between the cosmos and the earth. The first floor represents the roots of the tree and the Maya underworld, called Xibalba. The middle floor is the tree trunk, known as Middle World, home to humans and all their trappings. The top floor is the leaves and branches and the 13 heavens of the cosmic otherworld. ⊠ *Av. Héroes and Calle Mahatma Gandhi* ☎ *983/832–6838* ☒ *$5* ☉ *Tues.–Sun. 9–7.*

Where to Stay & Eat

$–$$$ ✗ **Sergio's Pizzas.** Locals rave about this pizzeria's grilled steaks, barbecued chicken (made with the owner's own sauce), and garlic shrimp, along with smoked-oyster and seafood pizzas. (Pasta is not the thing to order here.) ⊠ *Av. Alvaro Obregón 182, at Av. 5 de Mayo* ☎ *983/832–0882* ☰ *D, MC, V.*

¢ ✗ **Expresso Cafe.** At this bright, modern café, you get an appealing view of the placid Bay of Chetumal. Choose from more than 15 kinds of coffee as well as fresh salads, sandwiches, and chicken dishes. ⊠ *Blvd. Bahía 12* ☎ *983/832–2654* ☰ *No credit cards.*

$$ 🏨 **Los Cocos.** The jungle theme found in this hotel's outdoor restaurant—a popular local hangout—and lobby ends when you enter the rooms, which are comfortable and have many amenities. There's a pool in a large pleasant garden, and the waterfront is within easy walking distance. ⌧ *Av. Héroes 134, at Calle Chapultepec* ☎ *983/832–0544* 🖷 *983/832–0920* ⊕ *www. hotelloccocos.com* ⟿ *122 rooms* ♨ *Restaurant, minibars, cable TV, pool, bar, shops, meeting rooms, car rental* ▭ *AE, D, MC, V.*

$$ 🏨 **Holiday Inn Puerta Maya.** It may be small, but its staff works hard to provide luxury accommodations. The clublike lobby has dark-green leather furniture and lots of plants. In the light-filled guest rooms wood accents complement soft sunset colors; each room has a small terrace that overlooks the pool, which is itself surrounded by a garden with Maya sculptures. The hotel's location, directly across from the museum, is another perk. ⌧ *Av. Héroes 171* ☎ *983/835–0400* 🖷 *983/832–1676* ⊕ *www. holidayinn.com* ⟿ *85 rooms, 9 suites* ♨ *Restaurant, in-room safes, cable TV, pool, bar, travel services, free parking, no-smoking rooms* ▭ *MC, V.*

¢ 🏨 **Hotel Marlon.** This clean, comfortable hotel, done in pastel colors, is one of the best deals in town. There's plenty of cool air and lots of hot water. The pool is good, the restaurant is great, and the bar is small but sweet. The staff demonstrates what traditional Mexican hospitality is all about. ⌧ *Av. Juárez 87* ☎ *983/832–9411 or 983/832–9522* 🖷 *983/ 832–6555* ⊕ *www.hotelmarlon.com* ⟿ *50 rooms* ♨ *Restaurant, cable TV, pool, bar, car rental* ▭ *AE, MC, V.*

THE RÍO BEC ROUTE

The area known as the Río Bec Route enjoyed little attention for years, but the Mexican government opened it up by building a highway, preserving previously excavated sites, and uncovering more ruins. Visiting here has no less of a decidedly pioneer feel, however, because of the rustic conditions and continuing discoveries taking place.

Although most pyramids in Quintana Roo are built in the Peten style—an import from Guatemala whose chief characteristics are sloped sides and twin upper chambers—Río Bec is considered one of the principle Maya architectural styles. Temples done in this manner often have doorways carved like open mouths and stone roof combs reminiscent of latticework. Pyramids are steep and have narrow staircases that lead up to cone-shape tops.

The Río Bec Route continues beyond Quintana Roo's Valley of the Masks into Campeche. Xpujil, the first major site in Campeche, is 115 km (71 mi) west of Chetumal. Hotels and restaurants in the area are scarce, so it's best to make Chetumal your base for exploring.

Kohunlich

🔺 ★ ㉖ *42 km (26 mi) west of Chetumal on Carretera 186, 75 km (47 mi) east of Xpujil.*

Kohunlich (pronounced *ko*-hoon-lich) is renowned for the giant stucco masks on its principal pyramid, the **Edificio de los Mascarones** (Mask

Building). It also has one of Quintana Roo's oldest ball courts and the remains of a great drainage system at the **Plaza de las Estelas** (Plaza of the Stelae). Masks that are about 6 feet tall are set vertically into the wide staircases at the main pyramid, called **Edificio de las Estelas** (Building of the Stelae). First thought to represent the Maya sun god, they are now considered to be composites of the rulers and important warriors of Kohunlich. Another giant mask was discovered in 2001 in the building's upper staircase.

In 1902 loggers came upon Kohunlich, which was built and occupied during the Classic period by various Maya groups. This explains the eclectic architecture, which includes the Peten and Río Bec styles. Although there are 14 buildings to visit, it's thought that there are at least 500 mounds on the site waiting to be excavated. Digs have turned up 29 individual and multiple burial sites inside a residence building called **Temple de Los Viente-Siete Escalones** (Temple of the Twenty-Seven Steps). This site doesn't have a great deal of tourist traffic, so it's surrounded by thriving flora and fauna. ☎ *No phone* 🖾 *$4* ☉ *Daily 8–5.*

Where to Stay

★ **$$$$** 🏨 **Explorean Kohunlich.** At the edge of the Kohunlich ceremonial grounds, this ecological resort gives you the chance to have an adventure without giving up life's comforts. Daily excursions include trips to nearby ruins, lagoons, and forests for bird-watching, mountain biking, kayaking, rock climbing, and hiking. You return in the evening to luxurious, Mexican-style suites filled with natural textiles and woods. All guest quarters are strung along a serpentine jungle path; they're very private and have showers that open onto small back gardens. The pool and outdoor hot tub have views of the distant ruins. ⊠ *Carretera Chetumal–Escarega, Km 5.65 (same road as the ruins)* ☎ *55/5201–8350 in Mexico City, 877/397–5672 in U.S.* ⊕ *www.theexplorean.com* ⇗ *40 suites* ⚘ *Restaurant, fans, pool, outdoor hot tub, massage, sauna, boating, bicycles, hiking, bar, meeting room; no room TVs, no kids* ▤ *AE, DC, MC, V* ⧫❘ *AI.*

Dzibanché & Kinichná

🏛 **㉗** *1 km (½ mi) east of turnoff for Kohunlich on Carretera 186; follow signs for 24 km (15 mi) north to fork for Dzibanché (1½ km [1 mi] from fork) and Kinichná (3 km [2 mi] from fork).*

The alliance between the sister cities Dzibanché (place where they write on wood, pronounced zee-ban-*che*) and Kinichná (House of the Sun, pronounced kin-itch-*na*) was thought to have made them the most powerful cities in southern Quintana Roo during the Maya Classic period (AD 100–AD 1000). The fertile farmlands surrounding the ruins are still used today as they were hundreds of years ago, and the winding drive deep into the fields makes you feel as if you're coming upon something undiscovered.

Archaeologists have been making progress in excavating more and more ruins, albeit slowly. At **Dzibanché,** several carved wooden lintels have been discovered; the most perfectly preserved sample is in a supporting arch at the **Plaza de Xibalba** (Plaza of Xibalba). Also at the plaza is the **Templo del Búho** (Temple of the Owl), atop which a recessed tomb was found, the second discovery of its kind in Mexico (the first was at Palenque in Chiapas). In the tomb were magnificent clay vessels painted with white owls—messengers of the underworld gods. More buildings and three plazas have been restored as excavation continues. Several other plazas are surrounded by temples, palaces, and pyramids, all in the Peten style. The carved stone steps at **Edificio 13** and **Edificio 2** (Buildings 13 and 2) still bear traces of stone masks. A copy of the famed lintel of **Templo IV** (Temple IV), with eight glyphs dating from AD 618, is housed in the Museo de la Cultura Maya in Chetumal. (The original was replaced in 2003 because of deterioration.) Four more tombs were discovered at **Templo I** (Temple I). ☎ *No phone* 🎫 *$4* ⊙ *Daily 8–5.*

After you see Dzibanché, make your way back to the fork in the road and head to **Kinichná.** At the fork, you'll see the restored **Complejo Lamai** (Lamai Complex), administrative buildings of Dzibanché. Kinichná consists of a two-level pyramidal mound split into Acropolis B and Acropolis C, apparently dedicated to the sun god. Two mounds at the foot of the pyramid suggest that the temple was a ceremonial site. Here a giant Olmec-style jade figure was found. At its summit, Kinichná affords one of the finest views of any archaeological site in the area. ☎ *No phone* 🎫 *$4* ⊙ *Daily 8–5.*

THE CARIBBEAN COAST A TO Z

To research prices, get advice from other travelers, and book travel arrangements, visit www.fodors.com.

AIR TRAVEL

Almost everyone who arrives by air into this region flies into Cancún. Chetumal, however, has an airport on its southwestern edge, along Avenida Alvaro Obregón where it turns into Carretera 186. In Playa del Carmen, there's an air strip across from Plaza Antigua. Mexicana Airlines flies from Mexico City to Chetumal five times a week. Aerosaab, a charter company with four- and five-seat Cessnas, flies from Playa to Chichén Itzá and Isla Holbox. The five-hour Chichén Itzá tours costs $230. The three- to four-hour Isla Holbox tours cost $278. Aerosaab can be chartered for flights throughout the Riviera Maya and Costa Maya.

🛈 Airport Information **Aeropuerto de Chetumal** ⊠ Carretera 186, Chetumal ☎ 983/832-3525. **Aeropuerto Internacional Cancún** ⊠ Carretera Cancún–Puerto Morelos/Carretera 307, Km 9.5 ☎ 998/886-0028.

🛈 Carriers **Aerosaab** ☎ 984/873-0804 ⊕ www.aerosaab.com. **Mexicana** ☎ 800/531-7921 ⊕ www.mexicana.com.

BOAT & FERRY TRAVEL

Passenger-only ferries and two enormous speedboats depart from the dock at Playa del Carmen for the 45-minute trip to the main pier in Cozumel. They leave daily, approximately every hour on the hour 5 AM–11 PM, with no ferries at noon, 2, 8, or 10. Return service to Playa runs every hour on the hour 4 AM–10 PM, with no ferries at 5, 11 AM, 1, 7, or 9 PM. Call ahead, as the schedule changes often.

⚓Playa del Carmen passenger ferry ☎ 984/872–1508, 984/872–1588, or 984/872–0477.

BUS TRAVEL

The bus station in Chetumal (Avenida Salvador Novo 179) is served by Autobuses del Oriente (ADO), Caribe Express, and other lines. Buses run regularly from Chetumal to Cancún, Villahermosa, Mexico City, Mérida, Campeche City, and Veracruz, as well as Guatemala and Belize.

Buses traveling all points except Cancún stop at the terminal Avenida 20 and Calle 12. Buses headed to and from Cancún use the main bus terminal downtown (Avenida Juárez and Avenida 5). ADO runs express, first-class, and second-class buses to major destinations.

⚓ Bus Information ADO ☎ 984/873–0109. **Caribe Express** ☎ 984/832–7889.

CAR RENTAL

Most first-class hotels in Puerto Aventuras, Akumal, and Chetumal rent cars. If you're planning to stay in Puerto Morelos, it's better better to rent a car in Cancún, as there aren't many bargains in town. In Playa del Carmen, stick with the bigger rental agencies: Hertz, Budget, and Thrifty. If you want air-conditioning or automatic transmission, reserve your car at least one day in advance.

⚓ Major Agencies Budget ⊠ Continental Plaza, Playa del Carmen ☎ 984/873–0100. **Hertz** ⊠ Plaza Marina, Playa del Carmen ☎ 984/873–0702. **Thrifty** ⊠ Calle 8 between Avs. 5 and 10, Playa del Carmen ☎ 984/873–0119.

CAR TRAVEL

The entire 382-km (237-mi) coast from Punta Sam near Cancún to the main border crossing to Belize at Chetumal is traversable on Carretera 307—a straight, paved highway. Puerto Morelos, Playa del Carmen, Tulum, Puerto Felipe Carrillo, Bacalar, and Chetumal have gas stations.

Good roads that run into Carretera 307 from the west are Carretera 180 (from Mérida and Valladolid), Carretera 295 (from Valladolid), Carretera 184 (from central Yucatán), and Carretera 186 (from Villahermosa and, via Carretera 261, from Mérida and Campeche). There's an entrance to the *autopista* toll highway between Cancún and Mérida off Carretera 307 just south of Cancún. Approximate driving times are as follows: Cancún to Felipe Carrillo Puerto, 4 hours; Cancún to Mérida, 4½ hours (3½ hours on the autopista toll road, $27); Puerto Felipe Carrillo to Chetumal, 2 hours; Puerto Felipe Carrillo to Mérida, about 4½ hours; Chetumal to Campeche, 6½ hours.

Defensive driving is a must. Follow proper road etiquette—vehicles in front of you that have their left turn signal on are saying "pass me," not "I'm going to turn." Also, south of Tulum, keep an eye out for military and immigration checkpoints. Have your passport handy, be friendly and cooperative, and don't carry any items, such as firearms or drugs, that might land you in jail.

EMERGENCIES

In Puerto Morelos, there are two drugstores in town on either side of the gas station on Carretera 307. In Playa del Carmen, there's a pharmacy at the Plaza Marina shopping mall; several others are on Avenida 5 between Calles 4 and 12. There are two pharmacies on Avenida Juárez between Avenidas 20 and 25.

🚑 **Centro de Salud** ✉ Av. Juárez and Av. 15, Playa del Carmen ☎ 984/873-1230 Ext. 147. **Police** ✉ Av. Juárez between Avs. 15 and 20, Playa del Carmen ☎ 984/873-0291. **Red Cross** ✉ Av. Juárez and Av. 25, Playa del Carmen ☎ 984/873-1233.

ENGLISH-LANGUAGE MEDIA

Morgan's Tobacco Shop and Tequila Collection, both in Playa del Carmen, sell English-language magazines and newspapers.

🚩 **Stores Morgan's Tobacco Shop** ✉ Av. 5 and Calle 6, Playa del Carmen ☎ 984/873-2166. **Tequila Collection** ✉ Av. 5 between Calles 4 and 6, Playa del Carmen ☎ 984/873-0876.

INTERNET, MAIL & SHIPPING

Many of the more remote places on the Caribbean coast rely on e-mail and the Internet as their major forms of communication. In Playa del Carmen, Internet service is cheap and readily available. The best places charge $3 per half hour and include Cyberia Internet Café and Atomic Internet Café. In Tulum, try the Internet Club.

The Playa del Carmen *correos* (post office) is open weekdays 8–7. If you need to ship packages or important letters, go through the shipping company Estafeta.

🚩 **Cybercafés Atomic Internet Café** ✉ Av. 5 and Calle 8, Playa del Carmen. **Cyberia Internet Café** ✉ Calle 4 and Av. 15, Playa del Carmen. **Internet Club** ✉ Av. Oriente 89, Tulum.

🚩 **Services Correos** ✉ Av. Juárez, next to the police station, Playa del Carmen ☎ 983/873-0300. **Estafeta** ✉ Calle 20, Playa del Carmen ☎ 984/873-1008.

MONEY MATTERS

🚩 **Banks Banamex** ✉ Av. Juárez between Avs. 20 and 25, Playa del Carmen ☎ 984/873-0825. **Bancomer** ✉ Av. Juárez between Calles 25 and 30, Playa del Carmen ☎ 984/873-0356 ✉ Av. Alvaro Obregón 222, at Av. Juárez, Chetumal ☎ 984/832-5300. **Bancrecer** ✉ Av. 5 by the bus station, Playa del Carmen ☎ 984/873-1561. **Bital** ✉ Av. Juárez between Avs. 10 and 15, Playa del Carmen ☎ 984/873-0272 ✉ Av. 30 between Avs. 4 and 6, Playa del Carmen ☎ 984/873-0238. **Scotiabank Inverlat** ✉ Av. 5 between Avs. Juárez and 2, Playa del Carmen ☎ 984/873-1488.

TAXIS

You can hire taxis in Cancún to go as far as Playa del Carmen, Tulum, or Akumal, but the price is steep unless you have many passengers. Fares run about $65 or more to Playa alone; between Playa and Tulum or Akumal, expect to pay at least another $25–$35. It's much cheaper from Playa to Cancún, with taxi fare running about $30; negotiate before you hop into the cab. Getting a taxi along Carretera 307 can take a while. Ask your hotel to call one for you. You can walk to just about everything in Playa. If you need to travel along the highway or farther north than Calle 20, a reliable taxi service is Sitios Taxis.

🚖 Taxis **Sitios Taxis** ✉ Playa del Carmen ☎ 984/873-0032.

TELEPHONES

In Chetumal the government-run telephone office, TELMEX, is at Avenida Juárez and Calle Lazaro Cardenas. For long-distance and international calls, you might also try the booths on Avenida Héroes: one is on the corner of Ignacio Zaragoza, and the other is just opposite Avenida Efraín Aguilar, next to the tourist information booth.

You can find TELMEX phones that use phone cards in every town up and down the coast (buy the cards in gift shops and grocery stores). There are several long-distance calling stations in Playa del Carmen on Avenida 5 as well as in front of the post office on Avenida Juárez and at the corner of Avenidas Juárez and 5. Luxury hotels charge $1 a minute for calls made from your room, so many visitors buy phone cards and use phones outside their hotels.

TOURS

Although some guided tours are available in this area, the roads are quite good for the most part, so renting a car is an efficient and enjoyable alternative. Most of the sights along this stretch are natural, and you can hire a guide at the ruins. If you'd like someone else to do the planning and driving for you, contact Maya Sites Travel Services, which offers inexpensive personalized tours.

You can visit the ruins of Cobá and the Maya villages of Pac-Chen and Chi Much—deep in the jungle—with Alltournative Expeditions. The group offers other ecotours as well. ATV Explorer offers two-hour rides through the jungle on all-terrain vehicles; explore caves, see ruins, and snorkel in a cenote. Tours start at $38.50. Based in Playa del Carmen, Tierra Maya Tours runs trips to the ruins of Chichén Itzá, Uxmal, Palenque, and Tikal. It can also help you with transfers, tickets, and hotel reservations.

Tres Palmas runs a day tour to the Reserva de la Biosfera Sian Ka'an that includes a visit to a typical Maya family living in the biosphere, a tamale breakfast, a visit to the Maya ruins at Muyil, a jungle trek to a lookout point for bird-watching, a boat trip through the lagoon and mangrove-laden channels (where you can jump into one of the channels and float downstream), lunch on the beach beside the Maya ruins at Tulum, and a visit to nearby cenotes for a swim and snorkeling. The staff picks you up at your hotel; the fee of $129 per person includes a bilingual guide.

🚌 **Alltournative Expeditions** ✉ Av. 10 No. 1, Plaza Antigua, Playa del Carmen ☎ 984/873-2036 ⊕ www.alltournative.com. **ATV Explorer** ✉ Carretera 307, 1 km (½ mi) north of Xcaret ☎ 984/873-1626. **Maya Sites Travel Services** ☎ 719/256-5186 or 877/620-8715 ⊕ www.mayasites.com. **Tierra Maya Tours** ✉ Av. 5 and Calle 6, Playa del Carmen ☎ 984/873-1385. **Tres Palmas** ✉ Main plaza beside church, Puerto Morelos ☎ 998/871-0709, 044-998/845-4083 cell ⊕ www.trespalmasweb.com.

TRAVEL AGENCIES

There are more major travel agencies and tour operators along the coast than ever, and first-class hotels in Playa del Carmen, Puerto Aventuras, and Akumal usually have their own in-house travel services.

⁊ Local Agent Referrals Alltournative Expeditions ⊠ Av. 10 No. 1, Plaza Antigua, Playa del Carmen ☎ 984/873-2036. **IMC** ⊠ Plaza Antigua, Playa del Carmen ☎ 984/873-1439 🖷 984/873-1439 ⊕ www.imcplay.com. **Turistica Maya de Quintana Roo** ⊠ Holiday Inn Puerta Maya, Chetumal ☎ 984/832-0555 or 984/832-2058 🖷 984/832-9711.

VISITOR INFORMATION

The tourist information booths in Chetumal are open weekdays 8:30–2:30 and 6–9. In Playa del Carmen the booth is open Monday–Saturday 8 AM–9 PM.

⁊ Tourist Information Chetumal ⊠ Calles Cinco de Mayo and Carmen Ochoa ☎ 983/832-2031 ⊠ Calle 22 de Enero and Av. Reforma ☎ 983/832-6647. **Playa del Carmen** ⊠ Av. Juárez by the police station, between Calles 15 and 20, Playa del Carmen ☎ 983/873-2804 in Playa del Carmen, 888/955-7155 in U.S., 604/990-6506 in Canada, 800/731-6148 in U.K.

MÉRIDA &
YUCATÁN STATE

5

Updated by
Jane Onstott

**THE YUCATÁN REPRESENTS THE JUXTAPOSITION OF TWO POWERFUL CIV-
ILIZATIONS**—that of the Maya and that of transplanted Europeans.
Culturally, it is one of the richest parts of Mexico. Vestiges of the past
are evident in this land of oval, thatch-roofed adobe huts and sober Franciscan mission churches. Once-great cities, many abandoned at the
height of their power, rise above the low tropical forests that have engulfed them over more than a millennium. Mysterious caves harbor subterranean swimming holes; fishing villages hug beaches untouched by
the tourist industry.

In the midst of this exotic landscape stands the elegant city of Mérida,
for centuries the main stronghold of Spanish colonialism in the land of
the Maya. There is a marvelous eccentricity about Mérida. Fully urban,
with plenty of traffic, it nonetheless has a friendly, self-contented air that
evokes a small town more than a state capital. Unfortunately, many colonial buildings were lost to reckless "renovation" in the 20th century,
and the city, although sprawling, is hardly imposing. Tucked among the
newer and less-impressive facades, however, are some grand colonial structures adorned with iron grillwork, beautiful carved wooden doors, and
archways concealing gardens that recall the city's heyday as the wealthiest capital in Mexico.

Mérida is a city of obvious contrasts, from its varied architecture to its
population. The people of Mérida are increasingly aware and proud of
their Maya culture, and even today their ancestry is unmistakable: people are short, with square faces and almond-shaped eyes, and many women
wear traditional *huipiles* (we-*pill*-ays)—hand-embroidered, knee-length
tunics. Still, even in the outlying villages, residents can be seen wearing
hats and shoes made from modern synthetic materials as often as the
customary leather sandals and huano-palm-fiber hats from earlier eras.

Nearly 500 years after the Spanish conquest, the Maya are Mexico's
largest indigenous population, and many remain in the Yucatán, the land
of their ancestors. To this day the Maya in the most remote or isolated
villages may speak no Spanish, or just enough to get by.

One of the world's great ancient cultures, Maya civilization thrived
for about 1,500 years, although it was in a state of decline when the
conquistadores arrived in AD 1527. To discourage resistance to Catholic
conversion, the Spaniards superimposed Christian rituals and dogma
on existing beliefs whenever possible, creating the unique brand of ethnic Catholicism that's alive and well today. (Those defiant Maya who
resisted the new ideology were burned at the stake, drowned, and
hanged.)

Long incorrectly portrayed by archaeologists as docile and peace-lov-
ing, the irresolute Maya provided the Spaniards and the mainland Mexicans with one of their greatest challenges. Rebellious pockets of Maya
communities held out against the *dzulo'obs* (dzoo-loh-*obs*)—the upper
class, or outsiders—as late as the 1920s and '30s. And it's not just the
Maya who have traditionally resisted the impositions of outsiders. Yucatán tried to secede from the rest of Mexico in the 1840s, and Yucatecans
still think of themselves as *peninsulares* first, Mexicans second. Perhaps

Numbers in the text correspond to numbers in the margin and on the State of Yucatán and Mérida maps.

If you have 3 days

Spend two days in 🗺 **Mérida ❶–⓰**, savoring the city's unique character as you make your way among the historic churches and mansions and enjoy the parks and restaurants. (If you can plan around a Sunday, so much the better, as the city center is closed to traffic and cultural events are scheduled throughout the day.) Alternatively, spend a day seeing Mérida's sights and another day visiting Dzibilchaltún (take your bathing suit so you can swim in the sinkhole) and the idle port town of Progreso. On Day 3, drive or take a tour to one of Yucatán's most famous Maya ruins—either **Chichén Itzá ⓳** or **Uxmal ㉓**. Each is within about two hours of Mérida, making for an ideal day trip. Each site has lovely accommodations if you prefer to spend the night.

If you have 7 days

First explore the sights of 🗺 **Mérida ❶–⓰** (heading to Progreso and the low-key beach towns of the north coast if you want to see the sea), and then take two separate overnight excursions from the city. On Day 3 explore the ruins of 🗺 **Uxmal ㉓**, and spend the night at one of the hotels there. On Day 4 explore the Ruta Puuc—the series of lost cities south of Uxmal that includes **Kabah ㉔**, **Sayil ㉕**, and **Labná ㉖**, as well as the fascinating **Grutas de Loltún ㉗**—and then return to 🗺 Mérida through **Ticul ㉘**.

On Day 5, explore the charming town of **Izamal ⓱** en route to 🗺 **Chichén Itzá ⓳**, where there are a handful of great accommodations. On Day 6, visit **Grutas de Balancanchén ⓴** and then the colonial town of 🗺 **Valladolid ㉑**, where you can either shop and explore the colonial church and ex-monastery of Saint Bernard, or swim in one of two sinkholes: Cenote Zací, at the edge of town, or the lovely Cenote X-Keken (popularly called Cenote Dzitnup), outside town. From Valladolid you can either return to Mérida via the farming community of Tizimín, or spend the night in 🗺 Río Lagartos in order to visit **Parque Natural Ría Lagartos ㊱**. In either case, on Day 7 don't miss the Maya ruins of **Ek Balam ㉒**, a little less than halfway between Valladolid and Tizimín.

If you have 10 days

In addition to visiting the sights noted above, you may want to add beach days to your itinerary. An obvious choice is to extend your time in and around **Progreso ㉝** (seeing the ruins of **Dzibilchaltún ㉜** en route). A separate road from Mérida will deliver you to the equally laid-back town of **Celestún ㉛**, which is the departure point for **Parque Natural del Flamenco Mexicano,** a protected habitat for flocks of pink flamingos and other aquatic birds.

that's why people from other parts of Mexico refer to the easternmost part of their country as their Sister Republic of Yucatán.

It could well have been this independent attitude that induced Governor Salvador Alvarado, in 1915, to convene the first feminist congress in the country (and Latin America as well) here, with the idea of liberating women "from being social wards and from the traditions that have suppressed them for years." This congress, which Alvarado described as "brilliant," was so successful that it was followed by the second congress in Mexico City in 1921, when women asked for the right to vote. They were finally granted that right in 1953.

Francisco de Montejo's conquest of Yucatán took three gruesome wars, over a total of 24 years. "Nowhere in all America was resistance to Spanish conquest more obstinate or more nearly successful," wrote the historian Henry Parkes. Having procured a huge workforce of free indigenous labor, Spanish agricultural estates prospered. Mérida soon became a strategic administrative and military center, the gateway to Cuba and to Spain. By the 18th century, huge maize and cattle plantations flourished throughout the peninsula, and the wealthy *hacendados* (plantation owners), left largely to their own devices by the viceroys in faraway Mexico City, accumulated fortunes under a flagrantly feudal system. The social structure—based on Indian peonage—changed little as the economic base shifted to the export of dyewood; henequen, or sisal, a natural fiber used to make rope; and chicle, or gum arabic, formerly used to make chewing gum.

Insurrection came during the War of the Castes in the mid-1800s, when the enslaved indigenous people rose up with long-repressed furor and massacred thousands of whites. The United States, Cuba, and Mexico City finally came to the aid of the ruling elite, and between 1846 and 1850 the Indian population of Yucatán was effectively halved. Those Maya who did not escape into the remote jungles of neighboring Quintana Roo or Chiapas or get sold into slavery in Cuba found themselves, if possible, worse off than before under the dictatorship of Porfirio Díaz. The fruits of their labor can be seen today in the imposing French-style mansions that stretch along Mérida's Paseo Montejo.

Yucatán was then and still is a largely agricultural state, although the economic importance of tourism and the *maquiladoras* (assembly plants or factories, usually foreign-owned) has grown steadily in the last quarter century. These factories cut and assemble goods for such U.S. brand names as Gap and Liz Claiborne. Nearly 200 maquiladoras employ some 28,000 workers, producing everything from baby clothes to shoulder pads, turbine engines, and jewelry.

With some 1 million inhabitants, the capital accounts for more than a third of the state's population, but many still live in villages, maintaining conservative traditions and lifestyles. Apart from the goods produced by the maquiladoras for overseas markets, the state also exports honey, textiles, henequen, orange-juice concentrate, fresh fish, hammocks, and wood products.

Physically, too, Yucatán differs from the rest of the country. Its geography and wildlife have more in common with Florida and Cuba—with which it was probably once connected—than with the central Mexican plateau and mountains. A flat limestone slab possessing no significant rivers or lakes, it is rife with cenotes (sinkholes) both above the ground and below, caves with stalactites, and thick (but short and relatively dry)

5

Beaches

Folks don't come to Yucatán state for its beaches—not when long stretches of sugary sand and aquamarine water are just down the coast in Cancún and the Caribbean. The north coast of the peninsula does have some respectable beaches of its own, which are shared mainly by local children, fishermen, and the odd sunbather. However, this coastline suffered considerable damage in 2002's Hurricane Isidore, and quite a few beachfront properties remain closed.

Any storm damage to Progreso, where Mérida residents go to beat the heat, has long since been repaired. Unpretentious and affordable, Progreso comes to life on summer and holiday weekends, when it can be nearly as bustling as the Mexican Caribbean. Empty beaches stretch for about 64 km (40 mi) to the east, punctuated by short grassy dunes, small fishing villages, estuaries, and the salt flats that have been producing this precious commodity since way before Colombus and Cortés. Independent travelers interested in savoring the simple beach culture gravitate to these shores, while bird-watchers and other nature lovers may choose the equally rustic towns of Celestún, Río Lagartos, and San Felipe.

Bird-Watching

Rise before the sun and head for shallow water to see flamingos dance an intricate mating dance. From late winter into spring, thousands of bright pink and black flamingos crowd the estuaries of Ría Lagartos, coming from their "summer homes" in nearby Celestún as well as from northern latitudes, to mate and raise their chicks. The largest flocks of both flamingos and bird-watching enthusiasts can be found during these months, when thousands of the birds—90% of the entire flamingo population of the Western Hemisphere—come to Ría Lagartos to nest.

Although the long-legged creatures are the most famous and best-appreciated birds found in these two nature reserves, red, white, black, and buttonwood mangrove swamps are home to hundreds of other species. Of Ría Lagartos's estimated 350 different species, one-third are winter-only residents—the avian counterparts of Canadian and northern-U.S. "snowbirds." Twelve of the region's resident species are endemic: found nowhere else on earth. Ría Lagartos Expeditions now leads walks through the low deciduous tropical forest in addition to boat trips through the mangroves.

More than 400 bird species have been sighted in the Yucatán, inland as well as on the coast. Bird-watching expeditions can be organized in Mérida as well as Ría Lagartos and Celestún. November brings hundreds of professional ornithologists and bird-watching aficionados to the Yucatán for a weeklong conference and symposium with films, lectures, and field trips.

Yucatecan Cuisine

Yucatecan food is surprisingly diverse, and milder than you might expect. Anything that's too mild, however, can be spiced up in a jiffy with one of many varieties of chile sauce. The sour orange—large, green, and only slightly sour—is native to the region, and is also used to give many soups and sauces a unique flavor.

Typical snacks like *panuchos* (small, thick, fried rounds of cornmeal stuffed or topped with beans and sprinkled with shredded meat and cabbage), empanadas (turnovers of meat, fish, potatoes, or, occasionally, cheese or beans), and *salbutes* (fried tortillas smothered with diced turkey, pickled onion, and sliced avocado) are ubiquitous. You'll find them at lunch counters (*loncherías*), in the market, and on the menu of restaurants specializing in local food.

Some recipes made famous in certain Yucatecan towns have made their way to mainstream menus. *Huevos motuleños,* presumably a recipe from the town of Motul, are so yummy they're found on breakfast menus throughout the region, and even elsewhere in Mexico. The recipe is similar to huevos rancheros (fried eggs on soft corn tortillas smothered in a mild red sauce) with the addition of sliced ham, melted cheese, and peas. Likewise, *pollo ticuleño,* which originated in Ticul, is served throughout the Yucatán. It's a tasty casserole of layered tomato sauce, mashed potatoes or cornmeal, crispy tortillas, chicken, cheese, and peas.

Tik-n-xic (pronounced teak-en-*sheek*) is fun to say and even better to eat. This coastal delicacy consists of butterflied snapper rubbed with salt and *achiote* (an aromatic paste made from the ground seeds of the annatto plant, and used to color food red as well as to subtly season it), grilled over a wood fire, and garnished with tomatoes and onions. As throughout Mexico, *aguas frescas*—fruit-flavored waters—are refreshing on a typically hot day, as are the dark beers Montejo and Leon Negro. Xtabentún is a sweet thick liqueur made of anise and honey.

Hotels

Mérida has many and varied lodging choices, among them top-end chain establishments, classic older hotels housed in charming colonial or early-20th-century mansions, and basic lodging geared toward budget travelers less concerned with creature comforts. Accommodations outside Mérida fit the low-key, simple pace of the region, where internationally affiliated properties are the exception rather than the rule. Instead, charming former haciendas such as the Hacienda Xcanatun, between Mérida and Progreso, provide elegant albeit expensive bases from which to explore the countryside. If you don't want to blow your budget on luxury accommodations, there are plenty of simple, small hotels looked after by friendly proprietors.

Ruins

Maya ruins from the Classic period, about AD 100–AD 1000, are Yucatán's greatest claim to fame and are world renowned. The Maya city of Chichén Itzá, midway between Cancún and Mérida, was the first Yucatán ruin to be excavated and extensively restored for public viewing, in the late 1930s. Its main pyramid is one of the most familiar images of Mexico. Uxmal, south of Mérida, is, on a smaller scale, just as spectacular. Since the early 1990s, a combination of government interest in these ruins as a matter of national pride and Mexico's participation in the Mundo Maya program with four Central American nations has been fueling a restoration boom. (In addition, increased government funding has spurred a surge in excavations during the past few years.) Each of the archaeological sites along the Ruta Puuc (Puuc Route) south of Uxmal, though not large, has something striking to offer amateur archaeologists, and more-recently excavated sites such as Dzibilchaltún and Ek Balam invite travelers to explore where few people have set foot in the past few centuries.

Glyphs heralding royal births, deaths, and marriages as well as successful battles and celestial events were recorded on stelae, lintels, and murals; these are of crucial importance to scientists attempting to date the rise and fall of the Maya cities. Unfortunately, many other historical records were lost with the near total destruction of the Maya codices (or books) by early Catholic priests and bishops, such as Bishop Diego de Landa, who considered the writings heretical and even works of the devil.

But Maya temples are not the only ruins that tug at the imagination in Yucatán. Grandiose Spanish colonial churches, often built on the same site of stones scavenged from dismantled pyramids, dominate rural towns throughout the state. The opulence of a more recent era can be seen at haciendas where wealthy plantation owners grew corn and raised cattle and, later, produced a more lucrative crop, henequen. Originally, there were 500 haciendas; some plantations still operate on a small scale. Many of the lavish mansions have been left to decay since they were seized from their owners during the Mexican Revolution, but others have been restored as lovely inns, restaurants, and museums.

Shopping   Although Yucatecan artisans don't produce many different crafts, what items they do create are among the finest in the country. For the most part, Mérida is the best place in Yucatán to buy local handicrafts at reasonable prices. The main products include *hamacas* (hammocks), *guayaberas* (pleated dress shirts for men), leather sandals, huipiles, baskets, *jipis* (Panama hats made of huano palm fibers), leather goods, gold- and silver-filigree jewelry, masks, and piñatas.

Hammocks are one of the most popular craft items sold here. They are most often available in cotton or nylon. Nylon hammocks dry quickly and are therefore preferred for humid or wet climates. Cotton is soft and comfortable, but the colors fade faster. Double-threaded hammocks are sturdier and stretch less than single-threaded ones, a difference that can be identified by studying the density of the weave. Hammocks come in different sizes: *sencillo,* for one person (a rather tight fit); *doble,* very comfortable for one but crowded for two; *matrimonial* (also called king-size), which decently accommodates two; and *familiares* or *matrimoniales especiales,* which can theoretically sleep an entire family. (When more than one person shares a hammock, they should lie sideways in the hammock, not lengthwise.) For a good-quality matrimonial nylon or cotton hammock, expect to pay about $35. Sencillos go for about $22. Unless you are an expert, it's best to buy a hammock at one of the specialty shops in Mérida, many of which let you climb in to try the size. The proprietors will also give you tips on washing, storing, and hanging your hammock.

---

jungle. Wild ginger and spider lilies grow in profusion. Vast flamingo colonies nest at estuaries on the northern and western coasts, where undeveloped sandy beaches extend some 370 km (230 mi). Deer, turkeys, boars, ocelots, tapirs, and armadillos once flourished in this tropical climate (the average temperature is 28°C, or 82°F)—and they still survive in a few protected areas.

But it is, of course, the celebrated Maya ruins—including Chichén Itzá, Uxmal, and a spate of smaller sites—that bring most people to the State of Yucatán. Indeed, the Puuc hills south of Mérida have one of the highest concentrations of archaeological sites in the hemisphere. Most of the roads in this region are paved and two lane, many with potholes but otherwise trouble free. Local travel agencies offer many different tours of the sites.

Exploring Yucatán State

Mérida is the hub of Yucatán and the best base for exploring the rest of the state. From there, highways radiate in every direction. To the east, Carreteras 180 *cuota* and 180 *libre* are, respectively, the toll and free roads to Cancún. The toll road (which costs $24) has exits for the famous Chichén Itzá ruins and the low-key colonial city of Valladolid; the free road passes these and many smaller towns. Heading south from Mérida on Carretera 261 (Carretera 180 until the town of Umán), you come to Uxmal and the Ruta Puuc, a series of outstanding small ruins of relatively uniform style. Carretera 261 north from Mérida takes you to the seaport and beach resort of Progreso. To the west, the laid-back fishing village of Celestún—which borders on protected wetland—can be accessed by a separate highway from Mérida.

With the exception of the Mérida–Cancún toll highway, most roads in the state are narrow, paved, two-lane affairs that pass through small towns and villages. Rarely is traffic heavy on them, and they are in reasonably good shape, although potholes get worse as the rainy season progresses. The coastal highway between Progreso and Dzilám de Bravo was severely damaged in Hurricane Isidore in September of 2002. The section between Telchac Puerto and Dzilám de Bravo has not been entirely restored, and alternate routes are required in a few other stretches as well.

Getting around the state is fairly easy, either by public bus or car. There are many bus lines, and most have at least one round-trip run daily to the main archaeological sites and colonial cities. If you're visiting for the first time, a guided tour booked through one of the many Mérida travel agencies provides a good introduction to the state. If you're independent and adventurous, by all means jump on a bus or hire a rental car and strike out on your own. If opting for the latter, however, be sure to check the lights and spare tire before taking off, carry plenty of bottled water, and fill up the tank whenever you see a station. It's also best not to drive at night.

About the Restaurants

Dining out is a pleasure in Mérida. The city's 50-odd restaurants dish out a superb variety of cuisines—primarily Yucatecan, of course, but also Lebanese, Italian, French, Chinese, vegetarian, and Mexican—at very reasonable prices. And tony cafés have been sprouting up in atmospheric colonial buildings that lend a European air to casual dining. Generally, reservations are advised for $$$ restaurants, but only on weekends and in the high season. Casual but neat dress is acceptable at all Mérida restaurants. Avoid wearing shorts in the more expensive places.

Beach towns north of Mérida such as Progreso, as well as Río Lagartos to the east and Celestún to the west, serve fresh-caught seafood, although

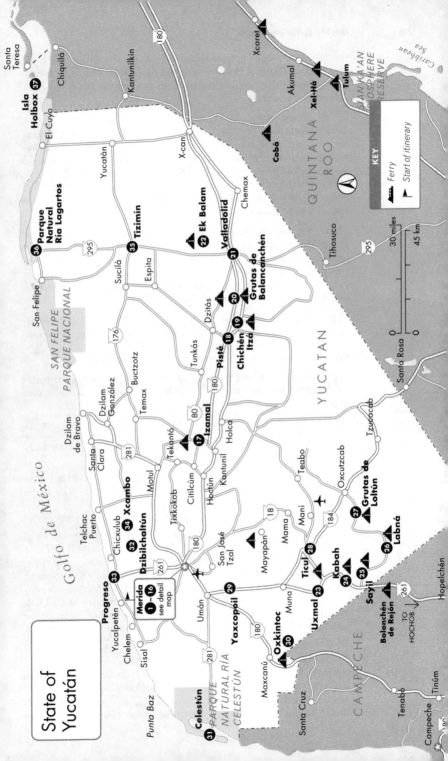

the dishes are usually prepared quite simply. A real gourmet dish is the blue crab at Celestún. However, you can't go wrong with most restaurants, whether they are thatch-roofed affairs along the beach or swank dining rooms in town.

About the Hotels

Yucatán State has 7,000 hotel rooms, which is about a third of the number of rooms in Cancún. As in the rest of Mexico, the facade rarely reveals the character of the hotel behind it so, if possible, check out the interior before booking. In general the public spaces in Mérida's hotels are prettier than the sleeping rooms. Most hotels have air-conditioning, and even many budget hotels have installed it in at least some rooms—but it's best to ask.

Location is very important: if you plan to spend most of your time enjoying Mérida, stay near the main square or along Calle 60. If you're a light sleeper, however, you may be better off staying in one of the highrises along or near Paseo Montejo, about a 20-minute stroll (but an easy cab ride) from the main square. Another option is to choose a room with double-pane windows to cut out traffic noise.

There are several charming and comfortable hotels near the major archaeological sites, and a couple of new, cozy, foreign-run bed-and-breakfasts in Progreso, which previously had only desultory digs. Elsewhere, expect modest to very basic accommodation.

WHAT IT COSTS In Dollars				
$$$$	**$$$**	**$$**	**$**	**¢**
RESTAURANTS over $25	$15–$25	$10–$15	$5–$10	under $5
HOTELS over $250	$150–$250	$75–$150	$50–$75	under $50

Restaurant prices are per person, for a main course at dinner, excluding tax and tip. Hotel prices are for a standard double room in high season, based on the European Plan (EP) and excluding service and 17% tax (15% Value Added Tax plus 2% hospitality tax).

Timing

Sunday is special in Yucatán. Mérida blocks off traffic downtown as what seems to be the city's entire population gathers in the *zócalo* (main square) and other parks and plazas to socialize and watch live entertainment. Cafés along this route are perfect places from which to watch the parade of people as well as folk dancers and singers. On Saturday nights between 7 PM and 1 AM, Calle 60 between Parque Santa Lucía and the main square comes alive. Restaurants set out tables in the streets, and these quickly fill with patrons eager to watch musicians playing free hip-hop, tango, salsa, or jazz.

Thousands of people, from international sightseers to Maya shamans, swarm to Chichén Itzá for the vernal equinox (the first day of spring), when the afternoon light creates a shadow that looks like a snake—meant to evoke the ancient Maya serpent god, Kukulcán—that moves slowly down the side of the main pyramid. The phenomenon also occurs on the autumnal equinox, but the rain clouds at that time of year sometimes block the sun, spoiling the effect.

Another good time to come is at the end of October, during Mérida's Otoño Cultural, the Autumn Cultural Festival, usually held in the last weeks of October or early November. During this two-week event, free or inexpensive classical-music concerts, dance performances, and art exhibits take place almost nightly at theaters and open-air venues around the city. Also at this time of year, Meridanos celebrate Hanal Pixan, meaning "food for departed souls." As well as putting up home altars for departed loved ones for the Feasts of All Saints and All Souls, November 1 and 2, residents erect altars in the main square and organize parades and other entertainment.

High season consists of the weeks around Christmas, Easter week, and the months of July and August. Rainfall is heaviest between June and October, bringing with it an uncomfortable humidity. The coolest months are November–January; April and May are usually the hottest.

MÉRIDA

Travelers to Mérida are a loyal bunch, content to return again and again to favorite restaurants, neighborhoods, and museums. The hubbub of the city can be frustrating, particularly after a peaceful stay on the coast or at one of the archaeological sites, but Mérida's merits far outweigh its flaws. Mérida is the cultural and intellectual center of the peninsula and its museums, shops, and attractions can provide great insight into the history and character of the Yucatán.

Most streets in Mérida are numbered, not named, and most run one-way. North–south streets have even numbers, which descend from west to east; east–west streets have odd numbers, which ascend from north to south. Street addresses are confusing because they don't progress in even increments by blocks; for example, the 600s may occupy two or more blocks. A particular location is therefore usually identified by indicating the street number and the nearest cross street, as in "Calle 64 and Calle 61," or "Calle 64 between Calles 61 and 63," which is written "Calle 64 x 61 y 63." Although it looks confusing at first glance, this system is actually extremely helpful.

Zócalo & Surroundings

The zócalo, the oldest part of town, has been dubbed the Centro Histórico (Historic Center) by city officials. The city has been restoring the colonial buildings in the area to their original splendor, and it's not uncommon to see work proceeding on facades on several streets at once.

A Good Walk

Start at the **zócalo** ❶ ►: see the **Casa de Montejo** ❷ (now a Banamex bank), on the south side; the **Palacio Municipal** ❹ and the **Centro Cultural de Mérida Olimpo** ❸, on the west side; the **Palacio del Gobierno** ❺, on the northeast corner, and, catercorner, the **Catedral de San Ildefonso** ❻; and the

Museo de Arte Contemporáneo ⑦ on the east side. Step out on Calle 60 from the cathedral and walk north to **Parque Hidalgo ⑧** and the **Iglesia de la Tercera Orden de Jesús ⑨**, which is across Calle 59. Continue north along Calle 60 for a short block to the **Teatro Peón Contreras ⑩**, which lies on the east side of the street; the entrance to the **Universidad Autónoma de Yucatán ⑪** is on the west side of Calle 60 at Calle 57. A block farther north on the west side of Calle 60 is the **Parque Santa Lucía ⑫**. From the park, walk north four blocks and turn right on Calle 47 for two blocks to **Paseo Montejo ⑬**. Once on this street, continue north for two long blocks to the **Palacio Cantón ⑭**. From here look either for a *calesa* (horse-drawn carriage) or cabs parked outside the museum to take you back past the zócalo to the **Mercado de Artesanías García Rejón ⑮** and the **Mercado Municipal ⑯**—or walk if you're up to it.

What to See

❷ **Casa de Montejo.** This stately palace sits on the south side of the plaza, on Calle 63. Francisco de Montejo—father and son—conquered the peninsula and founded Mérida in 1542; they built their "casa" 10 years later. The property remained with the family until the late 1970s, when it was restored by banker Agustín Legorreta and converted to a bank. Built in the French style, it represents the city's finest—and oldest—example of colonial plateresque architecture, which typically has elaborate ornamentation. A bas-relief on the doorway—the facade is all that remains of the original house—depicts Francisco de Montejo the younger, his wife, and daughter as well as Spanish soldiers standing on the heads of the vanquished Maya. Even if you have no banking to do, step into the building weekdays between 9 and 5 to glimpse the leafy inner patio.

❻ **Catedral de San Ildefonso.** Begun in 1561, St. Ildefonso is the oldest cathedral in Mexico and the second oldest on the North American mainland. It took several hundred Maya laborers, working with stones from the pyramids of the ravaged Maya city, 36 years to complete it. Designed in the somber Renaissance style by an architect who had worked on the Escorial in Madrid, its facade is stark and unadorned, with gunnery slits instead of windows, and faintly Moorish spires. Inside, the black Cristo de las Ampollas (Christ of the Blisters) occupies a side altar to the left of the main one. The statue is a replica of the original, which was destroyed during the Revolution; this is also when the gold that typically decorated Mexican cathedrals was carried off. According to one of many legends, the Christ figure burned all night yet appeared the next morning unscathed—except that it was covered with the blisters for which it is named. ✉ *Calles 60 and 61, Centro* ☎ *No phone* ☉ *Daily 7–11:30 and 4:30–8.*

❸ **Centro Cultural de Mérida Olimpo.** Referred to as simply Olimpo, this is the best venue in town for free cultural events. The beautiful porticoed cultural center was built adjacent to City Hall in late 1999, occupying what used to be a parking lot. The marble interior is a showcase for top international art exhibits, classical-music concerts, conferences, and theater and dance performances. Next door, a movie house renovated to its 1950s look, shows art films most nights: classics by such direc-

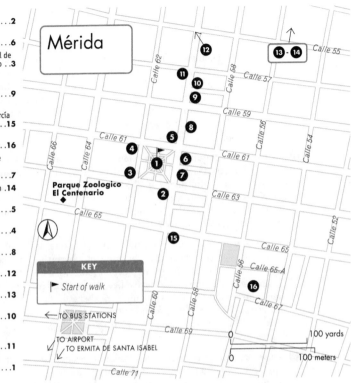

tors as Buñuel, Fellini, and Kazan. The complex also includes a book-store and a wonderful cybercafé-restaurant; 90-minute shows explaining the solar system are presented at the planetarium for \$3 (Tuesday–Saturday at 10, noon, 5, and 7; Sunday at 10 and noon). ⊠ *Calle 62 between Calles 61 and 63, Centro* ☎ *999/928–0000* ⊠ *Free* ⊙ *Tues.–Sun. 10–10.*

Ermita de Santa Isabel. At the southern end of the city stands the restored and beautiful Hermitage of St. Isabel. Built circa-1748 as part of a Je-suit monastery also known as the Hermitage of the Good Trip, it served as a resting place for colonial-era travelers heading to Campeche. One of the most peaceful places in the city, the chapel is an enchanting spot to visit at sunset (although it's usually closed) and perhaps a good des-tination for a ride in a calesa. Behind it, the huge and lush tropical gar-den, with its waterfall and footpaths, is usually unlocked during daylight hours. ⊠ *Calles 66 and 77, La Ermita* ☎ *No phone* ⊠ *Free* ⊙ *Church open only during Mass.*

❾ Iglesia de la Tercera Orden de Jesús. Just north of Parque Hidalgo is one of Mérida's oldest buildings and the first Jesuit church in the Yucatán. It was built in 1618 from the limestone blocks of a dismantled Maya temple, and faint outlines of ancient carvings are still visible on the west wall. Although a favorite place for society weddings because of its antiquity, the church interior is not very ornate.

The former convent rooms in the rear of the building now host the small **Pinoteca Juan Gamboa Guzmán,** a collection of artwork. The first room is dedicated to temporary exhibits; the second displays striking bronze sculptures of the Yucatán's indigenous people by its most celebrated 20th-century sculptor, Enrique Gottdiener. On the second floor are about 20 forgettable oil paintings—mostly of past governors and a few saints. ⊠ *Calle 59 between Calles 58 and 60, Centro* ☎ *No phone* 🖃 *$3* ⊙ *Tues.–Sat. 8–8, Sun. 8–2.*

⑮ Mercado de Artesanías García Rejón. Rows of stalls near the municipal market form the García Rejón Crafts Market. You'll find reasonable prices on straw and palm-fiber hats, hammocks, locally made liqueurs such as Xtabentún and mezcal, leather sandals, and jewelry. Postcards and other souvenirs can also be found. ⊠ *Calles 60 and 65, Centro* ☎ *No phone* ⊙ *Weekdays 9–6, Sat. 9–4, Sun. 9–1.*

★ ⑯ Mercado Municipal. Sellers of chiles, herbs, trinkets, and fruit occupy almost every patch of ground at the pungent labyrinthine municipal market. In the early morning the place is jammed with housewives and restaurateurs shopping for the freshest seafood and produce. Local pottery, embroidered clothes, men's guayabera dress shirts, hammocks, and straw bags can all be found at the Bazar de Artesanías Municipales within. ⊠ *Calles 56 and 67, Centro* ☎ *No phone* ⊙ *Mon.–Sat. dawn–dusk, Sun. 8–3.*

❼ Museo de Arte Contemporáneo. Originally designed as an art school but used until 1915 as a seminary, this enormous two-story building is full of light, just perfect for an art museum. It showcases the works of contemporary Yucatecan artists such as Gabriel Ramírez Aznar and Fernando García Ponce on the ground-floor and second-floor galleries. There's also a café (closed Sunday and Tuesday). ⊠ *Pasaje de la Revolución 1907, between Calles 58 and 60 on the main square, Centro* ☎ *999/928–3236 or 999/928–3258* 🖃 *$2* ⊙ *Wed.–Mon. 10–5:30.*

⑭ Palacio Cantón. The most compelling of the mansions on **Paseo Montejo,** the pale-peach palacio houses the air-conditioned **Museo de Antropología e Historia.** Designed by Enrique Deserti, who also did the blueprints for the Teatro Peón Contreras, the building has a grandiose air that seems more characteristic of a mausoleum than a home, but in fact it was built for a general between 1909 and 1911. There is marble everywhere, as well as Doric and Ionic columns and other Italianate Beaux Arts flourishes. From 1958 to 1967 the mansion served as the residence of the state governor; in 1977 it became a museum dedicated to the archaeology and history of the Maya. Although not as impressive as its counterparts in other Mexican cities, it's nonetheless an introduction to ancient Maya culture. Exhibits show conch shells, stones, and quetzal feathers used for trading and explain the Maya practice of dental mutilation and incrustation. ⊠ *Calle 43 and Paseo Montejo, Paseo Montejo* ☎ *999/923–0557* 🖃 *$3.50* ⊙ *Tues.–Sat. 8–8, Sun. 8–2.*

⑤ Palacio del Gobierno. Occupying the northeast corner of the main square, the seat of state government was built in 1885 on the site of the Casa Real (Royal House). The upper floor of the State House contains Fernando Castro Pacheco's vivid murals of the bloody history of the conquest of the Yucatán, painted in 1978. On the main balcony (visible from outside on the plaza) stands a reproduction of the Bell of Dolores Hidalgo, on which Mexican independence rang out on the night of September 15, 1810, in the town of Dolores Hidalgo in Guanajuato. On the anniversary of the event, the governor rings the bell to commemorate the occasion. ⊠ *Calle 61 between Calles 60 and 62, Centro* ☎ *999/930–3101* 🖃 *Free* ☉ *Daily 9–9.*

④ Palacio Municipal. The west side of the main square is occupied by City Hall, a 17th-century building painted pale yellow and trimmed with white arcades, balustrades, and the national coat of arms. Originally erected on the ruins of the last surviving Maya structure, it was rebuilt in 1735 and then completely reconstructed along colonial lines in 1928. It remains the headquarters of the local government, and houses the municipal tourist office. ⊠ *Calle 62 between Calles 61 and 63, Centro* ☎ *999/928–2020* ☉ *Daily 9–8.*

⑧ Parque Hidalgo. A half block north of the main plaza is this small cozy park, officially known as Plaza Cepeda Peraza. Historic mansions, now reincarnated as hotels and sidewalk cafés, line the south side of the park; at night, the area comes alive with marimba bands and street vendors. ⊠ *Calle 60 between Calles 59 and 61, Centro.*

⑫ Parque Santa Lucía. The rather plain park at Calles 60 and 55 draws crowds to its Thursday-night performances by local musicians and folk dancers; shows start at 9. The small church opposite the park dates from 1575 and was built as a place of worship for the African and Caribbean slaves who lived here. The churchyard functioned as the cemetery until 1821.

Parque Zoológico El Centenario. Mérida's greatest children's attraction, this large amusement complex features playgrounds, rides (including ponies and a small train), a roller-skating rink, snack bars, and cages with more than 300 native animals such as monkeys, birds, and reptiles. It also has picnic areas, pleasant wooded paths, and a small lake where you can rent rowboats. The French Renaissance–style arch (1921) commemorates the 100th anniversary of Mexican independence. ⊠ *Av. Itzaes between Calles 59 and 65 (entrances on Calles 59 and 65), Centro* ☎ *No phone* 🖃 *Free* ☉ *Daily 8–5.*

⑬ Paseo Montejo. North of downtown, this 10-block-long street was *the* place to reside in the late 19th century, when wealthy plantation owners sought to outdo each other with the opulence of their elegant mansions. Inside, the owners typically displayed imported Carrara marble and antiques, opting for the decorative styles popular in New Orleans, Cuba, and Paris rather than the style in Mexico City. (At the time there was more traffic by sea via the Gulf of Mexico and the Caribbean than there was overland across the lawless interior.) The broad boulevard, lined with tamarinds and laurels, has lost much of its former panache; many of the once-stunning mansions have fallen into disrepair. Others, however, are being restored as part of a citywide, privately funded beautification program.

🔟 **Teatro Peón Contreras.** This 1908 Italianate theater was built along the same lines as grand turn-of-the-20th-century European theaters and opera houses. In the early 1980s the marble staircase, dome, and frescoes were restored. Today, in addition to performing arts, the theater also houses the Centro de Información Turística, providing maps, brochures, and details about attractions in the city and state. A café serving cappucino and other coffees, plus snacks and light meals, spills out to a patio from inside the theater next to the information center. ⊠ *Calle 60 between Calles 57 and 59, Centro* ☎ *999/923–7354, 999/924–9290 tourist-information center* ⊙ *Theater daily 7 AM–1 AM; tourist-information center daily 8 AM–9 PM.*

⓫ **Universidad Autónoma de Yucatán.** The arabesque university plays a major role in the city's cultural and intellectual life. The folkloric ballet performs on the patio of the main building most Fridays at 9 PM ($3), and less often during the low season of September and October. A Jesuit college built in 1618 previously occupied the site; the present building, which dates from 1711, has crenellated Moorish ramparts and archways. Bulletin boards just inside the entrance announce upcoming cultural events. ⊠ *Calle 60 between Calles 57 and 59, Centro* ☎ *999/924–8000.*

❶ **Zócalo.** Meridanos traditionally refer to this main square as the Plaza de la Independencia, or the Plaza Principal. Whichever name you prefer, it's a good spot from which to begin a tour of the city. The plaza was laid out in 1542 on the ruins of T'hó, the Maya city demolished to make way for Mérida, and is still the focal point around which the most important public buildings cluster. *Confidenciales* (S-shape benches designed for tête-à-têtes), stationed under ancient, geometrically pruned laurel trees, invite lingering. Lampposts keep the park beautifully illuminated at night. ⊠ *Bordered by Calles 60, 62, 61, and 63, Centro.*

Where to Eat

★ **$$–$$$** ✕ **Alberto's Continental Patio.** The striking architecture of this dining spot dates from 1727, and was constructed on the site of a Maya temple. It's adorned with the original temple stones and mosaic floors from Cuba; the two air-conditioned dining rooms have handsome antiques, stone sculptures, and candles glowing in glass lanterns. A courtyard surrounded by rubber trees decked in white lights is ideal for starlit dining. There's lots of delicious Lebanese food: shish kebab, fried *kibi* (meatballs of ground beef, wheat germ, and spices), cabbage rolls, hummus, eggplant dip, and tabbouleh; and don't forget the almond pie and Turkish coffee. ⊠ *Calle 64 No. 482, at Calle 57, Centro* ☎ *999/928–5367* ▤ *AE, MC, V.*

★ **$$–$$$** ✕ **La Habichuela.** Custom-made hardwood furniture, marble floors, and lots of leaded-glass accents make this a favorite power-lunch spot for local businessmen; at night, it's filled with families and couples. The menu is inventive, and includes such appetizers as seafood crepes and salmon pâté;

the chicken breast stuffed with cheese and served with a rose-petal sauce is a standout entrée. The chocolate-mousse cake is the undisputed star of the dessert menu. Sax music lends a mellow air on weekend evenings. ⊠ *Calle 21 No. 416, at Calle 8 (about 20 mins by car from main square), Col. México Oriente* ☎ *999/926–3626* ▤ *AE, D, MC, V.*

$–$$$ ✕ **La Bella Epoca.** You'll pay for the ambience at this pretentious yet elegantly restored mansion, where sparkling crystal chandeliers hover overhead. Arrive for dinner before 8 PM to claim a table on one of the tiny balconies overlooking Parque Hidalgo. The ambitious handwritten menu includes French, Mexican, Middle Eastern, Yucatecan, vegetarian, and Maya dishes. The *sikil-pak* (a dip with ground pumpkin seeds, charbroiled tomatoes, and onions) and succulent *pollo pibil* (chicken baked in banana leaves) are both excellent. You can park in the hotel's lot—much easier than looking for street parking. ⊠ *Hotel del Parque, Calle 60 No. 497, between Calles 57 and 59, Centro* ☎ *999/928–1928* ▤ *AE, D, MC, V.*

★ **$–$$$** ✕ **Hacienda Teya.** This beautiful hacienda just outside the city has some of the best regional food in the area. Most patrons are well-to-do Meridanos enjoying a leisurely lunch, so you'll want to dress up a bit. A guitarist serenades from 2 to 5 on weekends. After a fabulous lunch of *cochinita pibil,* you can stroll in the orchard, or wander through the surrounding botanical gardens. If you find yourself wanting to stay longer, the hacienda also has six handsome lodging suites available. ⊠ *13 km (8 mi) east of Mérida on Carretera 180, Kanasín* ☎ *999/924–3800, 999/924–3880 in Mérida* ⌂ *Reservations essential* ▤ *AE, MC, V* ☺ *No dinner.*

$$ ✕ **Santa Lucía.** Opera music floats above black-and-white tile floors and red-draped tables in this century-old European-style bar-café-restaurant near the main plaza. Pizzas and calzones are the linchpins of the Italian menu; luscious pecan pies, cakes, and cookies beckon from behind the glass dessert case. The original art on the walls, much of which was done by the late Rudolfo Morales of Oaxaca, is for sale. ⊠ *Calle 60 No. 474A, Centro* ☎ *999/928–0704* ▤ *No credit cards.*

$–$$ ✕ **Hong Kong.** If you get tired of Mexican cuisine, head to this bustling eatery for some of Mérida's most authentic Chinese food. The wontons and egg rolls are served hot and crispy. The menu is full of chicken and shrimp dishes, but there are only a few vegetarian choices. Friday through Sunday (when only the $9 buffet is served until 5 PM) the place is jammed—and the clinking silverware and harried waiters are not conducive to lingering. ⊠ *Calle 31 No. 113, between Calles 22 and 24, Col. México* ☎ *999/926–1441 or 999/926–7439* ▤ *AE, D, MC, V.*

$–$$ ✕ **Pancho's.** In the evenings, this patio restaurant (which frames a small, popular local bar) is bathed in candlelight and the glow from tiny white lights decorating the tropical shrubs. The food, expensive by local standards, will seem familiar to anyone who's tried the sort of tacos-and-fajitas Mexican food usually served north of the border. Waiters—dressed in white muslin shirts and pants of the Revolution era—recommend the shrimp in tequila, and the tequila in general. Happy hour is 6 PM to 8 PM; afterwards there's live music on the tiny dance floor Wednesday–Saturday. ⊠ *Calle 59 No. 509, between Calles 60 and 62, Centro* ☎ *999/923–0942* ▤ *AE, D, MC, V.*

$–$$ ✕ **El Pórtico del Peregrino.** At the Pilgrim's Porch, a Mérida institution
Fodor'sChoice for 30 years, you can choose among three dining areas. Smokers get the
★ street view, while nonsmokers share the dining room stuffed with antiques (both these rooms have air-conditioning); groups gather on the
small, fern-draped interior patio. Start your meal with a warming, traditional lime soup before zeroing in on the *zarzuela de mariscos*—a yummy
dish containing lobster tails or crab claws (depending on the season),
squid, octopus, fish, and shrimp baked with white wine and garlic. Or
try the baked eggplant layered with Italian sauce, chicken, and grated
cheese. The homemade flan or coconut ice cream bathed in coffee
liqueur makes for a fine finish. ⊠ *Calle 57 No. 501, between Calles 60
and 62, Centro* ☎ 999/928–6163 ⊟ *AE, MC, V.*

$ ✕ **Los Almendros.** This two-salon Mérida institution, divided by a cov-
ered parking lot, provides a great introduction to Yucatecan cuisine. The
English-language menu has pictures and descriptions of each dish. Especially good choices include the pork sausage; the cochinita pibíl (pork
baked in banana leaves); and the *papadzules,* a concoction of tortillas,
green sauce, ground pumpkin seeds, and hard-cooked eggs. The house
sangria is tasty with or without alcohol. A musical trio plays romantic
traditional ballads daily between 2 and 5. ⊠ *Calle 50 No. 493, between
Calles 57 and 59, La Mejorada* ☎ 999/928–5459 *or 999/923–8135*
⊟ *AE, MC, V.*

$ ✕ **Amaro.** Statesman Andrés Quintana Roo was born in 1787 in this
historic home, which takes on a romantic glow at night with candlelit
tables on the open patio (bring a sweater—evenings can be chilly).
Meat, fish, and shellfish are served in moderation, but the emphasis is
on healthful drinks (locals rave about the agua de chaya, a thinned-down
juice made of a plant similar to spinach) and vegetarian dishes like eggplant curry and chaya soup. If you're missing your favorite comfort foods,
order a side of mashed potatoes or french fries, or a salad made with
fresh local veggies. ⊠ *Calle 59 No. 507, between Calles 60 and 62, Centro* ☎ 999/928–2451 ⊟ *MC, V.*

$ ✕ **Café La Habana.** Old-fashioned ceiling fans and a gleaming wood bar
contribute to the nostalgic feeling at this overwhelmingly popular café.
The aroma of fresh-ground coffee fills the air 24 hours a day. Sixteen
javas are offered (some spiked with spirits like Kahlúa or cognac), and
the menu has light snacks as well as some entrées, including tamales,
fajitas, and enchiladas. The waiters are friendly, and there are plenty of
them, although service is not always brisk. ⊠ *Calle 59 No. 511A, at
Calle 62, Centro* ☎ 999/928–6502 ⊟ *MC, V.*

$ ✕ **Ristorante & Pizzería Bologna.** Dine alfresco or inside the beautifully
restored old mansion, a few blocks off Paseo Montejo. Tables have fresh
flowers and cloth napkins; walls are adorned with pictures of Italy and
copper pots; and plants are everywhere. Most menu items are ordered
à la carte; among the favorites are the shrimp pizza and pizza *diabola,*
topped with salami, tomato, and chiles. The beef fillet—served solo or
draped in cheese or mushrooms—is served with baked potato and a med-
ley of mixed sautéed vegetables. ⊠ *Calle 21 No. 117A, near Calle 24,
Col. Izimná* ☎ 999/926–2505 ⊟ *AE, MC, V.*

¢–$ ✕ **Dante's.** Couples, families, and groups of students crowd this bustling coffeehouse on the second floor of one of Mérida's largest bookshops. The house specialty is crepes: there are 18 varieties with either sweet or savory fillings. Light entrées such as sandwiches, burgers, pizzas, and *molletes*—large open-faced rolls smeared with beans and cheese and then broiled—are also served, along with cappuccino, specialty coffees, beer, and wine. A small theater puts on evening comic sketches and live music from time to time, and puppet shows on Sunday at 10 AM. ⊠ *Prolongación Paseo Montejo 138B, Paseo Montejo* ☎ *999/927–7441* ▤ *No credit cards.*

¢–$ ✕ **La Vía Olimpo.** Lingering over coffee and a book is a pleasure at this smart Internet café; the outdoor tables are a great place to watch the nonstop parade—or the free Sunday performances—on the main square. In the colonial-era dining room, you can feast on *poc chuc* (pork marinated in sour-orange juice and spices), turkey sandwiches, or burgers and fries. Crepes are also popular, and there are lots of salads, smoothies, and juices if you're in the mood for lighter fare. The local intelligentsia keeps the venue hopping; it's open 24 hours Tuesday–Saturday. Spirits are also served. ⊠ *Calle 62 between Calles 63 and 61, Centro* ☎ *999/923–5843* ▤ *AE, MC, V.*

¢ ✕ **Alameda.** The building is old, and the decor couldn't be plainer. But you'll find good, hearty, and cheap fare at this always-popular spot. The most expensive main dish here costs about $4—but side dishes are extra, so if you want beans or potatoes with your eggs, you must order them à la carte. Middle Eastern and standard Yucatecan fare share the menu with vegetarian specialties: meat-free dishes include tabbouleh and spongy, lemon-flavor spinach turnovers. Shopkeepers linger over grilled beef shish kebab, pita bread, and coffee; some old couples have been coming in once a week for decades. Alameda closes at 7:30 PM. ⊠ *Calle 58 No. 474, near Calle 57, Centro* ☎ *999/928–3635* ▤ *No credit cards* ◷ *No dinner.*

Where to Stay

$$$–$$$$ ▥ **Hacienda Xcanatun.** The furnishings at this beautifully restored henequen hacienda include African and Indonesian antiques, locally made lamps, and oversize comfortable couches and chairs from Puebla. The rooms come with cozy sleigh beds, fine sheets, and fluffy comforters, and are decorated with art from Mexico, Cuzco, Peru, and other places the owners have traveled. Bathrooms are luxuriously large. An in-house restaurant serves a small menu of eclectic dishes. ⊠ *Carretera 261, Km 12, 8 mi north of Mérida, 97300* ☎ *999/941–0213 or 888/883–3633* ☏ *999/941–0319* ∰ *www.xcanatun.com* ⇆ *18 suites* ♨ *Restaurant, room service, fans, some in-room hot tubs, minibars, 2 pools, spa, steam room, 2 bars, laundry service, meeting room, airport shuttle, free parking; no room TVs* ▤ *AE, MC, V.*

$$$ ▥ **Hyatt Regency Mérida.** The city's first deluxe hotel is still among its most elegant. Rooms are regally decorated, with russet-hue quilts and rugs set off by blond-wood furniture and cream-color walls. There is a top-notch business center, and a beautiful marble lobby that comes alive with piano music from the popular Peregrina restaurant. ⊠ *Calle 60 No. 344, at*

Av. Colón, Paseo Montejo, 97000 ☎ 999/942–0202, 999/942–1234, or 800/233–1234 🖷 999/925–7002 ⊕ www.hyatt.com ⇆ 296 rooms, 4 suites ⚫ 2 restaurants, patisserie, room service, in-room data ports, minibars, cable TV with movies, 2 tennis courts, pool, gym, hot tub, massage, steam room, 2 bars, shops, baby-sitting, laundry service, concierge, concierge floor, Internet, business services, convention center, car rental, travel services, free parking, no-smoking rooms ⊟ AE, DC, MC, V.

$$–$$$ 🏨 **Fiesta Americana Mérida.** The facade of this posh hotel echoes the grandeur of the mansions on Paseo Montejo. The spacious lobby is filled with colonial accents and gleaming marble; there's also a 300-foot-high stained-glass atrium. Floral prints and larger-than-life proportions lend period elegance to the guest rooms, which are inspired by late-19th-century design, and which have such extras as balconies, bathtubs, hair dryers, and coffeemakers. Specially equipped rooms for people with disabilities are available, and guests on the business floor have access to the Fiesta Club for morning breakfast or afternoon appetizers. ✉ *Av. Colón 451, Paseo Montejo, 97127 ☎ 999/942–1111 or 800/343–7821 🖷 999/942–1122 ⊕ www.fiestaamericana.com ⇆ 323 rooms, 27 suites ⚫ Restaurant, coffee shop, room service, in-room data ports, minibars, cable TV with movies, golf privileges, tennis court, pool, gym, massage, bar, lounge, shops, baby-sitting, dry cleaning, laundry service, concierge, concierge floor, business services, car rental, travel services, free parking, no-smoking rooms ⊟ AE, D, DC, MC, V.*

$$ 🏨 **Casa del Balam.** This pleasant hotel two blocks from the zócalo is owned by the Barbachano family, pioneers of Yucatán tourism since the 1960s. The rooms here include colonial touches, like carved cedar doors and rocking chairs on the wide verandas; but they also have such modern-day conveniences as double-pane windows to keep out the noise. The rich decor and thoughtful details, like the hand-painted plates, make this place seem more like a home than a hotel. Guests have access to a golf and tennis club about 15 minutes away by car. ✉ *Calle 60 No. 488, Centro, 97000 ☎ 999/924–8844 or 800/624–8451 🖷 999/924–5011 ⊕ www.yucatanadventure.com.mx ⇆ 44 rooms, 3 suites ⚫ Restaurant, room service, minibars, refrigerators, cable TV, golf privileges, pool, bars, car rental, travel services, free parking, no-smoking rooms ⊟ AE, D, DC, MC, V.*

$$ 🏨 **Holiday Inn.** After suffering hurricane damage in late 2002, the Holiday Inn was extensively remodeled and is now nicer than ever. It's still the most light-filled hotel in Mérida, with floor-to-ceiling windows throughout the colorful lobby area and tiled dining room. Rooms and suites face an open courtyard and have comfy furnishings and marble bathrooms. Amenities include ironing boards, hair dryers, coffeemakers, alarm clocks, and more; be sure to ask about special rates, which can save you quite a bit. ✉ *Av. Colón 468, at Calle 60, Paseo Montejo, 97000 ☎ 999/942–8800 or 800/465–4329 🖷 999/942–8811 ⊕ www. basshotels.com ⇆ 197 rooms, 15 suites ⚫ Restaurant, café, room service, minibars, cable TV, tennis court, pool, bar, shop, baby-sitting, laundry service, concierge floor, Internet, business services, meeting rooms, airport shuttle, car rental, travel services, free parking, no-smoking rooms ⊟ AE, D, DC, MC, V.*

$$ ⌧ **Villa Mercedes.** This elegantly converted Art Nouveau home has been owned by the same local family since 1903. The hotel has gleaming marble floors, period furnishings, lush gardens and grounds, and a wonderful—although quite formal—restaurant. ⌧ *Av. Colón 500, between Calles 60 and 62, Paseo Montejo, 97000* ☏ *999/942–9000* 🖷 *999/942–9001* ⊕ *www.hotelvillamercedes.com.mx* ⟲ *91 rooms, 3 suites* ⌂ *Restaurant, room service, fans, cable TV, pool, exercise equipment, bar, laundry service, concierge, business services, meeting rooms, free parking* ⊟ *AE, MC, V.*

$ ⌧ **Best Western María del Carmen.** This modern hotel with its striking, salmon-color entrance caters to business travelers, tour groups, and those who desire secure parking. The main square, the market, and other major sights are within easy walking distance. Rooms have lacquered furniture and ornate Chinese lamps. ⌧ *Calle 63 No. 550, between Calles 68 and 70, Centro, 97000* ☏ *999/930–0390 or 800/528–1234* 🖷 *999/930–0393* ⊕ *www.bestwestern.com* ⟲ *86 rooms, 4 suites* ⌂ *Restaurant, room service, cable TV, pool, bar, shop, laundry service, meeting rooms, car rental, travel services, free parking, no-smoking rooms* ⊟ *AE, MC, V.*

$ ⌧ **Maison LaFitte.** Jazz and tropical music float quietly above this hotel's two charming patios, where you can sip a drink near the fountain or swim in the small swimming pool. Rooms are simple here and the bathrooms a bit cramped, but the staff is friendly and the location, a few blocks from the central plaza and surrounded by shops and restaurants, is ideal. Thursday through Saturday evenings a trio entertains on the pretty outdoor patio. ⌧ *Calle 60 No. 472, between Calles 53 and 55, Centro, 97000* ☏ *999/923–9159, 800/538–6802 in U.S. and Canada* ⟲ *30 rooms* ⌂ *Restaurant, room service, in-room safes, minibars, cable TV, pool, laundry service, Internet, travel services, free parking* ⊟ *MC, V* ⦿ *BP.*

¢–$ ⌧ **Casa Mexilio.** Four blocks from the main square is this eclectic B&B. Middle Eastern wall hangings, French tapestries, and colorful tile floors crowd the public spaces; individually decorated rooms have tile sinks and folk-art furniture. Some find the intimacy of this inn private and romantic, although others may find it a bit too small for their liking. A two-night minimum stay is required. ⌧ *Calle 68 No. 495, between Calles 57 and 59, Centro, 97000* ☏ *800/538–6802 in U.S. and Canada* 🖷 *999/928–2505* ⊕ *www.mexicoholiday.com* ⟲ *8 rooms, 1 penthouse* ⌂ *Dining room, pool; no a/c in some rooms, no room phones, no room TVs* ⊟ *MC, V* ⦿ *CP.*

¢–$ ⌧ **Gran Hotel.** Cozily situated on Parque Hidalgo, this legendary 1901 hotel is the oldest in the city, and it does look its age, with high ceilings, wrought-iron balcony and stair rails, and big old-fashioned room keys. Guest rooms are shabby-chic; beds are firm, if small. The tiny balconies that overlook the square won't open, so you might as well choose one of the quieter rooms at the rear without any windows at all. Fidel Castro chose one of these when he stayed here; Porfirio Díaz stayed in one of the corner suites, which have small living and dining areas. ⌧ *Calle 60 No. 496, Centro, 97000* ☏ *999/923–6963* 🖷 *999/924–7622* ⟲ *25 rooms, 7 suites* ⌂ *Restaurant, pizzeria, room service, fans, laundry service, free parking, some pets allowed* ⊟ *MC, D, V.*

¢–$ ⚏ **Medio Mundo.** A Lebanese-Uruguayan couple runs this B&B in a residential area downtown. The house has Mediterranean accents and spacious rooms that open off a long wrought-iron passageway. The original thick walls and tile floors are well preserved; rooms have custom-made hardwood furniture. A large patio in the back holds the breakfast nook, a small kidney-shape swimming pool, and an old mango tree. There's also a pond with a delightful waterfall and fountain surrounded by fruit and flowering trees. ⊠ *Calle 55 No. 533, between Calles 64 and 66, Centro, 97000* ⛨ *999/924–5472* ⊕ *www.hotelmediomundo.com* ⤳ *12 rooms* ⌂ *Dining room, pool, massage, laundry service, parking (fee); no a/c in some rooms, no room phones, no room TVs* ▭ *D, MC, V.*

★ ¢ ⚏ **Casa San Juan.** This homey B&B in a restored colonial mansion, just a few blocks from the zócalo, is popular with travelers who appreciate an informal friendly environment. Original design elements include 10-foot-high wooden doors and tiled floors. Guest rooms vary in size and are individually decorated; most have double beds and firm mattresses. Affable host Pablo da Costa, a hotelier from Cuba, can give you tips on visiting the city—in five languages. A two-night minimum stay is required. Guests are given front-door keys; if you're arriving in the afternoon, call ahead to make sure someone can let you in. ⊠ *Calle 62 No. 545A, between Calles 69 and 71, Centro, 97000* ⛨ *999/986–2937* ⛨ *999/986–2937* ⊕ *www.casasanjuan.com* ⤳ *8 rooms* ⌂ *Fans, travel services; no a/c in some rooms; no room phones, no room TVs* ▭ *AE, MC, V (when booked from the U.S, Canada, or Europe)* ⦿ *CP.*

★ ¢ ⚏ **Dolores Alba.** The newer wing of this comfortable, cheerful hotel has spiffy rooms with quiet yet strong air-conditioning, comfortable beds, and many amenities; rooms in this section have large TVs, balconies, and telephones. Although even the older and cheaper rooms have air-conditioning, they also have fans, which some people prefer to use. The pool is surrounded by lounge chairs and shaded by giant trees, and there's a comfortable restaurant and bar at the front of the property. Different meal plans packages are available, so be sure to ask when you make reservations. ⊠ *Calle 63 No. 464, between Calles 52 and 54, Centro, 97000* ⛨ *999/928–5650* ⊕ *www.doloresalba.com* ⤳ *95 rooms* ⌂ *Restaurant, some fans, pool, bar, free parking* ▭ *No credit cards* ⦿ *MAP, FP.*

¢ ⚏ **Posada Toledo.** This beautiful colonial house has retained its elegance with high ceilings, floors of Moorish-patterned tile, and old-fashioned carved furniture. The breakfast room is particularly lovely, with antique stained glass. Guest-room quality varies more than the rates would reflect, so inspect your room before checking in. Room 5 is an elegant two-room suite that was originally the mansion's master bedroom. If you're a light sleeper, ask for a room away from the courtyard. Breakfast only is served in the dining room. ⊠ *Calle 58 No. 487, at Calle 57, Centro, 97000* ⛨ *999/923–1690* ⛨ *999/923–2256* ⤳ *21 rooms, 1 suite* ⌂ *Dining room, fans, free parking; no a/c in some rooms* ▭ *MC, V.*

¢ ⚏ **Residencial.** Location is the major draw at this classy bright-pink hotel, a replica of a 19th-century French colonial mansion. It sits on Calle 59, the main entrance to town, and has gated parking. Its elegant dining room is more notable for its silk drapes and fine linen tablecloths than for its food. Rooms have powerful showers, comfortable beds, remote-control cable TV, and spacious closets. The small swimming pool in the central courtyard is pleasant for reconnoitering, but far from private. ⊠ *Calle 59 No. 589, at Calle 76, Centro, 97000* ☎ *999/924–3899 or 999/924–3099* 🖷 *999/924–0266* 🖙 *64 rooms, 2 suites* ⌂ *Restaurant, room service, cable TV, pool, bar, free parking* ▤ *D, MC, V.*

¢ 🖾 **Santa Ana.** A 10-minute walk from the main plaza, this trim little three-story hotel is great for those who like exercise: it has lots of stairs and no elevator. Rooms are decorated and tiled mainly in white, with blue accents. Bathrooms are small but stylish, with partial glass walls that function as shower screens. ⊠ *Calle 45 No. 503, between Calles 60 and 62, Centro, 97000* ☎ *999/923–3331* 🖷🖷 *999/923–3332* 🖙 *19 rooms* ⌂ *Cable TV, pool, free parking* ▤ *No credit cards.*

Nightlife & the Arts

Mérida has an active and diverse cultural life, which features free government-sponsored music and dance performances many evenings, as well as sidewalk art shows in local parks. At Parque de Santiago (Calles 59 and 72), old folks and lovers of 1940s ballads gather for dancing on Tuesday nights (at 9 PM). On Saturday evenings, the Fiesta Mexicana (corner of Paseo Montejo and Calle 47) hosts different musical and cultural events; more free music, dance, comedy, and regional handicrafts can be found at the Corazón de Mérida, on Calle 60 between the main plaza and Calle 55.

On Sunday, six blocks around the zócalo are closed off to traffic, and you can see performances—often mariachi and marimba bands or folkloric dancers—at Plaza Santa Lucía, Parque Hidalgo, and the main plaza. For a schedule of current performances, consult the tourist offices, the local newspapers, or the billboards and posters at the Teatro Peón Contreras or the Centro Cultural Olimpo.

Nightlife

BARS & NIGHTCLUBS

★ Part bar, restaurant, and stage show **Eladios** (⊠ Calle 24 No. 100, Col. Itzimná ☎ 999/927–2126), with its peaked palm-thatch room and ample dance floor, is a lively place often crammed with local families and couples even midweek. You can get free appetizers with your suds (there's a full menu of Yucatecan food as well), or just have a drink, enjoy the stage show, or dance. **El Nuevo Tucho** (⊠ Calle 60 No. 482, between Calles 55 and 57, Centro ☎ 999/924–12323) has live cabaret-style entertainment beginning at 4 PM, with no drink minimum and no cover. There's music for dancing in this cavernous—sometimes full, sometimes empty—venue.

Pancho's (⊠ Calle 59 No. 509, between Calles 60 and 62, Centro ☎999/923–0942), open daily 6 PM–2:30 AM, has a lively bar and a restaurant. It also has a small dance floor that attracts locals and foreigners for a mix of live salsa and western music.

Listen to sexy and romantic traditional ballads in a dark, smoky, small nightclub at **La Trova** (⊠ Calles 60 and 57, Centro ☎ 999/923–9500), where trios warm up after 9 PM. It's closed Sunday.

DANCE VENUES   **Azul Picante** (⌧ Calle 60 No. 484 altos, between Calles 55 and 57, Centro ☎ 999/924–2323) offers live tropical tunes nightly, and specializes in salsa. **Mambo Café** (⌧ Calle 21 between Calles 50 and 52, Plaza las Américas, Fracc. Miguel Hidalgo ☎ 999/987–7533) is the best place in town for dancing to DJ-spun salsa, merengue, cumbia, and other Latin beats. It's open from 9 PM Wednesday through Saturday. **Tequila Rock** (⌧ Prolongación Montejo at Av. Campestre, Centro ☎ 999/944–1828) is a disco that plays pop mixed with salsa and other dance music Tuesday through Saturday.

The Arts

FILM   **Cine Colón** (⌧ Av. Reforma 363A, Colón ☎ 999/925–4500) shows English action films with Spanish subtitles. Box-office hits are shown at **Cine Fantasio** (⌧ Calle 59 No. 492, at Calle 60, Centro ☎ 999/923–5431 or 999/925–4500), which has just one screen, but is the city's nicest theater. It was fully remodeled in 2002 after Hurricane Isidore. **Cine Hollywood** (⌧ Calle 50 Diagonal 460, Fracc. Gonzalo Guerrero ☎ 999/920–1089) is located within the popular Gran Plaza mall. International art films are shown most days at noon, 5, and 8 PM at **Teatro de Mérida** (⌧ Calle 60 between Calles 59 and 61, Centro ☎ 999/924–7687 or 999/924–9990).

FOLKLORIC   Paseo Montejo hotels such as the Fiesta Americana, Hyatt Regency, and
SHOWS   Holiday Inn stage dinner shows with folkloric dances; check with
★   concierges for schedules. The **Ballet Folklórico de Yucatán** (⌧ Calles 57 and 60, Centro ☎ 999/924–7260) presents a combination of music, dance, and theater every Friday at 9 PM at the university; tickets are $3. (Performances are every other Friday in the off-season, and there are no shows from August 1 to September 22 and the last two weeks of December.)

☾   On Saturday in the town of Ticopó, 21 km (13 mi) from Mérida off
Carretera 180, the **Teatro Indígena** (☎ 999/924–4465 information, 999/924–4465 tickets) is an extravaganza of local culture. Hundreds of men, women, and children from the town participate in the reenactment of daily rituals such as tortilla making and embroidery, and special events like funerals and religious processions. It's held Saturday at 4 PM (at 5 PM in the summer season, when the daylight lasts longer). Tickets ($12) can be purchased on-site or at any Omega photo store.

Sports & the Outdoors

Baseball

Baseball is played with enthusiasm between February and July at the **Centro Deportivo Kukulcán** (⌧ Calle 14 No. 17, Col. Granjas, across the street from the Pemex gas station and next to the Santa Clara brewery ☎ 999/940–0676). It's most common to buy your ticket at the on-site ticket booth the day of the game.

Bullfights

Bullfights are held sporadically late November–February and around holidays at the **Plaza de Toros** (⌧ Av. Reforma near Calle 25, Col. García Ginerés ☎ 999/925–7996). Seats in the shade go for between $15 and $30, depending on the fame of the bullfighter. You can buy tickets at the bullring or in advance at OXXO convenience stores. Check with the tourism office for the current schedule, or look for posters around town.

Golf

The 18-hole championship golf course at **Club de Golf La Ceiba** (✉ Carretera Mérida–Progreso, Km 14.5 ☎ 999/922–0053) is open to the public. It is about 16 km (10 mi) north of Mérida on the road to Progreso; greens fees are about $60, carts are an additional $25, and clubs can be rented. The pro shop is closed Monday.

Tennis

There are two cement public courts at **Estadio Salvador Alvarado** (✉ Calle 11 between Calles 23 and 60, Paseo Montejo ☎ 999/925–4856). Cost is $2 per hour during the day and $2.50 at night, when the courts are lighted. At the **Fiesta Americana Mérida** (✉ Av. Colón 451, Paseo Montejo ☎ 999/920–2194), guests have access to two lighted outdoor courts. The one cement tennis court at **Holiday Inn** (✉ Av. Colón 498, at Calle 60, Colón ☎ 999/942–8800) is lighted at night. The **Hyatt Regency Mérida** (✉ Calle 60 No. 344, Colón ☎ 999/942–0202) has two lighted cement outdoor courts.

Shopping

Malls

Mérida has several shopping malls, but the largest and nicest, **Gran Plaza** (✉ Calle 50 Diagonal 460, Fracc. Gonzalo Guerrero ☎ 999/944–7657), has more than 90 shops. It's just outside town, on the highway to Progreso (called Carretera a Progreso beyond the Mérida city limits). **Plaza Américas** (✉ Calle 21 No. 331, Col. Miguel Hidalgo ☎ No phone) is a pleasant mall where you'll find the Cineopolis movie theater complex. Tiny **Pasaje Picheta** is conveniently located right on the north side of the town square. It has a bus ticket information booth and an upstairs art gallery, as well as souvenir shops and a food court.

Markets

The **Mercado Municipal** (✉ Calles 56 and 67, Centro) has crafts, food, flowers, and live birds, among many other items. Guides often approach tourists near this market. They expect a tip and won't necessarily bring you to the best deals. You're better off visiting some specialty stores first to learn about the quality and types of hammocks, hats, and other crafts; then you'll have an idea of what you're buying—and what it's worth—if you want to bargain in the market.

Sunday brings an array of wares into Mérida; starting at 9 AM, the Handicrafts Bazaar, or **Bazar de Artesanías** (✉ At the main square, Centro), sells lots of huipiles and women's dresses as well as hats and costume jewelry. As its name implies, popular art, or handicrafts, are sold at the **Bazar de Artes Populares** (✉ Parque Santa Lucía, corner of Calles 60 and 55, Centro) beginning at 9 AM on Sunday, sometimes with work by local artists.

CloseUp

MÉRIDA'S MARKETS

MÉRIDA IS THE BEST PLACE on the Yucatán to shop, and making a round of the bustling local markets is worthwhile for local color even if you don't buy a thing. Start by picking up some sun protection for your head at El Becaleño, which produces Yucatán's fine Panama-style hats, often referred to as jipis. West of El Becaleño is the huge Mercado Municipal Lucas de Galvez, where you can find jewelry typical of the area. There isn't as much filigree being made as there once was, but the designs here are interesting and the quality is mostly good (usually 10-karat gold or gold-dipped; you have to hunt for 14-karat gold).

On the second floor of the municipal market are hammocks, guayaberas, and huipiles, cotton dresses, and blouses—some eyelet, others richly embroidered or decorated with silk ribbons. On the first floor are songbirds in cane cages,

mountains of mysterious fruits and vegetables, plastic water buckets, and dippers made of hollow gourds (made the same as they have been for a thousand years). Dozens of stalls sell the fabulous leather huaraches, some with tire-tread bottoms. They are sturdy and, once you break them in (some suggest soaking the sandals in water and allowing them to dry on your feet), quite comfortable.

Calle 65 between Calles 56 and 54 is piñata heaven: you'll find every imaginable shape and color, as well as the candy that goes inside them. Even if you're not shopping for the papier-mâché and color-paper party favorites, they make for great photos, although the street is always crowded.

HANDICRAFTS If you're interested in handicrafts, **Bazar García Rejón** (⊠ Calles 65 and 62, Centro) has rows of indoor stalls that sell items like leather goods, palm hats, and handmade guitars. Visit the government-run **Casa de las Artesanías** (⊠ Calle 63 No. 503A, between Calles 64 and 66, Centro ☎ 999/928–6676) for folk art from throughout Yucatán. There's a showcase of hard-to-find traditional filigree jewelry in silver, gold, and gold-dipped versions. **Casa de los Artesanos** (⊠ Calle 62 No. 492, between Calles 59 and 61, Centro ☎ 999/923–4523), just half a block from the main plaza, also sells Yucatecan handicrafts.

Miniaturas (⊠ Calle 59 No. 507A, Centro ☎ 999/928–6503) sells a delightful and diverse assortment of different crafts, but specializes in miniatures.

You can get hammocks made to order—choose from standard nylon and cotton, super-soft processed sisal, Brazilian-style (six stringed), or crocheted—at **El Xiric** (⊠ Calle 57-A No. 15, Pasaje Congreso, Centro ☎ 999/924–9906). You can also get Xtabentún liqueur, Panama hats, jewelry, black pottery, and woven goods from Oaxaca, as well as T-shirts and more commercial souvenirs.

Specialty Stores

BOOKS In addition to having a branch at all major shopping centers, **Librería**
★ **Dante** (⊠ Calle 62 No. 502, at Calle 61, Parque Principal Centro ☎ 999/
928-2611 ⊠ Calle 17 No. 138B, at Prolongación Paseo Montejo, Col.
Itzimná ☎ 999/927-7676) has several others downtown and on Paseo
Montejo. The stores carry lots of art and travel books, with at least a
small selection of English-language books. The Paseo Montejo store dou-
bles as a popular creperie and coffeehouse (*see* Where to Eat).

CLOTHING Pick up a Panama hat at **El Becaleño** (⊠ Calle 65 No. 483, between Calles
56 and 58, Centro ☎ 999/985-0581), and be sure to try your bargaining
skills.

You might not wear a guayabera to a business meeting as some men in
Mexico do, but the shirts are cool, comfortable, and attractive; for a
good selection, try **Camisería Canul** (⊠ Calle 62 No. 484, between Calles
57 and 59, Centro ☎ 999/923-0158).

Guayaberas Jack (⊠ Calle 59 No. 507A, between Calles 60 and 62, Centro ☎ 999/928-6002) has an excellent selection of guayaberas and typical women's cotton *filipinas* (house dresses) and blouses. They can be
made to order, but the shop closes daily at 2:30 PM. **Mexicanísimo**
(⊠ Calle 60 No. 496, at Parque Hidalgo, Centro ☎ 999/923-8132) sells
expensive designer cotton and linen clothing inspired by regional dress.

GALLERIES The **Casa de Cera** (⊠ Calle 74A No. 430E, between Calles 41 and 43,
Centro ☎ 999/920-0219) sells signed series of collectible indigenous
figures made of beeswax. The **Galería Casa Colón** (⊠ Av. Colón 507, Col.
García Ginerés ☎ 999/925-7952) highlights modern-day Mexican
painters in the setting of a colonial home.

LOCAL A great place to purchase hammocks is **El Aguacate** (⊠ Calle 58 No. 604,
SPECIALTIES at Calle 73, Centro ☎ 999/928-6429), a family-run outfit with many
sizes and designs. **El Hamaquero** (⊠ Calle 58 No. 572, between Calles
69 and 71, Centro ☎ 999/923-2117) has knowledgeable personnel
who let you try out the hammocks before you buy. **Tejidos y Cordeles
Nacionales** (⊠ Calle 56 No. 516B, between Calles 65 and 63, Centro
☎ 999/928-5561), the oldest hammock store in Mérida, is a family-
run, no-frills shop. **Tequilería Ajua** (⊠ Calle 56 No. 516B, at Calle 62,
Centro ☎ 999/924-1453) sells tequila, brandy, and mezcal as well as
Xtabentún.

JEWELRY **La Canasta** (⊠ Calle 60 No. 500, at Calle 61, Centro ☎ 999/928-
1978) has a good selection of filigree jewelry, both sterling silver and
gold-dipped. It also has lots of cotton blouses for women, and local
liqueurs. Shop for semiprecious stones and other gems, including diamonds, set in silver and gold at **Joyería Colonial** (⊠ Calle 60 between
Calle 61 and 63, Centro ☎ 999/923-5838). **Marcelino & Wiltrud**
(⊠ Calle 58 No. 487, at Calle 57, Centro ☎ 999/926-2008) sells carvings and stunning batiks of Maya gods and goddesses in addition to
one-of-a-kind gold jewelry. **Tane** (⊠ Hyatt Regency, Calle 60 No. 344,
at Av. Colón, Paseo Montejo ☎ 999/942-0202) is an outlet for

exquisite (and expensive) silver earrings, necklaces, and bracelets, some incorporating ancient Maya designs.

TO CHICHÉN ITZÁ & BEYOND

Although you can get to Chichén Itzá (120 km [74 mi] east of Mérida) along the shorter Carretera 180, it's far more scenic to follow Carretera 80 to Teya, then head south to Citilcúm, east past Izamal to Dzitás, and south again to Pisté. These roads have no signs but are the only paved roads going in these directions. Among the several villages you pass along Carretera 80 is Tixkokob, a Maya community famous for its hammock weavers.

Izamal

❿ *68 km (42 mi) southeast of Mérida.*

One of the best examples of a Spanish colonial town in the Yucatán, Izamal is nicknamed Ciudad Amarillo (yellow city) because its most important buildings are painted earth-tone yellow. It's also sometimes called "the city of three cultures," because of its combined pre-Hispanic, colonial, and contemporary influences. Calesas (horse-drawn carriages) surround the town's large main square, which fronts a lovely cathedral. The best ways to get a feel for this charming town are by hiring a calesa (drivers charge about $4.50 for a 35-minute tour, $6 per hour for longer) or simply lounging in the square and watching the passersby.

The drive to Izamal from Mérida takes less than an hour; take the Tixkokob road and follow the signs.

Fodor'sChoice ★ Facing the main plaza, the enormous 16th-century **Ex-Convento y Iglesia de San Antonio de Padua** (former monastery and church of St. Anthony of Padua) is perched on—and built from—the remains of a Maya pyramid devoted to Itzamná, god of the heavens. The monastery's ocher-color church, where Pope John Paul II led prayers in 1993, has a gigantic atrium (supposedly second in size only to the Vatican's) facing a colonnaded facade and rows of 75 white-trimmed arches. The Virgin of the Immaculate Conception, to whom the church is dedicated, is the patron saint of the Yucatán. A statue of Nuestra Señora de Izamal, or Our Lady of Izamal, was brought here from Guatemala in 1562 by Bishop Diego de Landa. Miracles are ascribed to her, and a yearly pilgrimage takes place in her honor. Frescoes of saints at the front of the church, which had once been plastered over, were rediscovered and refurbished in 1996.

Diagonally across from the massive cathedral, the small municipal market is worth a wander. It's a lot less frenetic than markets at major cities like Mérida. On the other side of the square, **Hecho a Mano** (✉ Calle 31 No. 308, Centro ☎ 988/954–0344), run by an American couple, sells a nice collection of framed photographs and handicrafts.

Kinich Kakmó pyramid is all that remains of the royal Maya city that flourished here between AD 250–600). Dedicated to the Maya god Zamná, the enormous structure is the largest of its kind in the state, covering about 10 acres. More remarkable for its size than for any remaining decoration, it's nonetheless an impressive monument, and you can scale it from stairs on the south face.

Where to Stay & Eat

¢ ✕ **Los Mestizos.** Most of the decor in this humble restaurant is orange—including the walls and ceiling fans. The short menu includes regional fare such as *salbutes* and *panuchos*—both typical appetizers of fried cornmeal, the latter stuffed with beans—as well as chicken and turkey dishes. There's a bit of a view of the church beyond the marketplace from the outdoor terrace. ⊠ *Calle 33 s/n, behind the market Centro* ☎ No phone ⊟ No credit cards.

¢ ▦ **Green River Inn.** Individual block units are sprinkled around this landscaped property. Rooms have a dollhouse look and are decorated with lots of pinks, blues, and purples. Small TVs are mounted on the walls. Each ground-floor room has a whimsical-looking but clean bath, and a small terrace with a metal folding table and chairs. ⊠ *Calle 39 No. 342 between Calles 38 and 40, 97540* ☎ *988/954–0453* ⊟ *988/ 954–0337* ⤶ *18 rooms* ⌂ *Fans, cable TV, minibars, pool, bar, free parking; no room phones* ⊟ No credit cards.

Pisté

⑱ *116 km (72 mi) southeast of Mérida.*

The town of Pisté serves as a base camp for travelers to Chichén Itzá. Hotels, campgrounds, restaurants, and handicrafts shops tend to be less expensive here than those at the ruins; they are strewn along the main street through town and impossible to miss.

Across from the Dolores Alba hotel, in town is the **Parque Ik Kil** (place of the winds). A $4 entrance fee is required if you want to swim in the lovely cenote here, open daily between 8 AM and 6 PM. If you're just going to eat in the adjacent restaurant, a sprawling place serving an international buffet ($15) to many bus tour groups, you don't need to pay the entrance fee. The site also has a swimming pool, bungalows inspired by Maya dwellings, and shops where artisans demonstrate their crafts. ⊠ *Carretera Mérida–Puerto Juárez, Km 112* ☎ *985/858–1525.*

Where to Stay

★ ¢ ▦ **Dolores Alba.** The best low-budget choice near the ruins is this family-run hotel, a longtime favorite of international travelers. Rooms have hard beds and chunky, colonial-style furniture. Two palapas with hammocks hang by one of the pools, and breakfast, lunch, and dinner are served family-style in the restaurant. A second pool with a rocky bottom simulates a natural reef. Free transportation to Chichén Itzá is provided, and there's a covered parking lot. Full board is available upon request. ⊠ *Carretera 180, Km 122, 3 km (2 mi) south of Chichén Itzá, 99751* ☎ *985/858–1555* ⊟ *999/928–3163* ⊕ *www.doloresalba.com* ⤶ *40 rooms* ⌂ *Restaurant, 2 pools, Internet, free parking; no room phones, no room TVs* ⊟ No credit cards.

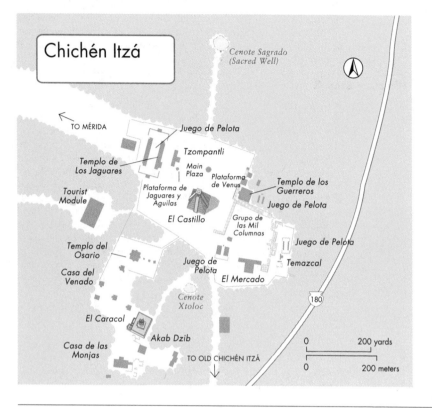

Chichén Itzá

Cenote Sagrado
(Sacred Well)

TO MÉRIDA

Juego de Pelota

Tzompantli

Templo de
Los Jaguares

Main
Plaza

Plataforma
de Venus

Templo de los
Guerreros

Tourist
Module

Plataforma de
Jaguares y
Aguilas

Juego de Pelota

El Castillo

Grupo de
las Mil
Columnas

Juego de Pelota

Templo del
Osario

Juego de
Pelota

Temazcal

Casa del
Venado

El Mercado

Cenote
Xtoloc

180

El Caracol

Akab Dzib

Casa de las
Monjas

TO OLD CHICHÉN ITZÁ

0   200 yards

0   200 meters

Chichén Itzá

120 km (74 mi) east of Mérida, 1 km (½ mi) east of Pisté.

Fodor'sChoice ★

One of the four most magnificent Maya ruins—along with Palenque in Chiapas in Mexico, Tikal in Guatemala, and Copán in Honduras—Chichén Itzá was the most important city in Yucatán from the 10th through the 12th century. Its architectural mélange shows the influence of several different Maya groups. As epigraphers have been able to translate many of the Chichén inscriptions, the site's history has become clearer to archaeologists.

At one time it was believed that Chichén Itzá was dominated by the Toltecs of central Mexico; now historians believe that the city was indeed influenced by trade with the north, although not by conquest. Chichén *was* altered by successive waves of inhabitants, and archaeologists are able to date the arrival of these waves by the changes in the architecture and information contained in inscriptions. However, the long gaps of time when the buildings seem to have been uninhabited remain a mystery.

The site is believed to have been first settled in AD 432, abandoned for an unknown period of time, then rediscovered in 868 by the Maya-speaking Itzás, who migrated north from the region of the Petén rain forest around Tikal, in what is now northern Guatemala. The latest data point to the city's having been refounded by not only the Itzás but also by two other groups—one from the Valley of Mexico (near present-day Mexico City) and another from Ek Balam. The trio formed a ruling triumvirate. The Itzás may have also abandoned the site, but they were the dominant group until 1224, when the city appears to have been abandoned for all time.

Chichén Itzá means "the mouth of the well of the Itzás." The enormity, grace, and functionality of this site are unforgettable. It encompasses approximately 6 square km (2½ square mi), though fewer than a quarter of the site's several hundred structures and buildings have been fully explored. It's divided into two parts, called Chichén Viejo (old) and Chichén Nuevo (new), although architectural motifs from the Classic period are found in both sections. A more convenient distinction is topographical, since there are two major complexes of buildings separated by a dirt path.

The martial, imperial architecture of the Itzás and the more cerebral architecture and astronomical expertise of the earlier Maya are married in the 98-foot-tall pyramid called **El Castillo**—The Castle—which dominates the site and rises above all the other buildings. Atop this structure is a temple dedicated to Kukulcán (also known as Quetzalcóatl), the legendary Toltec priest-king from Tula in the Valley of Mexico who was held to be an incarnation of the mystical plumed serpent. Open-jawed serpent statues adorn the balustrades of each stairway, and serpents reappear at the top of the temple as sculptured columns. At the spring and fall equinoxes, the afternoon light strikes one of these balustrades in such a way as to form a shadow representation of Kukulcán undulating out of his temple and down the pyramid to bless the fertile earth. (Thousands of people travel to Chichén Itzá to see this phenomenon, so if you're planning to witness it, you'll need to make hotel reservations many months in advance.) At the base of the temple on the northwest side, you can enter a passageway and climb a humid claustrophobic staircase to see two particularly ancient statues within—one of a jaguar and the other of a minor god, Chacmool. Each evening there's a sound-and-light show that highlights the architectural details in El Castillo and other buildings, though its accompanying narration is more dramatic than fact filled.

West of the temple is Chichén Itzá's largest **juego de pelota,** one of seven ball courts on the site. Its two parallel walls are each 272 feet long, with two stone rings on each side, and 99 feet apart. The game played here was something like soccer (no hands were used), but it had a religious and socio-political significance. Bas-relief carvings at the court depict a player being decapitated, the blood spurting from his neck fertilizing the earth. Other bas-reliefs show two teams of opposing players pitted against each other during the ball game.

Between the ball court and El Castillo stands the **Anexo del Templo de los Jaguares,** where bas-relief carvings represent several deities. On the bottom left column, Tlaloc's tears represent rain. In the central opening of the structure is a statue of Chacmool. West of the Jaguars' Temple is a **tzompantli,** a stone platform carved with rows of human skulls. These carvings are thought to depict the heads of enemies impaled on stakes.

One kilometer (½ mi) north of El Castillo at the end of a *sacbé* (white road), the **Cenote Sagrado** was used for human sacrifices. Some 37 skeletons have been recovered from the muddy bottom of the 65-yard-wide pool. Many archaeologists think the ritual sacrifices were carried out by local chiefs hundreds of years after Chichén Itzá was abandoned. Thousands of artifacts made of gold, jade, and other precious materials, most of them not of local provenance, have also been recovered from the sinkhole's brackish depths.

East of El Castillo is the **Grupo de las Mil Columnas,** or Group of the Thousand Columns. Part of this group, the **Templo de los Guerreros**—a masterful example of the Itzá influence at Chichén Itzá—was used as a meeting place for the high lords of the council that ruled the city. The temple-top sculpture of the reclining Chacmool—its head turned to the side, the offertory dish carved into its middle—is probably the most photographed symbol of the Maya. Murals of everyday village life and scenes of war are here, although climbing up to see them is no longer permitted.

To get to the less-visited cluster of structures at Chichén Nuevo, take the main path south from the Jaguars' Temple past El Castillo and turn right onto a small path opposite the ball court. Archaeologists have been restoring several buildings in this area, including the **Templo del Osario,** where several tombs with skeletons and offerings were found, and the northern part of the site, which was used for military training and barracks. The most impressive structure within this area is the astronomical observatory called **El Caracol.** The name, meaning the Snail, refers to the spiral staircase at the building's core. Built in several stages, El Caracol is one of the few round buildings constructed by the Maya. Judging by the eight tiny windows oriented toward the compass points, and the structure's alignment with the planet Venus, it was used for observing the heavens. Since astronomy was the province of priests and used to determine rituals and predict the future, the building undoubtedly served a religious function.

After leaving El Caracol, continue south several hundred yards to the **Grupo de las Monjas** (The Nunnery). Traditional to the Puuc style prevalent in southern Yucatán, the facades of this structure and of the adjacent annex are plain below their friezes, but richly decorated with masks above.

At Chichén Viejo, the architecture shows less outside influence. A combination of Puuc and Chenes Maya styles dominates, with playful latticework, masks, and gargoylelike serpents on the cornices. One highlight here is the Grupo de las Fechas, or Date Group, so named because of its complete series of hieroglyphic dates. If you ask, guides will lead you down the path by an old narrow-gauge railroad track to even more ruins, which are barely unearthed.

A fairly good restaurant and a great ice cream stand are in the entrance building, as are a gift shop and an ATM machine. A small museum includes information on the migration patterns of the ancient Maya and some small sculptures recovered from the site. The site draws some 3,000 visitors a day; most of the tour groups arrive in the morning. ☞ *$9 (includes museum and sound-and-light show, $4 on Sun.); parking $2; use of video camera $3* ⊙ *Daily 8–5; sound-and-light show Apr.–Oct., daily just after dusk.*

Where to Stay

$$–$$$ 🏨 **Hacienda Chichén.** A converted 16th-century hacienda with its own
FodorsChoice entrance to the ruins, this hotel once served as the headquarters for the
★ Carnegie expedition to Chichén Itzá. Rustic-chic cottages are simply but beautifully furnished in colonial Yucatecan style, with handwoven bedspreads and dehumidifiers; all of the ground-floor rooms have verandas, but only master suites have hammocks. There's a satellite TV in the library. An enormous old pool and a chapel now used for weddings grace the gardens. Meals are served on the patio overlooking the grounds, or in the air-conditioned restaurant. ⊠ *Carretera 180, Km 120* ☎ *985/ 851–0045, 999/924–2150 reservations, 800/624–8451* 🖨 *999/924– 5011* ⊕ *www.haciendachichen.com.mx* ➫ *24 rooms, 4 suites* ⚭ *Restaurant, some minibars, pool, bar, laundry service, free parking; no room phones, no room TVs* ☐ *AE, DC, MC, V.*

★ **$$–$$$** 🏨 **Mayaland.** This charming property is in a large garden, and close enough to the ruins to have its own entrance; you can actually see part of Chichén Viejo from here. Colonial-style guest rooms have decorative tiles; ask for one with a balcony, which doesn't cost extra. Bungalows have thatched roofs as well as wide verandas with hammocks. The simple Maya-inspired "huts" near the front of the property, built in the 1930s, are the cheapest option, but are for groups only. Snacks served poolside are an alternative to the rather expensive meals in the restaurants. ⊠ *Carretera 180, Km 120* ☎ *999/924–2099 or 800/235–4079* 🖨 *999/ 924–6290* 🖨 *985/851–0129* ⊕ *www.mayaland.com* ➫ *60 bungalows, 30 rooms, 10 suites* ⚭ *4 restaurants, room service, fans, minibars, cable TV, tennis court, 3 pools, volleyball, 2 bars, shop, laundry service, free parking* ☐ *AE, D, DC, MC, V.*

Grutas de Balancanchén

🔺 ⏱ ⑳ *6 km (4 mi) east of Chichén Itzá.*

The Balancanchén caves, whose Maya name translates as "throne of the jaguar," contain a shrine that remained virtually undisturbed from the time of the conquest until its discovery in 1959. Inside are some of the artifacts—mostly vases, jars, and incense burners—once used in sacred rituals. Although there are seven chambers, only three are open. You walk past tiers of stalactites and stalagmites; one group (according to the guides) forms the image of a sacred ceiba tree. You can also visit the underground cenote, filled with blind fish, where Maya priests worshipped at an altar to the gods of rain and water. In order to explore the shrine you must take one of the guided tours, which depart almost hourly. You need to be in fairly good shape for the tour and wear comfortable shoes; there's a lot of walking involved. Also at the site is a sound-and-light show that fancifully recounts Maya history. A small museum at the entrance is very informative. The caves are just 6 km (4 mi) from Chichén Itzá; you can catch a bus or taxi or arrange a tour at the Mayaland hotel. ⌨ *$4.50 (including tour), free Sun.; sound-and-light show $5; parking $2 extra* ☉ *Daily 9–5; tours leave daily at 11, 1, and 3 (English); 9, noon, 2, and 4 (Spanish); and 10 (French).*

Valladolid

➋ *44½ km (28 mi) east of Chichén Itzá.*

The second-largest city in the state of Yucatán, Valladolid (vay-ah-do-*lid*) is a picturesque provincial town, much smaller than Mérida. It has been enjoying growing popularity among travelers en route to or from Chichén Itzá or Río Lagartos who want a change from the more touristy, congested places. Montejo founded Valladolid in 1543 on the site of the Maya town of Sisal. The city suffered during the War of the Castes—when the Maya in revolt killed nearly all Spanish residents—and again during the Mexican Revolution.

Today, Valladolid is relatively placid. The center is mostly colonial, although it has many 19th-century structures. On the west side of the main square is a large church, **Iglesia de San Gervacio,** which was pillaged during the War of the Castes. Three longish blocks away is the ★ 16th-century, terra-cotta-color **Ex-Convento y Iglesia San Bernadino,** a Franciscan church and former monastery. If the priest is around, ask him to show you the 16th-century frescoes, protected behind curtains near the altarpiece. The lack of proportion in the human figures shows the initial clumsiness of indigenous artisans in reproducing the Christian saints.

☼ A beautiful sinkhole at the edge of town, large, round **Cenote Zací** (✉ Calles 36 and 37 ☎ 985/856–2107) is sometimes crowded with tourists and local boys clowning it up; if you're not up for a dip, visit the adjacent handicraft shop or the well-loved thatch-roofed restaurant. Leaves from the tall old trees surrounding the sinkhole float on the surface, but the water itself is quite clean. Five kilometers (3 mi) west of the main square and on the old highway to Chichén Itzá, you can ★ ☼ swim with the catfish in lovely mysterious **Cenote X-Keken** (popularly called Cenote Dzitnup), which is in a cave lit by a small natural skylight; admission is $3.

Valladolid is renowned for its **longaniza en escabeche**—a sausage dish, served in many of the restaurants facing the central square. There's a shop with Internet access diagonally across from the restaurants. In the shops and market you can find good buys on sandals, baskets, and Xtabentún liqueur.

SACRED CENOTES

O THE ANCIENT (and tradition-bound modern) Maya, holes in the ground—be they sinkholes (cenotes) or caves—are considered conduits to the world of the spirits. A source of water in a land of no surface rivers, sinkholes are of special importance. The domain of Chaac, god of rain and water, cenotes like Balancanchén, near Chichén Itzá, were used as prayer sites and shrines. Sacred objects and sacrificial victims were thrown in the sacred cenote at Chichén Itzá, and in others near large ceremonial centers in ancient times.

There are at least 2,800 known cenotes in the Yucatán. Rainwater sinks through the peninsula's thin soil and porous limestone to create underground rivers, while leaving the dry surface river-free.

Some pondlike sinkholes are found near ground level; most require a bit more effort to access, however. Near downtown

Valladolid, Cenote Zací is named for the Maya town conquered by the Spanish. It's a relatively simple saunter down a series of cement steps to reach the cool green water.

Lesser-known sinkholes are yours to discover, especially in the area labeled "zona de cenotes." To explore this area southeast of Mérida, you can hire a guide through the tourism office. Another option is to head directly for the ex-hacienda of Chunkanan, outside the village of the same name, about 30 minutes southeast of Mérida. There, former henequen workers will hitch their horses to tiny open railway carts to take you along the unused train tracks. The reward for this bumpy, sometimes dusty ride is a swim in several incredible cenotes.

Almost every local has a "secret" cenote; ask around, and perhaps you'll find a favorite of your own.

Where to Stay & Eat

$ ✕☰ **Ecotel Quinta Real.** This salmon-colored hotel is a mix of colonial and modern Mexico. Each whitewashed room is accented with one brightly colored wall; wrought-iron ceiling and wall fixtures; and substantial, hand-carved furniture. Junior suites have balconies and beautifully carved headboards but are not actually as nice as the standard rooms with terraces overlooking the orchard. There are a game room, arboretum, and duck pond, and the on-site restaurant ($–$$) has a substantial menu ranging from nachos and pizza to filet mignon and lobster. ⊠ Calle 40 No. 160A, at Calle 27, 97780 ☎☎985/856–6372 ☎985/ 856–3479 ⊕ www.ecotelquintareal.com.mx ⇆ 108 rooms, 4 suites ♨ Restaurant, room service, some minibars, cable TV, tennis court, pool, billiards, Ping-Pong, bar, car rental, laundry services, meeting room, free parking ⊟ AE, D, MC, V.

¢ ✕☰ **El Mesón del Marqués.** On the north side of the main square, this well-preserved, very old hacienda house was built around a lovely, colonnaded, open patio. The rooms, however, are less impressive; oddly, the smaller, older rooms touted as "colonial" seem to have more modern furnishings than those in the newer building. The charming restaurant ($–$$), in a courtyard with an old stone fountain and surrounded by porticoes, serves Yucatecan specialties such as pollo pibíl and several local sausage dishes. ⊠ *Calle 39 No. 203, 97780* ☎ *985/856–2073 or 985/856–3042* 🖷 *985/856–2280* ⊕ *www.mesondelmarques. com* ⟿ *73 rooms* ⚲ *Restaurant, room service, cable TV, pool, bar, shop, laundry services, free parking* ⊟ *AE.*

¢ ▦ **María de la Luz.** A worn but still somehow engaging budget hotel, the Mary of Light is conveniently situated on the main plaza. Motel style, it surrounds a shallow swimming pool surrounded by banana trees and tables for drinking or dining. The plain rooms are nothing to write home about, but consistently attract a diverse and bohemian clientele. The restaurant, where guests tend to gather, serves predictable but tasty Mexican dishes; pollo pibíl is a house specialty. You may be tempted to upgrade to the hotel's single suite—but it has the same uneventful decor, with a whirlpool tub and more beds of various sizes jammed in. ⊠ *Calle 42 No. 193C, 97780* ☎ *985/856–2071 or 985/856–1181* ⊕ *www. mariadelaluz.com.mx* ⟿ *68 rooms, 1 suite* ⚲ *Restaurant, pool, bar, free parking* ⊟ *MC, V.*

Ek Balam

🜚 ★ ㉒ *30 km (18 mi) north of Valladolid, off Carretera 295.*

The site of Ek Balam ("black jaguar"), a powerful city that was driven by an agricultural economy, opened to the public in 2000. The 45 structures in the main excavation field are surrounded by two concentric walls—a rare configuration in Maya sites—which are thought to have provided defense for the ruling elite. Prominent among them is the stunning, Chenes-style **Templo de los Frisas,** which is flanked by two smaller temples. A giant monster mask crowns the summit, which is embedded with marvelous glyphs and friezes. Along the friezes are stunning high-relief figures; those commonly referred to as angels because of their wings may have represented warriors in ceremonial dress.

The structure was a mausoleum for ruler Ukit Kan Lek Tok. Priceless funerary objects have been uncovered within, including pearls, thousands of perforated seashells, gold, jade, mother-of-pearl pendants, and small bone masks with moveable jaws.

Archaeologists have learned that the existing structure is superimposed upon earlier ones. At the bases at either end, the leader's name is inscribed on the forked tongue of a carved serpent. Ek Balam was a contemporary of Uxmal and Cobá. It may have been a satellite city to Chichén Itzá, which rose to power as Ek Balam waned. In the second phase of development, the Ek Balam leader Hun-Pik-Tok is thought to have been part of a ruling triumvirate with Chichén Itzá.

Along with the Impressive Temple of the Friezes, Ek Balam also has a ball court, stelae, and a variety of buildings with scenes, figures, and glyphs in carved stone or molded stucco. Although new-age groups sometimes converge on the site for prayers and seminars, it's usually quite sparsely visited, adding to the mystery and allure. 🝔 *$2* ☽ *Daily 8–5.*

Where to Stay

¢ 🏨 **Genesis Retreat.** Almost within shouting distance of the Ek Balam archaeological site, this singles-friendly retreat is new and inviting, albeit rustic. For no extra cost you can "adopt a family" for cultural exchange, language learning, or hammock- or tortilla-making classes. Tours to nearby ruins and sinkholes are reasonably priced, and a good way to meet other travelers. Modeled on typical dwellings of the region, cabins are simple stucco and wood structures with thatched roofs and rocking chairs and hammocks on their front porches. The on-site Chaya's restaurant emphasizes healthy food, primarily vegetarian options. ✉ *Domicilio Conocido* 🏬 *Calle 54 No. 197H, between Calles 37 and 39, Col. Bacalar, 97780 Valladolid* ☎ *985/852–7980* ⊕ *www.genesisretreat.com* ➱ *6 cabins, 3 tent-cabins* ⚭ *Restaurant, pool, airport shuttle, travel services; no a/c, no room phones, no room TVs* ▭ *No credit cards.*

UXMAL & THE RUTA PUUC

Passing through the large Maya town of Umán on Mérida's southern outskirts, you enter one of the Yucatán's least populated areas. The highway to Uxmal (ush-*mal*) and Kabah is relatively free of traffic and runs through uncultivated woodlands. The forest seems to become more dense beyond Uxmal, which was connected to a number of smaller ceremonial centers in ancient times by sacbéob (white roads). Several of these satellite sites—including Kabah, with its 250 masks; Sayil, with its majestic, three-story palace; and Labná, with its iconic, vaulted *puerta* (gateway)—are open to the public along a side road known as the Ruta Puuc, which winds its way eastward and eventually joins busy Carretera 184.

Along this route you'll also find the Grutas de Loltún, the Yucatán's largest known cave system, containing wall paintings and stone artifacts from Maya and pre-Maya times. You can make a loop to all these sites, ending in the little town of Ticul, which produces much of the pottery you'll see around the peninsula. There's daily transportation on the ATS bus line (*see* Bus Travel, *below*) to Uxmal, Labná, Xlapak, Sayil, Kabah, and Uxmal. For about $11, you can get transportation to each of these places, with 20–30 minutes to explore the lesser sites and 1 hour and 20 minutes to see Uxmal. A great value and convenience, this unguided tour leaves the second-class bus station daily at 8 AM and returns at 4.

Uxmal

🏛 ㉓ *78 km (48 mi) south of Mérida on Carretera 261.*

FodorśChoice ★ If Chichén Itzá is the most expansive Maya ruin in Yucatán, Uxmal is arguably the most elegant. The architecture here reflects the Late Classical renaissance of the 7th to the 9th century and is contemporary with that of Palenque and Tikal, among other great Maya cities of the southern highlands.

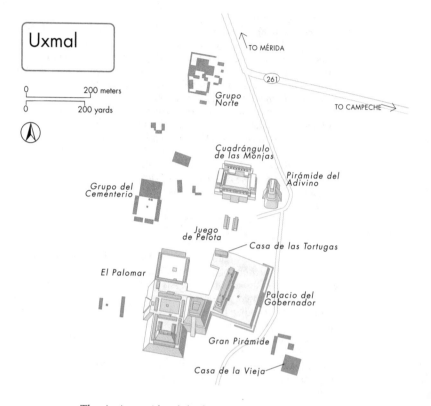

Uxmal

0 _____ 200 meters
0 _____ 200 yards

TO MÉRIDA
261
TO CAMPECHE

Grupo Norte

Cuadrángulo de las Monjas

Pirámide del Adivino

Grupo del Cementerio

Juego de Pelota

Casa de las Tortugas

El Palomar

Palacio del Gobernador

Gran Pirámide

Casa de la Vieja

The site is considered the finest and most extensively excavated example of Puuc architecture, which embraces such details as ornate stone mosaics and friezes on the upper walls, intricate cornices, rows of columns, and soaring vaulted arches. Although most of Uxmal hasn't been restored, three buildings in particular merit attention:

At 125 feet high, the **Pirámide del Adivino** is the tallest and most prominent structure at the site. Unlike most other Maya pyramids, which are stepped and angular, the Temple of the Magician has a softer and more refined round-corner design. This structure was rebuilt five times over hundreds of years, each time on the same foundation, so artifacts found here represent several different kingdoms. The pyramid has a stairway on its western side that leads through a giant open-mouthed mask to two temples at the summit. During restoration work in 2002, the grave of a high-ranking Maya official, a ceramic mask, and a jade necklace were discovered within the pyramid. Continuing excavations have revealed exciting new finds that are still being studied.

West of the pyramid lies the **Cuadrángulo de las Monjas,** considered by some to be the finest part of Uxmal. The name was given to it by the conquistadores because it reminded them of a convent building in Old Spain. According to research, what's called the Nunnery was actually the palace and living quarters of a high lord of Uxmal named Chaan Chak, which means "abundance of rain." You may enter the four buildings; each comprises a series of low, gracefully repetitive chambers that look onto a central patio. Elaborate and symbolic decorations—masks, geometric patterns, coiling snakes, and some phallic figures—blanket the upper facades.

Heading south from the Nunnery, you'll pass a small ball court before reaching the **Palacio del Gobernador,** which archaeologist Victor von Hagen considered the most magnificent building ever erected in the Americas. Interestingly, the palace faces east, while the rest of Uxmal faces west. Archaeologists believe this is because the palace was built to allow observation of the planet Venus. Covering 5 acres and rising over an immense acropolis, it lies at the heart of what may have been Uxmal's administrative center.

Today, you can watch a sound-and-light show at the site that recounts Maya legends. The colored light brings out details of carvings and mosaics that are easy to miss when the sun is shining. The show is performed nightly in Spanish; earphones ($2.50) provide an English translation. ✉ *Site, museum, and sound-and-light show $8.50 ($3.50 for foreigners on Sun.); parking $2; use of video camera $3* ☉ *Daily 8–5; sound-and-light show just after dusk.*

Where to Stay & Eat

$ ✕▦ **Villas Arqueológicas Uxmal.** Rooms in this pretty two-story Club Med

FodorsChoice property are small but functional, with wooden furniture and cozy twin

★ beds that fit nicely into alcoves. Half of the bright, hobbit-hole rooms have garden views. Since rooms are small, guests tend to hang out in the comfy library with giant-screen TV and lots of reading material, or at thatch-shaded tables next to the pool. The indoor restaurant ($$–$$$)—classy or old-Europe fussy, depending on your tastes—serves both regional fare and international dishes, like stuffed squid, chicken in tarragon, or roast chicken with french fries and steamed veggies. ✉ *Carretera 261, Km 76* ☎ *997/974–6020 or 800/258–2633* 🖷 *997/976–2040* ⊕ *www.clubmedvillas.com* ⇨ *40 rooms, 3 suites* ⚴ *Restaurant, in-room safes, tennis court, pool, billiards, bar, library, shop, laundry service, free parking; no room TVs* ▭ *AE, MC, V.*

$$$–$$$$ ▦ **Lodge at Uxmal.** The outwardly rustic, thatch-roofed buildings here have glossy red-tile floors, carved and polished hardwood doors and rocking chairs, and local weavings. The effect is comfortable yet luxuriant. All rooms have bathtubs and screened windows; suites have king-size beds and jet baths. Tennis and volleyball are available at the hotel's sister property, Hacienda Uxmal. ✉ *Carretera Uxmal, Km 78* ☎ *800/235–4079* 🖷 *998/884–4510 in Cancún* ⊕ *www.mayaland.com* ⇨ *40 suites* ⚴ *2 restaurants, fans, some in-room hot tubs, some minibars, cable TV, 2 pools, hot tub, bar, free parking* ▭ *AE, MC, V.*

$$ ▦ **Hacienda Uxmal.** The first hotel built in Uxmal, this pleasant colonial-style building has lovely floor tiles, ceramics, and iron grillwork. The rooms are fronted with wide, furnished verandas; the courtyard has two pools surrounded by gardens. Each room has an ample bathroom with tub, comfortable beds, and coffeemaker. Ask about packages that include free or low-cost car rentals, or comfortable minivans traveling to Mérida, Chichén, or Cancún. ⊠ *Carretera 261, Km 78* ☎ *997/976–2012 or 800/235–4079* 🖨 *997/976–2011, 998/884–4510 in Cancún* ⊕ *www.mayaland.com* ⇨ *80 rooms, 7 suites* ♨ *2 restaurants, room service, some in-room hot tubs, cable TV, 2 pools, billiards, bar, shop, laundry service, free parking* ▤ *AE, MC, V.*

Kabah

🏔 **24** *23 km (14 mi) south of Uxmal on Carretera 261.*

The most important buildings at Kabah, which means "lord of the powerful hand" in Maya, were built between AD 600 and AD 900, during the later part of the Classic era. A ceremonial center of almost Grecian beauty, it was once linked to Uxmal by a sacbé, at the end of which looms a great independent arch—now across the highway from the main ruins. The 151-foot-long **Palacio de Mascarones,** also known as Palace of the Masks, boasts a three-dimensional mosaic of 250 masks of inlaid stones. On the central plaza, you can see ground-level wells called "chultunes," which were used to store precious rainwater. 🎫 *$2.50* ⊙ *Daily 8–5.*

Sayil

🏔 **25** *9 km (5½ mi) south of Kabah on Carretera 31 E.*

Experts believe that Sayil, or "place of the red ants," flourished between AD 800 and AD 1000. It is renowned primarily for its majestic **Gran Palacio.** Built on a hill, the three-story structure is adorned with decorations of animals and other figures, and contains more than 80 rooms. The structure recalls Palenque in its use of multiple planes, columned porticoes, and sober cornices. Also on the grounds is a stela in the shape of a phallus—an obvious symbol of fertility. 🎫 *$2.50* ⊙ *Daily 8–5.*

Labná

🏔 **26** *9 km (5½ mi) south of Sayil on Carretera 31 E.*

The striking monumental structure at Labná (which means "old house" or "abandoned house") is a fanciful corbeled arch (also called the Maya arch, or false arch), with elaborate latticework and a small chamber on each side. One theory says the arch was the entrance to an area where religious ceremonies were staged. The site was used mainly by the military elite and royalty. 🎫 *$3* ⊙ *Daily 8–5.*

Grutas de Loltún

🏔 *19 km (12 mi) northeast of Labná.*

★ 🐚 **27** The Loltún ("stone flower" in Maya) is one of the largest known cave systems in the Yucatán. This series of caverns contains indigenous wall paintings, pottery, shells, and stone artifacts from as early as around 2500 BC, as well as stalactites and stalagmites. Some of the limestone formations have been given descriptive names such as Ear of Corn and Cathedral. Illuminated pathways meander a little over a kilometer (½ mi) through the caverns. You can enter only by joining one of the guided tours; they leave at 9:30, 12:30, and 3:30 (in Spanish), and 11 and 2 (in English). *$4.50 ☉ Daily 9–5.*

Ticul

28 *27 km (17½ mi) northwest of the Loltún Caves, 28 km (17 mi) east of Uxmal, 100 km (62 mi) south of Mérida.*

One of the larger towns in Yucatán, Ticul has a handsome 17th-century church and is a good base for exploring the Puuc region. Many descendants of the Xiu dynasty, which ruled Uxmal until the conquest, still live here. Industries include fabrication of huipiles and shoes, as well as
★ much of the pottery you see around the Yucatán. **Arte y Decoración Maya** (⊠ Calle 23 No. 269, between Calles 38 and 40 ☎ 997/972–1316) is a ceramics workshop that produces museum-quality replicas of archaeological pieces found throughout Mexico. The workshop also creates souvenir-quality pieces that are both more affordable and more easily transported.

> **off the beaten path**

MAYAPÁN – Those who are enamored of Yucatán and the ancient Maya may want to take a 42-km (26-mi) detour east of Ticul (or 43 km [27 mi] from Mérida) to Mayapán, the last of the major city-states on the peninsula, which flourished during the Postclassic era. It was demolished in AD 1450, presumably by war. It is thought that the city, with an architectural style reminiscent of Uxmal, was as big as Chichén Itzá, and there are more than 4,000 mounds to bear this out. At its height, the population could have been well over 12,000. A half dozen mounds have been excavated, including the palaces of Maya royalty and the temple of the benign god Kukulcán, where murals in vivid reds and oranges, plus stucco sculptures, have been uncovered. The ceremonial structures that were faithfully described in Bishop Diego de Landa's writings will look like they have jumped right out of his book when the work is completed. ⊠ *Off road to left before Telchaquillo; follow signs* *$2 ☉ Daily 8–5.*

Where to Stay & Eat

$ ✕ **Pizzería La Góndola.** The wonderful smells of fresh-baked bread and pizza waft from this small corner establishment between the market and the main square. Scenes of Old Italy and the Yucatán adorn bright yellow walls; clients pull their padded folding chairs up to yellow-tile tables, or take their orders to go. Pizza is the name of the game here, although tortas and pastas are also for sale. To drink, you can choose from beer, wine, and soft drinks. ⊠ *Calle 23 No. 208, at Calle 26A* ☎ 997/972–0112 ▤ *No credit cards ☉ Closed daily between 1–5 PM.*

¢–$ ✕ **Los Almendros.** This restaurant, one of the few in town open until 9 PM, is a good place to sample regional fare, including handmade tortillas. The *combinado yucateco* gives you a chance to try poc chuc and cochinita pibíl (two pork dishes) as well as *pavo relleno* (stuffed turkey) and sausage. The restaurant moved in 2003, and the new, fresh-looking building is often full of tour groups. There's a pool out back where you can swim—but do like mama says and wait at least a half hour after eating. ⊠ *Calle 22 s/n at Carretera Ticul–Chetumal* ☎ *997/972–0021* ☷ *V.*

¢ ▣ **Plaza.** There's not much to recommend the Plaza except that it's one of the town's tried-and-true lodgings and a block from the main plaza. It has clean bathrooms and firm mattresses, hammock hooks, telephones, fans, and TV. Choose a room with air-conditioning; the price difference is only about $4. A café and bar are in the works, which would at least get your out of the extremely plain rooms. ⊠ *Calle 23 No. 202, between Calles 26 and 26A* ☎ *997/972–0484* ☷ *997/972–0026* ⇱ *25 rooms, 5 suites* ♻ *Cable TV, free parking; no a/c in some rooms* ☷ *AE, MC, V (with 6% surcharge).*

Yaxcopoil

㉙ *50 km (31 mi) north of Uxmal on Carretera 261.*

Yaxcopoil (yash-co-po-*il*), a restored 17th-century hacienda, makes for a nice change of pace from the ruins. The main building, with its distinctive Moorish double arch at the entrance, has been used as a film set and is the best-known henequen plantation in the region. The great house's rooms—including library, kitchen, dining room, drawing room, and salons—are fitted with late-19th-century European furnishings. You can tour these, along with the chapel, and the storerooms and machine room used in the processing of henequen. In the museum you'll see pottery and other artifacts recovered from the still-unexplored, Classic-era Maya site for which the hacienda is named. ⊠ *Carretera 261, Km 186* ☎ *999/927–2606 or 999/950–1001* ⊟ *$4* ☉ *Mon.–Sat. 8–6, Sun. 9–1.*

Where to Stay

$$$$ ▣ **Hacienda Temozón.** These luxurious accommodations may seem to be in the middle of nowhere, but they're actually quite close to the ruins of Uxmal, the Ruta Puuc, and even Mérida. The converted henequen estate exudes luxury and grace, with mahogany furnishings, carved wooden doors, intricate mosaic floors in tile and stone, and a general air of genteel sophistication. Rooms have ceilings that are more than 20 feet high, with multiple ceiling fans, comfortable high beds with piles of pillows, armoires, and twin hammocks. Modern lighting and quiet, remote-controlled air-conditioning units add creature comforts to the rustic-style rooms. ⊠ *Carretera 261, Km 182, Temozón Sur, 97825* ☎ *999/923–8089 or 800/325–3589* ☷ *999/923–7963* ⊕ *www.luxurycollection.com* ⇱ *26 rooms, 1 suite* ♻ *Restaurant, room service, fans, some in-room hot tubs, minibars, cable TV, tennis court, pool, exercise equipment, bar, concierge, meeting rooms, car rental, free parking; no room TVs* ☷ *AE, DC, MC, V.*

Oxkintoc

🔺 **30** *50 km (31 mi) south of Mérida on Carretera 180*

The archaeological site of Oxkintoc (osh-kin-*tok*) is 5 km (3 mi) east of Maxcanú, off Carretera 180, and contains the ruins of an important Maya capital that dominated the region from about AD 300 to AD 1100. Little was known about Oxkintoc until excavations began here in 1987. Structures that have been excavated so far include two tall pyramids and a palace with stone statues of several ancient rulers. ✉ *Off Carretera 184, 1½ km (1 mi) west of Carretera 180* 🔲 *$2* ⊙ *Daily 8–5.*

PROGRESO & THE NORTH COAST

Various routes lead from Mérida to towns along the coast, which spreads across a distance of 380 km (236 mi). Separate roads connect Mérida with the former seaport of Sisal and the laid-back fishing village of Celestún, gateway to a flamingo reserve near the Campeche border. Carretera 261 leads due north from Mérida to the relatively modern but humble shipping port of Progreso, where Meridanos spend hot summer days and holiday weekends. To get to some of the small beach towns east of Progreso, head east on Carretera 176 out of Mérida and then cut north on one of the many access roads. Wide, white, and generally shadeless beaches here are peppered with bathers from Mérida during Holy Week and in summer—but are nearly vacant the rest of the year.

The terrain in this part of the peninsula is absolutely flat. Tall trees are scarce, because the region was almost entirely cleared for coconut palms in the early 19th century and again for henequen in the early 20th century. Local Maya people still tend some of the old fields of henequen, a spike-leafed agave plant, even though there is little profit to be made from the rope fiber it produces. Other former plantation fields are wildly overgrown with scrub, and are only identifiable by the low, white, stone walls that used to mark their boundaries. Many bird species make their home in this area, and butterflies swarm in profusion throughout the dry season.

Celestún

31 *90 km (56 mi) west of Mérida.*

This tranquil and humble fishing village sits at the end of a spit of land separating the Celestún estuary from the Gulf of Mexico. Celestún is the only point of entry to the **Parque Natural del Flamenco Mexicano,** a 100,000-acre wildlife reserve with extensive mangrove forests and one of the largest colonies of flamingos in North America. Clouds of the pink birds soar above the estuary all year, but the best months for seeing them in abundance are April through July. This is also the fourth-largest wintering ground for ducks of the Gulf-coast region, and more than 300 other species of birds, as well as a large sea-turtle population, make their home here. Conservation programs sponsored by the United States and Mexico protect the birds, as well as the endangered hawksbill and loggerhead marine tortoises, and other species such as the blue crab and crocodile.

The park is set among rocks, islets, and white-sand beaches. There's good fishing here, too, and several cenotes that are wonderful for swimming. Most Mérida travel agencies run boat tours of the *ría* (estuary) in the early morning or late afternoon, but it's not usually necessary to make a reservation in advance.

To see the birds, hire a fishing boat at the entrance to town (the boats hang out under the bridge leading into Celestún). A 75-minute tour for up to six people costs about $50, a two-hour tour around $75. Although popular with Mexican vacationers, the park's sandy beach is pleasant during the day but tends to get windy in the afternoon.

Where to Stay & Eat

$–$$$ ✕ **La Palapa.** Celestún's most popular seafood place has a conch-shell facade and is known for its *camarones a la palapa* (fried shrimp smothered in a garlic and cream sauce). Unless it's windy or rainy, most guests dine on the beachfront terrace. The menu has lots of fresh fish (including sea bass and red snapper), as well as crab, squid, and lobster. Although the restaurant's hours are 11 AM–7 PM, it sometimes closes early during the low season. ⊠ *Calle 12 No. 105, between Calles 11 and 13* ☎ *988/916–2063* ▤ *D, MC, V.*

$$$ ▦ **Hotel Eco Paraíso Xixim.** On an old coconut plantation outside town, this hotel offers classy comfort in thatched-roof bungalows along a shell-strewn beach. Each unit has two comfortable queen beds, tile floors, and attractive wicker, cedar, and pine furniture. The extra-large porch has twin hammocks and comfortable chairs. Biking and bird-watching tours as well as those to old haciendas or archaeological sites can be arranged; kayaks are available for rent. Vegetarian food is available for breakfast and dinner, included in the room price. ⊠ *Camino Viejo a Sisal, Km 10* ☎ *800/400–3333* ▤ *988/916–2111* ⊕ *www.ecoparaiso.com* ↩ *15 cabanas* ⚷ *Restaurant, fans, in-room safes, pool, beach, billiards, bar, library, Internet, no smoking rooms; no a/c, no room phones, no room TVs* ▤ *AE, MC, V* ▥❙ *MAP.*

$ ▦ **Hotel Sol y Mar.** Gerardo Vasquez, the friendly owner of this small hotel across from the town beach, also owns the local paint store—so it's no accident that the walls here are a lovely cool shade of green. The spacious rooms are sparsely furnished; each has two double beds, a table, chairs, and a tile bathroom. The more expensive rooms downstairs also have air-conditioning, TV, and tiny refrigerators. There's no restaurant, but La Palapa is across the street. ⊠ *Calle 12 No. 104, at Calle 10* ☎ *988/916–2166* ↩ *15 rooms* ⚷ *Fans, some refrigerators; no a/c in some rooms, no TV in some rooms* ▤ *No credit cards.*

Dzibilchaltún

🏛 ★ ㉜ *16 km (10 mi) north of Mérida.*

Dzibilchaltún (dzi-bil-chal-*tun*), which means "the place with writing on flat stones," is a sizable archaeological site in northern Yucatán. More than 16 square km (6 square mi) of land here are cluttered with thousands of mounds, platforms, piles of rubble, plazas, and stelae. It is also the longest continuously occupied city of this area, established around 500 BC in the Preclassic era and abandoned only when the conquistadores arrived in the 16th century. About equidistant from Mérida and Progreso, it had a marine and coastal economy and was more of an urban than a ceremonial center.

These days, Dzibilchaltún is significant because of the sculpture and ceramics, from all periods of Maya civilization, that have been unearthed here. The **Templo de las Siete Muñecas** ("temple of the seven dolls," circa AD 500) is one of a half dozen structures excavated to date. Low and trapezoidal, the temple exemplifies the Late Preclassic style, and predates such Puuc sites as Uxmal. The remains of stucco masks adorn each side, and there are vestiges of coiled-serpent sculptures representing Kukulcán. During the spring and fall equinoxes, sunbeams fall at the exact center of two windows opposite each other inside one of the temple rooms, an example of the highly precise mathematical calculations for which the Maya are known. Studies have found that a similar phenomenon occurs at the full moon between March 20 and April 20. The stone cube atop the temple and the open chapel built by the Spaniards for the Indians are additional points of interest. Twelve sacbéob lead to various groups of structures. Bones and ceremonial objects recovered by divers from the National Geographic Society between 1957 and 1959 suggest that the **Xlacah Cenote** was used for ceremonial offerings. These days, it's ideal for cooling off after walking around the ruins—so don't forget your swimsuit.

An excellent museum, **Pueblo Maya,** is at the entrance to the site. It's part of a national program that establishes museums devoted—and accessible—to the country's native peoples. It's fronted by a garden where several of the huge sculptures found on the site are displayed, along with botanical species common to the area. In the back, two *nas* (native huts) show what traditional Maya dwellings looked like. The museum's collection (labeled in English as well as in Spanish) includes figurines, bones, jewelry, and potsherds found in the cenote, as well as the seven crude dolls that gave the Temple of the Seven Dolls its name. It also traces the area's Hispanic history and highlights contemporary crafts from the region.

The easiest way to get to Dzibilchaltún is to get a *colectivo* taxi from Mérida's **Parque San Juan** (⊠ Calles 69 and 62, just a few blocks south of the Plaza Principal). The taxis depart whenever they fill up with passengers. Returns are a bit more dicey. If a colectivo taxi doesn't show up, you can take a more expensive regular taxi back to Mérida (it will cost you about $12–$15). You can also ask the regular taxi driver to drop you at the Mérida–Progreso highway, where you can catch a Mérida-bound bus for less than $2 ▱ *$5.50 (including museum)* ☉ *Daily 8–5.*

Progreso

㉝ *16 km (10 mi) north of Dzibilchaltún, 32 km (20 mi) north of Mérida.*

Progreso, the waterfront town closest to Mérida, is not particularly historic. It's also not terribly picturesque. On weekdays during most of the year the beaches are deserted, but when school is out (Easter week, July, and August) and on summer weekends it becomes a popular vacation spot for families from Mérida. More and more retired Canadians are also renting apartments here between December and April because of the low prices. Progreso has fine sand and shallow waters that extend quite far out, making for nice walks. Its water normally does not have the tantalizing clarity of the Caribbean off Quintana Roo, although sometimes it does acquire an aquamarine hue. Because it is so close to Mérida, many people come for the day only. It is, however, a perfectly pleasant overnight trip when skies are sunny, the sea is calm, and you have no expectations of wild nightlife. Several B&Bs that have cropped up in town over the past few years make fine places to stay.

Progreso has been the chief port of entry for the peninsula since its founding in 1872, when the shallow port at Sisal, to the southwest, proved inadequate for handling the large ships that were carrying henequen cargo. Since 1989 the 2-km-long (1-mi-long) pier has been extended 9 km (5½ mi) out to sea to accommodate the hoped-for cruise-ship business and to siphon some of the lucrative tourist trade from Cozumel, but only a trickle of cruise ships are berthing here these days.

Progreso's attractions include its malecón (waterfront walkway), Calle 19, which is lined with seafood restaurants. Fishermen sell their catch on the beach east of the city between 6 and 8 AM.

Some 120 km (74 mi) offshore, the Alacranes Reef is where divers can explore sunken ships. Pérez Island is part of Alacranes Reef; it supports a large population of sea turtles and seabirds.

Where to Stay & Eat

$–$$ ✕ **Le Saint Bonnet.** This thatched-roof restaurant and bar on the malecón is *the* place for locals. It gets its name from a French partner who has given all the dishes Gallic monikers; the shrimp St. Bonnet—jumbo shrimp stuffed with cheese, wrapped with bacon, breaded, fried, and served with crab sauce—is a perennial favorite. European and Chilean wines complement the meals, and the caramel crepes or chocolate mousse are perfect for dessert. A live band plays tropical music daily (except Monday) from 2:30 to 6:30 PM. ⊠ *Av. Malecón (Calle 19) 150D, at Calle 78* ☎ *969/935–2299* 🖃 *AE, MC, V.*

$ 🏠 **Casa Isidora.** A couple of Canadian English teachers have restored this grand, 100-year-old house a few blocks from the beach. Each guest room is individually decorated, but all have beautiful tile floors and a cozy beachy style; some have small private patios. Breakfast is served in the dining room or out on the back patio, where the small swimming pool is surrounded by cushioned chaise longues. Mexican and American bar food and lots of tequilas are served in the comely street-side bar. ⊠ *Calle 21 No. 116, 97320* 🖷🖷 *969/934–4595* ⊕ *www.casaisidora. com* 🖘 *6 rooms* ⸶ *Restaurant, café, fans, pool, bar, laundry service, Internet, free parking; no room TVs* ☰ *AE, MC, V* 🍽 *BP.*

$ 🏨 **Casa Quixote.** Fourteen-foot-high ceilings, lovely old tile floors, and eclectic, handmade room furnishings characterize this restored 1920s home–turned–B&B. Comfortable beds have carved wooden headboards and mosquito nets. One side of the house has less expensive rooms with room fans; pricier, air-conditioned rooms are on the other side. The American owners open their Saturday-night Texas-style barbecues to the public as well as guests (reservations required). Full breakfast is served outside near the small pool or in the second-floor dining room. ⊠ *Calle 23 No. 64, between Calles 48 and 50, 97320* ☎ *969/935–2909* 🖷 *969/ 935–5600* ⊕ *www.casaquixote.com* 🖘 *10 rooms, 2 suites, 1 apartment* ⸶ *Restaurant, fans, cable TV, pool; no a/c in some rooms, no room phones* ☰ *MC, V.*

Xcambo

🏛 ❸❹ *26 km (16 mi) east of Chicxulub, off the Progreso hwy. at Xtampu.*

Surrounded by a plantation where disease-resistant coconut trees are being developed, the Xcambo (*ish*-cam-bo) site is a couple of miles inland following the turnoff for Xtampu. It's also in the hometown of former governor Victor Cervera Pacheco, who, it is rumored, had given priority to its excavation. Salt, which was a much-sought-after item of trade in the ancient Maya world, was produced in this area and made it prosperous. Indeed, the bones of 600 former residents discovered in burial plots showed they had been healthier than the average Maya. Two plazas have been restored so far, surrounded by rather plain structures. The tallest temple is the **Xcambo,** also known as the Pyramid of the Cross. Ceramics found at the site indicate that the city traded with other Maya groups as far afield as Guatemala, Teotihuácan, and Belize. The Catholic church on-site was built by dismantling these ancient structures, and until recently, locals hauled off the cut stones to build fences and foundations. ⊠ *Turn off the Progreso hwy. at Xtampu* 🎫 *$2* ⊙ *Daily 8–5.*

Tizimín

❸❺ *108 km (67 mi) southeast of Dzilám de Bravo.*

Tizimín, renowned as the seat of an indigenous messianic movement during the 1840s Caste War, is at the junction of Carreteras 176 and 295. The town has a 17th-century church dedicated to the Three Wise Men, who are honored here during a festival that is held December 15–January 15.

If you are driving from Tizimín to the town of Río Lagartos, before you leave you can stop at the **Oficina del Reserva del Parque Natural Ría La-**

gartos (Flamingo Reserve Office; ✉ Calle 47 No. 415A, between Calles 52 and 54 ☎ 986/863–4390), open weekdays 9–2 and 6–9, for park information. (Don't worry if you miss it; there's an information station near the Parque Natural Ría Lagartos entrance.)

Parque Natural Ría Lagartos

★ ☾ ㊱ *115 km (71 mi) north Valladolid.*

This park, which encompasses a long estuary, was developed with eco-tourism in mind—although most of the alligators for which it and the village were named have long since been hunted into extinction. The real spectacle these days is the birds; more than 350 species nest and feed in the area, including flocks of flamingos, snowy and red egrets, white ibis, great white herons, cormorants, pelicans, and peregrine falcons. Fishing is good, too, and the protected hawksbill and green turtles lay their eggs on the beach at night.

You can make the 90-km (56-mi) trip from Valladolid (1½ hours by car or 2 hours by bus) as a day trip (add another hour if you're coming from Mérida; it's 3 hours from Cancún). Unless you're interested exclusively in the birds, it's nice to spend the night in Río Lagartos (the town is called *Río* Lagartos, and the park is *Ría* Lagartos) or nearby San Felipe. Buses leave Mérida and Valladolid regularly from the second-class terminals to either Río Lagartos or, 10 km (6 mi) west of the park, San Felipe.

The easiest way to book a trip is through Ría Lagartos Expeditions' Diego Núñez at the Isla Contoy restaurant where you can also eat a delicious meal of fresh seafood. Call ahead to reserve an English- or Italian-speaking guide. This boat trip will take you through the mangrove forests to the flamingo feeding grounds (where, as an added bonus, you can paint your face or body with supposedly therapeutic green mud). A 2½-hour tour, which accommodates five or six people, costs $42; the 3½-hour tour costs $65 per person. You can take a shorter boat trip for slightly less money, or a 2-hour, guided walking-and-boat tour ($25 for 1–6 passengers.) You can also hire a boat ($20 for 1–10 passengers) to take you to an area beach and pick you up at a designated time.

Where to Stay & Eat

★ $ ✕ **Isla Contoy.** Run by the amicable family that guides lagoon tours, this open-sided seafood shanty at the dock serves generous helpings of fish soup, fried fish fillets, shrimp, squid, and crab. If you've come with a group, order the combo for four (it can easily feed six, especially if you order a huge ceviche or other appetizer). The delicious platter comes with four shrimp crepes, fish stuffed with seafood, a seafood skewer, and one each of grilled, breaded, garlic-chile, and battered fish fillets (usually grouper or sea trout, whatever is freshest). There are also a few regional specialties and red-meat dishes. ✉ *Calle 19 No. 134, at Calle 14* ☎ *986/862–0000* ▭ *No credit cards.*

¢ ▭ **Hotel San Felipe.** This three-story white hotel in the beach town of San Felipe, 10 km (6 mi) west of Parque Natural Ría Lagartos, is basic (for example, toilets have no seats), but adequate. Each room has two twin beds or a double—some are mushy, some hard—and walls are decorated with regional scenes painted by the owner. The two most expensive rooms have private terraces with a marina view (ask for a hammock), and are worth the small splurge. The owner can arrange fly-fishing expeditions for tarpon. ⊠ *Calle 9 No. 13, between Calles 14 and 16, San Felipe* ☎ *986/862–2027* 🖷 *986/862–2036* ⇗ *18 rooms* ☖ *Restaurant, fans, free parking; no a/c in some rooms, no room TVs* ☰ *No credit cards.*

Isla Holbox

❸ *141 km (87 mi) northeast of Valladolid.*

The tiny Isla Holbox (25 km [16 mi] long) sits at the eastern end of the Ría Lagartos estuary and just across the Quintana Roo state line. A fishing fan's heaven because of the pompano, bass, barracuda, and shark thronging its waters, the island also pleases seekers of tranquillity who don't mind rudimentary accommodations (rooms and hammocks for rent) and simple palapa restaurants. Seabirds fill the air; the long sandy beach is strewn with seashells; and the swimming is good on the Gulf side.

To get here from Río Lagartos, take Carretera 176 to Kantunilkin and then head north on the unnumbered road for 44 km (27 mi) to Chiquilá. Continue by ferry to the island; schedules vary, but there are normally five crossings a day. The fare is $3 and the trip takes about 35 minutes. A car ferry makes the trip at 11 AM daily, returning at 5 PM. (You can also pay to leave your car in a lot in Chicquilá, in Quintana Roo.)

There are several less expensive lodgings in town for those who eschew air-conditioning and conventional beds in favor of fresh air and a hammock. Since it's a small island, it's easy to check several lodgings and make your choice. There are several restaurants near the zócalo on the beach, and hotel owners can help you set up a bird-watching expedition.

Where to Stay & Eat

$$ ✕🔟 **Villas Delfines.** This fisherman's lodge is expensive by island standards. Cabins are simple and have no TV or phone. Deluxe bungalows have wood floors (rather than cement), larger balconies, and a few more creature comforts, such as hair dryers and safes. All are on stilts with rounded palapa roofs, and have waterless, "eco-friendly" toilets. You can get your catch grilled in the restaurant ($–$$), and if you get tired of fishing you can rent a bike or kayak or arrange for a bird-watching trip. It's a 15-minute walk to the village's small main square. ⊠ *Domicilio Conocido* ☎ *998/874–4014, 998/884–8606 reservations* 🖷 *998/884–6342* ⊕ *www.holbox.com* ⇗ *20 cabins* ☖ *Restaurant, fans, some in-room safes, some minibars, beach, bicycles, Ping-Pong, volleyball, bar; no room phones, no room TVs* ☰ *AE, D, MC, V* ⫶❍⫶ *BP, MAP, AP.*

¢–$$ 🔟 **Los Mapaches.** A coconut's throw from the beach, this small enclave includes several thatched-roof bungalows and a second-floor, two-bedroom apartment. Each has wooden floors typical of coastal dwellings, and small patios or balconies overlooking small gardens. For an additional fee you can take Spanish lessons, arrange a fishing expedition, grab a free bike or a golf cart for touring the island, or just lounge in your hammock. Weekly and monthly rates are available. ⊠ *Av. Pedro Joaquin Coldwell s/n* 🕾 *984/875–2090* ⊕ *www.losmapaches.com* ➦*3 bungalows, 2 suites* ⚫ *Grill, fans, kitchens, kitchenettes, steam room, beach, bicycles, laundry service, Internet, travel services, some pets allowed; no a/c, no room phones, no room TVs* ▭ *MC, V.*

MÉRIDA & YUCATÁN STATE A TO Z

To research prices, get advice from other travelers, and book travel arrangements, visit www.fodors.com.

AIR TRAVEL

AIRPORT The Mérida airport, Aeropuerto Manuel Crescencio Rejón, is 7 km (4½ mi) west of the city on Avenida Itzaes, a 20- to 30-minute cab ride.

🗗 **Aeropuerto Manuel Crescencio Rejón** 🕾 999/946-1300 or 999/946-1340.

AIRPORT
TRANSFERS A private taxi from the airport costs about $8. Bus 79 (40¢) goes from the airport to downtown and vice versa, departing from Calle 67 between Calles 60 and 62 about every 25 minutes; the ride takes about 45 minutes. It's very inexpensive, but a hassle if you've got more than a day pack or small suitcase.

CARRIERS Aerocaribe, a subsidiary of Mexicana, has flights from Cancún, Cozumel, Mexico City, Oaxaca City, Tuxtla Gutiérrez, and Villahermosa, with additional service to Central America. Aeroméxico flies direct to Mérida from Miami with a stop (but no plane change) in Cancún. Aeroméxico's affiliate, AeroMaya, connects Chichén Itzá, Cozumel, Mérida, and Chetumal with Cancún. Aviacsa flies from Mérida to Mexico City, Villahermosa, and Monterrey with connects to Los Angeles, Las Vegas, Chicago, Miami, Ciudad Juárez, Houston, and Tijuana, among other destinations. Mexicana has direct flights to Cancún from Los Angeles and Miami, and a number of other connecting flights from Chicago and a number of other U.S. cities via Mexico City.

🗗 **Aerocaribe** 🕾 999/928-6790 ⊕ www.aerocaribe.com. **AeroMaya** 🕾 999/946-9450. **Aeroméxico** 🕾 999/920-1293 or 01800/021-4000 toll-free in Mexico ⊕ www.aeromexico.com. **Aviacsa** 🕾 999/925-6890, 01800/006-2200 toll-free in Mexico ⊕ www.aviacsa.com.mx. **Mexicana** 🕾 999/946-1332 ⊕ www.mexicana.com.mx.

BUS TRAVEL

Mérida's municipal buses run daily 5 AM–midnight. In the downtown area buses go east on Calle 59 and west on Calle 61, north on Calle 60 and south on Calle 62. You can catch a bus heading north to Progreso on Calle 56. There's no direct bus service from the hotels around the plaza to the long-distance bus station; however, taxis are reasonable.

There are several first-class bus lines offering deluxe buses with air-conditioning and comfortable seats. ADO and UNO have direct buses to Cancún, Chichén Itzá, Playa del Carmen, Tulum, Uxmal, Valladolid, and other Mexican cities, with intermediate service to Izamal.

They depart from the first-class CAME bus station. ADO and UNO also have direct buses to Cancún, Chetumal, and Playa del Carmen from their terminal at the Fiesta Americana hotel, on Paseo Montejo. Regional bus lines to intermediate or more out-of-the-way destinations leave from the second-class terminal. The most frequent destination of tourists using Autotransportes del Sureste (ATS), which departs from the second-class station, is Uxmal. Buses to Celestún depart from the Autobuses del Occidente station; those to Progreso are found at the Terminal de Autobuses a Progreso. Clase Elite/Nuevos Horizontes have first-class buses to destinations in Quintana Roo but depart from the second-class bus station.

🚍 : **ADO/UNO at Fiesta Americana** ⊠ Av. Colón 451, Paseo Montejo, Mérida ☏ 999/920-4444. **Autobuses de Occidente** ⊠ Calles 50 and 67, Centro Mérida ☏ 999/924-8391 or 999/924-9741. **CAME** ⊠ Calle 70 No. 555, at Calle 71, Centro Mérida ☏ 999/924-8391 or 999/924-9130. **Terminal de Autobuses a Progreso** ⊠ Calle 62 No. 524, between Calles 65 and 67, San Juan Mérida ☏ 999/924-8941 or 999/928-3965. **Terminal de Autobuses de 2da clase** ⊠ Calle 69 No. 544, between Calles 68 and 70, Centro Mérida ☏ 999/923-2287.

CAR RENTAL

The major international chains are represented in Mérida, with desks at the airport and either downtown or on Paseo Montejo, most often in the large hotels. Mundo Maya is part of the Mayaland group, owners of Mayaland hotel and tours, and sometimes offers combo packages.

🚗 **Major Agencies Budget** ⊠ Holiday Inn, Av. Colón No. 498, at Calle 60 Centro, Mérida ☏ 999/925-6877 Ext. 516 ⊠ airport ☏ 999/946-1323. **Hertz** ⊠ Fiesta Americana, Av. Colón 451, Paseo Montejo, Mérida ☏ 999/925-7595 ⊠ airport ☏ 999/946-1355. **Mundo Maya** ⊠ Calle 60 No. 486A, Centro, Mérida ☏ 999/926-3351. **Thrifty** ⊠ Calle 55 No. 508, at Calle 60, Centro, Mérida ☏ 999/923-2040 or 999/928-0966.

CAR TRAVEL

Driving in Mérida can be frustrating because of the narrow one-way streets and dense traffic. But having your own wheels is the best way to take excursions from the city. For more relaxed sightseeing, consider hiring a cab for short excursions. Most charge approximately $12 per hour. Carretera 180, the main road along the Gulf coast from the Texas border, passes through Mérida en route to Cancún. Mexico City is 1,550 km (961 mi) west, Cancún 320 km (198 mi) due east.

The autopista is a four-lane toll highway between Mérida and Cancún. Beginning at the town of Kantuníl, 55 km (34 mi) southeast of Mérida, it runs somewhat parallel to Carretera 180. The toll road cuts driving time between Mérida and Cancún—around 4½ hours on Carretera 180—by about an hour and bypasses about four dozen villages. Access to the toll highway is off old Carretera 180 and is clearly marked. The highway has exits for Valladolid and Pisté (Chichén Itzá), as well as rest stops and gas stations. Tolls between Mérida and Cancún total about $25.

CONSULATE

🚩 **United States** ⊠ Paseo Montejo 453, at Av. Colón, Centro, Mérida ☏ 999/925-5011.

EMERGENCIES

🔟 Doctors & Hospitals: English-speaking doctors can be found at **Centro de Especialidades Médicas** ⊠ Calle 60 No. 329, at Av. Colón, Centro, Mérida ☎ 999/920-4040. **Centro Médico de las Américas** ⊠ Calle 54 No. 365, between Calle 33A and Av. Pérez Ponce, Centro, Mérida ☎ 999/927-3199. **Clínica San Juan** ⊠ Calle 40 No. 238, Valladolid ☎ 985/856-2174 is near the main plaza.

🔟 Emergency Services **Fire, police, Red Cross, and general emergency** ☎ 060.

🔟 Pharmacies **Farmacia de Ahorros** ⊠ Calles 60 and 63, Centro, Mérida ☎ 999/928-5027. **Farmacia Arco Iris** ⊠ Calle 43 No. 207C, Valladolid ☎ 985/856-2188. **Farmacia Yza** ☎ 999/926-6666 information and delivery.

ENGLISH-LANGUAGE MEDIA

Librería Dante has a great selection of colorful books on Maya culture, although only a few are in English. There are many locations throughout town, including most of the malls, and there's also a large, happening shop–café–performance venue on Paseo Montejo. The Mérida English Library has novels and nonfiction in English; you can use the facilities free for five days before paying the $17 annual membership fee.

🔟 Bookstores **Librería Dante** ⊠ Calle 62 No. 502, at Calle 61 on the main plaza, Centro, Mérida ☎ 999/928-2611 ⊠ Calle 17 No. 138B, at Prolongación Paseo de Montejo, Centro, Mérida ☎ 999/927-7676. **Mérida English Library** ⊠ Calle 53 No. 524, between Calles 66 and 68, Centro, Mérida ☎ 999/924-8401.

MAIL, INTERNET & SHIPPING

Mérida's post office is open weekdays 8–3 and Saturday 9–1. You can, however, buy postage stamps at some handicrafts shops and newspaper and magazine kiosks. The Mex Post service can speed delivery, even internationally, though it costs more than regular mail. Cybercafés are ubiquitous, though particularly prevalent along Mérida's main square and Calles 61 and 63. Most charge $1–$3 per hour.

🔟 Cybercafés **Express Internet** ⊠ Café Express, Calle 60 No. 502, at Calle 59, Centro, Mérida ☎ 999/928-1691. **Phonet** ⊠ Calle 42 between Calles 39 and 41, main plaza, Valladolid ☎ No phone. **Vía Olimpo Café** ⊠ Calles 62 and 61, Centro, Mérida ☎ 999/923-5843.

🔟 Mail Service **Correo** ⊠ Calles 65 and 56, Centro, Mérida ☎ 999/928-5404 or 999/924-3590.

MONEY MATTERS

Most banks throughout Mérida are open weekdays 9–4. Banamex has its main offices, open weekdays 9–4 and Saturday 9–1:30, in the handsome Casa de Montejo, on the south side of the main square, with branches at the airport and the Fiesta Americana hotel. All have ATMs. Several other banks, including Bital, can be found on Calle 65 between Calles 62 and 60, and on Paseo Montejo.

🔟 Banks **Banamex** ⊠ Calle 59 No. 485, Mérida ☎ 01800/226-2639 toll-free in Mexico ⊠ Calle 26 No. 199D, Ticul ⊠ Calle 41 No. 206, Valladolid. **Banortel** ⊠ Calle 28 No. 31B, Izamal ☎ 988/954-0425 ⊠ Calle 58 No. 524, between Calles 63 and 65, Centro, Mérida ☎ 999/923-4572. **Bital** ⊠ Paseo Montejo 467A, Centro, Mérida ☎ 999/942-2378 ⊠ Calle 58 No. 524, between Calles 63 and 65, Centro, Mérida ☎ 999/923-4572. **Serfin** ⊠ Paseo Montejo 467A, Centro, Mérida ☎ 999/942-2378 ⊠ Calle 30 No. 150, at Calle 80, Progreso ☎ 969/935-0855.

TAXIS & CARRIAGES

Taxis charge beach-resort prices, which makes them a little expensive for this region of Mexico. They cruise the streets for passengers and are available at 13 taxi stands (*sitios*) around the city, or in front of major hotels like the Hyatt Regency, Holiday Inn, and Fiesta Americana. The minimum fare is $3, which should get you from one downtown location to another, or from downtown to Paseo Montejo or the first- or second-class bus stations.

You can hail horse-drawn calesas (horse-drawn carriages) along Calle 60. Their owners generally charge $11–$14 an hour. Bargaining is acceptable.

🗷 Taxi Company **Sitio 14** ☎ 999/924-5918.

TELEPHONES

Towns and cities of all sizes in Yucatán state have three-digit area codes (LADAs) and seven-digit phone numbers. However, many of the numbers in brochures and other literature—even business cards—are still written in the old style. Mérida's area code is 999. To convert an older number into a current one for local dialing, just deduct 9s from the area code and add them to the beginning of the number until you have a seven-digit phone number. For example, 99/24-87-88 becomes the local number 924-8788; the area code need not be used unless you are dialing Mérida from outside the city, in which case you would dial 01–999/924-8788.

Coin-operated phones are few and far between—most take only Ladatel cards, electronic phone cards you can buy at newsstands and pharmacies. Ladatel phone booths are at the airport and bus stations, in the main plaza, at Avenidas Reforma and Colón, and throughout the city. You can make both local and international direct calls at these public phones.

TOURS

Mérida has more than 50 tour operators, who generally go to the same places. Beware the *piratas* (street vendors) who stand outside the offices of reputable tour operators and offer to sell you a cheaper trip. They have been known to take your money and not show up; most also do not carry liability insurance.

A two- to three-hour group tour of the city, including museums, parks, public buildings, and monuments, costs $20 to $35 per person. Or you can pick up an open-air sightseeing bus at Parque Santa Lucía for $8 (departures are Monday–Saturday at 10, 1, 4, and 7 and Sunday at 10 and 1). Free guided tours are offered daily by the Municipal Tourist Office. These depart from City Hall, on the main plaza at 9:30 AM. Call 999/928-2020 Ext. 833 for information.

A day trip to Chichén Itzá, including guide service, entrance to the ruins, and lunch goes for $60–$70 and departs from Cancún or Mérida. For about the same price you can see the ruins of Uxmal and Kabah in the Puuc region. Early afternoon departures to Uxmal allow you to take in the sound-and-light show at the ruins and return by 11 PM for about

$63 (including dinner). Another option is a tour of Chichén Itzá followed by a drop-off in Cancún, for about $80. Most tour operators take credit cards.

If you don't have your own wheels, a great option for seeing the ruins of the Ruta Puuc is the unguided ATS tour that leaves Mérida at 8 AM from the second-class bus station. The tour stops for half an hour each at the ruins of Labná, Xlapak, Sayil, and Kabah, giving you just enough time to scan the plaques, climb a few crumbling steps, and poke your nose into a crevice or two. You get almost two hours at Uxmal before heading back to Mérida at 2:30 PM. The trip costs $9 per person, is unguided, and does not include entrance to the ruins.

Ecoturismo Yucatán leads kayaking tours out of Mérida that begin in Celestún and enable you to explore the mangroves and estuaries of the western coast. It also offers bird-watching and biking adventures, and custom trips to suit the needs and abilities of its clients. Ría Lagartos Expeditions' Diego Núñez conducts boat and walking tours of Parque Natural Ría Lagartos. He charges $42 for a 2½-hour tour, which accommodates five or six people. He usually can be found at the restaurant called Isla Contoy, which his family runs.

🗐 Tour Operators **Amigo Travel** ⊠ Av. Colón 508C, Col. García Ginerés, Mérida ☎ 999/920-0101 or 999/920-0107. **Ecoturismo Yucatán** ⊠ Calle 3 No. 235, between Calles 32A and 34, Col. Pensiones, Mérida ☎ 999/920-2772 ⊕ www.ecoyuc.com. **Mayaland Tours** ⊠ Calle Robalo 30, Sm 3, Cancún ☎ 998/887-2495 in Cancún, 01800/719-5465 toll-free from elsewhere in Mexico, 800/235-4079. **Ría Lagartos Expeditions** c/o Restaurant Isla Contoy ⊠ Calle 19 No. 12, Río Lagartos ☎ 998/862-0000. **Ricardía Tours** ☎ 999/923-6431. **Yucatán Trails** ⊠ Calle 62 No. 502, between Calles 57 and 59 ☎ 999/928-2582.

TRAIN TRAVEL

The Expreso Maya train is a private venture transporting passengers to and from one to four archaeological sites (Chichén Itzá, Uxmal, Edzná, and Palenque) aboard a train refurbished exclusively for this purpose. In addition to the Maya ruins, the train stops in a few major cities (Villahermosa, Mérida, Campeche) as well as laid-back Izamal, home of the beautiful St. Anthony of Padua Monastery and Church, and a little-visited sinkhole in Campeche state. One- to six-day tours are available. The shorter tours begin either at the Mérida or Palenque train stations; passengers for the five- or six-day tours are picked up at either the Villahermosa or Mérida airport. Per-person cost (based on double occupancy) ranges from $120 for the one-day Mérida–Izamal–Chichén Itzá tour to $1,450 for the full six-day tour ending in Mérida or Cancún. The train has four air-conditioned passenger cars with swivel seats, and dining, bar, snack, and luggage cars. Individual passengers are welcomed but a minimum number of passengers must be booked through tour operators for the train to depart as scheduled. Groups and conventions may book their own train cars.

🗐 **Expreso Maya** ⊠ Calle 1F No. 310, Fracc. Campestre, Mérida ☎ 999/944-9393 ⊕ www.expresomaya.com

TRAVEL AGENCIES

🔒 **Carmen Travel Service** ⊠ Hotel María del Carmen, Calle 63 No. 550, at Calle 68, Centro, Mérida ☎ 999/924–1212. **Viajes Valladolid** ⊠ Calle 42 No. 206, Valladolid ☎ 985/856–1881

VISITOR INFORMATION

The Mérida city, municipal, and state tourism departments are open daily 8–8. Those outside Mérida are generally open weekdays 9–7 and Saturday 9–1.

🔒 **City Tourist Information Center** ⊠ Calle 62 between Calles 61 and 63 on the ground floor of the Palacio Municipal, Centro, Mérida ☎ 999/928–2020 Ext. 133. **Dirección de Turismo** ⊠ Calles 40 and 41 Palacio Municipal, Valladolid ☎ 985/856–1865 Ext. 211. **Municipal Tourism Department** ⊠ Calles 61 and 60, Centro, Mérida ☎ 999/930–3101. **State Secretary of Tourism Office** ⊠ Teatro Peón Contreras, Calle 60 between Calles 57 and 59, Centro, Mérida ☎ 999/924–9290 or 999/924–9389.

CAMPECHE

6

BEST SNACK FROM THE SEA
The *camarones al coco* at La Pigua
restaurant ⇨*p.229*

MOST SECLUDED SWIMMING
Champotón's Cenote Azul ⇨*p.250*

PROTECTION AGAINST PIRATES
18th-century Fuerte de San Miguel ⇨*p.227*

BEAUTIFUL BLOSSOMS
120 orchid varieties at Reserva de la Biosfera
Calakmul ⇨*p.245*

TEMPLES AT EVERY TURN
Maya ruins along the Chenes Route ⇨*p.238*

Updated by
Jane Onstott

CAMPECHE IS THE PERFECT PLACE FOR ADVENTURE. It's the Yucatán's least-visited, most underrated corner, and its residents are friendly and welcoming. Receiving nowhere near as many tourists as the neighboring state of Yucatán, Campeche's colonial communities retain an air of innocence, and its protected biospheres, farmland, and jungle are unspoiled. In the forts of Campeche City, cannons still point across the Gulf of Mexico—historical relics that once protected the city from pirate attacks. Beyond its walls, the pyramids and ornate temples of ancient Maya kingdoms—some considered among the empire's most important—lie waiting in tropical forests.

The terrain of the state of Campeche varies from the northeastern flatlands to the rolling hills of the south. More than 60% is covered by jungles filled with precious mahogany and cedar. The Gulf Stream keeps temperatures at about 26°C (78°F) year-round; the humid, tropical climate feels even hotter, though evening breezes help cool things down. Campeche's economy relies on agriculture, fishing, logging, salt, tourism, and, since the 1970s, hydrocarbons—the state is Mexico's largest oil producer. At least 90 oil platforms sit on Campeche's coast, but the industry is most concentrated around Ciudad del Carmen, a business-oriented city with little to lure tourists.

Campeche City's Gulf location played a pivotal role in its history. Ah-Kim-Pech (Maya for "lord of the serpent tick," from which the name Campeche is derived)—was the capital of an Indian chieftainship long before the Spaniards arrived in 1517. In 1540, the conquerors—led by Francisco de Montejo and later by his son—established a real foothold at Campeche (originally called San Francisco de Campeche), using it as a base to conquer the peninsula.

At the time, Campeche City was the Gulf's only port and shipyard. So Spanish ships, loaded with cargoes of treasure plundered from Maya, Aztec, and other indigenous civilizations, dropped anchor here en route from Veracruz to Cuba, New Orleans, and Spain. As news of the riches spread, Campeche's shores were soon overrun with pirates. From the mid-1500s to the early 1700s, such notorious corsairs as Diego the Mulatto, Lorenzillo, Peg Leg, Henry Morgan, and Barbillas swooped in repeatedly from Tris—or Isla de Términos, as Isla del Carmen was then known—pillaging and burning the city and massacring its people.

Finally, after years of appeals to the Spanish crown, Campeche received funds to build a protective wall, with four gates and eight bastions, around the town center. For a while afterward, the city thrived on its exports, especially *palo de tinte*—a valuable dyewood more precious than gold because of demand by the nascent European textile industry—but also hardwoods, chicle, salt, and *henequen* (sisal hemp). But when the port of Sisal opened on the northern Yucatán coast in 1811, Campeche's monopoly on Gulf traffic ended, and its economy quickly declined. During the 19th and 20th centuries, Campeche, like most of the Yucatán peninsula, had little to do with the rest of Mexico. Left to their own devices, *Campechanos* lived in relative isolation until the petroleum boom of the 1970s brought businessmen from Mexico City, Europe, and the United States to its provincial doorstep.

Campeche City's history still shapes the community today. Remnants of its gates and bastions split the city into two main districts: the historical center (where relatively few people live) and the newer residential areas. Because the city was long preoccupied with defense, the colonial architecture is less flamboyant here than elsewhere in Mexico. The narrow flagstone streets reflect the confines of the city's walls; homes here emphasize the practical over the decorative. Over the centuries, as the city grew, some walls were torn down, bastions demolished, and landfill added to accommodate expansion. Yet an air of antiquity remains. Government decrees now ban the destruction of colonial structures, and an on-and-off beautification program keeps the city's one- and two-story building facades in good condition despite the damaging effects of humidity and salt air.

Most of the state's 700,000 residents live in villages and small towns. The most traditional and least-changed communities are in the northern part of the state, where Maya culture still holds sway. In other areas, Campeche's population has shifted dramatically in the last few generations. Many Guatemalan refugees have gone home, replaced by the Chol Maya homesteaders who relocated from Chiapas after the Zapatista uprising in 1994. Some newcomers settled on the southern edge of the Reserva de la Biosfera Calakmul, and land giveaways around sparsely populated Candelaria have drawn opportunity seekers from Durango, Zacatecas, Coahuila, and Michoacán. The petroleum industry in Ciudad del Carmen, Campeche's second-largest city, attracts businesspeople from other areas.

Campeche has few large cities, however. The countryside is covered with fields of tobacco, sugarcane, rice, indigo, maize, and cocoa as well as citrus groves. The sea is rich with shrimp, barracuda, swordfish, and other catch; in the wilder regions, including the Reserva de la Biosfera Calakmul, jaguars, deer, tapir, wild turkeys, howler monkeys, and armadillos roam in their natural habitat.

Exploring Campeche

Campeche City, the state's most accessible spot, makes a good hub for exploring other areas, many of which have only basic restaurants and primitive lodgings. Bring your Spanish-English dictionary; few outside the capital speak English, and you need at least a rudimentary grasp of Spanish. For purposes of exploration, the state's sights are arranged in three distinct regions.

The northern interior, along Carretera 261 and 180, contains the ruins of Edzná and other ancient cities and a handful of artisan villages that you can easily visit while traveling between Campeche City and Mérida or Uxmal.

Numbers in the text correspond to numbers in the margin and on the State of Campeche and Campeche City maps.

Although it may sound dauntingly ambitious to accomplish the Campeche City tour in one day, many sights described here can be seen in a few minutes. For a more leisurely approach, schedule two days. If you're venturing outside the city, plan to spend a minimum of two to five days, depending on how much you want to explore on and off the beaten path.

If you have
1 day

Almost all the interesting sights are within the city's compact historical district. You might start with a tram tour of the city's main sights. After the tour, explore **Parque Principal** ❷, stopping at the **Catedral** ❸ and at **Casa Seis** ❹, directly across the square. Take a lunch break at one of the restaurants or cafés around the main square; to see a bustling city market, head for the **Mercado Público Pedro Sainz de Baranda.** Everything closes for at least two hours between 2 and 4 for siesta, so you may want to head back to your hotel and indulge in this fine Mexican tradition. Or you can visit the tranquil botanical gardens in the **Baluarte de Santiago** ❻ (except on weekends, when it, too, closes during the midday nap). After siesta, when everything, including taxi service, returns to life, hop in a cab for a late-afternoon visit to the **Fuerte de San Miguel** and its Museum of Maya Culture. On the way back, join the locals on the **malecón** ⓮ to enjoy the sunset or a breezy walk. At 8:30 (on Tuesday, Friday, and Saturday, or nightly during holidays) head over to the **Puerta de Tierra** ❾ and the Baluarte San Francisco to view the historical light-and-sound show called "Place of the Sun." Afterward stop for a drink or late dinner on the elegant second-floor balcony of Casa Vieja, a restaurant overlooking the main square.

If you have
3 days

After a day in Campeche City, head inland the next morning to **Edzná** ㉑, a magnificently restored Maya ceremonial center an hour's ride from the city. On the way back, stop for a leisurely late-afternoon lunch at the glamorous restored hacienda **Uayamón.** Return to your Campeche City hotel, and gather for dinner with the locals at the fun, informal **Cenaduría de San Francisco,** famous for delicious fresh fruit juices and clove-spiked ham sandwiches. The next day, set out early for the **Hopelchén** ㉒ region, beyond Edzná, where you can explore one or two little-known Maya temples: **Hochob** ㉖, **Santa Rosa Xtampak** ㉔, and **Dzibilnocac** ㉕, as well as **Las Grutas de Xtacumbilxunaan** ㉓, one of the larger cave systems on the peninsula. From Hopelchén, it's as easy to continue north toward Ticul, Uxmal, or Mérida as it is to return to Campeche City.

If you have
7 days

With seven days, you can explore the southern part of the state in addition to the capital and the northern region. From Hopelchén—you can stay overnight there in very basic accommodations after spending a day exploring the area—drive three hours south to **Xpujil** ㉗ and the southern archaeological sites. To best experience the natural beauty of the rain forest and ruins, plan to spend two or three days here. **Becán** ㉘ and **Chicanná** ㉙ are within a couple of miles of Xpujil, and **Hormiguero** ㉛ and **Balamkú** ㉚ are not far off the highway, although in opposite directions. Local guides are recommended for visiting these sites, as well as for Calakmul, deep in the forests of the **Reserva de la Biosfera Calakmul** ㉜. From the Xpujil area, it's easy to return to Campeche City via the Escárcega–Champotón highway, with a stopover at **El Tigre** ㉝, a ruin two hours south of Escárcega. Or you can just as easily continue to the Caribbean coast, since you're right across the state line from Quintana Roo.

South of Campeche City, coast-hugging Carretera 180 leads to several small towns and fishing villages that have been all but eclipsed by the oil industry. From Champotón, among the largest communities, Carretera 261 continues due south, heading inland to meet with Carretera 186. This eastern-bound highway links Campeche with Chetumal, the Caribbean capital of Quintana Roo. En route are numerous Maya ruins, some a half mile or less off the highway, others deep in the biosphere and all but unreachable in rainy season. A two-lane highway now links Hopelchén, in the northeast, with the Chenes ruins in the south, off Carretera 186.

About the Restaurants

There's nothing fancy about Campeche's restaurants, but the regional cuisine is renowned throughout Mexico. Specialties include the fish and shellfish stews, cream soups, shrimp cocktails, squid and octopus, crab legs, *panuchos* (chubby rounds of fried cornmeal covered with refried beans and topped with chopped onion and shredded turkey or chicken). Because regional produce is plentiful (and foreign visitors scarce), most restaurants fall into the $ to $$ price categories. Casual attire—with the occasional exception of shorts—is fine in restaurants throughout Campeche, and reservations are not required. Despite such informality, service is usually quite attentive.

About the Hotels

Although the petroleum industry draws international business travelers to Campeche City and Ciudad del Carmen, the state's lodging choices trail those of other Mexican cities in both amenities and charm. Campeche City's hotels tend to be either moderately priced waterfront accommodations with basic amenities—air-conditioning, restaurants, bars, and swimming pools—or small downtown lodgings with thin mattresses, no-credit-card policies, and, for a small additional charge, ancient air-conditioning to supplement the ceiling fans. The best in the latter category are pleasant little hotels in refurbished early-20th-century buildings. Note that most of the less expensive hotels *include* the value-added tax in their quoted prices. That amount has been subtracted to provide a fair comparison with other hotels, so the quoted price may be slightly higher than that given here.

WHAT IT COSTS In Dollars				
$$$$	**$$$**	**$$**	**$**	**¢**
RESTAURANTS over $25	$15–$25	$10–$15	$5–$10	under $5
HOTELS over $250	$150–$250	$75–$150	$50–$75	under $50

Restaurant prices are per person, for a main course at dinner, excluding tax and tip. Hotel prices are for a standard double room on the European Plan (EP) and excluding service and 17% tax (15% Value Added Tax plus 2% hospitality tax). High season in Campeche is for holidays only, when you should expect to pay 20%–50% more.

Timing

Campechanos celebrate the Day of the Dead from October 31 to November 2. Festivities tend to be most colorful in the traditional small towns north of Campeche City, where graveyards are draped in flowers and lit with candles. In the capital, the dead are honored at home altars. At Campeche City's main plaza, municipalities from throughout the state create installations representative of their regions—with photos of deceased loved ones, flowers, incense, and favorite foods—to introduce visitors to this personal family event.

November also marks the end of the rainy season (the strongest rains fall July–September), when the hurricane threat has passed and both jungle and city foliage is at its most luxuriant. From November to March, the weather is hot but relatively dry. Both heat and humidity increase between March and June, although the rainy season brings little relief from the sweltering heat. Summer rains can cause mud slides and road closures, making it difficult to explore the more remote ruins. But some travelers thoroughly enjoy the heavy afternoon cloudbursts typical of the season. As elsewhere in Mexico, public transportation and hotels are especially crowded during the Christmas and Holy Week holidays.

CAMPECHE CITY

Campeche City has a lovely time-weathered air. There's no contrived, ultramodern tourist glitz here, just a friendly community by the sea (population 205,000). Residents are proud of their hometown's transformation from a rather run-down state capital to a United Nations' (UNESCO) historical site. Thanks to an on-and-off beautification campaign, more than 1,600 building facades have been restored, although paint in this humid climate peels readily, and upkeep is a constant challenge. Still, locals need little prompting to point out their city's beauty. In Mexico, a good-humored, open-minded attitude is described as *campechano*: quite a compliment. Perhaps this reputation accounts for the large number of Mexicans who vacation in Campeche. They represent by far the greatest number of tourists; most numerous are visitors from Mérida, Mexico City, and Puebla.

Although tourism isn't as integral to Campeche's economy as it is in Cancún or even Mérida, the city attracts its share of conventions, Mexican families on vacation, and bargain-seeking foreigners. Campeche City isn't a destination for the margarita-and-parasailing crowd. In fact, the city has no public beaches; instead, the bay is home to many small-time fishing operations. A peaceful, perfect city for wandering, Campeche's biggest appeal is its history—it's easy to imagine pirates swarming in from the sea.

Because it has been walled (though not successfully fortified) since 1686, most of the historic downtown is neatly contained in an area measuring five by nine blocks. Today, for the most part, streets running roughly north–south are even-numbered, and those running east–west are odd-numbered. The city is easily navigable—on foot, that is. Narrow cobblestone roads and lack of parking spaces can make driving frustrating, although drivers here are polite and mellow. Walking, on the other hand, is a pleasure. Though it's easy to take in Campeche in a day or two, a longer stay lets you absorb the traditional lifestyle—and maybe find a favorite café near the plaza.

On strategic corners surrounding the old city, or Viejo Campeche, stand the seven remaining *baluartes,* or bastions, in various stages of repair. These were once connected by a 3-km (2-mi) wall in a hexagonal fortification built to safeguard the city against ransacking pirates. Only bits of the wall still stand, and two stone archways—one facing the sea, the other the land—are all that remain of four gates that once provided the only access to Campeche. Although these walls provided some protection, it wasn't until 1771, when Fuerte de San Miguel was built on a hilltop outside town, that pirates finally stopped attacking the city.

Campeche was one of few walled cities in North and Central America and was built along the traditional lines of defensive Spanish settlements like Santo Domingo in the Dominican Republic, Cartagena in Colombia, and Portobello in Panama. The walls also served as a class demarcation. Within them lived the ruling elite. Outside were the barrios of blacks and mulattoes brought as slaves from Cuba, the Indians, and just about everyone else.

A Good Walk

The old city center is the best place to start a walking tour, beginning with the **Baluarte de la Soledad** ❶ ➤, which has a small Maya stelae museum. At the nearby **Parque Principal** ❷, the city's central plaza, view some of the Yucatán Peninsula's most stately Spanish colonial architecture, including the **Catedral de la Inmaculada Concepción** ❸ and, on the opposite side of the street, the **Casa Seis** ❹. On Calle 10 between Calles 51 and 53 is the **Mansión Carvajal** ❺, now home to government offices but still worth a peek inside. **Baluarte de Santiago** ❻ is about one block north and one west, on Calle 8 at the corner of Calle 51. Head away from the bay on Calle 51 several blocks to the small, well-fortified **Baluarte de San Pedro** ❼ at Circuito Baluartes Norte and Avenida Gobernadores. Walk south along Calle 18 to **Puerta de Tierra** ❽ and the

6

Archaeology

Of all the states in the peninsula, Campeche has the most buried Maya cities. These embrace a wealth of architectural styles, each characteristic of a different era. Elaborate geometric patterns and Chaac rain-god masks adorn Chenes-style facades typically found in central and southern Campeche. The giant zoomorphic masks surrounding doorways symbolize the open mouth of Itzamná; passing through the jaws of the creator-god was a symbolic act of rejuvenation for priests and some lucky ordinary people. The Río Bec style, found in the southern jungles, has several signature characteristics, including false stairways and round-edged lateral towers of equal height. Roof combs and an architectural trick called false perspective make the towers seem larger than they actually are. The Río Bec style borrowed its large platforms and plazas from the Petén style characteristic of northern Guatemala, but it can also be seen at several southern Campeche sites.

Visiting the ruins—with the exception of Edzná, just outside Campeche City—requires driving hundreds of highway miles to the most remote part of the Yucatán Peninsula. The two-lane roads are generally in fair condition, but have many potholes. Unlike the crowded, better-known sites such as Chichén Itzá, many ruins in Campeche attract only a handful of visitors. In the wilds of Calakmul, you can hang out with families of howler monkeys whose eerie roars sound much like those of the more elusive jaguar. Even at the more accessible sites, you can hear and see all manner of exotic birds and butterflies. Archaeological sites are open daily 8–5.

Architecture

Butter yellow, dill and olive green, tan, peach, and blue-gray—Campeche City's 16th- to 19th-century buildings are a palate of hues uncommonly subtle for Mexico. Usually trimmed in cream or white, the facades of one- and two-story houses and civic and religious structures in the heart of the once-walled city require constant maintenance. Many historic buildings now house hotels, photocopy stores, boutiques, bakeries, and schools, but UNESCO guidelines prohibit the use of neon signs, posters, and other modern trappings. The prevalence of well-preserved architecture from an earlier era makes this colonial city a good place to walk and an excellent backdrop for photos.

Another reason to photograph the inner city, and the reason that it survived arson and looting to be enjoyed by today's visitors, are the yards-thick walls that once surrounded the pirate-plagued port. Built after repeated sackings by bloodthirsty buccaneers from the 16th to 18th century, the hexagonal fortification originally enclosed the city—or at least the well-to-do. The remnants of these walls, along with seven of eight original bulwarks that have been restored or rebuilt, can all be seen in the city center. Two of four gates—which provided the only access to the old city—also remain. Facing the bay, but today several blocks from the seaside promenade, the Puerta del Mar was built to admit cargo-laden ships attempting to avoid last-minute looting by pirates lying in wait. On the inland side of the city, the old land gate is now the setting for elaborate if unsophisticated music and dance revues portraying the city's colorful heritage.

Dining Local seafood delicacies include the famous famously succulent baby shrimp from the coastal town of Champotón; *pan de cazón* (baby shark cooked, shredded, and layered with tortillas, tomato sauce, and black beans); red snapper wrapped in banana leaves; *camarones al coco* (fried shrimp with a crispy layer of coconut); *pulpo en su tinto* (octopus stewed and served in its own ink); and crayfish claws. Other popular dishes are *pollo alcaparrado* (chicken with a sauce of capers, olives, saffron, and chiles) and *papadzules* (tortillas stuffed with hard-boiled eggs and covered with a pumpkin and tomato sauce).

Fruits are served fresh, added to breads, made into liqueurs and conserves, or marinated in rum or vinegar. The most plentiful are mango, papaya, *zapote* (sapodilla), *sapote mamey* (a sweet, fleshy fruit the size of a mango), *guanabana* (soursop), tamarind, melon, pineapple, and coconut.

Ecotourism Ecotourism in Campeche is in its infancy; there's little infrastructure and few foreign tourists compared with those who visit Quintana Roo and Yucatán states. Nonetheless, state, federal, and private entities are working to preserve Campeche's wilderness. Southern Campeche contains one of the last primary growth rain forests in Mexico, legally protected under UNESCO's Man and the Biosphere program as the Reserva de la Biosfera Calakmul. It adjoins the much larger Reserva de la Biosfera Maya across the Guatemalan border, as well as a smaller reserve in Belize. Most of the conservation area is inaccessible except to locals and dedicated adventurers, who, à la Indiana Jones, are prepared to hire a local guide and begin bushwhacking. In the biosphere's most accessible sections, a few rutted roads lead to archaeological sites. Most impressive is Calakmul itself, home to orchids and jungle wildlife, including spider monkeys, peccaries, boa constrictors, and hundreds of species of birds.

The petroleum industry has taken its toll on parts of Campeche; as a result, the state has evolved into one of Mexico's most environmentally aware regions. Because it's primarily an agricultural society, Campeche hasn't undergone urban sprawl or global commercialization—meaning it still has something left to preserve. For the most part, the people of Campeche, with their cultural traditions of respect for the land, support ecotourism.

The conservation movement is in its infancy, but is already growing rapidly. Most ruins have ecologically sensitive restrooms, and members of the *ejidos* (land collectives) have participated in government-sponsored ecotourism workshops, seminars, and training courses.

Baluarte San Francisco; then take **Calle 59** ❾ past the **Iglesia y Ex-Convento de San Roque** ❿. Continuing to Calle 8, turn south (left) and proceed to **Baluarte de San Carlos** ⓫, at Calle 63, the bastion that once was connected to the Puerta de Tierra. From there, head to the **Ex-Templo de San José** ⓬ and then the **Iglesia de San Román** ⓭. Both are fine examples of colonial religious architecture. Finish the walk along the beachfront **malecón** ⓮.

What to See

⓫ Baluarte de San Carlos. Named for Charles II, King of Spain, this bastion, where Calle 8 curves around and becomes Circuito Baluartes, houses the **Museo de la Ciudad.** The free museum contains a small collection of historical artifacts, including several Spanish suits of armor and a beautifully inscribed silver scepter. Visit the basement dungeon where captured pirates were jailed, then head to the rooftop for an ocean view that's particularly stunning at sunset. ⊠ *Calle 8 between Calles 65 and 63, Circuito Baluartes, Centro* ☎ *No phone* ⬚ *Free* ⊙ *Tues.–Sun. 8–7.*

❼ Baluarte de San Pedro. Built in 1686 to protect the city from pirate attacks, this bastion's thick walls, flanked by watchtowers, now house a handicrafts-and-souvenir shop. It's also a satellite office for the Secretary of Tourism, which can book an English-speaking guide for you. Many tours to the ruins of Calakmul, Edzná, and other sites depart from here. ⊠ *Calles 18 and 51, Circuito Baluartes, Centro* ☎ *981/813–3788 (for guides only)* ⬚ *Free* ⊙ *Daily 9–1 and 5–8.*

❻ Baluarte de Santiago. The last of the bastions to be built (1704) has been transformed into the **X'much Haltún Botanical Gardens.** It houses more than 200 plant species, including the enormous *ceiba* tree, which had spiritual importance to the Maya, symbolizing a link between heaven, earth, and the underworld. Although the original bastion was demolished at the turn of the 20th century, and then rebuilt in the 1950s, the fort still resembles others in Campeche; it's a stone fortress with thick walls, watchtowers, and gunnery slits. ⊠ *Calles 8 and 49, Circuito Baluartes, Centro* ☎ *No phone* ⬚ *Free* ⊙ *Weekdays 9–9, Sat. 9–1 and 5–8, Sun. 9–1.*

★ ❶ Baluarte de la Soledad. Originally built to protect the **Puerta de Mar,** a sea gate that was one of four entrances to the city, this bastion stands on the west side of Parque Principal. Because it uses no supporting walls, it resembles a Roman triumphal arch. The largest of the bastions, it has comparatively complete parapets and embrasures that offer sweeping views of the cathedral, municipal buildings, and the old houses along Calle 8. Inside is the **Museo de las Estelas** with artifacts that include a well-preserved sculpture of a man wearing an owl mask, columns from Edzná and Isla Jaina, and at least a dozen well-proportioned Maya stelae from ruins throughout Campeche. ⊠ *Calles 8 between Calles 55 and 57, Centro* ☎ *No phone* ⬚ *$2.50* ⊙ *Tues.–Sun. 8–7:30.*

❾ Calle 59. Some of Campeche's finest homes once stood on this city street between Calles 8 and 18. Most were two stories high, with the ground floors serving as warehouses and the upper floors as residences. These days, behind the delicate grillwork and lace curtains, you can glimpse genteel scenes of Campeche life, with faded lithographs on the dun-color walls and plenty of antique furniture and gilded mirrors. The best-preserved houses are those between Calles 14 and 18; many closer to the sea have been remodeled or destroyed by fire. Campeche's INAH (Instituto Nacional de Antropología e Historia) office, between Calles 16 and 14, is an excellent example of one of Campeche City's fine old homes. Each month, INAH displays a different archaeological artifact in its

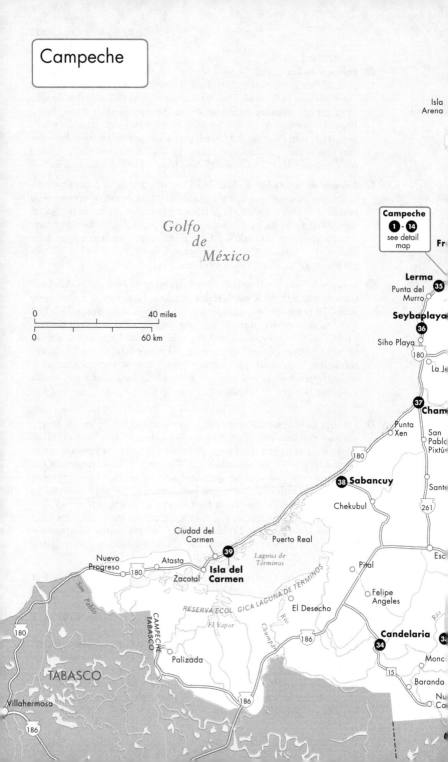

Campeche

Golfo
de
México

Isla
Arena

Campeche
1 · **14**
see detail
map

Fr

Lerma
Punta del
Murro

35

Seybaplaya

36

Siho Playa
180

La Je

37 Cham

Punta
Xen

San
Pablo
Pixtú

180

38 **Sabancuy**

Sante

261

Chekubul

Ciudad del
Carmen

Nuevo
Progreso   Atasta

180

Zacatal

39

Isla del
CARMEN

Puerto Real

Laguna de
Términos

Pital

Esc

Felipe
Angeles

San Pablo

TABASCO

Villahermosa

186

CAMPECHE
TABASCO

Palizada

RESERVA ECOL GICA LAGUNA DE TÉRMINOS

El Vapor

Río Chumpán

El Desecho

186

Candelaria

34

15

Monc

Baranda

Nu
Co

0   40 miles
0   60 km

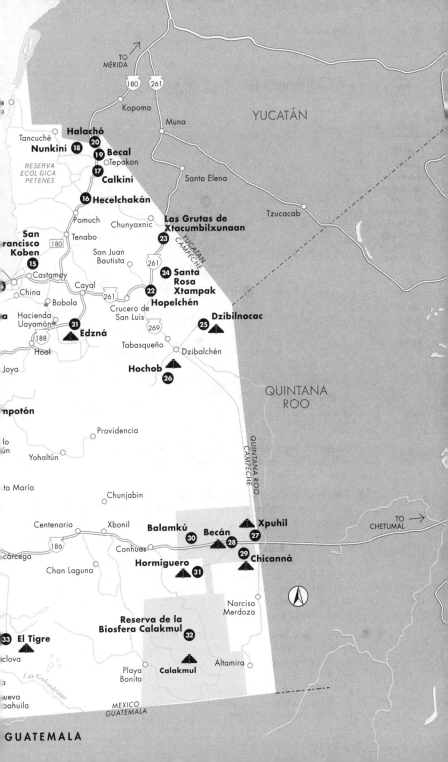

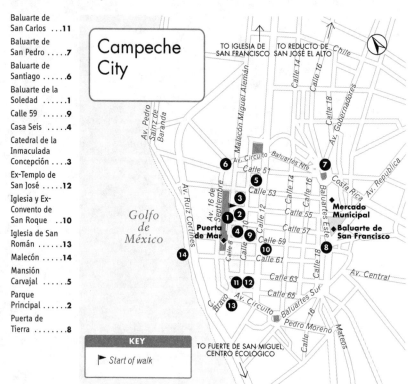

courtyard. Look for the names of the apostles carved into the lintels of houses between Calles 16 and 18, called "Calle de los Santos," or "street of saints."

❹ Casa Seis. One of the first colonial homes in Campeche is now a cultural center. It has been fully restored—rooms are furnished with original antiques and a few reproductions, creating an authentic replica of a typical colonial house. The original frescoes at the tops of the walls remain, some dating from 1500. The courtyard has Moorish architecture offset by 18th-century stained-glass windows; it's used as an area for exhibits, lectures, and performances. The small restaurant off the original kitchen area serves excellent local specialities daily 9–2 and 6–9. ⊠ *Calle 57 between Calles 10 and 8, Plaza Principal, Centro* ☎ *981/816–1782* ☜ *Free* ☉ *Daily 9–9.*

★ ❸ Catedral de la Inmaculada Concepción. It took two centuries (from 1650 to 1850) to finish the Cathedral of the Immaculate Conception, and as a result, it incorporates both neoclassical and Renaissance elements. The simple exterior is capped with two tall towers rising on each side of the gracefully curved stone entrance, and the fluted pilasters echo the towers' design. Sculptures of saints in niches resemble those found in French Gothic cathedrals. The interior is no less impressive, with its limestone nave supported by Doric columns, huge octagonal dome, and black-and-white marble floor. The high point, however, is the magnificent Holy Sepulchre, carved from ebony and decorated with a multitude of stamped silver angels. ⊠ *Calle 55 between Calles 8 and 10, Plaza Principal, Centro* ⊙ *Daily 6 AM–9 PM.*

Centro Ecológico de Campeche. High on a hill near the San Miguel Fort, this zoo, botanical garden, and playground offers guided flora and fauna tours, games and activities for children, and educational lectures. On weekends it becomes a favorite picnic spot for city dwellers seeking fresh air. ⊠ *Av. Escénica s/n, Col. Fuerte San Miguel* ☎ *No phone* 🎫 *Donation requested* ⊙ *Tues.–Fri. 9–1, weekends 10–4:30.*

⑫ Ex-Templo de San José. The Jesuits built this fine Baroque church in honor of Saint Joseph in 1756. Its block-long facade and portal are covered with blue-and-yellow Talavera tiles and crowned with seven narrow stone finials—resembling both the roof combs on many Maya temples and the combs Spanish women once wore in their elaborate hairdos. Next door is the **Instituto Campechano**, used for cultural events and art exhibitions. These events and exhibits are regularly held here Tuesday evening at 7 PM; at other times you can ask the guard (who should be somewhere on the grounds) to let you in. From the outside, you can admire Campeche's first lighthouse, built in 1864, now perched atop the right tower. ⊠ *Calles 10 and 65, Centro* ☎ *No phone.*

★ Fuerte de San Miguel. Near the city's southwest end, Avenida Ruíz Cortínez winds its way to this hilltop fort with its sweeping view of the Bay of Campeche. Built between 1779 and 1801 and dedicated to the archangel Michael, the fort was positioned to bombard enemy ships with its long-range cannons. As soon as it was completed, pirates stopped attacking the city. Its impressive cannons were fired only once, in 1842, when General Santa Anna used Fuerte de San Miguel to put down a revolt by Yucatecan separatists seeking independence from Mexico. The fort houses the **Museo de la Cultura Maya,** whose exhibits include the skeletons of long-ago Maya royals, complete with jewelry and pottery, which were found in Calakmul tombs. Also noteworthy are funeral vessels, masks, many wonderfully expressive figurines and whistles from Isla Jaina, stelae and stucco masks from the Maya ruins, and an excellent pottery collection. Although most information is in Spanish (computers have some information in English), that's no reason to skip these exhibits. The gift shop sells replicas of artifacts. ⊠ *Av. Francisco Morazán s/n, west of town center, Col. Fuerte San Miguel* ☎ *No phone* 🎫 *$2.50* ⊙ *Tues.–Sun. 9–8:30.*

Iglesia de San Francisco. Outside the city center in a residential neighborhood, the beautifully restored Church of Saint Francis is Campeche's oldest. It marks the spot where, some say, the first Mass on the North American continent was held in 1517—though the same claim has been made for Veracruz and Cozumel. One of Cortés's grandsons was baptized here, and the baptismal font still stands. ⊠ *Avs. Miguel Alemán and Mariano Escobedo, San Francisco* ⊙ *Daily 8–noon and 5–7.*

⑩ Iglesia y Ex-Convento de San Roque. With its elaborately carved main altarpiece and matching side altars framed in elaborate floral motifs, this long, narrow church adds to historic Calle 59's old-fashioned beauty. Built in 1565, it was originally called Iglesia de San Francisco; in addition to a statue of Saint Francis, humbler-looking saints peer out from behind glass in smaller niches. ⊠ *Calles 12 and 59, Centro* ☉ *Daily 8:30–noon and 5–7.*

⑬ Iglesia de San Román. Just outside the intramural boundary in the barrio of the same name, this church was built to house the *naboríos*—Indians brought by the Spaniards to aid in the conquest and work as household servants. Built in the early 16th century, the church became central to the lives of the Indians when an ebony image of Jesus, the "Black Christ," was brought from Italy in about 1575. The Indians had been skeptical of Christianity, but this Christ figure came to be associated with miracles. As legend has it, a ship that refused to carry the tradesman and his statue was wrecked, while the ship that accepted him reached Campeche in record time. To this day, the Feast of San Román—when worshippers carry a black-wood Christ and a silver filigree cross through the streets—remains a solemn but colorful affair. ⊠ *Calles 10 and Bravo, San Román* ☉ *Daily 7–1 and 3–7.*

★ ⑭ Malecón. A broad sidewalk more than 5 km (3 mi) long runs the length of Campeche's waterfront boulevard, from northeast of the Debliz hotel to the Justo Sierra Méndez monument at the southwest edge of downtown. With its landscaping, sculptures, rest areas, and fountains lit up at night in neon colors, the promenade attracts joggers, strollers, and families. On weekend nights, students turn the malecón into a party zone. Some of the city's best restaurants are across busy Avenida Ruíz Cortínez, which runs parallel to the walkway.

❺ Mansión Carvajal. Built in the early 20th century by one of the Yucatán's wealthiest plantation owners, this eclectic mansion logged time as the Hotel Señorial before becoming an office for the state-run Family Institute. The black-and-white tile floor, Art Nouveau staircase with Carrera marble steps and iron balustrade, and blue-and-white Moorish arcades are reminders of the city's heyday, when Campeche was the peninsula's only port. ⊠ *Calle 10 No. 584, between Calles 51 and 53, Centro* ☎ *981/816–7644* ⊡ *Free* ☉ *Weekdays 8–2.*

Mercado Municipal. To find the city's heart, visit its municipal market, where locals shop for seafood, produce, and housewares. Beside the market is a small yellow bridge aptly named **Puente de Perro**—four white plaster dogs guard the area. ⊠ *Av. Baluartes Este and Calle 53, Centro* ☉ *Daily dawn–dusk.*

★ ❷ Parque Principal. Also known as the Plaza de la Independencia, this central park hosts many events, including weekend concerts and dance performances. In its center is an old-fashioned gazebo with a pleasant café-bar where you can sit and watch city residents out for an evening stroll. ⊠ *Bounded by Calles 10, 8, 55, and 57, Centro.*

🕐 **⑧ Puerta de Tierra.** Old Campeche ends here; the Land Gate is the only one of the four city gates with its basic structure intact. The stone arch intercepts a stretch of the partially crenulated wall, 26 feet high and 10 feet thick, that once encircled the city. Walk the wall's full length to the **Baluarte San Juan** for excellent views of both the old and new cities. The staircase leads down to an old well, underground storage area, and dungeon. There is a two-hour light show ($2), accompanied by music and dance, at Puerta de Tierra; it's presented in Spanish with French and English subtitles. Shows are on Tuesday, Friday, and Saturday at 8:30 PM, and daily during spring, summer, and Christmas vacation periods. ✉ *Calles 18 and 59, Centro* ⊙ *Daily 8–9.*

🕐 **Reducto de San José el Alto.** This lofty *redoubt,* or stronghold, at the northwest end of town, is home to the **Museo de Armas y Barcos.** Displays focus on 18th-century weapons of siege and defense. Also look for ships in bottles, manuscripts, and religious art. The view is terrific from the top of the ramparts, which were used to spot invading ships. The "El Guapo" tram ($7) makes the trip daily at 9 AM, 11 AM, and 5 PM, departing from the east side of the main plaza. Visitors get about 10 minutes to admire the view before continuing to Fuerte de San Miguel and the main plaza. ✉ *Av. Escénica s/n, north of downtown, Reducto de San José* 📞 *No phone* 💲 *$2.20* ⊙ *Tues.–Sun. 8–8.*

Where to Eat

$$–$$$ ✕ **Hot Beach Pizza.** The two branches of this restaurant live up to their name: both are near the beach, and the pizza is hot. The most popular pie is the *mexicana,* with ham and hot jalapeño peppers. For vegetarians, there's a veggie version with fresh tomato, onion, and mild peppers. Open 2 PM–11 PM, Hot Beach delivers to your hotel room, or you can dine on-site. ✉ *Av. Resurgimiento 57, Malecón* 📞 *981/811–1133* ▭ *No credit cards* ✉ *Bajos Portales de San Francisco, San Francisco* 📞 *981/811–3131* ▭ *No credit cards.*

$–$$$ ✕ **Marganzo.** Traditional Campeche cuisine is served by a traditionally attired waitstaff at this colorful restaurant a half block south of the plaza. It's frequented equally by tour groups and locals out to lunch. The *pompano en escabeche* (fish marinated in sour orange juice and grilled with chiles) and the fresh shrimp dishes are good choices. Hours are 7 AM to 11 PM. ✉ *Calle 8 No. 267, between Calles 57 and 59, Centro* 📞 *981/ 811–3898* ▭ *MC, V.*

$–$$$
Fodor's Choice
★
✕ **La Pigua.** This spot is where local professionals go to linger over lunch. The seafood is delicious, and the setting is unusual: glass walls replicate an oblong Maya house, incorporating the profusion of plants outside into a design element. A truly ambitious lunch might start with a seafood cocktail, a plate of stone crab claws, or *camarones al coco* (coconut-encrusted shrimp), followed by fresh local fish, pampano, prepared in one of many ways. For dessert, the classic choice is *ate,* slabs of super-condensed mango, sweet potato, or other fruit or vegetable jelly served with Gouda cheese. It's open noon to 6. ✉ *Av. Miguel Alemán 179A, Col. San Martin* 📞 *981/811–3365* ▭ *AE, D, MC, V* ⊙ *No dinner.*

★ $ ✕ **Casa Vieja.** The menu here offers a rich mix of international dishes, including those from the owners' native lands: Cuba and Campeche. In addition to pastas, salads, and regional food, there's an extensive selection of aperitifs and digestifs. Whether you're having a meal or a sunset cocktail, try to snag a table on the outdoor balcony for a fabulous view overlooking Campeche's main plaza. The interior is usually warm and humid, with tropical music and brightly painted walls crammed with art. To get here look for the stairway on the plaza's east side. ⊠ *Calle 10 No. 319 Altos, between Calles 57 and 55, Centro* ☎ *981/811–8016* ▤ *No credit cards.*

$ ✕ **Sir Francis Drink.** Under the same management as La Pigua next door, this spot caters to a more laid-back crowd: if kids tire of adult conversation, they can romp on the brightly colored play equipment out front. Regional seafood and meat dishes are a specialty here. There's an extensive breakfast menu, with lots of fresh juices and shakes. For lunch, feast on octopus with golden garlic, *carne asada* (thin strips of grilled pork or beef) with steamed vegetables and rice, or *calamares Sir Francis Drink* (squid sautéed in olive oil with almonds and guajillo chiles). ⊠ *Av. Miguel Alemán 179, Col. San Martin* ☎ *981/816–4636* ▤ *MC, V* ⊗ *No dinner.*

★ ¢–$ ✕ **Cenaduría los Portales.** Campechano families come here to enjoy a light supper, perhaps a sandwich *claveteado* (a honey-and-clove-flavored ham or turkey sandwich) or panuchos, along with a typical drink such as *horchata* (rice water flavored with cinnamon). Although the place opens at 6 PM, most people come between 8 and midnight. Mark your choices on the paper menu: for tacos, "m" means "masa," or corn tortillas, while "h" stands for "harina," or flour. The dining area is a wide colonial veranda with tables decked out in checkered tablecloths. After eating, you can walk off your meal with a stroll around Plaza San Francisco. ⊠ *Calle 10 No. 86, at Portales San Francisco, 8 blocks northeast of Plaza Principal, San Francisco* ☎ *981/811–1491* ▤ *No credit cards* ⊗ *No lunch.*

¢–$ ✕ **La Parroquia.** The large entrance to La Parroquia, which faces Calle 55, is the best place in town for people-watching. Open 24 hours, this restaurant is a real locals' den—a comfortable family place with plastic tablecloths, a large menu, slow service, and televisions tuned to Mexican soccer. Feast on inexpensive fried pompano, breaded shrimp, *pan de cazón* (shredded shark layered with tortillas, tomato sauce, and black beans), or spaghetti, or just have a sandwich. Beer and tequila are also available. ⊠ *Calle 55 No. 8, between Calles 10 and 12, Centro* ☎ *981/816–2530* ▤ *No credit cards.*

¢–$ ✕ **Restaurant Campeche.** The open doorways of this bright, clean eatery look out onto the central plaza. Popular with locals and visitors in nearly equal proportions, the bustling restaurant serves hearty Mexican and regional dishes; its upholstered chairs provide relief from Campeche's ubiquitous hard wooden seats. The menu includes everything from burgers and fries to tacos and chicken mole (served in a chocolate-chile sauce). It's open from 6:30 AM to midnight. Breakfast items like pancakes and eggs are served all day, although the numbered specials are available in the morning only. For lunch or dinner try the *camarones tropi-*

cales, shrimp served with mango sauce, rice, and steamed veggies. ⊠ *Calle 57 at the main plaza, Centro* ☎ *981/816–2128* ⊟ *MC, V.*

¢ ✕ **Las Puertas.** Popular with students and java-lovers of all ages, this convivial café is at the back of a handicrafts-and-folk-art store. In additional to cappuccino and espresso, you can get cake, pastries, soft drinks, and light fare such as burritos. It's also an informal gallery, and the artwork on the walls is usually for sale. ⊠ *Calle 10 No. 256, between Calles 59 and 61, Centro* ☎ *981/811–4694* ⊟ *No credit cards.*

Where to Stay

$$ ▦ **Del Mar Hotel.** Rooms here are fairly plain, with understated furniture, blue and beige upholstery, tile floors, faux-rattan furniture, and tiny triangular balconies that overlook the pool or the bay across the street. The coffee shop, El Poquito, serves standard but tasty fare, and Lafitte's pirate-theme bar-restaurant—one of the city's most enduring nightlife spots—offers room service until 2 AM. There's a dearth of shade around the small pool, where swimmers are rarely seen. ⊠ *Av. Ruíz Cortínez 51, Centro, 24000* ☎ *981/811–9191* 🖷 *981/811–9192* ⊕ *www.delmarhotel.com.mx* ⇆ *138 rooms, 11 suites* ᾆ *Restaurant, coffee shop, room service, in-room data ports, some minibars, cable TV, pool, bar, nightclub, shop, laundry service, Internet, meeting rooms, car rental, travel services, free parking* ⊟ *AE, MC, V.*

$ ▦ **Baluartes.** Between the waterfront and the Puerta del Mar (gateway to the old city), the modern Baluartes has an attractive lounge area with plump, ocean-blue sofas surrounding small round tables. Many of the light-filled rooms have sea views; all are done in pastels with bright print bedspreads and accessories, and the comfy beds have firm mattresses and individual reading lamps. Although the rooms don't have balconies, their windows open, and floors two through four have views of the sea. Lacy palm trees with blue-and-white-striped trunks shade the plastic lounge chairs surrounding the large pool, which overlooks the ocean across the street. ⊠ *Av. 16 de Septiembre 128, Centro, 24000* ☎ *981/816–3911* 🖷 *981/816–2410* ⊕ *www.baluartes.com. mx* ⇆ *100 rooms* ᾆ *Restaurant, coffee shop, room service, in-room data ports, in-room safes, cable TV, pool, bar, nightclub, shop, laundry service, business services, meeting rooms, car rental, travel services, free parking* ⊟ *AE, MC, V.*

$ ▦ **Del Paseo.** A block from the ocean, this comely but fading hotel lies in the quiet neighborhood of San Román, about a 10-minute walk from the main square. Rooms are neither modern nor fancy, with painted rattan furniture and either one double bed or two tiny twins. Some have balconies. The hotel's draws are its central but quiet location, proximity to the malecón, and several handy businesses, including a beauty shop and a travel agency, which are available in the same complex. ⊠ *Calle 8 No. 215, San Román, 24000* ☎ *981/811–0077 or 981/811–0100* 🖷 *981/811–0097* ⊕ *www.hoteldelpaseo.8k.com* ⇆ *48 rooms, 2 suites* ᾆ *Restaurant, room service, in-room data ports, bar, shop, laundry service, Internet, business services, car rental, travel services, free parking* ⊟ *AE, MC, V.*

$ ⊞ **Francis Drake.** This small spiffy hotel sits right in the center of town. Its rooms offer few amenities, but their yellow walls, ocean-blue drapes, and bright patterned curtains and spreads lend a cheerful air. The restaurant is a bit sterile, and there is no bar or other place for guests to mingle. This is a good destination if you're looking for modest facilities without in-house social diversions. ⊠ *Calle 12 No. 207, between Calles 63 and 65, Centro, 24000* ☎ *981/811–5626 or 981/811–5628* 🖷 *981/811–5628* ⊕ *www.hotelfrancisdrake.com* ↩ *9 rooms, 15 suites* ⚐ *Restaurant, room service, some in-room data ports, some in-room safes, minibars, cable TV, shop, laundry service, free parking* ⊟ *AE, MC, V.*

$ ⊞ **Hotel Plaza Campeche.** This hotel is formal and elegant, with plush sofas and heavy floor-to-ceiling drapes in the lobby, and a rather fussy-looking restaurant. Rooms are pleasant and modern, with firm mattresses, digital air-conditioning units, and green tile work. All bathrooms have tubs. ⊠ *Calle 10 No. 126A, Centro, 24000* ☎ *981/811–9900* ↩ *82 rooms, 1 suite* ⚐ *Restaurant, café, fans, in-room data ports, cable TV, pool, bar, laundry service, business services, meeting room, free parking* ⊟ *MC, V.*

¢–$ ⊞ **Hotel América.** A converted colonial home, the aged America has scuffed black-and-white-checked floors offsetting white Moorish arches. There's a small, formal sitting area near the front door and a plainer but quieter place to gather or play cards on the second floor's central interior balcony. Breakfast is served at the umbrella-shaded tables on the ground-floor patio. Rooms themselves are simple and plain with local television only, and bamboo or pressed-wood furniture. This is one of the few hotels in the town center with parking, and you can check your e-mail for free at the front desk. ⊠ *Calle 10 No. 252, Centro, 24000* ☎ *981/816–4588 or 981/816–4576* 🖷 *981/816–0556* ⊕ *www.hotelamericacampeche.com* ↩ *49 rooms* ⚐ *Fans, free parking; no a/c in some rooms* ⊟ *AE, MC, V* ⁝◎⁝ *CP.*

¢ ⊞ **Colonial.** This romantic building dates from 1812 but was converted into a hotel in the 1940s, when its colorful tiles were added. Rooms vary, but all have thin mattresses, tile bathrooms with curtainless showers, and window screens. The original plumbing still works quite well. Rooms 16, 18, 27, and 28 have wonderful cathedral views at night. Rooms with air-conditioning cost a bit more, but even these are surprisingly inexpensive. The owners' refusal to modernize with phones, in-room TVs, or Internet access permits the rock-bottom prices. Public areas include a small sunroof and a second-floor sitting room. ⊠ *Calle 14 No. 122, between Calles 55 and 57, Centro, 24000* ☎ *981/816–2222 or 981/816–2630* ↩ *30 rooms* ⚐ *Fans; no a/c in some rooms, no room phones, no room TVs* ⊟ *No credit cards.*

¢ ⊞ **Debliz.** Northeast of the town center, this large hotel caters to tour groups. Although the rather faded exterior and the lobby look like those of an office building, the pool and deck areas—surrounded by bright pink and purple walls and hibiscus and bamboo plants—are more attractive. Rooms have modern wood furnishings, light tile floors, brown floral cotton bedspreads, and plush built-in headboards. Each room includes a small table and two chairs, but their tiny balconies have no furniture. You have to take a cab to the historical center—it's a bit too far to walk. ⊠ *Av. Diá Ordaz 55, Col. La Ermita, 24020* ☎ *981/815–2222* 🖷 *981/815–2277* 🖙 *137 rooms, 6 suites* ⌂ *Restaurant, snack bar, in-room data ports, cable TV, pool, bar, laundry service, meeting room, free parking* ⊟ *AE, MC, V.*

¢ 🖳 **Monkey Hostel.** While typically attracting a youthful international crowd, this friendly hostel overlooking the city's main plaza offers refuge for penny-pinching older travelers as well. It's got multilingual managers, a common kitchen and laundry facilities, a book exchange–library, and a busy Internet corner. If you're lucky enough to get them, the two private rooms are a super deal. Other accommodations include men's, women's, and coed dorm rooms, each with four bunk beds. Linens and storage boxes are provided. ⊠ *Calles 57 and 10, Centro 24000* ☎ *981/ 811–6500, 01800/CAM–PECHE toll-free outside Campeche City* ⊕ *www.hostalcampeche.com* 🖙 *2 private rooms without bath; 3 8-bed dorm rooms without bath* ⌂ *Dining room, fans, bicycles, laundry facilities, Internet, travel services; no a/c, no room phones, no room TVs* ⊟ *MC, V* 🍽 *CP.*

Nightlife & the Arts

Each Saturday evening from 7 to 10:30 PM, the streets around the main square are closed to traffic and filled with folk and popular dance performances, singers, comics, handicrafts, and food and drink stands. If you're in town on a Saturday evening, don't miss these weekly festivities, called *Campechanísimo* (which roughly translates as "Really Really Campeche")—the entertainment is often first-rate and always free. In December, concerts and other cultural events take place as part of the Festival del Centro Histórico. The Serenata Campechana is a free hour of *trova* (romantic trio music), held Thursday at 8:30 PM at Casa Seis. You can order snacks and nonalcoholic drinks on the back patio.

Bars & Discos

Campeche residents generally aren't big dancers, so their discos are mainly open on weekends. **Iguana Azul** (⊠ Calle 55 No. 11, between Calles 10 and 12, Centro ☎ 981/811–1311 or 981/816–2248), open daily after 6 PM, is a tranquil watering hole and a good place to have a few regional appetizers with drinks. There's one pool table.

Among the most enduring discos is **KY8** (⊠ Calle 8 between Calles 59 and 61, Centro ☎ No phone), open Friday and Saturday only, which plays disco music downstairs, with rock upstairs for the slightly older crowd. **Shooters** (⊠ Av. Resurgimiento at Calle Lazareto, Montecristo ☎ No phone) is a both a dance venue and an upper-end bar with billiards tables; it's popular with people who like being able to converse above the music. It's closed Monday.

Film

Cinema Hollywood (⊠ Lote 2, Manzana D, Zona Turística Ah Kim Pech, Centro ☎ 981/816–1452) is close to the malecón and Plaza Comercial Ah-Kim-Pech and has six large screens showing the latest blockbuster movies. Most are in English with Spanish subtitles.

Sports & Outdoors

Fishing and bird-watching are popular throughout the state of Campeche. Contact **Fernando Sansores** (✉ Calle 30 No. 1, Centro ☎☎ 981/828–0018) at the Snook Inn to arrange area sportfishing or wildlife photo excursions. **Francisco Javier Hernandez Romero** (✉ La Pigua restaurant, Av. Miguel Alemán 179A, Centro ☎ 981/811–3365) can arrange boat or fishing trips to the Reserva Ecológica Peténes. To enjoy a tour of Campeche Bay and the surrounding area, contact the **Marina Yacht Club** (✉ Av. Resurgimiento 120, Carretera a Lerma ☎☎ 981/816–1990). Times and duration of tours are per customer requests. Call ahead to make a reservation.

Shopping

Although Campeche's handicrafts have traditionally been limited to baskets, straw hats, embroidered cloth, and clay trinkets, a few stores provide stylish women's clothing and slightly more sophisticated souvenirs. Folk art is still rather limited, however, and most shops are dominated by ships in bottles, statues made of seashells, and mother-of-pearl and black-coral jewelry. Be aware that buying black coral is environmentally incorrect, since coral reefs take thousands of years to grow.

Districts & Malls

Visit the **Mercado Público Pedro Sainz de Baranda** (✉ Av. Circuito Baluartes Este between Calles 51 and 55, Centro) for food and craft items. Campeche City has two large modern shopping malls within walking distance of each other. **Plaza Comercial Ah-Kim-Pech** (✉ Avs. Pedro Sainz de Baranda and Ruíz Cortínez, Centro), on the waterfront, has boutiques, clothing, and souvenir shops, as well as a grocery store. Not far from Plaza Comercial Ah-Kim-Pech, **Plaza del Mar** (✉ Av. Ruíz Cortínez s/n, Centro) is closest to the center of town and home to a number of specialty stores. **Plaza Universidad** (✉ Avs. Agustín Melgar and Universidad, Universidad) has several good jewelry stores and boutiques.

Specialty Shops

CLOTHING **Códice** (✉ Calle 10 No. 256, between Calles 59 and 61, Centro ☎ 981/
★ 811–4694) carries an organic-looking line of women's dresses, skirts, and blouses made with muslin, cotton, and other natural fibers. They also have tasteful T-shirts and hats and bags made of dyed or natural palm fiber. Right on the main square, **Liz Minelli** (✉ Calle 10 No. 319A, Los Portales, Centro ☎ 981/811–6814) offers an impressive selection of glad rags for women, including swingy dresses in clingy materials. There are also short, ruffled tops and skirts and dresses in mixed fibers, as well as suits, jackets, jean jackets, ball gowns, and a selection of sexy undies.

CRAFTS In an old mansion, the government-run **Casa de Artesanía Tukulna**
★ (✉ Calle 10 No. 333, between Calles 59 and 61, Centro ☎ 981/816–9088) sells well-made embroidered dresses, blouses, pillow coverings, regional dress for men and women, hammocks, Campeche's famous Panama hats, posters, books on Campeche ecology in Spanish, jewelry,

baskets, and stucco reproductions of Maya motifs. The house is worth a visit if only to admire its arched doorways, black-and-white tile floors, and chandeliers. It's closed Sunday.

Veleros (✉ Plaza Comercial Ah-Kim-Pech, Centro ☎ 981/811–2446) is owned by craftsman David Pérez. It stocks miniature scale-model ships, seashells, figures of carved mahogany and cedar, furniture with nautical motifs, and jewelry made from sanded and polished bull's horn—a material that somewhat resembles tortoiseshell. It's closed Sunday. Pérez's first shop, **Artesanía Típica Naval** (✉ Calle 8 No. 259, Centro ☎ 981/816–5708), is still thriving, but it's much smaller and more cramped than the mall store.

LA RUTA DE LOS ARTESANOS

The so-called short route to Mérida (192 km, or 119 mi) takes you past several traditional villages where artisans produce the state's best-known handicrafts. Many pieces are made for distribution elsewhere, so there isn't a large selection for sale here, but viewing the places where they're produced provides a glimpse of the local way of life. Also along the Artists' Route are old Franciscan churches, abandoned haciendas, and small towns where life still revolves around the market and the central plaza. Don't count on finding many people who speak English, and note that villages mentioned offer little in the way of restaurants and accommodations.

San Francisco Koben

⓯ *30 km (19 mi) north of Campeche, along Carretera 180 toward Mérida.*

This town is famous in Campeche for a ceremonial ritual in which the townspeople unearth their dead on November 1, clean off their bones, and return them to their crypts wrapped in clean cloth. It's known the rest of the year for the preserves of mangoes and other fruits that you can buy from stands lining the highway. Hammocks, textiles, and hats are also for sale. Twenty-nine kilometers (18 mi) north on Carretera 180 is the village of Tenabo, where many of the fruit preserves are made. The town of Pomuch, famous for its breads, is north of Tenabo. Stop and try a *pichón* (a large ham-and-cheeseloaf), *budín* (which is similar to bread pudding), *pan de elote* (corn bread), or an *empanada de camote* (a sweet-potato turnover).

Hecelchakán

⓰ *60 km (37 mi) north of Campeche, along Carretera 180 toward Mérida.*

A faded but still vital 15th-century town with an idiosyncratic Franciscan church and former monastery, Hecelchakán (pronounced e-sell-cha-*kan*) is a good spot to observe a small town in action and see some colonial facades. Kiosks in front of the church dispense *cochinita pibíl*, pit-baked pork, a traditional morning snack served with hot tortillas, but these days, noisy video games nearby can disrupt the experience.

On the outskirts of town are several old haciendas, such as Chunkanán, as well as the village of Dzibalchén, where the Dzibalchén Verses (descriptions of Maya ceremonies and rituals) were written. The local church dates from 1768.

Hecelchakán's primary attraction is the **Museo Arqueológico del Camino Real.** In a 1660 house, this museum has an impressive collection of clay figurines from Isla Jaina and stelae of the Puuc style. It's worth the short detour off the highway. A diorama depicts the first *mestizos*, children of the shipwrecked Spanish soldier Gonzalo Guerrero and his Indian wife. Stone ax heads, arrow points, and other primitive tools and bowls are also on display. ⊠ *Main plaza* ☎ *No phone* 🗒 *$2.40* ☉ *Daily 8–7.*

The only accessible road to **Isla Jaina,** now part of the part of the Reserva Ecológica Peténes, starts in Hecelchakán. Some say the island is a giant Maya cemetery; others claim it's an ancient city whose inhabitants buried their dead beneath their homes. Isla Jaina is off-limits without prior written permission from the Instituto Nacional de Antropología e Historia (INAH) in Campeche. The easiest way to tour the island, however, is with **Espacios Naúticos** (⇨ Tours).

Where to Stay

$$ 🏨 **Hacienda Blanca Flor.** Although it's sometimes deserted midweek and off-season (you might want to bring your own party), this restored hacienda offers a good base for exploring the northern regions of Campeche. Surrounding the ancient open patio, rooms have screened windows and loud air-conditioning. There's an outdoor pool, but no poolside furniture, and the dining room has just one long table where everyone sits. Reservations must be made in advance through the Mérida office. ⊠, ☎ *999/925–7854 or 999/925–9655* 🖷 *999/925–9111* ✉ *hblancaf@prodigy.net.mx* 🛏 *20 rooms* ⚒ *Dining room, fans, pool, horseback riding, free parking; no room phones* ▭ *No credit cards.*

Calkiní

⑰ *24 km (15 mi) north of Hecelchakán.*

Among the most important towns along the Camino Real, Calkiní dates from the pre-Colombian Maya Ah-Canul dynasty. According to a indigenous documents from the epoch, the Ah-Canul chieftainship was founded here in 1443 after the destruction of the Postclassic kingdom of Mayapán, in what is now Yucatán state. The site chosen was beneath an enormous ceiba, a tree sacred to the Maya and frequently mentioned in their legends. The Ah-Canul was the most important dynasty at the time of the Conquest, when Maya fighters who rebelled against the Spanish leader Montejo were defeated in Mérida. Today the village of Calkiní is the jumping-off point for exploring the northeastern corner of Campeche.

Calkiní's major attraction is the **Parroquia de San Luis Obispo.** Franciscan friars built this church-fortress-convent beginning in 1561, and the Clarisas have used it as a cloistered convent since 1980. You can enter the church (even if the front gate is padlocked) by asking at the office around the right side of the building, but the convent itself is off-limits. Inside the church is an exquisite carved cedar altarpiece in burnished gold, red, and black along with a handsome pulpit carved with the symbols of the four Evangelists. The portal is plateresque—a 16th-century Spanish style whose elaborate ornaments suggest silver plate—and the rest of the structure is Baroque. Both are low-key versions of the styles, due to the typically sober Franciscan tradition. The shell motif above the doorway is also typically Franciscan. ⊠ *Off the town square* 🎫 *Free* 🕙 *Wed. and Fri.–Mon. 7–noon and 3–8, Thurs. 7 AM–9 PM.*

North of town is the village of Tepakán, home of **Cal-kin** (⊠ Carretera Calkiní–Tepakán, Km 1 ☎ 996/961–0232), the ceramics factory that produces the distinctive, hand-painted white, beige, and blue ceramics of Campeche. A four-piece place setting starts at $40. The factory's small store is open weekdays 8–5, Saturday 8–4.

Nunkiní

🔞 *28 km (17 mi) west of Calkiní, look for the sign for Santa Cruz.*

In this small traditional Maya village, women weave mats and rugs from the reeds of *huano* palm, incorporating traditional designs. The colorful church of San Diego Apóstol is here as well.

If you continue west to the village of Santa Cruz—there is only one road—for another 15 km (9 mi), you pass the remains of the 18th-century Santa Cruz hacienda. About 13 km (8 mi) farther is Tankuché, a good place to stop for sodas or simple provisions. Here the hacienda, despite efforts to restore it, sits in ruins. Machines once used to extract dye from Campeche wood remain on-site. Fourteen kilometers (9 mi) away is El Remate, a wonderful water hole surrounded by mangroves and sapodilla trees. *Palapas* (thatch-roofed huts) provide shade, and restrooms are available. The road continues to the Reserva Ecológica Peténes, where you can see flamingos, frigates, herons, and ibis in the mangroves. The final stop is the tiny fishing village of Isla Arena, where birds outnumber humans.

Becal

🔞 *10 km (6 mi) north of Calkiní.*

The town of Becal is noted for its famous *jipis*, known to most of the world as Panama hats. Local residents weave reeds of the huano palm in caves beneath their houses, where the humidity keeps the reeds flexible. As a result, the hats are so pliable that they can be rolled up in a suitcase with no harm done. First produced in the 19th century by the García family, the hats have become a village tradition. It's hard to resist photographing the statue of three giant hats in the center of the town plaza.

Buying jipis directly from the producers helps to sustain this craft and keep the tradition alive. The workshop of Mario Farfán Herrera at **Artesanía Becaleña** (⊠ Calle 30 No. 210A ☎ 996/431–4046) sells fine hats as well as baskets, jewelry boxes, lamp shades, and other objects made from palm fibers. Although Doña Chari of **Artesanías Chari** (✉ Calle 30 No. 231 ☎ No phone) is often off selling her wares in Campeche, her daughter attends the Calkiní shop and is happy to show you the cave where products are made. The **Sociedad de Artesanas Becaleñas** (✉ Calle 34 between Calles 33 and 35 ☎ No phone) sells souvenirs, hammocks, and more commercial-looking hats.

Halachó

⑳ *6 km (4 mi) north of Becal.*

Just across the Yucatán state line from Becal is the village of Halachó. Although not officially part of the Artists' Route, it's a worthwhile stop for those seeking handcrafted baskets, rugs, and bags. Halachó, which means "reed rats," was so named because it was founded on the shores of a lake (long since dried up), where rats once lived in abundance in the reeds along the shore. The centerpiece of Halachó is a magnificent white 18th-century mission church, **Iglesia Santiago Apóstol,** dedicated to the apostle James, patron saint of the conquistadores. Each year, standard-bearing pilgrims from surrounding towns and villages come to Halachó to pay homage at the equestrian statue of the saint, up a flight of stairs behind the altar. The church is open daily 8–noon and 3–8.

THE CHENES ROUTE

This is the longer way to reach the Yucatán capital of Mérida, passing by the Chenes ruins of eastern Campeche. Chenes-style temples are recognizable by their elaborate stucco facades decorated with geometric designs and giant earth god masks, often surrounding doorways shaped like the open mouths of monsters. It's a scenic route, leading through green hills with tall dark forests and valleys covered by low scrub, cornfields, and citrus orchards.

Edzná

FodorsChoice
★

㉑ *55 km (34 mi) southeast of Campeche City.*

The Maya ruin of Edzná, 55 km (34 mi) southeast of Campeche City off Carretera 261, deserves more recognition than it has received to date. Archaeologists consider it one of the peninsula's most important ruins because of the crucial transitional role it played among several architectural styles. Occupied from around 300 BC to AD 1450, Edzná grew from a humble agricultural settlement into a major political-religious center, reaching its pinnacle between AD 600 and AD 900. The city served as a trading center between the cities of the Petén region of Guatemala and the lowlands of northern Yucatán. The region's agricultural products were traded for hand-carved ritual objects and adornments from Guatemala.

Today the **Gran Acrópolis** (Great Acropolis) is surrounded by excavated buildings; it is dominated by the 102-foot **Pirámide de los Cinco Pisos.** The Five-Story Pyramid consists of five levels terminating in a tiny temple crowned by a roof comb. Hieroglyphs were carved into the vertical face of the 15 steps between each level, and numerous stelae depict the opulent attire and adornment of the ruling class—quetzal feathers, jade pectorals, and skirts of jaguar skin.

In 1992, Campeche archaeologist Antonio Benavides discovered that the Pirámide de los Cinco Pisos was constructed so that on certain dates the setting sun would illuminate the mask of the creator-god, Itzamná, inside one of the pyramid's rooms. This happens annually on May 1, 2, and 3, the beginning of the planting season for the Maya—then and now. It also occurs on August 7, 8, and 9, the days of harvesting and giving thanks. Near the pyramid's base, the **Templo de la Luna** (Temple of the Moon), **Templo del Sureste** (Southwest Temple), **Templo del Norte** (North Temple), and **Temezcal** (steam bath) surround a small plaza.

West of the Great Acropolis, the Puuc-style **Plataforma de las Navajas** (Platform of the Knives) was so named by a 1970 archaeological exploration that found a number of flint knives inside. To the south, four buildings surround a smaller structure called the **Pequeño Acrópolis.** Twin sun-god masks with huge protruding eyes, sharp teeth, and oversize tongues flank the **Templo de los Mascarones** (Temple of the Masks, or Building 414), adjacent to the Small Acropolis. The mask at bottom left (east) represents the rising sun, while the one on the right represents the setting sun.

If you're not driving, consider taking one of the inexpensive day trips offered by tour operators in Campeche; this is far easier than trying to get to Edzná by municipal buses. ✥ *Carretera 261 east from Campeche City for 44 km (27 mi) to Cayal, then Carretera 188 southeast for 18 km (11 mi)* 🕿 *No phone* 🎫 *$3.30* ☉ *Daily 8–5.*

Where to Stay

★ **$$$$** 🏨 **Hacienda Uayamón.** In the past, this elegant 1792 hacienda was, among other things, an ice factory. Abandoned in 1905, it was resurrected nearly a century later and transformed into a luxury hotel with an elegant restaurant. The original architecture and decor have been carefully preserved: the library has exposed beam ceilings, cane chairs, sisal carpets, and wooden bookshelves at least 12 feet high. Each casita has its own private garden, hot tub, and bathroom as well as a cozy bedroom. The remaining two walls of the machine house shelter the outdoor pool, and candles are still lit at the ruined chapel. ⊠ *9 km (5½ mi) north of Edzná* 🕿 *981/829–7527* 🖷 *981/829–7527* ⊕ *www. starwood.com* ⇥ *2 suites, 10 casitas* ↻ *Restaurant, fans, in-room safes, minibars, cable TV, pool, bar, free parking* ▭ *AE, MC, V.*

Hopelchén

㉒ *41 km (25 mi) north of the Edzná turnoff on Carretera 261, 153 km (95 mi) north of Xpujil.*

Since 1985, Hopelchén has been home to an immigrant colony of blond-haired, blue-eyed Mennonites who came from northern Mexico looking for arable land. They still speak a Dutch-German dialect, although those who do business with outsiders have learned Spanish. The

Campeche group makes and sells Mennonite cheese, which can be purchased in shops and restaurants throughout the state.

Otherwise, Hopelchén—the name means "place of the five wells"—is a traditional Maya town noted for the Iglesia de San Francisco, built in honor of St. Francis of Padua in 1667. Corn, beans, tobacco, fruit, squash, and henequen are cultivated in this rich agricultural center. If you want an ice cream cone, a magazine, or an old-fashioned treadle sewing machine, check out the general store called Escalante Heredia Hermanas right on the town square—it's also the place to make long-distance phone calls.

Where to Stay

¢ ⊡ **Los Arcos.** Those who want to stay the night and explore the Hopelchén area can check into this hostelry. Named for the arches that span the front of the hotel, Los Arcos has basic rooms facing a traditional colonial-style courtyard. There is a small restaurant in the lobby. ⊠ *Calle 23 s/n, Col. Centro* ☎ *996/822–0123* ⌫ *32 rooms* ⚭ *Restaurant, fans, free parking; no a/c, no room phones, no room TVs* ▭ *No credit cards.*

Las Grutas de Xtacumbilxunaan

❷❸ *34 km (21 mi) north of Hopelchén.*

Just short of the state line between Campeche and Yucatán and a few miles before Bolonchén de Rejón are the Grutas de Xtacumbilxunaan (pronounced shta-*cum*-bil-shu-nan), the "caverns of the hidden women" in Spanish and Maya—where legend says a Maya girl disappeared after going for water. In ancient times, cenotes (sinkholes) deep in the extensive cave system provided an emergency water source during droughts. Only a few chambers are open to the public, because the rock surfaces are dangerously slippery and the depth of the caverns is 240 feet. In the upper part of the caves, you can see delicate limestone formations that have been given whimsical names such as "Witch's Ball" and "Devil's Bridge." There are sometimes guides at the site who can show you around, but not always. ▱ *$2* ⊙ *Daily 9–2* ⊙ *closed Monday.*

Santa Rosa Xtampak

▲▲ ❷❹ *75 km (46 mi) from Campeche City; entrance at Carretera 261, Km 79, travel 30 km (19 mi) down signed side road; 25 km (16 mi) east of Hopelchén, 10 km (6 mi) south of Las Grutas de Xtacumbilxunaan.*

Believed to have been the political center of the Chenes empire, this extensive site also shows the influence of Puuc architecture. Although Xtampak was discovered in 1842, excavation didn't begin until 1995. It's believed that there are 100 structures in the area, although only 12 have been cleared. The most exciting find was the colossal **Palacio** in the western plaza. Inside, two inner staircases run the length of the structure, leading to different levels and ending in subterranean chambers. This combination is extremely rare in Maya temples. The **Casa de la Boca del Serpiente** (House of the Serpent's Mouth) is noteworthy for its perfectly preserved and integrated zoomorphic entrance. Here, the mouth

of the creator-god Itzamná stretches wide to reveal a perfectly proportioned inner chamber. ⊠ *East of Hopelchén on Dzibalchén–Chencho
road, watch for sign* ☎ *No phone* 💲 *$2.50* ⊙ *Daily 8–5.*

Dzibilnocac

 ㉕ *18 km (11 mi) northeast of Dzibalchén, 69 km (43 mi) southeast of
Hopelchén.*

To reach the rarely visited archaeological site of Dzibilnocac, you must
first get to the village of Dzibalchén by traveling south on Carretera 261.
From there, proceed north on a small side road to Vicente Guerrero,
also known as Iturbide, a farming community 19 km (12 mi) north—
literally at the end of the road. Each corner of the town square has a
small stone guardhouse built in 1850 during the War of the Castes, and
the road around them eventually turns into a dirt path that passes
houses and ends at the ruins. Dzibilnocac, which in Maya translates as
either "painted ceiling" or "great painted turtle," was a fair-size ceremonial center between AD 250 and AD 900, and represents the Chenes
architectural style typified by zoomorphic masks with Río Bec elements
such as rounded lateral towers and false stairways. Although there are
at least seven temple pyramids here, the only one that has been partially
excavated is the **Palacio Principal**, a Late Classic (AD 600–AD 800)
palace. Only one of the three towers remains intact; it contains a one-
room square temple with beautifully executed carvings of Chaac on the
outside walls. Under what remains of the middle tower, two small underground chambers can be accessed through a Maya arch. The farthest
tower has a roof comb sticking up from a mound of grass, trees, and
stones—an incongruous sight. ⊠ *South to Dzibalchén and then north
to Vicente Guerrero* ☎ *No phone* 💲 *Free* ⊙ *Daily 8–5.*

Hochob

 ㉖ *55 km (34 mi) south of Hopelchén, 15 km (9 mi) west of Dzibilnocac.*

The small Maya ruin of Hochob is an excellent example of the Chenes architectural style, which flowered in the Classic period from about
AD 100 to AD 1000. Most ruins in this area (central and southeastern
Campeche) were built on the highest possible elevation to prevent flooding during the rainy season, and Hochob is no exception. It rests high
on a hill overlooking the surrounding valleys. Another indication that
these are Chenes ruins is the number of *chultunes,* or cisterns, in the
area. Since work began at Hochob in the early 1980s, four temples
and palaces have been excavated at the site, including two that have
been fully restored. **Estructura II** has wonderfully preserved stucco carvings that are perfect examples of the intricate geometric designs of the
Chenes style. The doorway represents the open mouth of Itzamná, the
creator-god; above it are the eyes; to the side, the large earrings; fangs
are on either side of the base. Along both sides of the structure are
cascades of Chaac masks, and evidence of roof combs can be seen at
the top of the building. Ask the guard to show you the series of natural and man-made chultunes that extend back into the forest. ⊠ *South-*

west of Hopelchén on Dzibalchén–Chencho road ☎ *No phone* 💲 *Free* ⊙ *Daily 8–5.*

CARRETERA 186 TOWARD CHETUMAL

Campeche's archaeological sites, particularly those near the Quintana Roo border, are attracting more attention from scientists and travelers alike. Secluded yet accessible ruins are surrounded by tropical jungle—and for the most part are devoid of tourists. The vestiges of at least 10 little-known Maya cities lie hidden off Carretera 186 between Escárcega and Chetumal. Becán and the neighboring sites of Chicanná, Balamkú, and Xpujil are off Carretera 186 near the Quintana Roo border; Hormiguero is 25 km (16 mi) southwest of Xpujil. The road to Calakmul, near the Guatemala border south of Xpujil, has been paved (although it's still full of potholes), making parts of the Reserva de la Biosfera Calakmul more accessible.

You can see Xpujil, Becán, Hormiguero, and Chicanná in one rather rushed day by starting out early from Campeche City, or from Chetumal, in Quintana Roo. If you plan to see Calakmul, it's wise to spend the first night at Xpujil (after touring some or all of the ruins), arriving at Calakmul at dawn the next day. That provides the best chance to see wildlife, including armadillo, wild turkey, and families of howler and squirrel monkeys.

As late as 1950, southeastern Campeche was sparsely populated. After offering land to city-dwelling Campechanos without much success, the Mexican government began colonizing the area with settlers from Tabasco whose land had been seized by cattle barons. Later immigrants—also victims of the cattle industry—came from Veracruz, and when the Chicosen volcano erupted in Chiapas in the early 1980s, another wave of farmers appeared. The local people live an isolated existence in small communities; many rarely venture as far as the larger towns like Escárcega and the state capital. Their slash-and-burn technique of farming, which requires that sections of precious forests be burned down to make way for crops, is being replaced when possible by more environmentally friendly small industries such as beekeeping and pig farming. They have also learned organic farming methods that result in higher crop yields, so that they don't need to clear more land for agriculture.

The Pronatura program trains local people to work as guides in the ruins and biosphere. As a result, you can hire people with a strong knowledge of environmental education, Maya culture, ecotourism, the local flora and fauna, and basic English. Hiring a local guide not only enhances your own experience, but supports the local economy and preservation efforts. You can find English-speaking guides through the tourist office in Campeche City.

Two-lane Carretera 261 runs north from Xpujil, connecting to Hopelchén, west of Campeche City. Travelers can continue north from Xpujil to visit several Chenes-style ruins, from there returning to Campeche City or continuing north toward Yucatán state. Xpujil's tiny bus station has at least one bus per day to Escárcega, Hopelchén, Chetumal, and Campeche.

en route · If you're headed east from Champotón or Campeche toward the ruins of Xpujil, Chicanná, Becán, or Hormiguero, don't miss **La Teca**, a great truck stop and Mexican restaurant at the crossroads of Carreteras 186 and 261. Open 24 hours, the restaurant has an air-conditioned dining room and a large open-sided patio overlooking the highway. Both have TVs blaring nonstop and serve Yucatecan dishes such as smoked pork, breaded chicken, and spicy *pollo pibíl* (chicken baked in banana leaves). They're nicely presented—albeit on plastic plates—with refried beans, greasy french fries, pickled onions, and fresh salsa. ⊠ *Carretera 186, Km. 1, by the Pemex station.* ☎ 982/824–0635 ▭ No credit cards.

Xpujil

🏛 ㉗ *Carretera 186, Km 150; 300 km (186 mi) southeast of Campeche, 130 km (81 mi) south of Dzibilnocac, 125 km (78 mi) west of Chetumal.*

Xpujil (literally "cat's tail," pronounced ish-*poo*-hil) comprises several buildings on the north side of the highway and one other, **Estructura V**, to the south. Other building groups have yet to be excavated. Buildings I–IV demonstrate architectural elements of both the Chenes and Río Bec styles. The elaborately carved facades and doorways fashioned like monsters' mouths reflect the Chenes style, while the Río Bec style is seen in the three adjacent pyramid-towers, which are connected by a long platform. In **Edificio I**, all three towers were once crowned by false temples, and at the front of each are the remains of four vaulted rooms, each oriented toward one of the compass points and thought to have been used by priests and royalty. On the back side of the central tower is a huge mask of the rain god Chaac. 🎟 *$2.20* ☉ *Daily 8–5.*

Where to Stay & Eat

¢ ⨉🏨 **Hotel Calakmul.** Simple but pleasant rooms have bright peach walls, white tile floors, and bathrooms with hot water. Flowered curtains cover screened, wood-shuttered windows, and each unit has a ceiling fan. The original wooden cabins are cramped and rustic, but have mosquito nets and are a good bargain. With its peaked palapa roof and large windows overlooking tropical plants, the restaurant (¢–$) offers tasty, ample meals. Try the *mole poblano* (turkey leg topped with rich, spicy chocolate sauce) or the more straightforward fried chicken served with beans, rice, avocado, and tortillas. ⊠ *Carretera 186, Km 153, Xpujil* ☎ 983/871–6006 📠 983/871–6029 ⇨ *13 rooms, 9 cabanas without bath* ⌂ *Restaurant, fans; no room phones, no room TVs* ▭ *No credit cards.*

★ $$ 🏨 **Chicanná Ecovillage Resort.** Rooms in this comfortable jungle lodge are in two-story stucco duplexes with thatch roofs. Each ample unit has a tile floor, an overhead fan, screened windows, a wide porch or balcony with a table and chairs, and one king or two double beds with bright cotton bedspreads. There's a library with a television and VCR, and a small pool filled with rainwater and surrounded by flowering plants. There is no phone or fax at the hotel; both are available in nearby Xpujil. For reservations, contact the Del Mar Hotel in Campeche City.

✉ *Carretera 186, Km 144, 9 km (5½ mi) north of village of Xpujil* ☎ *981/ 811–9191 for reservations* 🖶 *981/811–9192* ⤳ *32 rooms* ⚴ *Restaurant, fans, pool, bar, library, laundry service, meeting room, free parking; no a/c, no room phones, no room TVs* ▭ *AE, MC, V.*

Becán

⛰ ★ ㉘ *7 km (4½ mi) west of Xpujil, Carretera 186, Km 145.*

Becán (which some translate as "road of the serpent" and others as "canyon of water," referring to the site's surrounding moat) is thought to have been an important city within the Río Bec group, inhabited from around 600 BC. The moat, ½ km (¼ mi) long and ½ km (¼ mi) deep, is an unusual feature among ancient Maya cities; entrance to the city was through one of seven gateways. Archaeologists believe the moat served defensive purposes, and recent investigations have established that Becán was often under siege—most likely from neighboring Calakmul. However, the constant skirmishes didn't hinder the construction of at least 84 main buildings during its golden age, from AD 600 to AD 1000. The most interesting is **Estructura VIII,** whose underground passages lead to small subterranean rooms and to a concealed staircase that reaches the top of the temple. One of several buildings surrounding a central plaza, **Estructura VIII,** has lateral towers and a giant zoomorphic mask on its central facade. Experts believe the building was used for self-mutilation rites and other religious rituals. Hire a guide to get the most out of your visit. ☼ *Daily 8–5.*

Chicanná

⛰ ㉙ *Carretera 186, Km 141; 3 km (2 mi) east of Becán.*

Thought to have been a satellite community of the larger, more commercial city of Becán, Chicanná ("house of the serpent's mouth") was also in its prime during the Late Classic period. Of the four buildings surrounding the main plaza, **Estructura II,** on the east side, is the most impressive. On its intricate facade are well-preserved sculpted reliefs and faces with long twisted noses, symbols of Chaac. In typical Chenes style, the doorway represents the mouth of the creator-god Itzamná; surrounding the opening are large crossed eyes, fierce fangs, and earrings to complete the stone mask, which still bears traces of blue and red pigments. 🎟 *$3* ☼ *Daily 8–5.*

Balamkú

⛰ ㉚ *Carretera 186, Km 95; about 60 km (37 mi) west of Xpujil.*

Near the western boundary of the Reserva de la Biosfera Calakmul is the Templo del Jaguar, famous for the intricate molded stucco and polychrome frieze discovered here in 1995. Dated to AD 550–AD 650 (in the Classic period), this dazzling work is nearly 56 feet long and 13 feet high. On the middle panel, the aquatic symbols—two frogs and two crocodiles—represent the fertility of the earth; jaguars represent war. Above this are representations of the god and below, figures relating to the *infra-*

mundo, or underworld. Three subterranean chambers are symbolic entrances to the world of the dead. In places you can still see the original red and black paint. The fresco is enclosed to protect it from the elements, and flash cameras are prohibited. You can view other structures here, including remnants of residences up a path to the left as you enter the site, but they're anticlimactic in comparison to the impressive fresco. 🖭 *$2* ☉ *Daily 8–5.*

Hormiguero

③ *14 km (9 mi) southeast of Xpujil.*

Hormiguero is Spanish for "anthill," referring both to the looters' tunnels that honeycombed the ruins when archaeologists discovered them and to the number of large anthills in the area. The buildings here were constructed roughly between 400 BC and AD 1100 in the Río Bec style, with rounded lateral towers and ornamental stairways, the latter built to give an illusion of height. The site has five temples, two of which have been excavated to reveal ornate facades covered with zoomorphic figures whose mouths are the doorways. **Estructura II,** the largest structure on the site, has a beautifully preserved carved facade, rounded corners, and false staircases. **Estructura V** has some admirable Chaac masks arranged in a cascade atop a pyramid. 🖭 *$2.50* ☉ *Daily 8–5.*

Reserva de la Biosfera Calakmul

③ *Entrance at Carretera 186, Km 65; 107 km (66 mi) southwest of*
Fodor'sChoice *Xpujil.*
★

Remote Calakmul (meaning "two adjacent towers") is in the isolated region near the Guatemala border. The area surrounding the ancient Maya city was declared a protected biosphere reserve in 1989. Covering 1.8 million acres, Calakmul is the second-largest reserve of its kind in Mexico after Sian Ka'an in Quintana Roo. Within its border, all kinds of flora and fauna thrive, including some endangered species. Among them are five of Mexico's six remaining species of wildcats, spider and howler monkeys, hundreds of exotic birds—Calakmul is perfect for bird-watching—and 120 varieties of orchids, including a rare species of black orchid. There are some 350 species of butterflies and 75 different reptiles; luckily, the venomous snakes tend to be active only at night. There's no dearth of insects either, so don't forget the bug repellent.

The Escárcega–Chetumal highway (Carretera 186) runs right through the reserve—it's about 50 km (31 mi) from this highway to the excavations along a potholed narrow road. Although structures will be excavated, the dense jungle surrounding them is being left in its natural state. Arrangements for an English-speaking tour guide should be made beforehand with the Campeche City tourist office or through the Del Mar Hotel, which administers Chicanná Ecovillage near Xpujil. Camping is permitted near the entrance gate (there are latrines and water for washing; bring your own food and drinking water). Be sure to tip the caretakers, and if it's rainy, ask if you can use their roomy storage structure as a shelter.

Archaeologists and anthropologists estimate that the region may once have been inhabited by more than 50,000 Maya; to date, they've mapped more than 6,250 structures of all sizes, including what may be the peninsula's largest Maya building, Templo II. More than 180 stelae have been found, as have twin pyramids that face each other across a plaza, similar to those at Tikal in Guatemala. However, Calakmul's towering, early-Petén-style temples, with their long, sloping sides, are a bit bulky compared to Tikal's more graceful pyramids.

Perhaps the most monumental discovery that's been made so far at Calakmul has been the remains of royal ruler Garra del Jaguar (Jaguar Claw); his body had been wrapped (but not embalmed) in a shroud of palm leaf, lime, and fine cloth, and locked away in a royal tomb since about AD 700. The 1994 find is the first known example of this type of burial in the Maya world. The royal tomb's contents, along with other items from the site—including fabulous stelae, jewelry, and jade funeral masks—are on display at the Fuerte de San Miguel's Museum of Maya Culture, in Campeche City. In an adjacent crypt, a young woman and child were entombed together, as well. The woman, whose identity is not known, was found wearing fine jadeite jewelry and an elaborate polychrome, wood-and-stucco headdress.

Experts believe Calakmul was founded no earlier than 1000 BC, and was the likely capital city of the mighty Serpent Head dynasty. The glyph with this symbol has been found on stelae in other cities of the ancient Maya empire, suggesting that Calakmul dominated a large number of tributary city-states. It reached the pinnacle of its political power between the years 542 and 695, in the Classic period. Some stelae indicate that the new heads of tributary cities were obligated to journey to Calakmul to be formally consecrated in their duties by the leader of the Serpent Head lineage. Epigraphists also have discovered inscriptions relating the defeat of Calakmul's most famous ruler, Garra del Jaguar, at the hands of archrival Tikal in AD 695. After that, the city's rulers decided to forge an alliance with groups to the north, most importantly with Río Bec.

From the entrance gate, it's a 50-km (31-mi) drive along a pitted paved road to the parking area. (Signs and common sense recommend a 30-kph [19-mph] speed limit, so allow about 90 minutes for the journey.) The site is shrouded in tropical deciduous forest, but paths with signposts lead to several temples. Choose from the short, medium, or long paths, all of which include the impressive **Templo II** and **Templo VII**—twin pyramids separated by an immense plaza. Templo II, at 175 feet, is the tallest structure found here so far. Getting to the top involves climbing many steps, which—because Calakmul gets few visitors—can be more slippery than those at places like Chichén Itzá and Uxmal. It's worth the effort, though, because the view from the top is spectacular. If you look south, you can gaze into Guatemala.

You can also ascend **Templo I**, which is only slightly shorter than Templo II. There's a stela at the base of the pyramid overlooking the plaza. Parts of temples are scattered around one of the rain-forest paths—a state likely attributable to "grave robbers" who made off with the choicest pieces. When you see a flat stela with no decoration, it likely indicates that the facade was simply cut away from the rest of the stone for easier transport.

Upon entering the biosphere, you must register your vehicle and pay an entrance fee. About halfway to the ruins is another checkpoint; primitive camping is permitted here. Farther on is the official entrance site with restrooms and a tiny bookstore. Bring your own food and water. ✉ 97 km (60 mi) east of Escárcega to the turnoff at Cohuas, then 50 km (31 mi) south to Calakmul 🎟 $4 per car (more for larger vehicles), plus $4 per person ⊘ Daily 8–5.

Where to Stay

$ ⌂ **Puerta Calakmul.** Designed and built by a master woodworker and architect, these rustic cabins are tucked away in the forest on the edge of the Calakmul biosphere. Built with natural wood and stone from the area, the cabins combine earthiness and sophistication with their cement floors, rough cotton drapes, comfortable beds, pounded tree-bark lamp shades, blue tile showers, and screened-in porches. Small ponds and sitting areas complete the Garden of Eden setting, and nearby trails allow for hiking in the woods. ✉ Carretera 186, Km 98.5, inside entrance to Calakmul biosphere 📞 998/887–8916 ✉ puertacalakmul@hotmail. com ➡ 15 cabanas ⚙ Fans, restaurant, pool; no a/c, no room phones, no room TVs ▭ No credit cards.

El Tigre

⛰ ㉝ 46 km (28 mi) south of Candelaria.

This port on the Candelaria River, inhabited since at least 300 BC, was historically known as Itzankanac, capital of the province of Acalán. Now called El Tigre, in reference to the nearby community of that name, Itzankanac was an important trading city that connected the Campeche coast with the Petén. Spanish conquistador Hernán Cortés passed through this area on his expedition to Honduras, and it was here that he supposedly hanged Cuauhtémoc, the last Aztec emperor. El Tigre archaeological site consists of a 656-foot-long ceremonial plaza surrounded by four structures, which, despite the obviously planned organization of the plaza, have no unifying style. Some stucco masks found here have anthropomorphic features, while others are more realistic, although the facial figures are far from classic Maya, causing much speculation about their meaning and origin. The site is currently under excavation, and a large pyramid (**Edificio IV**) is being studied and restored. Visible through the treetops from the ceremonial plaza, it's not as far away as it looks and is definitely worth closer inspection. El Tigre is more than three hours from Campeche by car, so most folks overnight in Candelaria. From there it's a 90-minute drive. Alternatively, you can arrange a trip by river (about three hours each way, $150) through the Autel Jardines hotel. 🎟 $2.50 ⊘ Daily 8–5.

Candelaria

🏛 **③** *95 km (59 mi) west of Reserva de la Biosfera Calakmul.*

Bird-watching and fly-fishing in Lake Salsipuedes and Vieja Lagoon in the Candelaria River basin are what make this spot an increasingly popular, though out-of-the-way, destination. Primarily an agricultural hub producing corn and sugarcane, Candelaria is also a good starting point for a visit to El Tigre. Or, if you're departing from Campeche City, you might spend the night in Candelaria after your visit to the ruins.

Where to Stay & Eat

¢–$ ✕ **Comedor los Reyes.** With a thatched roof, lilac walls, an ocher cement floor and matching oilcloths, this unassuming little place almost lives up to its name as the "diner of kings." Order the delicious *pellizcadas* (thick rounds of lightly fried cornmeal topped with melted cheese, chopped onion, and black beans), or one of the daily specials. There's much more on the menu, too, including more recognizable items like burritos and enchiladas. Mainly locals eat here, so don't expect English menus or explanations. Happily, almost anything you point to on the menu should be a winner. It's open from 7 AM. ⊠ *Calle 27 s/n, Col. Acalán* ☎ *982/826–0574* ▭ *No credit cards.*

¢–$ 🏨 **Autel Jardines.** Offering the most comfortable accommodations in town, this motel-like lodging has a parking place outside each unit. Heavy curtains block the tropical sun, and air-conditioning units are effective, if somewhat noisy. The restaurant is open only during peak vacation periods, and the dance club only on Saturday night. Suites are no larger than standard rooms but have cozy pillow-top mattresses and coverlets, DVD players, small refrigerators, and room safes. With advance notice, owner Manuel Valladares Hernández can make arrangements for a river tour, fly-fishing, or a visit to El Tigre. ⊠ *Calle 27 No. 1, Col. Acalán* ☎ *982/826–0064* 🖷 *981/816–0075* ⊕ *www.auteljardines.com* 🛏 *28 rooms, 2 suites ᘓ Restaurant, some fans, pool, exercise equipment, bar, dance club, laundry service, free parking; no a/c in some rooms* ▭ *AE, MC, V.*

CARRETERA 180 TO VILLAHERMOSA

Heading southwest from Campeche, Carretera 180 hugs the coast, offering views of narrow beaches and the Gulf of Mexico. Most of the beaches are simply solitary stretches of narrow sand with no services and no bathers. Still, there's nothing to stop you from pulling off the road for a walk along the shore. The deep-green sea here is so shallow that the Continental Shelf is almost visible at low tide. Waves are rare and the current runs at a nearly imperceptible 0.3 knots.

Lerma

㉟ *13 km (8 mi) southwest of Campeche City.*

ᘓ Playa Bonita, the most popular bathing spot southwest of Campeche City, is at the far end of this rural village. The sandy beach has lockers, changing rooms, showers, and several snack bars. It's lonely on week-days but crowded on weekends and holidays, when the rocky coves fronting homes at the beach's north end fill up with families. A basketball court and soccer field and children's play equipment are available for those who prefer nonaquatic exercise. Roving vendors sell mangoes and sweets, but most families bring picnics. You can rent tables, chairs, and palapas for shade. Public buses to Lerma depart daily 6 AM–11 PM from the market in Campeche City (Circuito Baluartes, between Calles 53 and 55). If you're driving, be aware that there's no sign specifying Playa Bonita. Turn toward the sea at the Lerma sign and again at the first traffic cir-cle. You'll need to pay 50¢ per car to get in.

Seybaplaya

36 *About 7 km (4½ mi) southwest of Lerma.*

Dozens of identical, turquoise-and-white fiberglass motor launches line the beach at the traditional fishing port of Seybaplaya. Its palm-fringed setting is among the prettiest seascapes on the Campeche coast. Snorkel-ing is good here, as a number of large coral heads are just offshore, along with an underwater cemetery for boats. For a challenge, climb the huge staircase that juts up the mountain, ending at a giant statue of Jesus with outstretched arms. The view is incredible, but be warned: it's quite a hike. A couple of miles north along the beach road is Payucán—a beach with fine white sand and lots of herons, sandpipers, pelicans, and other seabirds—and Punta del Morro, a huge seaside cavern created by cen-turies of erosion. The sound of crashing waves echoes off the cavern's walls, adding to its drama.

About 9 km (5½ mi) southwest is Siho Playa, a rocky beach and the old home of the pirate Henry Morgan. Here the sea is quite calm and stays shallow for about 10 yards. Three kilometers (2 mi) southwest is the Costa Blanca beach, with shells, birds, and calm surf.

Where to Stay

$$ ⊡ **Tucán Siho-Playa.** Just less than halfway between Seybaplaya and Champotón, the Tucán has a mainly Mexican and European clientele. Rooms are simply furnished and let in plenty of light—a contrast to the dark, low-ceilinged hallways. Each room has a tiled floor, a wall made of rock, and a small balcony (ask for chairs). There's a large rectangular pool; a sandy little beach is surrounded by rocks and has a few indi-vidual palapas for shade. ⊠ *Carretera Libre Campeche–Champotón, Km 35, 24400* ☎ *982/823–1200 or 982/823–1202* ⊜ *982/823–1203* ⊕ *www.hoteles-tucan.com* ⇨ *70 rooms, 4 suites* ⚒ *Restaurant, room service, some minibars, cable TV, pool, exercise equipment, beach, bil-liards, Ping-Pong, playground, meeting room, free parking* ⊟ *MC, V.*

Champotón

37 *35 km (22 mi) southwest of Seybaplaya.*

Carretera 180 curves through a series of hills before reaching Cham-potón's immensely satisfying vista of open sea. This is an appealing little town with palapas at the water's edge, and plenty of swimmers and boats. The Spaniards dubbed the outlying bay the Bahía de la Mala Pelea, or "bay of the evil battle," because it was here that the troops of the Spanish conqueror and explorer Hernández de Córdoba were first trounced, in 1517, by pugnacious Indians armed with arrows, slingshots, and darts. The famous battle is commemorated with a small reenactment each year on March 21.

The 17th-century church of Nuestra Señora de la Inmaculada Concepción is the site for a festival honoring the Virgin Mary (Our Lady of the Immaculate Conception). The festival culminates each year on December 8. On that day the local fishermen carry the saint from the church to their boats for a seafaring parade. In the middle of town are the ruins of the Fortín de San Antonio. The Champotón area is ideal for bird-watching and fishing. More than 35 kinds of fish, including shad, snook, and bass, live in Río Champotón. The mangroves and swamps are home to cranes and other waterfowl. The town is primarily an agricultural hub—its most important exports are lumber and honey, as well as coconut, sugarcane, bananas, avocados, corn, and beans.

★ About a dozen small seafood restaurants make up **Los Cockteleros,** an area 5 km (3 mi) north of the center of Champotón. This is where Campechanos head on weekends to munch fried fish and slurp down seafood cocktails. The open-air palapa eateries are near the beach and are open daily during daylight hours.

Approximately 15 km (9 mi) southwest of Champotón, Punta Xen is a beautiful beach popular for its calm, clean water. It's a long stretch of deserted sand interrupted only by birds and seashells. Across the highway are a few good, basic restaurants.

★ The Expreso Maya train (⇨ the write-up in the Yucatán chapter for details) makes one of its few stops at **Cenote Azul,** a sinkhole about 1½ hours from the town of Champotón. The train stops a few hundred yards from stairs to the sinkhole, which is just outside the small community of Miguel Colorado. Infrastructure for getting to and from this private, special spot is still not in place, but those interested in visiting and swimming at this isolated spot can contact the Champotón tourism office (☎ 982/828–0343, 982/828–0067 Ext. 207) to arrange transportation or get driving directions. A second sinkhole, Cenote de los Patos, is a short but rather rugged walk from the first. Both are gorgeous and isolated, though; most find the hike well worth it. The dirt road from Miguel Colorado may be impassable for two-wheel-drive vehicles during the rainy season.

Where to Stay & Eat

$ ✕ **Las Brisas.** A favorite with locals, this is the best place in town for fresh fish, shrimp, and octopus. Open until 6 PM, Las Brisas is on the main street by the water, overlooking the bay. ⊠ *Av. Eugenio Echeverría Castellot s/n between Calles 18 and 16* ☎ *982/828–0515* ▭ *No credit cards* ☉ *No dinner.*

¢ ✕⊞ **Geminis.** Not far from the town's main plaza, this modest hotel is about as fancy as Champotón gets. In other words, it's quite plain, as reflected in the modest room rates. Some mattresses are mushy, others are firm; all have orange chenille spreads. The louvered windows have no screens to keep the bugs out, and TVs are tiny. Rooms surround a largish pool with a few tables and chairs. The popular restaurant, La Casona ($), serves varied breakfasts, homemade soups, and seafood. There's karaoke in the adjoining bar on weekend nights. ✉ *Calle 30 No. 10* ☎ *982/828–0008* 🖷 *982/828–0094* ➥ *42 rooms* 🚻 *Restaurant, fans, cable TV, pool, bar, free parking; no a/c in some rooms, no room phones* ⊟ *No credit cards.*

¢ ⊞ **Snook Inn.** Like its competition, Geminis, the Snook Inn is all business. Many clients are hunters or fishermen who have clan, the hotel's longtime owners and outdoor enthusiasts. The clean, kidney-shaped pool has both a slide and a diving board, and it's surrounded by the two-story, L-shaped, 1960s-era hotel. Simple rooms have remote-control TVs, tile floors, unadorned walls, and hammock hooks in the walls (bring your own hammock). The parking area is quite small. ✉ *Calle 30 No. 1* 🖷🖷 *982/828–0018* ➥ *19 rooms* 🚻 *Cable TV, pool, laundry service, free parking* ⊟ *No credit cards.*

Sabancuy

🟤 *47 km (29 mi) west of Champotón.*

A launching point for exploring the Laguna de Términos and its many estuaries and mangroves, Sabancuy is the final village before high-tension lines start to follow the coastal highway and oil country starts. Most travelers here are European or Mexican, the former sometimes on escorted tours. An unnamed secondary road (pitted with potholes, which makes for slow going at times) leads to the ruins of El Tigre.

Where to Stay & Eat

$ ✕ **Viaductoplaya Restaurant Bar Turístico.** Menus in Spanish and German give you a clue about who frequents this large seaside shanty. Mexican favorites like grilled chicken are on the menu, but the restaurant's strength is clearly seafood, including shrimp, squid, and fish. The *ensaladas,* which usually means salads, are really ceviche (fish or seafood cured in lime, with chopped chile, cilantro, and onions). Waiters recommend the fresh fish fillet stuffed with seafood or with shrimp and cheese. Beer, wine, and liquor are available. ✉ *Carretera Carmen–Champotón, Km 77.5* ☎ *982/825–0008* ⊟ *No credit cards.*

¢ ⊞ **Hotel Sabancuy Plaza.** Though unassuming, the Plaza offers the best accommodations in town. The better rooms, higher up in the four-story building, have tiny balconies overlooking the estuary and rusty rooftops— but no chairs where you can sit while taking in the so-so view. Tiled rooms have blue printed drapes and bedspreads, wood headboards, and reasonably strong air-conditioning units. ✉ *South side of plaza principal* ☎ *982/825–0081* ➥ *35 rooms* 🚻 *Free parking; no room phones, no TV in some rooms* ⊟ *No credit cards.*

Isla del Carmen

③⑨ *147 km (91 mi) south of Champotón.*

It was on this barrier island protecting the lagoon from the Gulf that pirates who raided Campeche regularly hid out from the mid-1500s to their expulsion in the early 18th century. The island has served as a depot for everything from dyewoods and textiles to hardwoods, chicle, and shrimp. Today, oil is the big export; the area produces about 80% of Mexico's petroleum.

A major hub and the second-largest city in Campeche, Ciudad del Carmen is, frankly, no place for tourists. But if you're headed toward Tabasco, Veracruz, Chiapas, or other points west or south of Campeche, you might decide to pass through. Most other out-of-towners are Mexican and foreign business travelers.

The city is short on sights and long on franchise restaurants like KFC, Pizza Hut, and Bennigan's. Parts of the bay are polluted, and the city is battling social problems such as prostitution, which is reflected in the cheap, ugly motels advertised as "men's clubs." Be prepared to pay higher prices for a safe hotel room than you would in Campeche City or other, more tourist-oriented, cities. Ciudad del Carmen is actually not on the island but on the adjoining peninsula's east end. The island is connected by two bridges to the mainland.

Locals recommend Puerto Real, 30 km (19 mi) north of town along the Campeche highway, as a good spot to find bathrooms, showers, and several restaurants that are lively only on holidays and warm-weather weekends.

Where to Stay & Eat

$$–$$$ ✕ **El Cactus.** Carnivores will be happy here, where meaty entrées are the best menu choices. Rib-eye steak and filet mignon are served with baked potato and sautéed vegetables; the bone-marrow soup and the cheese pie are also popular. The restaurant's exterior resembles an adobe house with—of course—cacti growing at the doorway. Inside, whitewashed stucco walls, wood furnishings, and quiet background music are conducive to closing business deals. ⌂ *Calle 31 No. 132, at Calle 50, Col. Cuauhtémoc (next to Hotel Lino)* ☎ *938/382–4986* ⊟ *AE, MC, V.*

$$$ 🏨 **Holiday Inn.** This low-rise hotel offers all the amenities you'd expect from a Holiday Inn, including alarm clocks, coffeemakers, and hair dryers. The lobby is all business, with plenty of couches here and there for conversing with colleagues. Off the lobby are a pool, a shop, an unremarkable bar, and an airy restaurant. Most rooms have king-size beds and small patios or terraces. There's a golf course not far away. ⌂ *Calle 31 No. 274, between Av. Periférica and Calle 56, 24170* ☎ *938/381–1500 or 800/465–4329* 🖷 *938/382–0520* ⊕ *www.holiday-inn.com* 🛏 *100 rooms, 6 suites* ⌂ *Restaurant, snack bar, room service, in-room safes, some minibars, cable TV, pool, gym, bar, lounge, shop, laundry service, concierge floor, business services, meeting rooms, airport shuttle, free parking, no-smoking rooms* ⊟ *AE, MC, V.*

$ 🏨 **Lossandes.** A friendly low-rise surrounding a swimming pool, this place is a good choice for business travelers seeking comfortable, if simple, accommodations. The tennis court is in good condition, and each room has a tub. Rooms on the third floor at the back are the quietest. ⊠ *Av. Periférica Norte 67, 24167* ☎ *938/382–2400* 🖷 *938/382–2388* ⊕ *www. lossandes.com.mx* 🛏 *95 rooms* ⚐ *Restaurant, room service, cable TV, pool, tennis court, gym, laundry service, Internet, meeting rooms, free parking* ⊟ *AE, D, MC, V.*

CAMPECHE A TO Z

To research prices, get advice from other travelers, and book travel arrangements, visit www.fodors.com.

AIR TRAVEL

AIRPORT Campeche's Aeropuerto Internacional Alberto Acuña Ongay is 16 km (10 mi) north of downtown. Aeropuerto Internacional de Ciudad del Carmen is in the eastern sector of the city itself.

🚺 Airport Information **Aeropuerto Internacional Alberto Acuña Ongay** ☎ 981/ 816-3109.

Aeropuerto Internacional de Ciudad del Carmen ⊠ Prolongación Calle 31, 1 block from Plaza Comercial Aviación ☎ 938/382-8001 or 938/382-1510.

AIRPORT Taxis are the only means of transportation to and from the Campeche
TRANSFERS airport. A ride in a private cab to or from the city center costs around $7. At the airport you pay your fare ahead of time at the ticket booth outside the terminal; a dispatcher then directs you to your cab. Cabs from Ciudad del Carmen's airport cost about $9.

CARRIER Aeroméxico has daily flights from Mexico City to Campeche City.
🚺 **Aeroméxico** ☎ 981/816-6656 or 981/816-5678 in Campeche City, 01800/021-4000 toll-free in Mexico, 800/237-6639.

BUS TRAVEL

Within Campeche City, buses run along Avenida Ruíz Cortínez and cost the equivalent of about 30¢.

ADO, a first-class line, runs buses from Campeche City to Mérida, Villahermosa, and Ciudad del Carmen almost every hour, with less frequent departures for Cancún, Chetumal, Oaxaca, and other destinations. Adjacent to the ADO station, the second-class bus station has service on Unión de Camioneros to intermediate points throughout the Yucatán Peninsula, as well as less desirable service to Chetumal, Ciudad del Carmen, Escárcega, Mérida, Palenque, Tuxtla Gutiérrez, and Villahermosa.

In Ciudad del Carmen, the ADO bus station has departures for Campeche City many times a day, with fewer departures to Villahermosa, Mérida, and other points in southern Mexico. In eastern Campeche near Calakmul, several buses leave the Xpujil ADO bus station each day for Escárcega and Campeche City; there is one night bus for Hopelchén.

For destinations to (and from) major destinations within the Yucatán peninsula, purchase tickets with a credit card by phone through Ticketbus; make sure to ask from which station the bus departs.

ADO ✉ Av. Gobernadores 289, at Calle 45, along Carretera 261 to Mérida, Campeche City ☎ 981/816-2802 or 981/816-2381 ✉ Periférica s/n and Av. Francisco Villa, Ciudad del Carmen ☎ 938/382-0680 ✉ Carretera 186 s/n, Xpujil ☎ 983/871-6027. **Ticketbus** ☎ 01800/702-8000 toll-free in Mexico.

Unión de Camioneros ✉ Calle Chile and Av. Gobernadores, Campeche City ☎ 981/816-2332.

CAR RENTAL

Agencies Budget ✉ Calle 31 No. 117, between Calles 42 and 42A, Col. Cuauhtémoc, Ciudad del Carmen ☎ 938/382-7844. **Localiza** ✉ Hotel Baluartes, Av. 16 de Septiembre 128, Campeche City ☎ 981/811-3187. **Maya Rent-a-Car** ✉ Del Mar Hotel, Av. Ruíz Cortínez and Calle 59, Campeche City ☎ 981/816-0670 or 981/816-2233.

CAR TRAVEL

Campeche City is about 2 to 2½ hours from Mérida along the 160-km (99-mi) *via corta* (short way), Carretera 180. The alternative route, the 250-km (155-mi) *via larga* (long way), Carretera 261, takes 3 to 4 hours, but passes the major Maya ruins of Uxmal, as well as those of Kabah and Sayil.

A toll road from Campeche City to Champotón costs $4.50 one way and shortens the drive from 65 km (40 mi) to 45 km (28 mi). Look for the Carretera 180 CUOTA sign when leaving the city. Carretera 180 continues to Ciudad del Carmen (90 minutes to 2 hours); the bridge toll entering or leaving Ciudad del Carmen is about $3. From Champotón, Carretera 261 heads inland to Escárcega (about 2 hours from Campeche City to Escárcega), where you pick up Carretera 186 west to Xpujil (about 157 km, or 97 mi—a drive of just under 2 hours). From Xpujil it's about 140 km (87 mi) to Chetumal, on the coast of Quintana Roo. All of these, including Carretera 261, which connects Xpujil and Hopelchén in northeastern Campeche, are two-lane highways in reasonably good condition. If you're headed to Mérida, you can continue north on Carretera 261 from Hopelchén.

E-MAIL

Cybercafés have popped up all over Campeche City; try Ciber Club downtown. Some Campeche City lodgings and most of Ciudad del Carmen's business hotels have Internet access. Average cost is $1–$2 per hour.

Services Ciber Club ✉ Calle 67 No. 1B Altos, Campeche City ☎ 981/811-3577. **Compuniverso** ✉ Centro Comercial Plaza Real Norte, Avs. Periférica Norte and Concordia, Ciudad del Carmen ☎ 938/384-3677.

EMERGENCIES

Doctors & Hospitals If you're in luck you'll find an English-speaking doctor at **Hospital Manuel Campos** ✉ Av. Boulevard s/n, Campeche City ☎ 981/816-2409 or 981/811-1709.

Clínica Campeche ✉ Av. Central No. 72, Centro Campeche City ☎ 981/816-5612. Social Security Clinic ✉ Avs. López Mateos and Talamantes, Campeche City ☎ 981/816-
1855 or 981/816-5202.

🏥 Emergency Services **General Emergencies** ☎ 060. **Police** ✉ Av. Resurgimiento
77, Col. Lazareto, Campeche City ☎ 981/816-2309. **Red Cross** ✉ Av. Las Palmas at Calle
Ah-Kim-Pech s/n, Campeche City ☎ 981/815-2411.

🏥 24-Hour Pharmacy **Clínica Campeche** ✉ Av. Central 65, near the Social Security
Clinic, Campeche City ☎ 981/816-5612. **Clínica de Hospital Manuel Campos** ✉ Av.
Boulevard s/n, Campeche City ☎ 981/811-1709 Ext. 138.

MAIL & SHIPPING

The *correo* in Campeche City is open weekdays 8–8, Saturday 9–1. For
important letters or packages, it's best to use the DHL courier service.

🏤 Mail Services **Correo** ✉ Av. 16 de Septiembre between Calles 53 and 55, Campeche
City ☎ 981/816-2134. **DHL** ✉ Av. Miguel Alemán 140, Campeche City ☎ 981/816-0382.

MONEY MATTERS

Campeche City banks will change traveler's checks and currency weekdays 9–4. Almost without exception, banks in towns and cities have ATMs,
most are open 24 hours. You get a great exchange rate using the ATM,
but don't forget there's an international transaction fee, usually $2–$8.

🏦 Banks **Banamex** ✉ Calle 29 No. 103, Champotón ☎ 01800/021-2345 toll-free in Mexico. **Bancomer** ✉ Av. 16 de Septiembre 120, Campeche City ☎ 981/816-6622. **Banorte**
✉ Calle 8 No. 237, between Calles 53 and 55, Campeche City ☎ 981/811-0370. **Scotiabank Inverlet** ✉ Calle 31 No. 10, near main plaza, Ciudad del Carmen ☎ 938/382-
4115.

TAXIS

You can hail taxis on the street in Campeche City; there are also stands
by the bus stations, the cathedral, and the market. The minimum fare
is $2; it's $2.50 from the center to the bus station and $4 to the airport.
Add 50¢ for radio taxis or after 11 PM.

🚕 Radio Taxis ✉ Campeche City ☎ 981/816-1113 or 981/816-6666.

TELEPHONES

LONG-DISTANCE   TELMEX phones that take the electronic Ladatel cards are found
CALLS   throughout the capital. In smaller towns these phones are usually found
at bus stations and main plazas. Using such phones is both the easiest
and cheapest way to make calls—local or international—in Mexico. If
you plan to chat awhile, however, make sure to purchase a 100-peso
Ladatel card, the largest denomination.

TOURS

Guided trolley tours of historic Campeche City leave from Calle 10 on
the Plaza Principal on the hour between 9 and noon and again between
5 and 8. Trips are sporadic in the off-season, and it's always best to dou-
ble-check schedules at the municipal tourist office next to the cathedral.
You can buy tickets here ahead of time, or on board the trolley. The one-
hour tour costs $7; if English-speakers request it, guides will do their
best to speak the language. For the same price, the green "El Guapo"
trolley makes unguided trips to Reducto de San José at 9, 10, 11, noon,

and 5. There are only about 10 minutes to admire the view. Take the Super Guapo tram hourly between 9 and noon or 5 to 8 in the afternoon to visit Fuerte de San Miguel. The tour doesn't allow enough time to visit the museum, but you can linger to see the worthwhile exhibits before calling for a taxi or walking downhill to catch a downtown bus en route from Lerma.

Several tour operators can guide you to ruins throughout the state. Chito Tours and Intermar are recommended by the state's tourism department and offer tours and/or transportation to Calakmul, Edzná, and other ruins, as well as tours of Campeche City. Ask whether guide service is included; if not, ask the tour operator to arrange for an English-speaking guide at the ruins. Emerald Planet is an ecotourism outfitter that works closely with Pronatura, an ecology-oriented nonprofit organization active in Chiapas and the Yucatán.

For rappelling, spelunking, or mountain-bike tours, contact Expediciones Ecoturísticos de Campeche. For tours of Isla Jaina, the source of an enormous cache of figurines depicting all stations and occupations of pre-Hispanic residents, contact Hector Solis of Espacios Naúticos. If you like, augment the island tour with breakfast, lunch, or swimming at the beach. This operator, based at the Club de Yates de Campeche (yacht club), also offers waterskiing, bay tours, snorkeling, and sportfishing.

🚩 Fees & Schedules **Chito Tours** ⊠ Calle 51 No. 9, Int. C, between Calles 57 and 59, Centro, Campeche City ☎ 981/811–4700. **Emerald Planet** ⊠ 2602 Timberwood Dr., No. 16, Fort Collins, CO 80528 ☎ 888/883–0736 ⊕ www.emeraldplanet.com. **Espacios Naúticos** ⊠ Av. Resurgimiento 120, Campeche City ☎ 981/816–1990. **Expediciones Ecoturísticos de Campeche** ⊠ Calle 12 No. 168A, Centro, Campeche City ☎ 981/816–6373 or 981/816–1310. **Intermar** ⊠ Hotel Baluartes, Av. 16 de Septiembre 128, Campeche City ☎ 981/816–9006 or 981/811–3447 ⊕ www.emeraldplanet.com.

TRAVEL AGENCIES

🚩 Local Agents **American Express/VIPs** ⊠ Prolongación Calle 59, Edificio Belmar, Depto. 5, Centro Campeche City ☎ 981/811–1010 or 981/811–1000. **Intermar Campeche** ⊠ Av. 16 de Septiembre 128, Campeche City ☎ 981/811–3447.

VISITOR INFORMATION

The state tourism office is open daily 8–9. The municipal tourist office is open weekdays 9–3 and 6–9, weekends 9–9.

🚩 **Municipal Tourist Office** ⊠ Calle 55 between Calles 8 and 10, Campeche City ☎ 981/811–3989 or 981/811–3990. **State Tourist Office** ⊠ Av. Ruíz Cortínez s/n, Plaza Moch Couoh, across from Gobierno, Campeche City ☎ 981/811–9229 🖷 981/816–6767.

UNDERSTANDING CANCÚN

A PLACE APART

The Yucatán Peninsula has captivated travelers since the early Spanish explorations. "A place of white towers, whose glint could be seen from the ships—temples rising tier on tier," is how the expeditions' chroniclers described the peninsula, then thought to be an island. Rumors of a mainland 10 days west of Cuba were known to Columbus, who obstinately hoped to find "a very populated land," and one that was richer than any he had yet discovered. Subsequent explorers and conquistadores met with more resistance there than in almost any other part of the New World, and this rebelliousness continued for centuries.

Largely because of their geographic isolation, Yucatecans tend to preserve ancient traditions more than many other indigenous groups in the country. This can be seen in such areas as housing (the use of the ancient Maya thatched hut, or *na*); dress (*huipiles* have been made and worn by Maya women for centuries); and occupation (most modern-day Maya are farmers, just as their ancestors were). Maya culture is also evident in today's Yucatecan language (although it has evolved, it is still very similar to what was spoken in the area 500 years ago); and religion. Ancient deities persist, particularly in the form of gods associated with agriculture, such as the *chacs,* or rain gods, and festivals to honor the seasons and benefactor spirits maintain the traditions of old.

This vast peninsula encompasses 113,000 square km (43,630 square mi) of a flat limestone table covered with sparse topsoil and scrubby jungle growth. Geographically, it comprises the states of Yucatán, Campeche, and Quintana Roo, as well as Belize and a part of Guatemala (these two countries are not discussed in this book). Still one of the least-Hispanicized (or Mexicanized) regions of the country, Yucatán catapulted into the tourist's vocabulary with the creation of its most precious man-made asset, Cancún.

Mexico's most popular resort destination owes its success to its location on the superb eastern coastline of the Yucatán Peninsula, which is washed by the exquisitely colored and translucent waters of the Caribbean. The area is also endowed with a semitropical climate, unbroken stretches of beach, and the world's second-longest barrier reef, which separates the mainland from Cozumel. Cancún and, to a lesser extent, Cozumel incarnate the success formula for sun-and-sand tourism: luxury hotels, sandy beaches, water sports, nightlife, and restaurants that specialize in international fare.

Although Cancún is no longer less expensive than its Caribbean neighbors, it can be reached via more nonstop flights and it offers a far richer culture. Cancún's popularity has allowed the peninsula's Maya ruins—long a mecca for archaeology enthusiasts—to become satellite destinations of their own. The proximity of such compelling sites as Chichén Itzá, Uxmal, and Tulum allows Cancún's visitors to explore the vestiges of one of the most brilliant civilizations in the ancient world without having to journey too far from their base.

Yucatán offers a diversity of other charms, too. The waters of the Mexican Caribbean are clearer and bluer than those of the Pacific; many of the beaches are unrivaled. Scuba diving (in natural sinkholes, caves, and along the impressive barrier reef), snorkeling, deep-sea fishing, and other water sports attract growing numbers of tourists—who can also bird-watch, camp, spelunk, and shop for Yucatán's splendid handicrafts. There is a broad spectrum of settings and accommodations to choose from: the pricey strip of hotels along Cancún's Boulevard Kukulcán; the less showy properties on Cozumel, beloved of scuba divers; and the relaxed ambience of Isla Mujeres, where most lodgings consist of rustic bungalows with ceiling fans and hammocks.

There are also the cities of Yucatán. Foremost is Mérida, wonderfully unaltered by time, where Moorish-inspired, colonnaded colonial architecture blends handsomely with turn-of-the-19th-century pomposity. In Mérida, café life remains an art, and the Maya still live proudly as Maya. Campeche, one of the few walled cities in North America, possesses an eccentric charm; it is slightly out of step with the rest of the country and not the least bothered by the fact. Down on the border with Belize stands Chetumal, a modest commercial center that is pervaded by the hybrid culture of coastal Central America and the pungent smell of the sea. Progreso, at the other end of the peninsula on the Gulf of Mexico, is Chetumal's northern counterpart, an overgrown fishing village–turned–commercial port. Hotels in these towns, although for the most part not as luxurious as the beach resort properties, range from the respectable if plain 1970s buildings to the undated fleabags so popular with filmmakers and writers exploring the darker side of Mexico (for example, *Under the Volcano,* by Malcolm Lowry). As a counterpoint to this, the Yucatán countryside now shines with magnificently restored haciendas turned into luxury lodgings.

The peninsula is also rich in wildlife. Iguanas, lizards, tapirs, deer, armadillos, and wild boars thrive on this alternately parched and densely foliated plain. Flamingos and herons, manatees and sea turtles, their once-dwindling numbers now rising in response to Mexico's newly awakened ecological consciousness, find idyllic watery habitats in and above the coastline's mangrove swamps, lagoons, and sandbars, acres of which have been made into national parks. Both Ría Lagartos and the coast's Reserva de la Biosfera Sian Ka'an sparkle with Yucatán's natural beauty. Orchids, bougainvillea, and poinciana are ubiquitous. And while immense palm groves and forests of precious hardwood trees slowly succumb to fire and disease, the region's edible tropical flora—coconuts, limes, papaya, bananas, and oranges—remains a succulent ancillary to the celebrated Yucatecan cuisine.

But it may be the colors of Yucatán that are most remarkable. From the stark-white sun-bleached sand, the sea stretches out like some immense canvas painted in bands of celadon green, pale aqua, and deep dusty blue. At dusk the sea and the horizon meld in the sumptuous glow of lavender sunsets, the sky just barely tinged with periwinkle and violet. Inland, the beige, gray, and amber stones of ruined temples are set off by riotous greenery. The colors of newer structures are equally intoxicating: the tawny, gray-brown thatched roofs of traditional huts; the creamy pastels and white arches, balustrades, and porticoes of colonial mansions. Cascades of dazzling red, pink, orange, and white flowers spill into courtyards and climb up the sides of buildings.

The Yucatán is historically colorful, too. From the conquistadores' first landfall off Cape Catoche in 1517, to the bloody skirmishes that wiped out most of the Indians, to the razing of Maya temples and burning of their sacred books, the peninsula was a battlefield. Pirates wreaked havoc off the coast of Campeche for centuries. Half the Indian population was killed during the 19th-century uprising known as the War of the Castes, when the enslaved indigenous population rose up and massacred thousands of Mexicans; Yucatán was attempting to secede from Mexico, and dictator Porfirio Díaz sent in his troops. These events, like the towering Maya civilization, have left their mark throughout the peninsula: in its archaeological museums, its colonial monuments, and the opulent mansions of the hacienda owners who enslaved the natives to cultivate their henequen.

But despite the violent conflicts of the past, the people of Yucatán treat today's visitors with hospitality and friendliness, especially outside the beach resorts. If you learn a few words of Spanish, you will be rewarded with an even warmer welcome.

— Updated by Patricia Alisau
and Shelagh McNally

CANCÚN AT A GLANCE

Cancún

Origin: "Cancún" is Maya for "pit of snakes."

State: Quintana Roo is the most easterly state in Mexico. Until 1974, it was a territory where dissidents were sent to be eaten alive by mosquitoes and die of malaria; only after Cancún was built and became a successful tourist destination did it become a recognized state. It covers 50,212 square km (19,382 square mi), and represents 2.6% of Mexico's landmass.

Common traffic signs: *Obedezca las señales* (Obey the signs); *No maltrate las señales* (Do not mistreat the signs); *No deje piedras sobre el pavimento* (Do not leave rocks on the road).

What's nearby: Cancún is 847 km (526 mi) away from Miami; that's closer than Mexico City, which is 1,300 km (808 mi) away. Closest of all, however, is Cuba, which is just 90 km (48 mi) away.

Flag: The Mexican flag was formed in 1821 by the Ejército Trigarante (Army of the Three Guarantees), after the Mexicans won their independence from Spain. Each color stands for one part of the agreement. Green is for independence; white is for religion; red is for union. The flag of Quintana Roo symbolizes the ocean and forests of the state.

Mayor: The first municipal president took charge when the seat of the Municipality Government was established on April 10, 1975.

Legal system: There are three judicial levels: the Lower Court, the High Court, and the Supreme Court. As the interpreter of civil law, the Supreme Court is the highest court, and has 11 judges.

And you thought American politics were complicated: There are 11 main political parties: CDPPN (Democratic Convergence National Political Party); PAN (National Action Party); PARM (Authentic Revolutionary Mexican Party); PAS (Social Alliance Party); PCD (Democratic Center Party); PDS (Social Democracy Party); PRD (Party of the Democratic Revolution); PRI (Institutional Revolutionary Party); PSN (Nationalist Society Party); PT (Labor Party); PVEM (Green Ecological Mexican Party). At present, the PRI is the party in power.

Population: 400,000. Prior to 1974 there were only 117 people living in the area.

Density: 296 inhabitants per square kilometer.

Language: Spanish and Maya. English is used in the tourist areas.

Sunshine: Cancún has 285 days of sunshine per year.

Ethnic groups: 60% of the inhabitants of Cancún come from Yucatán, Campeche, and Quintana Roo; 24% of the population comes from Guerrero, Tabasco, Veracruz, and Mexico City; and the remaining 16% are natives of Cancún or foreigners.

Visitors: In 2002, 2,802,113 tourists arrived at Cancún's international airport; 2.1 million cruise tourists arrived in Cozumel.

Contribution to Western cuisine: Gum was first invented using the sap from the chicle tree found in Quintana Roo.

Contribution to romance: Cancún is the sixth most popular place in the world to get married or have a honeymoon. Four witnesses are required for each ceremony, though.

Religion: There are over 29 gods in the Maya religion. Among the most important are Itzamná, the creator-god, the feathered serpent called "Kukulcán," and Chaac, the god of rain.

CHRONOLOGY

11,000 BC Hunters and gatherers settle in Yucatán.

Preclassic Period: 2000 BC–AD 100

2,000 BC Maya ancestors in Guatemala begin to cultivate corn and build permanent dwellings.

1500–900 BC The powerful and sophisticated Olmec civilization develops along the Gulf of Mexico in the present-day states of Veracruz and Tabasco.

Primitive farming communities develop in Yucatán.

900–300 BC Olmec iconography and social institutions strongly influence the Maya populations in neighboring areas. The Maya adopt the Olmecs' concepts of tribal confederacies and small kingships as they move across the lowlands.

600 BC Edzná is settled. It will be inhabited for nearly 900 years before the construction of the large temples and palaces found there today.

400 BC–AD 100 Dzibilchaltún develops as an important center in Komchen, an ancient state north of present-day Mérida. Becán, in southern Campeche, is also settled.

300 BC Major construction begins in the Maya lowlands as the civilization begins to flourish.

300 BC–AD 200 New architectural elements, including the corbeled arch and roof comb, develop in neighboring Guatemala and gradually spread into the Yucatán.

300 BC–AD 900 Edzná becomes a city; increasingly large temple-pyramids are built.

Classic Period: AD 100–AD 1000

The calendar and the written word are among the achievements that mark the beginning of the Classic period. The architectural highlight of the period is large, stepped pyramids with frontal stairways topped by limestone and masonry temples, arranged around plazas and decorated with stelae (stone monuments), bas-reliefs, and frescoes. Each Maya city is painted a single bright color, often red or yellow.

200–600 Economy and trade flourish. Maya culture achieves new levels of scientific sophistication and some groups become warlike.

250–300 A defensive fortification ditch and earthworks are built at Becán.

300 The first structures are built at San Gervasio on Cozumel.

300–600 Kohunlich rises to dominate the forests of southern Quintana Roo.

400–1100 Cobá grows to be the largest city in the eastern Yucatán.

432 The first settlement is established at Chichén Itzá.

6th Century Influenced by the Toltec civilization of Teotihuacán in Central Mexico, larger and more elaborate palaces, temples, ball courts, roads, and fortifications are built in southern Maya cities, including Becán, Xpujil, and Chicanná in Campeche.

600–900 Northern Yucatán ceremonial centers become increasingly important as centers farther south reach and pass developmental climax; the influence of Teotihuacán wanes. Three new Maya architectural styles develop: Puuc (exemplified by Chichén Itzá and Edzná) is the dominant style; Chenes (in northern Campeche) is characterized by ornamental facades with serpent masks; and Río Bec features small palaces with high towers exuberantly decorated with serpent masks.

850–950 The largest pyramids and palaces of Uxmal are built. By 975, however, Uxmal and most other Puuc sites are abandoned.

Postclassic Period: AD 1000–AD 1521

900–1050 The great Classic Maya centers of Guatemala, Honduras, and southern Yucatán are abandoned. The reason for their fall remains one of archaeology's greatest mysteries.

circa 920 The Itzá, a Maya tribe from the Petén rain forest in Guatemala, establish themselves at Champotón and then at Chichén Itzá.

987–1007 The Xiu, a Maya clan from the southwest, settle near the ruins of Uxmal.

1224 An Itzá dynasty known as Cocomes emerges as a dominant group in northern Yucatán, building its capital at Mayapán.

1263–1440 Mayapán, under the rule of Cocomes aided by Canul mercenaries from Tabasco, becomes the most powerful city-state in Yucatán. The league of Mayapán—including the key cities of Uxmal, Chichén Itzá, and Mayapán—is formed in northern Yucatán. Peace reigns for almost two centuries. To guarantee the peace, the rulers of Mayapán hold members of other Maya royal families as lifelong hostages.

1441 Maya cities under Xiu rulers sack Mayapán, ending centralized rule of the peninsula. Yucatán henceforth is governed as 18 petty provinces, with constant internecine strife. The Itzá return to Lake Petén Itzá in Guatemala and establish their capital at Tayasal (modern-day Flores), one of the last un-Christianized Maya capitals, which will not be conquered by the Spanish until 1692.

15th Century The last ceremonial center on Cancún island is abandoned. Other Maya communities are developing along the Caribbean coast.

1502 A Maya canoe is spotted during Columbus's fourth voyage.

1511 Spanish sailors Jerónimo de Aguilar and Gonzalo Guerrero are shipwrecked off Yucatán's Caribbean coast and taken to a Maya village on Cozumel.

1517 Fernández de Córdoba discovers Isla Mujeres.

Trying to sail around Yucatán, which he believes to be an island, Córdoba lands at Campeche, marking the first Spanish landfall on the mainland. He is defeated by the Maya at Champotón.

1518 Juan de Grijalva sights the island of Cozumel but does not land there.

1519 Hernán Cortés lands at Cozumel, where he rescues Aguilar. Guerrero chooses to remain on the island with his Maya family.

Colonial Period: 1521–1821

1527, 1531 The Spanish make unsuccessful attempts to conquer Yucatán.

1540 Francisco de Montejo founds Campeche, the first Spanish settlement in Yucatán.

1541 Another takeover is attempted—unsuccessfully—by the Spanish.

1542 Maya chieftains surrender to Montejo at T'ho; 500,000 Indians are killed during the conquest of Yucatán. Indians are forced into labor under the *encomienda* system, by which conquistadores are charged with their subjugation and Christianization. The Franciscans contribute to this process.

Mérida is founded on the ruins of T'ho.

1543 Valladolid is founded on the ruins of Zací.

1546 A Maya group attacks Mérida, resulting in a five-month-long rebellion.

1562 Bishop Diego de Landa burns Maya codices at Maní.

1600 Cozumel is abandoned after smallpox decimates the population.

1686 Campeche's city walls are built for defense against pirates.

1700 182,500 Indians account for 98% of Yucatán's population.

1736 The Indian population of Yucatán declines to 127,000.

1761 The Cocomes uprising near Sotuta leads to the death of 600 Maya.

1771 The Fuerte (fort) de San Miguel is completed on a hill above Campeche, ending the pirates' reign of terror.

1810 The Port of Sisal opens, ending Campeche's ancient monopoly on peninsular trade and its economic prosperity.

Postcolonial/Modern Period: 1821–Present

1821 Mexico wins independence from Spain by diplomatic means. Various juntas vie for control of the new nation, resulting in frequent military coups.

1823 Yucatán becomes a Mexican state encompassing the entire peninsula.

1839–42 American explorer John Lloyd Stephens visits Yucatán's Maya ruins and describes them in two best-selling books.

1840–42 Yucatecan separatists revolt in an attempt to secede from Mexico. The Mexican government quells the rebellion, reduces the state of Yucatán to one-third its previous size, creates the federal territories of Quintana Roo and Campeche, and recruits Maya soldiers into a militia to prevent further disturbance.

1846 Following years of oppression, violent clashes between Maya militiamen and residents of Valladolid launch the War of the Castes. The entire non-Indian population of Valladolid is massacred.

1848 Rebels from the Caste War settle in the forests of Quintana Roo, creating a secret city named Chan Santa Cruz. An additional 20 refugee families settle in Cozumel, which has been almost uninhabited for centuries. By 1890 Cozumel's population numbers 500, Santa Cruz's 10,000.

1850 Following the end of the Mexican War with the United States in 1849, the Mexican army moves into the Yucatán to end the Indian uprising. The Maya flee into the unexplored forests of Quintana Roo. Military attacks, disease, and starvation reduce the Maya population of the Yucatán Peninsula to fewer than 10,000.

1863 Campeche achieves statehood.

1872 The city of Progreso is founded.

1880–1914 Yucatán's monopoly on henequen, enhanced by plantation owners' exploitation of Maya peasants, leads to its golden age as one of the wealthiest states in Mexico. Prosperity will last until the beginning of World War II.

Waves of Middle Eastern immigrants arrive in Yucatán and become successful in commerce, restaurants, cattle ranching, and tourism.

Payo Obispo (present-day Chetumal) is founded on the site of a long-abandoned Spanish colonial outpost.

1901 The Cult of the Talking Cross reaches the height of its popularity in Chan Santa Cruz (later renamed Felipe Carrillo Puerto). The Cruzob Indians continue to resist the Mexican army.

U.S. consul Edward Thompson buys Chichén Itzá for $500 and spends the next three years dredging the Sacred Cenote for artifacts.

1902 Mexican president Porfirio Díaz asserts federal jurisdiction over the Territory of Quintana Roo to isolate rebellious pockets of Indians and increase his hold on regional resources.

1915 The War of the Castes reaches an uneasy truce after the Mexican Army leaves the Cruzob Indians to rule Quintana Roo as an independent territory.

1915–24 Felipe Carrillo Puerto, Socialist governor of Yucatán, institutes major reforms in land distribution, labor, women's rights, and education during Mexican Revolution.

1923–48 A Carnegie Institute team led by archaeologist Sylvanus Moreley restores the ruins of Chichén Itzá.

1934–40 President Lázaro Cárdenas implements significant agrarian reforms in Yucatán.

1935 Chan Santa Cruz rebels in Quintana Roo relinquish Tulum and sign a peace treaty.

1940–70   With the collapse of the world henequen markets, Yucatán gradually becomes one of the poorest states in Mexico.

1968   The Mexican government selects Cancún as the site of the country's largest tourist resort.

1974   Quintana Roo achieves statehood. The first resort hotels at Cancún open for business.

1988   Hurricane Gilbert shuts down Cancún hotels and devastates the north coast of the Yucatán. The reconstruction is immediate. Within three years, the number of hotels on Cancún triples.

1993   Under the guise of an environmentalist platform, Quintana Roo's newly elected governor Mario Villanueva begins systematically selling off state parks and federally owned land to developers.

1994   Mexico joins the United States and Canada in NAFTA (North American Free Trade Association), which will phase out tariffs over a 15-year period.

        Institutional Revolutionary Party (PRI) presidential candidate Luis Donaldo Colosio is assassinated while campaigning in Tijuana. Ernesto Zedillo, generally thought to be more of a technocrat and "old boy"–style PRI politician, replaces him and wins the election.

        Zedillo, blaming the economic policies of his predecessor, devalues the peso in December.

1995   Recession sets in as a result of the peso devaluation. The former administration is rocked by scandals surrounding the assassinations of Colosio and another high-ranking government official; ex-president Carlos Salinas de Gortari moves to the United States.

        Quintana Roo governor Mario Villanueva is suspected of using his office to smuggle drugs into the state.

1996   Mexico's economy, bolstered by a $28 billion bailout led by the United States, turns around, but the recovery is fragile. The opposition National Action Party (PAN), which is committed to conservative economic policies, gains strength. New details emerge of scandals within the former administration.

1997   Mexico's top antidrug official is arrested on bribery charges. Nonetheless, the United States recertifies Mexico as a partner in the war on drugs. Party elections are scheduled for midyear. When Mexican environmentalists discover that Villanueva has sold the turtle sanctuary on Xcacel beach to a Spanish hotel chain, they begin an international campaign to save the site; Greenpeace stages a protest on the beach.

1998   Mexican author Octavio Paz dies.

        U.S. Congress demands an investigation into the office of Mario Villanueva. Villanueva is refused entry into the United States when the DEA reveals that it has an open file on his activities.

1999   Raúl Salinas, brother of former Mexican president Carlos Salinas di Gortari (in exile in Ireland), is sentenced for the murder of a PRI leader.

Joaquin Hendricks, a retired military officer, is elected the new governor of Quintana Roo. Although he is thought to be an enemy of Mario Villanueva, the ex-governor sanctions Hendricks's rise to power. The Mexican government decides to arrest Villanueva on drug charges; Villanueva disappears.

2000   Spurning the long-ruling PRI, Mexicans elect opposition candidate Vicente Fox president.

Fox government implements the "Financial Strengthening Program 2000–2001" as part of an economic reform and vows to clean up corruption. Fox also appeals to the United Nation for help in reducing the country's long-standing human rights problems—mostly associated with political corruption—and promises to launch an investigation.

2001   Ex-governor Mario Villanueva is captured, aided by DEA agents. A bitter dispute erupts over the election of PAN candidates. The old guard, led by the PRI, demands a reelection. The PAN wins for a second time.

Fox's Human Rights Commission presents a 3,000-page report concluding that federal, state, and municipal authorities have been guilty of abducting and torturing citizens over the past three decades, beginning with a massacre of student protesters in 1968. The report sets off a backlash against political activists.

2002   Fox continues to clean house, charging 25 prominent public officials after uncovering a network that aided and abetted drug traffickers and organized-crime groups.

Fox urges President Bush to legalize the millions of Mexicans who work in the United States illegally. He reveals that money sent home to Mexico by workers in the United States is Mexico's second-largest source of income. Bush promises to begin work on a new immigration policy.

The presidency of the Gulf of Mexico States Accord was transferred from Jeb Bush, Governor of Florida, to Joaquin Hendricks, Governor of Quintana Roo. It is primarily a figurehead role.

Pope John Paul II comes to Mexico to beatify two Mexican Indian martyrs, Juan Bautista and Jacinto de los Angeles, after declaring Juan Diego the first Indian saint in the Americas.

Hurricane Isidore hits Mérida and dozens of smaller coastal communities, destroying buildings, tearing down power lines, and uprooting thousands of trees. More than 300,000 people are left homeless; many towns are still recovering today.

2003   Mexico's foreign minister closes the country's first high-level human rights office on the same day Amnesty International releases a report criticizing the government's role in the killings and disappearances of more than 300 women in Ciudad Juárez. Another independent inquiry investigating the massacre of student protesters before the 1968 Mexico City Olympics is closed and the Zapatista (Indian rights revolutionaries) from Chiapas begin protesting over human rights violations.

In July, voters held Fox to account, cutting back by 51 the number of seats the PAN holds in the lower house of Mexico's Congress.

Quintana Roo registers 8% growth, and 3,013,708 foreign tourists come through its borders.

SPANISH VOCABULARY

Words and Phrases

	English	Spanish	Pronunciation
Basics			
	Yes/no	Sí/no	see/no
	Please	Por favor	pohr fah-**vohr**
	May I?	¿Me permite?	meh pehr-**mee**-teh
	Thank you (very much)	(Muchas) gracias	(**moo**-chas) **grah**-see-as
	You're welcome	De nada	deh **nah**-dah
	Excuse me	Con permiso/perdón	con pehr-**mee**-so/ pehr-**dohn**
	Pardon me/ what did you say?	¿Perdón?/Mande?	pehr-**dohn**/**mahn**-deh
	Could you tell me . . . ?	¿Podría decirme . . . ?	po-**dree**-ah deh-**seer**-meh
	I'm sorry	Lo siento	lo see-**en**-to
	Good morning!	¡Buenos días!	**bway**-nohs **dee**-ahs
	Good afternoon!	¡Buenas tardes!	**bway**-nahs **tar**-dess
	Good evening!	¡Buenas noches!	**bway**-nahs **no**-chess
	Goodbye!	¡Adiós!/ ¡Hasta luego!	ah-dee-**ohss**/ ah-stah-**lwe**-go
	Mr./Mrs.	Señor/Señora	sen-**yor**/sen-**yohr**-ah
	Miss	Señorita	sen-yo-**ree**-tah
	Pleased to meet you	Mucho gusto	**moo**-cho **goose**-to
	How are you?	¿Cómo está usted?	**ko**-mo es-**tah** oo-**sted**
	Very well, thank you.	Muy bien, gracias.	**moo**-ee bee-**en**, **grah**-see-as
	And you?	¿Y usted?	ee oos-**ted**
	Hello (on the phone)	Diga	**dee**-gah

Numbers

1		un, uno	oon, **oo**-no
2		dos	dohs
3		tres	tress
4		cuatro	**kwah**-tro
5		cinco	**sink**-oh

6	seis	saice
7	siete	see-**et**-eh
8	ocho	**o**-cho
9	nueve	new-**eh**-veh
10	diez	dee-**es**
11	once	**ohn**-seh
12	doce	**doh**-seh
13	trece	**treh**-seh
14	catorce	ka-**tohr**-seh
15	quince	**keen**-seh
16	dieciséis	dee-**es**-ee-**saice**
17	diecisiete	dee-**es**-ee-see-**et**-eh
18	dieciocho	dee-**es**-ee-**o**-cho
19	diecinueve	dee-**es**-ee-new-**ev**-eh
20	veinte	**vain**-teh
21	veinte y uno/ veintiuno	**vain**-te-oo-noh
30	treinta	**train**-tah
32	treinta y dos	train-tay-**dohs**
40	cuarenta	kwah-**ren**-tah
50	cincuenta	seen-**kwen**-tah
60	sesenta	sess-**en**-tah
70	setenta	set-**en**-tah
80	ochenta	oh-**chen**-tah
90	noventa	no-**ven**-tah
100	cien	see-**en**
200	doscientos	doh-see-**en**-tohss
500	quinientos	keen-**yen**-tohss
1,000	mil	meel
2,000	dos mil	dohs meel

Days of the Week

Sunday	domingo	doh-**meen**-goh
Monday	lunes	**loo**-ness
Tuesday	martes	**mahr**-tess
Wednesday	miércoles	me-**air**-koh-less
Thursday	jueves	hoo-**ev**-ess
Friday	viernes	vee-**air**-ness

| Saturday | sábado | **sah**-bah-doh |

Useful Phrases

Do you speak English?	¿Habla usted inglés?	**ah**-blah oos-**ted** in-**glehs**
I don't speak Spanish	No hablo español	no **ah**-bloh es-pahn-**yol**
I don't understand (you)	No entiendo	no en-tee-**en**-doh
I understand (you)	Entiendo	en-tee-**en**-doh
I don't know	No sé	no seh
I am American/British	Soy americano (americana)/inglés(a)	soy ah-meh-ree-**kah**-no (ah-meh-ree-**kah**-nah)/in-**glehs**(ah)
My name is . . .	Me llamo . . .	meh **yah**-moh
Yes, please/No, thank you	Sí, por favor/No, gracias	**see** pohr fah-**vor**/no **grah**-see-ahs
Yesterday/today/tomorrow	Ayer/hoy/mañana	ah-**yehr**/oy/mahn-**yah**-nah
This morning/afternoon	Esta mañana/tarde	**es**-tah mahn-**yah**-nah/**tar**-deh
Tonight	Esta noche	**es**-tah **no**-cheh
This/Next week	Esta semana/la semana que entra	**es**-tah seh-**mah**-nah/lah seh-**mah**-nah keh **en**-trah
This/Next month	Este mes/el próximo mes	**es**-teh mehs/el **prok**-see-moh mehs
How?	¿Cómo?	**koh**-mo
When?	¿Cuándo?	**kwahn**-doh
What?	¿Qué?	keh
What is this?	¿Qué es esto?	keh es **es**-toh
Why?	¿Por qué?	por **keh**
Who?	¿Quién?	kee-**yen**
Where is . . . ?	¿Dónde está . . . ?	**dohn**-deh es-**tah**
the train station?	la estación del tren?	la es-tah-see-**on** del **train**
the subway station?	la estación del metro?	la es-ta-see-**on** del **meh**-tro
the bus stop?	la parada del autobus?	la pah-**rah**-dah del oh-toh-**boos**
the bank?	el banco?	el **bahn**-koh
the hotel?	el hotel?	el oh-**tel**
the post office?	la oficina de correos?	la oh-fee-**see**-nah deh-koh-**reh**-os
the museum?	el museo?	el moo-**seh**-oh

the hospital?	el hospital?	el ohss-pee-**tal**
the bathroom?	el baño?	el **bahn**-yoh
Here/there	Aquí/allá	ah-**key**/ah-**yah**
Open/closed	Abierto/cerrado	ah-bee-**er**-toh/ ser-**ah**-doh
Left/right	Izquierda/derecha	iss-key-**er**-dah/ dare-**eh**-chah
Straight ahead	Todo recto	**toh**-doh-**rec**-toh
Is it near/far?	¿Está cerca/lejos?	es-**tah** sehr-kah/ **leh**-hoss
I'd like . . .	Quisiera . . .	kee-see-**ehr**-ah
a room	una habitación	**oo**-nah ah-bee- tah-see-**on**
the key	la llave	lah **yah**-veh
a newspaper	un periódico	oon pehr-ee-**oh**- dee-koh
a stamp	un sello	**say**-oh
How much is this?	¿Cuánto cuesta?	**kwahn**-toh **kwes**-tah
A little/a lot	Un poquito/ mucho	oon poh-**kee**-toh/ **moo**-choh
More/less	Más/menos	mahss/**men**-ohss
I am ill	Estoy enfermo(a)	es-**toy** en-**fehr**- moh(mah)
Please call a doctor	Por favor llame un medico	pohr fah-**vor** ya- meh oon **med**-ee-koh
Help!	¡Ayuda!	ah-**yoo**-dah

On the Road

Avenue	Avenida	ah-ven-**ee**-dah
Broad, tree-lined boulevard	Paseo	pah-**seh**-oh
Highway	Carretera	car-reh-**ter**-ah
Port; mountain pass	Puerto	poo-**ehr**-toh
Street	Calle	**cah**-yeh
Waterfront promenade	Paseo marítimo	pah-**seh**-oh mahr-**ee**-tee-moh

In Town

Cathedral	Catedral	cah-teh-**dral**
Church	Iglesia	**tem**-plo/ee-**glehs**- see-ah
City hall, town hall	Ayuntamiento	ah-yoon-tah-me- **yen**-toh

Door, gate	Puerta	poo-**ehr**-tah
Main square	Plaza Mayor	plah-thah mah-**yohr**
Market	Mercado	mer-**kah**-doh
Neighborhood	Barrio	**bahr**-ree-o
Tavern, rustic restaurant	Mesón	meh-**sohn**
Traffic circle, roundabout	Glorieta	glor-ee-**eh**-tah
Wine cellar, wine bar, wine shop	Bodega	boh-**deh**-gah

Dining Out

	de . . .	yah deh
A bottle of . . .	Una bottella de . . .	**oo**-nah bo-**teh**-yah deh
A glass of . . .	Un vaso de . . .	oon **vah**-so deh
Bill/check	La cuenta	lah **kwen**-tah
Breakfast	El desayuno	el deh-sah-**yoon**-oh
Dinner	La cena	lah **seh**-nah
Menu of the day	Menú del día	meh-**noo** del **dee**-ah
Fork	El tenedor	ehl ten-eh-**dor**
Is the tip included?	¿Está incluida la propina?	es-**tah** in-cloo-**ee**-dah lah pro-**pee**-nah
Knife	El cuchillo	el koo-**chee**-yo
Large portion of tapas	Ración	rah-see-**ohn**
Lunch	La comida	lah koh-**mee**-dah
Menu	La carta, el menú	lah **cart**-ah, el meh-**noo**
Napkin	La servilleta	lah sehr-vee-**yet**-ah
Please give me . . .	Por favor déme . . .	pohr fah-**vor** **deh**-meh
Spoon	Una cuchara	**oo**-nah koo-**chah**-rah

INDEX

NOTES

To TULUM:
$61

8AM
9³⁰AM
10³⁰AM
11AM

[KM 7
[CARRETERA TULUM - Boca Paila
[CABAÑAS TULUM

TIKETBUS.COM.MX

NOTES

NOTES

NOTES

NOTES

NOTES

NOTES

FODOR'S KEY TO THE GUIDES

America's guidebook leader publishes guides for every kind of traveler.
Check out our many series and find your perfect match.

FODOR'S GOLD GUIDES

America's favorite travel-guide series offers the most detailed insider reviews of hotels, restaurants, and attractions in all price ranges, plus great background information, smart tips, and useful maps.

COMPASS AMERICAN GUIDES

Stunning guides from top local writers and photographers, with gorgeous photos, literary excerpts, and colorful anecdotes. A must-have for culture mavens, history buffs, and new residents.

FODOR'S CITYPACKS

Concise city coverage in a guide plus a foldout map. The right choice for urban travelers who want everything under one cover.

FODOR'S EXPLORING GUIDES

Hundreds of color photos bring your destination to life. Lively stories lend insight into the culture, history, and people.

FODOR'S TRAVEL HISTORIC AMERICA

For travelers who want to experience history firsthand, this series gives in-depth coverage of historic sights, plus nearby restaurants and hotels. Themes include the Thirteen Colonies, the Old West, and the Lewis and Clark Trail.

FODOR'S POCKET GUIDES

For travelers who need only the essentials. The best of Fodor's in pocket-size packages for just $9.95.

FODOR'S FLASHMAPS

Every resident's map guide, with dozens of easy-to-follow maps of public transit, restaurants, shopping, museums, and more.

FODOR'S CITYGUIDES

Sourcebooks for living in the city: thousands of in-the-know listings for restaurants, shops, sports, nightlife, and other city resources.

FODOR'S AROUND THE CITY WITH KIDS

Up to 68 great ideas for family days, recommended by resident parents. Perfect for exploring in your own backyard or on the road.

FODOR'S HOW TO GUIDES

Get tips from the pros on planning the perfect trip. Learn how to pack, fly hassle-free, plan a honeymoon or cruise, stay healthy on the road, and travel with your baby.

FODOR'S LANGUAGES FOR TRAVELERS

Practice the local language before you hit the road. Available in phrase books, cassette sets, and CD sets.

KAREN BROWN'S GUIDES

Engaging guides—many with easy-to-follow inn-to-inn itineraries—to the most charming inns and B&Bs in the U.S.A. and Europe.

SEE IT GUIDES

Illustrated guidebooks that include the practical information travelers need, in gorgeous full color. Thousands of photos, hundreds of restaurant and hotel reviews, actual prices, and ratings for attractions all in one indispensable package. Perfect for travelers who want the best value, packed in a fresh, easy-to-use, colorful layout.

OTHER GREAT TITLES FROM FODOR'S

Baseball Vacations, The Complete Guide to the National Parks, Family Vacations, Golf Digest's Places to Play, Great American Drives of the East, Great American Drives of the West, Great American Vacations, Healthy Escapes, National Parks of the West, Skiing USA.